WILEY CIA

EXAM REVIEW

VOLUME 1

Internal Audit Activity's Role
in Governance, Risk, and Control

WILEY CIA EXAM REVIEW

VOLUME 1

Internal Audit Activity's Role in Governance, Risk, and Control

THIRD EDITION

S. RAO VALLABHANENI

WILEY

JOHN WILEY & SONS, INC.

Published by John Wiley & Sons, Inc., Hoboken, New Jersey.
Published simultaneously in Canada.

For general information on our other products and services, or technical support, please contact our Customer Care Department within the United States at 800-762-2974, outside the United States at 317-572-3993 or fax 317-572-4002.

Wiley also publishes its books in a variety of electronic formats. Some content that appears in print may not be available in electronic books. For more information about Wiley products, visit our Web site at www.wiley.com.

ISBN: 978-0-471-71883-3 (Set)

ISBN: 978-0-471-71879-6

10 9 8 7

CONTENTS

ABOUT THE WEB SITE

This site contains the Institute of Internal Auditors' (IIA's) new and revised International Standards for the Professional Practice Framework (IPPF) for internal auditing (standards). The new standards became effective on January 1, 2011. The Certified Internal Auditor (CIA) Exam questions will be aligned to the new standards effective six months from the date January 1, 2011.

The major purpose in releasing this online document now is to provide the CIA Exam candidate an interim solution to study the IIA's new standards and new/modified questions until the IIA's new content specifications (including the new standards) become available.

The address for the Web site is www.wiley.com/go/ciavolone.

PREFACE

The Certified Internal Auditor (CIA) Examination is a program of the Institute of Internal Auditors (IIA), Inc. The CIA examination certifies a person as a professional internal auditor and is intended to measure the knowledge, skills, and competency required in the field of internal auditing. The Certified Internal Auditor designation is the mark of an expert in internal auditing. The new exam, effective from May 2004, tests knowledge at two levels of comprehension—proficiency and awareness—as indicated in the IIA's content specifications outlines (*www.theiia.org*). These levels require allocating more preparation time to proficiency-level topics and less time to awareness-level topics.

A series of four-volume review guides have been prepared for the candidate to utilize for all four parts of the new CIA exam. There is a one-to-one relationship between the four-volume books and the four parts of the exam; that is, one volume covers one part of the exam.

Each volume includes a comprehensive coverage of the subject matter (theory) followed by hundreds of previous CIA exam multiple-choice questions with answers and explanations (practice). The structure and topics of the book matches the content specifications as closely as possible. In Volume 1, a total of 597 questions have been included from previous CIA exams and other sources. The actual CIA exam for each part consists of 125 multiple-choice questions to be completed in 3½ hours. The breakdown of questions by chapter is

Chapter 1	243 questions
Chapter 2	32 questions
Chapter 3	51 questions
Chapter 4	21 questions
Chapter 5	184 questions
Chapter 6	66 questions
Total	597 questions

The objective of this book is to provide single-source, comprehensive review materials to assist the CIA exam candidate in successfully preparing for the exam. Major highlights of these review books include

- Easy to navigate, comprehend, learn, and apply the subject matter since it was written from a student's perspective in a textbook style and format.
- It contains fully developed theories and concepts with complete thoughts as opposed to mere outlines. The candidate needs to know more than outlines to pass the difficult CIA exam.
- The theoretical topic at the beginning of each chapter is shown with a range of percentages to indicate the relative weights given to that topic in the exam. Candidates are expected to plan their study time in proportion to the relative weights suggested. A clear linkage is provided between theory and practice presented in the same chapter, in the same book, to provide consistency.
- The multiple-choice questions are organized in the same sequence as the theoretical topics for quick and easy access to the subject matter and for better integration between theory and practice. Each answer is labeled with its subject area and is identified with its source (i.e., CIA, CBM, and Author). The author is S. Rao Vallabhaneni.
- Greater use of comparisons and contrasts of subject matter make the key concepts come alive by providing lasting impressions. These comparisons show interrelationships between key concepts.
- The four volumes offer full coverage of all the IIA's *Standards*, all of the Practice Advisories, and the Code of Ethics in their entirety, issued as of February 2003.
- A total of 4,013 multiple-choice questions are provided in all four volumes together.

These books focus on the student—the candidate preparing for the CIA exam. They provide a positive learning experience for candidates by helping them to remember what they read and recall the subject matter through the use of tree diagrams, line drawings, memory aids (which is what), tables, charts, and graphic text boxes. In other words, an attempt has been made to bring life to static words through visual aids. *The positive learning experience system provided through visual aids and memories will enable candidates to form long-lasting study impressions of the subject matter in their minds.* In short, these books are student-focused and learning-oriented.

The needs of the students have been recognized. Learning is made easier, more convenient, and more enjoyable for our customer, the student. A great deal of planning and thought went into the creation of these books with the single goal of making the student's study program (whether individual or group) relatively easier, more relevant, and meaningful. It is hoped that these books meet or exceed the student's expectations in terms of quality, content coverage, and presentation of the subject matter.

We were excited and challenged while writing these books, and we hope that you too will be excited to study, remember, and achieve lifelong benefit from them. We believe that the knowledge gained from these books will remain with the candidate even after passing the CIA exam, assisting on-the-job as reference material, as well as a training source.

Our goal is to be responsive to the CIA exam candidate's needs and provide customer (student) satisfaction through continuous quality improvement. This goal can be met only through timely feedback from the candidate. Please help us to serve you better—your input counts.

How to Use This Book

Volume 1 covers "The Internal Audit Activity's Role in Governance, Risk, and Control" (Part I). It has six chapters: Chapter 1 deals with complying with the IIA's *Attribute Standards*. Chapter 2 addresses establishing a risk-based plan to determine the priorities of the internal audit activity. Chapter 3 covers understanding of internal audit activity's role in organizational governance. Chapter 4 focuses on performing other internal audit roles and responsibilities. Chapter 5 discusses governance, risk, and control knowledge elements. Chapter 6 explains audit engagement planning.

We suggest a sequential approach, that is, study the theory first and then answer the multiple-choice questions. Both the theory and the practice are highly integrated, and the theory provides good input and clear framework to the practice. Since some theoretical topics are covered in multiple chapters, it is strongly advised that students read all the theory chapters first, followed by the practice questions. Also, note that a practice question can be grouped into multiple chapters in the same part or even multiple parts due to overlapping coverage of the subject matter.

Exam-Taking Tips and Techniques

The types of questions a candidate can expect to see in the CIA exam are objective, multiple-choice questions. Answering multiple-choice questions requires a good amount of practice and effort.

The following tips and techniques will be helpful in answering the multiple-choice questions:

- Stay with your first impression of the correct choice.
- Know the subject area or topic. Don't read too much into the question.
- Remember that questions are independent of specific country, products, practices, vendors, hardware, software, or industry.
- Read the last sentence of the question first followed by all choices and then the body of the question. Underline or circle the keywords.
- Read the question twice or read the underlined or circled keywords twice, and watch for tip-off words, such as **not, except, all, every, always, never, least, or most,** which denote absolute conditions.
- Do not project the question into your organizational environment, practices, policies, procedures, standards, and guidelines. The examination is focussing on the IIA's Professional Standards and Publications and on the CIA's exam syllabus (i.e., content specifications).
- Try to eliminate wrong choices quickly by striking or drawing a line through the choices or other ways convenient to you.
- When you get down to two semifinal choices, take a big-picture approach. For example, if choice A and D are the semifinalists, and choice D could be a part of choice A, then select choice A; or if choice D could be a more complete answer, then select choice D.
- Don't spend too much time on one question. If you are not sure of an answer, move on, and go back to it if time permits. The last resort is to guess the answer. There is no penalty for guessing the wrong answer.
- Transfer all questions to the answer sheet either after each question is answered individually or in small groups of ten or fifteen questions. Allocate sufficient time to do this task since this is a very important one. Place the right answer on the correct dot of the answer sheet.

Remember that success in the examination depends on your time management skills, preparation effort levels, education and experience, memory recall of the subject matter, and decision-making skills.

Administrative Matters

We encourage the new, prospective candidate to write directly to the Institute of Internal Auditors, 247 Maitland Avenue, Altamonte Springs, Florida 32701-4201 USA to obtain a copy of the CIA program "Information for Candidates" brochure. This brochure contains everything the candidate needs to know about the CIA exam (i.e., application form, exam fees, exam dates, and exam sites). Phone: 407-937-1100, Fax: 407-937-1111. Web site: www.theiia.org.

Your comments are important to us in order to improve quality and presentation of future editions. Please send us your feedback through the Web site at www.srvbooks.com. Thank you.

Acknowledgments

The author is indebted to the following sources and individuals who helped to improve the quality of this book: Angela Philips Woodward, Director of Certification at The Institute of Internal Auditors, Altamonte Springs, Florida, for providing great assistance during the writing of these books. Special thanks for providing previous CIA exam questions, answers, and explanations, and IIA *Standards* and other sources of material. The author also wishes to thank the publishers of the *Certified Business Manager (CBM) Examination Preparation Guides,* Volumes 1 through 6, Thomson Learning (South-Western), Mason, Ohio, 2003–2004 (www.apbm.org).

CIA EXAM CONTENT SPECIFICATIONS

The CIA exam tests a candidate's knowledge of current internal auditing practices and understanding of internal audit issues, risks, and controls. The exam is offered in four parts, each part consisting of 125 multiple-choice questions. The following is a breakdown of topics for Part 1 (Volume 1).

Part I: The Internal Audit Activity's Role in Governance, Risk, and Control

A. Comply with the IIA's *Attribute Standards* (15–25%)

1. Define purpose, authority, and responsibility of the internal audit activity
   a. Determine if the purpose, authority, and responsibility of internal audit activity are clearly documented and approved
   b. Determine if the purpose, authority, and responsibility of internal audit activity are communicated to the engagement clients
   c. Demonstrate an understanding of the purpose, authority, and responsibility of the internal audit activity
2. Maintain independence and objectivity
   a. Foster independence
      (1) Understand organizational independence
      (2) Recognize the importance of organizational independence
      (3) Determine if the internal audit activity is properly aligned to achieve organizational independence
   b. Foster objectivity
      (1) Establish policies to promote objectivity
      (2) Assess individual objectivity
      (3) Maintain individual objectivity
      (4) Recognize and mitigate impairments to independence and objectivity
3. Determine if the required knowledge, skills, and competencies are available
   a. Understand the knowledge, skills, and competencies that an internal auditor needs to possess
   b. Identify the knowledge, skills, and competencies required to fulfill the responsibilities of the internal audit activity
4. Develop and/or procure necessary knowledge, skills, and competencies collectively required by internal audit activity
5. Exercise due professional care
6. Promote continuing professional development
   a. Develop and implement a plan for continuing professional development for internal audit staff
   b. Enhance individual competency through continuing professional development
7. Promote quality assurance and improvement of the internal audit activity
   a. Establish and maintain a quality assurance and improvement program
   b. Monitor the effectiveness of the quality assurance and improvement program
   c. Report the results of the quality assurance and improvement program to the board or other governing body
   d. Conduct quality assurance procedures and recommend improvements to the performance of the internal audit activity
8. Abide by and promote compliance with the IIA Code of Ethics

B. Establish a Risk-Based Plan to Determine the Priorities of the Internal Audit Activity (15–25%)

1. Establish a framework for assessing risk
2 Use the framework to

a. Identify sources of potential engagements (e.g., audit universe, management request, regulatory mandate)
b. Assess organization-wide risk
c. Solicit potential engagement topics from various sources
d. Collect and analyze data on proposed engagements
e. Rank and validate risk priorities

3. Identify internal audit resource requirements
4. Coordinate the internal audit activity's efforts with

a. External auditor
b. Regulatory oversight bodies
c. Other internal assurance functions (e.g., health and safety department)

5. Select engagements

a. Participate in the engagement selection process
b. Select engagements.
c. Communicate and obtain approval of the engagement plan from board

C. Understand the Internal Audit Activity's Role in Organizational Governance: IIA's *Performance Standards* (10–20%)

1. Obtain board's approval of audit charter
2. Communicate plan of engagements
3. Report significant audit issues
4. Communicate key performance indicators to board on a regular basis
5. Discuss areas of significant risk
6. Support board in enterprise-wide risk assessment
7. Review positioning of the internal audit function within the risk management framework within the organization
8. Monitor compliance with the corporate code of conduct/business practices
9. Report on the effectiveness of the control framework
10. Assist board in assessing the independence of the external auditor
11. Assess ethical climate of the board
12. Assess ethical climate of the organization
13. Assess compliance with policies in specific areas (e.g., derivatives)
14. Assess organization's reporting mechanism to the board
15. Conduct follow-up and report on management response to regulatory body reviews
16. Conduct follow-up and report on management response to external audit
17. Assess the adequacy of the performance measurement system, achievement of corporate objective
18. Support a culture of fraud awareness and encourage the reporting of improprieties

D. Perform Other Internal Audit Roles and Responsibilities (0–10%)

1. Ethics/Compliance

a. Investigate and recommend resolution for ethics/compliance complaints
b. Determine disposition of ethics violations
c. Foster healthy ethical climate
d. Maintain and administer business conduct policy (e.g., conflict of interest)
e. Report on compliance

2. Risk Management

a. Develop and implement an organization-wide risk and control framework
b. Coordinate enterprise-wide risk assessment
c. Report corporate risk assessment to board
d. Review business continuity planning process

3. Privacy

a. Determine privacy vulnerabilities
b. Report on compliance

4. Information or physical security

a. Determine security vulnerabilities
b. Determine disposition of security violations
c. Report on compliance

E. Governance, Risk, and Control Knowledge Elements (15–25%)

1. Corporate governance principles
2. Alternative control frameworks
3. Risk vocabulary and concepts
4. Risk management techniques
5. Risk/control implications of different organizational structures
6. Risk/control implications of different leadership styles
7. Change management
8. Conflict management
9. Management control techniques
10. Types of control (preventive, detective, input, output)

F. Plan Engagements (15–25%)

1. Initiate preliminary communication with engagement client
2. Conduct a preliminary survey of the area of engagement

a. Obtain input from engagement client
b. Perform analytical reviews
c. Perform benchmarking
d. Conduct interviews
e. Review prior audit reports and other relevant documentation
f. Map processes
g. Develop checklists

3. Complete a detailed risk assessment of the area (prioritize or evaluate risk/control factors)
4. Coordinate audit engagement efforts with

a. External auditor
b. Regulatory oversight bodies

5. Establish/refine engagement objectives and identify/finalize the scope of engagement
6. Identify or develop criteria for assurance engagements (criteria against which to audit)
7. Consider the potential for fraud when planning an engagement

a. Be knowledgeable of the risk factors and red flags of fraud
b. Identify common types of fraud associated with the engagement area
c. Determine if risk of fraud requires special consideration when conducting an engagement

8. Determine engagement procedures
9. Determine the level of staff and resources needed for the engagement
10. Establish adequate planning and supervision of the engagement
11. Prepare engagement work program

1 COMPLY WITH THE IIA'S *ATTRIBUTE STANDARDS* (15–25%)

THEORY

1.1 Managing an Internal Audit Function

The internal audit director needs to comply with the IIA's *Attribute Standards*, which say that the chief audit executive is responsible for properly managing the department so that: audit work fulfills the general purposes and responsibilities approved by senior management and accepted by the board, resources of the internal auditing department are efficiently and effectively employed, and audit work conforms to the *Standards*.

(a) **Internal Audit Charter.** The basic policy statement under which the internal auditing department functions is the internal audit department charter. A written audit charter establishes the internal auditing department's position in the organization's hierarchy. The department functions independently of all other departments in the organization. The audit charter should describe the organizational status that the director of internal auditing should report to the chief executive officer (CEO) but have access to the board of directors. A dual reporting relationship exists here: reporting administratively (solid line) to the president or CEO, reporting functionally (dotted line) to the audit committee of the board of directors. The hierarchy of the audit director's reporting relationship is depicted in Exhibit 1.1.

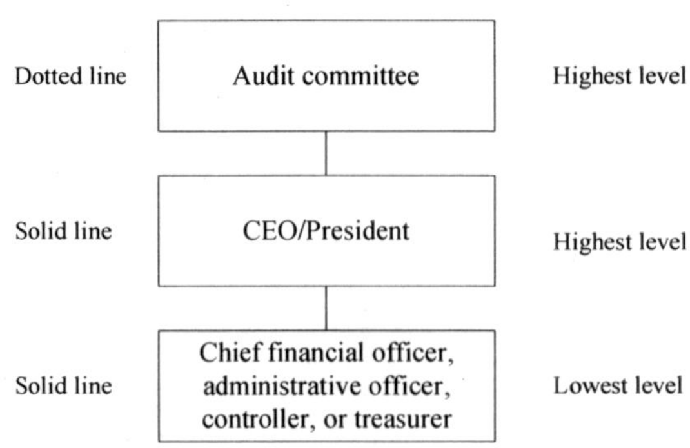

Exhibit 1.1: Hierarchy of the audit director's reporting relationship

The *charter* should describe the purpose, authority, and responsibility of the internal auditing department.

(i) **Purpose.** The mission or purpose of the internal auditing department is to

- Review organization's activities to determine whether it is efficiently and effectively carrying out its function of controlling in accordance with management instructions, policies, and procedures.
- Determine the adequacy and effectiveness of the system of internal controls in all areas of activity.
- Review the reliability and integrity of financial information and the means used to identify, measure, classify, and report such information.
- Review the means of safeguarding assets and, as appropriate, verify the existence of such assets.
- Appraise the economy and efficiency with which resources are employed, identify opportunities to improve operating performance, and recommend solutions to problems where appropriate.
- Review operations and plans to ascertain whether results are consistent with established objectives and goals, and whether the operations and plans are being carried out as intended.
- Coordinate audit efforts, where appropriate, with those of the external auditors.
- Review the planning, design, development, implementation, and operation of relevant computer-based systems to determine whether
  - Adequate controls are incorporated in the systems,
  - Thorough system testing is performed at appropriate stages,
  - System documentation is complete and accurate, and
  - The needs of the users are met.
- Conduct periodic audits of computer centers and make postinstallation evaluations of relevant data processing systems to determine whether those systems meet their intended purposes and objectives.
- Participate in the planning and performance of audits of acquisitions. Follow up to ensure the proper accomplishment of the audit objective.
- Report to those members of management who should be informed, or who should take corrective action, the results of audit examinations, the audit opinions formed, and the recommendations made.
- Evaluate the plans or actions taken to correct reported conditions for satisfactory disposition of audit findings. If corrective action is considered unsatisfactory, hold further discussions to achieve acceptable disposition.
- Provide adequate follow-up to ensure that proper corrective action is taken and that it is effective.

KEY CONCEPTS TO REMEMBER: INTERNAL AUDITING DEPARTMENT CHARTER

- The audit charter, audit director's reporting relationship, and the presence of an audit committee composed of all directors from the outside will enhance the internal auditing department's independence and objectivity.
- The internal auditing department's charter is the official source of authority to contact with units outside the organization (i.e., suppliers, customers, and other divisions of the firm).

(ii) **Authority.** In carrying out its duties, the internal auditing department will have full, free, and unrestricted access to records, personnel, and physical properties relevant to the performance of an audit. The internal auditors have no authority over nor responsibility for the activities they audit. The audit director should have direct access to the audit committee since it tends to enhance internal auditing's independence and objectivity. Independence permits internal auditors to reach the impartial and unbiased judgments essential to the proper conduct of audits.

(iii) **Responsibility.** The internal auditing department accomplishes its purpose of assisting management by reviewing, examining, and evaluating activities and furnishing analyses, appraisals, and reporting findings and recommendations. This audit responsibility cannot relieve any operating manager of the requirement for ensuring proper control within his or her area of concern.

The internal auditing department also has the responsibility to perform audit work with due professional care with appropriate education, experience, certification, professional image and attitude, and personal integrity.

(b) **Planning.** The director of internal auditing should establish plans to carry out the responsibilities of the internal auditing department (IIA *Standard* 520). These plans should be consistent with the charter and with the goals for the organization. The planning process involves establishing goals, audit work schedules, staffing plans and financial budgets, and activity reports. During audit planning, internal auditors should review all relevant information.

(i) **Risk models/risk analysis.** Risk models or risk analysis is often used in conjunction with development of long-range audit schedules. Although quantitative risk assessment is the basis for audit planning work, the key input in the evaluation of risk is judgment of the internal auditor. Some factors to be considered during risk analysis include: financial exposure and potential loss of assets, results of prior audits, major operating changes, damage to assets, and failure to comply with laws and regulations. Skills available on the audit staff are not a risk factor since missing skills can be obtained from elsewhere.

The director should allocate the audit work schedule to managers based on risk analysis performed by auditors and skill analysis of the audit managers. This approach will ensure that each manager receives an appropriate share of both the work schedule and resources.

KEY CONCEPTS TO REMEMBER: AUDIT TIME BUDGETS

When many audits are over budget, when there is no evidence of progressive reviews by supervisors, and when a quality assurance program does not exist, the audit director should ensure that decisions to revise time budgets for an audit are made immediately after the preliminary survey. This is to control audit projects and avoid time-budget overruns. Time budgets should not be revised after the fieldwork is done or audit reports are being prepared since it is too late in the audit cycle, and not much can be done to prevent or correct the problem situation.

(ii) **Audit plan.** The *audit plan* should include: a detailed schedule of areas to be audited during the coming year; an estimate of the time required for each audit, risk, exposure, and potential loss to the organization; and the approximate starting date for each audit.

Audit Scope

The scope of the internal auditing function should not include reviewing the strategic management process, assessing the quality of management decision making both qualitatively and quantitatively, and reporting the results to the audit committee. Strategic planning and decision making are the basic duties of senior management, and auditors may not be qualified to perform such reviews.

Internal audit goals should be available and measurable. Examples of goals include training hours completed, audit hours completed against plans, number of audits completed against plan, number of locations or divisions audited, percentage of company activities audited, and number of auditors certified. Comparison of the audit plan to actual audit activity will indicate whether the audit department has met its goal of implementing broader audit coverage.

The requirements for staffing level, education, training, and audit research should be included in the annual plan for the department. The operating plan for the department should include a prioritized listing of all audits, staffing, a detailed expense budget, and the targeted start date and completion date of each audit along with measurability criteria. "Audit work schedules" is one factor for a direct input to the department's financial budget.

The most likely source for planning staffing requirements would be discussions of audit needs with executive management and the audit committee. The least likely sources would be: reviewing audit staff education and training records, reviewing audit staff size and composition of similar-size companies in the same industry, and interviewing the existing audit staff.

The long-range schedule is an audit-planning tool that is general in nature and is used to ensure adequate audit coverage over time. Requirements of a long-range audit plan include that it be consistent with the department's charter, be capable of being accomplished, and contains a list of auditable activities.

KEY CONCEPTS TO REMEMBER: AUDIT PLANNING

- The audit charter is a long-term document, but is not a planning tool.
- The audit schedule is a long-range planning tool.
- The audit department budget is a midrange planning tool.
- The audit program is a short-range planning tool.
- When auditors are transferred from an operating department of the company, they should not be assigned to an audit of their previous department.

(iii) **Audit assignment.** Documentation needed to plan an audit assignment should include evidence that resources needed to complete the audit were considered. When the audit director makes audit assignments for inclusion in the work schedule, those assignments should be based on the relative risk of the auditable areas.

For example, if audit resources are scarce and no audits were done before, cash management and credit policy area should be given first priority over: (1) corporate code of ethics and conflict-of-interest policy, (2) employee time-reporting system, or (3) budget preparation and forecasts.

Criteria should be established when the audit resources are limited and a decision has to be made to choose between two operating departments for scheduling an audit. The most important criteria to be considered are: major changes in operations in one of the departments, more opportunities to achieve operating benefits in one of the departments than in the other, and the potential loss is significantly greater in one department than the other. Least important criteria are whether the audit staff has recently added an individual with experience in one of the auditable areas.

(iv) **Activity reports.** Activity reports submitted periodically by the audit director to management and to the board should compare performance with audit work schedules. This requires comparing audits completed with audits planned.

(c) **Policies and Procedures.** The director of internal auditing should provide written policies and procedures to guide the audit staff (IIA *Standard* 530). An audit policies and procedures manual is most essential for guiding the audit staff in maintaining daily compliance with the department's standards of performance; and least important to audit quality control reviews, auditor position/job descriptions, and auditor performance appraisals.

(i) **Audit manual.** The need to issue formal manuals will largely depend on the size of the department. As a rule of thumb, any department that has more than five staff members, or whose auditors work alone, should probably have one. The audit department manual should address such things as administrative matters (e.g., progress reports, time and attendance, travel), adherence to department's guidelines, relationships with auditees, auditing techniques, reporting audit results, working paper standards (whether paper media, electronic media, or a combination). The manual should not stifle the creativity and initiative of the auditor.

Written policies and procedures should give consideration to the structure and size of the department and the complexity of the audit work performed. For example, the policies for a large internal audit department should be in considerable detail since many people are involved, which leads to many interpretations and confusion. For a small department, too much detail is not necessary.

(ii) **Staff meetings.** Staff meetings should be conducted periodically to improve communications. Internal audit staff members should be afforded an appropriate means through which they can discuss problems and receive updates regarding departmental policies through periodic staff meetings. The audit director should directly address rumors affecting the audit department and the company in regularly scheduled staff meetings.

(iii) **Conflict of interest.** Independence of the internal auditor is best promoted when there is a policy that requires auditors to report to the director any situation in which a conflict of interest or bias on the part of the individual auditor is present.

(iv) **Audit reports.** A report issued by an internal auditor should contain an expression of opinion when an opinion will improve communications with the reader of the report. Due professional care requires that the auditor's opinions be based on sufficient factual evidence that warrants the expression of the opinions. Due care does not require the performance of extensive audit examination. It calls for reasonable work.

The audit director or designee is responsible for the distribution of the audit report. Internal auditing reports should be distributed to those members of the organization who are able to ensure that audit results are given due consideration. For high-level managers of the organization, that requirement can be satisfied with summary reports.

The type of audit report (final, interim, or combination), the form of communication (oral, written, or combination), the type of audience to receive the audit report (internal management, external auditors, or combination), and the type of participants (by job title in the audit and the auditee department) to attend the entrance conference and the exit audit conference should be spelled out in the audit department policies and procedures manual.

For example: (1) An audit report with routine findings in the accounts payable department should be distributed to the accounts payable supervisor, the accounts payable manager, the division general manager, the external auditor, and the corporate controller, but not to the audit committee or senior management. (2) If an audit is done in the sales department, a copy of the audit report should be sent to the sales director and vice president of marketing. (3) Attendees to be invited for the exit conference for an audit of an automated accounts receivable system would include the head of the audit team, the manager of the accounts receivable department, and the manager of information technology (IT).

An audit policy should require that final audit reports would not be issued without a management response. However, when an audit with significant findings is complete except for management's response, the best alternative is to issue an interim report regarding the important issues noted. This is because time is of the essence here.

The final audit report should be reviewed, approved, and signed by the director of internal auditing or his designee. When illegal acts are being performed by several of the highest-ranking officers for the company, the audit report should be addressed to the audit committee of the board of directors.

(v) **Follow-up.** The audit director should ensure follow-up of prior audit findings and recommendations to determine if corrective action was taken and is achieving the desired results. If the auditor finds that no corrective action has been taken on a prior audit finding that is still valid, the auditor should determine whether management or the board has assumed the risk of not taking corrective action.

There will be circumstances where, upon reviewing the results of the audit report with the audit committee, executive management decides to accept the risk of not implementing corrective action on certain audit findings. The best alternative for the internal audit director is that internal audit responsibility has been discharged, and no further audit action is required.

(d) **Personnel Management and Development.** The director of internal auditing should establish a program for selecting and developing the human resources of the internal auditing department. A well-developed set of selection criteria is a key factor to the success of an audit department's human resource program.

(i) **Hiring.** The audit staff should include members proficient in applying internal auditing standards, procedures, and techniques. When hiring an entry-level audit staff, the most likely predictors of the applicant's success as an auditor would be the ability to organize and express thoughts well; the least likely predictors would be: grade point average on college accounting courses, ability to fit well socially into a group, and the level of detail knowledge of the company. When hiring an auditor, reasonable assurance should be obtained as to each prospective auditor's qualifications and proficiency. It should include obtaining college transcript(s), checking an applicant's references, and determining previous job experience.

If one auditor has a thorough understanding of internal auditing techniques, accounting, and principles of management, and has limited knowledge of economics and computer science, it would be appropriate to hire the person if other auditors possess sufficient knowledge of economics and computer science.

The audit director should hire auditors who collectively have the knowledge and skills needed to complete all internal audit assignments. The audit director is responsible for: developing formal job descriptions for the audit staff, selecting qualified individuals, and performing an annual review of each auditor's performance.

The audit director may hire a professional engineer who applied for a position in the audit department of a high-technology firm in spite of the lack of knowledge of internal auditing standards.

The capabilities of individual staff members are key features in the effectiveness of an internal auditing department. Job descriptions should be used as a primary consideration when staffing the department.

The audit department usually hires a management trainee. The most appropriate staffing control for hiring the management trainees is a plan for recruiting, selecting, and training. This plan would give a clear picture to the trainee about his movement within the company over a period of time.

(ii) **Selection criteria.** The audit director should establish the evaluation criteria for the selection of new internal audit staff members. Criteria would be an appreciation of the fundamentals of accounting, an understanding of management principles, and the ability to recognize deviations from good business practices. Criteria would not include proficiency in computerized operations and the use of computers in auditing.

(iii) **Performance criteria.** The audit director should establish guidelines for evaluating the performance of audit staff members. These guidelines include: (1) the evaluator should justify very high and very low evaluations because of their impact on the employee, (2) evaluations should be made annually or more frequently to provide the employee feedback about competence, and (3) the first evaluation should be made shortly after commencing work to serve as an early guide to the new employee. But the evaluator should not use standard evaluation comments because there are so many employees whose performance is completely satisfactory. The performance appraisal system for evaluating an auditor should include specific accomplishments directly related to the performance of the audit program.

(iv) **Continuing education.** The director of audit is responsible for establishing continuing education and training opportunities to develop the human resources of the audit department. The main purpose of audit department training is to achieve both individual and departmental goals in training. Continuing education is a form of ongoing training.

(e) **External Auditors.** The director of internal auditing should coordinate internal and external audit efforts to minimize duplication of audit work and to increase the effectiveness of audit work.

EXAMPLE: Coordination between internal and external auditors

Background. *A parent company has many domestic and foreign subsidiaries, which are audited by different external auditors with direct assistance provided by internal auditors. The foreign subsidiary's external audit firms like to rely on some of the work performed by the parent company's external audit firm.*

Situation 1. *When the subsidiary's external audit firm asked the internal audit director for copies of the parent company's external audit firm's working paper, the internal audit director should notify the parent company's external audit firm of the situation and request that either they provide the working papers or authorize the director to do so. This is because: (1) the internal audit director has copies of audit programs and selected working papers produced by each external audit firm, and (2) a part of the parent company's external audit was conducted by the internal audit department.*

Situation 2. *When the foreign subsidiary's external auditors have requested copies of the internal audit working papers in order to place reliance on the internal audit work performed, then the internal audit director should comply with the request.*

SOURCE: CIA Examination.

(f) **Quality Assurance.** The director of internal auditing should establish and maintain a quality assurance program to evaluate the operations of the internal auditing department. The standard calls for three elements for the quality assurance program: supervision, internal reviews, and external reviews. The audit department should have periodic quality assurance reviews.

(i) **Supervision.** Supervision is a continuing process beginning with planning and ending with conclusion of the audit assignment. The best control over the work on which audit opinions are based is supervisory review of all audit work. The director is responsible for providing appropriate audit supervision. Internal audits should be properly supervised in order to produce professional audits of consistently high quality.

Periodic and formal *internal reviews* of the audit department by members of the audit department staff primarily serve the needs of the director of internal auditing, not the board of directors, not the audit staff, and not the executive management.

The peer review process can be performed internally or externally. A distinguishing feature of the *external review* is its objective to provide an independent evaluation.

AUDIT QUALITY CONTROL SYSTEM: ESSENTIAL ELEMENTS

Importance of Audit Quality

A high-quality job greatly increases the probability that audit results will be relied on and recommended improvements will be seriously considered and implemented. The audit organization's reputation for consistent high-quality work helps ensure that decision makers will more readily and more assuredly accept findings and implement recommendations.

The quality control system should define principles, policies, and procedures that will achieve the consistent quality of work that the organization expects. The quality should be built-in at every stage of the audit, that is, from planning to follow-up.

Preaudit Quality Review

Selecting those jobs that will make a contribution: doing the right job. Each audit job requires resources that could have been used on another job. Most audit organizations have must-do jobs. They also have considerable latitude in using the rest of their resources to seek a balanced portfolio—based on needs, capability, and resources. In exercising that latitude, audit staff should be able to answer questions such as: Is the job selection a wise one? Does it respond appropriately to a request or to user needs? Does the job help build staff capability? Are the benefits of the job greater than could have been obtained if other work were done? How do you know?

Ensuring the quality of each assignment: doing the job right. Doing a job right requires efficient use of resources and high effectiveness. Key questions include: Are assignment objectives clear and responsive to customer needs? Is the assignment scoped to meet objectives? Is the audit methodology appropriate? Is job planning adequate? Are staff motivated and well supervised? Are assignment results effectively communicated?

INTERNAL AUDIT AND TOTAL QUALITY MANAGEMENT

An audit assignment can go wrong at any stage. It can be ill conceived, improperly directed, poorly planned, or badly implemented, and its results can be ineffectively communicated. For a variety of reasons, it can fail to meet its customers' needs.

An appropriate quality control system identifies or flags those factors that could jeopardize the quality of an audit and establishes processes or procedures that promptly identify and correct problems before they occur. For example, it will be more effective to correct a planning-related problem in the planning phase than to correct it in a later phase (e.g., reporting phase).

(ii) **Accomplishing intended results.** Audit work is performed for a wide variety of reasons—to accomplish a range of objectives. Most jobs seek results that improve the auditee's operation. The right job done the right way provides the best opportunity to get desired results for the auditor and the audit organization. Were the results of our work used? Did we have a beneficial impact? Did we make the difference our work sought? If staff members can answer those questions positively, they are providing the quality service that stakeholders can expect every time.

(iii) **Demonstrating consistent quality.** Care is taken to build quality into audit job selection, planning, performance, reporting, and follow-up. Individual jobs are to be given a final quality check before the report is issued. But how well have all those audit policies, procedures, and processes actually worked? Are you satisfied that they were followed, fit together, and accomplished intended results? Can we satisfy peers that the organization's work is of high quality, meeting applicable professional standards (IIA)?

The final quality check consists of two tests: (1) an independent verification of the evidence supporting the product (referencing) and (2) product review. Questions to answer include

- Have the working papers received appropriate supervisory review?
- Are facts and figures correctly reported as determined by satisfactory evidence in the working papers or by independent mathematical or other checks?

Referencer Alert

The referencer should also be alert to pertinent evidence in the working papers that either contradicts or calls into question facts or statements in the report (negative assurance). Such observations should be noted for management consideration.

- Are findings adequately supported by the facts in the working papers?
- Do conclusions and recommendations flow logically from the findings?
- Have the auditee's views been accurately reported, and are points made in rebuttal accurate and adequately supported?
- Has a qualified person who is not involved in the assignment examined highly technical data? Are the results of that examination documented in the working papers?

A checklist for an audit product review (Audit Report) ensures that

- Higher-level managers are satisfied with the overall quality of the product (i.e., audit report).
- The message is sound, addresses the objectives, and meets the customers' needs.
- The message is consistent with prior positions.
- Key units of the audit organization had an opportunity to review the product and agreed with the message.
- The auditee's views are appropriately reflected and key differences have been adequately addressed.

(g) **Postaudit Quality Review.** The postaudit quality review provides top managers with an independent assessment of the extent to which the audit organization complies with professional standards and its own policies and procedures. In reviewing compliance with professional standards and policies and procedures, these questions should be answered.

- Are policies clearly stated and are they achievable? Do they cover key matters on which guidance would be helpful?
- Are policies unnecessarily prescriptive, or do they leave room for using initiative and objectivity in meeting assignment objectives?
- Are policies and procedures readily accessible by the audit staff?
- Has the audit staff been adequately trained in the organization's policies and procedures?
- How is compliance with policies and procedures assessed?

Reviewing individual assignments provides valuable feedback to managers on how well-selected auditable units consistently achieve the expected quality. The number and type of assignments selected for testing should provide a reasonable basis for making this assessment. In reviewing individual assignments, these questions should be answered.

- Was the audit team collectively qualified for the tasks required? Did individual staff members meet applicable continuing professional education requirements?
- Do the working papers indicate any unresolved questions concerning external or personal impairments to independence?

INTERNAL AUDIT AND TOTAL QUALITY MANAGEMENT

An effective quality control system needs to do more than ensure the quality with which work was performed. It also needs to determine what the work accomplished and how customers and stakeholders viewed the result. This can be done by system approaches such as surveys of customers and stakeholders, recommendation tracking and reporting system, and auditor performance measurements and award/reward systems.

- Was there adequate evidence that a determination was made of applicable standards and that they were complied with?
- Were assignment objectives clear and responsive to requesters' or auditees' needs? Was the assignment scope adequate? Was methodology appropriate? Were data sources, methodology, and data collection instruments tested? Was a detailed audit plan prepared?
- Was the assignment plan effectively implemented? Were deviations from the plan consistent with professional standards and appropriate to assignment objectives? Were the working papers adequately document, summarized, indexed, and reviewed?
- Was there evidence that supervision was timely, adequate, and responsive to audit staff needs and professional development?
- Were applicable internal controls identified, tested, and appropriately relied on?
- Was compliance with laws and regulations applicable to assignment objectives appropriately tested?
- Were findings and conclusions supported in the working papers, and was the evidence relevant, competent, and sufficient?
- Were auditees' positions on findings and recommendations obtained and appropriately handled in report development and presentation?
- Was the audit report timely?
- Did conclusions follow reasonably from the findings?
- Were recommendations responsive to the root cause of deficiencies detected? Were they clearly achievable and cost-effective?
- Was there adequate evidence that the facts in the report were independently referenced? Were the referencer's questions appropriately handled?
- Was the report reviewed for logic and consistency of positions taken?[1]

1.2 *International Standards for the Professional Practice of Internal Auditing (Standards)*

Internal auditing is an independent, objective assurance and consulting activity designed to add value and improve an organization's operations. It helps an organization accomplish its objectives by bringing a systematic, disciplined approach to evaluate and improve the effectiveness of risk management, control, and governance processes.

Internal audit activities are performed in diverse legal and cultural environments; within organizations that vary in purpose, size, complexity, and structure; and by persons within or outside the organization. While differences may affect the practice of internal auditing in each environment, compliance with the *International Standards for the Professional Practice of Internal Auditing* is essential if the responsibilities of internal auditors are to be met. If internal auditors are prohibited by laws or regulations from complying with certain parts of the *Standards*, they should comply with all other parts of the *Standards* and make appropriate disclosures.

---

[1] ***An Audit Quality Control System: Essential Elements*** *(Washington, DC: U.S. General Accounting Office, August 1993).*

Assurance services involve the internal auditor's objective assessment of evidence to provide an independent opinion or conclusions regarding a process, system, or other subject matter. The nature and scope of the assurance engagement are determined by the internal auditor. There are generally three parties involved in assurance services: (1) the person or group directly involved with the process, system, or other subject matter—the process owner, (2) the person or group making the assessment—the internal auditor, and (3) the person or group using the assessment—the user.

Consulting services are advisory in nature, and are generally performed at the specific request of an engagement client. The nature and scope of the consulting engagement are subject to agreement with the engagement client. Consulting services generally involve two parties: (1) the person or group offering the advice—the internal auditor, and (2) the person or group seeking and receiving the advice—the engagement client. When performing consulting services, the internal auditor should maintain objectivity and not assume management responsibility.

The four purposes of the *Standards* are to

1. Delineate basic principles that represent the practice of internal auditing as it should be.
2. Provide a framework for performing and promoting a broad range of value-added internal audit activities.
3. Establish the basis for the *evaluation* of internal audit performance.
4. Foster improved organizational processes and operations.

The *Standards* consist of *Attribute Standards, Performance Standards,* and *Implementation Standards.* The *Attribute Standards* address the characteristics of organizations and parties performing internal audit activities. The *Performance Standards* describe the nature of internal audit activities and provide quality criteria against which the performance of these services can be evaluated. While the *Attribute and Performance Standards* apply to all internal audit services, the *Implementation Standards* apply to specific types of engagements.

There is one set of *Attribute and Performance Standards*; however, there are multiple sets of *Implementation Standards*: a set for each of the major types of internal audit activity. The *Implementation Standards* have been established for assurance (A) and consulting (C) activities.

The *Standards* are part of the Professional Practices Framework. The Professional Practices Framework includes the Definition of Internal Auditing, the Code of Ethics, the *Standards*, and other guidance. Guidance regarding how the *Standards* might be applied is included in Practice Advisories that are issued by the Professional Issues Committee.

1.3 IIA's *Attribute Standards*

(a) Purpose, Authority, and Responsibility

1000—Purpose, Authority, and Responsibility—The purpose, authority, and responsibility of the internal audit activity should be formally defined in a charter, consistent with the Standards, and approved by the board.

1000.A1—The nature of assurance services provided to the organization should be defined in the audit charter. If assurances are to be provided to parties outside the organization, the nature of these assurances should also be defined in the charter

1000.C1—The nature of consulting services should be defined in the audit charter.

IIA's Practice Advisory 1000-1: Internal Audit Charter

Nature of This Practice Advisory

Internal auditors should consider these suggestions when adopting an internal audit charter. This guidance is not intended to represent all the considerations that may be necessary when adopting a charter, but simply a recommended set of items that should be addressed. *Compliance with Practice Advisories is optional.*

1. The purpose, authority, and responsibility of the internal audit activity should be defined in a charter. The chief audit executive (CAE) should seek approval of the charter by senior management as well as acceptance by the board. The approval of the charter should be documented in the governing body minutes. The charter should (a) establish the internal audit activity's position within

the organization; (b) authorize access to records, personnel, and physical properties relevant to the performance of engagements; and (c) define the scope of internal audit activities.

2. The internal audit activity's charter should be in writing. A written statement provides formal communication for review and approval by management and for acceptance by the board. It also facilitates a periodic assessment of the adequacy of the internal audit activity's purpose, authority, and responsibility. Providing a formal, written document containing the charter of the internal audit activity is critical in managing the auditing function within the organization. The purpose, authority, and responsibility should be defined and communicated to establish the role of the internal audit activity and to provide a basis for management and the board to use in evaluating the operations of the function. If a question should arise, the charter also provides a formal, written agreement with management and the board about the role and responsibilities of the internal audit activity within the organization.
3. The CAE should periodically assess whether the purpose, authority, and responsibility, as defined in the charter, continue to be adequate to enable the internal audit activity to accomplish its objectives. The result of this periodic assessment should be communicated to senior management and the board.

IIA's Practice Advisory 1000.C1-1: Principles Guiding the Performance of Consulting Activities of Internal Auditors

Nature of This Practice Advisory

The definition of internal auditing states: "Internal auditing is an independent, objective assurance and consulting activity designed to add value and improve an organization's operations. It helps an organization accomplish its objectives by bringing a systematic, disciplined approach to evaluate and improve the effectiveness of risk management, control, and governance processes." Internal auditors are reminded that the *Attribute and Performance Standards* relate to internal auditors performing both assurance and consulting engagements.

This advisory focuses on broad parameters to be considered in all consulting engagements. Consulting may range from formal engagements, defined by written agreements, to advisory activities, such as participating in standing or temporary management committees or project teams. Internal auditors are expected to use professional judgment to determine the extent to which the guidance provided in this advisory should be applied in each given situation. Special consulting engagements, such as participation in a merger or acquisition project, or in emergency engagements, such as disaster recovery activities, may require departure from normal or established procedures for conducting consulting engagements.

Internal auditors should consider these guiding principles when performing consulting engagements. This guidance is not intended to represent all the considerations that may be necessary in performing a consulting engagement and internal auditors should take extra precautions to determine that management and the board understand and agree with the concept, operating guidelines, and communications required for performing consulting services. *Compliance with Practice Advisories is optional. This guidance is repeated in Part 1 and Part 2 for proper coverage of the subject matter.*

1. **Value proposition.** The value proposition of the internal audit activity is realized within every organization that employs internal auditors in a manner that suits the culture and resources of that organization. That value proposition is captured in the definition of internal auditing and includes assurance and consulting activities designed to add value to the organization by bringing a systematic, disciplined approach to the areas of governance, risk, and control.
2. **Consistency with internal audit definition.** A disciplined, systematic evaluation methodology is incorporated in each internal audit activity. The list of services can generally be incorporated into the broad categories of assurance and consulting. However, the services may also include evolving forms of value-adding services that are consistent with the broad definition of internal auditing.
3. **Audit activities beyond assurance and consulting.** There are multiple internal auditing services. Assurance and consulting are not mutually exclusive and do not preclude other auditing services, such as investigations and nonauditing roles. Many audit services will have both an assurance and consultative (advising) role.

4. **Interrelationship between assurance and consulting.** Internal audit consulting enriches value-adding internal auditing. While consulting is often the direct result of assurance services, it should also be recognized that assurance could also be generated from consulting engagements.
5. **Empower consulting through the internal audit charter.** Internal auditors have traditionally performed many types of consulting services, ranging from the analysis of controls built into developing systems, analysis of security products, serving on task forces to analyze operations and make recommendations, and so forth. The board (or audit committee) should empower the internal audit activity to perform additional services where they do not represent a conflict of interest or detract from its obligations to the committee. That empowerment should be reflected in the internal audit charter.
6. **Objectivity.** Consulting services may enhance the auditor's understanding of business processes or issues related to an assurance engagement and do not necessarily impair the auditor's or the internal audit activity's objectivity. Internal auditing is not a management decision-making function. Decisions to adopt or implement recommendations made as a result of an internal audit advisory service should be made by management. Therefore, internal audit objectivity should not be impaired by the decisions made by management.
7. **Internal audit foundation for consulting services.** Much of consulting is a natural extension of assurance and investigative services and may represent informal or formal advice, analysis, or assessments. The internal audit activity is uniquely positioned to perform this type of consulting work based on (a) its adherence to the highest standards of objectivity and (b) its breadth of knowledge about organizational processes, risks, and strategies.
8. **Communication of fundamental information.** A primary internal audit value is to provide assurance to senior management and audit committee directors. Consulting engagements cannot be rendered in a manner that masks information that in the CAE's judgment should be presented to senior executives and board members. All consulting is to be understood in that context.
9. **Principles of consulting understood by the organization.** Organizations must have ground rules for the performance of consulting services that are understood by all members of an organization. These rules should be codified in the audit charter approved by the audit committee and promulgated in the organization.
10. **Formal consulting engagements.** Management often engages outside consultants for formal consulting engagements that last a significant period of time. However, an organization may find that the internal audit activity is uniquely qualified for some formal consulting tasks. If an internal audit activity undertakes to perform a formal consulting engagement, the internal audit group should bring a systematic, disciplined approach to the conduct of the engagement.
11. **CAE responsibilities.** Consulting services permit the CAE to enter into dialog with management to address specific managerial issues. In this dialog, the breadth of the engagement and time frames is made responsive to management needs. However, the CAE retains the prerogative of setting the audit techniques and the right of reporting to senior executives and audit committee members when the nature and materiality of results pose significant risks to the organization.
12. **Criteria for resolving conflicts or evolving issues.** An internal auditor is first and foremost an internal auditor. Thus, in the performance of all services, the internal auditor is guided by the IIA's Code of Ethics and the *Attribute and Performance Standards* of the *International Standards for the Professional Practice of Internal Auditing (Standards).* Any unforeseen conflicts or activities should be resolved consistent with the Code of Ethics and *Standards.*

IIA's Practice Advisory 1000.C1-2: Additional Considerations for Formal Consulting Engagements

Nature of This Practice Advisory

This Practice Advisory is similar in subject matter to Practice Advisory 1000.C1-1, which discusses the Principles Guiding the Performance of Consulting Services, and both advisories are useful to internal auditors in performing consulting activities. The definition of internal auditing states: "Internal auditing is an independent, objective assurance and *consulting* activity designed to add value and improve an organization's operations. It helps an organization accomplish its objectives by bringing a systematic, disciplined approach to evaluate and improve the effectiveness of risk management, control, and governance processes." Internal auditors are reminded that the *Attribute and Performance Standards* relate to internal auditors performing both assurance and consulting engagements.

This Practice Advisory focuses on broad parameters to be considered in formal consulting engagements. Consulting may range from formal engagements, defined by written agreements, to advisory activities, such as, participating in standing or temporary management committees or project teams. Internal auditors are expected to use professional judgment to determine the extent to which the guidance provided in this advisory should be applied in each given situation. Special consulting engagements, such as participation in a merger or acquisition project and in an emergency engagement (e.g., a review of disaster recovery activities), may require departure from normal or established procedures for conducting consulting engagements.

Internal auditors should consider these suggestions when performing formal consulting engagements. This guidance is not intended to represent all the considerations that may be necessary in performing a consulting engagement and internal auditors should take extra precautions to determine that management and the board understand and agree with the concept, operating guidelines, and communications required for performing formal consulting services. *Compliance with Practice Advisories is optional. This guidance is repeated in Part 1 and Part 2 for proper coverage of the subject matter.*

Definition of Consulting Services

1. The Glossary in the *International Standards for the Professional Practice of Internal Auditing (Standards)* defines "consulting services" as: "Advisory and related client service activities, the nature and scope of which are agreed with the client and which are intended to add value and improve an organization's governance, risk management, and control processes without the internal auditor assuming management responsibility. Examples include counsel, advice, facilitation, and training."
2. The CAE should determine the methodology to use for classifying engagements within the organization. In some circumstances, it may be appropriate to conduct a "blended" engagement that incorporates elements of both consulting and assurance activities into one consolidated approach. In other cases, it may be appropriate to distinguish between the assurance and consulting components of the engagement.
3. Internal auditors may conduct consulting services as part of their normal or routine activities as well as in response to requests by management. Each organization should consider the type of consulting activities to be offered and determine if specific policies or procedures should be developed for each type of activity. Possible categories could include

    - Formal consulting engagements—Planned and subject to written agreement
    - Informal consulting engagements—Routine activities, such as participation on standing committees, limited-life projects, ad hoc meetings, and routine information exchange
    - Special consulting engagements—Participation on a merger and acquisition team or system conversion team
    - Emergency consulting engagements—Participation on a team established for recovery or maintenance of operations after a disaster or other extraordinary business event or a team assembled to supply temporary help to meet a special request or unusual deadline

4. Auditors generally should not agree to conduct a consulting engagement simply to circumvent, or to allow others to circumvent, requirements that would normally apply to an assurance engagement if the service in question is more appropriately conducted as an assurance engagement. This does not preclude adjusting methodologies where services once conducted as assurance engagements are deemed more suitable to being performed as a consulting engagement.

Independence and Objectivity in Consulting Engagements (Standard 1130.C1)

5. Internal auditors are sometimes requested to provide consulting services relating to operations for which they had previous responsibilities or had conducted assurance services. Prior to offering consulting services, the CAE should confirm that the board understands and approves the concept of providing consulting services. Once approved, the internal audit charter should be amended to include authority and responsibilities for consulting activities, and the internal audit activity should develop appropriate policies and procedures for conducting such engagements.

6. Internal auditors should maintain their objectivity when drawing conclusions and offering advice to management. If impairments to independence or objectivity exist prior to commencement of the consulting engagement, or subsequently develop during the engagement, disclosure should be made immediately to management.
7. Independence and objectivity may be impaired if assurance services are provided within one year after a formal consulting engagement. Steps can be taken to minimize the effects of impairment by assigning different auditors to perform each of the services, establishing independent management and supervision, defining separate accountability for the results of the projects, and disclosing the presumed impairment. Management should be responsible for accepting and implementing recommendations.
8. Care should be taken, particularly involving consulting engagements that are ongoing or continuous in nature, so that internal auditors do not inappropriately or unintentionally assume management responsibilities that were not intended in the original objectives and scope of the engagement.

Due Professional Care in Consulting Engagements (Standards 1210.C1, 1220.C1, 2130.C1, and 2201.C1)

9. The internal auditor should exercise due professional care in conducting a formal consulting engagement by understanding the
   - Needs of management officials, including the nature, timing, and communication of engagement results
   - Possible motivations and reasons of those requesting the service
   - Extent of work needed to achieve the engagement's objectives
   - Skills and resources needed to conduct the engagement
   - Effect on the scope of the audit plan previously approved by the audit committee
   - Potential impact on future audit assignments and engagements
   - Potential organizational benefits to be derived from the engagement
10. In addition to the independence and objectivity evaluation and due professional care considerations just described, the internal auditor should
    - Conduct appropriate meetings and gather necessary information to assess the nature and extent of the service to be provided.
    - Confirm that those receiving the service understand and agree with the relevant guidance contained in the internal audit charter, internal audit activity's policies and procedures, and other related guidance governing the conduct of consulting engagements. The internal auditor should decline to perform consulting engagements that are prohibited by the terms of the internal audit charter, conflict with the policies and procedures of the internal audit activity, or do not add value and promote the best interests of the organization.
    - Evaluate the consulting engagement for compatibility with the internal audit activity's overall plan of engagements. The internal audit activity's risk-based plan of engagements may incorporate and rely on consulting engagements, to the extent deemed appropriate, to provide necessary audit coverage to the organization.
    - Document general terms, understandings, deliverables, and other key factors of the formal consulting engagement in a written agreement or plan. It is essential that both the internal auditor and those receiving the consulting engagement understand and agree with the reporting and communication requirements.

Scope of Work in Consulting Engagements (Standards 2010.C1, 2110.C1 and C2, 2120.C1 and C2, 2201.C1, 2210.C1, 2220.C1, 2240.C1, and 2440.C2)

11. As observed, internal auditors should reach an understanding about the objectives and scope of the consulting engagement with those receiving the service. Any reservations about the value, benefit, or possible negative implications of the consulting engagement should be communicated to those receiving the service. Internal auditors should design the scope of work to ensure that professionalism, integrity, credibility, and reputation of the internal audit activity will be maintained.

12. In planning formal consulting engagements, internal auditors should design objectives to meet the appropriate needs of management officials receiving these services. In the case of special requests by management, internal auditors may consider these actions if they believe that the objectives that should be pursued go beyond those requested by management.
    - Persuade management to include the additional objectives in the consulting engagement; or
    - Document the fact that the objectives were not pursued and disclose that observation in the final communication of consulting engagement results; and
    - Include the objectives in a separate and subsequent assurance engagement.
13. Work programs for formal consulting engagements should document the objectives and scope of the engagement as well as the methodology to be used in satisfying the objectives. The form and content of the program may vary depending on the nature of the engagement. In establishing the scope of the engagement, internal auditors may expand or limit the scope to satisfy management's request. However, the internal auditor should be satisfied that the projected scope of work will be adequate to meet the objectives of the engagement. The objectives, scope, and terms of the engagement should be periodically reassessed and adjusted during the course of the work.
14. Internal auditors should be observant of the effectiveness of risk management and control processes during formal consulting engagements. Substantial risk exposures or material control weaknesses should be brought to the attention of management. In some situations, the auditor's concerns should also be communicated to executive management, the audit committee, and/or the board of directors. Auditors should use professional judgment (a) to determine the significance of exposures or weaknesses and the actions taken or contemplated to mitigate or correct these exposures or weaknesses and (b) to ascertain the expectations of executive management, the audit committee, and board in having these matters reported.

Communicating the Results of Consulting Engagements (Standards 2410.C1 and 2440.C1)

15. Communication of the progress and results of consulting engagements will vary in form and content depending on the nature of the engagement and the needs of the client. Reporting requirements are generally determined by those requesting the consulting service and should meet the objectives as determined and agreed to with management. However, the format for communicating the results of the consulting engagement should clearly describe the nature of the engagement and any limitations, restrictions, or other factors about which users of the information should be made aware.
16. In some circumstances, the internal auditor may conclude that the results should be communicated beyond those who received or requested the service. In such cases, the internal auditor should expand the reporting so that results are communicated to the appropriate parties. When expanding the reporting to other parties, the auditor should conduct these steps until satisfied with the resolution of the matter.
    - Determine what direction is provided in the agreement concerning the consulting engagement and related communications.
    - Attempt to convince those receiving or requesting the service to expand voluntarily the communication to the appropriate parties.
    - Determine what guidance is provided in the internal audit charter or audit activity's policies and procedures concerning consulting communications.
    - Determine what guidance is provided in the organization's code of conduct, code of ethics, and other relative policies, administrative directives, or procedures.
    - Determine what guidance is provided by the IIA's *Standards* and Code of Ethics, other standards or codes applicable to the auditor, and any legal or regulatory requirements that relate to the matter under consideration.
17. Internal auditors should disclose to management, the audit committee, board, or other governing body of the organization the nature, extent, and overall results of formal consulting engagements along with other reports of internal auditing activities. Internal auditors should keep executive management and the audit committee informed about how audit resources are being deployed. Neither detailed reports of these consulting engagements nor the specific results and recommendations are required to be communicated. But an appropriate description of these types of en-

gagements and their significant recommendations should be communicated and is essential in satisfying the internal auditor's responsibility in complying with Standard 2060, Reporting to the Board and Senior Management.

Documentation Requirements for Consulting Engagements (Standard 2330.C1)

18. Internal auditors should document the work performed to achieve the objectives of a formal consulting engagement and support its results. However, documentation requirements applicable to assurance engagements do not necessarily apply to consulting engagements.
19. Auditors are encouraged to adopt appropriate record retention policies and address related issues, such as ownership of consulting engagement records, in order to protect the organization adequately and to avoid potential misunderstandings involving requests for these records. Situations involving legal proceedings, regulatory requirements, tax issues, and accounting matters may call for special handling of certain consulting engagement records.

Monitoring of Consulting Engagements (Standard 2500.C1)

20. The internal audit activity should monitor the results of consulting engagements to the extent agreed on with the client. Varying types of monitoring may be appropriate for differing types of consulting engagements. The monitoring effort may depend on factors such as management's explicit interest in the engagement or the internal auditor's assessment of the project's risks or value to the organization.

(b) **Independence and Objectivity**

1100—Independence and Objectivity—The internal audit activity should be independent, and internal auditors should be objective in performing their work.
1110—Organizational Independence—The chief audit executive should report to a level within the organization that allows the internal audit activity to fulfill its responsibilities.

1110.A1—The internal audit activity should be free from interference in determining the scope of internal auditing, performing work, and communicating results.

1120—Individual Objectivity—Internal auditors should have an impartial, unbiased attitude and avoid conflicts of interest.
1130—Impairments to Independence or Objectivity—If independence or objectivity is impaired in fact or appearance, the details of the impairment should be disclosed to appropriate parties. The nature of the disclosure will depend on the impairment.

1130.A1—Internal auditors should refrain from assessing specific operations for which they were previously responsible. Objectivity is presumed to be impaired if an ***internal*** auditor provides assurance services for an activity for which the ***internal*** auditor had responsibility within the previous year.
1130.A2—Assurance engagements for functions over which the chief audit executive has responsibility should be overseen by a party outside the internal audit activity.
1130.C1—Internal auditors may provide consulting services relating to operations for which they had previous responsibilities.
1130.C2—If internal auditors have potential impairments to independence or objectivity relating to proposed consulting services, disclosure should be made to the engagement client prior to accepting the engagement.

IIA's Practice Advisory 1100-1: Independence and Objectivity

Nature of This Practice Advisory

Internal auditors should consider these suggestions when evaluating independence and objectivity. This guidance is not intended to represent all the considerations that may be necessary when conducting such an evaluation, but simply a recommended set of items that should be addressed. *Compliance with Practice Advisories is optional.*

1. Internal auditors are independent when they can carry out their work freely and objectively. Independence permits internal auditors to render the impartial and unbiased judgments essential to the proper conduct of engagements. It is achieved through organizational status and objectivity.

IIA's Practice Advisory 1110-1: Organizational Independence

Nature of This Practice Advisory

Internal auditors should consider these suggestions when evaluating organizational independence. This guidance is not intended to represent all the considerations that may be necessary during such an evaluation, but simply a recommended set of items that should be addressed. *Compliance with Practice Advisories is optional.*

1. Internal auditors should have the support of senior management and of the board so that they can gain the cooperation of engagement clients and perform their work free from interference.
2. The CAE should be responsible to an individual in the organization with sufficient authority to promote independence and to ensure broad audit coverage, adequate consideration of engagement communications, and appropriate action on engagement recommendations.
3. Ideally, the CAE should report functionally to the board and administratively to the chief executive officer of the organization.
4. The CAE should have direct communication with the board. Regular communication with the board helps assure independence and provides a means for the board and the CAE to keep each other informed on matters of mutual interest.
5. Direct communication occurs when the CAE regularly attends and participates in meetings of the board, which relate to its oversight responsibilities for auditing, financial reporting, organizational governance, and control. The CAE's attendance and participation at these meetings provide an opportunity to be appraised of strategic business and operational developments and to raise high-level risk, systems, procedures, or control issues at an early stage. The opportunity is also provided to exchange information concerning the plans and activities of the internal auditing activity. The CAE should meet privately with the board, at least annually.
6. Independence is enhanced when the board concurs in the appointment or removal of the CAE.

IIA's Practice Advisory 1110-2: Chief Audit Executive (CAE) Reporting Lines

Nature of This Practice Advisory

Internal auditors should consider this guidance when establishing or evaluating the reporting lines and relationships with organizational officials to whom the CAE reports. This guidance is not intended to represent all the considerations that may be necessary during such an evaluation, but simply a recommended set of items that should be considered. *Compliance with Practice Advisories is optional.*

1. The IIA's *International Standards for the Professional Practice of Internal Auditing (Standards)* require that the CAE report to a level within the organization that allows the internal audit activity to fulfill its responsibilities. The IIA believes strongly that to achieve necessary independence, the CAE should report functionally to the audit committee or its equivalent. For administrative purposes, in most circumstances, the CAE should report directly to the chief executive officer of the organization. The next descriptions of what the IIA considers "functional reporting" and "administrative reporting" are provided to help focus the discussion in this Practice Advisory.

    - **Functional reporting.** The functional reporting line for the internal audit function is the ultimate source of its independence and authority. As such, the IIA recommends that the CAE report functionally to the audit committee, board of directors, or other appropriate governing authority. In this context, report functionally means that the governing authority would

        - Approve the overall charter of the internal audit function.
        - Approve the internal audit risk assessment and related audit plan.
        - Receive communications from the CAE on the results of the internal audit activities or other matters that the CAE determines are necessary, including private meetings with the CAE without management present.
        - Approve all decisions regarding the appointment or removal of the CAE.
        - Approve the annual compensation and salary adjustment of the CAE.

- Make appropriate inquiries of management and the CAE to determine whether there are scope or budgetary limitations that impede the ability of the internal audit function to execute its responsibilities.

- **Administrative reporting.** Administrative reporting is the reporting relationship within the organization's management structure that facilitates the day-to-day operations of the internal audit function. Administrative reporting typically includes

  - Budgeting and management accounting
  - Human resource administration, including personnel evaluations and compensation
  - Internal communications and information flows
  - Administration of the organization's internal policies and procedures

2. This advisory focuses on considerations in establishing or evaluating CAE reporting lines. Appropriate reporting lines are critical to achieve the independence, objectivity, and organizational stature for an internal audit function necessary to effectively fulfill its obligations. CAE reporting lines are also critical to ensuring the appropriate flow of information and access to key executives and managers that are the foundations of risk assessment and reporting of results of audit activities. Conversely, any reporting relationship that impedes the independence and effective operations of the internal audit function should be viewed by the CAE as a serious scope limitation, which should be brought to the attention of the audit committee or its equivalent.
3. This advisory also recognizes that CAE reporting lines are impacted by the nature of the organization (public or private as well as relative size); common practices of each country; growing complexity of organizations (joint ventures, multinational corporations with subsidiaries); and the trend toward internal audit groups providing value-added services with increased collaboration on priorities and scope with their clients. Accordingly, while the IIA believes that there is an ideal reporting structure with functional reporting to the audit committee and administrative reporting to the CEO, other relationships can be effective if there are clear distinctions between the functional and administrative reporting lines and appropriate activities are in each line to ensure that the independence and scope of activities are maintained. Internal auditors are expected to use professional judgment to determine the extent to which the guidance provided in this advisory should be applied in each given situation.
4. The *Standards* stress the importance of the CAE reporting to an individual with sufficient authority to promote independence and to ensure broad audit coverage. The *Standards* are purposely somewhat generic about reporting relationships, however, because they are designed to be applicable at all organizations regardless of size or any other factors. Factors that make "one size fits all" unattainable include organization size and type of organization (private, governmental, corporate). Accordingly, the CAE should consider these attributes in evaluating the appropriateness of the administrative reporting line.

   - Does the individual have sufficient authority and stature to ensure the effectiveness of the function?
   - Does the individual have an appropriate control and governance mind-set to assist the CAE in their role?
   - Does the individual have the time and interest to actively support the CAE on audit issues?
   - Does the individual understand the functional reporting relationship and support it?

5. The CAE should also ensure that appropriate independence is maintained if the individual responsible for the administrative reporting line is also responsible for other activities in the organization, which are subject to internal audit. For example, some CAEs report administratively to the chief financial officer, who is also responsible for the organization's accounting functions. The internal audit function should be free to audit and report on any activity that also reports to its administrative head if it deems that coverage appropriate for its audit plan. Any limitation in scope or reporting of results of these activities should be brought to the attention of the audit committee.
6. Under the recent move to a stricter legislative and regulatory climate regarding financial reporting around the globe, the CAE's reporting lines should be appropriate to enable the internal audit activity to meet any increased needs of the audit committee or other significant stakeholders. Increasingly, the CAE is being asked to take a more significant role in the organization's governance

and risk management activities. The reporting lines of the CAE should facilitate the ability of the internal audit activity to meet these expectations.

7. Regardless of which reporting relationship the organization chooses, several key actions can help ensure that the reporting lines support and enable the effectiveness and independence of the internal auditing activity.

   - **Functional reporting**
     - The functional reporting line should go directly to the audit committee or its equivalent to ensure the appropriate level of independence and communication.
     - The CAE should meet privately with the audit committee or its equivalent, without management present, to reinforce the independence and nature of this reporting relationship.
     - The audit committee should have the final authority to review and approve the annual audit plan and all major changes to the plan.
     - At all times, the CAE should have open and direct access to the chair of the audit committee and its members; or the chair of the board or full board if appropriate.
     - At least once a year, the audit committee should review the performance of the CAE and approve the annual compensation and salary adjustment.
     - The charter for the internal audit function should clearly articulate both the functional and administrative reporting lines for the function as well as the principal activities directed up each line.
   - **Administrative reporting**
     - The administrative reporting line of the CAE should be to the CEO or another executive with sufficient authority to afford it appropriate support to accomplish its day-to-day activities. This support should include positioning the function and the CAE in the organization's structure in a manner that affords appropriate stature for the function within the organization. Reporting too low in an organization can negatively impact the stature and effectiveness of the internal audit function.
     - The administrative reporting line should not have ultimate authority over the scope or reporting of results of the internal audit activity.
     - The administrative reporting line should facilitate open and direct communications with executive and line management. The CAE should be able to communicate directly with any level of management, including the CEO.
     - The administrative reporting line should enable adequate communications and information flow such that the CAE and the internal audit function have an adequate and timely flow of information concerning the activities, plans, and business initiatives of the organization.
     - Budgetary controls and considerations imposed by the administrative reporting line should not impede the ability of the internal audit function to accomplish its mission.

8. CAEs should also consider their relationships with other control and monitoring functions (risk management, compliance, security, legal, ethics, environmental, external audit) and facilitate the reporting of material risk and control issues to the audit committee.

IIA's Practice Advisory 1110.A1-1: Disclosing Reasons for Information Requests

Nature of This Practice Advisory

Internal auditors should consider these suggestions when requested to disclose reasons for information requests. This guidance is not intended to represent all the considerations that may be necessary, but simply a recommended set of items that should be addressed. *Compliance with Practice Advisories is optional.*

1. At times, an internal auditor may be asked by the engagement client or other parties to explain why a document that has been requested is relevant to an engagement. Disclosure or nondisclosure during the engagement of the reasons why documents are needed should be determined based on the circumstances. Significant irregularities may dictate a less open environment than would normally be conducive to a cooperative engagement. However, that is a judgment that should be made by the chief audit executive in light of the specific circumstances.

IIA's Practice Advisory 1120-1: Individual Objectivity

Nature of This Practice Advisory

Internal auditors should consider these suggestions when evaluating individual objectivity. This guidance is not intended to represent all the considerations that may be necessary during such an evaluation, but simply a recommended set of items that should be addressed. *Compliance with Practice Advisories is optional.*

1. Objectivity is an independent mental attitude that internal auditors should maintain in performing engagements. Internal auditors are not to subordinate their judgment on audit matters to that of others.
2. Objectivity requires internal auditors to perform engagements in such a manner that they have an honest belief in their work product and that no significant quality compromises are made. Internal auditors are not to be placed in situations in which they feel unable to make objective professional judgments.
3. Staff assignments should be made so that potential and actual conflicts of interest and bias are avoided. The chief audit executive should periodically obtain from the internal auditing staff information concerning potential conflicts of interest and bias. Staff assignments of internal auditors should be rotated periodically whenever it is practicable to do so.
4. The results of internal audit work should be reviewed before the related engagement communications are released to provide reasonable assurance that the work was performed objectively.
5. It is unethical for an internal auditor to accept a fee, gift, or entertainment from an employee, client, customer, supplier, or business associate. Accepting a fee, gift, or entertainment may create an appearance that the auditor's objectivity has been impaired. The appearance that objectivity has been impaired may apply to current and future engagements conducted by the auditor. The status of engagements should not be considered as justification for receiving fees, gifts, or entertainment. The receipt of promotional items (i.e., pens, calendars, or samples) that are available to employees and the general public and that have minimal value should not hinder internal auditors' professional judgments. Internal auditors should report the offer of all material fees or gifts immediately to their supervisors.
6. The internal audit activity should adopt a policy that addresses its commitment to conduct activities so as to avoid conflicts of interest and to disclose any activities that could result in a possible conflict of interest.

IIA's Practice Advisory 1130-1: Impairments to Independence or Objectivity

Nature of This Practice Advisory

Internal auditors should consider these suggestions when evaluating impairments to independence or objectivity. This guidance is not intended to represent all the considerations that may be necessary during such an evaluation, but simply a recommended set of items that should be addressed. *Compliance with Practice Advisories is optional.*

1. Internal auditors should report to the CAE any situations in which a conflict of interest or bias is present or may reasonably be inferred. The CAE should then reassign such auditors.
2. A scope limitation is a restriction placed on the internal audit activity that precludes the audit activity from accomplishing its objectives and plans. Among other things, a scope limitation may restrict the
    - Scope defined in the charter
    - Internal audit activity's access to records, personnel, and physical properties relevant to the performance of engagements
    - Approved engagement work schedule
    - Performance of necessary engagement procedures
    - Approved staffing plan and financial budget
3. A scope limitation along with its potential effect should be communicated, preferably in writing, to the board.

4. The CAE should consider whether it is appropriate to inform the board regarding scope limitations that were previously communicated to and accepted by the board. This may be necessary particularly when there have been organization, board, senior management, or other changes.

IIA's Practice Advisory 1130.A1-1: Assessing Operations for Which Internal Auditors Were Previously Responsible

Nature of This Practice Advisory

Internal auditors should consider these suggestions when faced with a situation where the auditors have been assigned to assess an operation for which they were previously responsible. This guidance is not intended to represent all the considerations that may be necessary during such an evaluation, but simply a recommended set of items that should be addressed. *Compliance with Practice Advisories is optional.*

1. Internal auditors should not assume operating responsibilities. If senior management directs internal auditors to perform nonaudit work, it should be understood that they are not functioning as internal auditors. Moreover, objectivity is presumed to be impaired when internal auditors perform an assurance review of any activity for which they had authority or responsibility within the past year. This impairment should be considered when communicating audit engagement results.
    - If internal auditors are directed to perform nonaudit duties that may impair objectivity, such as preparation of bank reconciliations, the chief audit executive should inform senior management and the board that this activity is not an assurance audit activity, and, therefore, audit-related conclusions should not be drawn.
    - In addition, when operating responsibilities are assigned to the internal audit activity, special attention must be given to ensure objectivity when a subsequent assurance engagement in the related operating area is undertaken. Objectivity is presumed to be impaired when internal auditors audit any activity for which they had authority or responsibility within the past year. These facts should be clearly stated when communicating the results of an audit engagement relating to an area where an auditor had operating responsibilities.
2. At any point that assigned activities involve the assumption of operating authority, audit objectivity would be presumed to be impaired with respect to that activity.
3. Persons transferred to or temporarily engaged by the internal audit activity should not be assigned to audit those activities they previously performed until a reasonable period of time (at least one year) has elapsed. Such assignments are presumed to impair objectivity, and additional consideration should be exercised when supervising the engagement work and communicating engagement results.
4. The internal auditor's objectivity is not adversely affected when the auditor recommends standards of control for systems or reviews procedures before they are implemented. The auditor's objectivity is considered to be impaired if the auditor designs, installs, drafts procedures for, or operates such systems.
5. The occasional performance of nonaudit work by the internal auditor, with full disclosure in the reporting process, would not necessarily impair independence. However, it would require careful consideration by management and the internal auditor to avoid adversely affecting the internal auditor's objectivity.

IIA's Practice Advisory 1130.A1-2: The Internal Auditor's Responsibility for Other (Nonaudit) Functions

Nature of This Practice Advisory

This guidance is offered to internal auditors faced with accepting responsibility for nonaudit, operational functions or duties. Acceptance of such responsibilities can impair independence and objectivity and, if possible, should be avoided. This guidance is not intended to represent all the considerations that may be necessary in evaluating such responsibilities or assignments. *Compliance with Practice Advisories is optional.*

1. Some internal auditors have been assigned or accepted nonaudit duties due to a variety of business reasons that make sense to management of the organization. Internal auditors are more frequently

being asked to perform roles and responsibilities that may impair independence or objectivity. Given the increasing demand on organizations, both public and private, to develop more efficient and effective operations and to do so with fewer resources, some internal audit activities are being directed by their organization's management to assume responsibility for operations that are subject to periodic internal auditing assessments.

2. When the internal audit activity or individual internal auditor is responsible for, or management is considering assigning, an operation that it might audit, the internal auditor's independence and objectivity may be impaired. The internal auditor should consider these factors in assessing the impact on independence and objectivity.

   - The requirements of the IIA's Code of Ethics and *International Standards for the Professional Practice of Internal Auditing (Standards)*
   - Expectations of stakeholders that may include the shareholders, board of directors, audit committee, management, legislative bodies, public entities, regulatory bodies, and public interest groups
   - Allowances and/or restrictions contained in the internal audit activity charter
   - Disclosures required by the *Standards*
   - Subsequent audit coverage of the activities or responsibilities accepted by the internal auditor

3. Internal auditors should consider these factors to determine an appropriate course of action when presented with the opportunity of accepting responsibility for a nonaudit function.

   A. The IIA's Code of Ethics and *Standards* require the internal audit activity to be independent and internal auditors to be objective in performing their work.

      - If possible, internal auditors should avoid accepting responsibility for nonaudit functions or duties that are subject to periodic internal auditing assessments. If this is not possible, then

        - Impairment to independence and objectivity are required to be disclosed to appropriate parties, and the nature of the disclosure depends on the impairment.
        - Objectivity is presumed to be impaired if an auditor provides assurance services for an activity for which the auditor had responsibility within the previous year.
        - If on occasion management directs internal auditors to perform nonaudit work, it should be understood that they are not functioning as internal auditors.

   B. Expectations of stakeholders, including regulatory or legal requirements, should be evaluated and assessed in relation to the potential impairment.

   C. If the internal audit activity charter contains specific restrictions or limiting language regarding the assignment of nonaudit functions to the internal auditor, then these restrictions should be disclosed and discussed with management. If management insists on such an assignment, the auditor should disclose and discuss this matter with the audit committee or appropriate governing body. If the charter is silent on this matter, the guidance noted in the points below should be considered. All the points noted below are subordinated to the language of the charter.

   D. **Assessment.** The results of the assessment should be discussed with management, the audit committee, and/or other appropriate stakeholders. A determination should be made regarding a number of issues, some of which affect one another.

      - The significance of the operational function to the organization (in terms of revenue, expenses, reputation, and influence) should be evaluated.
      - The length or duration of the assignment and scope of responsibility should be evaluated.
      - Adequacy of separation of duties should be evaluated.
      - The potential impairment to objectivity or independence or the appearance of such impairment should be considered when reporting audit results.

E. **Audit of the Function and Disclosure.** Given that the internal audit activity has operational responsibilities and that operation is part of the audit plan, there are several avenues for the auditor to consider.

- The audit may be performed by a contracted, third-party entity, by external auditors, or by the internal audit function. In the first two situations, impairment of objectivity is minimized by the use of auditors outside the organization. In the latter case, objectivity would be impaired.
- Individual auditors with operational responsibility should not participate in the audit of the operation. If possible, auditors conducting the assessment should be supervised by, and report the results of the assessment to, those whose independence or objectivity is not impaired.
- Disclosure should be made regarding the operational responsibilities of the auditor for the function, the significance of the operation to the organization (in terms of revenue, expenses, or other pertinent information), and the relationship of those who audited the function to the auditor.
- Disclosure of the auditor's operational responsibilities should be made in the related audit report and in the auditor's standard communication to the audit committee or other governing body.

(c) **Proficiency and Due Professional Care**

1200—Proficiency and Due Professional Care—Engagements should be performed with proficiency and due professional care.
1210—Proficiency—Internal auditors should possess the knowledge, skills, and other competencies needed to perform their individual responsibilities. The internal audit activity collectively should possess or obtain the knowledge, skills, and other competencies needed to perform its responsibilities.

1210.A1—The chief audit executive should obtain competent advice and assistance if the internal audit staff lacks the knowledge, skills, or other competencies needed to perform all or part of the engagement.
1210.A2—The internal auditor should have sufficient knowledge to identify the indicators of fraud but is not expected to have the expertise of a person whose primary responsibility is detecting and investigating fraud.
1210.A3—Internal auditors should have knowledge of key information technology risks and controls and available technology-based audit techniques to perform their assigned work. However, not all internal auditors are expected to have the expertise of an internal auditor whose primary responsibility is information technology auditing.
1210.C1—The chief audit executive should decline the consulting engagement or obtain competent advice and assistance if the internal audit staff lacks the knowledge, skills, or other competencies needed to perform all or part of the engagement.

1220—Due Professional Care—Internal auditors should apply the care and skill expected of a reasonably prudent and competent internal auditor. Due professional care does not imply infallibility.

1220.A1—The internal auditor should exercise due professional care by considering the

- Extent of work needed to achieve the engagement's objectives
- Relative complexity, materiality, or significance of matters to which assurance procedures are applied
- Adequacy and effectiveness of risk management, control, and governance processes
- Probability of significant errors, irregularities, or noncompliance
- Cost of assurance in relation to potential benefits

1220.A2—In exercising due professional care, the internal auditor should consider the use of computer-assisted audit tools and other data analysis techniques.
1220.A3—The internal auditor should be alert to the significant risks that might affect objectives, operations, or resources. However, assurance procedures alone, even when performed with due professional care, do not guarantee that all significant risks will be identified.

1220.C1—The internal auditor should exercise due professional care during a consulting engagement by considering the

- Needs and expectations of clients, including the nature, timing, and communication of engagement results
- Relative complexity and extent of work needed to achieve the engagement's objectives
- Cost of the consulting engagement in relation to potential benefits

1230—Continuing Professional Development—Internal auditors should enhance their knowledge, skills, and other competencies through continuing professional development.

IIA's Practice Advisory 1200-1: Proficiency and Due Professional Care

Nature of This Practice Advisory

Internal auditors should consider these suggestions when performing engagements. This guidance is not intended to represent all the considerations that may be necessary, but simply a recommended set of items that should be addressed. *Compliance with Practice Advisories is optional.*

1. Professional proficiency is the responsibility of the CAE and each internal auditor. The CAE should ensure that persons assigned to each engagement collectively possess the necessary knowledge, skills, and other competencies to conduct the engagement properly.
2. Internal auditors should comply with professional standards of conduct. The IIA's Code of Ethics extends beyond the definition of internal auditing to include two essential components.
   - Principles that are relevant to the profession and practice of internal auditing: integrity, objectivity, confidentiality, and competency; and
   - Rules of conduct that describe behavior norms expected of internal auditors. These rules are an aid to interpreting the principles into practical applications and are intended to guide the ethical conduct of internal auditors.

IIA's Practice Advisory 1210-1: Proficiency

Nature of This Practice Advisory

Internal auditors should consider these suggestions when evaluating proficiency. This guidance is not intended to represent all the considerations that may be necessary during such an evaluation, but simply a recommended set of items that should be addressed. *Compliance with Practice Advisories is optional.*

1. Each internal auditor should possess certain knowledge, skills, and other competencies.
   - Proficiency in applying internal audit standards, procedures, and techniques is required in performing engagements. "Proficiency" means the ability to apply knowledge to situations likely to be encountered and to deal with them without extensive recourse to technical research and assistance.
   - Proficiency in accounting principles and techniques is required of auditors who work extensively with financial records and reports.
   - An understanding of management principles is required to recognize and evaluate the materiality and significance of deviations from good business practices. "An understanding" means the ability to apply broad knowledge to situations likely to be encountered, to recognize significant deviations, and to be able to carry out the research necessary to arrive at reasonable solutions.
   - An appreciation is required of the fundamentals of subjects such as accounting, economics, commercial law, taxation, finance, quantitative methods, and information technology. "An appreciation" means the ability to recognize the existence of problems or potential problems and to determine the further research to be undertaken or the assistance to be obtained.
2. Internal auditors should be skilled in dealing with people and in communicating effectively. Internal auditors should understand human relations and maintain satisfactory relationships with engagement clients.

3. Internal auditors should be skilled in oral and written communications so that they can clearly and effectively convey such matters as engagement objectives, evaluations, conclusions, and recommendations.
4. The CAE should establish suitable criteria of education and experience for filling internal audit positions, giving due consideration to scope of work and level of responsibility. Reasonable assurance should be obtained as to each prospective auditor's qualifications and proficiency.
5. The internal audit staff should collectively possess the knowledge and skills essential to the practice of the profession within the organization. An annual analysis of an audit department's knowledge and skill sets should be performed to help identify areas of opportunity that can be addressed by continuing professional development, recruiting, or cosourcing.
6. Continuing professional development is essential to help ensure an audit staff remains proficient. See Practice Advisory 1230-1 for specifics related to continuing professional development.
7. The CAE should obtain assistance from experts outside the internal audit activity to support or complement areas where the activity is not fully proficient. See Practice Advisory 1210.A1-1 for more specifics related to obtaining services to support or complement the internal audit activity.

IIA's Practice Advisory 1210.A1-1: Obtaining Services to Support or Complement the Internal Audit Activity

Nature of This Practice Advisory

Internal auditors should consider these suggestions when contemplating acquiring additional services to support the internal audit activity. This guidance is not intended to represent all the considerations that may be necessary, but simply a recommended set of items that should be addressed. *Compliance with Practice Advisories is optional.*

1. The internal audit activity should have employees or use outside service providers who are qualified in disciplines such as accounting, auditing, economics, finance, statistics, information technology, engineering, taxation, law, environmental affairs, and such other areas as needed to meet the internal audit activity's responsibilities. Each member of the internal audit activity, however, need not be qualified in all disciplines.
2. An outside service provider is a person or firm, independent of the organization, who has special knowledge, skill, and experience in a particular discipline. Outside service providers include, among others, actuaries, accountants, appraisers, environmental specialists, fraud investigators, lawyers, engineers, geologists, security specialists, statisticians, information technology specialists, the organization's external auditors, and other auditing organizations. An outside service provider may be engaged by the board, senior management, or the CAE.
3. Outside service providers may be used by the internal audit activity in connection with, among other things

   - Audit activities where a specialized skill and knowledge are required such as information technology, statistics, taxes, language translations, or to achieve the objectives in the engagement work schedule
   - Valuations of assets such as land and buildings, works of art, precious gems, investments, and complex financial instruments
   - Determination of quantities or physical condition of certain assets such as mineral and petroleum reserves
   - Measuring the work completed and to be completed on contracts in progress
   - Fraud and security investigations
   - Determination of amounts by using specialized methods, such as actuarial determinations of employee benefit obligations
   - Interpretation of legal, technical, and regulatory requirements
   - Evaluating the internal audit activity's quality improvement program in accordance with Section 1300 of the *International Standards for the Professional Practice of Internal Auditing (Standards)*
   - Mergers and acquisitions
   - Consulting on risk management and other matters

4. When the CAE intends to use and rely on the work of an outside service provider, the CAE should assess the competency, independence, and objectivity of the outside service provider as it relates to the particular assignment to be performed. This assessment should also be made when the outside service provider is selected by senior management or the board, and the CAE intends to use and rely on the outside service provider's work. When the selection is made by others and the CAE's assessment determines that he or she should not use and rely on the work of an outside service provider, the results of the assessment should be communicated to senior management or the board, as appropriate.
5. The CAE should determine that the outside service provider possesses the necessary knowledge, skills, and other competencies to perform the engagement. When assessing competency, the CAE should consider
    - Professional certification, license, or other recognition of the outside service provider's competency in the relevant discipline
    - Membership of the outside service provider in an appropriate professional organization and adherence to that organization's code of ethics
    - The reputation of the outside service provider; this may include contacting others familiar with the outside service provider's work
    - The outside service provider's experience in the type of work being considered
    - The extent of education and training received by the outside service provider in disciplines that pertain to the particular engagement
    - The outside service provider's knowledge and experience in the industry in which the organization operates
6. The CAE should assess the relationship of the outside service provider to the organization and to the internal audit activity to ensure that independence and objectivity are maintained throughout the engagement. In performing the assessment, the CAE should determine that there are no financial, organizational, or personal relationships that will prevent the outside service provider from rendering impartial and unbiased judgments and opinions when performing or reporting on the engagement.
7. In assessing the independence and objectivity of the outside service provider, the CAE should consider
    - The financial interest the provider may have in the organization
    - The personal or professional affiliation the provider may have to the board, senior management, or others within the organization
    - The relationship the provider may have had with the organization or the activities being reviewed
    - The extent of other ongoing services the provider may be performing for the organization
    - Compensation or other incentives that the provider may have
8. If the outside service provider is also the organization's external auditor and the nature of the engagement is extended audit services, the CAE should ascertain that work performed does not impair the external auditor's independence. "Extended audit services" refers to those services beyond the requirements of audit standards generally accepted by external auditors. If the organization's external auditors act or appear to act as members of senior management, management, or as employees of the organization, then their independence is impaired. Additionally, external auditors may provide the organization with other services, such as tax and consulting. Independence, however, should be assessed in relation to the full range of services provided to the organization.
9. The CAE should obtain sufficient information regarding the scope of the outside service provider's work. This is necessary in order to ascertain that the scope of work is adequate for the purposes of the internal audit activity. It may be prudent to have these and other matters documented in an engagement letter or contract. The CAE should review with the outside service provider
    - Objectives and scope of work
    - Specific matters expected to be covered in the engagement communications
    - Access to relevant records, personnel, and physical properties
    - Information regarding assumptions and procedures to be employed

- Ownership and custody of engagement working papers, if applicable
- Confidentiality and restrictions on information obtained during the engagement
- Where applicable, compliance with the IIA's *Standards* and the audit department's standards for working practices should be referenced in the engagement letter.

10. Where the outside service provider performs internal audit activities, the CAE should specify and ensure that the work complies with the *Standards* and the audit department's standards for working practices. In reviewing the work of an outside service provider, the CAE should evaluate the adequacy of work performed. This evaluation should include a sufficiency of information obtained to afford a reasonable basis for the conclusions reached and the resolution of significant exceptions or other unusual matters.
11. When the CAE issues engagement communications, and an outside service provider was used, the CAE may, as appropriate, refer to such services provided. The outside service provider should be informed and, if appropriate, concurrence should be obtained prior to such reference being made in engagement communications.

IIA's Practice Advisory 1210.A2-1: Identification of Fraud

Nature of This Practice Advisory

Internal auditors should consider these suggestions in connection with the identification of fraud. This guidance is not intended to represent all the considerations that may be necessary, but simply a recommended set of items that should be addressed. *Compliance with Practice Advisories is optional.* This guidance is repeated in Part 1 and Part 2 for proper coverage of the subject matter.

1. Fraud encompasses an array of irregularities and illegal acts characterized by intentional deception. It can be perpetrated for the benefit of or to the detriment of the organization and by persons outside as well as inside the organization.
2. Fraud designed to benefit the organization generally produces such benefit by exploiting an unfair or dishonest advantage that also may deceive an outside party. Perpetrators of such frauds usually accrue an indirect personal benefit. Examples of frauds designed to benefit the organization include

    - Sale or assignment of fictitious or misrepresented assets
    - Improper payments, such as illegal political contributions, bribes, kickbacks, and payoffs to government officials, intermediaries of government officials, customers, or suppliers
    - Intentional, improper representation or valuation of transactions, assets, liabilities, or income
    - Intentional, improper transfer pricing (e.g., valuation of goods exchanged between related organizations). By purposely structuring pricing techniques improperly, management can improve the operating results of an organization involved in the transaction to the detriment of the other organization.
    - Intentional, improper related-party transactions in which one party receives some benefit not obtainable in an arm's-length transaction
    - Intentional failure to record or disclose significant information to improve the financial picture of the organization to outside parties
    - Prohibited business activities, such as those that violate government statutes, rules, regulations, or contracts
    - Tax fraud

3. Fraud perpetrated to the detriment of the organization generally is for the direct or indirect benefit of an employee, outside individual, or another organization. Some examples are

    - Acceptance of bribes or kickbacks
    - Diversion to an employee or outsider of a potentially profitable transaction that would normally generate profits for the organization
    - Embezzlement, as typified by the misappropriation of money or property, and falsification of financial records to cover up the act, thus making detection difficult
    - Intentional concealment or misrepresentation of events or data
    - Claims submitted for services or goods not actually provided to the organization

4. Deterrence of fraud consists of those actions taken to discourage the perpetration of fraud and limit the exposure if fraud does occur. The principal mechanism for deterring fraud is control. Primary responsibility for establishing and maintaining control rests with management.
5. Internal auditors are responsible for assisting in the deterrence of fraud by examining and evaluating the adequacy and the effectiveness of the system of internal control, commensurate with the extent of the potential exposure/risk in the various segments of the organization's operations. In carrying out this responsibility, internal auditors should, for example, determine whether

    - The organizational environment fosters control consciousness.
    - Realistic organizational goals and objectives are set.
    - Written policies (e.g., codes of conduct) exist that describe prohibited activities and the action required whenever violations are discovered.
    - Appropriate authorization policies for transactions are established and maintained.
    - Policies, practices, procedures, reports, and other mechanisms are developed to monitor activities and safeguard assets, particularly in high-risk areas.
    - Communication channels provide management with adequate and reliable information.
    - Recommendations need to be made for the establishment or enhancement of cost-effective controls to help deter fraud.

6. When an internal auditor suspects wrongdoing, the appropriate authorities within the organization should be informed. The internal auditor may recommend whatever investigation is considered necessary in the circumstances. Thereafter, the auditor should follow up to see that the internal audit activity's responsibilities have been met.
7. Investigation of fraud consists of performing extended procedures necessary to determine whether fraud, as suggested by the indicators, has occurred. It includes gathering sufficient information about the specific details of a discovered fraud. Internal auditors, lawyers, investigators, security personnel, and other specialists from inside or outside the organization are the parties who usually conduct or participate in fraud investigations.
8. When conducting fraud investigations, internal auditors should

    - Assess the probable level and the extent of complicity in the fraud within the organization. This can be critical to ensuring that the internal auditor avoids providing information to or obtaining misleading information from persons who may be involved.
    - Determine the knowledge, skills, and other competencies needed to carry out the investigation effectively. An assessment of the qualifications and the skills of internal auditors and of the specialists available to participate in the investigation should be performed to ensure that engagements are conducted by individuals having appropriate types and levels of technical expertise. This should include assurances on such matters as professional certifications, licenses, reputation, and the fact that there is no relationship to those being investigated or to any of the employees or management of the organization.
    - Design procedures to follow in attempting to identify the perpetrators, extent of the fraud, techniques used, and cause of the fraud.
    - Coordinate activities with management personnel, legal counsel, and other specialists as appropriate throughout the course of the investigation.
    - Be cognizant of the rights of alleged perpetrators and personnel within the scope of the investigation and the reputation of the organization itself.

9. Once a fraud investigation is concluded, internal auditors should assess the facts known in order to

    - Determine if controls need to be implemented or strengthened to reduce future vulnerability
    - Design engagement tests to help disclose the existence of similar frauds in the future
    - Help meet the internal auditor's responsibility to maintain sufficient knowledge of fraud and thereby be able to identify future indicators of fraud

10. Reporting of fraud consists of the various oral or written, interim or final communications to management regarding the status and results of fraud investigations. The chief audit executive has the responsibility to report immediately any incident of significant fraud to senior management and the board. Sufficient investigation should take place to establish reasonable certainty that a fraud has occurred before any fraud reporting is made. A preliminary or final report may be desirable at

the conclusion of the detection phase. The report should include the internal auditor's conclusion as to whether sufficient information exists to conduct a full investigation. It should also summarize observations and recommendations that serve as the basis for such decision. A written report may follow any oral briefing made to management and the board to document the findings.

11. Section 2400 of the *International Standards for the Professional Practice of Internal Auditing (Standards)* provides interpretations applicable to engagement communications issued as a result of fraud investigations. Additional interpretive guidance on reporting of fraud is

    - When the incidence of significant fraud has been established to a reasonable certainty, senior management and the board should be notified immediately.
    - The results of a fraud investigation may indicate that fraud has had a previously undiscovered significant adverse effect on the financial position and results of operations of an organization for one or more years on which financial statements have already been issued. Internal auditors should inform senior management and the board of such a discovery.
    - A written report or other formal communication should be issued at the conclusion of the investigation phase. It should include all observations, conclusions, recommendations, and corrective action taken.
    - A draft of the proposed final communications on fraud should be submitted to legal counsel for review. In those cases in which the internal auditor wants to invoke client privilege, consideration should be given to addressing the report to legal counsel.

12. Detection of fraud consists of identifying indicators of fraud sufficient to warrant recommending an investigation. These indicators may arise as a result of controls established by management, tests conducted by auditors, and other sources both within and outside the organization.
13. In conducting engagements, the internal auditor's responsibilities for detecting fraud are to

    - Have sufficient knowledge of fraud to be able to identify indicators that fraud may have been committed. This knowledge includes the characteristics of fraud, the techniques used to commit fraud, and the types of fraud associated with the activities reviewed.
    - Be alert to opportunities, such as control weaknesses, that could allow fraud. If significant control weaknesses are detected, additional tests conducted by internal auditors should include tests directed toward identification of other indicators of fraud. Some examples of indicators are unauthorized transactions, override of controls, unexplained pricing exceptions, and unusually large product losses. Internal auditors should recognize that the presence of more than one indicator at any one time increases the probability that fraud may have occurred.
    - Evaluate the indicators that fraud may have been committed and decide whether any further action is necessary or whether an investigation should be recommended.
    - Notify the appropriate authorities within the organization if a determination is made that there are sufficient indicators of the commission of a fraud to recommend an investigation.

14. Internal auditors are not expected to have knowledge equivalent to that of a person whose primary responsibility is detecting and investigating fraud. Also, audit procedures alone, even when carried out with due professional care, do not guarantee that fraud will be detected.

IIA's Practice Advisory 1210.A2-2: Responsibility for Fraud Detection

Nature of This Practice Advisory

Internal auditors should consider these suggestions in relation to the responsibility for fraud detection. This guidance is not intended to represent all the considerations that may be necessary, but simply a recommended set of items that should be addressed. *Compliance with this Practice Advisory is optional. This guidance is repeated in Part 1 and Part 2 for proper coverage of the subject matter.*

1. Management and the internal audit activity have differing roles with respect to fraud detection. The normal course of work for the internal audit activity is to provide an independent appraisal, examination, and evaluation of an organization's activities as a service to the organization. The objective of internal auditing in fraud detection is to assist members of the organization in the effective discharge of their responsibilities by furnishing them with analyses, appraisals, recommen-

dations, counsel, and information concerning the activities reviewed. The engagement objective includes promoting effective control at a reasonable cost.

2. Management has a responsibility to establish and maintain an effective control system at a reasonable cost. To the degree that fraud may be present in activities covered in the normal course of work as defined above, internal auditors have a responsibility to exercise "due professional care" as specifically defined in *Standard 1220* with respect to fraud detection. Internal auditors should have sufficient knowledge of fraud to identify the indicators that fraud may have been committed, be alert to opportunities that could allow fraud, evaluate the need for additional investigation, and notify the appropriate authorities.
3. A well-designed internal control system should not be conducive to fraud. Tests conducted by auditors, along with reasonable controls established by management, improve the likelihood that any existing fraud indicators will be detected and considered for further investigation.

IIA's Practice Advisory 1220-1: Due Professional Care

Nature of This Practice Advisory

Internal auditors should consider these suggestions when evaluating due professional care. This guidance is not intended to represent all the considerations that may be necessary during such an evaluation, but simply a recommended set of items that should be addressed. *Compliance with Practice Advisories is optional.*

1. Due professional care calls for the application of the care and skill expected of a reasonably prudent and competent internal auditor in the same or similar circumstances. Professional care should, therefore, be appropriate to the complexities of the engagement being performed. In exercising due professional care, internal auditors should be alert to the possibility of intentional wrongdoing, errors and omissions, inefficiency, waste, ineffectiveness, and conflicts of interest. They should also be alert to those conditions and activities where irregularities are most likely to occur. In addition, they should identify inadequate controls and recommend improvements to promote compliance with acceptable procedures and practices.
2. Due care implies reasonable care and competence, not infallibility or extraordinary performance. Due care requires the auditor to conduct examinations and verifications to a reasonable extent, but does not require detailed reviews of all transactions. Accordingly, internal auditors cannot give absolute assurance that noncompliance or irregularities do not exist. Nevertheless, the possibility of material irregularities or noncompliance should be considered whenever an internal auditor undertakes an internal auditing assignment.

IIA's Practice Advisory 1230-1: Continuing Professional Development

Nature of This Practice Advisory

Internal auditors should consider these suggestions in connection with continuing professional development. This guidance is not intended to represent all the considerations that may be necessary during such an evaluation, but simply a recommended set of items that should be addressed. *Compliance with Practice Advisories is optional.*

1. Internal auditors are responsible for continuing their education in order to maintain their proficiency. They should keep informed about improvements and current developments in internal audit standards, procedures, and techniques. Continuing education may be obtained through membership and participation in professional societies; attendance at conferences, seminars, college courses, and in-house training programs; and participation in research projects.
2. Internal auditors are encouraged to demonstrate their proficiency by obtaining appropriate professional certification, such as the Certified Internal Auditor designation and other designations offered by the IIA.
3. Internal auditors with professional certifications should obtain sufficient continuing professional education to satisfy requirements related to the professional certification held.
4. Internal auditors not currently holding appropriate certifications are encouraged to pursue an educational program that supports efforts to obtain professional certification.

(d) **Quality Assurance and Improvement Program**

1300—Quality Assurance and Improvement Program—The chief audit executive should develop and maintain a quality assurance and improvement program that covers all aspects of the internal audit activity and continuously monitors its effectiveness. *This program includes periodic internal and external quality assessments and ongoing internal monitoring. Each part of the program* should be designed to help the internal auditing activity add value and improve the organization's operations and to provide assurance that the internal audit activity is in conformity with the *Standards* and the Code of Ethics.

1310—Quality Program Assessments—The internal audit activity should adopt a process to monitor and assess the overall effectiveness of the quality program. The process should include both internal and external assessments.

1311—Internal Assessments—Internal assessments should include ongoing reviews of the performance of the internal audit activity; and periodic reviews performed through self-assessment or by other persons within the organization, with knowledge of internal audit practices and the *Standards.*

1312—External Assessments—External assessments, such as quality assurance reviews, should be conducted at least once every five years by a qualified, independent reviewer or review team from outside the organization.

1320—Reporting on the Quality Program—The chief audit executive should communicate the results of external assessments to the board.

1330—Use of "Conducted in Accordance with the Standards"—Internal auditors are encouraged to report that their activities are "conducted in accordance with the *International Standards for the Professional Practice of Internal Auditing*" *(Standards).* However, internal auditors may use the statement only if assessments of the quality improvement program demonstrate that the internal audit activity is in compliance with the *Standards.*

1340—Disclosure of Noncompliance—Although the internal audit activity should achieve full compliance with the *Standards* and internal auditors with the Code of Ethics, there may be instances in which full compliance is not achieved. When noncompliance impacts the overall scope or operation of the internal audit activity, disclosure should be made to senior management and the board.

IIA's Practice Advisory 1300-1: Quality Assurance and Improvement Program

Nature of This Practice Advisory

Internal auditors should consider these suggestions when developing or assessing quality programs. This guidance is not intended to represent all the procedures necessary for comprehensive quality programs or their assessment, but is simply a recommended set of quality assessment practices. *Compliance with Practice Advisories is optional.*

Overview of a quality assurance and improvement program (QA&IP). The CAE is responsible for establishing an internal audit activity whose scope of work includes all the activities in the *Standards* and in the IIA's definition of internal auditing (*Standard*–Introduction–P. 3, first paragraph). To ensure that this occurs, *Standard 1300* requires that the CAE develop and maintain a quality assurance and improvement program (QA&IP)

Implementing a QA&IP. The CAE should be accountable for implementing processes that are designed to provide reasonable assurance to the various stakeholders of the internal audit activity that it

- Performs in accordance with its charter, which should be consistent with the *International Standards for the Professional Practice of Internal Auditing* and the Code of Ethics
- Operates in an effective and efficient manner
- Is perceived by those stakeholders as adding value and improving the organization's operations

These processes should include appropriate supervision, periodic internal assessments and ongoing monitoring of quality assurance, and periodic external assessments.

Nature and scope of a QA&IP. The QA&IP should be sufficiently comprehensive to encompass all aspects of operation and management of an internal audit activity, as found in the *Standards* and best practices of the profession. The QA&IP processes should be performed by or under direct supervision of the CAE. Except in small internal audit activities, the CAE would usually delegate most

QA&IP responsibilities to subordinates. In large or complex environments (e.g., numerous business units and/or locations), the CAE should establish a formal QA&IP function independent of the audit and consulting segments of the internal audit activity. This independent function should be headed by an audit executive. This executive (and limited staff) would not normally perform all of the QA&IP responsibilities, but would administer and monitor these activities.

Key elements of a QA&IP. The QA&IP should be structured to achieve an optimum level of professional competence and reviews should be administered, to the extent practicable, independently of the functions and activities being reviewed. These key elements of the internal audit activity—performed by, or administered by a person or functional unit under the direction of, the CAE—should be considered for the QA&IP function.

- Oversee the development and implementation of internal audit policies/procedures; administer/maintain the internal audit activity's policy/procedure manual
- Assist the CAE and audit management with budgeting and financial administration for the internal audit activity
- Maintain and update the comprehensive audit risk universe, including gathering and incorporating new information impacting the universe; overseeing the division of responsibilities among internal audit, external audit, and other evaluation and investigation functions
- Administer the general operation of the system for evaluation of audit risk and long-range planning—assisting the CAE and audit management in this area
- Assist with the overall scheduling process for audit and consulting engagements and the associated time tracking
- Assist internal audit management in the acquisition, maintenance, and employment of audit tools and other use of technology
- Administer external recruitment and the internal audit activity's participation in the organization's internal staff rotation and management development programs
- Oversee the training/development of staff—for example, selection or development of training courses, and administration of the related career planning and performance evaluation processes, including the tracking system for professional development of individual staff members
- Oversee the system(s) for internal audit statistics/metrics and for postaudit and other surveys (e.g., of the customers and other stakeholders of the internal audit activity)
- Administer/monitor quality assurance and process improvement activities, including formal internal and external quality assessments
- Oversee/administer information gathering and preparation of the periodic summary reports by the internal audit activity to senior management and the audit committee (including reports of the results of internal and external quality assessments)
- Administer/maintain the comprehensive follow-up database for recommendations and action plans resulting from internal audit engagements and the work of external auditors and other internal evaluation and investigation functions
- Assist the CAE, audit management, and internal audit staff in keeping current with the *Standards*, other changes and emerging best practices of the internal audit profession, regulatory matters, and other emerging issues and opportunities—under the direction of internal audit management

The words "assist, administer, oversee, monitor, and maintain" are intended to indicate that the person(s) working in the QA&IP function would not necessarily perform much of this work. It would be assigned—either ad hoc for particular tasks or on a longer-term basis—to other internal audit executives and staff, but would be overseen, administered, and so on, through the QA&IP.

IIA's Practice Advisory 1310-1: Quality Program Assessments

Nature of This Practice Advisory

Internal auditors should consider these suggestions when developing or assessing quality programs. This guidance is not intended to represent all the procedures necessary for comprehensive quality programs or their assessment, but is simply a recommended set of quality assessment practices. *Compliance with Practice Advisories is optional.*

Monitoring quality programs. Means ongoing and periodic assessments of the entire spectrum of audit and consulting work performed by the internal audit activity, and is not limited to assessing its Quality Assurance and Improvement Program (QA&IP)—see Practice Advisory 1300-1. These ongoing and periodic assessments should be comprised of rigorous, comprehensive processes, both routine, continuous supervision and testing of performance of audit and consulting work and periodic validations of compliance with the *Standards*. Monitoring should also include ongoing measurements and analyses of performance metrics (e.g., audit plan accomplishment, cycle time, recommendations accepted, and customer satisfaction). If the results of these assessments indicate areas for improvement by the internal audit activity, the improvements should be implemented by the CAE through the QA&IP.

Definition and timing of assessments.

- Ongoing internal assessments (the term "internal assessments" is synonymous with the terms "internal review" and "self-assessment" used elsewhere in the Practice Advisories) should be an integral part of the day-to-day supervision, review, and measurement of the internal audit activity, as set forth in Practice Advisory 1311-1, Paragraphs 2 and 3.
- Periodic internal assessments should be completed as set forth in Practice Advisory 1311-1, Paragraphs 4 and 5.
- Periodic external assessments of the internal audit activity, by an individual or team having a high level of competence and experience in the internal audit profession, should be performed in accordance with Practice Advisories 1312-1 and 1312-2.
- The requirement that internal audit activities conduct ongoing and periodic internal assessments became effective as of January 1, 2002. In addition, at least one external assessment is required during the five years commencing on that date and at least once during each five-year period thereafter. The requirement for a periodic internal assessment may be waived for the year in which an external assessment is performed.

Assessing quality programs. Assessments should evaluate and conclude on the quality of the internal audit activity and lead to recommendations for appropriate improvements. Assessments of quality programs should include evaluation of

- Compliance with the *Standards* and Code of Ethics, including timely corrective actions to remedy any significant instances of noncompliance
- Adequacy of the internal audit activity's charter, goals, objectives, policies, and procedures
- Contribution to the organization's governance, risk management, and control processes
- Compliance with applicable laws, regulations, and government or industry standards
- Effectiveness of continuous improvement activities and adoption of best practices
- Whether the auditing activity adds value and improves the organization's operations

Continuous improvement. All quality assessment and improvement efforts should include appropriate, timely modification of resources, technology, processes, and procedures as indicated by monitoring and assessment activities.

Communicating results. To provide accountability and transparency, the CAE should share the results of external and, as appropriate, internal quality program assessments with the various stakeholders of the activity, such as senior management, the board, and external auditors.

IIA's Practice Advisory 1311-1: Internal Assessments

Nature of This Practice Advisory

Internal auditors should consider these suggestions when performing internal assessments within the internal audit activity. This guidance is not intended to represent all the procedures necessary for comprehensive internal assessments, but is simply a recommended set of internal assessment practices. *Compliance with Practice Advisories is optional.*

Overview of a quality assurance and improvement program (QA&IP). The CAE is responsible for establishing an internal audit activity whose scope of work includes all the activities in the *Standards* and in the IIA's definition of internal auditing (*Standards* – Introduction – P. 3, first paragraph). To ensure that this occurs, *Standard 1300* requires that the CAE develop and maintain a Quality Assurance and Improvement Program (QA&IP). The QA&IP should include both ongoing and periodic internal assessments (the term "internal assessments" is synonymous with the terms "internal review" and "self-assessment" used elsewhere in the Practice Advisories). These ongoing and periodic assessments should cover the entire spectrum of audit and consulting work performed by the internal audit activity and should not be limited to assessing its QA&IP—see Practice Advisory 1300-1.

Ongoing internal assessments. Are usually incorporated into the routine policies and practices used to manage the internal audit activity and should be conducted by means of such processes and tools as

- Engagement supervision as described in Practice Advisory 2340-1,"Engagement Supervision"
- Checklists and other means to provide assurance that processes adopted by the internal audit activity (e.g., in an audit and procedures manual) are being followed
- Feedback from audit customers and other stakeholders
- Project budgets, timekeeping systems, audit plan completion, cost recoveries
- Analyses of other performance metrics, (such as cycle time and recommendations accepted)

Conclusions should be developed as to the quality of ongoing performance, and follow-up action should be taken to ensure appropriate improvements are implemented.

Periodic internal assessments. Usually represent nonroutine, special-purpose reviews and compliance testing. They should be designed to assess (1) compliance with the internal audit activity's charter, the *International Standards for the Professional Practice of Internal Auditing,* and the Code of Ethics, and (2) the efficiency and effectiveness of the activity in meeting the needs of its various stakeholders. The IIA's *Quality Assessment Manual*, or a comparable set of guidance and tools, should serve as the basis for periodic internal assessments.

Periodic assessments may

- Include more in-depth interviews and surveys of stakeholder groups
- Be performed by members of the internal audit activity (self-assessment)
- Be performed by Certified Internal Auditors (CIAs), or other competent audit professionals, currently assigned elsewhere in the organization
- Encompass a combination of self-assessment and preparation of materials subsequently reviewed by CIAs or other competent audit professionals
- Include benchmarking of the internal audit activity's practices and performance metrics against relevant best practices of the internal auditing profession

A periodic internal assessment, performed within a short time prior to an external assessment, can serve to facilitate and reduce the cost of an external assessment. If the external assessment takes the form of a "self-assessment with independent validation" (New Practice Advisory 1312-2), the periodic internal assessment can serve as the self-assessment portion of this process.

Conclusions should be developed as to the quality of performance and appropriate action initiated to achieve improvements and conformity to the *Standards,* as necessary.

The CAE should establish a structure for reporting results of periodic reviews that maintains appropriate credibility and objectivity. Generally, those assigned responsibility for conducting ongoing and periodic reviews should report to the CAE while performing the reviews and should communicate their results directly to the CAE.

Communicating results. The CAE should share the results of internal assessments, necessary action plans, and their successful implementation with appropriate persons outside the activity, such as senior management, the board, and external auditors.

IIA's Practice Advisory 1312-1: External Assessments

Nature of This Practice Advisory

Internal auditors should consider these suggestions when planning and contracting for an external assessment of their internal audit activity. This guidance is not intended to represent all the considerations necessary for an external assessment but simply a recommended set of high-level considerations with respect to the external assessment. *Compliance with Practice Advisories is optional.*

Overview of a quality assurance and improvement program (QA&IP). The CAE is responsible for establishing an internal audit activity whose scope of work includes all the activities in the *Standards* and in the IIA's definition of internal auditing (*Standards* – Introduction – P. 3, first paragraph). To ensure that this occurs, *Standard 1300* requires that the CAE develop and maintain a Quality Assurance and Improvement Program (QA&IP). The QA&IP should include a periodic external assessment, conducted at least once every five years by a qualified, independent reviewer or review team. These external assessments should cover the entire spectrum of audit and consulting work performed by the internal audit activity and should not be limited to assessing its QA&IP—see Practice Advisory 1300-1.

General considerations. External assessments of an internal audit activity should appraise and express an opinion as to the internal audit activity's compliance with the *Standards for the Professional Practice of Internal Auditing* and, as appropriate, should include recommendations for improvement. These reviews can have considerable value to the chief audit executive and other members of the internal audit activity. Only qualified persons (Paragraph 5, below) should perform such reviews.

An external assessment is required within five years of January 1, 2002. *Earlier adoption of the new **Standard** requiring an external review is highly recommended.* Organizations that have had external reviews prior to that date are encouraged to have their next external review within five years of their last review.

On completion of the review, **a formal communication should be provided** to the board (as defined in the Glossary to the *Standards*) and to senior management.

Qualifications for external reviewers. External reviewers, including those who validate self-assessments (New Practice Advisory 1312-2), should be independent of the organization and of the internal audit activity. The review team should consist of individuals who are competent in the professional practice of internal auditing and the external assessment process. To be considered as candidates to be external assessors, qualified individuals could include IIA quality assurance reviewers, regulatory examiners, consultants, external auditors, other professional service providers, and internal auditors from outside the organization whose internal audit activity is the subject of the external assessment.

Independence. The individual or organization that undertakes to perform the external assessment, the members of the assessment team, and any other individuals who participate in the assessment should be free from any obligation to, or interest in, the organization whose internal audit activity is the subject of the external assessment or the personnel of such organization. Particular considerations relating to independence of external assessors include

- Individuals who perform the assessment must be independent of the organization whose internal audit activity is the subject of the assessment and must not have either a real or apparent conflict of interest. "Independent of the organization" means not a part of, or under the control of, the organization to which the internal auditing activity belongs. In the selection of an external reviewer, consideration should be given to a possible real or apparent conflict of interest that the reviewer may have due to present or past relationships with the organization or its internal auditing activity.
- Individuals who are in another department of that subject organization or in a related organization, although organizationally separate from the internal audit activity, are not considered independent for purposes of conducting an external assessment. A "related organization" may be a parent organization, an affiliate in the same group of entities, or an entity with regular oversight, supervision, or quality assurance responsibilities with respect to the organization whose internal audit activity is the subject of the external assessment.
- Reciprocal peer review arrangements among three or more organizations (e.g., within an industry or other affinity group, regional association, or other group of organizations) may be structured in a manner that alleviates independence concerns, but care must be taken to ensure that the issue of independence does not arise. Reciprocal peer reviews between two organizations would not pass the independence test.
- To overcome concerns that there may be an appearance or reality of impairment of independence in instances such as those discussed in this paragraph, one or more independent individuals could be part of the external assessment team, or scheduled to participate subsequently, to independently validate the work of that external assessment team.

Integrity and objectivity. *Integrity* requires the review team to be honest and candid within the constraints of confidentiality. Service and the public trust should not be subordinated to personal gain and advantage. *Objectivity* is a state of mind and a quality that lends value to a review team's services. The principle of objectivity imposes the obligation to be impartial, intellectually honest, and free of conflicts of interest.

Competence. Performing and communicating the results of an external assessment require the exercise of professional judgment. Accordingly, an individual serving as an external assessor should

- Be a competent, certified audit professional (e.g., CIA, CPA, CA, or CISA), who possesses current, in-depth knowledge of the *Standards.*
- Be well versed in the best practices of the profession.
- Have at least three years of recent experience in the practice of internal auditing at a management level.
- External assessment team leaders and independent validators (Practice Advisory 1312-2) should have an additional level of competence and experience, such as that gained from working previously as a team member on an external quality assessment, successful completion of the IIA's quality assessment training course or similar training, and CAE or comparable senior internal audit management experience.

The review team should include members with information technology expertise and relevant industry experience. Individuals with expertise in other specialized areas may assist the external review team. For example, specialists in enterprise risk management, statistical sampling, operations monitoring systems, or control self-assessment may participate in certain segments of the review.

Approval by management and the board. The CAE should involve senior management and the board in the selection process for an external reviewer and obtain their approval.

Scope of external assessments. The external assessment should consist of a broad scope of coverage that includes these elements of the internal audit activity

- Compliance with the *Standards*, the IIA's Code of Ethics, and the internal audit activity's charter, plans, policies, procedures, practices, and applicable legislative and regulatory requirements
- Expectations of the internal audit activity expressed by the board, executive management and operational managers
- Integration of the internal audit activity into the organization's governance process, including the attendant relationships between and among the key groups involved in that process
- Tools and techniques employed by the internal audit activity
- Mix of knowledge, experience, and disciplines within the staff, including staff focus on process improvement
- Determination as to whether the audit activity adds value and improves the organization's operations

Communicating results. The preliminary results of the review should be discussed with the CAE during and at the conclusion of the assessment process. Final results should be communicated to the CAE or other official who authorized the review for the organization, preferably with copies sent directly to appropriate members of senior management and the board.

The communication should include

- An opinion on the internal audit activity's compliance with the *Standards* based on a structured rating process. The term "compliance" means that the practices of the internal audit activity, taken as a whole, satisfy the requirements of the *Standards*. Similarly, "noncompliance" means that the impact and severity of the deficiencies in the practices of the internal audit activity are so significant that they impair the internal audit activity's ability to discharge its responsibilities. The degree of "partial compliance" with individual *Standards*, if relevant to the overall opinion, should also be expressed in the report on the independent assessment. The expression of an opinion on the results of the external assessment requires the application of sound business judgment, integrity, and due professional care.
- An assessment and evaluation of the use of best practices, both those observed during the assessment and others potentially applicable to the activity
- Recommendations for improvement, where appropriate

- Responses from the CAE that include an action plan and implementation dates

The CAE should communicate the results of the review to appropriate members of senior management and to the board, if not already copied directly, as well as the specifics of planned remedial actions for significant issues and subsequent information as to accomplishment of those planned actions.

IIA's Practice Advisory 1312-2: External Assessments Self Assessment with Independent Validation

Nature of This Practice Advisory

Internal auditors should consider these suggestions when planning and contracting for an external assessment of their internal audit activity. This guidance is not intended to represent all the considerations necessary for an external assessment but simply a recommended set of high-level considerations with respect to the external assessment. *Compliance with Practice Advisories is optional.*

Overview of a quality assurance and improvement program (QA&IP). The chief audit executive (CAE) is responsible for establishing an internal audit activity whose scope of work includes all the activities in the *Standards* and in the IIA's definition of internal auditing (*Standards* – Introduction – P. 3, first paragraph). To ensure that this occurs, *Standard* 1300 requires that the CAE develop and maintain a Quality Assurance and Improvement Program (QA&IP). The QA&IP should include a periodic external assessment, conducted at least once every five years by a qualified, independent reviewer or review team. These external assessments should cover the entire spectrum of audit and consulting work performed by the internal audit activity and should not be limited to assessing its QA&IP—see Practice Advisory 1300-1.

Self-assessment with independent validation. In response to concerns that an external assessment by an independent individual or team may be onerous for smaller internal audit activities, the IIA has provided an alternative process, a "self-assessment with independent [external] validation," with these features.

- A comprehensive and fully documented self-assessment process, which should emulate the external assessment process, at least with respect to evaluation of compliance with the *Standards*
- An independent on-site validation by a qualified reviewer
- Economical time and resource requirements—for example, the primary focus would be on compliance with the *Standards*. Attention to other areas such as benchmarking, review and consultation as to employment of best practices, and interviews with senior and operating management (whose views and concerns the CAE and staff of the internal audit activity already know) may be reduced or omitted.
- Otherwise, the same requirements and criteria as set forth in Practice Advisory 1312-1 would apply for
    - General considerations
    - Qualifications of the independent validator (external reviewer)
    - Independence, integrity and objectivity, competence, approval by management and the board, scope (except for areas such as employment of tools, techniques, other best practices, career development, and value-adding activities)
    - Communication of results (including remedial actions and their accomplishment)

A team under the direction of the CAE should perform and fully document the self-assessment process. The IIA's *Quality Assessment Manual* contains an outline of the process, including guidance and tools for the self-assessment. A draft report, similar to that for an external assessment, should be prepared.

A qualified, independent validator should perform limited tests of the self-assessment so as to validate the results and express an opinion about the indicated level of the activity's conformity to the *Standards*. This independent validation should follow the process outlined in the IIA's *Quality Assessment Manual* or a similar comprehensive process.

Upon completion of the independent validation, including a rigorous review of the self-assessment team's evaluation of compliance with the *Standards* and the Code of Ethics

- The independent validator should review the draft report mentioned in Paragraph 3, above, and attempt to reconcile unresolved issues (if any).
- If in agreement with the evaluation of compliance with the *Standards* and Code of Ethics, the independent validator should add wording (as needed) to the report, concurring in the evaluation and, to the extent deemed appropriate, in the report's findings, conclusions, and recommendations.
- If not in agreement with that evaluation, the independent evaluator should add dissenting wording to the report, specifying the points of disagreement with it and, to the extent deemed appropriate, with the significant findings, conclusions, and recommendations in the report.
- Alternatively, the independent validator may prepare a separate independent validation report, concurring or expressing disagreement as outlined above, to accompany the report of the self-assessment.
- The final report(s) of the self-assessment with independent validation should then be signed by the self-assessment team and the independent validator and issued by the CAE to senior management and the board.

While a full external review achieves maximum benefit for the activity and should be included in the activity's quality program, the self-assessment with independent validation provides an alternative means of complying fully with this *Standard 1312*. However, insofar as possible, in order to achieve optimum quality assurance and process-improvement benefits, an internal audit activity should consider the self-assessment with independent validation as an interim measure and endeavor to obtain a full external assessment during subsequent periods.

IIA's Practice Advisory 1320-1: Reporting on the Quality Program

Nature of This Practice Advisory

Internal auditors should consider these suggestions when reporting on the quality program. This guidance is not intended to represent all the considerations that may be necessary, but simply a recommended set of items that should be addressed. *Compliance with Practice Advisories is optional.*

Upon completion of an external assessment, the review team should issue a formal report containing an opinion on the internal audit activity's compliance with the *Standards* (see Practice Advisory 1312-1). The report should also address compliance with the internal audit activity's charter and other applicable standards and include appropriate recommendations for improvement. The report should be addressed to the person or organization requesting the assessment. The chief audit executive should prepare a written action plan in response to the significant comments and recommendations contained in the report of external assessment. Appropriate follow-up is also the CAE's responsibility.

The evaluation of compliance with the *Standards* is a critical component of an external assessment. The review team should acknowledge the *Standards* in order to evaluate and opine on the internal audit activity's compliance. However, as noted in Practice Advisory 1310-1, there are additional criteria that should be considered in evaluating the performance of an internal audit activity.

IIA's Practice Advisory 1330-1: Use of "Conducted in Accordance with the *Standards*"

Nature of This Practice Advisory

Internal auditors should consider these suggestions when using the phrase "conducted in accordance with the *International Standards for the Professional Practice of Internal Auditing*." This guidance is not intended to be all-inclusive, but simply to supplement the *Standards. Compliance with Practice Advisories is optional.*

General considerations. External and internal assessments of an internal audit activity should be performed to appraise and express an opinion as to the internal audit activity's compliance with the *International Standards for the Professional Practice of Internal Auditing* and the Code of Ethics and, as appropriate, should include recommendations for improvement.

An external assessment is required within five years of January 1, 2002. Earlier adoption of the new *Standard* requiring an external review is highly recommended. Organizations that have had external reviews are encouraged to have their next external review within five years of their last review.

Use of compliance phrase. The compliance phrase to be used may be: "in compliance with the *Standards*," or "in conformity to the *Standards*," or "in accordance with the *Standards*." Use of the compliance phrase requires an external assessment at least once during each five-year period, along with periodic internal assessments, which have concluded that the internal audit activity is in compliance with the *Standards* and Code of Ethics. Initial use of the compliance phrase is not appropriate until an external review, performed within the past five years, has demonstrated that the internal audit activity is in compliance with the *Standards* and the Code of Ethics. Instances of noncompliance that impact the overall scope or operation of the internal audit activity, including failure to obtain an external assessment by January 1, 2007, should be disclosed to senior management and the board.

Prior to the internal audit activity's use of the compliance phrase, any instances of noncompliance that have been disclosed by a quality assessment (internal or external) and that impair the internal audit activity's ability to discharge its responsibilities

- Should be adequately remedied.
- The remedial actions should be documented and reported to the relevant assessor(s), to obtain concurrence that the noncompliance has been adequately remedied.
- The remedial actions and agreement of the relevant assessor(s) therewith should be reported to senior management and the board.

1.4. IIA's Code of Ethics

Introduction

The purpose of the IIA's Code of Ethics is to promote an ethical culture in the profession of internal auditing.

Internal auditing is an independent, objective assurance and consulting activity designed to add value and improve an organization's operations. It helps an organization accomplish its objectives by bringing a systematic, disciplined approach to evaluate and improve the effectiveness of risk management, control, and governance processes.

A code of ethics is necessary and appropriate for the profession of internal auditing, founded as it is on the trust placed in its objective assurance about risk management, control, and governance. The IIA's Code of Ethics extends beyond the definition of internal auditing to include two essential components.

- Principles that are relevant to the profession and practice of internal auditing;
- Rules of Conduct that describe behavior norms expected of internal auditors. These rules are an aid to interpreting the Principles into practical applications and are intended to guide the ethical conduct of internal auditors.

The Code of Ethics together with the IIA's *Professional Practices Framework* and other relevant Institute pronouncements provide guidance to internal auditors serving others. "Internal auditors" refers to Institute members, recipients of or candidates for IIA professional certifications, and those who provide internal auditing services within the definition of internal auditing.

Applicability and enforcement. This Code of Ethics applies to both individuals and entities that provide internal auditing services.

For Institute members and recipients of or candidates for IIA professional certifications, breaches of the Code of Ethics will be evaluated and administered according to the Institute's Bylaws and Administrative Guidelines. The fact that a particular conduct is not mentioned in the Rules of Conduct does not prevent it from being unacceptable or discreditable, and therefore, the member, certification holder, or candidate can be liable for disciplinary action.

Principles. Internal auditors are expected to apply and uphold these principles.

Integrity. The integrity of internal auditors establishes trust and thus provides the basis for reliance on their judgment.

Objectivity. Internal auditors exhibit the highest level of professional objectivity in gathering, evaluating, and communicating information about the activity or process being examined. Internal auditors make a balanced assessment of all the relevant circumstances and are not unduly influenced by their own interests or by others in forming judgments.

Confidentiality. Internal auditors respect the value and ownership of information they receive and do not disclose information without appropriate authority unless there is a legal or professional obligation to do so.

Competency. Internal auditors apply the knowledge, skills, and experience needed in the performance of internal auditing services.

Rules of Conduct

1. Integrity
   Internal auditors

   1.1 Shall perform their work with honesty, diligence, and responsibility.
   1.2 Shall observe the law and make disclosures expected by the law and the profession.
   1.3 Shall not knowingly be a party to any illegal activity, or engage in acts that are discreditable to the profession of internal auditing or to the organization.
   1.4 Shall respect and contribute to the legitimate and ethical objectives of the organization.

2. Objectivity
   Internal auditors

   2.1 Shall not participate in any activity or relationship that may impair or be presumed to impair their unbiased assessment. This participation includes those activities or relationships that may be in conflict with the interests of the organization.
   2.2 Shall not accept anything that may impair or be presumed to impair their professional judgment.
   2.3 Shall disclose all material facts known to them that, if not disclosed, may distort the reporting of activities under review.

3. Confidentiality
   Internal auditors

   3.1 Shall be prudent in the use and protection of information acquired in the course of their duties.
   3.2 Shall not use information for any personal gain or in any manner that would be contrary to the law or detrimental to the legitimate and ethical objectives of the organization.

4. Competency
   Internal auditors

   4.1 Shall engage only in those services for which they have the necessary knowledge, skills, and experience.
   4.2 Shall perform internal auditing services in accordance with the *Standards for the Professional Practice of Internal Auditing.*
   4.3 Shall continually improve their proficiency and the effectiveness and quality of their services.

MULTIPLE-CHOICE QUESTIONS (1-243)

IIA's *Attribute Standards*

1. According to the IIA *Standards*, which of the following is **not** included in the scope of the internal audit function?

a. Appraising the economy and efficiency with which resources are employed.
b. Reviewing the strategic management process, assessing the quality of management decision making both quantitatively and qualitatively, and reporting the results to the audit committee.
c. Reviewing the means of safeguarding assets and, as appropriate, verifying the existence of such assets.
d. Reviewing operations or programs to ascertain whether results are consistent with established objectives and goals and whether the operations or programs are being carried out as planned.

2. An internal auditor is auditing the financial operations of an organization. Which of the following is not specified by the IIA *Standards* for inclusion in the scope of the audit?

a. Reviewing the reliability and integrity of financial information.
b. Reviewing systems established to ensure compliance with appropriate policy, plans, procedures, and other types of authority.
c. Appraising economy, efficiency, and effectiveness of the employment of resources.
d. Reviewing the financial decision-making process.

3. The audit committee of an organization has charged the director of internal auditing with bringing the department into full compliance with the IIA *Standards*. The director's first task is to develop a charter. Identify the item that should be included in the statement of objectives.

a. Report all audit findings to the audit committee every quarter.
b. Notify governmental regulatory agencies of unethical business practices by organization management.
c. Determine the adequacy and effectiveness of the organization's systems of internal controls.
d. Submit departmental budget variance reports to management every month.

4. A charter is being drafted for a newly formed internal auditing department. Which of the following **best** describes the appropriate organizational status that should be incorporated into the charter?

a. The director of internal auditing should report to the chief executive officer but have access to the board of directors.
b. The director of internal auditing should be a member of the audit committee of the board of directors.
c. The director of internal auditing should be a staff officer reporting to the chief financial officer.
d. The director of internal auditing should report to an administrative vice president.

5. If an auditee's operating standards are vague and thus subject to interpretation, the auditor should

a. Seek agreement with the auditee as to the standards to be used to measure operating performance.
b. Determine best practices in this area and use them as the standard.
c. Interpret the standards in their strictest sense because standards are otherwise only minimum measures of acceptance.
d. Omit any comments on standards and the auditee's performance in relationship to those standards, because such an analysis would be meaningless.

6. In which of the following situations does the auditor potentially lack objectivity?

a. An auditor reviews the procedures for a new electronic data interchange (EDI) connection to a major customer before it is implemented.
b. A former purchasing assistant performs a review of internal controls over purchasing four months after being transferred to the internal auditing department.
c. An auditor recommends standards of control and performance measures for a contract with a service organization for the processing of payroll and employee benefits.
d. A payroll accounting employee assists an auditor in verifying the physical inventory of small motors.

7. Which of the following actions would be a violation of auditor independence?

a. Continuing on an audit assignment at a division for which the auditor will soon be responsible as the result of a promotion.
b. Reducing the scope of an audit due to budget restrictions.
c. Participating on a task force which recommends standards for control of a new distribution system.
d. Reviewing a purchasing agent's contract drafts prior to their execution.

8. Which of the following activities would **not** be presumed to impair the independence of an internal auditor?

I. Recommending standards of control for a new information system application.
II. Drafting procedures for running a new computer application to ensure that proper controls are installed.
III. Performing reviews of procedures for a new computer application before it is installed.

a. I only.
b. II only.
c. III only.
d. I and III.

9. Which of the following is **not** a true statement about the relationship between internal auditors and external auditors?

a. Oversight of the work of external auditors is the responsibility of the director of internal auditing.
b. There may be periodic meetings between internal and external auditors to discuss matters of mutual interest.
c. There may be an exchange of audit reports and management letters between internal and external auditors.
d. Internal auditors may provide audit programs and work papers to external auditors.

10. A quality assurance program of an internal audit department provides reasonable assurance that audit work conforms to applicable standards. Which of the following activities are designed to provide feedback on the effectiveness of an audit department?

I. Proper supervision.
II. Proper training.
III. Internal reviews.
IV. External reviews.

a. I, II, and III only.
b. II, III, and IV only.
c. I, III, and IV only.
d. I, II, III, and IV.

Items 11 and 12 are based on the following:

An internal audit team recently completed an audit of the company's compliance with its lease-versus-purchase policy concerning company automobiles. The audit report noted that the basis for several decisions to lease rather than purchase automobiles had not been documented and was not auditable. The report contained a recommendation that operating management ensure that such lease agreements not be executed without proper documentation of the basis for the decision to lease rather than buy. The internal auditors are about to perform follow-up work on this audit report.

11. The primary purpose for performing a follow-up review is to

a. Ensure timely consideration of the internal auditors' recommendations.
b. Ascertain that appropriate action was taken on reported findings.
c. Allow the internal auditors to evaluate the effectiveness of their recommendations.
d. Document what management is doing in response to the audit report and close the audit file in a timely manner.

12. Assume that senior management has decided to accept the risk involved in failure to document the basis for lease-versus-purchase decisions involving company automobiles. In such a case, what would be the auditors' reporting obligation?

a. The auditors have no further reporting responsibility.
b. Management's decision and the auditors' concern should be reported to the company's board of directors.
c. The auditors should issue a follow-up report to management clearly stating the rationale for the recommendation that the basis for lease-versus-purchase decisions be properly documented.
d. The auditors should inform the external auditor and any responsible regulatory agency that no action has been taken on the finding in question.

13. Auditors realize that at times corrective action is not taken even when agreed to by the appropriate parties. This should lead an internal auditor to

a. Decide the extent of necessary followup work.
b. Allow management to decide when to follow-up, since it is management's ultimate responsibility.
c. Decide to conduct follow-up work only if management requests the auditor's assistance.
d. Write a follow-up audit report with all findings and their significance to the operations.

14. In publicly held companies, management often requires the internal auditing department's involvement with quarterly financial statements that are made public and/or used internally. Which one of the following is generally **not** a reason for such involvement?

a. Management may be concerned about its reputation in the financial markets.
b. Management may be concerned about potential penalties that could occur if quarterly financial statements that are made public are misstated.
c. The Standards state that internal auditors should be involved with reviewing quarterly financial statements.
d. Management may perceive that having quarterly financial information examined by the internal auditors enhances its value for internal decision making.

15. During testing of the effectiveness of inventory controls, the auditor makes a note in the working papers that most of the cycle count adjustments for the facility involved transactions of the machining department. The machining department also had generated an extraordinary number of cycle count adjustments in comparison to other departments last year. The auditor should

a. Interview management and apply other audit techniques to determine whether transaction controls and procedures within the machining department are adequate.
b. Do no further work because the concern was not identified by the analytical procedures designed in the audit program.
c. Notify internal audit management that fraud is suspected.
d. Place a note in the working papers to review this matter in detail during the next review.

16. Developing an audit finding involves comparing the condition to the relevant standard or criterion. Which of the following choices best represents an appropriate standard or criterion to support a finding?

a. A quality standard operating procedure (number and date) for the department.
b. An internal accounting control principle, cited and copied from a public accounting reference.
c. A sound business practice, based on the internal auditor's knowledge and experience obtained during many audit assignments within the company.
d. All of the above.

17. An internal audit director for a large manufacturing company is considering revising the department's audit charter with respect to the minimum educational and experience qualifications required. The audit director wants to require all staff auditors to possess specialized training in accounting and a professional auditing certification such as the Certified Internal Auditor (CIA) or the Chartered Accountant (CA). One of the **disadvantages** of imposing this requirement would be

a. The policy might negatively affect the department's ability to perform quality examinations of the company's financial and accounting systems.
b. The policy would not promote the professionalism of the department.
c. The policy would prevent the department from using outside consultants when the department did

not have the skills and knowledge required in certain audit situations.

d. The policy could limit the range of activities that could be audited by the department due to the department's narrow expertise and backgrounds.

18. An organization was in the process of establishing its new internal audit department. The controller had no previous experience with internal auditors. Due to this lack of experience, the controller advised the applicants that they would be reporting to the external auditors. However, the new director of internal audit would have free access to the controller to report anything important. The controller would convey the director's concerns to the board of directors. Which of the following is true?

a. The internal audit department will be independent because the director has direct access to the board of directors.
b. The internal audit department will not be independent because the director reports to the external auditors.
c. The internal audit department will not be independent because the controller has no experience with internal auditors.
d. The internal audit department will not be independent because the company did not specify that the applicants must be Certified Internal Auditors.

Items 19 and 20 are based on the following:

During a year-end planning meeting with senior management, the director of internal auditing learns that a recent draft audit report on one of the company's inventory costing systems had provoked a discussion in the accounting area. The audit report proposed a relatively large adjustment due to an error in the local inventory system. The auditor's conclusion stated that six other production facilities using the same costing system would require similar inventory adjustments. The total required adjustment for all seven locations represented a material adjustment to the financial statements, according to the chief financial officer (CFO). The CFO questioned the method used by the auditor to calculate the amount of the inventory adjustment and asked the director of internal auditing to delay processing the audit report until all aspects of the finding had been fully considered. The director of internal auditing reports directly to the CFO. The audit committee has not been apprised of this audit because the audit report is still in draft stage awaiting management comment.

19. Assuming that there is a meeting later the same day with the audit committee of the board, which of the following is **not** a responsibility of the director of internal auditing?

a. Inform the audit committee of senior management's decisions on all significant audit findings.
b. Highlight significant audit findings and recommendations and report on the approved audit work schedule.
c. Inform the audit committee of the outcome of earlier meetings with the CFO and the options being considered for recording the inventory adjustment.
d. Attempt to resolve the inventory issue before reporting the finding to the audit committee.

20. Which of the following actions should the director take?

a. Schedule audits to review the inventory costing systems at all locations after year-end.
b. Recall all copies of the draft audit report sent out for management review and response.
c. Tell the representatives of senior management that distorting financial reports is not acceptable.
d. Offer to review the basis for the conclusion about the inventory valuation at all locations.

21. An inexperienced internal auditor notified the senior auditor of a significant variance from the auditee's budget. The senior told the new auditor not to worry as the senior had heard that there had been an unauthorized work stoppage that probably accounted for the difference. Which of the following statements is most appropriate?

a. The new auditor should have investigated the matter fully and not bothered the senior.
b. The senior used proper judgment in curtailing what could have been a wasteful investigation.
c. The senior should have halted the audit until the variance was fully explained.
d. The senior should have aided the new auditor in formulating a plan for accumulating appropriate evidence.

22. The IIA *Standards* state that internal auditors are "responsible for continuing their education in order to maintain their proficiency." Which of the following is correct regarding the continuing education requirements of the practicing internal auditor?

a. Internal auditors are required to obtain 40 hours of continuing professional development each year and a minimum of 120 hours over a three-year period.
b. CIAs have formal requirements that must be met in order to continue as a CIA.
c. Attendance, as an officer or committee member, at formal Institute of Internal Auditors meetings does not meet the criteria of continuing professional development.
d. In-house programs meet continuing professional development requirements only if they have been preapproved by the Institute of Internal Auditors.

23. A significant part of the auditor's working papers will be the conclusions reached by the auditor regarding the audit area. In some situations, the supervisor might not agree with the conclusions and will ask the staff auditor to perform more work. Assume that after subsequent work is performed, the staff auditor and the supervisor continue to disagree on the conclusions documented in the working paper developed by the staff auditor. Which of the following audit department responses would **not** be appropriate?

a. Both the staff auditor and the supervisor document their reasons for reaching different conclusions. Retain the rationale of both parties in the working papers.
b. Note the disagreement and retain the notice of disagreement and follow-up work in the audit working papers.
c. Present both conclusions to the director of internal auditing for resolution. The director may resolve the matter.
d. Present both conclusions in the audit report and let management and the auditee react to both.

24. The IIA *Standards* specify that supervision of the work of internal auditors be "carried out continuously." Which of the following statements regarding supervision is correct?

I. "Continuously" indicates that supervision should be performed throughout the planning, examination, evaluation, report, and follow-up stages of the audit.
II. Supervision should also be extended to training, time reporting, and expense control, as well as similar administrative matters.
III. The extent and nature of supervision needs to be documented, preferably in the appropriate working papers.

a. I only.
b. I and III only.
c. II only.
d. I, II, and III.

25. It would be appropriate for internal auditing departments to use consultants with expertise in health care benefits when the internal auditing department is

a. Conducting an audit of the organization's estimate of its liability for postretirement benefits, which include health care benefits.
b. Comparing the cost of the organization's health care program with other programs offered in the industry.
c. Training its staff to conduct an audit of health care costs in a major division of the organization.
d. All of the above.

26. An auditor has uncovered facts that could be interpreted as indicating unlawful activity on the part of an auditee. The auditor decides not to inform senior management of these facts since he cannot prove that an irregularity occurred. The auditor, however, decides that if questions are raised regarding the omitted facts, they will be answered fully and truthfully. In taking this action, the auditor

a. Has not violated the Code of Ethics or the *Standards* because confidentiality takes precedence over all other standards.
b. Has not violated the Code of Ethics or the Standards because the auditor is committed to answering all questions fully and truthfully.
c. Has violated the Code of Ethics because unlawful acts should have been reported to the appropriate regulatory agency to avoid potential "aiding and abetting" by the auditor.
d. Has violated the *Standards* because the auditor should inform the appropriate authorities in the organization if fraud may be indicated.

27. A new staff auditor was told to perform an audit in an area with which the auditor was not familiar. Because of time constraints, there was no supervision of the audit. The auditor was given the assignment because it represented a good learning experience, but the area was clearly beyond the auditor's competence. Nonetheless, the auditor prepared comprehensive working papers and reported the results to management. In this situation

a. The audit department violated the IIA *Standards* by hiring an auditor without proficiency in the area.
b. The audit department violated the IIA *Standards* by not providing adequate supervision.
c. The director of internal auditing has not violated the Code of Ethics since the code does not address supervision.
d. The IIA's *Standards* and the Code of Ethics were followed by the audit department.

28. Management has requested the internal auditing department to perform an operational audit of the telephone marketing operations of a major division and to recommend procedures and policies for improving management control over the operation. The auditor should

a. Not accept the engagement because recommending controls would impair future objectivity of the department regarding this auditee.
b. Not accept the engagement because audit departments are presumed to have expertise on accounting controls, not marketing controls.
c. Accept the engagement, but indicate to management that recommending controls would impair audit independence so management knows that future audits of the area would be impaired.
d. Accept the audit engagement because independence would not be impaired.

29. A new staff auditor has been assigned to an audit of the cash management operations of the organization. The staff auditor has no background in cash management, and this is the auditor's first audit. Under which of the following conditions would the internal auditing department be in compliance with the *Standards* regarding knowledge and skills?

a. The senior auditor is skilled in the area and closely supervises the staff auditor.
b. The staff auditor performs the work and prepares a report that is reviewed in detail by the director of audit.
c. Both a. and b.
d. Neither a. nor b.

30. Communication skills are important to internal auditors. According to the *Standards*, the auditor should be able to effectively convey all of the following to the auditee **except:**

a. The audit objectives designed for a specific auditable entity.
b. The audit evaluations based on a preliminary survey of an auditable entity.
c. The risk assessment used in selecting the area for audit investigation.
d. Recommendations that are generated in relationship to a specific auditable entity.

31. Internal auditing is unique in that its scope often encompasses all areas of an organization. Thus, it is not possible for each internal auditor to possess detailed competence in all areas that might be audited. Which of the following competencies is required by the IIA *Standards* for every internal auditor?

a. Taxation and law as it applies to operation of the organization.
b. Proficiency in accounting principles.
c. Understanding of management principles.
d. Proficiency in computer systems and databases.

32. The IIA *Standards* would **not** require the director of internal auditing to

a. Contribute resources for the annual audit of financial statements.

b. Coordinate audit work with that of the external auditors.
c. Communicate to senior management and the board the results of evaluations of the coordination between internal and external auditors.
d. Communicate to senior management and the board the results of evaluations of the performance of external auditors.

33. Follow-up activity may be required to ensure that corrective action has taken place for certain findings. The internal audit department's responsibility to perform follow-up activities as required should be defined in the
a. Internal auditing department's written charter.
b. Mission statement of the audit committee.
c. Engagement memo issued prior to each audit assignment.
d. Purpose statement within applicable audit reports.

34. As a particular audit is being planned in a high-risk area, the director of internal auditing determines that the available staff does not have the requisite skills to perform the assignment. The best course of action consistent with audit planning standards would be to
a. Not perform the audit, since the requisite skills are not available.
b. Use the audit as a training opportunity and let the auditors learn as the audit is performed.
c. Consider using external resources to supplement the needed knowledge, skills, and disciplines and complete the assignment.
d. Perform the audit but limit the scope in light of the skill deficiency.

35. According to the IIA *Standards*, internal auditors must be objective in performing audits. Assume that the internal audit director received an annual bonus as part of that individual's compensation package. The bonus may impair the audit director's objectivity if
a. The bonus is administered by the board of directors or its salary administration committee.
b. The bonus is based on dollar recoveries or recommended future savings as a result of audits.
c. The scope of internal auditing work is reviewing control rather than account balances.
d. All of the above.

36. A company is planning to develop and implement a new computerized purchase order system in one of its manufacturing subsidiaries. The vice president of manufacturing has requested that internal auditors participate on a team consisting of representatives from finance, manufacturing, purchasing, and marketing. This team will be responsible for the implementation effort. Eager to take on this high-profile project, the Director of Auditing assigns a senior auditor to the project to assist "as needed." Assuming the senior auditor performed all of the following activities, which one of the following would impair objectivity if asked to review the purchase order system on a postaudit basis?
a. Helping to identify and define control objectives.
b. Testing for compliance with system development standards.
c. Reviewing the adequacy of systems and programming standards.
d. Drafting operating procedures for the new system.

37. An internal audit department is currently undergoing its first external quality assurance review since its formation three years ago. From interviews with a few of the staff auditors, the review team is informed of certain auditor activities that occurred over the past year. Which of the following activities could affect the quality assurance review team's evaluation of the objectivity of the internal audit department?
a. One internal auditor told the review team that, during the payroll audit, the payroll manager approached him. The manager indicated he was looking for an accountant to prepare his financial statements for his part-time business. The internal auditor agreed to perform this work for a reduced fee during nonwork hours.
b. During the audit of the company's construction of a building addition to the corporate office, the vice-president of facilities management gave the auditor a commemorative mug with the company's logo. These mugs were distributed to all employees present at the groundbreaking ceremony.
c. After reviewing the installation of a data processing system, the auditor made recommendations on standards of control. Three months after completing the audit, the auditee requested the auditor's review of certain procedures for adequacy. The auditor agreed and performed this review.
d. An auditor's participation was requested on a task force to reduce the company's inventory losses from theft and shrinkage. This is the first consulting assignment undertaken by the audit department. The auditor's role is to advise the task force on appropriate control techniques.

38. A medium-size publicly owned corporation operating in Country X has grown to a size that the directors of the corporation believe warrants the establishment of an internal auditing department. Country X has legislated internal auditing requirements for government-owned companies. The company changed the corporate bylaws to reflect the establishment of the internal auditing department. The directors decided that the director of internal auditing must be a Certified Internal Auditor and will report directly to the newly established audit committee of the board of directors. Which of the items discussed above will contribute the most to the new audit director's independence?
a. The establishment of the internal auditing department is documented in corporate bylaws.
b. Legislated internal auditing requirements in Country X.
c. The fact that the director will report to the audit committee of the board of directors.
d. The fact that the director is to be a Certified Internal Auditor.

39. An internal auditor reports directly to the board of directors. The auditor discovered a material cash shortage. When questioned, the person responsible explained that the cash was used to cover sizable medical expenses for a child and agreed to replace the funds. Because of the corrective action, the internal auditor did not inform management. In this instance, the auditor
a. Has organizational independence but not objectivity.

b. Has both organizational independence and objectivity.
c. Does not have organizational independence but has objectivity.
d. Does not have either organizational independence or objectivity.

40. During a purchasing audit, the internal auditor finds that the largest blanket purchase order is for tires, which are expensed as vehicle maintenance items. The fleet manager requisitions tires against the blanket order for the company's 400-vehicle service fleet based on a visual inspection of the cars and trucks in the parking lot each week. Sometimes the fleet manager picks up the tires, but she always signs the receiving report for payment. Vehicle service data are entered into a maintenance database by the mechanic after the tires are installed. Which would be the best course of action for the auditor in these circumstances?

a. Determine whether the number of tires purchased can be reconciled to maintenance records.
b. Count the number of tires on hand and trace them to the related receiving reports.
c. Select a judgmental sample of requisitions and verify that the fleet manager signs each one.
d. Compare the number of tires purchased under the blanket purchase order with the number of tires purchased in the prior year for reasonableness.

41. Auditors need to determine if management has established criteria to determine if goals and objectives have been accomplished. If the auditor determines such criteria are inadequate or nonexistent, which of the following actions would be appropriate?

I. Report the inadequacies to the appropriate level of management and recommend appropriate courses of action.
II. Recommend alternative sources of criteria to management such as acceptable industry standards.
III. Formulate criteria the auditor believes to be adequate and perform the audit and report in relationship to the alternative criteria.

a. I only.
b. I and II only.
c. I, II, and III.
d. II only.

42. Several members of senior management have questioned whether the internal audit department should report to the newly established quality audit function as part of the total quality management process within the company. The director of internal auditing has reviewed the quality standards and the programs that the quality audit manager have proposed. The director's response to senior management should include

a. Changing the applicable standards for internal auditing within the company to provide compliance with quality audit standards.
b. Changing the qualification requirements for new staff members to include quality audit experience.
c. Estimating departmental cost savings from eliminating the internal auditing function.
d. Identifying appropriate liaison activities with the quality audit function to ensure coordination of audit schedules and overall audit responsibilities.

43. Internal auditors are often called on either to perform or to assist the external auditor in performing a due diligence review. A due diligence review is

a. A review of interim financial statements as directed by an underwriting firm.
b. An operational audit of a division of a company to determine if divisional management is complying with laws and regulations.
c. A review of operations as requested by the audit committee to determine whether the operations comply with audit committee and organizational policies.
d. A review of financial statements and related disclosures in conjunction with a potential acquisition.

Items 44 through 47 are based on the following:

The director of internal auditing of a midsize internal auditing organization was concerned that management might outsource the internal auditing function. Therefore, the manager adopted a very aggressive program to promote the internal auditing department within the organization. The manager planned to present the results to management and the audit committee and recommend modification of the Internal Audit Charter after using the new program. The following lists six actions the audit manager took to promote a positive image within the organization:

1. Audit assignments concentrated on economy and efficiency audits. The audits focused solely on cost savings, and each audit report highlighted potential costs to be saved. Negative findings were omitted. The focus on economy and efficiency audits was new, but the auditees seemed very happy.
2. Drafts of all audit reports were carefully reviewed with the auditee to get their input. Their comments were carefully considered when developing the final audit report.
3. The information technology auditor participated as part of a development team to review the control procedures to be incorporated into a major computer application under development.
4. Given limited resources, the audit manager performed a risk analysis to determine which locations to audit. This was a marked departure from the previous approach of ensuring that all operations are reviewed at least every three years.
5. In order to save time, the manager no longer required that a standard internal control questionnaire be completed for each audit.
6. When the auditors found that management and the auditee had not developed specific criteria or data to evaluate the operations of the auditee, the audit team was instructed to perform research, develop specific criteria, review the criteria with the auditee, and, if acceptable, use that criteria to evaluate the auditee's operations. If the auditee disagreed with the criteria, a negotiation took place until acceptable criteria could be agreed on. The audit report commented on the auditee's operations in conjunction with the agreed-on criteria.

44. Which of the following elements of Action 1 taken by the audit manager would be considered a violation of the IIA *Standards*?

I. The type of audits was changed before modifying the charter and going to the audit committee.
II. Negative findings were omitted from the audit reports.
III. Cost savings and recommendations were highlighted in the report.

a. I and II.
b. I and III.
c. I only.
d. II and III.

45. Considering Actions 2, 3, and 4 that were taken, which would be considered a violation of the IIA *Standards*?

a. Actions 2, 3, and 4.
b. Action 4 only.
c. Action 2 and 3 only.
d. None of the actions.

46. Is Action 5 a violation of the IIA *Standards*?

a. Yes. Internal control should be evaluated on every audit, but the internal control questionnaire is not the mandated approach to evaluate the controls.
b. No. Auditors may omit necessary procedures if there is a time constraint. It is a matter of audit judgment.
c. Yes. Internal control should be evaluated on every audit engagement, and the internal control questionnaire is the most efficient method to do so.
d. No. Auditors are not required to fill out internal control questionnaires on every audit.

47. Regarding Action 6, which of the following elements of the action would be considered a violation of the IIA *Standards*?

a. Failing to report the lack of criteria to appropriate level of management.
b. Developing a set of criteria to present to the auditee as a basis for evaluating the auditee's operations.
c. Commenting on the agreed-on criteria.
d. All of the above.

48. Given the acceptance of the cost savings audits and the scarcity of internal audit resources, the audit manager also decided that follow-up action was not needed. The manager reasoned that cost savings should be sufficient to motivate the auditee to implement the auditor's recommendations. Therefore, follow-up was not scheduled as a regular part of the audit plan. Does the audit manager's decision violate the *Standards*?

a. No. The Standards do not specify whether follow-up is needed.
b. Yes. The Standards require the auditors to determine whether the auditee has appropriately implemented all of the auditor's recommendations.
c. Yes. Scarcity of resources is not a sufficient reason to omit follow-up action.
d. No. When there is evidence of sufficient motivation by the auditee, there is no need for follow-up action.

49. Reporting to senior management and the board is an important part of the auditor's obligation. Which of the following items is **not** required to be reported to senior management and/or the board?

a. Subsequent to the completion of an audit, but prior to the issuance of an audit report, the audit senior in charge of the audit was offered a permanent position in the auditee's department.
b. An annual report summary of the department's audit work schedule and financial budget.
c. Significant interim changes to the approved audit work schedule and financial budget.
d. An audit plan was approved by senior management and the board. Subsequent to the approval, senior management informed the audit director not to perform an audit of a division because the division's activities were very sensitive.

50. It has been established that an internal auditing charter is one of the more important factors positively affecting the internal auditing department's independence. The IIA *Standards* help clarify the nature of the charter by providing guidelines as to the contents of the charter. Which of the following is **not** suggested in the *Standards* as part of the charter?

a. The department's access to records within the organization.
b. The scope of internal auditing activities.
c. The length of tenure for the internal auditing director.
d. The department's access to personnel within the organization.

51. The preliminary survey indicates that severe staff reductions at the audit location have resulted in extensive amounts of overtime among accounting staff. Department members are visibly stressed and very vocal about the effects of the cutbacks. Accounting payrolls are nearly equal to prior years, and many key controls, such as segregation of duties, are no longer in place. The accounting supervisor now performs all operations within the cash receipts and posting process, and has no time to review and approve transactions generated by the remaining members of the department. Journal entries for the last six months since the staff reductions show increasing numbers of prior month adjustments and corrections, including revenues, cost of sales, and accruals that had been misstated or forgotten during month-end closing activity. The auditor should

a. Discuss these findings with audit management to determine whether further audit work would be an efficient use of audit resources at this time.
b. Proceed with the scheduled audit but add audit personnel based on the expected number of findings and anticipated lack of assistance from local accounting management.
c. Research temporary helps agencies and evaluates the cost and benefit of outsourcing needed services.
d. Suspend further audit work because the findings are obvious and issue the audit report.

52. Auditors realize that at times corrective action is not taken even when agreed to by the appropriate parties. This should lead an internal auditor to

a. Decide the extent of necessary follow-up work.
b. Allow management to decide when to followup, since it is management's ultimate responsibility.
c. Decide to conduct follow-up work only if management requests the auditor's assistance.
d. Write a follow-up audit report with all findings and their significance to the operations.

53. Which of the following actions would be a violation of independence?

a. Continuing on an audit assignment at a division for which the auditor will soon be responsible as the result of a promotion.
b. Reducing the scope of an audit due to budget restrictions.
c. Participating on a task force that recommends standards for control of a new distribution system.
d. Reviewing a purchasing agent's contract drafts prior to execution.

54. Management has requested the audit department to conduct an audit of the implementation of its recently developed company code of conduct. In preparing for the audit, the auditor reviews the newly developed code, compares it with several others for comparable companies, and concludes that the newly developed code has severe deficiencies. Based on this conclusion, the auditor should

a. Plan an audit for the implementation of management's code of conduct and also for compliance with the "best practices" from the other codes since this represents the best available criteria.
b. Report the nature of the deficiencies in a formal report to management.
c. Inform management of the problems with the existing code and report that it would be inappropriate to conduct an audit until the code is revised to incorporate the "best practices" from industry.
d. Conduct the audit as requested by management, reporting only noncompliance with the code.

55. Internal auditing standards assign the responsibility for providing appropriate audit supervision to the

a. Audit committee.
b. Director of internal auditing.
c. Audit supervisor.
d. Senior auditor.

56. The IIA *Standards* require that the director of internal auditing seek the approval of management and acceptance by the board of a formal written charter for the internal auditing department. The purpose of this charter is to

a. Protect the internal auditing department from undue outside influence.
b. Establish the purpose, authority, and responsibility of the internal auditing department.
c. Clearly define the relationship between internal and external auditing.
d. Establish the director's status as a staff executive.

57. The primary criteria for determining the adequacy of working papers can be found in the

a. IIA *Standards*.
b. Institute's Code of Ethics.
c. Statement of Responsibilities of Internal Auditing.
d. Foreign Corrupt Practices Act.

58. Based on the IIA *Standards*, an internal auditing department's staff development program will be deficient if individual employees are

a. Given a large variety of tasks to perform.
b. Expected to study current events on an independent basis.
c. Assigned to a different supervisor on each job.
d. Formally evaluated once every two years.

59. The IIA *Standards* require written policies and procedures to guide the audit staff. Which of the following statements is **false** with respect to this requirement?

a. The form and content of written policies and procedures should be appropriate to the size of the department.
b. All internal audit departments should have a detailed policies and procedures manual.
c. Formal administrative and technical audit manuals may not be needed by all internal auditing departments.
d. A small internal auditing department may be managed informally through close supervision and written memos.

Items 60 and 61 are based on the following:

Paragraph 1: The production department has the newest production equipment available because of a fire that required the replacement of all equipment.

Paragraph 2: The members of the production department have become completely comfortable with the state-of-the-art technology over the past year and a half. As a result, the production department has become an industry leader in production efficiency and effectiveness.

Paragraph 3: The production department produces an average of 25 units per worker per shift. The defect rate is 1%.

Paragraph 4: The industry average productivity is 20 units per worker per shift. The industry defect rate is 3%.

60. Which paragraph would be characterized as the attribute described in the IIA *Standards* as "Criteria"?

a. 1
b. 2
c. 3
d. 4

61. Which paragraph would be characterized as the attribute described in the IIA *Standards* as "Condition"?

a. 1
b. 2
c. 3
d. 4

62. A relatively new internal auditor is completing an audit report. The final report should most appropriately be signed by

a. The auditor because of a greater level of detail knowledge of the report.
b. The auditor and the person in charge of the area being audited to indicate review of the report.
c. The director of internal auditing.
d. The chairman of the audit committee of the board of directors.

63. An auditor often faces special problems when auditing a foreign subsidiary. Which of the following statements is **false** with respect to the conduct of international audits?

a. The IIA *Standards* do not apply outside of the United States.
b. The auditor should determine whether managers are in compliance with local laws.
c. There may be justification for having different company policies in force in foreign branches.
d. It is preferable to have multilingual auditors conduct audits at branches in non–English-speaking nations.

64. The interpretation related to quality assurance given by the IIA *Standards* is that
a. Quality assurance reviews can provide senior management and the audit committee with an assessment of the internal auditing function.
b. Appropriate follow-up to an external review is the responsibility of the internal auditing director's immediate supervisor.
c. The internal auditing department is primarily measured against the Institute's Code of Ethics.
d. Continual supervision is limited to the planning, examination, evaluation report, and follow-up process.

65. An internal auditor fails to discover an employee fraud during an audit. The nondiscovery is most likely to suggest a violation of the IIA *Standards* if it was the result of a
a. Failure to perform a detailed audit of all transactions in the area.
b. Determination that any possible fraud in the area would not involve a material amount.
c. Determination that the cost of extending audit procedures in the area would exceed the potential benefits.
d. Presumption that the internal controls in the area were adequate and effective.

66. Which of the following will best promote the independence of the internal auditing function?
a. A quality control system within the internal auditing function designed to ensure that departmental objectives are met.
b. Direct lines of communication between the audit committee and the director of internal auditing.
c. A written charter that reflects the concepts contained in the Statement of Responsibilities of Internal Auditing.
d. Direct reporting responsibilities to the company's chief financial officer.

67. The charter of a newly formed internal auditing department contains the following statement: "The organizational status of the internal auditing department will be sufficient to permit the accomplishment of its audit responsibilities." From the following relationships, select the best reporting lines that would promote the accomplishment of the intended organizational status. Solid line to
a. Board of directors, dotted line to vice president of finance.
b. President, dotted line to board of directors.
c. Controller, dotted line to board of directors.
d. Vice president, finance, dotted line to board of directors.

68. According to the IIA *Standards*, the purpose of an internal auditor's review for effectiveness of the system of internal control is to ascertain if
a. The system is functioning as intended.
b. The system is functioning efficiently and economically.
c. The organization's goals and objectives have been achieved.
d. Financial and operating data are reliable.

69. The best description of the purpose of internal auditing is that it
a. Furnishes members of the organization with information needed to effectively discharge their responsibilities.
b. Reviews the reliability and integrity of financial and operating information.
c. Reviews the means of safeguarding assets and, as appropriate, verifies the existence of such assets.
d. Appraises the economy and efficiency with which resources are employed.

70. The director of a newly formed internal auditing department is seeking management approval of a charter. What is the authoritative source for seeking such approval?
a. The IIA *Standards,* which clearly place that responsibility on the director.
b. The appropriate Practice Advisories, which require the director to take that course of action.
c. The Code of Ethics, which requires internal auditors to document company policy.
d. According to the IIA *Standards*, no approval is necessary.

71. According to the IIA *Standards*, the staff of a newly developed internal auditing department should include
a. Members with bachelor's degrees in accounting and related fields.
b. Members possessing appropriate professional designations.
c. Members proficient in applying internal auditing standards, procedures, and techniques.
d. Members with prior internal audit experience.

72. According to the IIA *Standards*, which of the following **best** describes the nature of opinions that are appropriate for internal audit reports?
a. Opinions are generally the auditor's subjective judgments concerning why deficiencies exist.
b. Opinions are the auditor's evaluations of the effects of the findings on the activities reviewed.
c. Opinions are conclusions that the auditor has reached concerning the appropriateness of the auditee's objectives.
d. Opinions should only involve the fairness of the auditee's financial statements.

73. The director of internal auditing is concerned that a recently disclosed fraud was not uncovered during the last audit of cash operations. A review of the work papers indicated that the fraudulent transaction was not included in a properly designed statistical sample of transactions tested. Which of the following applies to this situation?
a. Because cash operation is a high-risk area, 100% testing of transactions should have been performed.
b. The internal auditor acted with due professional care since an appropriate statistical sample of material transactions was tested.
c. Fraud should not have gone undetected in a recently audited area.
d. Extraordinary care is necessary in the performance of a cash operations audit and the auditor should be held responsible for the oversight.

74. In the course of their work, internal auditors must be alert for fraud and other forms of white-collar crime. The important characteristic that **distinguishes** fraud from other varieties of white-collar crime is that

a. Fraud encompasses an array of irregularities and illegal acts that involve intentional deception.
b. Unlike other white-collar crimes, fraud is always perpetrated against an outside party.
c. White-collar crime is usually perpetrated for the benefit of an organization, whereas fraud benefits an individual.
d. White-collar crime is usually perpetrated by outsiders to the detriment of an organization, whereas fraud is perpetrated by insiders to benefit the organization.

75. During an audit of purchasing, internal auditors found several violations of company policy concerning competitive bidding. The same condition had been reported in an audit report last year, and corrective action had not been taken. Which of the following **best** describes the appropriate action concerning this repeat finding?
a. The audit report should note that this same condition had been reported in the prior audit.
b. During the exit interview, management should be made aware that a finding from the prior report had not been corrected.
c. The director of internal auditing should determine whether management or the board has assumed the risk of not taking corrective action.
d. The director of internal auditing should determine whether this condition should be reported to the independent auditor and any regulatory agency.

76. Internal auditing is responsible for assisting in the prevention of fraud by
a. Informing the appropriate authorities within the organization and recommending whatever investigation is considered necessary in the circumstances when wrongdoing is suspected.
b. Establishing the systems designed to ensure compliance with the organization's policies, plans, and procedures, as well as applicable laws and regulations.
c. Examining and evaluating the adequacy and the effectiveness of control, commensurate with the extent of the potential exposure/risk in the various segments of the organization's operations.
d. Determining whether operating standards have been established for measuring economy and efficiency, and whether these standards are understood and are being met.

77. Which of the following combination of participants would be **most** appropriate to attend an exit conference?
a. The responsible internal auditor and representatives from management who are knowledgeable regarding detailed operations and those who can authorize implementation of corrective action.
b. The director of internal audit and the executive in charge of the activity or function audited.
c. Staff auditors who conducted the fieldwork and operating personnel in charge of the daily performance of the activity or function audited.
d. Staff auditors who conducted the fieldwork and the executive in charge of the activity or function audited.

78. An internal audit of sales contracts revealed that a bribe had been paid to secure a major contract. It was considered possible that a senior executive had authorized the bribe. Which of the following **best** describes the proper distribution of the completed audit report?
a. The report should be distributed to the chief executive officer and the appropriate regulatory agency.
b. The report should be distributed to the board of directors, the chief executive officer, and the independent auditor.
c. The director of internal auditing should provide the board of directors a copy of the report and decide whether further distribution is appropriate.
d. The report should be distributed to the board of directors, the appropriate law enforcement agency, and the appropriate regulatory agency.

79. The IIA *Standards* define "relevant evidence" as
a. Factual, adequate, and convincing.
b. Reliable and the best attainable through the use of appropriate audit techniques.
c. Consistent with the audit objectives and supports audit findings and recommendations.
d. Information that helps the organization meets its goals.

80. Which is the lowest organizational level to which the internal auditing department should address the final report of the operational audit of the production department?
a. The audit committee of the board of directors.
b. The chief executive officer.
c. The vice president of production.
d. The first-line supervisor.

81. Which of the following is **not** ordinarily an objective of a quality assurance review? To determine compliance with
a. Applicable laws and regulations.
b. The general standards for the professional practice of internal auditing.
c. The specific standards for the professional practice of internal auditing.
d. The goals of the internal audit function.

82. According to the IIA *Standards*, the independence of internal auditors is achieved through
a. Staffing and supervision.
b. Continuing education and due professional care.
c. Human relations and communications.
d. Organizational status and objectivity.

83. According to the IIA *Standards*, an internal auditor should possess proficiency in
a. Management principles.
b. The fundamentals of such subjects as accounting, economics, and finance.
c. Computerized information systems.
d. Applying internal auditing standards, procedures, and techniques.

84. Which of the following audit committee activities would be of the greatest benefit to the internal auditing department?
a. Review and approval of audit programs.
b. Assurance that the external auditor will rely on the work of the internal auditing department whenever possible.
c. Review and endorsement of all internal audit reports prior to their release.
d. Support for appropriate follow-up of recommendations made by the internal auditing department.

85. Which of the following relationships best depicts the appropriate dual reporting responsibility of the internal auditor? Administratively to the

a. Board of directors, functionally to the chief executive officer.
b. Controller, functionally to the chief financial officer.
c. Chief executive officer, functionally to the board of directors.
d. Chief executive officer, functionally to the external auditor.

86. According to the IIA *Standards*, the documentation required to plan an internal auditing project should include evidence that the

a. Expected findings were clearly identified.
b. Internal auditing department's resources are effectively and efficiently employed.
c. Planned audit work will be completed on a timely basis.
d. Resources needed to perform the audit have been considered.

87. The IIA *Standards* require an internal auditor to exercise due professional care in performing internal audits. This includes

a. Establishing direct communication between the director of internal auditing and the board of directors.
b. Evaluating established operating standards and determining whether those standards are acceptable and are being met.
c. Accumulating sufficient evidence so that the auditor can give absolute assurance that irregularities do not exist.
d. Establishing suitable criteria of education and experience for filling internal audit positions.

88. The director of internal auditing for a large retail organization reports to the controller and is responsible for designing and installing computer applications relating to inventory control. Which of the following is the major limitation of this arrangement?

a. It prevents the audit organization from devoting full time to auditing.
b. Auditors generally do not have the required expertise to design and implement such systems.
c. It potentially affects the director's independence and thereby lessens the value of audit services.
d. Such arrangements are unlawful because the director participates in incompatible functions.

89. According to the IIA *Standards*, the internal auditing department's goals should specify

a. Audit work schedules and activities to be audited.
b. Policies and procedures to guide the audit staff.
c. Measurement criteria and target dates for completion.
d. Staffing plans and financial budgets.

90. According to the IIA *Standards*, internal auditors should possess the knowledge, skills, and disciplines essential to the performance of internal auditing. This means that all internal auditors should be proficient in applying

a. Internal auditing standards.
b. Quantitative methods.
c. Management principles.
d. Structured systems analysis.

91. Coordination of internal and external auditing can reduce the overall audit costs. According to the IIA *Standards*, who is responsible for coordinating internal and external audit efforts?

a. Director of internal auditing.
b. External auditor.
c. Audit committee of the board of directors.
d. Management.

92. You have been asked to be a member of a peer review team. In assessing the independence of the internal audit department being reviewed, you should consider all of the following factors **except:**

a. Access to and frequency of communications with the board of directors or its audit committee.
b. The criteria of education and experience considered necessary when filling vacant positions on the audit staff.
c. The degree to which auditors assume operating responsibilities.
d. The scope and depth of audit objectives for the audits included in the review.

93. The IIA *Standards* require that, in most cases, an internal auditing department have documented policies and procedures to ensure the consistency and quality of audit work. The exception to this requirement is directly related to

a. Departmentalization.
b. Division of labor.
c. Span of control.
d. Authority.

94. The director of internal auditing routinely provides activity reports to the board as part of the board meeting agenda each quarter. Senior management has asked to review the director's board presentation before each board meeting so that any issues or questions can be discussed beforehand. The director should

a. Provide the activity reports to senior management as requested and discuss any issues that may require action to be taken.
b. Not provide activity reports to senior management because such matters are the sole province of the board.
c. Disclose only those matters in the activity reports to the board that pertain to expenditures and financial budgets of the internal auditing department.
d. Provide information to senior management that pertains only to completed audits and findings available in published audit reports.

95. An auditor finds a situation where there is some suspicion, but no evidence, of potential misstatement. The standard of due professional care would be violated if the auditor

a. Identified potential ways in which an error could occur and ranked the items for audit investigation.
b. Informed the audit manager of the suspicions and asked for advice on how to proceed.
c. Did not test for possible misstatement because the audit program had already been approved by audit management.

d. Expanded the audit program, without the auditee's approval, to address the highest-ranked ways in which a misstatement may have occurred.

96. Which of the following combination of participants would be **most** appropriate to attend an exit conference?

a. The responsible internal auditor and representatives from management who are knowledgeable of detailed operations and those who can authorize implementation of corrective action.
b. The director of internal auditing and the executive in charge of the activity or function audited.
c. Staff auditors who conducted the fieldwork and operating personnel in charge of the daily performance of the activity or function audited.
d. Staff auditors who conducted the fieldwork and the executive in charge of the activity or function audited.

97. An internal audit director initiated an audit of the corporate code of ethics and the environment for ethical decision making. Which of the following would **most** likely be considered **inappropriate** regarding the scope and/or recommendations of the audit?

a. A review of the corporate code of ethics and a comparison to other corporate codes.
b. A survey of corporate employees, asking general questions regarding the ethical quality of corporate decision making.
c. Administration of an anonymous "ethics test" to determine if employees know of unethical behavior or have acted unethically themselves.
d. A survey of the board of directors to determine members' level of support for a corporate code of ethics.

98. Which of the following statements is **true** regarding coordination of internal and external audit efforts?

a. The director of internal audit should not give information about illegal acts to an external auditor because external auditors may be required to report the matter to the board and/or regulatory agencies.
b. Ownership and the confidentiality of the external auditor's working papers prohibit their review by internal auditors.
c. The director of internal audit should determine that appropriate follow-up and corrective action was taken by management where required on matters discussed in the external auditor's management letter.
d. If internal auditors provide assistance to the external auditors in connection with the annual audit, the audit work is not subject to the Standards for the Professional Practice of Internal Auditing.

99. An auditor's objectivity could be compromised in all of the following situations **except:**

a. A conflict of interest.
b. Auditee familiarity with auditor due to lack of rotation in assignments.
c. Auditor assumption of operational duties on a temporary basis.
d. Reliance on outside expert opinion when appropriate.

100. The IIA *Standards* require that the internal audit director establish and maintain a quality assurance program to evaluate the operations of the internal audit department. All of the following are considered elements of a quality assurance program **except:**

a. Annual appraisals of individual internal auditors' performance.
b. Internal reviews of audits completed.
c. Supervision of audit work.
d. External reviews to assess compliance with standards

101. Auditing standards state that "reports may include recommendations for potential improvements." Which of the following would be a **valid** justification for omitting recommendations in an audit report? The auditor

a. May not always understand the true cause of the finding being reported.
b. Does not have sufficient time to formulate a recommendation due to audit budget pressures.
c. Can avoid the confrontation by letting management solve its own problems.
d. May lose independence by being perceived as making operational decisions.

102. When evaluating the independence of an internal audit department, a quality review team considers several factors. Which of the following factors has the **least** amount of influence when judging an internal audit department's independence?

a. Criteria used in making auditors assignments.
b. The extent of auditor training in communications skills.
c. Relationship between audit working papers and audit report.
d. Impartial and unbiased audit judgments.

103. As used in the IIA *Standards* when discussing audit planning or risk assessment, the term "risk" is best defined as the probability that

a. An internal auditor will fail to detect a material error or event that causes financial statement or internal reports to be misstated or misleading.
b. An event or action may adversely affect the organization.
c. Management will, either knowing or unknowingly, make decisions that increase the potential liability of the organization.
d. Financial statements and/or internal records will contain material error.

104. Which of the following statements is **not** true regarding risk assessment as the term is used in internal auditing?

a. Risk assessment is a judgmental process of assigning dollar values to the perceived level of risk found in an auditable activity. These values allow directors to select the auditees most likely to result in identifiable audit savings.
b. The audit director should incorporate information from a variety of sources into the risk assessment process, including discussions with the board, management, external auditors, and review of regulations, and analysis of financial/operating data.
c. Risk assessment is a systematic process of assessing and integrating professional judgments about

probable adverse conditions and/or events, providing a means of organizing an internal audit schedule.
   d. As a result of an audit or preliminary survey, the audit director may revise the level of assessed risk of an auditee at any time, making appropriate adjustments to the work schedule.

105. A director of internal auditing has to determine how an organization can be divided into auditable activities. Which of the following is an auditable activity?
   a. A procedure.
   b. A system.
   c. An account.
   d. All of the above.

106. When determining the number and experience level of the internal audit staff to be assigned to an audit, the director should consider all of the following **except** the:
   a. Complexity of the audit assignment.
   b. Available audit resources.
   c. Training needs of internal auditors.
   d. Lapsed time since the last audit.

107. The IIA *Standards* require an auditor to have the knowledge, skills, and disciplines essential to perform an internal audit. Which of the following correctly describes the level of knowledge or skill required by the *Standards*? Auditors must have
   a. Proficiency in applying knowledge of auditing standards and procedures to specific situations without extensive recourse to technical research and assistance.
   b. Proficiency in applying knowledge of accounting and computerized information systems to specific or potential problems.
   c. An understanding of broad techniques used in supporting and developing audit findings and the ability to research the proper audit procedures to be used in any audit situation.
   d. A broad appreciation for accounting principles and techniques when auditing the financial records and reports of the organization.

108. An audit manager responsible for the supervision and review of other auditors needs the necessary skills and knowledge. Which of the following does **not** describe a skill or knowledge necessary to supervise a particular audit assignment?
   a. The ability to review and analyze an audit program to determine if the proposed audit procedures will result in evidence relevant to the audit's objectives.
   b. Ensuring that an audit report is supported and accurate relative to the evidence documented in the working papers of the audit.
   c. Using risk assessment and other judgmental processes to develop an audit plan and schedule for the department and present the plan to the audit committee.
   d. Determining that staff auditors have completed the audit procedures and that audit objectives have been met.

109. You have been asked to be a member of a peer review team. In assessing the independence of the internal audit department being reviewed, you should consider all of the following factors **except:**
   a. Access to and frequency of communications with the board of directors or its audit committee.
   b. The criteria of education and experience considered necessary when filling vacant positions on the audit staff.
   c. The degree to which auditors assume operating responsibilities.
   d. The scope and depth of audit objectives for the audits included in the review.

110. A written charter, approved by the board of directors, that outlines the internal audit department's purpose, authority, and responsibility is primarily meant to enhance the department's
   a. Due professional care.
   b. Stature within the organization.
   c. Relationship with management.
   d. Independence.

111. In the past, the internal auditing department of XYZ Company designed and installed computerized systems for the company. A newly appointed member of the audit committee has questioned the auditing department's independence due to its performance of that activity. Which of the following actions would **best** satisfy the committee's concern regarding independence?
   a. The internal audit department should continue to design and install other computer systems as long as the internal audit staff possesses the expertise to do so.
   b. The internal audit department should refrain from designing and installing any computer systems for their organization in the future.
   c. The internal audit department should not assign those internal auditors who designed and installed the payroll system to audit the payroll area.
   d. The internal audit department should refrain from operating and drafting procedures for any of its organization's systems.

112. A professional engineer applied for a position in the internal auditing department of a high-technology firm. The engineer became interested in the position after observing several internal auditors while they were auditing the engineering department. The director of internal auditing
   a. Should not hire the engineer because of the lack of knowledge of internal auditing standards.
   b. May hire the engineer in spite of the lack of knowledge of internal auditing standards.
   c. Should not hire the engineer because of the lack of knowledge of accounting and taxes.
   d. May hire the engineer because of the knowledge of internal auditing gained in the previous position.

113. Specific airline ticket information, including fare class, purchase date, and lowest available fare options, as prescribed in the company's travel policy, is obtained and reported to department management when employees purchase airline tickets from the company's authorized travel agency. Such a report provides information for
   a. Quality of performance in relation to the company's travel policy.
   b. Identifying costs necessary to process employee business expense report data.

c. Departmental budget-to-actual comparisons.
d. Supporting employer's business expense deductions.

114. Audit policy requires that final reports will not be issued without a management response. An audit with significant findings is complete except for management's response. Evaluate the following courses of action and select the **best** alternative.
a. Issue an interim report regarding the important issues noted.
b. Modify audit policy to allow a specific time period for the management response.
c. Wait for management response and issue audit report.
d. Discuss situation with the external auditors.

115. Audit findings often emerge by a process of comparing "what should be" with "what is." Findings are based on the attributes of criteria, condition, and cause and effect. From the following descriptions, which one most appropriately describes the effect of the audit finding?
a. Reason for the difference between the expected and actual conditions.
b. Factual evidence found during the course of the examination.
c. Risk or exposure encountered because of the condition.
d. Standards, measures, or expectations used in making the evaluation.

116. Management asserted that the performance standards the auditors used to evaluate operating performance were inappropriate. Written performance standards that had been established by management were vague and had to be interpreted by the auditor. In such cases, auditors may meet their due care responsibility by
a. Assuring them that their interpretations are reasonable.
b. Assuring themselves that their interpretations are in line with industry practices.
c. Establishing agreement with auditees as to the standards needed to measure performance.
d. Incorporating management's objections in the audit report.

117. The IIA *Standards* require the director of internal auditing to establish and maintain a quality assurance program to evaluate the operations of the internal audit department. Which of the following relates **most** directly to the objective of maintaining high quality in all audits?
a. Required supervisory review of all audit programs, working papers, and draft audit reports.
b. Required coordination with external auditors.
c. Required compliance with the Code of Ethics of the Institute of Internal Auditors.
d. Required educational standards for all members of the professional audit staff.

118. An audit supervisor would challenge whether audit evidence is sufficient to support the conclusion that journal entries are properly prepared and approved if the working papers included
a. A note stating the controller's assurance those journal entries are always looked at by the accounting supervisor before entry into the computer system.
b. A copy of a handwritten schedule of standard and appended nonstandard journal entries for the most recent month showing the initials of the preparer for each entry and the summary approval of the controller at the top.
c. A copy of a computer-generated list of automated and nonstandard journal entries initialed by the controller showing the auditor's references to system reports and monthly reconciliations.
d. A cross-reference to another section of the working papers containing sufficient evidence for this conclusion.

119. The internal auditing department has concluded a fraud investigation that revealed a previously undiscovered materially adverse impact on the financial position and results of operations for two years on which financial statements have already been issued. The director of internal auditing should immediately inform
a. The external audit firm responsible for the financial statements affected by the discovery.
b. The appropriate governmental or regulatory agency.
c. Appropriate management and the audit committee of the board of directors.
d. The internal accounting function ultimately responsible for making corrective journal entries.

120. According to the IIA *Standards*, internal auditing has a responsibility for helping to deter fraud. Which of the following **best** describes how this responsibility is generally met?
a. By coordinating with security personnel and law enforcement agencies in the investigation of possible frauds.
b. By testing for fraud in every audit and following up as appropriate.
c. By assisting in the design of control systems to prevent fraud.
d. By evaluating the adequacy and effectiveness of controls in light of the potential exposure or risk.

121. An internal auditor observes that a receivables clerk has physical access to and control of cash receipts. The auditor worked with the clerk several years before and has a high level of trust in the individual. Accordingly, the auditor notes in the working papers that controls over receipts are adequate. Is the auditor in compliance with the *Standards*?
a. Yes, reasonable care has been taken.
b. No, irregularities were not noted.
c. No, alertness to conditions where irregularities are most likely was not shown.
d. Yes, the working papers were annotated.

122. Which of the following most seriously compromises the independence of the internal auditing department?
a. Internal auditors frequently draft revised procedures for departments whose procedures they have criticized in an audit report.
b. The director of internal auditing has dual reporting responsibility to the firm's top executive and the board of directors.
c. The internal auditing department and the firm's external auditors engage in joint planning of total audit coverage to avoid duplicating each other's work.

d. The internal auditing department is included in the review cycle of the firm's contracts with other firms before the contracts are executed.

123. An internal auditor has uncovered illegal acts that were committed by a member of senior management. According to the IIA *Standards*, such information

a. Should be excluded from the internal auditor's report and discussed orally with the senior manager.
b. Must be immediately reported to the appropriate government authorities.
c. May be disclosed in a separate report and distributed to all senior management.
d. May be disclosed in a separate report and distributed to the company's audit committee of the board of directors.

124. The internal auditing department for a chain of retail stores recently concluded an audit of sales adjustments in all stores in the southeast region. The audit revealed that several stores are costing the company an estimated $85,000 per quarter in duplicate credits to customers' charge accounts. The audit report, published eight weeks after the audit was concluded, included the internal auditors' recommendations to store management that should prevent duplicate credits to customers' accounts. Which of the following standards for reporting has been disregarded in the above case?

a. The follow-up actions were not adequate.
b. The auditors should have implemented appropriate corrective action as soon as the duplicate credits were discovered.
c. Auditor recommendations should not be included in the report.
d. The report was not timely.

125. During an audit of the organization's accounts payable function, an internal auditor plans to confirm balances with suppliers. What is the source of authority for such contacts with units outside the organization?

a. Internal auditing department policies and procedures.
b. The IIA *Standards*.
c. The Statement of Responsibilities of Internal Auditing.
d. The internal auditing department's charter.

126. The director of internal auditing is responsible for establishing a program to develop the human resources of the internal auditing department. According to the IIA *Standards*, this program should include

a. Continuing education opportunities and performance appraisals.
b. Counseling and an established career path.
c. An established training plan and a charter.
d. Job descriptions and competitive salary increases.

127. The IIA *Standards* require the performance of periodic internal reviews by members of the internal auditing staff. This function is designed to primarily serve the needs of

a. The audit committee.
b. The director of internal auditing.
c. Management.
d. The internal auditing staff.

128. According to the IIA *Standards*, which of the following is the correct listing of information that must be included in a fraud report?

a. Purpose, scope, results, and, where appropriate, an expression of the auditor's opinion.
b. Criteria, condition, and cause and effect.
c. Background, findings, and recommendations.
d. Findings, conclusions, recommendations, and corrective action.

129. An internal auditor reported a suspected fraud to the director of internal auditing. The director turned the entire case over to the security department. Security failed to investigate or report the case to management. The perpetrator continued to defraud the organization until being accidentally discovered by a line manager two years later. Select the most appropriate action for the audit director.

a. The director's actions were correct.
b. The director should have periodically checked the status of the case with Security.
c. The director should have conducted the investigation.
d. The director should have discharged the perpetrator.

130. An internal auditor has just completed an audit of a division and is in the process of preparing the audit report. According to the IIA *Standards*, the findings in the audit report should include

a. Statements of opinion about the cause of a finding.
b. Pertinent factual statements concerning the control weaknesses that were uncovered during the course of the audit.
c. Statements of both fact and opinion developed during the course of the audit.
d. Statements dealing with potential future events that may be helpful to the audited division.

131. According to the IIA *Standards*, supervision of an audit assignment should include

a. Determining that audit working papers adequately support the audit findings.
b. Assigning staff members to the particular engagement.
c. Determining the scope of the audit.
d. Appraising each auditor's performance on at least an annual basis.

132. Which of the following reporting structures would **best** depict the internal audit organizational guidelines contained in the IIA *Standards*?

a. Administratively to the board of directors, functionally to the chief executive officer.
b. Administratively to the controller, functionally to the chief financial officer.
c. Administratively to the chief executive officer, functionally to the board of directors.
d. Administratively to the chief executive officer, functionally to the external auditor.

133. As the director of internal auditing for your organization, you have developed a plan that includes a detailed schedule of areas to be audited during the coming year, an estimate of the time required for each audit, and the approximate starting date of each audit. The scheduling of specific audits was based on the time elapsed since the last audit in each area. The plan is inadequate because it fails to

a. Cite authoritative support, such as the IIA *Standards*, for such a plan.

b. Consider factors such as risk, exposure, and potential loss to the organization.
c. State whether all audit resources had been committed to the plan.
d. Seek management approval of the plan.

134. The audit committee can serve several important purposes, some of which directly benefit internal auditing. The most significant benefit provided by the audit committee to the internal auditor is

a. Protecting the independence of the internal auditor from undue management influence.
b. Reviewing annual audit plans and monitoring audit results.
c. Approving audit plans, scheduling, staffing, and meeting with the internal auditor as needed.
d. Reviewing copies of the internal control procedures for selected company operations and meeting with company officials to discuss them.

135. The IIA *Standards* indicate that independence permits internal auditors to render the impartial and unbiased judgments essential to the proper conduct of audits. Which of the following would **best** promote independence?

a. A policy that requires internal auditors to report to the director any situation in which a conflict of interest or bias on the part of the individual auditor is present or may reasonably be inferred.
b. An internal audit department policy that prevents it from recommending standards of controls for systems that it audits.
c. An organizational policy that allows internal audits of sensitive operations to be "contracted out" to other audit providers.
d. An organizational policy that prevents personnel transfers from operating activities to the internal audit department.

136. The IIA *Standards* require written policies and procedures to guide the audit staff. Which of the following statements is false with respect to this requirement?

a. The form and content of written policies and procedures should be appropriate to the size of the department.
b. All internal audit departments should have a detailed policies and procedures manual.
c. Formal administrative and technical audit manuals may not be needed by all internal auditing departments.
d. A small internal auditing department may be managed informally through close supervision and written memos.

137. According to the IIA *Standards*, the director of internal auditing should establish goals that have two basic qualities. Select the correct traits of internal auditing goals.

a. Measurable and attainable.
b. Budgeted and approved.
c. Planned and attainable.
d. Requested and approved.

138. Internal audit reports should contain the purpose, scope, and results. The audit results should contain the criteria, condition, effect, and cause of the finding. The cause can best be described as

a. Factual evidence which the internal auditor found.
b. Reason for the difference between the expected and actual conditions.
c. The risk or exposure because of the condition found.
d. Resultant evaluations of the effects of the findings.

139. According to the IIA *Standards*, internal auditing reports should be distributed to those members of the organization who are able to ensure that audit results are given due consideration. For higher-level members of the organization, that requirement can usually be satisfied with

a. Interim reports.
b. Summary reports.
c. Oral reports.
d. Final written reports only.

140. If an internal auditor finds that no corrective action has been taken on a prior audit finding that is still valid, the IIA *Standards* states that the internal auditor should

a. Restate the prior finding along with the findings of the current audit.
b. Determine whether management or the board has assumed the risk of not taking corrective action.
c. Seek the board's approval to initiate corrective action.
d. Schedule a future audit of the specific area involved.

141. Internal auditing is responsible for reporting fraud to senior management or the board when

a. The incidence of fraud of a material amount has been established to a reasonable certainty.
b. Suspicious activities have been reported to internal auditing.
c. Irregular transactions have been identified and are under investigation.
d. The review of all suspected fraud-related transactions is complete.

142. According to the IIA *Standards*, the role of internal auditing in the investigation of fraud includes all of the following **except:**

a. Assessing the probable level and extent of complicity in the fraud within the organization.
b. Designing the procedures to follow in attempting to identify the perpetrators, extent of the fraud, techniques used, and cause of the fraud.
c. Coordinating activities with management personnel, legal counsel, and other appropriate specialists throughout the investigation.
d. Interrogating suspected perpetrators of the fraud.

143. After completing an investigation, internal auditing has concluded that an employee has stolen a material amount of cash receipts. A draft of the proposed report on this finding should be reviewed by

a. Legal counsel.
b. The audit committee of the board of directors.
c. The president of the organization.
d. The external auditor.

144. The IIA *Standards* specify that final audit reports should be reviewed and approved by the

a. Auditee or the person to whom the auditee reports.
b. Auditor in charge.
c. Internal auditing director or designee.
d. Chief financial officer.

145. According to the IIA *Standards*, internal auditors should review the means of physically safeguarding assets from losses arising from

a. Misapplication of accounting principles.
b. Procedures that are not cost justified.
c. Exposure to the elements.
d. Underutilization of physical facilities.

146. The IIA *Standards* state that the director of internal auditing should have direct communication with the board. Such communication is often accomplished through the board's audit committee. Which of the following **best** describes why the charter for internal auditing should provide for direct access to the audit committee?

a. Such access is required by law for publicly traded companies.
b. Direct access to the audit committee tends to enhance internal auditing's independence and objectivity.
c. With direct access, the director of internal auditing is in a better position to affect policy decisions.
d. The audit committee must authorize implementation of audit recommendations that involve financial reporting.

147. According to the IIA *Standards*, a report issued by an internal auditor should contain an expression of opinion when

a. The area of the audit is the financial statements.
b. The internal auditors' work is to be used by external auditors.
c. A full-scope audit has been conducted in an area.
d. An opinion will improve communications with the reader of the report.

Items 148 and 149 are based on the following:

As an internal auditor for a multinational chemical company, you have been assigned to perform an operational audit at a local plant. This plant is similar in age, sizing, and construction to two other company plants that have been cited recently for discharge of hazardous wastes. In addition, you are aware that chemicals manufactured at the plant release toxic by-products.

148. Assume that you have evidence that the plant is discharging hazardous wastes. As a Certified Internal Auditor, what is the appropriate reporting requirement in this situation?

a. Send a copy of your audit report to the appropriate regulatory agency.
b. Ignore the issue; the regulatory inspectors are better qualified to assess the danger.
c. Issue an interim report to the appropriate levels of management.
d. Note the issue in your working papers, but do not report it.

149. Identify your responsibility for detection of a hazardous waste discharge problem.

a. You have no responsibility; it is the concern of the appropriate governmental agency.
b. You are responsible for ensuring compliance with company policies and procedures.
c. Operational audits do not require a determination of compliance with laws and regulations.
d. You are required by the *Standards* to determine compliance with laws and regulations.

150. The IIA *Standards* define competent information as

a. Supporting the audit findings and being consistent with the audit objectives.
b. Assisting the organization in meeting prescribed goals.
c. Factual, adequate, and convincing so that a prudent person would reach the same conclusion as auditor.
d. Reliable and the best available through the use of appropriate audit techniques.

151. Adequate internal controls are most likely to be present if

a. Management has planned and organized in a manner that provides reasonable assurance that the organization's objectives and goals will be achieved efficiently and economically.
b. Management has exercised due professional care in the design of operating and functional systems.
c. Operating and functional systems are designed, installed, and implemented in compliance with law.
d. Management has designed, installed, and implemented efficient operating and functional systems.

152. A company's management accountants prepared a set of reports for top management. These reports detail the funds expended and the expenses incurred by each department for the current reporting period. The function of internal auditing would be to

a. Ensure against any and all noncompliance of reporting procedures.
b. Review the expenditure items and match each item with the expenses incurred.
c. Determine if there are any employees expending funds without authorization.
d. Identify inadequate controls that increase the likelihood of unauthorized expenditures.

153. Independence permits internal auditors to render impartial and unbiased judgments. The **best** way to achieve independence is through

a. Individual knowledge and skills
b. Organizational status and objectivity
c. Supervision within the organization
d. Organizational knowledge and skills

154. When faced with an imposed scope limitation, the director of internal auditing should

a. Refuse to perform the audit until the scope limitation is removed.
b. Communicate the potential effects of the scope limitation to the audit committee of the board of directors.
c. Increase the frequency of auditing the activity in question.
d. Assign more experienced personnel to the engagement.

155. Which of the following is **not** a requirement of a long-range plan for the internal auditing department?

a. To be consistent with the department's charter.
b. To be capable of being accomplished.
c. To include a list of auditable activities.
d. To include the basics of the audit program.

156. To avoid being the apparent cause of conflict between an organization's top management and the audit committee, the director of internal auditing should

a. Submit copies of all audit reports to both top management and the audit committee.
b. Strengthen the independence of the department through organizational status.
c. Discuss all reports to top management with the audit committee first.
d. Request board acceptance of policies that include internal auditing relationships with the audit committee.

157. According to the IIA *Standards*, internal auditors should possess all of the following **except:**

a. Proficiency in applying internal audit standards.
b. An understanding of management principles.
c. The ability to exercise good interpersonal relations.
d. The ability to conduct training sessions in quantitative methods.

158. Which of the following aspects of evaluating the performance of staff members would be considered as a violation of good personnel management techniques?

a. The evaluator should justify very high and very low evaluations because of their impact on the employee.
b. Evaluations should be made annually or more frequently to provide the employee feedback about competence.
c. The first evaluation should be made shortly after commencing work to serve as an early guide to the new employee.
d. Because there are so many employees whose performance is completely satisfactory, it is preferable to use standard evaluation comments.

159. According to the IIA *Standards* concerning due professional care, an internal auditor should

a. Consider the relative materiality or significance of matters to which audit procedures are applied.
b. Emphasize the potential benefits of an audit without regard to the cost.
c. Consider whether established operating standards are being met and not whether those standards are acceptable.
d. Select procedures that are likely to provide absolute assurance those irregularities do not exist.

160. Which of the items below would most likely reflect differences between the policies of a relatively small and relatively large internal auditing operation? The policies for the large operation should

a. Spell out scope and status of internal auditing.
b. Contain the authority to carry out audits.
c. Be specific as to activities to be followed.
d. Be in considerable detail.

161. An audit committee of the board of directors of a corporation is being established. Which of the following would normally be a responsibility of the committee?

a. Approval of the selection and dismissal of the internal auditing director.
b. Development of the annual internal audit schedule.
c. Approval of internal audit programs.
d. Determination of findings appropriate for specific internal audit reports.

162. While performing a construction audit, the auditor suspects that the structural steel used does not conform to contract specifications. The internal auditing department does not have an engineer on the staff. According to the IIA *Standards*, the appropriate course of action is to

a. Assign a dollar value to the difference and prepare a deficiency finding.
b. Ask a company or consulting engineer to determine whether the steel conforms to the contract specifications.
c. Ask the construction superintendent to explain why there is a difference.
d. Require suspension of contract payments until the difference is resolved.

163. The charter of the internal auditing department should

a. Authorize access to records, personnel, and physical properties relevant to the performance of audits.
b. Provide recommended formats to report significant audit findings and recommendations.
c. Describe audit programs to be carried out.
d. Define the audit department's work schedule, staffing plan, and financial budget.

164. According to the IIA *Standards*, activity reports submitted periodically to management and to the board should

a. Summarize planned audit activities.
b. Compare performance with audit work schedules.
c. Provide detail on financial budgets.
d. Detail projected staffing needs.

165. An internal auditing director is establishing the evaluation criteria for the selection of new internal audit staff members. According to the IIA *Standards*, which of the following would be an **inappropriate** item to list?

a. An appreciation of the fundamentals of accounting.
b. An understanding of management principles.
c. The ability to recognize deviations from good business practice.
d. Proficiency in computerized operations and the use of computers in auditing.

166. The person responsible for audit report distribution should be

a. The director of internal auditing or designee.
b. The audit committee of the board of directors.
c. The vice president responsible for the area being audited.
d. The audit supervisor of the audit being performed.

167. The IIA *Standards* require that the internal auditing department provide assurance that internal audits are properly supervised in order to

a. Produce professional audits of consistently high quality.
b. Assure high productivity of audit reporting.
c. Provide for the efficient training of the audit staff.
d. Determine that the audit program is followed without deviation.

168. An exit conference helps ensure that

a. The objectives of the audit and the scope of the audit work are known by the auditee.

b. The auditee understands the audit program.
c. There have been no misunderstandings or misinterpretations of fact.
d. The list of persons who are to receive the final report are identified.

169. You transferred from the treasury department to the internal auditing department of the same company last month. The chief financial officer of the company has suggested that since you have significant knowledge in this area, it would be a good idea for you to immediately begin an audit of the treasury department. In this circumstance you should

a. Accept the audit engagement and begin work immediately.
b. Discuss the need for such an audit with your former superior, the treasurer.
c. Suggest that the audit be performed by another member of the internal auditing staff.
d. Offer to prepare an audit program but suggest that interviews with your former coworkers be conducted by other members of the internal auditing staff.

170. Which of the following is the most appropriate method of reporting disagreement between the auditor and the auditee concerning audit findings and recommendations?

a. State the auditor's position because the report is designed to provide the auditor's independent view.
b. State the auditee's position because management is ultimately responsible for the activities reported.
c. State both positions and identify the reasons for the disagreement.
d. State neither position. If the disagreement is ultimately resolved, there will be no reason to report the previous disagreement. If the disagreement is never resolved, the disagreement should not be reported, because there is no mechanism to resolve it.

171. Which of the following does **not** describe one of the functions of audit working papers?

a. Facilitates third-party reviews.
b. Aids in the planning, performance, and review of audits.
c. Provides the principal evidential support for the auditor's report.
d. Aids in the professional development of the operating staff.

172. Which of the following statements most correctly reflects the director of internal auditing's responsibilities for personnel management and development as reflected in the IIA *Standards*?

a. The director is responsible for selecting qualified individuals but has no explicit responsibility for providing ongoing educational opportunities for the internal auditor.
b. The director is responsible for performing an annual review of each internal auditor's performance but has no explicit responsibility for counseling internal auditors on their performance and professional development.
c. The director is responsible for selecting qualified individuals but has no explicit responsibility for the preparation of job descriptions.
d. The director is responsible for developing formal job descriptions for the audit staff but has no explicit responsibility for administering the corporate compensation program.

173. During the year-end physical inventory process, the auditor observed over $1.2 million worth of items staged in the shipping area and marked "Sold—Do Not Inventory." The customer had been on credit hold for three months because of bankruptcy proceedings, but the sales manager had ordered the shipping supervisor to treat the inventory as sold for physical inventory purposes. The auditor noted the terms of sale were "FOB Warehouse." After confirming no change in corporate policy, the auditor should

a. Recommend that the inventory staged in the shipping area be counted and included along with the rest of the physical inventory results.
b. Make test counts and trace the results to appropriate records to ensure that the cost is properly relieved from inventory.
c. Follow up with appropriate procedures to ensure that the inventory staged in the shipping area appears on related invoicing documentation.
d. Request copies of the signed bills of lading to include with working papers for this physical inventory.

174. According to the IIA *Standards*, the organizational status of the internal auditing department

a. Should be sufficient to permit the accomplishment of its audit responsibilities.
b. Is best when the reporting relationship is direct to the board of directors.
c. Requires the board's annual approval of the audit schedules, plans, and budgets.
d. Is guaranteed when the charter specifically defines its independence.

175. Which of the following best defines an audit opinion?

a. A summary of the significant audit findings.
b. The auditor's professional judgment of the situation that was reviewed.
c. Conclusions that must be included in the audit report.
d. Recommendations for corrective action.

176. "Due care implies reasonable care and competence, not infallibility or extraordinary performance." This statement makes which of the following unnecessary?

a. The conduct of examinations and verifications to a reasonable extent.
b. The conduct of extensive examinations.
c. The reasonable assurance that compliance does exist.
d. The consideration of the possibility of material irregularities.

177. Management asserted that the performance standards the auditors used to evaluate operating performance were inappropriate. Written performance standards that had been established by management were vague and had to be interpreted by the auditor. In such cases, auditors may meet their due care responsibility by

a. Assuring them that their interpretations are reasonable.
b. Assuring themselves that their interpretations are in line with industry practices.
c. Establishing agreement with auditees as to the standards needed to measure performance.
d. Incorporating management's objections in the audit report.

178. Which of the following is **not** a true statement about the relationship between internal auditors and external auditors?
a. External auditors must assess the competence and objectivity of internal auditors.
b. There may be periodic meetings between internal and external auditors to discuss matters of mutual interest.
c. There may be an exchange of audit reports and management letters.
d. Internal auditors may provide audit programs and working papers to external auditors.

179. In recent years, which two factors have changed the relationship between internal auditors and external auditors so that internal auditors are partners rather than subordinates?
a. The increasing liability of external auditors and the increasing professionalism of internal auditors.
b. The increasing professionalism of internal auditors and the evolving economics of external auditing.
c. The increased reliance on computerized accounting systems and the evolving economics of external auditing.
d. The globalization of audit entities and the increased reliance on computerized accounting systems.

Items 180 and 181 are based on the following:

After using the same public accounting firm for several years, the board of directors retained another public accounting firm to perform the annual financial audit in order to reduce the annual audit fee. The new firm has now proposed a onetime audit of the cost-effectiveness of the various operations of the business. The director of internal auditing has been asked to advise management in making a decision on the proposal.

180. An argument can be made that the internal auditing department would be better able to perform such an audit because
a. External auditors may not possess the same depth of understanding of the company as the internal auditors.
b. Internal auditors are required to be objective in performing audits.
c. Audit techniques used by internal auditors are different from those used by external auditors.
d. Internal auditors will not be vitally concerned with fraud and waste.

181. Additional criteria that should be considered by management in evaluating the proposal would include all the following **except:**
a. Existing expertise of internal auditing staff.
b. Overall cost of the proposed audit.
c. The need to develop in-house expertise.
d. The external auditor's required adherence to the single audit concept.

182. To improve audit efficiency, internal auditors can rely on the work of external auditors if it is
a. Performed after the internal audit.
b. Primarily concerned with operational objectives and activities.
c. Coordinated with the internal audit.
d. Conducted in accordance with the IIA Code of Ethics.

Items 183 and 184 are based on the following:

You are the internal audit director of a parent company that has foreign subsidiaries. Independent external audits performed for the parent company are not conducted by the same firm that conducts the foreign subsidiary audits. Since your department occasionally provides direct assistance to both external firms, you have copies of audit programs and selected working papers produced by each firm.

183. The foreign subsidiary's audit firm would like to rely on some of the work performed by the parent company's audit firm, but it needs to review the working papers first. The audit firm has asked you for copies of the parent company's audit firm working papers. Select the most appropriate response to the foreign subsidiary's auditors.
a. Provide copies of the working papers without notifying the parent company's audit firm.
b. Notify the parent company's audit firm of the situation and request that either they provide the working papers or authorize you to do so.
c. Provide copies of the working papers and notify the parent company's audit firm that you have done so.
d. Refuse to provide the working papers under any circumstances.

184. The foreign subsidiary's audit firm wants to rely on an audit of a function at the parent company. The audit was conducted by the internal auditing department. To place reliance on the work performed, the foreign subsidiary's auditors have requested copies of the working papers. Select the most appropriate response to the foreign subsidiary's auditors.
a. Provide copies of the working papers.
b. Ask the parent company's audit firm if it is appropriate to release the working papers.
c. Ask the audit committee for permission to release the working papers.
d. Refuse to provide the working papers under any circumstances.

185. The director of internal auditing plans to meet with the independent outside auditor to discuss joint efforts regarding an upcoming audit of the company's pension plan. The independent outside auditor has performed all audit work in this area in the past. The director's objective is to
a. Determine if audit work in this area could not be performed exclusively by internal auditing.
b. Coordinate the pension audit so as to fulfill the scope of work and not duplicate work of the independent outside auditor.
c. Ascertain which account balances have been tested by the independent outside auditor so that internal

auditing may test the internal controls to determine the reliability of these balances.
d. Determine whether the independent outside auditor's audit techniques, methods, and terminology should be used by internal auditing in this area to conform with past audit work or if the independent outside auditor should use techniques consistent with other internal auditors.

IIA's Code of Ethics

186. A Certified Internal Auditor (CIA) is working in a noninternal audit position as the director of purchasing. The CIA signs a contract to procure a large order from the supplier with the best price, quality, and performance. Shortly after signing the contract, the supplier presents the CIA with a gift of significant monetary value. Which of the following statements regarding the acceptance of the gift is correct?
a. Acceptance of the gift would be prohibited only if it were noncustomary.
b. Acceptance of the gift would violate the IIA Code of Ethics and would be prohibited for a CIA.
c. Since the CIA is no longer acting as an internal auditor, acceptance of the gift would be governed only by the organization's code of conduct.
d. Since the contract was signed before the gift was offered, acceptance of the gift would not violate either the IIA Code of Ethics or the organization's code of conduct.

187. An auditor who is nearly finished with an audit discovers that the director of marketing has a gambling habit. The gambling issue is not directly related to the existing audit, and there is pressure to complete the current audit. The auditor notes the problem and passes the information on to the director of internal audit but does no further follow-up. The auditor's actions would
a. Be in violation of the IIA Code of Ethics for withholding meaningful information.
b. Be in violation of the *Standards* because the auditor did not properly follow-up on a red flag that might indicate the existence of fraud.
c. Not be in violation of either the IIA Code of Ethics or *Standards.*
d. Both a. and b.

188. As used by the internal auditing profession, the IIA *Standards* refer to all of the following **except:**
a. Criteria by which the operations of an internal audit department are evaluated and measured.
b. Criteria that dictate the minimum level of ethical actions to be taken by internal auditors.
c. Statements intended to represent the practice of internal auditing, as it should be.
d. Criteria that are applicable to all types of internal audit departments.

189. Which of the following situations would be a violation of the IIA Code of Ethics?
a. An auditor was subpoenaed in a court case in which a merger partner claimed to have been defrauded by the auditor's company. The auditor divulged confidential audit information to the court.
b. An auditor for a manufacturer of office products recently completed an audit of the corporate marketing function. Based on this experience, the auditor spent several hours one Saturday working as a paid consultant to a hospital in the local area that intended to conduct an audit of its marketing function.
c. An auditor gave a speech at a local IIA chapter meeting outlining the contents of a program the auditor had developed for auditing electronic data interchange (EDI) connections. Several auditors from major competitors were in the audience.
d. During an audit, an auditor learned that the company was about to introduce a new product that would revolutionize the industry. Because of the probable success of the new product, the product manager suggested that the auditor buy additional stock in the company, which the auditor did.

190. In applying the standards of conduct set forth in the Code of Ethics, internal auditors are expected to
a. Exercise their individual judgment.
b. Compare them to standards in other professions.
c. Be guided by the desires of the auditee.
d. Use discretion in deciding whether to use them or not.

191. During an audit of a manufacturing division of a defense contractor, the auditor came across a scheme that looked like the company was inappropriately adding costs to a cost-plus governmental contract. The auditor discussed the manner with senior management, which suggested that the auditor seek an opinion from legal counsel. The auditor did so. Upon review of the government contract, legal counsel indicated that the practice was questionable, but did offer the opinion that the practice was not technically in violation of the government contract. Based on legal counsel's decision, the auditor decided to omit any discussion of the practice in the formal audit report that went to management and the audit committee, but did informally communicate legal counsel's decision to management. Did the auditor violate the IIA's Code of Ethics?
a. No. The auditor followed up the matter with appropriate personnel within the organization and reached a conclusion that no fraud was involved.
b. No. If a fraud is suspected, it should be resolved at the divisional level where it is taking place.
c. Yes. It is a violation because all important information, even if resolved, should be reported to the audit committee.
d. Yes. Internal legal counsel's opinion is not sufficient. The auditor should have sought advice from outside legal counsel.

192. An internal auditor recently terminated from a company due to downsizing has found a job with another company in the same industry. Which of the following disclosures made by the internal auditor to the new organization would constitute a violation of the IIA's Code of Ethics?
a. The auditor used the audit risk approach that was used by the auditor's former employer in determining audit priorities in the new job.
b. The new audit department does not utilize probability-proportional-to-size (PPS) sampling, and the auditor believes PPS sampling has advantages for many of the types of audits conducted by the new employer. The auditor conducts training

sessions and develops forms to implement sampling in the same manner as the previous employer.
c. While at the previous firm, the auditor conducted a great deal of research to identify "best practices" for the management of the treasury function as part of an audit for that firm. Since most of the research was done at home and during nonoffice hours, the auditor retained much of the research and plans to use it in conducting an audit of the treasury function at the new employer.
d. None of the above represents a violation of the Code.

193. Which of the following could be an organization factor that might adversely affect the ethical behavior of the director of internal auditing?
a. The director reports directly to an independent audit committee of the board of directors.
b. The director of internal auditing is not assigned any operational responsibilities.
c. A director of internal auditing may not be appointed or approved without concurrence of the board of directors.
d. The director's annual bonuses are based on dollar recoveries or recommended future savings as a result of audits.

194. The code of ethics of a professional organization sets forth
a. Broad standards of conduct for the members of the organization.
b. The organizational details of the profession's governing body.
c. A list of illegal activities that are proscribed to the members of the profession.
d. The criteria by which the performance of professional activities is to be evaluated and measured.

195. The IIA's Code of Ethics identifies three personal characteristics that form the foundation on which the entire Code rests. Which is **not** one of these three personal characteristics?
a. Objectivity.
b. Diligence.
c. Probity.
d. Honesty.

196. Under the IIA's Code of Ethics' provisions with respect to gifts and fees, which of the following would be acceptable for an internal auditor to receive?
a. A pen received from the sales manager of a subsidiary with the imprinted name of the company's product and a phone number.
b. A dinner and baseball tickets from the manager of a department being audited. The tickets are usually made available to employees of the audited department.
c. A dinner and baseball tickets from the manager of a department that has never been audited and for which there are no plans for a future audit. The tickets are usually made available to employees of that department.
d. A bottle of whiskey from the corporate treasurer.

197. A Certified Internal Auditor is found to have committed a very serious violation of the Code of Ethics of the IIA. Which of the following describes the disciplinary action most likely to be imposed by the Institute? The CIA will
a. Be required to take up to 40 hours of appropriate continuing professional education courses.
b. Be required to retake the CIA Examination.
c. Forfeit his or her membership in the Institute.
d. Be assessed a fine not to exceed $1,000.

198. Which of the following actions by an internal auditor would violate the IIA's Code of Ethics?
a. Attendance at an educational program offered by an auditee to all employees.
b. Acceptance of airline tickets from an auditee.
c. Disclosure, in an audit opinion, of all material facts relevant to the audit area.
d. Disposal of stock in the company prior to learning of a business downturn.

199. An internal auditor for XYZ company is auditing the revenues and operating expenses of a shopping mall managed by ABC company. ABC is the operating partner of this joint venture with XYZ. The internal auditor discovers numerous audit exceptions where some credits will be due to each party. Which of the following should the auditor report in this situation?
a. Only those audit exceptions where credit is due to XYZ.
b. If requested by ABC, detailed information on credits due ABC.
c. Only those audit exceptions where credit is due ABC.
d. All material audit exceptions and provide ABC with a net amount due.

200. Which of the following actions by an auditor would violate the IIA's Code of Ethics?
a. An audit of an activity managed by the auditor's spouse.
b. A material financial investment in the company.
c. Use of a company car.
d. A significant ownership interest in a nonrelated business.

201. Through an audit of the credit department, the director of internal auditing became aware of a material misstatement of the year-end accounts receivable balance. The external auditor has completed the audit without detecting the misstatement. What should the director do in this situation?
a. Inform the external auditor of the misstatement.
b. Report the misstatement to management when the external auditor presents his report.
c. Exclude the misstatement from the internal audit report since the external auditor is responsible for expressing an opinion on the financial statements.
d. Perform additional audit work on account receivable balances to benefit the external auditor.

202. A Certified Internal Auditor who is judged by the board of directors of the IIA to be in violation of the provisions of the IIA's Code of Ethics shall be subject to
a. Suspension as a Certified Internal Auditor for a minimum of one year.
b. Completion of additional continuing professional development hours to retain the Certified Internal Auditor designation.

c. Suspension as a Certified Internal Auditor indefinitely until reinstatement by the board.
d. Forfeiture of the Certified Internal Auditor designation.

203. In a review of warranty programs for new products introduced by a company with low and declining profits, an auditor has determined, and management has acknowledged, that the company will be unable to fulfill promised warranty coverage. The auditor should

a. Inform appropriate regulatory authorities.
b. Inform customers.
c. Inform the audit committee.
d. Resign from the employer.

204. A Certified Internal Auditor is found to have committed a violation of the Code of Ethics of the IIA. The violation is **not** serious enough to warrant the maximum disciplinary action. The most likely result is that the CIA will

a. Be required to take up to 24 hours of appropriate continuing professional education courses.
b. Lose his or her CIA designation permanently unless subsequent reinstatement is approved by the board of directors of the IIA.
c. Be prohibited from engaging in the practice of internal auditing for a period not to exceed 60 days.
d. Receive from the Institute's board of directors a written censure, which outlines the consequences of repeated similar actions.

205. Internal auditors should be prudent in their relationships with persons and organizations external to their employers. Which of the following activities would most likely **not** adversely affect internal auditors' ethical behavior?

a. Accepting compensation from professional organizations for consulting work.
b. Serving as consultants to competitor organizations.
c. Serving as consultants to suppliers.
d. Discussing audit plans or results with external parties.

206. A primary purpose for establishing a code of conduct within a professional organization is to

a. Reduce the likelihood that members of the profession will be sued for substandard work.
b. Ensure that all members of the profession perform at approximately the same level of competence.
c. Demonstrate acceptance of responsibility to the interests of those served by the profession.
d. Require members of the profession to exhibit loyalty in all matters pertaining to the affairs of their organization.

207. An auditor discovers some material inefficiency in a purchasing function. The purchasing manager happens to be the auditor's next-door neighbor and best friend. In accordance with the Code of Ethics, the auditor should

a. Objectively include the facts of the case in the audit report.
b. Not report the incident because of loyalty to the friend.
c. Include the facts of the case in a special report submitted only to the friend.
d. Not report the friend unless the activity is illegal.

208. Which of the following actions could be construed as a violation of the IIA's Code of Ethics?

a. Failing to report to management information that would be material to management's judgment.
b. Rendering an opinion on internal financial statements.
c. Turning a case over to the security department when an auditor suspects fraud, but has no proof.
d. Including an internal control problem in a report, when it has been corrected prior to completion of the audit.

209. Which of the following would constitute a violation of the IIA's Code of Ethics?

a. Janice has accepted an assignment to audit the electronics manufacturing division. Janice has recently joined the internal auditing department. But she was senior auditor for the external audit of that division and has audited many electronics companies during the past two years.
b. George has been assigned to do an audit of the warehousing function six months from now. George has no expertise in that area but accepted the assignment anyway. He has signed up for continuing professional education courses in warehousing, which will be completed before his assignment begins.
c. Jane is content with her career as an internal auditor and has come to look at it as a regular 9-to-5 job. She has not engaged in continuing professional education or other activities to improve her effectiveness during the last three years. However, she feels she is performing the same quality work she always has.
d. John discovered an internal financial fraud during the year. The books were adjusted to properly reflect the loss associated with the fraud. John discussed the fraud with the external auditor when the external auditor reviewed working papers detailing the incident.

210. Which of the following would be permissible under the IIA's Code of Ethics?

a. Disclosing confidential, audit-related information that is potentially damaging to the organization in a court of law in response to a subpoena.
b. Using audit-related information in a decision to buy stock issued by the employer corporation.
c. Accepting an unexpected gift from an employee whom you have praised in a recent audit report.
d. Not reporting significant findings about illegal activity to the audit committee because management has indicated it will handle the issue.

211. During an audit, an employee with whom you have developed a good working relationship informs you that she has some information about top management that would be damaging to the organization and may concern illegal activities. The employee does not want her name associated with the release of the information. Which of the following actions would be considered **inconsistent** with the IIA's Code of Ethics and *Standards*?

a. Assure the employee that you can maintain her anonymity and listen to the information.
b. Suggest the person consider talking to legal counsel.

c. Inform the individual that you will attempt to keep the source of the information confidential and will look into the matter further.
d. Inform the employee of other methods of communicating this type of information.

212. An internal auditor for a large regional bank holding company was asked to serve on the board of directors of a local bank. The bank competes in many of the same markets as the bank holding company, but focuses more on consumer financing than on business financing. In accepting this position, the auditor

I. Violates the IIA Code of Ethics because serving on the board may be in conflict with the best interests of the auditor's employer.
II. Violates the IIA Code of Ethics because the information gained while serving on the board of directors of the local bank may influence recommendations regarding potential acquisitions.

a. I only.
b. II only.
c. I and II.
d. Neither I nor II.

213. The director of internal auditing has been appointed to a committee to evaluate the appointment of the external auditors. The engagement partner for the external accounting firm wants the director to join him for a week of hunting at his private lodge. The director should
a. Accept, assuming both their schedules allow it.
b. Refuse on the grounds of conflict of interest.
c. Accept as long as it is not charged to company time.
d. Ask the comptroller if this would be a violation of the company's code of ethics.

214. In a review of travel and entertainment expenses, a Certified Internal Auditor questioned the business purposes of an officer's reimbursed travel expenses. The officer promised to compensate for the questioned amounts by not claiming legitimate expenses in the future. If the officer makes good on the promise, the internal auditor
a. Can ignore the original charging of the nonbusiness expenses.
b. Should inform the tax authorities in any event.
c. Should still include the finding in the audit report.
d. Should recommend that the officer forfeit any frequent flyer miles received as part of the questionable travel.

215. The standards of conduct set forth in the IIA's Code of Ethics
a. Provide basic principles in the practice of internal auditing.
b. Are guidelines to assist internal auditors in dealing with auditees.
c. Are rules that must be obeyed in all circumstances.
d. Provide a general understanding of the responsibility of internal auditing.

216. Today's internal auditor will often encounter a wide range of potential ethical dilemmas, not all of which are explicitly addressed by the Institute of Internal Auditors' Code of Ethics. If the auditor encounters such a dilemma, the auditor should always
a. Seek counsel from an independent attorney to determine the personal consequences of potential actions.
b. Consider all parties affected and the potential consequences of actions, and take an action consistent with the objectives of internal auditing and the concepts embodied in the Institute of Internal Auditors' Code of Ethics.
c. Seek the counsel of the audit committee before deciding on an action.
d. Act consistently with the code of ethics adopted by the organization even if such action would not be consistent with the IIA's Code of Ethics.

217. An internal auditor has been assigned to audit a foreign subsidiary. The auditor is aware that the social climate of the country is such that "facilitating payments" (bribes) are often used to make things happen and are an accepted part of that society. The auditor has completed an audit of the division and has found significant weaknesses relating to important controls. The division manager offers the auditor a substantial "facilitating payment" to omit the audit findings from the audit report with a provision that the auditor could revisit the division in six months so the auditor could verify that the problem areas had been properly addressed. The auditor should
a. Not accept the payment since such acceptance would be in conflict with the Code of Ethics.
b. Not accept the payment, but omit the findings as long as there is a verification visit in six months.
c. Accept the offer since it is consistent with the ethical concepts of the country in which the division is doing business.
d. Accept the payment because it has the effect of doing the greatest good for the greatest number; the auditor is better off, the division is better off, and the organization is better off because there is strong motivation to correct the deficiencies found by the auditor.

218. A certified internal auditor (CIA), who performs financial, operational, and information systems audits, is now facing an ethical dilemma. During an audit, he discovered several illegal activities conducted by senior management of his firm. What should the auditor do now?
a. Comply with the Institute of Management Accountant's (IMA's) Code of Ethics and Standards
b. Comply with the American Institute of Certified Public Accountant's (AICPA's) Code of Ethics and Standards
c. Comply with the Institute of Internal Auditor's (IIA's) Code of Ethics and Standards
d. Comply with the Information Systems and Audit Control Association's (ISACA's) Code of Ethics and Standards

Items 219 and 220 are based on the following:

A staff auditor has been assigned to the treasury audit for the second consecutive year. The auditor confirmed investment securities held by a brokerage house and realized that several large securities were improperly used as collateral for personal loans a few years ago by the current treasurer. Last year the staff auditor had mistakenly signed off on the audit steps involving the confirmations and verification of the securities without completing all of the steps. The audit manager also mistakenly signed off on the review last year. When the error was detected this year, the audit manager commented that "it was an error, but the loan has been repaid, and the securities returned. We have corrected the control weakness, and I'm positive it will not happen again. Pursuit of this issue will be an embarrassment to everyone involved. Leave it as it is."

219. Which of the following should be considered by the staff auditor when deciding whether to report the situation or not?

a. Securities were used improperly as collateral.
b. The mistake in signing off work that was not done.
c. The repayment of loans and return of the securities.
d. The correction of the control weakness.

220. As a staff auditor, which of the following actions would be considered a violation of the IIA *Standards* or Code of Ethics?

a. Inform the audit manager that you will be including the information in your working papers as an audit finding.
b. Discuss the matter with the audit director without further discussion with the audit manager.
c. Disclose the matter to the external auditor without further discussion.
d. Resign from the audit department and company if further action is not taken on the matter.

221. Which of the following situations would **most** likely be considered a violation of the IIA's Code of Ethics and thus the *Standards*?

a. As director of internal auditing you have become perplexed as to how to resolve a particular disagreement between you and auditee management regarding the finding and recommendation in a very sensitive audit area. Unsure as to what to do, you discuss the detail of the finding and your proposed recommendation with a fellow audit director you know from your work in the IIA's local chapter.
b. After researching and developing the proposed yearly audit plan, your company audit charter requires that, as director, you present the plan to the audit committee for its approval and suggestions.
c. Your audit manager has just removed your most significant finding and recommendation from your audit report. Being the in-charge auditor, you have voiced your opposition to the removal and have explained that you know the reported condition exists. Although you agree that, technically, the audit lacks sufficient evidence to support the finding, management cannot explain the condition and your audit finding is the only reasonable conclusion.
d. Because your department lacks skill and knowledge in a specialty area, your audit director has engaged the services of an expert consultant. As audit manager, you have been asked to review the expert's approach to the assignment. You are knowledgeable regarding the area under review but are hesitant to accept the assignment because you lack the expertise to judge the validity of the expert's conclusion.

222. Internal auditors sometimes express opinions in audit reports in addition to stating facts. Due professional care requires that the auditor's opinions be

a. Based on sufficient factual evidence that warrants the expression of the opinions.
b. Based on experience and not biased in any manner.
c. Expressed only when requested by the auditee or executive management.
d. Limited to the effectiveness of controls and the appropriateness of accounting treatments.

223. An accounting association established a code of ethics for all members. Identify the association's primary purpose for establishing the code of ethics.

a. To outline criteria for professional behavior to maintain standards of competence, morality, honesty, and dignity within the association.
b. To establish standards to follow for effective accounting practice.
c. To provide a framework within which accounting policies could be effectively developed and executed.
d. To outline criteria that can be utilized in conducting interviews of potential new accountants.

224. During an audit, a Certified Internal Auditor (CIA) learned that certain individuals in the organization were involved in industrial espionage for the benefit of the organization. According to the IIA's Code of Ethics, identify the auditor's course of action.

a. Report the facts to the appropriate individuals within the organization.
b. No action is required since this condition is not detrimental to the organization.
c. Note the condition in the working papers but refrain from reporting it because it benefits the organization.
d. Report the condition to the appropriate government regulatory agency.

225. An organization has recently placed a former operating manager in the position of director of internal auditing. The new director is not a member of the IIA and is not a CIA. Henceforth, the internal auditing department will be run strictly by the director's standards, not the IIA's. All four staff auditors are members of the IIA, but they are not CIAs. According to the Code of Ethics, what is the **best** course of action for the staff auditors?

a. The Code does not apply because the auditors are not CIAs.
b. The auditors should adopt suitable means to comply with the IIA *Standards*.
c. The auditors must exhibit loyalty to the organization and ignore the IIA *Standards*.
d. The auditors must resign their jobs to avoid improper activities.

226. A primary purpose for establishing a code of conduct within a professional organization is to

a. Reduce the likelihood that members of the profession will be sued for substandard work.
b. Ensure that all members of the profession perform at approximately the same level of competence.
c. Demonstrate acceptance of responsibility to the interests of those served by the profession.

d. Require members of the profession to exhibit loyalty in all matters pertaining to the affairs of their organization.

227. While performing an operational audit of the firm's production cycle, an internal auditor discovers that, in the absence of specific guidelines, some engineers and buyers routinely accept vacation trips paid for by certain of the firm's vendors. Other engineers and buyers will not accept even a working lunch paid for by a vendor. Which of the following actions should the internal auditor take?

a. None. The engineers and buyers are professionals. It is inappropriate for an internal auditor to interfere in what is essentially a personal decision.
b. Informally counsel the engineers and buyers who accept the vacation trips. This helps prevent the possibility of kickbacks, while preserving good auditor/auditee relations.
c. Formally recommend that the organization establish a corporate code of ethics. Guidelines of acceptable conduct within which individual decisions may be made should be provided.
d. Issue a formal deficiency report naming the personnel who accept vacations but make no recommendations. Corrective action is the responsibility of management.

228. You work for an organization that has adopted a conflict-of-interest policy that prohibits any activity contrary to the best interests and well-being of the organization. Which of the following statements should be included in the policy to illustrate unacceptable behavior?

a. Serving as a member of the board of directors of nonprofit organization dedicated to preservation of the environment.
b. Serving as an elected official (part-time) of a local government.
c. Providing a mailing list of company employees to a relative who is offering training that might benefit the organization.
d. Teaching (part-time) at a local university.

229. The Code of Ethics requires IIA members to exercise three particular qualities in the performance of their duties. These qualities are

a. Honesty, objectivity, and diligence.
b. Timeliness, sobriety, and clarity.
c. Knowledge, skill, and discipline.
d. Punctuality, loyalty, and dignity.

230. According to the Code of Ethics, the IIA board of directors may take action against a CIA whose work is dishonest by

a. Requesting that the CIA be fired by the employing company.
b. Reporting the dishonest act to legal authorities.
c. Having the CIA's employer issue a reprimand.
d. Revoking the auditor's CIA designation.

231. Which of the following involves a violation of the Institute of Internal Auditors' Code of Ethics?

a. An auditor informed a friend in an operating department of the expected closing of that department.
b. Unlike other employees, the auditors always fly first-class to maintain the appearance of independence.
c. With the consent of senior management, an auditor accepted a gift from an auditee department that was given as a reward for finding a major inefficiency.
d. An auditor accepted a promotional calendar from the sales manager.

232. The board of directors of the IIA has been informed that a CIA was tried and convicted of tax evasion. The probable consequences for this person are

a. Immediate revocation of the CIA designation by the Internal Auditing Standards Board.
b. Nothing; the act was performed outside of the normal line of work.
c. Censure by the director of professional practices of the Institute.
d. Review by the board of directors and forfeiture of the CIA designation.

233. An internal auditing director learns that a staff auditor has provided confidential information to a relative. Both the director and staff auditor are Certified Internal Auditors (CIAs). Although the auditor did not benefit from the transaction, the relative used the information to make a significant profit. The most appropriate way for the director to deal with this problem is to

a. Verbally reprimand the auditor.
b. Summarily discharge the auditor and notify the IIA.
c. Take no action since the auditor did not benefit from the transaction.
d. Inform the IIA's board of directors and take the personnel action required by company policy.

234. During the course of an audit, an auditor discovers that a clerk is embezzling company funds. Although this is the first embezzlement ever encountered and the organization has a security department, the auditor decides to personally interrogate the suspect. If the auditor is violating the IIA's Code of Ethics, the rule violated is most likely

a. Failing to show due diligence.
b. Lack of loyalty to the organization.
c. Lack of competence in this area.
d. Failing to comply with the law.

235. The director of internal auditing of a company is aware of a material inventory shortage caused by internal control deficiencies at one manufacturing plant. The shortage and related causes are of sufficient magnitude to impact the external auditor's report. Based on the IIA's Code of Ethics, identify the director's most appropriate course of action

a. Say nothing; guard against interfering with the independence of the external auditors.
b. Discuss the issue with management and take appropriate action to ensure that the external auditors are informed.
c. Inform the external auditors of the possibility of a shortage but allow them to make an independent assessment of the amount.
d. Report the shortages to the board of directors and allow the board to report it to the external auditor.

236. Which of the following statements is **not** appropriate to include in a manufacturer's conflict-of-interest policy? An employee shall not

a. Accept money, gifts, or services from a customer.
b. Participate (directly or indirectly) in the management of a public agency.
c. Borrow from or lend money to vendors.
d. Use company information for private purposes.

237. A firm's code of ethics contains the following statement: "Employees shall not accept gifts or gratuities over $50 in value from persons or firms with whom our organization does business." This provision is designed to prevent

a. Diversion of the firm's securities by an employee.
b. Excessive sales allowances granted by an employee.
c. Failure by an employee to record cash collections.
d. Participation by an employee in a working lunch funded by one of the firm's suppliers.

238. A code of conduct was developed several years ago and distributed by a large financial institution to all its officers and employees. Identify the best audit approach to provide the audit committee with the highest level of comfort about the code of conduct.

a. Fully evaluate the comprehensiveness of the code and compliance therewith, and report the results to the audit committee.
b. Fully evaluate company practices for compliance with the code, and report to the audit committee.
c. Review employee activities for compliance with provisions of the code, and report to the audit committee.
d. Perform tests on various employee transactions to detect potential violations of the code of conduct.

239. A review of an organization's code of conduct revealed that it contained comprehensive guidelines designed to inspire high levels of ethical behavior. The review also revealed that employees were knowledgeable of its provisions. However, some employees still did not comply with the code. What element should a code of conduct contain to enhance its effectiveness?

a. Periodic review and acknowledgment by all employees.
b. Employee involvement in its development.
c. Public knowledge of its contents and purpose.
d. Provisions for disciplinary action in the event of violations.

240. The best reason for establishing a code of conduct within an organization is that such codes

a. Are required by the Foreign Corrupt Practices Act.
b. Express standards of individual behavior for members of the organization.
c. Provide a quantifiable basis for personnel evaluations.
d. Have tremendous public relations potential.

Items 241 through 243 are based on the following:

A company with a whistle-blowing hotline has received an anonymous tip that three senior internal auditors are in violation of the IIA Code of Ethics. The company has adopted the IIA Code as a part of its corporate ethical code. Among the allegations against the auditors were the following:

1. Auditor 1 has a part-time job outside of office hours as a visiting professor at a local community college.
2. Auditor 1 owns stock in the employer company.
3. Auditor 1 told his next-door neighbor to start looking for a new job because an audit of the executive office indicated that the neighbor's division was going to be closed down in about six months.
4. Auditor 2 received an item of value from a local nonprofit organization of purchasing agents for whom he gave a speech.
5. Auditor 2 received an item of value from a customer of the employer.
6. Auditor 2 has a part-time job as president of a local charitable organization.
7. Auditor 2 shared audit techniques with auditors from another company while attending a professional meeting.
8. A buyer accepted a kickback of $500 to give bid amounts to a supplier to enable that supplier to bid the contract. Auditor 2 omitted this information from the audit report since the contract amount was not material to the financial statements.
9. Auditor 3 received royalties from a publisher for authoring a professional book on internal auditing.
10. Auditor 3 has a part-time job as a real estate broker, and his real estate firm recently received a commission from the employer company.
11. Auditor 3 received an item of value from a fellow employee in the same company whose department has never been audited and whose department is not scheduled to be audited in the foreseeable future.
12. Auditor 3 did not include in an audit report that the bottlenecks in a shipping department were caused by the absence of the supervisor. The supervisor was the auditor's friend and neighbor who had a hospitalized child requiring him to miss work off and on for several weeks.

241. How many of the allegations about Auditor 1 represent violations of the IIA's Code of Ethics?

a. None.
b. One.
c. Two.
d. Three.

242. How many of the allegations about Auditor 2 represent violations of the IIA's Code of Ethics?

a. One.
b. Two.
c. Three.
d. Four.

243. How many of the allegations about Auditor 3 represent violations of the IIA's Code of Ethics?

a. One.
b. Two.
c. Three.
d. Four.

MULTIPLE-CHOICE ANSWERS AND EXPLANATIONS

1. b	51. a	101. a	151. a	201. a
2. d	52. a	102. b	152. d	202. d
3. c	53. a	103. b	153. b	203. c
4. a	54. b	104. a	154. b	204. d
5. a	55. b	105. d	155. d	205. a
6. b	56. b	106. d	156. d	206. c
7. a	57. a	107. a	157. d	207. a
8. d	58. d	108. c	158. d	208. a
9. a	59. b	109. b	159. a	209. c
10. c	60. d	110. d	160. d	210. a
11. b	61. c	111. b	161. a	211. a
12. a	62. c	112. b	162. b	212. c
13. a	63. a	113. a	163. a	213. b
14. c	64. a	114. a	164. b	214. c
15. a	65. d	115. c	165. d	215. a
16. d	66. b	116. c	166. a	216. b
17. d	67. b	117. a	167. a	217. a
18. b	68. a	118. a	168. c	218. c
19. c	69. a	119. c	169. c	219. a
20. d	70. a	120. d	170. c	220. c
21. d	71. c	121. c	171. d	221. a
22. b	72. b	122. a	172. d	222. a
23. d	73. b	123. d	173. a	223. a
24. d	74. a	124. d	174. a	224. a
25. d	75. c	125. d	175. b	225. b
26. d	76. c	126. a	176. b	226. c
27. b	77. a	127. b	177. c	227. c
28. d	78. c	128. d	178. a	228. c
29. a	79. c	129. b	179. b	229. a
30. c	80. d	130. b	180. a	230. d
31. c	81. a	131. a	181. d	231. a
32. a	82. d	132. c	182. c	232. d
33. a	83. d	133. b	183. b	233. d
34. c	84. d	134. a	184. a	234. c
35. b	85. c	135. a	185. b	235. b
36. d	86. d	136. b	186. b	236. b
37. a	87. b	137. a	187. c	237. b
38. c	88. c	138. b	188. b	238. a
39. a	89. c	139. b	189. d	239. d
40. a	90. a	140. b	190. a	240. b
41. c	91. a	141. a	191. a	241. b
42. d	92. b	142. d	192. d	242. b
43. d	93. c	143. a	193. d	243. c
44. a	94. a	144. c	194. a	
45. d	95. c	145. c	195. c	
46. d	96. a	146. b	196. a	
47. a	97. d	147. d	197. c	
48. c	98. c	148. c	198. b	
49. a	99. d	149. d	199. d	1st: __/243 = __%
50. c	100. a	150. d	200. a	2nd: __/243 = __%

IIA's *Attribute Standards*

1. (b) The scope of the internal audit function does not include an assessment of the company's strategic management process. Choices (a), (c), and (d) are incorrect. Each of these is included in the scope of internal auditing as stated in the IIA Standards.

Subject Area: Comply with the IIA's *Attribute Standards*—professionalism. Source: CIA 593, II-2.

2. (d) This element of the audit is not included in the IIA *Standards.* Choice (a) is incorrect. Reviewing the reliability and integrity of financial information is the basic element of the audit. Choice (b) is incorrect. The Statement includes compliance and there are compliance aspects in financial operations. Choice (c) is incorrect. The auditor would review the economy, efficiency, and effectiveness of the financial functions.

Subject Area: Comply with the IIA's *Attribute Standards*—professionalism. Source: CIA 1192, II-1.

3. **(c)** This is a primary function of any internal auditing department. Choice (a) is incorrect. Only significant audit findings should be discussed with the audit committee. Choice (b) is incorrect. Internal auditors are not required to report deficiencies in regulatory compliance to the appropriate agencies. However, IIA members and Certified Internal Auditors (CIAs) may not knowingly be involved in illegal acts. Choice (d) is incorrect. This is not a primary objective of the internal auditing department. It is a budgetary control that management may require on a periodic basis.

Subject Area: Comply with the IIA's *Attribute Standards*—professionalism. Source: CIA 1192, II-7.

4. **(a)** This arrangement provides for the most operating flexibility and independence. Choice (b) is incorrect. That would place the director in a position of operational control. Choice (c) is incorrect. It is not the best choice; it limits influence and independence. Choice (d) is incorrect. It is not the best choice; it limits influence and independence.

Subject Area: Comply with the IIA's *Attribute Standards*—professionalism. Source: CIA 1190, I-2.

5. **(a)** This is what is required by the IIA's *Standards*. Choice (b) is incorrect. The auditor should seek to understand the operating standards as they are applied to the organization. Choice (c) is incorrect. Agreement is necessary. Choice (d) is incorrect. The auditor should first seek to gain an understanding with the auditee on the appropriate standards.

Subject Area: Comply with the IIA's *Attribute Standards*—professionalism. Source: CIA 597, I-39.

6. **(b)** The IIA S*tandards* say that persons transferred to the internal auditing department should not be assigned to audit those activities they previously performed until a reasonable period of time has elapsed. Choice (a) is incorrect. The IIA *Standards* says the internal auditor's objectivity is not adversely affected when the auditor reviews procedures before they are implemented. Choice (c) is incorrect. *Standards* say the internal auditor's objectivity is not adversely affected when the auditor recommends standards of control for systems before they are implemented. Choice (d) is incorrect. Use of staff from other areas to assist the internal auditor does not impair objectivity, especially when the staff is from outside of the area being audited.

Subject Area: Comply with the IIA's *Attribute Standards*—professionalism. Source: CIA 597, I-45.

7. **(a)** The IIA *Standards* specifies that an auditor who has been promoted to an operating department should not continue on an audit of the new department. Choice (b) is incorrect. The *Standards* state that budget restrictions do not constitute a violation of an auditor's independence. Choice (c) is incorrect. The *Standards* state that an auditor may participate on a task force that recommends new systems. However, designing, installing, or operating such systems might impair objectivity. Choice (d) is incorrect. The *Standards* state that an auditor may review contracts prior to their execution.

Subject Area: Comply with the IIA's *Attribute Standards*—professionalism. Source: CIA 597, I-52.

8. **(d)** Choices (a) and (c) are are incorrect. They are presumed not to impair independence per the IIA *Standards*. Choice (b) is incorrect. This is presumed to impair independence per the *Standards*.

Subject Area: Comply with the IIA's *Attribute Standards*—professionalism. Source: CIA 597, I-62.

9. **(a)** Oversight of external audit work is generally the responsibility of the board. Choices (b) and (c) are incorrect. When internal auditors are assigned to assist in the external audit, they are allowed to share relevant information with the external auditors. Choice (d) is incorrect. If the external auditor plans to rely on the work of an internal auditor, the work must be reviewed and tested. This would require access to both programs and workpapers.

Subject Area: Comply with the IIA's *Attribute Standards*—professionalism. Source: CIA 1196, III-35.

10. **(c)** The purpose of a quality assurance program is to evaluate the operations of the internal audit department. The IIA *Standards* note that a program should include supervision, internal reviews, and external reviews. Choice (a), (b), and (d) are incorrect. Proper training is an important component of maintaining a current staff, but does not provide feedback.

Subject Area: Comply with the IIA's *Attribute Standards*—professionalism. Source: CIA 1196, III-31.

11. **(b)** This is what the IIA *Standards* require. Choice (a) is incorrect. it is not the best answer. It implies that the auditor's recommendations, not the findings, are the most important elements of the report. Choice (c) is incorrect. It is not the best choice. This implies that the auditor's recommendations, not findings, are primary. Choice (d) is incorrect. It implies that processes in the internal auditing activity are primary.

Subject Area: Comply with the IIA's *Attribute Standards*—professionalism. Source: CIA 596, I-1.

12. **(a)** When senior management has assumed such risk, reporting to the board is only required for significant findings. There is no indication that the failure to document several decisions is significant enough to report to the board. Choice (b) is incorrect. See explanation given in Choice (a). Choice (c) is incorrect. Senior management has already indicated that it understands and has accepted the related risk. Choice (d) is incorrect. Reporting to anyone outside the organization is not required or appropriate.

Subject Area: Comply with the IIA's *Attribute Standards*—professionalism. Source: CIA 596, I-2.

13. **(a)** The IIA *Standards* state that the nature, timing and extent of follow-up should be determined by the director of internal auditing. Choices (b) and (c) are incorrect. The IIA *Standards* state that follow-up work is not management's responsibility. Choice (d) is incorrect. The auditor has to provide an opinion as to the decision made with regard to lack of action.

Subject Area: Comply with the IIA's *Attribute Standards*—professionalism. Source: CIA 596, I-3.

14. **(c)** This material does not exist in the IIA *Standards*. Choices (a), (b), and (d) are incorrect. These are reasons that management desires internal audit involvement.

Subject Area: Comply with the IIA's *Attribute Standards*—professionalism. Source: CIA 596, I-5.

15. **(a)** The *Standards* call for follow-up when analytical procedures identify unexpected results. Choice (b) is incorrect. The audit program is a guide, but it does not restrict the auditor from pursuing information unknown at the time that the program was written. Choice (c) is incorrect. The facts belie an indication of fraud. Choice (d) is incorrect. The risk of a material error caused by the machining department's activity is not addressed by delaying appropriate audit procedures.

Subject Area: Comply with the IIA's *Attribute Standards*—professionalism. Source: CIA 596, I-62.

16. (d) Provided that the auditee agrees with the standard or criterion, any of the above choices is appropriate. Choice (a) is incorrect. Standard operating procedures are an appropriate source. Choice (b) is incorrect. Textbook references are appropriate authority for standards and criteria. Choice (c) is incorrect. Sound business practice is valid as a criterion as long as the auditee agrees.

Subject Area: Comply with the IIA's *Attribute Standards*—professionalism. Source: CIA 596, I-63.

17. (d) The mix of audit skills in an audit staff affects the range of activities that can be audited. Auditing departments that comprise only people trained in accounting probably would be better able to examine financial and accounting systems than engineering systems, for example. As a result, departments should strive for an appropriate balance of experience, training, and ability in order to audit a range of activities within their respective organizations. Choice (a) is incorrect. Auditing departments that hired only CIAs or CAs and individuals possessing accounting degrees would be better equipped to audit certain operations, for example, financial and accounting systems, than others that did not have these minimum standards. Choice (b) is incorrect. A charter which set minimum professional standards, that is, CIA or CA, for its department's auditors would promote professionalism. Choice (c) is incorrect. The impact of this requirement would not affect whether consultants were used. Standard states that when auditors do not possesses adequate knowledge and skills in certain required area consultants should be used.

Subject Area: Comply with the IIA's *Attribute Standards*—professionalism. Source: CIA 596, I-64.

18. (b) According to the IIA's *Standards*, "the director of the internal auditing department should be responsible to an individual in the organization with sufficient authority to promote independence." External auditors are not individuals in the organization. Choice (a) is incorrect. The internal audit department will not have direct access to the board of directors. The access is indirect, via the controller. According to the *Standard*s, the "director should have direct communication with the board." Choice (c) is incorrect. Whether the controller has experience with internal auditors or not does not affect the audit department's independence. Choice (d) is incorrect. Although desirable, the Certified Internal Auditor designation is not mandatory for a person to become an internal auditor. A CIA would, of course, insist on internal audit department independence.

Subject Area: Comply with the IIA's *Attribute Standards*—professionalism. Source: CIA 596, I-65.

19. (c) There is no provision for the discussion of the meeting or the related options for handling the necessary transaction in the *Standards*. Choice (a) is incorrect. The *Standards* prescribe informing the board of management's decision on significant audit findings. Choice (b) is incorrect. The *Standards* prescribe highlighting significant audit findings and recommendations and reporting on the approved audit work schedule. Choice (d) is incorrect. The auditor does not yet know if this is actually a problem that can adversely affect the organization.

Subject Area: Comply with the IIA's *Attribute Standards*—professionalism. Source: CIA 596, I-66.

20. (d) Because the case indicates that the amount of the inventory adjustment is in question, this would be the appropriate step for the audit director to take. Choices (a) and (c) are incorrect. Reviews after year-end will not address the current year's financial reporting integrity. Choice (b) is incorrect. The director of internal auditing cannot do this and maintain independence.

Subject Area: Comply with the IIA's *Attribute Standards*—professionalism. Source: CIA 596, I-67.

21. (d) The IIA *Standards* provide that unexpected results from applying analytical auditing procedures should be investigated since unexplained results could indicates a potential error or irregularity. The variance was not adequately investigated or explained. Choices (a) and (b) are incorrect. The *Standards* provide that the extent of supervision should vary with the proficiency of the auditor. It is not inappropriate for an inexperienced auditor to refer this to the senior. Choice (c) is incorrect. The variance does need explanation and the rest of the audit can continue.

Subject Area: Comply with the IIA's *Attribute Standards*—professionalism. Source: CIA 596, I-69.

22. (b) In order to maintain the CIA designation, the CIA must commit to a formal program of continuing professional development (CPD) and report to the Certification Department of the IIA. Choice (a) is incorrect. There are no formal "hours" requirements for internal auditors contained in the *Standards*. The intent of the *Standards* is to ensure that internal auditors maintain their technical competence. Choice (c) is incorrect. Attendance at professional meetings does meet the criteria of continuing education. Choice (d) is incorrect. Prior approval by the IIA is not necessary for CPD courses.

Subject Area: Comply with the IIA's *Attribute Standards*—professionalism. Source: CIA 1195, I-43.

23. (d) This would not be an appropriate response. The director of internal auditing should determine the most reasonable conclusion and present that to the auditee and management. The issue of disagreements on the working papers should not necessarily affect the reporting to management unless the director of internal auditing believes that both conclusions are equally appropriate and it would enhance management's understanding to be presented with both. Choices (a) and (b) are incorrect. Both would be an appropriate response. Choice (c) is incorrect. This is an appropriate response since the director of internal auditing is ultimately responsible for the supervision of the audit staff as well as the quality of the working papers.

Subject Area: Comply with the IIA's *Attribute Standards*—professionalism. Source: CIA 1195, I-41.

24. (d) All of the statements are correct according to the IIA *Standards*. Choices (a), (b), and (c) are incorrect. They are partial answers.

Subject Area: Comply with the IIA's *Attribute Standards*—professionalism. Source: CIA 1195, I-39.

25. (d) All of the above items are appropriate uses of consultants. Choice (a) is incorrect. This would be an appropriate use of such experts according to the *Standards*. However, choices (b) and (c) also describe appropriate uses of consultants. Choice (b) is incorrect. This is an example of an operational audit and would be an appropriate use of such experts according to the *Standards*. However, Choice (a) and (c) also describe appropriate uses of consultants. Choice (c) is incorrect. This would be an appropriate example of training. However, Choice (a) and (b) also describe appropriate uses of consultants.

Subject Area: Comply with the IIA's *Attribute Standards*—professionalism. Source: CIA 1195, I-18.

26. (d) The IIA *Standards* indicate that the auditor should inform the appropriate authorities in the organization if there are sufficient indicators of the commission of a fraud. Choices (a) and (b) are incorrect. The action does violate the Code of Ethics. Choice (c) is incorrect. The action does violate the Code of Ethics, but the auditor should report the unlawful activities to the appropriate personnel within the organization, not to a regulatory agency.

Subject Area: Comply with the IIA's *Attribute Standards*—professionalism. Source: CIA 1195, I-53.

27. (b) The IIA *Standards* require the director to ensure that audit work conforms to the *Standards*. The *Standards* require the department to provide adequate supervision depending on the proficiency of the auditor. Choice (a) is incorrect. The *Standards* do not require all auditors to be proficient in all areas. The department should have an appropriate mix of skills. Choice (c) is incorrect. Although the Code does not address supervision directly, it does require the director to follow the *Standards*. Choice (d) is incorrect. See responses given for choices (b) and (c)

Subject Area: Comply with the IIA's *Attribute Standards*—professionalism. Source: CIA 1195, I-54.

28. (d) The auditor should accept the engagement, assign staff with sufficient control knowledge, and make recommendations where appropriate. This would not impair objectivity. Choice (a) is incorrect. The auditor should accept the engagement. Recommending controls is not considered a violation of the auditor's independence or objectivity. Choice (b) is incorrect. The auditor should accept the engagement. Auditors should have control knowledge that is not limited to accounting controls. Choice (c) is incorrect. The audit is not impaired by making control recommendations.

Subject Area: Comply with the IIA's *Attribute Standards*—professionalism. Source: CIA 1195, I-47.

29. (a) The internal audit department would, in composite, have the requisite skills to perform the audit. The other key element is that the staff auditor is carefully supervised such that significant deviations from good business practices would be noted. Choice (b) is incorrect. The audit would not be conducted in accordance with the *Standards* because the staff auditor might not have noted significant deviations to include in the audit report. The review by the director at the time the report is generated would be too late. Choice (c) is incorrect. Response (b) would not meet the *Standards*. Choice (d) is incorrect. Response (a) would be consistent with the *Standards*.

Subject Area: Comply with the IIA's *Attribute Standards*—professionalism. Source: CIA 1195, I-48.

30. (c) The risk assessment process is not normally communicated to the auditee. Choice (a) is incorrect. Auditors should be proficient in communicating audit objectives. Choice (b) is incorrect. Auditors should be proficient in communicating audit evaluations. Choice (d) is incorrect. Auditors should be proficient in communicating audit recommendations.

Subject Area: Comply with the IIA's *Attribute Standards*—professionalism. Source: CIA 1195, I-49.

31. (c) An understanding of management principles is required of all internal auditors. Choice (a) is incorrect. Such skills should be included within the staff, but not required for each auditor. Choice (b) is incorrect. Detailed knowledge of accounting is required only for those auditors who work extensively with financial records and reports. Choice (d) is incorrect. An appreciation of computerized information systems is required, but this is less expertise than is needed for proficiency.

Subject Area: Comply with the IIA's *Attribute Standards*—professionalism. Source: CIA 1195, I-14.

32. (a) According to the IIA *Standards,* "The director *may agree* to perform work...in connection with (the) annual audit...." Choice (b) is incorrect. According to the IIA *Standards,* "Actual coordination [of audit efforts] should be the responsibility of the director of internal auditing." Choice (c) is incorrect. According to the IIA *Standards*, "The director of internal auditing should communicate to senior management and the board the results of evaluations of coordination with external auditors." Choice (d) is incorrect. According to the IIA *Standards,* "The director should communicate to senior management and the board...any relevant comments about the performance of external auditors."

Subject Area: Comply with the IIA's *Attribute Standards*—professionalism. Source: CIA 596, I-59.

33. (a) Responsibility for follow-up should be defined in the internal auditing department's written charter. Choice (b) is incorrect. Follow-up is not specified in the content of the audit committee's mission statement. Choice (c) is incorrect. This memo may contain a statement about responsibility for follow-up, but such a statement should be based on the wording and authority of the departmental charter. Choice (d) is incorrect. Follow-up authority and responsibility may be cited in applicable audit reports, but the definition should be first contained in the departmental charter.

Subject Area: Comply with the IIA's *Attribute Standards*—professionalism. Source: CIA 596, I-60.

34. (c) Proper planning includes documented determination of resources including consideration of supplementation. Choice (a) is incorrect. The director is responsible for staffing each assignment as needed to meet the audit responsibilities Choice (b) is incorrect. Training is to be properly supervised, and the department does not have anyone with knowledge in this area to provide supervision. Choice (d) is incorrect because it is not the **best** course of action. If the requisite skills are not accessible through supplementation, this might be necessary, but the resource constraint should be communicated to management in an interim report.

Subject Area: Comply with the IIA's *Attribute Standards*—professionalism. Source: CIA 1194, I-12.

35. **(b)** According to the IIA *Standards*, objectivity may be impaired if the bonus is based on dollar recoveries or recommended future savings as a result of audits. A bonus based on either of these criteria could unduly influence the type of audits performed or the recommendations made. Choice (a) is incorrect. According to the IIA *Standards*, objectivity is not impaired if the bonus is administered by the board of directors or its salary administration committee. Use of a board compensation committee would be an environmental factor, which would enhance the director's independence and objectivity. Choice (c) is incorrect. According to the IIA *Standards*, objectivity is not impaired if the scope of internal auditing work is reviewing control rather than account balances. Compensation packages are often tied to financial results. If the scope of work was reviewing account balances, the director might be unduly influenced to report results, which would be favorable to his bonus. In contrast, there would be less inducement if the scope of work were limited to reviewing controls. Choice (d) is incorrect since only one answer is correct.

Subject Area: Comply with the IIA's *Attribute Standards*—professionalism. Source: CIA 1194, I-49.

36. **(d)** According to the IIA *Standards*, "the internal auditor's objectivity is not impaired when the auditor recommends standards of control for systems or reviews procedures before they are implemented. Designing, installing, and operating systems are not audit functions. Also, the drafting of procedures for systems is not an audit function. Performing such activities is presumed to impair audit objectivity." Internal auditors are not independent if they cannot do their work objectively. Choice (a) is incorrect. According to the IIA *Standards*, an internal auditor's objectivity would not be impaired when performing such tasks as helping to identify and define control objectives. Identifying and defining control objectives are necessary parts of any audit. The auditor's familiarity with the process of documenting systems and integrating recommendations into systems of control would be helpful to management in developing new systems. As long as the auditor's involvement did not cross over in operating areas, which are the responsibility of management, the auditor's objectivity would not be compromised. Choice (b) is incorrect. According to the IIA *Standards*, testing for compliance with system development standards would be a standard procedure for any system under development. Participation in this area would not place the auditor in an operating capacity. Consequently, this would not impair the auditor's objectivity. Choice (c) is incorrect. According to the IIA *Standards*, reviewing the adequacy of systems and programming standards would be standard procedures in performing a review of systems under development. Participation in this area would not place the auditor in an operating capacity. Consequently, this would not impair the auditor's objectivity.

Subject Area: Comply with the IIA's *Attribute Standards*—professionalism. Source: CIA 1194, I-50.

37. **(a)** According to the IIA *Standards*, internal auditors should be independent of the activities they audit. Accepting a fee or gift from an auditee would impair the auditor's objectivity. As a result, the auditor might feel obligated to render a more favorable result than would be warranted if the auditor maintained professional objectivity. Choice (b) is incorrect. According to the IIA *Standards*, the receipt of promotional items, such as pens, calendars, or samples available to the general public that have minimal value, would not impair the auditor's objectivity. Under these circumstances, it is unlikely that the receipt of these items would unduly influence the auditor to render a more favorable opinion than warranted under the circumstances. Choice (c) is incorrect. According to the IIA *Standards*, reviewing the installation of a data processing system would not impair the auditor's objectivity. Reviewing and documenting systems are necessary parts of auditing a system under development. As long as the auditor did not assume any operating responsibilities, for example, documenting operating procedures, the auditor's objectivity would not be compromised. Choice (d) is incorrect. According to the IIA *Standards*, participation in a task force and advising on control techniques would not impair the auditor's objectivity. As long as the auditor refrained from performing operating functions such as designing or installing operating systems or drafting detailed control procedures, the auditor's objectivity would not be compromised.

Subject Area: Comply with the IIA's *Attribute Standards*—professionalism. Source: CIA 1194, I-51.

38. **(c)** The IIA *Standards* state "It [independence] is achieved through organizational status and objectivity." The auditor is reporting to the highest level possible. Choice (a) is incorrect. The IIA *Standards* state "It [independence] is achieved through organizational status and objectivity," which is more directly related to the reporting level of the director. Choice (b) is incorrect. The IIA *Standards* state "It [independence] is achieved through organizational status and objectivity." Independence is not ensured by regulations. Choice (d) is incorrect. The IIA *Standards* state "It [independence] is achieved through organizational status and objectivity." A CIA designation will ensure a better auditor, but does not guarantee independence.

Subject Area: Comply with the IIA's *Attribute Standards*—professionalism. Source: CIA 1194, I-56.

39. **(a)** Because the auditor reports directly to the board of directors, he has organizational independence. Choice (b) is incorrect. Because the auditor reports directly to the board of directors, he has independence and therefore objectivity. Choice (c) is incorrect. The auditor has objectivity because he reports directly to the board of directors. He is, however, not exercising objectivity because he is trying to avoid conflict. Choice (d) is incorrect. The auditor has organizational independence because he reports directly to the board of directors (the highest level in the organization). The auditor has not exercised his independence because, although he can render any opinion he wants, he has lost his objectivity by adjusting his opinion.

Subject Area: Comply with the IIA's *Attribute Standards*—professionalism. Source: CIA 1194, I-61.

40. **(a)** Based on the control weakness and the potential for fraud, the auditor should look for other indicators of fraud or verify that no fraud has occurred. Choice (b) is incorrect. Tracing the tires on hand to the receiving reports would not reveal a fraud since manager signs the receiving report. Choice (c) is incorrect. Testing for signed requisitions would not necessarily reveal whether fraud is present. The manager is the signor. Choice (d) is incorrect. While the comparison may provide useful information, it would be less conclusive than Choice (a). If a fraud existed, it could have occurred last year also. The need for tires may vary.

Subject Area: Comply with the IIA's *Attribute Standards*—professionalism. Source: CIA 1194, I-70.

41. (c) All three responses would be appropriate according to the IIA *Standards.*

Subject Area: Comply with the IIA's *Attribute Standards*—professionalism. Source: CIA 1195, I-70.

42. (d) Coordination of audit efforts and the efficiency of audit activities should be primary responsibilities of the director of internal auditing. Choice (a) is incorrect. Adopting the full set of quality auditing standards for the internal auditing function would duplicate functions within the organization. Choice (b) is incorrect. The issue is the reporting relationship of internal auditing, not the qualifications of audit staff. Choice (c) is incorrect. Sufficient information in not given to conclude that the internal audit function should be eliminated.

Subject Area: Comply with the IIA's *Attribute Standards*—professionalism. Source: CIA 595, I-25.

43. (d) This is a broad definition of due diligence reviews per the IIA's *Standards.* Choice (a) is incorrect. Although the underwriter may use the reviews, the underwriter does not direct them. Choice (b) is incorrect. The due diligence review is not an operational audit. Choice (c) is incorrect. It is not a review for compliance with company policies.

Subject Area: Comply with the IIA's *Attribute Standards*—professionalism. Source: CIA 595, I-52.

44. (a) The audit manager dramatically changed the nature of the audit function without consulting with the audit committee, management, or the audit department charter. A second violation is the omission of negative findings. Choice (b) is incorrect. Highlighting potential cost savings is appropriate for an audit report. Choice (c) is incorrect. Item II is also a violation. Choice (d) is incorrect. Highlighting cost savings is appropriate.

Subject Area: Comply with the IIA's *Attribute Standards*—professionalism. Source: CIA 595, I-36.

45. (d) None of the actions constitutes a violation of the *Standards.* Action 2 is consistent with the IIA's *Standards. Action 3* is consistent with the IIA's *Standards.* Action 4 is consistent with the IIA's *Standards* on planning the audit. Auditors are not required to review all operations, unless mandated by law, within a specific time frame. Choices (a), (b), and (c) are incorrect. See reasons given in Choice (d).

Subject Area: Comply with the IIA's *Attribute Standards*—professionalism. Source: CIA 595, I-37.

46. (d) Auditors are not required to perform control evaluations and are certainly not required to fill out standard internal control questionnaires. Choice (a) is incorrect. Internal control evaluations are not required on every audit. Choice (b) is incorrect. Auditors cannot omit necessary procedures because of a time constraint. Choice (c) is incorrect. It is not a violation of the *Standards.*

Subject Area: Comply with the IIA's *Attribute Standards*—professionalism. Source: CIA 595, I-38.

47. (a) This is a violation of the *Standards,* which require that the lack of established criteria should be reported to the appropriate levels of management. This would normally be one level above the auditee. The negotiated formulation of the criteria may result in the correct criteria, but it should be discussed with, and communicated to, the appropriate level of management. Choice (b) is incorrect because, according to the *Standards,* auditors may formulate criteria they believe is adequate. Choice (c) is incorrect. Auditors should comment on the quality of operations in comparison with suitable criteria. The problem in this situation was the manner in which the criteria were formulated. Choice (d) is incorrect because of the responses given for choices (a), (b), and (c).

Subject Area: Comply with the IIA's *Attribute Standards*—professionalism. Source: CIA 595, I-39.

48. (c) The IIA *Standards* require follow-up action. Lack of resources is not a sufficient reason. Choice (a) is incorrect. Follow-up is required. Choice (b) is incorrect. Follow-up is to see that actions are taken, not just that the auditor's recommendations have been implemented. Choice (d) is incorrect. Follow-up is required.

Subject Area: Comply with the IIA's *Attribute Standards*—professionalism. Source: CIA 595, I-40.

49. (a) This would not have to be communicated. The audit work was done. The director of internal auditing would have to determine that there was no impairment of the independence of the senior's work. If there was none, the report could be issued without reporting the personnel change. Choices (b) and (c) are incorrect. This is a standard part of the required reporting to senior management and the board. Choice (d) is incorrect. The audit plan had been approved by both senior management and the board. The change dictated by senior management should be reported to the board.

Subject Area: Comply with the IIA's *Attribute Standards*—professionalism. Source: CIA 595, I-58.

50. (c) This is not included in the IIA *Standards.* Choices (a), (b), and (d) are incorrect. These are suggested by the *Standards.*

Subject Area: Comply with the IIA's *Attribute Standards*—professionalism. Source: CIA 595, I-60.

51. (a) Additional planning is necessary to align the audit effort to the circumstances and address the responsibilities of the audit department. Choice (b) is incorrect. It is not clear at this point what additional audit work will be necessary. Choice (c) is incorrect. Management has not accepted this plan of action. Choice (d) is incorrect. This action would not address applicable standards of the auditor or the audit department, including objectivity, due professional care, and performance of audit work standards.

Subject Area: Comply with the IIA's *Attribute Standards*—professionalism. Source: CIA 595, I-70.

52. (a) The IIA *Standards* states that the director of internal auditing should determine the nature, timing, and extent of follow-up. Choices (b) and (c) are incorrect. The *Standards* state that follow-up work is not management's responsibility. Choice (d) is incorrect. The auditor has to provide an opinion as to the decision made with regard to lack of action.

Subject Area: Comply with the IIA's *Attribute Standards*—professionalism. Source: CIA 1194, I-7.

53. (a) The IIA Professional Standard specifies that an auditor who has been promoted to an operating department should not continue on an audit of his or her new department. Choice (b) is incorrect. The Standard states that budget restrictions do not constitute a violation of an auditor's independence. Choice (c) is incorrect. The Standard states that an auditor may participate on a task force that recommends new systems. However, designing, installing, or operating such systems might impair objectivity. Choice (d) is incorrect. The Standard states that an auditor may review contracts prior to their execution.

Subject Area: Comply with the IIA's *Attribute Standards*—professionalism. Source: CIA 1194, I-8.

54. (b) This would be the best solution. The auditor is responsible for reporting deficiencies in criteria to management. Choice (a) is incorrect. It is not appropriate to conduct an audit for compliance with criteria that have never been communicated to auditees. Choice (c) is incorrect. It is okay to inform management and discuss whether now is the best time to conduct the audit. But it is not inappropriate to conduct the audit if management wants feedback on the implementation of its code. Choice (d) is incorrect. The auditor needs to communicate deficiencies in criteria to management. Just reporting on the implementation of the current code would be deficient.

Subject Area: Comply with the IIA's *Attribute Standards*—professionalism. Source: CIA 595, I-55.

55. (b) Per the IIA *Standards*, the director of internal auditing is responsible for providing appropriate audit supervision. Choice (a) is incorrect. Although the audit committee may determine whether due care is being exercised by the audit director, audit supervision is not the committee's responsibility. Choice (c) is incorrect. Although the audit supervisor may act on behalf of the director, the director is ultimately responsible for audit supervision. Choice (d) is incorrect. It is the senior or in-charge auditor who is in need of supervision, for which the director is responsible.

Subject Area: Comply with the IIA's *Attribute Standards*—professionalism. Source: CIA 1190, I-28.

56. (b) This is the purpose established by *Standards*. Choice (a) is incorrect. While a charter may help to do this, this option is not the best choice. Choice (c) is incorrect. It is not the best choice. Choice (d) is incorrect. While a charter may help to do this, this option is not the best choice. Subject Area: Comply with the IIA's *Attribute Standards*—professionalism. Source: CIA 1190, I-1.

57. (a) The IIA *Standards* address this aspect of working paper content. Choice (b) is incorrect. The Code of Ethics does not address working papers. Choice (c) is incorrect. The Statement of Responsibilities of Internal Auditing does not address working papers. Choice (d) is incorrect. The Foreign Corrupt Practices Act does not deal with workpaper content.

Subject Area: Comply with the IIA's *Attribute Standards*—professionalism. Source: CIA 590, I-18.

58. (d) The IIA *Standards* states that each auditor must be formally evaluated at least annually. Choice (a) is incorrect. Diversified tasks enhance an auditor's experience by allowing him to become familiar with various components of the audit. Choice (b) is incorrect. Internal auditors must be aware of current events in the field. Independent study is one means of accomplishing this. Choice (c) is incorrect. Rotating supervisors is desirable because it helps to broaden on-the-job training.

Subject Area: Comply with the IIA's *Attribute Standards*—professionalism. Source: CIA 1190, I-3.

59. (b) The form and content of written policies and procedures should be appropriate to the size and structure of the department and the complexity of its work. A small department may be managed informally. Choices (a), (c), and (d) are incorrect. They are true statements.

Subject Area: Comply with the IIA's *Attribute Standards*—professionalism. Source: CIA 1190, I-4.

60. (d) Paragraph 4 describes the standards by which the production department is measured. These are the "criteria," and they are the standards, measures, or expectations used in making an evaluation and/or verification ("what **should** exist"). Choice (a) is incorrect. Paragraph 1 explains the reason that the firm's productivity is greater than is the industry average. This is the attribute called "Cause," and it is the reason for the difference between the expected and actual conditions ("**why** the difference exists"). Choice (b) is incorrect. Paragraph 2 describes the result of the firm's access to state-of-the-art technology. This attribute is called "Effect," and it is the risk or exposure the auditee organization and/or others encounter because the condition is not the same as the criteria ("the **impact** of the difference"). In this case the effect is positive, rather than negative. Choice (c) is incorrect. Paragraph 3 describes the actual productivity extant within the firm. This attribute is called "Condition," and it is the factual evidence that the internal auditor found in the course of the examination ("what **does** exist").

Subject Area: Comply with the IIA's *Attribute Standards*—professionalism. Source: CIA 590, I-34.

61. (c) Paragraph 3 is the statement of "Condition." Choice (a) is incorrect. Paragraph 1 is the statement of "Cause." Choice (b) is incorrect. Paragraph 2 is the statement of "Effect." Choice (d) is incorrect. Paragraph 4 is the statement of "Criteria."

Subject Area: Comply with the IIA's *Attribute Standards*—professionalism. Source: CIA 590, I-35.

62. (c) The director of internal auditing has ultimate responsibility for the quality of reports issued by the internal auditing group and should signify formal approval of the report by his or her signature. Choice (a) is incorrect. Although the internal auditor performing the audit has much detail knowledge, the final audit report should be signed by the head of the internal audit department who has performed an objective review of the findings and recommendations. Choice (b) is incorrect. The person in charge of the area being reviewed will indicate his or her review of the report through a written reply. Choice (d) is incorrect. The chair of the audit committee is responsible for reviewing the ongoing activities of the internal auditing group and should not be directly involved in the preparation and review of the audit report.

Subject Area: Comply with the IIA's *Attribute Standards*—professionalism. Source: CIA 590, I-36.

63. (a) The IIA *Standards* are not limited to U.S. locations. Choices (b), (c), and (d) are incorrect. They are true.

Subject Area: Comply with the IIA's *Attribute Standards*—professionalism. Source: CIA 1190, I-5.

64. (a) This is the correct answer based on the IIA *Standards*. Choice (b) is incorrect. Standard 560.04.5: Appropriate follow-up is the director's responsibility. Choice (c) is incorrect. The key criterion should be an assessment of the department to the *Standards*. Choice (d) is incorrect. It also includes training, employee performance evaluations, time and expense control, and similar administrative areas.

Subject Area: Comply with the IIA's *Attribute Standards*—professionalism. Source: CIA 1190, I-6.

65. (d) Although the IIA *Standards* state that "the internal auditor should consider . . . the adequacy and effectiveness of internal control," the *Standards* make clear that this consideration must be based on an examination and evaluation, not just an assumption. Choice (a) is incorrect. The *Standards* state "Due care . . . does not require detailed audits of all transactions." Choice (b) is incorrect. The *Standards* state: "the relative materiality . . . of matters to which audit procedures are applied" is a legitimate consideration. Choice (c) is incorrect. The *Standards* state that "the internal auditor should consider . . . the cost of auditing in relation to potential benefits."

Subject Area: Comply with the IIA's *Attribute Standards*—professionalism. Source: CIA 1190, I-49.

66. (b) The IIA *Standards* note that access to the board helps assure independence and provides a means for the board and director to keep each other informed on matters of mutual interest. Choice (a) is incorrect. While this is important, it is not the best choice. Choice (c) is incorrect. While this is important, it is not the best choice. Choice (d) is incorrect. Since much of internal auditing involves evaluating activities directly under the control of this officer, independence might be hampered by such an arrangement.

Subject Area: Comply with the IIA's *Attribute Standards*—professionalism. Source: CIA 590, I-3.

67. (b) Direct reporting to top executive, dotted line to board. Choices (a) and (d) are incorrect. Solid line should be to a top executive. Choice (c) is incorrect. Internal auditing department should not be responsible to controller.

Subject Area: Comply with the IIA's *Attribute Standards*—professionalism. Source: CIA 590, I-4.

68. (a) The IIA *Standards* state that effectiveness of the system of internal control is to ascertain whether the system is functioning as intended. Choice (b) is incorrect. It defines the purpose of the review for adequacy of the system of internal control. Choice (c) is incorrect. It defines the purpose of the review of the quality of performance. Choice (d) is incorrect. It defines one of the objectives of internal control.

Subject Area: Comply with the IIA's *Attribute Standards*—professionalism. Source: CIA 590, I-5.

69. (a) Service to all members of the organization is the pervasive theme of the introduction to the *Standards*. Choices (b), (c), and (d) are incorrect. Each has just one of the specific activities outlined in the *Standards*.

Subject Area: Comply with the IIA's *Attribute Standards*—professionalism. Source: CIA 590, I-6.

70. (a) This is the correct answer per the IIA *Standards*. Choice (b) is incorrect. Professional Standards Bulletins are not authoritative sources. Choice (c) is incorrect. The Code makes no such requirement. Choice (d) is incorrect. This is not true.

Subject Area: Comply with the IIA's *Attribute Standards*—professionalism. Source: CIA 590, I-7.

71. (c) This is the correct answer based on the IIA *Standards*. Choice (a) is incorrect. The level of formal education will vary according to position requirements or departmental needs. Choice (b) is incorrect. Some entry-level positions require less than two years' experience, which is one of the prerequisites for many certification programs. Choice (d) is incorrect. Some of the staff positions may not require previous audit experience.

Subject Area: Comply with the IIA's *Attribute Standards*—professionalism. Source: CIA 590, I-8.

72. (b) This is the nature of opinions per the IIA *Standards*. Choice (a) is incorrect. It is not the best answer. Opinions should be solidly based and involve more than is given here. Choice (c) is incorrect. It is not the best answer. Auditors usually take the auditee's objectives as given. Choice (d) is incorrect. Opinions in internal audit reports are not limited to the fairness of financial statements.

Subject Area: Comply with the IIA's *Attribute Standards*—professionalism. Source: CIA 590, I-40.

73. (b) This is the correct answer based on the IIA *Standards*, "The possibility of material irregularities or noncompliance should be considered whenever the internal auditor undertakes an internal auditing assignment." Choice (a) is incorrect. "Due care requires the auditor to conduct examinations and verification to a reasonable extent, but does not require detailed audits of all transactions." Choice (c) is incorrect. "The internal auditor cannot give absolute assurance that noncompliance or irregularities do not exist." Choice (d) is incorrect. "Due care implies reasonable care and competence, not infallibility or extraordinary performance."

Subject Area: Comply with the IIA's *Attribute Standards*—professionalism. Source: CIA 590, I-44.

74. (a) This is in accord with the IIA *Standards*. Choice (b) is incorrect. Fraud may be perpetrated against the organization. Choice (c) is incorrect. Fraud may be for the benefit of an organization. Choice (d) is incorrect. Parts of this statement may or may not be true.

Subject Area: Comply with the IIA's *Attribute Standards*—professionalism. Source: CIA 590, I-47.

75. (c) This action meets the requirements of the *Standards*. Choices (a) and (b) are incorrect. These actions are insufficient. Choice (d) is incorrect. This action would be inappropriate.

Subject Area: Comply with the IIA's *Attribute Standards*—professionalism. Source: CIA 590, I-42.

76. (c) The principal means of preventing fraud is internal control; the internal auditor's role is related to evaluating the control. Choice (a) is incorrect. This response relates to the internal auditor's obligation for reporting suspected fraud, not for preventing fraud. Choice (b) is incorrect. Management, not internal auditing, is responsible for establishing these systems. Choice (d) is incorrect. The standards referred to relate to operational efficiency, not to prevention of fraud.

Subject Area: Comply with the IIA's *Attribute Standards*—professionalism. Source: CIA 590, II-46.

77. (a) This is the option most in line with what is suggested by the *Standards*. Choice (b) is incorrect. These executives may not be knowledgeable enough about details. Choice (c) is incorrect. These persons might not have the necessary perspectives and/or authority. Choice (d) is incorrect. The staff auditor might lack the proper perspective and may be "overmatched."

Subject Area: Comply with the IIA's *Attribute Standards*—professionalism. Source: CIA 590, II-37.

78. (c) This is basically what the *Standards* require. Choices (a), (b), and (d) are incorrect. Outside distribution is probably not appropriate.

Subject Area: Comply with the IIA's *Attribute Standards*—professionalism. Source: CIA 590, II-38.

79. (c) This defines relevant information. Choice (a) is incorrect. This defines sufficient information. Choice (b) is incorrect. This defines competent information. Choice (d) is incorrect. This defines useful information.

Subject Area: Comply with the IIA's *Attribute Standards*—professionalism. Source: CIA 590, II-16.

80. (d) The stem identifies the first-line position as the lowest-level persons "who are in a position to take corrective action or insure that corrective action is taken." In any case, the foremen are in a position "to insure that audit results are given due consideration." As a result, the foremen should each receive a full final audit report. Since the foreman's position is the lowest report-receiving organizational level, this response is correct. Choice (a) is incorrect. Audit committees usually do not require the full audit report to be submitted to them. Instead, they ordinarily ask for a summary of the audit report. This summary is sometimes nothing more than the summary referred to in the *Standards*. The audit committee may ask for the full audit report. If it does, however, it is the highest organizational level to receive it. Three lower levels, which may or must receive the full final audit report, are identified in the other responses. Choice (b) is incorrect. The chief executive officer (CEO) qualifies as one of those "higher-level members in the organization" who "may receive only a summary report." Like the audit committee, the CEO can request the full audit report. If the CEO does receive the full report, however, this represents a high organizational level. Two of the other three responses identify lower organizational levels that receive the full final audit report. Choice (c) is incorrect. The vice president of production is the head of the audited unit. As such, he or she should receive the complete final audit report. There are organizational levels lower than the unit head that "are in a position to take corrective action or insure that corrective action is taken." One such organizational level is identified among the other three responses.

Subject Area: Comply with the IIA's *Attribute Standards*—professionalism. Source: CIA 590, II-32.

81. (a) This is not an objective of the *Standards*. Choices (b), (c), and (d) are incorrect. Each one is an objective under the *Standards*.

Subject Area: Comply with the IIA's *Attribute Standards*—professionalism. Source: CIA 590, II-10.

82. (d) Organizational status and objectivity permit internal auditors to render the impartial and unbiased judgments essential to the proper conduct of audits. Choice (a) is incorrect. Staffing and supervision relate to the professional proficiency of the internal auditing department. Choice (b) is incorrect. Continuing education and due professional care is related to the professional proficiency of the internal auditor. Choice (c) is incorrect. Human relations and communications relate to the professional proficiency of the internal auditor.

Subject Area: Comply with the IIA's *Attribute Standards*—professionalism. Source: CIA 590, II-3.

83. (d) The *Standards* specify, in the area of applying internal auditing standards, procedures, and techniques, that an internal auditor should possess the ability to "apply knowledge to situations likely to be encountered and to deal with them without extensive recourse to technical research and assistance." Choice (a) is incorrect. The *Standards* specify only an understanding of management principles. Choice (b) is incorrect. The *Standards* specify only an appreciation of the fundamentals of such subjects as accounting, economics, and finance. Choice (c) is incorrect. The *Standards* specify only an appreciation of the fundamentals of computerized information systems.

Subject Area: Comply with the IIA's *Attribute Standards*—professionalism. Source: CIA 590, II-4.

84. (d) The audit committee can lend considerable weight to the recommendations of internal auditing. Choice (a) is incorrect. Review and approval of audit programs is the responsibility of internal audit supervision. Choice (b) is incorrect. External audit's reliance on the work of internal auditing is the subject of an AICPA pronouncement. Choice (c) is incorrect. Review and approval of internal audit reports is the responsibility of the director of internal auditing or designee.

Subject Area: Comply with the IIA's *Attribute Standards*—professionalism. Source: CIA 590, II-5.

85. (c) This is an ideal reporting relation. Choice (a) is incorrect. Reversed. Choice (b) is incorrect. This reporting responsibility would not be independent when reporting to controller. Choice (d) is incorrect. Internal auditor does not report to external auditor.

Subject Area: Comply with the IIA's *Attribute Standards*—professionalism. Source: CIA 590, II-6.

86. (d) The *Standards* require that resources needed to perform the audit have been considered. Choices (a), (b), and (c) are incorrect. The *Standards* do not require them.

Subject Area: Comply with the IIA's *Attribute Standards*—professionalism. Source: CIA 590, II-7.

87. (b) Within the definition of due professional care, the *Standards* include the evaluation of operating standards for acceptability and determining whether they are being met. Choice (a) is incorrect. Communication between the director of internal auditing and the board of directors is part of the Independence standard, not the Due Professional Care standard. Choice (c) is incorrect. The amount of audit time and effort required to give absolute assurance that there are no irregularities would be so great that the audit costs would exceed the benefits. Choice (d) is incorrect. Criteria for filling internal audit positions relate to the Staffing standard; they do not relate directly to the performance of an audit.

Subject Area: Comply with the IIA's *Attribute Standards*—professionalism. Source: CIA 1190, II-49.

88. (c) Choice (c) is the correct answer. Independence would be adversely affected since internal auditors would be expected to review systems for which the director and the director's immediate superior were responsible. Choice (a) is incorrect. It is not the best choice. Choice (b) is incorrect.

Auditors often have the required expertise. Choice (d) is incorrect. Such arrangements are not illegal.

Subject Area: Comply with the IIA's *Attribute Standards*—professionalism. Source: CIA 1190, II-1.

89. (c) The *Standards* specify that goals should include measurement criteria and targeted dates of completion. Choice (a) is incorrect. Planning does include specifying audit work schedules and the activities to be audited. However, the goals for the internal auditing department do not ordinarily include this information. The goals tend to be broader in scope. Choice (b) is incorrect. The department's goals are separate from its policies and procedures should be based on goals. Choice (d) is incorrect. Staffing plans include the number of auditors required for an engagement, and the knowledge, skills, and disciplines required, as partly determined from audit work schedules. Goals do not include budgets, either. Instead, goals should be achievable within relevant budget constraints.

Subject Area: Comply with the IIA's *Attribute Standards*—professionalism. Source: CIA 1190, II-2.

90. (a) Auditors should have a proficiency in applying internal auditing standards. Choices (b), (c), and (d) are incorrect. Only an appreciation is required.

Subject Area: Comply with the IIA's *Attribute Standards*—professionalism. Source: CIA 1190, II-4.

91. (a) The *Standards* specify that the director of internal auditing is responsible for coordination. Choices (b), (c), and (d) by definition are incorrect.

Subject Area: Comply with the IIA's *Attribute Standards*—professionalism. Source: CIA 1190, II-5.

92. (b) These criteria are related to skill, not independence. Choice (a) is incorrect. Communication is related to independence. Choice (c) is incorrect. Assumption of operating duties is related to independence. Choice (d) is incorrect. The scope and depth of the audit objectives reflect on the department's independence.

Subject Area: Comply with the IIA's *Attribute Standards*—professionalism. Source: CIA 596, I-48.

93. (c) With a small audit department, substantial direct supervision can be provided by the audit director. Choice (a) is incorrect. Departmentalization can improve communications among team members, but sufficient direct supervision may be lacking if spans of control are large. Choice (b) is incorrect. Division of labor produces highly specialized individuals, but formalized guidance is necessary for newer employees if the department is large. Choice (d) is incorrect. The audit director is the ultimate authority for the internal auditing department, but direct supervision by this individual will be lacking in a large department. Formal policies are needed.

Subject Area: Comply with the IIA's *Attribute Standards*—professionalism. Source: CIA 596, III-2.

94. (a) Activity reports should be submitted periodically to both senior management and the board; no distinction between the contents of the reports is necessary except in extraordinary situations requiring confidentiality. Choice (b) is incorrect. This is not included in the provisions of the *Standards*. Choice (c) is incorrect. Financial budget information is only part of the provisions established in the *Standards*; there is no need to restrict the information to this subject. Choice (d) is incorrect. The *Standards* do not provide for limiting information in this manner.

Subject Area: Comply with the IIA's *Attribute Standards*—professionalism. Source: CIA 595, III-23.

95. (c) This would violate the IIA *Standards* because the auditor has not acted on audit evidence that indicated that the audit should be expanded. Choice (a) is incorrect. This action would be consistent with the *Standards* on due professional care. Choice (b) is incorrect. This action would be consistent with the *Standards* on due professional care. Choice (d) is incorrect. The auditor does not need the auditee's approval to expand the audit test.

Subject Area: Comply with the IIA's *Attribute Standards*—professionalism. Source: CIA 1195, I-56.

96. (a) This is the option most in line with what is suggested by the IIA *Standards*. Choice (b) is incorrect. These executives may not be knowledgeable enough about details. Choice (c) is incorrect. These persons might not have the necessary perspectives and/or authority. Choice (d) is incorrect. The staff auditor might lack the proper perspective and may be "overmatched."

Subject Area: Comply with the IIA's *Attribute Standards*—professionalism. Source: CIA 1195, I-56.

97. (d) Not much benefit is gained by surveying the board of directors since members' views will be biased for this audit. Choice (a) is incorrect. This would be included in the "normal scope" of this type of audit. Choice (b) is incorrect. Surveys of employees are not prohibited by the *Standards*. Choice (c) is incorrect. Ethics Test is not prohibited by the *Standards*.

Subject Area: Comply with the IIA's *Attribute Standards*—professionalism. Source: CIA 594 I-9.

98. (c) The *Standards* place the responsibility for the evaluation of corrective action on the director of internal audit. Choice (a) is incorrect. The *Standards* state that information on illegal acts should be communicated to the external auditor. Choice (b) is incorrect. Both internal and external audit standards allow review of each other's working papers to evaluate scope, quality of work, and so on. Choice (d) is incorrect. All work done by internal auditors should be done in accordance with the *Standards*.

Subject Area: Comply with the IIA's *Attribute Standards*—professionalism. Source: CIA 594, I-15.

99. (d) Auditors sometimes must rely on outside experts; the *Standards* allow this reliance. Choice (a) is incorrect. A conflict of interest compromises objectivity. Choice (b) is incorrect. An auditor's familiarity with the auditee can compromise objectivity. Choice (c) is incorrect. Assuming operational duties compromises an auditor's objectivity.

Subject Area: Comply with the IIA's *Attribute Standards*—professionalism. Source: CIA 594 I-16.

100. (a) Individual appraisal is part of personnel management. Choice (b) is incorrect. Internal review is part of quality assurance. Choice (c) is incorrect. Supervision is part of quality assurance. Choice (d) is incorrect. External review is part of quality assurance.

Subject Area: Comply with the IIA's *Attribute Standards*—professionalism. Source: CIA 594 I-17.

101. (a) The true cause of a finding may require additional expertise and may be determinable only through additional management study. Choice (b) is incorrect. If the finding is significant enough to report, time must be found to determine what action would solve the deficiency. Choice (c) is incorrect. Avoiding honest differences of opinion is not an acceptable reason for deleting a recommendation. Choice (d) is incorrect. Recommendations do not impair an auditor's independence. Management is responsible for decision making and implementing suggestions or formulating new solutions.

Subject Area: Comply with the IIA's *Attribute Standards*—professionalism. Source: CIA 594 I-18.

102. (b) Training is a factor of skill, not independence. Choice (a) is incorrect. How auditors are assigned is a factor related to independence: does the auditor have personal relationships with operating personnel, work experience with the auditee, and so forth? Choice (c) is incorrect. If significant findings found in the working papers are left out of the report, independence is brought into question. Choice (d) is incorrect. Unbiased judgment is a factor of independence.

Subject Area: Comply with the IIA's *Attribute Standards*—professionalism. Source: CIA 594, I-37.

103. (b) This is the correct answer based on the IIA *Standards*. Choice (a) is incorrect. This is the definition of audit risk used in external auditing. Choice (c) is incorrect. This could be used as a definition of management decision making risk, but the answer has no defined term. Choice (d) is incorrect. This answer is the definition of financial statement error.

Subject Area: Comply with the IIA's *Attribute Standards*—professionalism. Source: CIA 594, I-55.

104. (a) Risk assessment does not necessarily involve the assignment of dollar values and is not intended to identify the audit area with the greatest dollar savings (Standard 520, Planning). Choice (b) is incorrect. Risk assessment includes information from many sources. Choice (c) is incorrect. Risk assessment is systematic and provides a means for development of an audit schedule. Choice (d) is incorrect. Risk assessments may be revised on the basis of new information.

Subject Area: Comply with the IIA's *Attribute Standards*—professionalism. Source: CIA 594, I-56.

105. (d) Procedures, systems, and accounts can all be auditable activities according to the *Standards*. Choices (a), (b), and (c) are incorrect. Each choice is a part of Choice (d).

Subject Area: Comply with the IIA's *Attribute Standards*—professionalism. Source: CIA 594, I-57.

106. (d) It is a part of the audit scheduling, not auditor selection for audit assignment. Choices (a), (b), and (c) are incorrect. Each choice is included as a factor in the *Standards*.

Subject Area: Comply with the IIA's *Attribute Standards*—professionalism. Source: CIA 594, I-58.

107. (a) Proficiency in the application of the *Standards* is required. Choice (b) is incorrect. An appreciation, not proficiency, in accounting and computerized information systems is required. Choice (c) is incorrect. Proficiency, not an understanding, of audit techniques is required. Choice (d) is incorrect. Proficiency, not a broad understanding, of accounting principles is required when auditing financial records.

Subject Area: Comply with the IIA's *Attribute Standards*—professionalism. Source: CIA 594, I-67.

108. (c) This is a requirement of the director of auditing, not an audit manager. Choices (a), (b), and (d) are incorrect. Each is a list skill of an audit manager.

Subject Area: Comply with the IIA's *Attribute Standards*—professionalism. Source: CIA 594, I-68.

109. (b) This criterion is related to skill, not independence. Choice (a) is incorrect. Communication is related to independence. Choice (c) is incorrect. Assumption of operating duties is related to independence. Choice (d) is incorrect. The scope and depth of the audit objectives reflects on the department's independence.

Subject Area: Comply with the IIA's *Attribute Standards*—professionalism. Source: CIA 594, I-69.

110. (d) A charter establishes the department's independence from management. Choice (a) is incorrect. Due care is a function of audit work, not the charter. Choice (b) is incorrect. Although stature within the organization may be increased, the main function of the charter is to establish the department's independence not stature. Choice (c) is incorrect. The department's relationship with management is a function of professionalism; the charter establishes independence, not a working relationship.

Subject Area: Comply with the IIA's *Attribute Standards*—professionalism. Source: CIA 594, I-70.

111. (b) The IIA *Standards* state "Internal auditors are independent when they carry out their work freely and objectively. Independence permits internal auditors to render the impartial and unbiased judgments essential to the proper conduct of audits. It is achieved through organizational status and objectivity." Furthermore, the *Standards* state: "Designing, installing, and operating systems are not audit functions. Also, the drafting of procedures for systems is not an audit function. Performing such activities is presumed to impair audit objectivity." Accordingly, it would be inappropriate for the internal audit department to continue to design and install other computer systems, regardless of the expertise of the audit staff in such areas, because such functions impair independence. Choice (a) is incorrect. According to the IIA *Standards*, refraining from designing and installing any systems would enhance independence and is therefore an appropriate action. Choice (c) is incorrect. The *Standards* state that "objectivity is presumed to be impaired when internal auditors audit any activity for which they had authority or responsibility." Assigning internal auditors other than those who designed and installed the payroll system to audit the payroll system slightly enhances independence. However, this is not the best answer, as it does not address the ongoing independence concern the audit committee has voiced. Choice (d) is incorrect. This is discussed in the *Standards*.

Subject Area: Comply with the IIA's *Attribute Standards*—professionalism. Source: CIA 1193, I-4.

112. (b) Internal auditing standards are required to be known by the department collectively. Individual internal auditing staff members may, however, bring special skills to the department instead of specific knowledge of internal auditing standards. Choice (a) is incorrect. Each new employee of an internal auditing department is not required to have knowledge of internal auditing standards. It is required that the department collectively has this knowledge. Choice (c) is incorrect. Each individual internal auditor is not required to have knowledge of accounting or taxes. Choice (d) is incorrect. What knowledge that was acquired by observing is irrelevant to the skills necessary for internal auditing.

Subject Area: Comply with the IIA's *Attribute Standards*—professionalism. Source: CIA 1193, I-5.

113. (a) Reporting provides feedback on these options as prescribed in the travel policy. Choice (b) is incorrect. Travel department information is preliminary; employees may change tickets and routings prior to their trip. Choice (c) is incorrect. In this type of system, airline tickets would normally be charged to employee accounts receivable; departmental charges would be initiated by the expense report transaction. Choice (d) is incorrect. Documentation for the employer's business expense deduction would include that filed with the employee business expense report that also establishes the business purpose of such expenditures.

Subject Area: Comply with the IIA's *Attribute Standards*—professionalism. Source: CIA 1193, I-8.

114. (a) Interim report should be issued regarding the significant issues noted. Choices (b) and (c) are incorrect. Significant audit findings should be timely communicated. Choice (d) is incorrect. Significant audit findings should be timely communicated to audit committee.

Subject Area: Comply with the IIA's *Attribute Standards*—professionalism. Source: CIA 1193, I-41.

115. (c) The risk or exposure encountered represents the effect of the audit finding. Choice (a) is incorrect. The reason for the difference between expected and actual conditions represents the cause of the finding. Choice (b) is incorrect. Factual evidence represents the condition. Choice (d) is incorrect. Standards, measures, or expectations represent the criteria for the audit findings.

Subject Area: Comply with the IIA's *Attribute Standards*—professionalism. Source: CIA 1193, I-42.

116. (c) This is what the *Standards* require in such cases. Choices (a) and (b) are incorrect. The assertions are self-serving. Choice (d) is incorrect. Noting differences in interpretation in the audit report, in and of itself, is not due care. Due care has to do with how the audit is performed and the report written.

Subject Area: Comply with the IIA's *Attribute Standards*—professionalism. Source: CIA 1193, I-50.

117. (a) The purpose of supervisory review is to assure quality. Choice (b) is incorrect. This relates to efficiency more than quality. Choice (c) is incorrect. This relates only indirectly to the quality of audits. Choice (d) is incorrect. This relates directly to the quality of audits but is not as effective a control as supervisory review.

Subject Area: Comply with the IIA's *Attribute Standards*—professionalism. Source: CIA 1193, II-21.

118. (a) This evidence suggests that the auditor did not confirm this information or follow up with testing. Choice (b) is incorrect. This evidence shows the source and approval of journal entry information. Choice (c) is incorrect. This evidence shows testing based on computer-based reports and manual reconciliations. Choice (d) is incorrect. This evidence demonstrates efficiency by referencing work already done in another section of the working papers.

Subject Area: Comply with the IIA's *Attribute Standards*—professionalism. Source: CIA 1193, II-22.

119. (c) The *Standards* require this path for reporting; it is management's decision to make further disclosure. Choices (a), (b), and (d) are incorrect. The *Standards* do not require such reporting.

Subject Area: Comply with the IIA's *Attribute Standards*—professionalism. Source: CIA 1193, II-47.

120. (d) This is how the responsibility is met according to the *Standards*. Choice (a) is incorrect. This involves detection, not deterrence. Choice (b) is incorrect. Testing for fraud in every audit is not required. Choice (c) is incorrect. This is not the primary means as described in the standards.

Subject Area: Comply with the IIA's *Attribute Standards*—professionalism. Source: CIA 593, I-47.

121. (c) The *Standards* require alertness for irregularities and knowledge of high-risk areas. Choice (a) is incorrect because the *Standards* also call for alertness. Choice (b) is incorrect. There is no indication that irregularities should occur. Choice (d) is incorrect. Following instructions by rote is unacceptable. Professional judgment and alertness must be used.

Subject Area: Comply with the IIA's *Attribute Standards*—professionalism. Source: CIA 593, I-44.

122. (a) Choice (a) is the correct answer. If the auditing department drafts procedures, it will be in the position of auditing its own work during the next audit cycle. Choice (b) is incorrect. This type of dual reporting enhances the internal auditing department's independence, since it protects auditors from the potentially disastrous effect of unwarranted displeasure on the part of the chief executive officer. Choice (c) is incorrect. "Independence" refers to the internal auditing department's relationship with management, not with the external auditors. While the internal auditing department should not allow its audit plans to be dictated by the external auditors, close cooperation eliminates wasteful duplication and permits an efficient division of labor. Choice (d) is incorrect. This policy is a good example of "preemptive auditing" and affords an opportunity to evaluate the adequacy of controls and audit trails in the proposed contracts.

Subject Area: Comply with the IIA's *Attribute Standards*—professionalism. Source: CIA 593, I-3.

123. (d) Improper or illegal acts that are committed by senior management may be disclosed in a separate report and distributed to the audit committee of the board of directors or to a similar high-level entity within the organization. Choice (a) is incorrect. Although improper or illegal acts may be disclosed in a separate report, the internal auditor should not discuss such information with those individuals who have committed such acts. Choice (b) is incorrect. In general, internal auditors are responsible to their organization's management rather than outside agencies. In the case of fraud, statutory filings with regulatory agencies may be required. Choice (c) is incorrect. Since it is a member of senior management who has committed the illegal acts, it would not be appropriate for the internal auditor to disclose this information to senior management. Instead, such information should be communicated to those individuals in the organization to whom senior management report.

Subject Area: Comply with the IIA's *Attribute Standards*—professionalism. Source: CIA 593, I-38.

124. (d) The report, which was not published until eight weeks after the audit was concluded, was not issued in a timely fashion, given the significance of the findings and the need for prompt, effective action. Choice (a) is incorrect. There is not enough information to evaluate the effectiveness of follow-up. Choice (b) is incorrect. Auditors may properly make recommendations for potential improvements but should not implement corrective action. Choice (c) is incorrect. Auditor recommendations are one of the recommended elements of an audit finding.

Subject Area: Comply with the IIA's *Attribute Standards*—professionalism. Source: CIA 593, I-40.

125. (d) The charter should prescribe internal auditing's relationships to other units within the organization and to those outside. Choice (a) is incorrect. Departmental policies and procedures guide the audit staff in the consistent compliance with the department's standards of performance. Choice (b) is incorrect. The *Standards* do not contain an element of authority for individual departments. Choice (c) is incorrect. The *Standards* recommend a formal charter to outline the authority of individual departments.

Subject Area: Comply with the IIA's *Attribute Standards*—professionalism. Source: CIA 593, II-5.

126. (a) The IIA *Standards* require that the program include these attributes as well as written job descriptions and counseling. Choice (b) is incorrect. Counseling is an attribute, but an automatic established career path is not. Choice (c) is incorrect. Planning is an overall part of the development program, but a charter is not specified. Choice (d) is incorrect. Written job descriptions are required by the *Standards*, but salary increases are not mentioned.

Subject Area: Comply with the IIA's *Attribute Standards*—professionalism. Source: CIA 593, II-6.

127. (b) Internal quality assurance reviews primarily serve the needs of the director of internal auditing, but can also provide senior management and the board with an assessment of the internal auditing department. This is specified in the *Standards*. Choice (a) is incorrect. The audit committee is an indirect beneficiary by knowing the effectiveness of the overall internal auditing function. Choice (c) is incorrect. Management is an indirect beneficiary, as is the audit committee. Choice (d) is incorrect. The audit staff also benefits (but not a primary beneficiary) by having deficiencies addressed more promptly.

Subject Area: Comply with the IIA's *Attribute Standards*—professionalism. Source: CIA 593, II-7.

128. (d) A written report should be issued at the conclusion of the investigation phase. It should include all findings, conclusions, recommendations, and corrective action taken. This is the list provided by the *Standards*. Choice (a) is incorrect. This is the list of information to include in a final written report at the conclusion of an audit examination, which may not include fraud. Since this definition does not include "corrective action," it is incomplete. Choice (b) is incorrect. This is a correct listing of the elements comprising "Findings." A fraud report includes more than findings, so this answer is incomplete. Choice (c) is incorrect. The inclusion of background is recommended but not required for inclusion in a final audit report. There is no mention of it in a fraud report. This list leaves out "conclusions" and "corrective action," so it is incomplete.

Subject Area: Comply with the IIA's *Attribute Standards*—professionalism. Source: CIA 593, II-50.

129. (b) The director should have periodically checked the status of the case with security. Follow-up is specified by the *Standards*. Choice (a) is incorrect. According to the IIA *Standards*, the director should have ensured that the internal auditing department's responsibilities were met. Choice (c) is incorrect. A security department would generally have more expertise in the investigation of a fraud. Choice (d) is incorrect. The fraud was only suspected when reported to the director. Immediate discharge would have violated the suspect's rights. In addition, the director would not normally have the authority to discharge an employee in an audited area.

Subject Area: Comply with the IIA's *Attribute Standards*—professionalism. Source: CIA 593, II-44.

130. (b) The IIA *Standards* state "Findings are pertinent statements of fact." Audit findings must be factual evidence regarding control strengths and weaknesses that the auditor has found during the course of his or her examination. Choice (a) is incorrect. Audit findings must be statements of fact rather than statements representing an auditor's opinion. Opinions represent the auditor's evaluations of the effects of audit findings on the activities reviewed. Choice (c) is incorrect. Audit findings cannot be both facts and opinions. They must only describe facts or conditions that exist. Choice (d) is incorrect. Audit findings deal with present, not future, factual conditions or events.

Subject Area: Comply with the IIA's *Attribute Standards*—professionalism. Source: CIA 593, II-37.

131. (a) The IIA *Standards* specify that supervision includes determining that working papers adequately support audit findings. Choice (b) is incorrect. Staffing engagements is not a supervisory function; it is a planning function. Choice (c) is incorrect. Determining audit scope is not a supervisory function; it is a planning function. Choice (d) is incorrect. Appraising performance on an annual basis is not a supervisory function of a specific assignment; it is part of the management of the internal auditing department.

Subject Area: Comply with the IIA's *Attribute Standards*—professionalism. Source: CIA 1192, I-14.

132. (c) The chief executive officer has the highest authority to promote independence and to ensure broad audit coverage, adequate consideration of audit reports, and appropriate action on audit recommendations. This is an ideal reporting relation per the *Standards*. Choice (a) is incorrect. It is the reverse of the recommended structure. Choice (b) is incorrect. This arrangement would not be independent when reporting to controller. Choice (d) is incorrect. An internal auditor does not report to an external auditor.

Subject Area: Comply with the IIA's *Attribute Standards*—professionalism. Source: CIA 1192, I-2.

133. (b) The IIA *Standards* state that audit priorities should be based on financial exposure, potential loss and risk, requests from management, and opportunities to achieve operating benefits as well as the date and results of the last audit. Choice (a) is incorrect. While the *Standards* provide authoritative support for work schedules, there is no requirement to cite them. Choice (c) is incorrect. To the contrary, the *Standards* suggest keeping the plan flexible in the event of unanticipated needs. Choice (d) is incorrect. Activity reports should be submitted to management periodically, but there is no requirement for seeking approval of the annual work schedule.

Subject Area: Comply with the IIA's *Attribute Standards*—professionalism. Source: CIA 1192, I-5.

134. (a) Maintaining independence allows the auditor to perform necessary duties. Choices (b), (c), and (d) are incorrect. They are a benefit, but not most significant.

Subject Area: Comply with the IIA's *Attribute Standards*—professionalism. Source: CIA 1192, I-6.

135. (a) Such a policy is called for by the IIA *Standards* to promote independence. Choice (b) is incorrect. The *Standards* specifically indicate that this is a part of internal auditing's responsibilities and that it would not cause an independence problem. Choice (c) is incorrect. It is not the best choice. Choice (d) is incorrect. The *Standards* specifically provide for such transfers. However, the *Standards* note that transfers should not be assigned to audit those activities they previously performed until a reasonable period of time has elapsed.

Subject Area: Comply with the IIA's *Attribute Standards*—professionalism. Source: CIA 1192, I-7.

136. (b) The form and content of written policies and procedures should be appropriate to the size and structure of the department and the complexity of its work. A small department may be managed informally. Choices (a), (c), and (d) are incorrect. They are true statements.

Subject Area: Comply with the IIA's *Attribute Standards*—professionalism. Source: CIA 1192, I-8.

137. (a) The IIA *Standards* require that goals be capable of accomplishment within given plans and budgets and that they be measurable. Choice (b) is incorrect. Goals should be attainable within budget constraints. However, approval of goals is not mentioned in this portion of the *Standards*. Choice (c) is incorrect. The establishment of goals is part of the overall planning process for the internal auditing department. Choice (d) is incorrect. Goals are not generally requested, but instead they are established by the director of internal auditing.

Subject Area: Comply with the IIA's *Attribute Standards*—professionalism. Source: CIA 1192, I-10.

138. (b) "Cause" is the reason for the difference between the expected and actual condition. Choice (a) is incorrect. Factual evidence represents the condition. Choice (c) is incorrect. Risk or exposure is the effect. Choice (d) is incorrect. Resultant evaluations are the conclusions.

Subject Area: Comply with the IIA's *Attribute Standards*—professionalism. Source: CIA 1192, I-44.

139. (b) Summary reports that highlight audit results are appropriate for higher-level management. Choice (a) is incorrect. Interim reports are used to communicate urgent information, changes in audit scope, and audit progress. Choice (c) is incorrect. Only interim reports may be oral. The final report must be written. Choice (d) is incorrect. Higher-level management is often too busy to read an entire report.

Subject Area: Comply with the IIA's *Attribute Standards*—professionalism. Source: CIA 1192, I-45.

140. (b) This is the correct answer per the IIA *Standards*. Choices (a), (c), and (d) are incorrect by definition.

Subject Area: Comply with the IIA's *Attribute Standards*—professionalism. Source: CIA 1192, I-47.

141. (a) If the incidence of significant fraud has been established with reasonable certainty, the auditor is responsible for reporting such to senior management or the board. Choice (b) is incorrect. No reporting is required when suspicious acts are reported to the auditor. Choice (c) is incorrect. Irregular transactions under investigation would not require reporting until the investigation phase is completed. Choice (d) is incorrect. Reporting should occur sooner. See Choice (a).

Subject Area: Comply with the IIA's *Attribute Standards*—professionalism. Source: CIA 1192, II-49.

142. (d) Internal auditors are not normally trained in the interrogation of suspected perpetrators and therefore should leave such activity to security or law enforcement specialists. Choice (a) is incorrect. This can be critical to ensuring that internal auditors avoid providing information to or obtaining misleading information from persons who may be involved. Choice (b) is incorrect. This is a responsibility assigned by the *Standards* and will be useful when determining what controls to recommend preventing future occurrences of similar fraud. Choice (c) is incorrect. This is a responsibility assigned by the *Standards* and will tend to ensure a complete and thorough investigation.

Subject Area: Comply with the IIA's *Attribute Standards*—professionalism. Source: CIA 1192, II-50.

143. (a) Review by legal counsel reduces the possibility of inclusion (and dissemination) of a statement for which the accused employee could sue the organization. Choice (b) is incorrect. The audit committee should receive a final draft of the report only after it has been reviewed and approved by legal counsel. Choice (c) is incorrect. If appropriate, the president may receive a final draft of the report after it has been reviewed and approved by legal counsel. Choice (d) is incorrect. If it is customary to send the outside auditors copies of all internal audit reports, it should be a final report that has been reviewed and approved by legal counsel.

Subject Area: Comply with the IIA's *Attribute Standards*—professionalism. Source: CIA 1192, II-46.

144. (c) The IIA *Standards* state that audit reports should be reviewed and approved by a director or designee. Choice (a) is incorrect. The *Standards* state that final reports should be reviewed by director or designee. Choice (b) is incorrect. Auditor in charge would not be correct unless designated by director of internal audit. Choice (d) is incorrect. Audit reports should be reviewed by director or designee prior to distribution.

Subject Area: Comply with the IIA's *Attribute Standards*—professionalism. Source: CIA 1192, II-43.

145. (c) Choice (c) is the correct answer. Internal auditors should review the means used to safeguard assets from various types of losses such as those resulting from theft, fire, improper, or illegal activities, and exposure to elements. Choice (a) is incorrect. Misapplication of accounting principles relates to the reliability of information and not physical safeguards. Choice (b) is incorrect.

Procedures that are not cost justified relate to efficiency of operations. Choice (d) is incorrect. Underutilization of facilities relates to efficiency of operation.

Subject Area: Comply with the IIA's *Attribute Standards*—professionalism. Source: CIA 1192, II-5.

146. (b) This is the primary reason why the *Standards* require direct access to the board. Choice (a) is incorrect. Access to audit committees by the internal auditor is not required by law for publicly traded companies. Choice (c) is incorrect. Internal auditing serves the organization and does not necessarily influence policy decisions. Choice (d) is incorrect. The board sets policy, management authorizes implementation of audit recommendations.

Subject Area: Comply with the IIA's *Attribute Standards*—professionalism. Source: CIA 1192, II-6.

147. (d) According to the IIA *Standards*, a report should contain an opinion where appropriate. The criterion of appropriateness is improvement in communications. Choice (a) is incorrect. The area of the audit is irrelevant for decisions about whether or not an overall opinion is appropriate. Choice (b) is incorrect. Whether the internal auditors' work is to be used by external auditors is irrelevant, particularly since the external auditor cannot depend on an overall opinion but must examine the detail and form his or her own opinion. Choice (c) is incorrect. An overall opinion is not a mandatory requirement.

Subject Area: Comply with the IIA's *Attribute Standards*—professionalism. Source: CIA 592, I-43.

148. (c) Suspected wrongdoing should be reported to the appropriate levels of management. Choice (a) is incorrect. Internal auditors are not responsible for notifying outside authorities of suspected wrongdoing. Choice (b) is incorrect. The *Standards* require internal auditors to determine whether the organization is complying with applicable laws. Choice (d) is incorrect. The *Standards* on due professional care require the reporting of violations of laws or regulations, that is, wrongdoing.

Subject Area: Comply with the IIA's *Attribute Standards*—professionalism. Source: CIA 592, I-43.

149. (d) Determination of compliance is required by the IIA *Standards*. Choice (a) is incorrect. This is contrary to the *Standards*. Choice (b) is incorrect. The *Standards* specify compliance with all laws and regulations having a significant impact. Choice (c) is incorrect. The IIA *Standards* apply to financial and operational audits.

Subject Area: Comply with the IIA's *Attribute Standards*—professionalism. Source: CIA 592, I-46.

150. (d) Competent information is reliable and the best available through the use of appropriate audit techniques. Choice (a) is incorrect. Relevant information supports audit findings and is consistent with audit objectives. Choice (b) is incorrect. Useful information assists the organization in meeting goals. Choice (c) is incorrect. Sufficient information is factual, adequate, and convincing to a prudent person.

Subject Area: Comply with the IIA's *Attribute Standards*—professionalism. Source: CIA 592, I-24.

151. (a) The purpose of the review for adequacy of the system of internal control is to ascertain whether the system established provides reasonable assurance that the organization's objectives and goals will benefit efficiently and economically. Choice (b) is incorrect. Due professional care of the design of a system does not necessarily provide adequate control. Choice (c) is incorrect. Compliance with law and policy is just one aspect of the scope of activity covered by controls. Choice (d) is incorrect. This answer does not include the factors needed.

Subject Area: Comply with the IIA's *Attribute Standards*—professionalism. Source: CIA 592, I-14.

152. (d) Internal auditors are responsible for identifying inadequate controls, for appraising managerial effectiveness, and for pinpointing common risks. Choice (a) is incorrect. The *Standards* do not require internal auditors to be omniscient or to be ensurers against any and all noncompliance of reporting procedures. Choice (b) is incorrect. There is no expected match of funds flows with expense items in a single time period. Choice (c) is incorrect. This would be a function of the personnel and or finance departments.

Subject Area: Comply with the IIA's *Attribute Standards*—professionalism. Source: CIA 592, I-20.

153. (b) Organizational status and objectivity provides for the achievement of independence. Choice (a) is incorrect. Individual knowledge and skills allow individual auditors to achieve professional proficiency. Choice (c) is incorrect. Supervision allows the internal auditing department to achieve professional proficiency. Choice (d) is incorrect. Organizational knowledge and skills allow the internal auditing department to achieve professional proficiency.

Subject Area: Comply with the IIA's *Attribute Standards*—professionalism. Source: CIA 592, I-2.

154. (b) The scope limitation and its potential effects should be communicated to the audit committee of the board of directors. Choice (a) is incorrect. The audit may be conducted under a scope limitation. Choice (c) is incorrect. A scope limitation would not necessarily cause the need for more frequent audits. Choice (d) is incorrect. A scope limitation would not necessarily cause the need for more experienced personnel.

Subject Area: Comply with the IIA's *Attribute Standards*—professionalism. Source: CIA 592, I-3.

155. (d) This item is an element of the planning of the audit, and not a requirement of the long-term plan. Choices (a), (b), and (c) are incorrect. Each one is a requirement.

Subject Area: Comply with the IIA's *Attribute Standards*—professionalism. Source: CIA 592, I-7.

156. (d) To clearly establish the purpose, authority, and responsibility of the internal auditing department, a formal written charter, which would include department policies, should be approved by the board. Choice (a) is incorrect. It is impractical because of time constraints of top management and the audit committee. Choice (b) is incorrect. Organizational stature, by itself, is not enough to avoid seeming to cause conflict. Choice (c) is incorrect. It is impractical because of time constraints of top management and the audit committee.

Subject Area: Comply with the IIA's *Attribute Standards*—professionalism. Source: CIA 592, II-2.

157. (d) Choice (d) is the correct answer. Internal auditors need only an appreciation of the broad nature and fundamentals of quantitative methods. That does not suggest sufficient knowledge to teach the methods to others. Choice (a) is incorrect. An internal auditor should possess a sound understanding of the nature of internal auditing, including the *Standards*. Choice (b) is incorrect. A sound understanding of the broad aspects of management theory is expected. Choice (c) is incorrect. Internal auditors must possess the ability to communicate effectively; interpersonal skills are an essential element of that ability.

Subject Area: Comply with the IIA's *Attribute Standards*—professionalism. Source: CIA 592, II-5.

158. (d) This impersonal technique degrades the evaluation process and gives it an air of impersonality. Choice (a) is incorrect. The evaluator should justify giving very high or very low evaluation. Choice (b) is incorrect. Annual evaluations are a minimum. Choice (c) is incorrect. This practice serves to advise the employee early as to the acceptability of performed work.

Subject Area: Comply with the IIA's *Attribute Standards*—professionalism. Source: CIA 592, II-6.

159. (a) The exercise of due professional care includes consideration of materiality. Choice (b) is incorrect. The auditor should consider the cost/benefit ratio before beginning an audit. Choice (c) is incorrect. The auditor should evaluate the acceptability of standards as well as whether they are being met. Choice (d) is incorrect. Due care does not require absolute assurance.

Subject Area: Comply with the IIA's *Attribute Standards*—professionalism. Source: CIA 1191, I-49.

160. (d) The larger staff will normally have longer spans of control and/or levels of supervision. Detail policies are necessary for effective communication, coordination, and consistency of operation of larger audit staffs. Choice (a) is incorrect. The *Standards* clearly state "in a large internal auditing department more formal and comprehensive policies and procedures are essential." Choice (b) is incorrect. This is covered in the department's charter. Choice (c) is incorrect. It is the same as Choice (a).

Subject Area: Comply with the IIA's *Attribute Standards*—professionalism. Source: CIA 1191, I-8.

161. (a) This is a recommended responsibility of audit committees. Choice (b) is incorrect. This activity is an operational function of the audit director and the audit staff. It is submitted to the committee. Choice (c) is incorrect. This activity is a technical responsibility of the audit staff. Choice (d) is incorrect. This function is a field operation of the audit staff.

Subject Area: Comply with the IIA's *Attribute Standards*—professionalism. Source: CIA 1191, I-4.

162. (b) The *Standards* require the internal auditing department to possess or acquire the knowledge, skills, and disciplines necessary to carry out its audit responsibilities. Choice (a) is incorrect. Dollar impact is only a part of the potential problem. The *Standards* on due professional care and on sufficient knowledge, skills, and disciplines require further research. Choice (c) is incorrect. Since the internal auditing department has no engineering expertise, there is no basis from which to judge the accuracy of the superintendent's statements. Choice (d) is incorrect. Such an action is not within the authority of internal auditing.

Subject Area: Comply with the IIA's *Attribute Standards*—professionalism. Source: CIA 1191, II-1.

163. (a) The charter defines the purpose, authority, and responsibility of the internal auditing department. Choice (b) is incorrect. Specific instructions, such as report format, would be covered by the internal auditing manual or individual policies. Choice (c) is incorrect. Annual audit work schedules, not a charter, would describe planned audit programs. Choice (d) is incorrect. The audit department's work schedule, staffing plan, and financial budget are approved annually and are not a part of the charter.

Subject Area: Comply with the IIA's *Attribute Standards*—professionalism. Source: CIA 1191, II-5.

164. (b) Comparisons of performance with audit work schedules are a major purpose of activity reports. Choice (a) is incorrect. Planned audit activities make up the audit work schedule and are used in comparisons to actual performance. Choice (c) is incorrect. Financial budget detail provides only a partial basis for the activity report. Choice (d) is incorrect. Projected staffing needs provide a basis for financial budgets.

Subject Area: Comply with the IIA's *Attribute Standards*—professionalism. Source: CIA 1191, II-7.

165. (d) The IIA *Standards* state that "an appreciation is required." Also, many audit staffs have a specialized IT audit operation that handles complex computer-related audits. Choice (a) is incorrect. The *Standards* require only an appreciation of accounting unless the auditor is required to work extensively with financial records and reports. Choice (b) is incorrect. An understanding of management principles is required per the *Standards*. Choice (c) is incorrect. The *Standards* require knowledge beyond the ability to recognize deviations; thus a lesser requirement would be acceptable.

Subject Area: Comply with the IIA's *Attribute Standards*—professionalism. Source: CIA 1191, II-8.

166. (a) The director of internal auditing is the most appropriate individual to make the decision as to report distribution. Choice (b) is incorrect. This committee is a recipient of the reports. Choice (c) is incorrect. This individual would not be knowledgeable of potential recipients. Choice (d) is incorrect. This individual is an audit technician, engaged in the performance of the audit, not audit administration.

Subject Area: Comply with the IIA's *Attribute Standards*—professionalism. Source: CIA 1191, II-43.

167. (a) The supervisor is the keystone to this effort. Choice (b) is incorrect. There must also be an assurance of quality. Choice (c) is incorrect. Training is a part of the supervision but is not the overall objective. Choice (d) is incorrect. In some cases, the audit program should be deviated from. This also is only a part of the supervisory responsibility.

Subject Area: Comply with the IIA's *Attribute Standards*—professionalism. Source: CIA 1191, II-46.

168. (c) The clarification of matters of fact is one of the reasons for an exit interview with the auditee. Choice (a) is incorrect. Both audit objectives and the scope of audit work are properly covered with the auditee during the preliminary survey. Choice (b) is incorrect. It is not important that the auditee understand the audit program. Choice (d) is incorrect. The identification of persons who are to receive the final report occurs much earlier than the exit conference. With rare exceptions, the list is determined during the preliminary survey.

Subject Area: Comply with the IIA's *Attribute Standards*—professionalism. Source: CIA 591, I-45.

169. (c) This response would avoid the lack of objectivity inherent in auditing activities, which the auditor so recently performed. This response conforms with the IIA *Standards*. Choice (a) is incorrect. The proposed engagement directly violates the *Standards* on objectivity. Objectivity would be presumed to be impaired in this circumstance. Choice (b) is incorrect. Subordinating your judgment on audit matters to that of others does not maintain the independent mental attitude defined in the *Standards*. Choice (d) is incorrect. This response still violates the *Standards* since the preparation of the audit program offers significant opportunities for bias to occur.

Subject Area: Comply with the IIA's *Attribute Standards*—professionalism. Source: CIA 591, II-4.

170. (c) Both positions should be reported, and the reasons for the disagreement should be identified. Choice (a), (b), and (c) are incorrect. Both positions in each answer should be reported, and the reasons for the disagreement should be identified.

Subject Area: Comply with the IIA's *Attribute Standards*—professionalism. Source: CIA 591, II-42.

171. (d) While audit work papers may aid in the professional development of auditor staff, that is not a primary function. Choices (a), (b), and (c) are incorrect. They all describe primary functions of audit work papers.

Subject Area: Comply with the IIA's *Attribute Standards*—professionalism. Source: CIA 591, II-29.

172. (d) Developing job descriptions is the responsibility of the director as presented in the *Standards*. Responsibility for administering the corporate compensation program is not presented in the *Standards* since this responsibility normally resides in the human resources (personnel) area. Choice (a) is incorrect. The director's responsibility for continuing education is clearly defined in the *Standards*. Choice (b) is incorrect. The director's responsibility for providing counsel on performance and professional development is identified in the *Standards*. Choice (c) is incorrect. The director's responsibility for the preparation of written job descriptions is explicitly stated in the Standards.

Subject Area: Comply with the IIA's *Attribute Standards*—professionalism. Source: CIA 591, II-9.

173. (a) Given these circumstances, excluding the inventory from the physical count would inflate revenues and profitability for the current period. The physical inventory process is a periodic control to ensure that sales-related controls are effective. Choices (b), (c), and (d) are incorrect. The inventory has not been sold and transacted according to established procedures.

Subject Area: Comply with the IIA's *Attribute Standards*—professionalism. Source: CIA 1193, I-9.

174. (a) It is the definition of the organizational status. Choice (b) is incorrect. The department still needs day to day support. The department should still report into management. Choice (c) is incorrect. The board's concurrence is suggested, not its approval. Choice (d) is incorrect. Most charters have a statement on independence; however, they need support to accomplish their responsibilities.

Subject Area: Comply with the IIA's *Attribute Standards*—professionalism. Source: CIA 593, II-3.

175. (b) The audit opinion is the auditor's professional judgment of the situation under review. It is based on the audit findings. Choice (a) is incorrect. While significant audit findings are summarized in the audit report, this does not constitute an audit opinion. An audit opinion is the auditor's professional judgment of the situation under review. Choice (c) is incorrect. The *Standards* do not require that audit reports include opinions. However, the opinion is a desirable component of the audit report. Choice (d) is incorrect. Recommendations for corrective action are separate from the audit opinion, since the opinion is the auditor's professional judgment of the situation.

Subject Area: Comply with the IIA's *Attribute Standards*—professionalism. Source: CIA 1192, I-46.

176. (b) The *Standards* do not require extensive and detailed audits of all transactions. Choices (a), (c), and (d) are incorrect. The *Standards* specifically identify these items.

Subject Area: Comply with the IIA's *Attribute Standards*—professionalism. Source: CIA 592, I-50.

177. (c) This is what the IIA *Standards* require in such cases. Choices (a) and (b) are incorrect. The *Standards* do not require such action. Choice (d) is incorrect. Noting differences in interpretation in the audit report, in and of itself, is not due care. Due care has to do with how the audit is performed and the report written.

Subject Area: Comply with the IIA's *Attribute Standards*—professionalism. Source: CIA 592, I-48.

178. (a) External auditors are required to assess these traits *only* when they determine that the work may have a bearing on their audit procedures (i.e., they rely on the work of the internal auditors). Choices (b) and (c) are incorrect. When internal auditors are assigned to assist in the external audit, they are allowed to share relevant information with the external auditors. Choice (d) is incorrect. If the external auditor plans to rely on the work of an internal auditor, the work must be reviewed and tested. This would require access to both programs and working papers.

Subject Area: Comply with the IIA's *Attribute Standards*—professionalism. Source: CIA 594, III-1.

179. (b) Includes the two primary factors: (1) taking the CIA exam increases the professionalism of internal auditors, and (2) reducing external audit fees is becoming more critical than ever. Choices (a), (c), and (d) are incorrect. Increased liability of external auditors would probably have the opposite effect. Computerized accounting systems and globalization of audit entities would have no significant on the relative roles of external and internal auditors.

Subject Area: Comply with the IIA's *Attribute Standards*—professionalism. Source: CIA 594, III-90.

180. (a) Internal auditors are more familiar with the organization, including systems, people, and objectives. Choice (b) is incorrect. Both internal and external auditors are required to be objective. Choice (c) is incorrect. Internal and external auditors use the same techniques. Choice (d) is incorrect. Internal auditors will be concerned with fraud and waste.

Subject Area: Comply with the IIA's *Attribute Standards*—professionalism. Source: CIA 592, I-9.

181. (d) Choice (d) is the correct answer. The single audit concept is not always pertinent. Choice (a) is incorrect. If the expertise exists it might be more economical to use the internal auditing department. Choice (b) is incorrect. Overall costs must be considered in relation to the potential savings. Choice (c) is incorrect. Training and the enhanced effectiveness of the internal auditing department are important considerations.

Subject Area: Comply with the IIA's *Attribute Standards*—professionalism. Source: CIA 592, I-10.

182. (c) Coordinating internal and external audit work helps to prevent duplication in coverage, thereby improving internal audit efficiency. Choice (a) is incorrect. This may lead to duplication in audit coverage. Choice (b) is incorrect. Internal auditing encompasses both financial and operational objectives and activities. Therefore, internal auditing coverage could also be provided by external audit work, which included primarily financial objectives and activities. Choice (d) is incorrect. External auditing work is conducted in accordance with generally accepted auditing standards.

Subject Area: Comply with the IIA's *Attribute Standards*—professionalism. Source: CIA 592, II-3.

183. (b) It is your responsibility to ensure proper coordination with external auditors and minimize duplication of effort. However, you must also respect the confidentiality of the external auditor's work. Choice (a) is incorrect. The working papers are the property of the parent company's audit firm, and their confidentiality should be respected. Choice (c) is incorrect. The working papers are the property of the parent company's audit firm and their confidentiality should be respected. The external auditors should give prior authorization for the release of their working papers. Choice (d) is incorrect. It is your responsibility to ensure proper coordination with external auditors and minimize duplication of effort.

Subject Area: Comply with the IIA's *Attribute Standards*—professionalism. Source: CIA 592, II-8.

184. (a) The working papers are the property of your company. It is your responsibility as internal audit director to ensure proper coordination with external auditors and minimize duplication of effort. Choices (b) and (c) are incorrect. The working papers are the property of your company. It is your responsibility as internal audit director to maintain security of the working papers and coordinate efforts with external auditors. Choice (d) is incorrect. It is your responsibility as internal audit director to ensure proper coordination with external auditors and minimize duplication of effort.

Subject Area: Comply with the IIA's *Attribute Standards*—professionalism. Source: CIA 592, II-9.

185. (b) According to the IIA *Standards*, the director of internal auditing should coordinate internal and external audit efforts. Choice (a) is incorrect. The independent outside auditor is not permitted to delegate certain work to the internal auditors such as the verification of material account balances within a pension plan. Choice (c) is incorrect. Testing internal controls to determine the reliability of tested account balances is an example of duplicate work. Choice (d) is incorrect. The *Standards* state that common understanding of audit techniques, methods, and terminology is involved in audit coordination. Therefore, common techniques should be used; it is not a case of either one technique or the other.

Subject Area: Comply with the IIA's *Attribute Standards*—professionalism. Source: CIA 591, I-21.

IIA's Code of Ethics

186. (b) As long as an individual is a Certified Internal Auditor, he or she should be guided by the profession's Code of Ethics in addition to the organization's code of conduct. Article V of the Code of Ethics would preclude such a gift because it could be presumed to have influenced the individual's decision. Choice (a) is incorrect. Acceptance of the gift could easily be presumed to have impaired independence and thus would not be acceptable. Choice (c) and (d) are incorrect. There is not sufficient information given to judge possible violations of the organization's code of conduct. However, the action could easily be perceived as a kickback.

Subject Area: Comply with the IIA's *Attribute Standards*—the Code of Ethics. Source: CIA 597, I-64, I-66.

187. (c) There is no violation of either the Code of Ethics or the *Standards*. See responses (a) and (b). Choice (a) is incorrect. The auditor is not withholding information because he or she has passed the information along to the director of internal audit. The information may be useful in a subsequent audit in the marketing area. Choice (b) is incorrect. The auditor has documented a red flag that may be important in a subsequent audit. This does not violate the *Standards*. Choice (d) is incorrect. Choice (c) is the only correct answer.

Subject Area: Comply with the IIA's *Attribute Standards*—the Code of Ethics. Source: CIA 597, I-66.

188. (b) The Code of Ethics defines the minimum ethical standards for the internal auditor. Choice (a) is incorrect. This is the definition of the IIA *Standards*. Choice (c) is incorrect. The *Standards* define the practice of internal auditing *as it should be*. Choice (d) is incorrect. The *Standards* are applicable across all industries and types of internal audit organizations.

Subject Area: Comply with the IIA's *Attribute Standards*—the Code of Ethics. Source: CIA 597, I-60.

189. (d) Article VIII states that members and CIAs shall not use confidential information for any personal gain. Choice (a) is incorrect. Article II prohibits members and CIAs from being party to illegal activities. Failure to comply with a subpoena would be illegal. Choice (b) is incorrect. A part-time job would not be a problem since it was not with a competitor or supplier. Choice (c) is incorrect. Giving a speech is not a violation of the Code of Ethics. In fact, the IIA's motto is "progress through sharing."

Subject Area: Comply with the IIA's *Attribute Standards*—the Code of Ethics. Source: CIA 597, I-70.

190. (a) The Code of Ethics contains basic principles that require individual judgment to apply. Choice (b) is incorrect. While the comparison might be interesting, it would not help determine how to apply the code. Choice (c) is incorrect. Application might not be in the best interest of the auditee. Choice (d) is incorrect. Judgment may be applied to their use, but not to whether to use them.

Subject Area: Comply with the IIA's *Attribute Standards*—the Code of Ethics. Source: CIA 596, I-17.

191. (a) Although an argument should be made that it would make common sense to bring the issue to both the audit committee and management, there is no evidence that the auditor is deliberately withholding information. Therefore, there is no violation of the Code of Ethics. Choice (b) is incorrect. Material fraud, if suspected, should be brought to the attention of management. However, in this case, the auditor did enough work to alleviate the suspicion of fraud. Choice (c) is incorrect. It is not a violation. The auditor did not deliberately withhold important information. Choice (d) is incorrect. The auditor has gathered sufficient information. Internal legal counsel opinion would appear to be sufficient.

Subject Area: Comply with the IIA's *Attribute Standards*—the Code of Ethics. Source: CIA 595, I-53.

192. (d) All the three choices are not violated. Choice (a) is incorrect. This could be viewed as general information about "best practices" and is acceptable to carry to the next employer. Choice (b) is incorrect. The auditor is applying knowledge of a commonly used, standard audit technique. It is not confidential information. Choice (c) is incorrect. This information could be viewed as part of continuing education of the auditor. As long as it is general information about "best practices," it is acceptable to carry it to the next employer.

Subject Area: Comply with the IIA's *Attribute Standards*—the Code of Ethics. Source: CIA 595, I-57.

193. (d) This could taint the director's objectivity and promote unethical behavior. Choices (a), (b), and (c) are incorrect. These arrangements should strengthen independence and promote ethical behavior.

Subject Area: Comply with the IIA's *Attribute Standards*—the Code of Ethics. Source: CIA 1190, I-45.

194. (a) A profession's code of ethics summarizes principles or standards of conduct that govern the members of the profession. Choice (b) is incorrect. This response describes the by-laws of a professional organization. Choice (c) is incorrect. Certain actions may not be illegal, yet are contrary to an organization's code of ethics (e.g., a CIA attempting to perform a service for which he or she does not possess the necessary competence). Choice (d) is incorrect. This response, a paraphrase from the foreword to the Standards for the Professional Practice of Internal Auditing, implies more emphasis on adequacy of procedures than is normally contained within a code of ethics.

Subject Area: Comply with the IIA's *Attribute Standards*—the Code of Ethics. Source: CIA 1190, I-46.

195. (c) This is not a personal characteristic mentioned in the Code of Ethics. Choices (a), (b), and (d) are incorrect. These characteristics are mentioned in the Code.

Subject Area: Comply with the IIA's *Attribute Standards*—the Code of Ethics. Source: CIA 1190, I-47.

196. (a) Small promotional items, such as pens that are available to the general public and are of minimal value, are not likely to hinder the auditor's professional judgment. Choice (b) is incorrect. Gifts may not be accepted, under Article IV. Choice (c) is incorrect. The manager may think that a gift will ward off future audits. Choice (d) is incorrect. Gifts may not be accepted, under Article IV.

Subject Area: Comply with the IIA's *Attribute Standards*—the Code of Ethics. Source: CIA 1190, I-48.

197. (c) The Code of Ethics specifically mentions forfeiture of IIA membership as a possible penalty for violation of its provisions. Choice (a) is incorrect. The IIA board of directors is not authorized to require continuing professional education as a sanction for misconduct. Choice (b) is incorrect. The board is not authorized to require retaking of the CIA Examination as a sanction for misconduct. Choice (d) is incorrect. The board has no authority to assess a monetary fine.

Subject Area: Comply with the IIA's *Attribute Standards*—the Code of Ethics. Source: CIA 1190, I-50.

198. (b) Without consent by appropriate senior management, acceptance of any gift is prohibited (Article II of the Code of Ethics). Choice (a) is incorrect. Because continuing education is encouraged and because the program is open to all employees, there is no violation. Choice (c) is incorrect. The auditor is required to reveal all material facts in his or her opinion. Choice (d) is incorrect. A violation would occur only if confidential information were used for personal gain. In this case, no information was known.

Subject Area: Comply with the IIA's *Attribute Standards*—the Code of Ethics. Source: CIA 590, I-45.

199. (d) To neither overstate nor understate the audit exceptions, all material claims should be presented with a net amount owing either party. Either an overstatement or understatement of audit claims would violate the Code of Ethics, Article II. Choice (a) is incorrect. To report only those audit exceptions in favor of XYZ would inflate the amount due XYZ by the credits due ABC (Code of Ethics, Article II). Choice (b) is incorrect. It is not necessary to perform audit work on behalf of ABC. However, detailed information on the credits due XYZ plus any amounts due ABC would probably expedite the audit claim. Choice (c) is incorrect. To report only that audit exceptions in favor of ABC would not give benefits to the auditor's company, XYZ (Code, Article II).

Subject Area: Comply with the IIA's *Attribute Standards*—the Code of Ethics. Source: CIA 590, I-46.

200. (a) Auditing a spouse may create a conflict of interest and would prejudice the ability to carry out an assignment objectively (Code of Ethics, Article II). Choice (b) is incorrect. An investment in the employer creates no conflict. Choice (c) is incorrect. Use of a company car is accepted business practice. Choice (d) is incorrect. An ownership interest in a nonrelated business does not create a conflict of interest.

Subject Area: Comply with the IIA's *Attribute Standards*—the Code of Ethics. Source: CIA 590, II-41.

201. (a) Per the Code of Ethics, Article VI, "Certified Internal Auditors shall reveal such material facts known to them which, if not revealed, could either distort the report of the results of operations under review or conceal unlawful practice." Choice (b) is incorrect. The internal auditor should cooperate with the external auditor and coordinate audit efforts with professional conduct. Choice (c) is incorrect. Although an internal auditor's main focus may be on internal controls and operating efficiencies, a material misstatement must be reported as per the Code, Article VI. Choice (d) is incorrect. The external auditor should determine what work the internal auditor should perform in order that the external auditor may express an opinion per the Statement on Auditing Standards (SAS No. 9).

Subject Area: Comply with the IIA's *Attribute Standards*—the Code of Ethics. Source: CIA 590, II-43.

202. (d) is the correct answer, as per the last sentence in the "Applicability" section of the Code. Choice (a) is incorrect. There are no provisions for suspensions in the Code.

Choice (b) is incorrect. There are no provisions in the Code for continuing professional development (CPD) hours to be completed for ethics violations. Choice (c) is incorrect. There are no provisions for suspension in the Code.

Subject Area: Comply with the IIA's *Attribute Standards*—the Code of Ethics. Source: CIA 590, II-44.

203. (c) Article II of the Code of Ethics requires loyalty to the employer, which in this case requires reporting to the employer. Choices (a) and (b) are incorrect. Reporting findings outside the organization violates Article II of the Code of Ethics. Choice (d) is incorrect. Resignation is not required. Loyalty to the employer is required by Article II.

Subject Area: Comply with the IIA's *Attribute Standards*—the Code of Ethics. Source: CIA 590, I-41.

204. (d) Censure is the disciplinary action prescribed by Professional Standards for the least serious misconduct cases. Choice (a) is incorrect. The IIA board of directors is not authorized to require continuing professional education as a sanction for misconduct. Choice (b) is incorrect. Forfeiture of the CIA designation is imposed only for the most serious misconduct cases. Choice (c) is incorrect. The board has no authority to prohibit a person from practicing internal auditing.

Subject Area: Comply with the IIA's *Attribute Standards*—the Code of Ethics. Source: CIA 1190, II-50.

205. (a) Professional organizations usually do not deal with auditors' employees and are not in competition with them. They also normally do not reveal or use confidential information to the detriment of employers. Choices (b) and (c) are incorrect. There could be a conflict of interest and could involve misuse of confidential information. Choice (d) is incorrect. This could result in misuse of confidential information.

Subject Area: Comply with the IIA's *Attribute Standards*—the Code of Ethics. Source: CIA 1190, II-45.

206. (c) This is a distinguishing mark of a profession. Choice (a) is incorrect. Although this may be a result of establishing a code of conduct, it is not the primary purpose. To consider it so would be self-serving. Choice (b) is incorrect. A code of conduct may help to establish minimum standards of competence, but it would be impossible to legislate equality of competence by all members of a profession. Choice (d) is incorrect. There are situations where responsibility to the public at large may conflict with, and be more important than, loyalty to one's organization.

Subject Area: Comply with the IIA's *Attribute Standards*—the Code of Ethics. Source: CIA 1190, II-46.

207. (a) Article II requires the auditor to be loyal to his or her employer. Choices (b), (c), and (d) are incorrect by definition.

Subject Area: Comply with the IIA's *Attribute Standards*—the Code of Ethics. Source: CIA 1190, II-47.

208. (a) Article VI requires auditors to report any information that is material to management. Choice (b) is incorrect. This is acceptable for internal use only. Choice (c) is incorrect. This is acceptable as long as the auditor is careful not to state any final conclusions that are not supported by factual evidence. Choice (d) is incorrect. This is typically done.

Subject Area: Comply with the IIA's *Attribute Standards*—the Code of Ethics. Source: CIA 1190, II-48.

209. (c) This would be a violation of Article X of the Code, which requires auditors to continually strive for improvement in their proficiency and the effectiveness of their audits. Choice (a) is incorrect. There is no professional conflict of interest per se. However, the auditor should be aware of potential conflicts. Choice (b) is incorrect. George has committed to obtaining the needed expertise before conducting the audit. Choice (d) is incorrect. The information was disclosed as part of the normal process of cooperation between the internal and external auditor. Since the books were adjusted, it would be expected that the external auditor would inquire as to the nature of the adjustment.

Subject Area: Comply with the IIA's *Attribute Standards*—the Code of Ethics. Source: CIA 595, I-43.

210. (a) Auditors must exhibit loyalty to the organization, but not be a party to any illegal activity. Thus, auditors must comply with legal subpoenas. Choice (b) is incorrect. Article VIII prohibits auditors from using audit information for personal gain. Choice (c) is incorrect. Article V prohibits auditors form accepting gifts from other employees that might be presumed to impair the auditor's professional judgment. Choice (d) is incorrect. Article II prohibits auditors from knowingly being a party to any illegal or improper activity. The *Standards* specifies that significant findings of illegal account should be reported to the audit committee.

Subject Area: Comply with the IIA's *Attribute Standards*—the Code of Ethics. Source: CIA 1196, I-32.

211. (a) The Code of Ethics and *Standards* do not provide for strict confidentiality of information. Choice (b) is incorrect. This option is allowable, and an attorney can provide legal confidentiality. Choice (c) is incorrect. This option is allowable, but is not a guarantee of confidentiality. Choice (d) is incorrect. To maintain confidentiality, the employee can be directed to other options to provide the information.

Subject Area: Comply with the IIA's *Attribute Standards*—the Code of Ethics. Source: CIA 1196, I-33.

212. (c) The action may represent a violation of the Code of Ethics for both of the reasons given. Choice (a) is incorrect. It clearly violates the IIA's Code, Article IV, but statement II is also correct. Choice (b) is incorrect. It could cause a conflict of the type described and would be considered a discreditable act (Article III). However, statement I is also correct. Choice (d) is incorrect. It is a violation of the Code.

Subject Area: Comply with the IIA's *Attribute Standards*—the Code of Ethics. Source: CIA 1196, I-43.

213. (b) The director has to avoid conflict of interest or activities that might prejudice his or her ability to carry out assigned duties. The director may not accept anything of value that might impair professional judgment. Reference to Code of Ethics, sections IV and V. Choices (a,) c), and (d) are incorrect per the Code of Ethics.

Subject Area: Comply with the IIA's *Attribute Standards*—the Code of Ethics. Source: CIA 596, I-61.

214. (c) The IIA's Code of Ethics, Article IX, requires CIA's to reveal all material facts that could conceal unlawful practices. Choice (a) is incorrect. The auditor cannot ignore the matter since it is an ethical issue. Choice (b) is incorrect. The *Standards* require the director of internal auditing to distribute audit reports to those members of the organization who can take appropriate action. Choice (d) is incorrect because management should determine what constitutes just compensation.

Subject Area: Comply with the IIA's *Attribute Standards*—the Code of Ethics. Source: CIA 596, I-68.

215. (a) This is part of the introduction to *the IIA Code of Ethics.* Choices (b) and (c) are incorrect. They are part of internal auditing standards. Choice (d) is incorrect. This is the purpose of the Statement of Responsibilities.

Subject Area: Comply with the IIA's *Attribute Standards*—the Code of Ethics. Source: CIA 596, I-70.

216. (b) This is consistent with the concepts embodied in the IIA Code of Ethics. The last sentence of the Code clearly indicates that the auditor needs to uphold the objectives of the IIA. Choice (a) is incorrect. The auditor must act consistently with the spirit embodied in the IIA Code of Ethics. It would not be practical to seek the advice of legal counsel for all ethical decisions. Ethics is a moral and professional concept, not just a legal concept. Choice (c) is incorrect. It would not be practicable to seek management advice for all potential dilemmas. Further, the advice might not be consistent with the profession's standards. Choice (d) is incorrect. If the company's standards are not consistent with, or as high as, the profession's standards, the professional internal auditor is held to the standards of the profession.

Subject Area: Comply with the IIA's *Attribute Standards*—the Code of Ethics. Source: CIA 1195, I-51.

217. (a) This is consistent with the IIA's Code of Ethics. See Article V of the Code. Choice (b) is incorrect. This would be inconsistent with the *Standards* adopted by the profession. Choice (c) is incorrect. The internal auditor is guided by the profession's standards, not the customs of individual countries or regions. Choice (d) is incorrect. The action is explicitly prohibited by the Code of Ethics.

Subject Area: Comply with the IIA's *Attribute Standards*—the Code of Ethics. Source: CIA 1195, I-52.

218. (c) A CIA, whether he is performing financial, operational, and information systems audits, should follow and comply with the IIA's Code of Ethics and Standards since he is certified with that institute and being a professional with that organization. Choice (a) is incorrect because certified management accountants (CMAs) will follow and comply with the IMA's Code of Ethics and Standards. Choice (b) is incorrect because certified public accountants (CPAs) will follow and comply with the AICPA's Code of Ethics and Standards. Choice (d) is incorrect because certified information systems auditors (CISAs) will follow and comply with the ISACA's Code of Ethics and Standards.

Subject Area: Comply with the IIA's Attribute Standards—the Code of Ethics. Source: Author.

219. (a) Securities were improperly used; the fact that they are not now should not prevent the internal reporting of the situation. Choices (b), (c), and (d) are incorrect. Each choice is a fact, but not relevant to the decision as to what to whether to report the improper use of the securities. An auditor may want to include the information in the report, but whether to report should not be based on this information.

Subject Area: Comply with the IIA's *Attribute Standards*—the Code of Ethics. Source: CIA 594, I-29.

220. (c) It is the director of internal auditing who is responsible to communicate with the external auditor. Choice (a) is incorrect. Including facts in the working papers is not a violation of the Code of Ethics. Choice (b) is incorrect. Additional discussion with the audit manager is not necessary before discussion with the director of internal audit. Choice (d) is incorrect. Resigning is an option always available to the auditor without a Code of Ethics violation.

Subject Area: Comply with the IIA's *Attribute Standards*—the Code of Ethics. Source: CIA 594, I-30.

221. (a) The Code of Ethics requires confidentiality. Choice (b) is incorrect. Approval of audit committee or management is required by the *Standards*. Choice (c) is incorrect. The *Standards* require sufficient evidence to support findings. Choice (d) is incorrect. The *Standards* allow use of "experts" when needed.

Subject Area: Comply with the IIA's *Attribute Standards*—the Code of Ethics. Source: CIA 594, I-66.

222. (a) This is what is required by the Code of Ethics of the IIA. Choice (b) is incorrect. There is no specific requirement for this. Choices (c) and (d) are incorrect. Each is too constraining.

Subject Area: Comply with the IIA's *Attribute Standards*—the Code of Ethics. Source: CIA 592, I-49.

223. (a) This is the primary purpose of the Code of Ethics. Choice (b) is incorrect. The Code of Ethics was not designed to serve as standards for effective accounting. Choice (c) is incorrect. The Code does not provide the framework within which accounting policies are developed. Choice (d) is incorrect. The primary purpose of the Code of Ethics is not for interviewing new accountants.

Subject Area: Comply with the IIA's *Attribute Standards*—the Code of Ethics. Source: CIA 1193, II-44.

224. (a) CIAs must not knowingly be a party to any illegal or improper act. Also, reporting within the organization is the proper action. Choice (b) is incorrect. CIAs must not knowingly be a party to any illegal or improper act. The fact that this activity is improper and, probably, illegal requires the CIA to report it. Choice (c) is incorrect. CIAs must not knowingly be a party to any illegal or improper act. The fact that this activity is improper and, probably, illegal requires the CIA to report it. Merely noting the condition in the audit working papers does not constitute "reporting" it. Choice (d) is incorrect. CIAs are not required to voluntarily reveal illegal or improper acts to outside individuals or organizations. They should try to work within their organizations.

Subject Area: Comply with the IIA's *Attribute Standards*—the Code of Ethics. Source: CIA 593, I-45.

225. (b) The IIA's Code of Ethics, Standard of Conduct VII, requires members and CIAs to adopt suitable means to comply with the *Standards*. Choice (a) is incorrect. The Code of Ethics applies to IIA members and CIAs. Choice (c) is incorrect. Loyalty to the organization must be exhibited, but a member or CIA must follow the *Standards*. Choice (d) is incorrect. The Code of Ethics says nothing about resignation to avoid improper activities.

Subject Area: Comply with the IIA's *Attribute Standards*—the Code of Ethics. Source: CIA 1193, II-45.

226. (c) This is a distinguishing mark of a profession. Choice (a) is incorrect. Although this may be a result of establishing a code of conduct, it is not the primary purpose. To consider it so would be self-serving. Choice (b) is incorrect. A code of conduct may help to establish minimum standards of competence, but it would be impossible to legislate equality of competence by all members of a profession. Choice (d) is incorrect. There are situations where responsibility to the public at large may conflict with, and be more important than, loyalty to one's organization.

Subject Area: Comply with the IIA's *Attribute Standards*—the Code of Ethics. Source: CIA 1193, I-45.

227. (c) Any discipline or organization aspiring to professionalism or unity of direction needs an organizational code of ethical conduct. Choice (a) is incorrect. Internal auditors are charged with the responsibility of evaluating that which they examine and of making recommendations, where appropriate. Choice (b) is incorrect. Management is charged with the responsibility of making any corrections necessary within their department. Choice (d) is incorrect. Internal auditors should make recommendations whenever practicable.

Subject Area: Comply with the IIA's *Attribute Standards*—the Code of Ethics. Source: CIA 592, I-44.

228. (c) Even though the training could benefit the organization, the relative (and you, albeit indirectly) stands to benefit from company information. Choice (a) is incorrect. Serving on a nonprofit organization is unlikely to cause a conflict of interest. Choice (b) is incorrect. Although a conflict might arise, it is not inevitable. Choice (d) is incorrect. Teaching is not considered in conflict with the interests of most organizations.

Subject Area: Comply with the IIA's *Attribute Standards*—the Code of Ethics. Source: CIA 592, II-48.

229. (a) The first Standard of Conduct states these qualities. Choice (b) is incorrect. Timeliness and sobriety are not mentioned. Choice (c) is incorrect. They are not mentioned in the Code of Ethics. Choice (d) is incorrect. Punctuality is not mentioned in the Code of Ethics.

Subject Area: Comply with the IIA's *Attribute Standards*—the Code of Ethics. Source: CIA 592, II-49.

230. (d) The IIA board of directors may revoke his CIA designation if it is established that he violated the Code of Ethics. Choice (a) is incorrect. This would be at the discretion of his employer. Choice (b) is incorrect. The Code of Ethics contains no provision for reporting him to legal authorities. Further, it has not been established that the broke a law. Choice (c) is incorrect. The Code of Ethics contains no provision to require the employer to issue a reprimand.

Subject Area: Comply with the IIA's *Attribute Standards*—the Code of Ethics. Source: CIA 592, II-50.

231. (a) This is a violation of Article VIII. Choice (b) is incorrect. Article II emphasizes loyalty to the organization. Fraternization might be discouraged. Choice (c) is incorrect. Article IV permits the acceptance of a gift with the consent of senior management. Choice (d) is incorrect. Under Article IV, gifts of minimal value that are available to the general public are not likely to hinder professional judgment.

Subject Area: Comply with the IIA's *Attribute Standards*—the Code of Ethics. Source: CIA 1191, I-48.

232. (d) The sanction must be imposed by the board. This act is probably severe enough to warrant forfeiture of the CIA designation. Choice (a) is incorrect. Sanctions against CIAs must be imposed by the board of directors. Choice (b) is incorrect. The CIA violated the law and performed an act discreditable to the profession. Choice (c) is incorrect. Sanctions against CIAs must be imposed by the board of directors.

Subject Area: Comply with the IIA's *Attribute Standards*—the Code of Ethics. Source: CIA 1192, I-48.

233. (d) Since the IIA Code of Ethics (Article VIII) was violated, the IIA should be notified. In addition, company policy must be followed. Choice (a) is incorrect. The auditor has violated the Code of Ethics standard regarding use of confidential information. The IIA should be notified. Choice (b) is incorrect. Summary discharge may not be in accordance with company personnel policies. Choice (c) is incorrect. The auditor was negligent in the use of confidential information and violated the Code of Ethics. Some action is warranted.

Subject Area: Comply with the IIA's *Attribute Standards*—the Code of Ethics. Source: CIA 1192, I-49.

234. (c) The Code of Ethics requires members and CIAs to refrain from undertaking services that cannot be reasonably completed with professional competence. Choice (a) is incorrect. Diligence does not override professional competence or use of good judgment. Choice (b) is incorrect. Loyalty would be better exhibited by consulting professionals in interrogation and knowing your limits of competence. Choice (d) is incorrect. The auditor may violate the suspect's civil rights due to inexperience, but that is not a certainty.

Subject Area: Comply with the IIA's *Attribute Standards*—the Code of Ethics. Source: CIA 592, I-47.

235. (b) The Code of Ethics calls for compliance with the *Standards,* which charge the director with coordination with external auditors and exchanging information. In addition, the Code requires that all material facts known be revealed. Since this impacts the external auditor's work, in which the internal auditors are participating, the situation must be divulged. Choice (a) is incorrect. This is a material fact that could distort a report of operations if not revealed. Choice (c) is incorrect. The shortage is known and the external auditors should be told more than that there is a possibility. Choice (d) is incorrect. The audit director should discuss the issue with management first and later with the board of directors. The audit director can report these issues directly with the external auditors.

Subject Area: Comply with the IIA's *Attribute Standards*—the Code of Ethics. Source: CIA 1192, II-47.

236. (b) Generally, there should be no prohibition from public service. This is a right, if not a duty, of all citizens. Choices (a), (c), and (d) are incorrect. They are a classic part of most conflict-of-interest policies.

Subject Area: Comply with the IIA's *Attribute Standards*—the Code of Ethics. Source: CIA 593, II-42.

237. (b) The direct beneficiary of excessive sales allowances is the buyer. Choice (a) is incorrect. The first person benefited by a diversion of the firm's securities is the thieving employee. The stated provision of the Code of Ethics is designed to prevent a vendor from an inordinate benefit. Choice (c) is incorrect. Employees who operate cash registers are in a position to keep cash from sales and to fail to record the transaction. Since this action first benefits the thief, the stated provision of the Code of Ethics is not designed to prevent this. Choice (d) is incorrect. Participation in a working lunch funded by a vendor is an acceptable practice.

Subject Area: Comply with the IIA's *Attribute Standards*—the Code of Ethics. Source: CIA 1193, I-43.

238. (a) Evaluating the code for appropriate provisions, compliance therewith, and reporting the results would provide the audit committee with the greatest level of comfort. Choices (b), (c), and (d) are incorrect. Comprehensiveness of the code should also be evaluated.

Subject Area: Comply with the IIA's *Attribute Standards*—the Code of Ethics. Source: CIA 1193, I-44.

239. (d) Compliance is more likely if employees know they will be taken to task for violations. Choice (a) is incorrect. That would ensure employee knowledge of the code; that is not the issue here. Choice (b) is incorrect. That would ensure employee acceptance of the code; that is not an issue here. Choice (c) is incorrect. Public knowledge might impact the behavior of professionals, but it is not likely to help in the case of general employees.

Subject Area: Comply with the IIA's *Attribute Standards*—the Code of Ethics. Source: CIA 1193, II-46.

240. (b) In addressing ethical conduct, codes of conduct provide a model of conduct for individuals within an organization. Choice (a) is incorrect. Codes of conduct are not required by the Foreign Corrupt Practices Act. Choice (c) is incorrect. Codes of conduct do not provide a quantifiable basis for personnel evaluations. Choice (d) is incorrect. Public relations value may accrue, but it is not the best reason for establishing a code of conduct.

Subject Area: Comply with the IIA's *Attribute Standards*—the Code of Ethics. Source: CIA 590, I-43.

241. (b) According to the IIA Code of Ethics (Articles II, IV, V, VIII, and X), telling the neighbor about a plant closing (item 3) is the only violation. Choices (a), (c), and (d) are incorrect. They are not violations of the Code.

Subject Area: Comply with the IIA's *Attribute Standards*—the Code of Ethics. Source: CIA 1194, I-52.

242. (b) According to the IIA Code of Ethics (Articles II, IV, V, VIII, and X), receiving an item of value from a customer of the employer (item 5) and failure to disclose a kickback (item 8) are the only violations. Choices (a), (c), and (d) are incorrect. They do not violate the IIA's Code of Ethics.

Subject Area: Comply with the IIA's *Attribute Standards*—the Code of Ethics. Source: CIA 1194, I-53.

243. (c) According to the IIA Code of Ethics (Articles II, IV, V, VI, VIII, and X), receiving royalties from a book publisher (item 9) is the only action that is not a violation, and the other three (items 10, 11, and 12) are clear violations. Choices (a), (b), and (d) are incorrect. They do not violate the IIA's Code of Ethics.

Subject Area: Comply with the IIA's *Attribute Standards*—the Code of Ethics. Source: CIA 1194, I-54.

2 ESTABLISH A RISK-BASED PLAN TO DETERMINE THE PRIORITIES OF THE INTERNAL AUDIT ACTIVITY (15—25%)

THEORY

2.1 Managing the Internal Audit Activity

2000—Managing the Internal Audit Activity—The chief audit executive should effectively manage the internal audit activity to ensure it adds value to the organization.

IIA's Practice Advisory 2000-1: Managing the Internal Audit Activity

Nature of This Practice Advisory

Internal auditors should consider these suggestions in connection with managing the internal audit activity. This guidance is not intended to represent all the considerations that may be necessary, but simply a recommended set of items that should be addressed. *Compliance with Practice Advisories is optional.*

The chief audit executive is responsible for properly managing the internal audit activity so that

- Audit work fulfills the general purposes and responsibilities described in the charter, approved by the board and senior management as appropriate.
- Resources of the internal audit activity are efficiently and effectively employed.
- Audit work conforms to the *International Standards for the Professional Practice of Internal Auditing (Standards).*

2.2 Planning

2010—Planning—The chief audit executive should establish risk-based plans to determine the priorities of the internal audit activity, consistent with the organization's goals.

2010.A1—The internal audit activity's plan of engagements should be based on a risk assessment, undertaken at least annually. The input of senior management and the board should be considered in this process.

2010.C1—The chief audit executive should consider accepting proposed consulting engagements based on the engagement's potential to improve management of risks, add value, and improve the organization's operations. Those engagements that have been accepted should be included in the plan.

IIA's Practice Advisory 2010-1: Planning

Nature of This Practice Advisory

Internal auditors should consider these suggestions when planning for the internal audit activity. This guidance is not intended to represent all the considerations that may be necessary, but simply a recommended set of items that should be addressed. *Compliance with Practice Advisories is optional.*

1. Planning for the internal audit activity should be consistent with its charter and with the goals of the organization. The planning process involves establishing

    - Goals
    - Engagement work schedules
    - Staffing plans and financial budgets
    - Activity reports

2. The goals of the internal audit activity should be capable of being accomplished within specified operating plans and budgets and, to the extent possible, should be measurable. They should be accompanied by measurement criteria and targeted dates of accomplishment.
3. Engagement work schedules should include
   - What activities are to be performed
   - When they will be performed
   - The estimated time required, taking into account the scope of the engagement work planned and the nature and extent of related work performed by others
4. Matters to be considered in establishing engagement work schedule priorities should include
   - The dates and results of the last engagement
   - Updated assessments of risks and effectiveness of risk management and control processes
   - Requests by the board and senior management
   - Current issues relating to organizational governance
   - Major changes in enterprise's business, operations, programs, systems, and controls
   - Opportunities to achieve operating benefits
   - Changes to and capabilities of the audit staff; the work schedules should be sufficiently flexible to cover unanticipated demands on the internal audit activity

IIA's Practice Advisory 2010-2: Linking the Audit Plan to Risk and Exposures

Nature of This Practice Advisory

The organization's risk strategy should be reflected in the design of the internal audit activity's plan. A coordinated approach should be applied to leverage synergies between the organization's risk management and internal audit processes. Additional considerations beyond those contained in this advisory may be necessary. *Compliance with Practice Advisories is optional.*

1. Any organization faces a number of uncertainties and risks that can both negatively and positively affect the organization. Risk can be managed in a number of different ways, including acceptance, avoidance, transfer, and control. Internal controls are a common method for reducing the potential negative impact of risk and uncertainty.
2. The internal audit activity's audit plan should be designed based on an assessment of risk and exposures that may affect the organization. Ultimately, key audit objectives are to provide management with information to mitigate the negative consequences associated with accomplishing the organization's objectives, as well as an assessment of the effectiveness of management's risk management activities. The degree or materiality of exposure can be viewed as risk mitigated by establishing control activities.
3. The audit universe can include components from the organization's strategic plan. By incorporating components of the organization's strategic plan, the audit universe will consider and reflect the overall business objectives. Strategic plans also likely reflect the organization's attitude toward risk and the degree of difficulty to achieving planned objectives. The audit universe will normally be influenced by the results of the risk management process. The organization's strategic plan should have been created considering the environment in which the organization operates. These same environmental factors would likely impact the audit universe and assessment of relative risk.
4. Changes in management direction, objectives, emphasis, and focus should be reflected in updates to the audit universe and related audit plan. It is advisable to assess the audit universe on at least an annual basis to reflect the most current strategies and direction of the organization. In some situations, audit plans may need to be updated frequently (e.g., quarterly) in response to changes in the organization's environment of management activities.
5. Audit work schedules should be based on, among other factors, an assessment of risk priority and exposure. Prioritizing is needed to make decisions for applying relative resources based on the significance of risk and exposure. A variety of risk models exist to assist the chief audit executive in prioritizing potential audit subject areas. Most risk models utilize risk factors to establish the priority of engagements, such as: financial impact; asset liquidity; management competence; quality of internal controls; degree of change or stability; time of last audit engagement; complexity; employee, and government relations; and so on. In conducting audit engagements, methods and techniques for testing and validating exposures should be reflective of the risk materiality and likelihood of occurrence.

6. Management reporting and communication should convey risk management conclusions and recommendations to reduce exposures. For management to fully understand the degree of exposure, it is critical that audit reporting identify the criticality and consequence of the risk exposure to achieving objectives.

2.3 Communication and Approval

2020—Communication and Approval—The chief audit executive should communicate the internal audit activity's plans and resource requirements, including significant interim changes, to senior management and to the board for review and approval. The chief audit executive should also communicate the impact of resource limitations.

IIA's Practice Advisory 2020-1: Communication and Approval

Nature of This Practice Advisory

Internal auditors should consider these suggestions when communicating and seeking approval of the internal audit activity plans and resources. This guidance is not intended to represent all the considerations that may be necessary, but simply a recommended set of items that should be addressed. *Compliance with Practice Advisories is optional.*

1. The chief audit executive (CAE) should submit annually to the board for approval, and to senior management as appropriate, a summary of the internal audit activity's work schedule, staffing plan, and financial budget. The CAE should also submit all significant interim changes for approval and information. Engagement work schedules, staffing plans, and financial budgets should inform senior management and the board of the scope of internal auditing work and of any limitations placed on that scope.
2. The approved engagement work schedule, staffing plan, and financial budget, along with all significant interim changes, should contain sufficient information to enable the board to ascertain whether the internal audit activity's objectives and plans support those of the organization and the board.

2.4 Resource Management

2030—Resource Management—The chief audit executive should ensure that internal audit resources are appropriate, sufficient, and effectively deployed to achieve the approved plan.

IIA's Practice Advisory 2030-1: Resource Management

Nature of This Practice Advisory

Internal auditors should consider these suggestions when evaluating internal audit resources. This guidance is not intended to represent all the considerations that may be necessary during such an evaluation, but simply a recommended set of items that should be addressed. *Compliance with Practice Advisories is optional.*

1. Staffing plans and financial budgets, including the number of auditors and the knowledge, skills, and other competencies required to perform their work, should be determined from engagement work schedules, administrative activities, education and training requirements, and audit research and development efforts.
2. The chief audit executive (CAE) should establish a program for selecting and developing the human resources of the internal audit activity. The program should provide for
   - Developing written job descriptions for each level of the audit staff
   - Selecting individuals who are qualified and competent regarding the areas being audited and in applying internal auditing skills
   - Training and providing continuing educational opportunities for each internal auditor
   - Establishing annual performance objectives for internal auditors
   - Appraising each internal auditor's performance at least annually
   - Providing counsel to internal auditors on their performance and professional development
3. The CAE should consider using persons from cosourcing arrangements, other consultants, or company employees from other departments to provide specialized or additional skills where needed.

2.5 Policies and Procedures

2040—Policies and Procedures—The chief audit executive should establish policies and procedures to guide the internal audit activity.

IIA's Practice Advisory 2040-1: Policies and Procedures

Nature of This Practice Advisory

Internal auditors should consider these suggestions when establishing policies and procedures. This guidance is not intended to represent all the considerations that may be necessary, but simply a recommended set of items that should be addressed. *Compliance with Practice Advisories is optional.*

The form and content of written policies and procedures should be appropriate to the size and structure of the internal audit activity and the complexity of its work. Formal administrative and technical audit manuals may not be needed by all internal auditing entities. A small internal audit activity may be managed informally. Its audit staff may be directed and controlled through daily, close supervision and written memoranda. In a large internal audit activity, more formal and comprehensive policies and procedures are essential to guide the audit staff in the consistent compliance with the internal audit activity's standards of performance.

2.6 Coordination

2050—Coordination—The chief audit executive should share information and coordinate activities with other internal and external providers of relevant assurance and consulting services to ensure proper coverage and minimize duplication of efforts.

IIA's Practice Advisory 2050-1: Coordination

Nature of This Practice Advisory

Internal auditors should consider these suggestions when coordinating activities with other providers of relevant assurance and consulting services. This guidance is not intended to represent all the considerations that may be necessary, but simply a recommended set of items that should be addressed. *Compliance with Practice Advisories is optional.*

1. Internal and external auditing work should be coordinated to ensure adequate audit coverage and to minimize duplicate efforts. The scope of internal auditing work encompasses a systematic, disciplined approach to evaluate and improve the effectiveness of risk management, control, and governance processes. The scope of internal auditing work is described within Section 2100 of the *International Standards for the Professional Practice of Internal Auditing (Standards).* However, the external auditors' ordinary examination is designed to obtain sufficient evidential matter to support an opinion on the overall fairness of the annual financial statements. The scope of the work of external auditors is determined by their professional standards, and they are responsible for judging the adequacy of procedures performed and evidence obtained for purposes of expressing their opinion on the annual financial statements.
2. Oversight of the work of external auditors, including coordination with the internal audit activity, is the responsibility of the board. Actual coordination should be the responsibility of the chief audit executive (CAE). The CAE will require the support of the board to achieve effective coordination of audit work.
3. In coordinating the work of internal auditors with the work of external auditors, the CAE should ensure that work to be performed by internal auditors in fulfillment of Section 2100 of the *Standards* does not duplicate the work of external auditors, which can be relied on for purposes of internal auditing coverage. To the extent that professional and organizational reporting responsibilities allow, internal auditors should conduct engagements in a manner that allows for maximum audit coordination and efficiency.
4. The CAE may agree to perform work for external auditors in connection with their annual audit of the financial statements. Work performed by internal auditors to assist external auditors in fulfilling their responsibility is subject to all relevant provisions of the *Standards*.
5. The CAE should make regular evaluations of the coordination between internal and external auditors. Such evaluations may also include assessments of the overall efficiency and effectiveness of internal and external auditing functions, including aggregate audit cost.
6. In exercising its oversight role, the board may request the CAE to assess the performance of external auditors. Such assessments should ordinarily be made in the context of the CAE's role of coordinating internal and external auditing activities, and should extend to other performance matters only at the

specific request of senior management or the board. Assessments of external auditors' performance should be based on sufficient information to support the conclusions reached. Assessments of the external auditors' performance with respect to the coordination of internal and external auditing activities should reflect the criteria described in this Practice Advisory.

7. Assessments of the performance of external auditors extending to matters beyond coordination with the internal auditors may address additional factors, such as

    - Professional knowledge and experience
    - Knowledge of the organization's industry
    - Independence
    - Availability of specialized services
    - Anticipation of and responsiveness to the needs of the organization
    - Reasonable continuity of key engagement personnel
    - Maintenance of appropriate working relationships
    - Achievement of contract commitments
    - Delivery of overall value to the organization

8. The CAE should communicate the results of evaluations of coordination between internal and external auditors to senior management and the board along with, as appropriate, any relevant comments about the performance of external auditors.
9. External auditors may be required by their professional standards to ensure that certain matters are communicated to the board. The CAE should communicate with external auditors regarding these matters so as to have an understanding of the issues. These matters may include

    - Issues that may affect the independence of the external auditors
    - Significant control weaknesses
    - Errors and irregularities
    - Illegal acts
    - Management judgments and accounting estimates
    - Significant audit adjustments
    - Disagreements with management
    - Difficulties encountered in performing the audit

10. Coordination of audit efforts involves periodic meetings to discuss matters of mutual interest.

    - **Audit coverage.** Planned audit activities of internal and external auditors should be discussed to ensure that audit coverage is coordinated and duplicate efforts are minimized. Sufficient meetings should be scheduled during the audit process to ensure coordination of audit work and efficient and timely completion of audit activities and to determine whether observations and recommendations from work performed to date require that the scope of planned work be adjusted.
    - **Access to each other's audit programs and working papers.** Access to the external auditors' programs and working papers may be important in order for internal auditors to be satisfied as to the acceptability for internal audit purposes of relying on the external auditors' work. Such access carries with it the responsibility for internal auditors to respect the confidentiality of those programs and working papers. Similarly, access to the internal auditors' programs and working papers should be given to external auditors in order for external auditors to be satisfied as to the acceptability, for external audit purposes, of relying on the internal auditors' work.
    - **Exchange of audit reports and management letters.** Internal audit final communications, management's responses to those communications, and subsequent internal audit activity follow-up reviews should be made available to external auditors. These communications assist external auditors in determining and adjusting the scope of work. In addition, the internal auditors need access to the external auditors' management letters. Matters discussed in management letters assist internal auditors in planning the areas to emphasize in future internal audit work. After review of management letters and initiation of any needed corrective action by appropriate members of management and the board, the CAE should ensure that appropriate follow-up and corrective action have been taken.
    - **Common understanding of audit techniques, methods, and terminology.**

- The CAE should understand the scope of work planned by external auditors and should be satisfied that the external auditors' planned work, in conjunction with the internal auditors' planned work, satisfies the requirements of Section 2100 of the *Standards*. Such satisfaction requires an understanding of the level of materiality used by external auditors for planning and the nature and extent of the external auditors' planned procedures.
- The CAE should ensure that the external auditors' techniques, methods, and terminology are sufficiently understood by internal auditors to enable the CAE to (1) coordinate internal and external auditing work; (2) evaluate, for purposes of reliance, the external auditors' work; and (3) ensure that internal auditors who are to perform work to fulfill the external auditors' objectives can communicate effectively with external auditors.
- The CAE should provide sufficient information to enable external auditors to understand the internal auditors' techniques, methods, and terminology to facilitate reliance by external auditors on work performed using such techniques, methods, and terminology. It may be more efficient for internal and external auditors to use similar techniques, methods, and terminology to effectively coordinate their work and to rely on the work of one another.

IIA's Practice Advisory 2050-2: Acquisition of External Audit Services

Nature of This Practice Advisory

This guidance should be considered by chief audit executives (CAEs) when requested or assigned responsibility for acquisition of external audit services. This guidance may also be useful to the audit committee and to financial management if they are charged with obtaining external audit services. The considerations contained in this Practice Advisory are not intended to represent a complete listing of all considerations that may be necessary in every situation. CAEs should adapt and adjust this guidance as necessary to fit the specific circumstances under consideration. This Practice Advisory is particularly well suited for use in acquisition of external audit services for audits of the financial statements, but it may also be useful in obtaining external audit services for other types of engagements. See PA 2050-1, "Coordination," for guidance related to "coordinating" internal and external audit activities. *Compliance with Practice Advisories is optional.*

1. The internal auditor's participation in the selection, evaluation, and retention of the organization's external auditors may vary from no role in the process, to advising management or the audit committee, assistance or participation in the process, management of the process, or auditing the process. Since IIA *International Standards for the Professional Practice of Internal Auditing (Standards)* require internal auditors to "share information and coordinate activities with other internal and external providers of relevant assurance and consulting services," it is advisable for internal auditors to have some role or involvement in the selection or retention of the external auditors and in the definition of scope of work.
2. A board- or audit committee–approved policy can facilitate the periodic request for external audit services and position such exercises as normal business activities so that the current service providers do not view a decision to request proposals as a signal that the organization is dissatisfied with current services. If a specific policy does not exist, the internal auditor should determine if such services are subject to any other existing procurement policies of the organization. In the absence of appropriate policies, the internal auditor should consider facilitating development of appropriate policies.
3. Appropriate policies for selection or retention of external audit services should consider addressing the following attributes:
    - Board or audit committee approval of the policy
    - Nature and type of services covered by the policy
    - Duration of contract, frequency of the formal request for services, and/or determination to retain the existing service providers
    - Participants or members of the selection and evaluation team
    - Any critical or primary criteria that should be considered in the evaluation
    - Limitations on service fees and procedures for approving exceptions to the policy
    - Regulatory or other governing requirements unique to specific industries or countries
4. A board policy may also address the acquisition of services other than just financial statement audits that may be offered by external audit firms. Those may include

- Tax services
- Consulting and other nonaudit services
- Internal audit outsourcing and/or cosourcing services
- Other outsourced or cosourced services
- Special services, such as agreed-on service engagements
- Valuation, appraisal, and actuarial services
- Temporary services such as recruiting, bookkeeping, technology services
- Legal services provided by external audit firms

5. Appropriate documentation should be retained concerning a periodic, formal decision to retain the existing service providers and forego or delay requests to other potential service providers.
6. A plan should be developed for the selection process that identifies the selection committee participants, key deliverables and target dates for each phase of the process, candidates from whom to request proposals, nature and extent of services to be requested, and how information will be communicated to potential candidates. Often, at the start of the selection process, an organization may conduct a comprehensive meeting with all potential candidates in which management makes a formal presentation to cover pertinent information for the service request and supplies the candidates with a formal information package or report describing the services being requested. This general meeting can be followed with individual, on-site meetings for each candidate and include appropriate management representatives. Other combinations of meetings and information packages are also practical or appropriate for special situations.
7. A two-phased request may be necessary to facilitate a screening process to narrow or reduce the field of potential service providers to a reasonable number of final candidates. Initial information requests should be focused on obtaining appropriate statements of qualifications, including background and other general information about the potential candidates. Information should be obtained, such as history of the firm, size of the firm, resources available, firm philosophy and audit approach, special expertise, local or servicing office that would handle the engagement, related industry experience, and biographies of key team members that would be assigned to the engagement.
8. After the initial screening process, those candidates selected to advance to the next phase should be sent a second request for information that provides more specifics about the services requested. A detailed service request that itemizes deliverables expected and key target dates should be developed. Candidates should be requested to provide specific details, including pricing for the services. A timetable for the remainder of the process can be supplied that schedules dates for delivery of the additional information requested, meetings for presentations by the candidates to the selection committee, and a date for the final selection. The detailed service request should be specific for each of the services requested and should indicate whether the services may be awarded as one package or split between multiple candidates.
9. It may be appropriate to compare and summarize the attributes of the candidates by key criteria and provide it in a format that facilitates consistent evaluation of all the service providers. Questions may be supplied that stimulate thought processes and focus the evaluation on key criteria. An evaluation form can facilitate collection of each participant's analysis and conclusions about each of the candidates. Background information, such as the organization's past history with the various candidates, type of services previously provided, and fee history, can provide the selection team with an appropriate perspective to begin the evaluation.
10. Service arrangements for external audit engagements should be documented in a written agreement and signed by both the service provider and the engagement client.
11. If the selection process results in a change in the service providers, appropriate transition plans should be developed to facilitate a smooth and orderly change. Notifications to appropriate parties, including regulatory bodies, if required, should be communicated in a timely manner.
12. Internal auditors should determine how the organization monitors ongoing service activities from external auditors. Compliance with the terms of service contracts and other agreements should be assessed on a periodic basis. Assessment of the independence of the external auditors should include internal audit participation, be performed at least annually, and be communicated to the audit committee.

2.7 Reporting to the Board and Senior Management

2060—Reporting to the Board and Senior Management—The chief audit executive should report periodically to the board and senior management on the internal audit activity's purpose, authority, responsibility, and performance relative to its plan. Reporting should also include significant risk exposures and control issues, corporate governance issues, and other matters needed or requested by the board and senior management.

IIA's Practice Advisory 2060-1: Reporting to Board and Senior Management

Nature of This Practice Advisory

Internal auditors should consider these suggestions when reporting to the board and senior management. This guidance is not intended to represent all the considerations that may be necessary, but simply a recommended set of items that should be addressed. *Compliance with Practice Advisories is optional.*

1. The chief audit executive (CAE) should submit activity reports to senior management and to the board periodically throughout the year. Activity reports should highlight significant engagement observations and recommendations and should inform senior management and the board of any significant deviations from approved engagement work schedules, staffing plans, and financial budgets, and the reasons for them.
2. Significant engagement observations are those conditions that, in the judgment of the CAE, could adversely affect the organization. Significant engagement observations may include conditions dealing with irregularities, illegal acts, errors, inefficiency, waste, ineffectiveness, conflicts of interest, and control weaknesses. After reviewing such conditions with senior management, the CAE should communicate significant engagement observations and recommendations to the board, whether they have been satisfactorily resolved or not.
3. Management's responsibility is to make decisions on the appropriate action to be taken regarding significant engagement observations and recommendations. Senior management may decide to assume the risk of not correcting the reported condition because of cost or other considerations. The board should be informed of senior management's decisions on all significant observations and recommendations.
4. The CAE should consider whether it is appropriate to inform the board regarding previously reported significant observations and recommendations in those instances when senior management and the board assumed the risk of not correcting the reported condition. This may be particularly necessary when there have been organization, board, senior management, or other changes.
5. In addition to subjects covered above, activity reports should also compare (a) actual performance with the internal audit activity's goals and audit work schedules and (b) expenditures with financial budgets. Reports should explain the reason for major variances and indicate any action taken or needed.

IIA's Practice Advisory 2060-2: Relationship with the Audit Committee

Nature of This Practice Advisory

Internal auditors should consider these suggestions regarding the relationship between the internal audit activity and the audit committee of the governing body. This guidance is not intended to represent all necessary considerations, but merely summarizes key information concerning appropriate relationships between audit committees and internal auditing. *Compliance with Practice Advisories is optional.*

1. The term "audit committee," as used in this document, refers to the governance body that is charged with oversight of the organization's audit and control functions. Although these fiduciary duties are often delegated to an audit committee of the board of directors, the information in this Practice Advisory is also intended to apply to other oversight groups with equivalent authority and responsibility, such as trustees, legislative bodies, owners of an owner-managed entity, internal control committees, or full boards of directors.
2. The Institute of Internal Auditors (IIA) recognizes that audit committees and internal auditors have interlocking goals. A strong working relationship with the audit committee is essential for each to fulfill its responsibilities to senior management, board of directors, shareholders, and other outside parties. This Practice Advisory summarizes the IIA's views concerning the aspects and attributes of an appro-

priate relationship between an audit committee and the internal audit function. The IIA acknowledges that audit committee responsibilities encompass activities that are beyond the scope of this advisory, and in no way intends it to be a comprehensive description of audit committee responsibilities.

3. Three areas of activities are key to an effective relationship between the audit committee and the internal audit function, chiefly through the chief audit executive (CAE).

    - Assisting the audit committee to ensure that its charter, activities, and processes are appropriate to fulfill its responsibilities
    - Ensuring that the charter, role, and activities of internal audit are clearly understood and responsive to the needs of the audit committee and the board
    - Maintaining open and effective communications with the audit committee and the chairperson

Audit Committee Responsibilities

4. The CAE should assist the committee in ensuring that the charter, role, and activities of the committee are appropriate for it to achieve its responsibilities. The CAE can play an important role by assisting the committee to periodically review its activities and suggesting enhancements. In this way, the CAE serves as a valued advisor to the committee on audit committee and regulatory practices. Examples of activities that the CAE can undertake are

    - Review the charter for the audit committee at least annually and advise the committee whether the charter addresses all responsibilities directed to the committee in any terms of reference or mandates from the board of directors
    - Review or maintain a planning agenda for the audit committee's meeting that details all required activities to ascertain whether they are completed and that assists the committee in reporting to the board annually that it has completed all assigned duties
    - Draft the audit committee's meeting agenda for the chairman's review, facilitate the distribution of the material to the audit committee members, and write up the minutes of the audit committee meetings
    - Encourage the audit committee to conduct periodic reviews of its activities and practices compared with current best practices to ensure that its activities are consistent with leading practices
    - Meet periodically with the chairperson to discuss whether the materials and information being furnished to the committee are meeting their needs
    - Ask the audit committee if any educational or informational sessions or presentations would be helpful, such as training new committee members on risk and controls
    - Ask the committee whether the frequency and time allotted to the committee are sufficient

Internal Audit Activity's Role

5. The CAE's relationship to the audit committee should revolve around a core role of the CAE ensuring that the audit committee understands, supports, and receives all assistance needed from the internal audit function. The IIA supports the concept that sound governance is dependent on the synergy generated among the four principal components of effective corporate governance systems: boards of directors, management, internal auditors, and external auditors. In that structure, internal auditors and audit committees are mutually supportive. Consideration of the work of internal auditors is essential for the audit committee to gain a complete understanding of an organization's operations. A primary component of the CAE's role with the committee is to ensure this objective is accomplished and the committee views the CAE as their trusted advisor. The CAE can perform a number of activities to accomplish this role.

    - Request that the committee review and approve the internal audit charter on an annual basis. (A model internal audit department charter is available on the IIA's Web site at http://www.theiia.org/ecm/guide-ia.cfm?doc_id=383.)
    - Review with the audit committee the functional and administrative reporting lines of internal audit to ensure that the organizational structure in place allows adequate independence for internal auditors. (Practice Advisory 1110-2, "Chief Audit Executive [CAE] Reporting Lines")
    - Incorporate in the charter for the audit committee to review hiring decisions of the CAE, including appointment, compensation, evaluation, retention, and dismissal.

- Incorporate in the charter for the audit committee to review and approve proposals to outsource any internal audit activities.
- Assist the audit committee in evaluating the adequacy of the personnel and budget, and the scope and results of the internal audit activities, to ensure that there are no budgetary or scope limitations that impede the ability of the internal audit function to execute its responsibilities.
- Provide information on the coordination with and oversight of other control and monitoring functions (e.g., risk management, compliance, security, business continuity, legal, ethics, environmental, external audit).
- Report significant issues related to the processes for controlling the activities of the organization and its affiliates, including potential improvements to those processes, and provide information concerning such issues through resolution.
- Provide information on the status and results of the annual audit plan and the sufficiency of department resources to senior management and the audit committee.
- Develop a flexible annual audit plan using an appropriate risk-based methodology, including any risks or control concerns identified by management, and submit that plan to the audit committee for review and approval as well as periodic updates.
- Report on the implementation of the annual audit plan, as approved, including as appropriate any special tasks or projects requested by management and the audit committee.
- Incorporate into the internal audit charter the responsibility for the internal audit department to report to the audit committee on a timely basis any suspected fraud involving management or employees who are significantly involved in the internal controls of the company. Assist in the investigation of significant suspected fraudulent activities within the organization and notify management and the audit committee of the results.
- Audit committees should be made aware that quality assessment reviews of the internal audit activity be done every five years in order for the audit activity to declare that it meets the IIA's *International Standards for the Professional Practice of Internal Auditing (Standards).* Regular quality assessment reviews will provide assurance to the audit committee and to management that internal auditing activities conform to the *Standards.*

Communications with the Audit Committee

6. While not to diminish any of the activities noted above, in a large part the overall effectiveness of the CAE and audit committee relationship will revolve around the communications between the parties. Today's audit committees expect a high level of open and candid communications. If the CAE is to be viewed as a trusted advisor by the committee, communications is the key element. Internal auditing, by definition, can help the audit committee accomplish its objectives by bringing a systematic, disciplined approach to its activities, but unless there is appropriate communications, it is not possible for the committee to determine this. The CAE should consider providing communications to the audit committee in the following areas:

   - Audit committees should meet privately with the CAE on a regular basis to discuss sensitive issues.
   - It should provide an annual summary report or assessment on the results of the audit activities relating to the defined mission and scope of audit work.
   - It should issue periodic reports to the audit committee and management summarizing results of audit activities.
   - It should keep the audit committee informed of emerging trends and successful practices in internal auditing.
   - Together with external auditors, the CAE should discuss fulfillment of committee information needs.
   - It should review information submitted to the audit committee for completeness and accuracy.
   - It should confirm there is effective and efficient work coordination of activities between internal and external auditors. It also should determine if there is any duplication between the work of the internal and external auditors and give the reasons for such duplication.

MULTIPLE-CHOICE QUESTIONS (1-32)

1. What should the audit strategy be?
a. It should be knowledge based.
b. It should be cycle based.
c. It should be request based.
d. It should be risk based.

2. Which one of the following items includes the other three items?
a. Inherent risk.
b. Control risk.
c. Audit risk.
d. Detection risk.

3. Which of the following would **not** be considered in performing a risk analysis exercise?
a. System complexity.
b. Results of prior audits.
c. Auditor skills.
d. System changes.

4. During a computer risk assessment process, which of the following would **not** be considered an auditable activity?
a. Application software.
b. Systems software.
c. Print software.
d. Telecommunications software.

Items 5 and 6 are based on the following:

Management is concerned with a recent increase in expenditures and lower profits at a division and has asked the internal audit department to perform an operational audit of the division. Management would like to have the audit completed as quickly as possible and has asked the internal audit department to allocate all possible resources to the task. The director of internal audit is concerned with the time pressure since the internal audit department is heavily involved in a major legal compliance audit that had been requested by the audit committee.

5. Which of the following comments are correct regarding the assessment of risk associated with the two projects?

I. Activities requested by the audit committee should always be considered higher risk than those requested by management.
II. Activities with higher dollar budgets should always be considered higher risk than those with lower dollar budgets.
III. Risk should always be measured by the potential dollar or adverse exposure to the organization.

a. I only.
b. II only.
c. III only.
d. I and III.

6. Which of the following factors would be considered the **least** important in deciding whether existing internal audit resources should be moved from the ongoing legal compliance audit to the management-requested division audit?
a. A financial audit of the division by the external auditor a year ago.
b. The potential of fraud associated with the legal compliance audit.
c. The increase in expenditures at the division for the past year.
d. The potential for significant regulatory fines associated with the legal compliance audit.

7. When gathering data, an audit team identified both subjective and objective criteria for measuring audit risk. Which one of the following risk factors is most objective?
a. Prior audit findings.
b. Size of the audit unit.
c. Comfort with operating management.
d. Changes in staff, systems, or the environment.

8. The director of internal auditing was reviewing recent reports that had recommended additional audits because of risk and exposure to the company. Which of the following represents the greatest risk to the company and should be the next assignment?
a. Three prenumbered receiving reports were missing.
b. Several purchase orders were issued without purchase requisitions.
c. Payment had been made for routine inventory items without a purchase order or receiving report.
d. Several times cash receipts had been held over an extra day before depositing.

Items 9 through 12 are based on the following:

The audit process is one of critical thinking, analysis, and careful evaluation. All mechanical procedures are integrated into a larger context of thoughtful inquiry. All audits include a description and analysis of internal controls. Auditees are selected in a number of ways, with risk being the primary basis for selection. The departments being considered for possible audit in the coming year and attributes of those departments are listed below.

Department	*Assets*	*Annual Costs*	*Probability of Loss*
Production A	$ 50,000	$ 700,000	10%
Production B	5,000,000	10,000,000	1%
Production C	1,000,000	1,000,000	1%
Purchasing	50,000	150,000	10%
Marketing	50,000	500,000	10%
Shipping	60,000	100,000	50%
Security	10,000	100,000	90%
Travel	6,000	30,000	50%

All of these departments except two are on the potential list of auditees because of a risk analysis performed by the audit director. Production Department A is on the list because the president thinks too many bottlenecks occur in that department. The marketing department is on the list because the chief of security received an anonymous phone call accusing a marketing manager of accepting substantial financial kickbacks from a media outlet. Internal controls seem adequate in all departments, with the possible exception of marketing.

9. Which department would most likely need a pure operational (nonfinancial) audit?
a. Production A.
b. Production C.
c. Purchasing.
d. Marketing.

10. What is the audit director's most logical definition of risk of loss to be used in selecting auditees?
a. Amount of risk exposure times the probability of loss.

b. Amount of annual costs in department.
c. Probability of loss.
d. Amount of assets in a department.

11. The internal auditing department is assigned responsibility for investigating fraud by its charter. If obtaining access to outside media outlet records and personnel were not possible, the best action an auditor could take to investigate the allegation of marketing kickbacks would be to

a. Search for unrecorded liabilities from media outlets.
b. Obtain a list of approved media outlets.
c. Develop a financial/behavioral profile of the suspect.
d. Vouch any material past charge-off of receivables.

12. If there is fraud in the marketing department, which of the following would be beyond the scope of the auditor's responsibility?

a. Informing the wrongdoer of his or her legal rights.
b. Determining the effects of the wrongdoing.
c. Discussing the wrongdoing with an appropriate level of management.
d. Including the wrongdoing in a report that will go to the audit committee.

13. Which of the following auditable activities represents the greatest risk to a postmerger manufacturing corporation and would therefore most likely be subjected to an audit?

a. Combining imprest funds.
b. Combining purchasing functions.
c. Combining legal functions.
d. Combining marketing functions.

14. In planning an audit, the internal auditor should design audit objectives and procedures to address the risk associated with the activity. Risk is defined as

a. The risk that the balance or class of transactions and related assertions contain misstatements that could be material to the financial statements.
b. The probability that an event or action may adversely affect the activity under audit.
c. The failure to adhere to organizational policies, plans, and procedures, or not complying with relevant laws and regulations.
d. The failure to accomplish established objectives and goals for operations or programs.

Items 15 through 21 are based on the following:

Two major retail companies, both publicly traded and operating in the same geographic area, have recently merged. Both companies are approximately the same size and have audit departments. Company B has invested heavily in information technology and has electronic data interchange (EDI) connections with its major vendors.

The audit committee has asked the internal auditors from both companies to analyze risk areas that should be addressed after the merger. The director of internal auditing of Company B has suggested that the two audit groups have a planning meeting to share audit programs, scope of audit coverage, and copies of audit reports that were delivered to their audit committees. Management has also suggested that the auditors review the compatibility of the companies' two computer systems and control philosophy for individual store operations.

15. Which of the following would be the **least** important risk factor when considering the ability to integrate the two companies' computer systems?

a. The number of programmers and systems analysts employed by each company.
b. The extent of EDI connections with vendors.
c. The compatibility of existing operating systems and database structures.
d. The size of company databases and the number of database servers used.

16. During the first meeting, a disagreement occurs over the approach taken regarding store compliance. The audit director for Company B questions Company A's extensive use of store compliance testing, stating that the approach is neither responsive to materiality concepts nor an appropriate application of risk assessment. Company A's audit director presents the following reasoning:

I. You have misconstrued materiality. Materiality is not based only on the size of individual stores; it is also based on the control structure that affects the whole organization.
II. Any deviation from a prescribed control procedure is, by definition, material.
III. The only way to ensure that a material amount of the company's control structure is covered is to comprehensively audit all stores.

Which of the statements by the audit director of Company A are valid?

a. I only.
b. I and II only.
c. III only.
d. I, II, and III.

17. The audit director for Company B decides to review selected store compliance audit reports issued by the internal audit department of Company A. Upon reviewing the reports, the director comments that most items included in the report are inappropriate because they are very minor and cannot be considered material. The director states that such reports would not be tolerated by the management of Company B. Which of the following assertions by the audit director of Company A are valid?

I. These are the kinds of reports we have provided since the company has been in operation, and they have served our company well.
II. The reports are consistent with management's control philosophy and are an integral part of the overall control environment.
III. Materiality is in the eyes of the beholder. Any deviation is considered material by my management.

a. I only.
b. II only.
c. III only.
d. II and III.

18. In analyzing the differences between the two companies, the audit director of Company A notes that Company A has a formal corporate code of ethics while Company B does not. The code of ethics covers such things as purchase agreements and relationships with vendors as well as a host of other issues to guide individual behavior within the firm.

Which of the following statements regarding the existence of the code of ethics in Company A can be logically inferred?

I. Company A exhibits a higher standard of ethical behavior than does Company B.
II. Company A has established objective criteria by which an individual's actions can be evaluated.
III. The absence of a formal corporate code of ethics in Company B would prevent a successful audit of ethical behavior in that company.

a. I and II.
b. II only.
c. III only.
d. II and III.

19. Company A's audit director, who is also a CIA, faces an ethical dilemma. For an audit in process, persuasive evidence indicates that a top manager has been involved in insider trading. The extent and type of trading is such that the trading would be considered fraudulent. However, the findings were encountered as a side issue of another audit and are not considered relevant to the compatibility of the computer systems. Regarding this finding, which of the following is the audit director's most appropriate action?

a. Discontinue audit work associated with the insider trading and report the preliminary findings to the company's external legal counsel for their investigation. Report the legal counsel findings to management.
b. Discontinue audit work associated with the insider trading. Report the preliminary findings to the chairperson of the audit committee and recommend an investigation.
c. Continue work on the insider trading sufficient to conclusively establish whether fraudulent activity has taken place, then report the findings to the chairperson of the audit committee. Report the matter to government officials if appropriate action is not taken.
d. Discontinue audit work associated with the insider trading since it is not an integral part of the existing audit and the audit committee has established higher priority work for the auditors.

20. The two organizations agree to share data on store operations. The data reveal that three stores in Company A are characterized by

- Significantly lower gross margins,
- Higher-than-average sales volume, and
- Higher levels of employee bonuses.

The three stores are part of a set of six that are managed by a relatively new section manager. In addition, the store managers of the three stores are also relatively new. The **most** likely cause of the observed data is

a. The relative inexperience of the store managers.
b. Problems with employee training and employee ability to meet customer needs.
c. Fraudulent activity whereby goods are taken from the stores thus results in the lower gross margins.
d. Promotional activities that offer large discounts coupled with the payment of commissions to employees who reach targeted sales goals.

21. Assume the auditor concludes that the most reasonable explanation of the observed data in the prior question is that inventory fraud is taking place in the three stores. Which of the following audit activities would provide the **most** persuasive evidence that fraud is taking place?

a. Use an integrated test facility (ITF) to compare individual sales transactions with test transactions submitted through the ITF. Investigate all differences.
b. Interview the three individual store managers to determine if their explanations about the observed differences are the same, and then compare their explanations to that of the section manager.
c. Schedule a surprise inventory audit to include a physical inventory. Investigate areas of inventory shrinkage.
d. Take a sample of individual store prices and compare them with the sales entered on the cash register for the same items.

22. The first phase of the risk assessment process is to identify and catalog the auditable activities of the organization. Which of the following would **not** be considered an auditable activity?

a. The agenda established by the audit committee for one of its quarterly meetings.
b. General ledger account balances.
c. Computerized information systems.
d. Statutory laws and regulations as they affect the organization.

23. The director of internal auditing for an organization has just completed a risk assessment process, identified the areas with the highest risks, and assigned an audit priority to each. Which of the following conclusions logically follows from such a risk assessment and are consistent with the IIA *Standards?*

I. Items should be quantified as to risk in the rank order of quantifiable dollar exposure to the organization.
II. The risk priorities should be in order of major control deficiencies.
III. The risk process, though quantified, is the result of professional judgments about both exposures and probability of occurrences.

a. I only.
b. III only.
c. II and III only.
d. I, II, and III.

24. Which of the following represents appropriate internal audit action in response to the risk assessment process?

I. The low-risk areas may be delegated to the external auditor, but the high-risk areas should be performed by the internal auditing function.
II. The high-risk areas should be integrated into an audit plan along with the high-priority requests of management and the audit committee.
III. The risk analysis should be used in determining an annual audit work plan; therefore the risk analysis should be performed only on an annual basis.

a. I only.
b. II only.
c. III only.
d. I and III only.

25. The internal auditor is considering performing risk analysis, as a basis for determining which areas of the organization ought to be examined. Which one of the following statements is correct regarding risk analysis?

a. The extent to which management judgments are required in an area could serve as a risk factor in assisting the auditor in making a comparative risk analysis.
b. The highest risk assessment should always be assigned to the area with the largest potential loss.
c. The highest risk assessment should always be assigned to the area with highest probability of occurrence.
d. Risk analysis must be reduced to quantitative terms in order to provide meaningful comparisons across an organization.

26. The director of internal auditing set up a computerized spreadsheet to facilitate the risk assessment process involving a number of different divisions in the organization. The spreadsheet included the following factors:

- Pressure on divisional management to meet profit goals.
- Complexity of operations.
- Competence of divisional personnel.
- The dollar amount of subjectively influenced accounts in the division, such as accounts where management's judgment can affect the expense. Example: postretirement benefits.

The director used a group meeting of audit managers to reach a consensus on the competence of divisional personnel. Other factors were assessed as high, medium, or low by either the director or an audit manager who had audited the division. The director assigned a weight ranging from 0.5 to 1.0 to each factor and then computed a composite risk score. Which of the following statements is correct regarding the risk assessment process?

a. The risk analysis would not be appropriate because it mixes both quantitative and qualitative factors, thereby making expected values calculation impossible.
b. Assessing factors at discrete levels such as high, medium, and low is inappropriate for the risk assessment process because the ratings are not quantifiable.
c. The weighting is subjective and should have been determined through a process such as multiple regression analysis.
d. Using a subjective group consensus to assess personnel competence is appropriate.

27. Corporate management has just implemented a policy that every department must downsize by immediately cutting 10% of each department's staff and budget. The director of internal auditing has reacted to the organization's recent plans for "downsizing" (reducing the size of staff across the board) by notifying the audit managers that the time allocated for all jobs must be cut by 10%. Which of the following statements regarding the director's action and potential manager's action would be correct?

a. The director's action should result in approximately the same amount of risk coverage as the previous audit plan, but reduced by 10%.
b. Individual audit managers can attain 90% of the previously defined audit coverage by uniformly cutting audit procedures by 10%.
c. The director should have reprioritized risks and cut out specific audit engagements, rather than cutting 10% across the board.
d. All of the above.

28. Risk models or risk analysis is often used in conjunction with development of long-range audit schedules. The key input in the evaluation of risk is

a. Previous audit results.
b. Management concerns and preferences.
c. Specific requirements of the *Standards*.
d. Judgment of the internal auditor.

29. Directors may use a tool called "risk analysis" in preparing work schedules. Which of the following would **not** be considered in performing a risk analysis?

a. Financial exposure and potential loss.
b. Skills available on the audit staff.
c. Results of prior audits.
d. Major operating changes.

30. Factors that should be considered when evaluating audit risk in a functional area include

1. Volume of transactions.
2. Degree of system integration.
3. Years since last audit.
4. Significant management turnover.
5. (Dollar) value of "assets at risk."
6. Average value per transaction.
7. Results of last audit.

Factors that **best** define materiality of audit risk are

a. 1 through 7.
b. 2, 4, and 7.
c. 1, 5, and 6.
d. 3, 4, and 6.

31. In an audit of a purchasing department, which of the following generally would be considered a risk factor?

a. Purchase specifications are developed by the department requesting the material.
b. Purchases are made against blanket or open purchase orders for certain types of items.
c. Purchases are made from parties related to buyers or other company officials.
d. There is a failure to rotate purchases among suppliers included on an approved vendor list.

32. Employees using personal computers have been reporting occupational injuries and claiming substantial workers' compensation benefits. Working papers of an operational audit to determine the extent of company exposure to such personal injury liability should include

a. Analysis of claims by type of equipment and extensiveness of use by individual employees.
b. Confirmations from insurance carriers as to claims paid under workers' compensation policies in force.
c. Reviews of documentation supporting purchases of personal computers.
d. Listings of all personal computers in use and the employees who are assigned to use them.

MULTIPLE-CHOICE ANSWERS AND EXPLANATIONS

1. d __ __	8. c __ __	15. a __ __	22. a __ __	29. b __ __
2. c __ __	9. a __ __	16. a __ __	23. b __ __	30. c __ __
3. c __ __	10. a __ __	17. b __ __	24. b __ __	31. c __ __
4. c __ __	11. c __ __	18. b __ __	25. a __ __	32. a __ __
5. c __ __	12. a __ __	19. b __ __	26. d __ __	
6. a __ __	13. b __ __	20. d __ __	27. c __ __	1st: __/32 __%
7. b __ __	14. b __ __	21. c __ __	28. d __ __	2nd: __/32 __%

1. (d) Audits should be planned and conducted according to the risk level; that is, high-risk auditable areas should be reviewed first, followed by medium-risk areas, which are followed by low-risk areas. The medium- and low-risk auditable areas should be reviewed only when audit resources are available. Choices (a), (b), and (c) are incorrect because they do not consider risk as explicitly as choice (d).

Subject Area: Establishing a risk-based plan—audit priorities. Source: Author.

2. (c) Audit risk is the risk that the auditor may unknowingly fail to appropriately modify his or her opinion on financial statements that are materially misstated. It is the product of the other three risks: It is equal to inherent risk multiplied by control risk, which is multiplied by detection risk. Audit risk is an all-inclusive term here. Choice (a) is incorrect. Inherent risk is the susceptibility of a management assertion to a material misstatement, assuming that there are no related internal control structure policies or procedures. Choice (b) is incorrect. Control risk is the risk that a material misstatement in a management assertion will not be prevented or detected on a timely basis by the entity's internal control structure policies or procedures. Choice (d) is incorrect. Detection risk is the risk that the auditor will not detect a material misstatement present in a management assertion.

Subject Area: Establishing a risk-based plan—audit priorities. Source: Author.

3. (c) Auditor skills become a consideration during audit scheduling. Risk analysis is done prior to the start of an audit, where factors such as system complexity, system changes, and results of prior audit are very important to consider. These factors determine whether an auditable area is high risk, medium risk, or low risk. Choices (a), (b), and (d) are incorrect. They are considered in performing a risk analysis exercise.

Subject Area: Establishing a risk-based plan—audit priorities. Source: Author.

4. (c) The audit resources should be allocated to those areas where the risk level is the highest. Print software is low risk compared to the other three types of software to be reviewed by an auditor. Choices (a), (b), and (d) are incorrect. They are auditable activities to audit due to their high-risk nature.

Subject Area: Establishing a risk-based plan—audit priorities. Source: Author.

5. (c) This is the basic definition of risk given in the IIA *Standards* (Item III). Choice (a) is incorrect. Requests from management and the audit committee should both be considered by the internal audit department. Although an audit committee request is important, it is not always more important, nor does it always imply higher risk (item I). Choice (b) is incorrect. Risk is measured by the potential exposure to the organization. The size of the departmental budget is an important determinant, but is not a sufficient determinant (item II). Choice (d) is incorrect since it contains both correct and incorrect answers.

Subject Area: Establishing a risk-based plan—audit priorities. Source: CIA 597, I-1.

6. (a) The results of a financial audit would be the least relevant factor in prioritizing the auditor's tasks because the financial audit will not resolve the question asked by management. Also, the financial audit was prior to the recent problems. Choice (b) is incorrect. Fraud is one of the major factors to be considered in analyzing risk and identifying audit activities. Choice (c) is incorrect. The increase in expenditures provides a benchmark for potential exposure or loss to the organization. Choice (d) is incorrect. Fines imposed by regulatory agencies could represent a significant risk.

Subject Area: Establishing a risk-based plan—audit priorities. Source: CIA 597, I-2.

7. (b) The IIA *Standards* state, "Objective reports are factual. ..." Sawyer states, "Every categorical statement, every figure, every reference must be based on hard evidence."[1] The size of the audit unit is a fact, and not affected by the auditor's impressions and feelings. Choice (a) is incorrect. Assessment of prior audit findings is dependent on the auditor's impressions and feelings. Choice (c) is incorrect. Comfort with operating management is dependent on the auditor's impressions and feelings. Choice (d) is incorrect. Assessment of changes in staff systems or the environment is dependent on the auditor's impressions and feelings.

Subject Area: Establishing a risk-based plan—audit priorities. Source: CIA 596, II-8.

8. (c) There is a great risk when cash payments can be made with no authorization. Several possible types of fraud could be occurring. Choice (a) is incorrect. This is an important item, but most important items include whether cash disbursements are properly controlled and payment will not be made without verification of receipt. The receipts could have been voided and destroyed. Choice (b) is incorrect. Some types of purchases do not require purchases requisitions, such as routine inventory acquisition. There is some risk in this, but it is not the greatest risk posed in the problem. Choice (d) is incorrect. Unless other controls are missing, the largest risk would be the loss of a day's receipts. This is a risk, but not the greatest risk.

Subject Area: Establishing a risk-based plan—audit priorities. Source: CIA 590, I-11.

---

[1] ***Sawyer's Internal Auditing,*** *5th ed. (Altamonte Springs, FL: The Institute of Internal Auditors, Altamonte Springs, FL 2003)*

9. (a) A department causing production bottlenecks would seem to have problems with efficiency and effectiveness, and would thus warrant an operational audit. Choice (b) is incorrect. There is no information given that would indicate that production C was particularly inefficient or ineffective. Choice (c) is incorrect. There is nothing to indicate that purchasing has been particularly inefficient or ineffective. Choice (d) is incorrect. There is nothing to indicate that marketing has been particularly inefficient or ineffective.

Subject Area: Establishing a risk-based plan—audit priorities. Source: CIA 1194, I-1.

10. (a) Risk is a combination of the amount of assets exposed to risk times the probability of a loss occurring. Choice (b) is incorrect. Annual cost is not a sufficient reason to conduct an audit. The amount of costs at risk times the probability of loss would be a better risk measure. Choice (c) is incorrect. The probability of loss is not sufficient reason to conduct an audit. If only a few assets are involved (i.e., a petty cash fund), then audit resources can best be utilized elsewhere. Choice (d) is incorrect. Quantity of assets is not a sufficient reason to conduct an audit. The amount of assets at risk times the probability of loss would be a better risk measure.

Subject Area: Establishing a risk-based plan—audit priorities. Source: CIA 1194, I-2.

11. (c) Developing a financial/behavioral profile may corroborate illegal income and provide a basis for tracing illegal payments. Choice (a) is incorrect. The issue is not unrecorded liabilities but direct financial kickbacks, which will not be determined by this action. Choice (b) is incorrect. Although helpful in identifying possible sources of kickbacks, this action would not corroborate the allegation. Choice (d) is incorrect. Past charge-offs of receivables have no relation to kickbacks from a media outlet to a marketing manager.

Subject Area: Establishing a risk-based plan—audit priorities. Source: CIA 1194, I-3.

12. (a) Informing the wrongdoer of legal rights is the responsibility of legal authorities. Choice (b) is incorrect. This is a part of the auditor's responsibility with respect to the discovery of fraud. Choices (c) and (d) are incorrect. Both are part of the auditor's responsibility.

Subject Area: Establishing a risk-based plan—audit priorities. Source: CIA 1194, I-4.

13. (b) Of all the four choices, the purchasing function typically represents significant risk for a manufacturing operation. In a merger of two manufacturers' purchasing functions, that auditable area can be a source of even more significant risk. Choice (a) is incorrect. The usual size of imprest funds will not likely result in risk that matches a purchasing operation. Choice (c) is incorrect. Legal functions typically do not represent the magnitude of risk that a purchasing operation has. Choice (d) is incorrect. Marketing functions may have identifiable risks but typically not as much as purchasing operations.

Subject Area: Establishing a risk-based plan—audit priorities. Source: CIA 1194, I-9.

14. (b) The IIA *Standards* specifically define risk as: "the probability that an event or action may adversely affect the activity under audit." Choice (a) is incorrect. This is the AICPA's definition of inherent risk for financial statement audit purposes. Choices (c) and (d) are incorrect. They are listed in the *Standards* as types of adverse action that can result from unmitigated risk.

Subject Area: Establishing a risk-based plan—audit priorities. Source: CIA 1194, I-11.

15. (a) This is the least risky area because the number of analysts and programmers may be more of a reflection of operating philosophy (buying new applications versus developing them). This philosophy is unlikely to affect the probability of the event adversely affecting the operations. See IIA *Standards* for a description of risk and materiality concepts. Choice (b) is incorrect. This is a risk area because one of the companies has little experience with dealing with EDI, and the complexity of computer communications in an EDI environment creates risk for those companies that have not yet established strong communication controls. Choice (c) is incorrect. This is a high-risk factor because the two different systems must be made compatible to achieve the economy of objectives and strategic plans of a merged organization. The conversion from one systems or database structure to another is risky because data or applications may be lost or modified. Employees will have to be retrained on the surviving system. There is always increased risk of error when people are not familiar with a computer system. Choice (d) is incorrect. This is a heavy risk factor for all the reasons discussed in choice (c).

Subject Area: Establishing a risk-based plan—audit priorities. Source: CIA 1196, I-11 to 19.

16. (a) Materiality is defined by the potential impact of an item on the organization and is not limited to items that can be assessed only in quantitative terms. Choice (b) is incorrect. There may be some control failures of a minor nature that would not be considered material. Choice (c) is incorrect. Sampling approaches may be used to comprehensively cover the control structure of an organization. Choice (d) is incorrect. Responses II and III are not correct. See choices (b) and (c).

Subject Area: Establishing a risk-based plan—audit priorities. Source: CIA 1196, I-11 to 19.

17. (b) This could be very consistent with management's philosophy and would be considered part of the overall control environment. Detailed internal audit review can be an integral part of an organization's control structure. Choice (a) is incorrect. It is difficult ever to justify an audit approach or reporting style based on tradition. It may indicate the audit director is not in touch with management or that management may not be adopting its control philosophy to substantive changes in the environment. Choice (c) is incorrect. There is a "user" component of materiality, but it would be difficult to consider every situation or deviation as material. Choice (d) is incorrect. See choices (a) and (c).

Subject Area: Establishing a risk-based plan—audit priorities. Source: CIA 1196, I-11 to 19.

18. (b) A formalized corporate code of ethics presents objective criteria by which actions can be evaluated and would thus serve as criteria against which activities could be evaluated. Choice (a) is incorrect. Response I is not correct. The existence of a corporate code of ethics, by itself, does not ensure higher standards of ethical behavior. It must be complemented by follow-up policies and monitoring activities to ensure adherence to the code. Choice (c) is incorrect.

Standards of ethical behavior, which would influence individual actions, can occur in other places than the corporate code of ethics. For example, there may be defined policies regarding purchasing activities that may serve the same purpose as a code of ethics. These policies also serve as criteria against which activities may be evaluated. Choice (d) is incorrect. See response given for choice (c).

Subject Area: Establishing a risk-based plan—audit priorities. Source: CIA 1196, I-11 to 19.

19. **(b)** The audit director's preliminary findings should be immediately reported to the audit committee, rather than management, because the audit committee is considered an organization one level above where the alleged fraud is taking place. Choice (a) is incorrect. This response would not be appropriate because the internal auditors are not in a position to engage external legal counsel. Further, the findings should not be reported to management since they might be involved. Choice (c) is incorrect. The *Standards* clearly indicate that the auditors report the suspected fraud to the appropriate levels of the organization to determine whether an investigation is undertaken. The auditors may not be in the best position to determine whether the trading is fraudulent and certainly are not in a position to report the information to government officials. Choice (d) is incorrect. This would not be acceptable because the IIA's Code of Ethics clearly indicates that auditors cannot be associated with any illegal or inappropriate behavior. Ignoring their findings would violate that standard of conduct.

Subject Area: Establishing a risk-based plan—audit priorities. Source: CIA 1196, I-11 to 19.

20. **(d)** This is the one explanation that could be supported by all the data elements and would thus form a hypothesis for subsequent audit testing. Choice (a) is incorrect. This might be a potential explanation for one store but is unlikely to occur at all three stores. Choice (b) is incorrect. Although this might be a problem, the data tend to contradict it. Sales are increasing, which would indicate customer satisfaction. Choice (c) is incorrect. There is not enough evidence to indicate that fraud might be present. In order for this hypothesis to hold true, there would have to be significant amounts of inventory shrinkage. This does not explain higher sales and bonuses.

Subject Area: Establishing a risk-based plan—audit priorities. Source: CIA 1196, I-11 to 19.

21. **(c)** If this type of fraud was occurring, it would result in inventory shrinkage. The surprise inventory count would be an effective audit technique. Choice (a) is incorrect. The ITF provides evidence only on the correctness of computer processing. It would not be relevant to the hypothesized rationale for the operating data. Choice (b) is incorrect. Interviews provide a weak form of evidence and would be better if the auditor first has substantive documentary evidence. Choice (d) is incorrect. The problem is with inventory shrinkage, not whether items are appropriately keyed in or scanned in at the cash register.

Subject Area: Establishing a risk-based plan—audit priorities. Source: CIA 1196, I-11 to 19.

22. **(a)** The audit committee's agenda for an audit committee meeting would not be an auditable activity, but may contain audit activities conducted by the audit function. Choices (b), (c), and (d) are incorrect because these are auditable activities specifically identified in the IIA *Standards*.

Subject Area: Establishing a risk-based plan—audit priorities. Source: CIA 1195, I-7.

23. **(b)** This is the essence of the risk process per the IIA *Standards*. Choice (a) is incorrect. Risk represents the probability that an event or action may adversely affect the organization. Although it may be most convenient to quantify those risks into dollars for ranking purposes, it is not required that they be quantified. Choice (c) is incorrect. The risk priorities do not necessarily mean there are major control deficiencies in the area. The auditor may use the exposures as a basis to evaluate controls, but the controls may be in place. Choice (d) is incorrect. Items I and II are incorrect. See the responses in choices (a) and (c).

Subject Area: Establishing a risk-based plan—audit priorities. Source: CIA 1195, I-12.

24. **(b)** The annual audit plan should integrate the risk analysis with requests from management and the audit committee. Choice (a) is incorrect. The *Standards* incorporate the concept of coordinating work with the external auditor. There may be a number of factors that affect the choice of work performed by the external auditors. However, there is no prohibition regarding high-risk or low-risk items. Choice (c) is incorrect. The risk analysis should be updated for changes as they occur during the year. Choice (d) is incorrect. Items I and III are not correct as noted in the responses to choices (a) and (c).

Subject Area: Establishing a risk-based plan—audit priorities. Source: CIA 1195, I-13.

25. **(a)** According to the *Standards*, the auditor could appropriately consider the extent of management judgments and accounting estimates as a risk factor. Choice (b) is incorrect. Risk analysis should consider both the potential loss (or damages) and the probability of occurrence. An area with the largest potential loss may have a very low expected loss. Choice (c) is incorrect. Risk analysis should consider both the potential loss (or damages) and the probability of occurrence. An area with a high probability of occurrence may have a very small risk of potential loss associated with it. Choice (d) is incorrect. Although it may be preferable in many circumstances to reduce items to quantitative terms, the concept of risk analysis is not limited to quantitative measures.

Subject Area: Establishing a risk-based plan—audit priorities. Source: CIA 1195, I-15.

26. **(d)** Audit managers have the experience to make such judgments. Group consensus tends to eliminate the extreme judgments that might occur with a single evaluator and would be an acceptable method. Choice (a) is incorrect. Risk analysis should consider all appropriate factors and need not be limited to quantitative or expected value calculations. Choice (b) is incorrect. High, medium, and low may be the most precise measures available for the audit department and would therefore be acceptable assessments for the risk analysis process. Choice (c) is incorrect. Subjective analysis is acceptable. It would be difficult to use multiple regression analysis to obtain a weighted average for the risk-weighting model because no criterion value exists to determine the weightings.

Subject Area: Establishing a risk-based plan—audit priorities. Source: CIA 1195, I-17.

27. (c) This would be the preferred response and should enable the auditor to develop an optimum plan to cover the maximum amount of risk with the more limited resources. Choice (a) is incorrect. Cutting all jobs by 10% does not necessarily mean that the risks addressed will drop by 10%. The auditor should reprioritize the audit schedule to ensure the optimum coverage of risk with the more limited resources. Choice (b) is incorrect. A uniform 10% reduction in audit procedures or audit scope may result in gathering insufficient evidence across a number of audit areas. The managers should consider cutting the scope of each audit to better address the major risks in the auditable unit. Choice (d) is incorrect. Only choice (c) is correct.

Subject Area: Establishing a risk-based plan—audit priorities. Source: CIA 1195, I-42.

28. (d) In assessing the magnitude of risk associated with any factor in a risk model, informed judgment by the auditor is required. Choice (a) is incorrect. The informed judgment of the internal auditor is still required to assess the magnitude of risk posed by previous audit results. Choice (b) is incorrect. To assess the risk posed by management concerns, informed judgment of the internal auditor is required. Choice (c) is incorrect. The *Standards* do not specify the basic input risk analyses.

Subject Area: Establishing a risk-based plan—audit priorities. Source: CIA 1191, II-6.

29. (b) This does not involve risk associated with potential auditees. Choices (a), (c), and (d) are incorrect, because these are the factors that should definitely be considered in risk analysis.

Subject Area: Establishing a risk-based plan—audit priorities. Source: CIA 591, II-11.

30. (c) Factors 1, 5, and 6 can all be quantified into values, which can be measured into materiality. Choice (a) is incorrect. Although all items are used to define audit risk, not all factors are used to define materiality of audit risk. Choice (b) is incorrect. Factors 2 and 4 cannot be quantified into materiality. Choice (d) is incorrect. Factors 3 and 4 cannot be quantified into materiality.

Subject Area: Establishing a risk-based plan—audit priorities. Source: CIA 1191, II-13.

31. (c) This invariably involves high risk. Choice (a) is incorrect. It is a normal procedure; purchasing reviews the specifications only. Choice (b) is incorrect. It is normal procedure for high-use items. Choice (d) is incorrect. An approved vendor list is often maintained as a control factor to help ensure that purchases are made only from reliable vendors. However, rotation is not usually appropriate.

Subject Area: Establishing a risk-based plan—audit priorities. Source: CIA 1193, II-11.

32. (a) Claims analysis is an appropriate inclusion since it enables identification of the importance of the two key factors (equipment in use and time spent by employees at such equipment) in leading to claims. Choice (b) is incorrect. This procedure fails to identify exposure to risks; it only supports claims paid by the carrier under the worker's compensation policies. Choice (c) is incorrect. Documentation supporting purchases of personal computers cannot customarily be expected to address risk assessments. Choice (d) is incorrect. These data fail to indicate the risks associated with extent of usage and with type of equipment.

Subject Area: Establishing a risk-based plan—audit priorities. Source: CIA 593, I-20.

3 UNDERSTAND THE INTERNAL AUDIT ACTIVITY'S ROLE IN ORGANIZATIONAL GOVERNANCE (10–20%)

THEORY

3.1 Nature of Work

2100—Nature of Work—The internal audit activity *should* evaluate and contribute to the improvement of risk management, control, and governance *processes using a systematic and disciplined approach.*

IIA's Practice Advisory 2100-1: Nature of Work

Nature of This Practice Advisory

Internal auditors should consider these suggestions when evaluating the nature of the internal audit activity's work. This guidance is not intended to represent all the considerations that may be necessary during such an evaluation, but simply a recommended set of items that should be addressed. *Compliance with Practice Advisories is optional.*

1. The scope of internal auditing work encompasses a systematic, disciplined approach to evaluating and improving the *adequacy* and *effectiveness* of risk management, control, and governance processes and the quality of performance in carrying out assigned responsibilities. The purposes of evaluating the adequacy of the organization's existing risk management, control, and governance processes is to provide: (1) reasonable assurance that these processes are functioning as intended and will enable the organization's objectives and goals to be met, and (2) recommendations for improving the organization's operations, in terms of both efficient and effective performance. Senior management and the board might also provide general direction as to the scope of work and the activities to be audited.
2. *Adequacy* of risk management, control, and governance processes is present if management has planned and designed processes in a manner that provides reasonable assurance that the organization's objectives and goals will be achieved efficiently and economically. Efficient performance accomplishes objectives and goals in an accurate, timely, and economical fashion. Economical performance accomplishes objectives and goals with minimal use of resources (i.e., cost) commensurate with the risk exposure. Reasonable assurance is provided if the most cost-effective measures are taken in the design and implementation stages to reduce risks and restrict expected deviations to a tolerable level. Thus, the design process begins with the establishment of objectives and goals. This is followed by connecting or interrelating concepts, parts, activities, and people in such a manner as to operate together to achieve the established objectives and goals.
3. *Effectiveness* of risk management, control, and governance processes is present if management directs processes in such a manner as to provide reasonable assurance that the organization's objectives and goals will be achieved. In addition to accomplishing the objectives and planned activities, management directs by authorizing activities and transactions, monitoring resulting performance, and verifying that the organization's processes are operating as designed.
4. Broadly, management is responsible for the sustainability of the whole organization and accountability for the organization's actions, conduct, and performance to the owners, other stakeholders, regulators, and general public. Specifically, the primary objectives of the overall management process are to achieve

- Relevant, reliable, and credible financial and operating information
- Effective and efficient use of the organization's resources
- Safeguarding of the organization's assets
- Compliance with laws, regulations, ethical and business norms, and contracts
- Identification of risk exposures and use of effective strategies to control them
- Established objectives and goals for operations or programs

5. Management plans, organizes, and directs the performance of sufficient actions to provide reasonable assurance that objectives and goals will be achieved. Management periodically reviews its objectives and goals and modifies its processes to accommodate changes in internal and external conditions. Management also establishes and maintains an organizational culture, including an ethical climate, that understands risk exposures and implements effective risk strategies for managing them.
6. *Control* is any action taken by management to enhance the likelihood that established objectives and goals will be achieved. Controls may be preventive (to deter undesirable events from occurring), detective (to detect and correct undesirable events that have occurred), or directive (to cause or encourage a desirable event to occur). The concept of a system of control is the integrated collection of control components and activities that are used by an organization to achieve its objectives and goals.
7. Internal auditors evaluate the whole management process of planning, organizing, and directing to determine whether reasonable assurance exists that objectives and goals will be achieved. Internal auditors should be alert to actual or potential changes in internal or external conditions that affect the ability to provide assurance from a forward-looking perspective. In those cases, internal auditors should address the risk that performance may deteriorate.
8. These internal auditing evaluations, in the aggregate, provide information to appraise the overall management process. All business systems, processes, operations, functions, and activities within the organization are subject to the internal auditors' evaluations. The comprehensive scope of work of internal auditing should provide reasonable assurance that management's

   - Risk management system is effective
   - System of internal control is adequate, effective, and efficient
   - Governance process is effective by establishing and preserving values, setting goals, monitoring activities and performance, and defining the measures of accountability

3.2 Risk Management

2110—Risk Management—The internal audit activity should assist the organization by identifying and evaluating significant exposures to risk and contributing to the improvement of risk management and control systems.

2110.A1—The internal audit activity should monitor and evaluate the effectiveness of the organization's risk management system.
2110.A2—The internal audit activity should evaluate risk exposures relating to the organization's governance, operations, and information systems regarding the

- Reliability and integrity of financial and operational information
- Effectiveness and efficiency of operations
- Safeguarding of assets
- Compliance with laws, regulations, and contracts

2110.C1—During consulting engagements, internal auditors should address risk consistent with the engagement's objectives and be alert to the existence of other significant risks.
2110.C2—Internal auditors should incorporate knowledge of risks gained from consulting engagements into the process of identifying and evaluating significant risk exposures of the organization.

IIA's Practice Advisory 2110-1: Assessing the Adequacy of Risk Management Processes

Nature of This Practice Advisory

Internal auditors may be charged with the responsibility for providing assurance to management and the audit committee on the adequacy of the organization's risk management processes. This responsibility would require the auditor to formulate an opinion on whether the organization's risk management process is sufficient to protect the assets, reputation, and ongoing operations of the organization. This advisory provides guidance on the major risk management objectives that the auditor should consider in formulating an opinion on the adequacy of the organization's risk management process. This Practice Advisory covers only the assessment and reporting of the effectiveness of the organization's risk management process. Other Practice Advisories will address controls and consulting issues in greater depth. This advisory recognizes that an organization's risk management process is an important business process that can and should be evaluated in a manner similar to other strategically important processes. *Compliance with Practice Advisories is optional.*

1. Risk management is a key responsibility of management. To achieve its business objectives, management should ensure that sound risk management processes are in place and functioning. Boards and audit committees have an oversight role to determine that appropriate risk management processes are in place and that these processes are adequate and effective. Internal auditors should assist both management and the audit committee by examining, evaluating, reporting, and recommending improvements on the adequacy and effectiveness of management's risk processes. Management and the board are responsible for their organization's risk management and control processes. However, internal auditors acting in a consulting role can assist the organization in identifying, evaluating, and implementing risk management methodologies and controls to address those risks.
2. Developing assessments and reports on the organization's risk management processes are normally a high audit priority. Evaluating management's risk processes is different from the requirement that auditors use risk analysis to plan audits. However, information from a comprehensive risk management process, including the identification of management and board concerns, can assist the internal auditor in planning audit activities.
3. Each organization may choose a particular methodology to implement its risk management process. The internal auditor should ascertain whether the methodology is understood by key groups or individuals involved in corporate governance, including the board and audit committee. Internal auditors must satisfy themselves that the organization's risk management processes address five key objectives to formulate an opinion on the overall adequacy of the risk management processes. The five key objectives of a risk management process are

    - Risks arising from business strategies and activities are identified and prioritized.
    - Management and the board have determined the level of risks acceptable to the organization, including the acceptance of risks designed to accomplish the organization's strategic plans.
    - Risk mitigation activities are designed and implemented to reduce, or otherwise manage, risk at levels that were determined to be acceptable to management and the board.
    - Ongoing monitoring activities are conducted to periodically reassess risk and the effectiveness of controls to manage risk.
    - The board and management receive periodic reports of the results of the risk management processes. The corporate governance processes of the organization should provide periodic communication of risks, risk strategies, and controls to stakeholders.

4. Internal auditors should recognize that there could be significant variations in the techniques used by various organizations for their risk management practices. Risk management processes should be designed for the nature of an organization's activities. Depending on the size and complexity of the organization's business activities, risk management processes can be

    - Formal or informal
    - Quantitative or subjective
    - Embedded in the business units or centralized at a corporate level

    The specific process used by an organization must fit that organization's culture, management style, and business objectives. For example, the use of derivatives or other sophisticated capital markets products by the organization would require the use of quantitative risk management tools. Smaller, less complex organizations may use an informal risk committee to discuss the organization's risk profile and to initiate periodic actions. The auditor should determine that the methodology chosen is both comprehensive and appropriate for the nature of the organization's activities.
5. Internal auditors should obtain sufficient evidence to satisfy themselves that the five key objectives of the risk management processes are being met in order to form an opinion on the adequacy of risk man-

agement processes. In gathering such evidence, the internal auditor should consider these types of audit procedures.

- Research and review reference materials and background information on risk management methodologies as a basis to assess whether the process used by the organization is appropriate and represents best practices for the industry.
- Research and review current developments, trends, industry information related to the business conducted by the organization, and other appropriate sources of information to determine risks and exposures that may affect the organization and related control procedures used to address, monitor, and reassess those risks.
- Review corporate policies, board, and audit committee minutes to determine the organization's business strategies, risk management philosophy and methodology, appetite for risk, and acceptance of risks.
- Review previous risk evaluation reports by management, internal auditors, external auditors, and any other sources that may have issued such reports.
- Conduct interviews with line and executive management to determine business unit objectives, related risks, and management's risk mitigation and control monitoring activities.
- Assimilate information to independently evaluate the effectiveness of risk mitigation, monitoring, and communication of risks and associated control activities.
- Assess the appropriateness of reporting lines for risk monitoring activities.
- Review the adequacy and timeliness of reporting on risk management results.
- Review the completeness of management's risk analysis and actions taken to remedy issues raised by risk management processes, and suggest improvements.
- Determine the effectiveness of management's self-assessment processes through observations, direct tests of control and monitoring procedures, testing the accuracy of information used in monitoring activities, and other appropriate techniques.

Review risk-related issues that may indicate weakness in risk management practices and, as appropriate, discuss with management, the audit committee, and the board of directors. If the auditor believes that management has accepted a level of risk that is inconsistent with the organization's risk management strategy and policies, or that is deemed unacceptable to the organization, the auditor should refer to *Standard* 2600, *Management's Acceptance of Risks,* and any related guidance for additional direction.

IIA's Practice Advisory 2100-7: The Internal Auditor's Role in Identifying and Reporting Environmental Risks

Nature of This Practice Advisory

The purpose of this Practice Advisory is to provide guidance to internal audit organizations on risk and independence issues related to environmental auditing activities. Internal auditors should be alert to the potential risks that may result from the organizational placement and reporting relationships of environmental auditors. This Practice Advisory suggests the minimum safeguards to ensure that important environmental issues are reported on a timely basis and to the appropriate level. The risks related to environmental noncompliance, fines and penalties, and other mismanagement may result in significant losses for the organization. *Compliance with Practice Advisories is optional. This guidance is repeated in Part 1 and Part 2 for proper coverage of the subject matter.*

Potential Risks

1. The chief audit executive (CAE) should include the environmental, health, and safety (EH&S) risks in any entity-wide risk management assessment and assess the activities in a balanced manner relative to other types of risk associated with an entity's operations. Among the risk exposures that should be evaluated are: organizational reporting structures; likelihood of causing environmental harm, fines, and penalties; expenditures mandated by Environmental Protection Agency (EPA) or other governmental agencies; history of injuries and deaths; record of losses of customers; and episodes of negative publicity and loss of public image and reputation.
2. If the CAE finds that the management of the EH&S risks largely depends on an environmental audit function, the CAE needs to consider the implications of that organizational structure and its effects on

operations and the reporting mechanisms. If the CAE finds that the exposures are not adequately managed and residual risks exist, that conclusion would normally result in changes to the internal audit activity's plan of engagements and further investigations.

3. The majority of environmental audit functions report to their organization's environmental component or general counsel, not to the CAE. The typical organizational models for environmental auditing fall into one of these scenarios.

    - The CAE and environmental audit chief are in separate functional units with little contact with each other.
    - The CAE and environmental audit chief are in separate functional units and coordinate their activities.
    - The CAE has responsibility for auditing environmental issues.

4. According to an IIA flash report on environmental auditing issues

    - About one-half of the environmental auditors seldom meet with a committee of the governing board, and only 40% have some contact with the CAE.
    - Seventy percent of the organizations reported that environmental issues are not regularly included on the agenda of the governing board.
    - About 40% of the organizations reported that they had paid fines or penalties for environmental violations in the past three years. Two-thirds of the respondents described their environmental risks as material.

5. The Environmental, Health, and Safety Auditing Roundtable (new name is the Auditing Roundtable) commissioned Richard L. Ratliff of Utah State University and a group of researchers to perform a study of environmental, health, and safety auditing. The researchers' findings related to the risk and independence issues follow.

    - The EH&S audit function is somewhat isolated from other organizational auditing activities. It is organized separately from internal auditing, only tangentially related to external audits of financial statements, and reports to an EH&S executive, rather than to the governing board or to senior management. This structure suggests that management believes EH&S auditing to be a technical field that is best placed within the EH&S function of the organization.
    - With that organizational placement, EH&S auditors could be unable to maintain their independence, which is considered one of the principal requirements of an effective audit function. EH&S audit managers typically report administratively to the executives who are responsible for the physical facilities being audited. Thus, poor EH&S performance would reflect badly on the facilities management team, who would therefore try to exercise their authority and influence over what is reported in audit findings, how audits are conducted, or what is included in the audit plan. This potential subordination of the auditors' professional judgment, even when only apparent, violates auditor indepen-dence and objectivity.
    - It is also common for written audit reports to be distributed no higher in the organization than to senior environmental executives. Those executives may have a potential conflict of interest, and they may curtail further distribution of EH&S audit findings to senior management and the governing board.
    - Audit information is often classified as either (a) attorney-client privilege or attorney work product, (b) secret and confidential, or (c) if not confidential, then closely held. This results in severely restricted access to EH&S audit information.

Suggestions for the Chief Audit Executive

6. The CAE should foster a close working relationship with the chief environmental officer and coordinate activities with the plan for environmental auditing. In those instances where the environmental audit function reports to someone other than the CAE, the CAE should offer to review the audit plan and the performance of engagements. Periodically, the CAE should schedule a quality assurance review of the environmental audit function if it is organizationally independent of the internal audit activity. That review should determine if the environmental risks are being adequately addressed. An EH&S audit program could be either (a) compliance-focused (i.e., verifying compliance with laws, regulations, and the entity's own EH&S policies, procedures, and performance objectives), or (b)

management systems-focused (i.e., providing assessments of management systems intended to ensure compliance with legal and internal requirements and the mitigation of risks), or (c) a combination of both approaches.

7. The CAE should evaluate whether the environmental auditors who are not part of the CAE's organization are in compliance with recognized professional auditing standards and a recognized code of ethics. The Board of Environmental, Health, & Safety Auditor Certifications (BEAC) as well as the IIA publish practice standards and ethical codes.
8. The CAE should evaluate the organizational placement and independence of the environmental audit function to ensure that significant matters resulting from serious risks to the enterprise are reported up the chain of command to the audit or other committee of the governing board. The CAE should also facilitate the reporting of significant EH&S risk and control issues to the audit (or other board) committee.

3.3 Control

2120—Control—The internal audit activity should assist the organization in maintaining effective controls by evaluating their effectiveness and efficiency and by promoting continuous improvement.

2120.A1—Based on the results of the risk assessment, the internal audit activity should evaluate the adequacy and effectiveness of controls encompassing the organization's governance, operations, and information systems. This should include

- Reliability and integrity of financial and operational information
- Effectiveness and efficiency of operations
- Safeguarding of assets
- Compliance with laws, regulations, and contracts

2120.A2—Internal auditors should ascertain the extent to which operating and program goals and objectives have been established and conform to those of the organization.
2120.A3—Internal auditors should review operations and programs to ascertain the extent to which results are consistent with established goals and objectives to determine whether operations and programs are being implemented or performed as intended.
2120.A4—Adequate criteria are needed to evaluate controls. Internal auditors should ascertain the extent to which management has established adequate criteria to determine whether objectives and goals have been accomplished. If adequate, internal auditors should use such criteria in their evaluation. If inadequate, internal auditors should work with management to develop appropriate evaluation criteria.
2120.C1—During consulting engagements, internal auditors should address controls consistent with the engagement's objectives and be alert to the existence of any significant control weaknesses.
2120.C2—Internal auditors should incorporate knowledge of controls gained from consulting engagements into the process of identifying and evaluating significant risk exposures of the organization.

IIA's Practice Advisory 2120.A1-1: Assessing and Reporting on Control Processes

Nature of This Practice Advisory

Internal auditors should consider this guidance when assessing the effectiveness of an organization's system of controls and reporting that judgment to senior management and the board of directors. The audit work performed during the year should obtain sufficient information to enable an evaluation of the system of controls and the formulation of an opinion. *Compliance with Practice Advisories is optional.*

1. One of the tasks of a board of directors is to establish and maintain the organization's governance processes and obtain assurances concerning the effectiveness of the risk management and control processes. Senior management's role is to oversee the establishment, administration, and assessment of that system of risk management and control processes. The purpose of that multifaceted system of control processes is to support people of the organization in the management of risks and the achievement of the established and communicated objectives of the enterprise. More specifically, those control processes are expected to ensure, among other things, that these conditions exist.
    - Financial and operational information is reliable and possesses integrity.
    - Operations are performed efficiently and achieve effective results.

- Assets are safeguarded.
- Actions and decisions of the organization are in compliance with laws, regulations, and contracts.

2. Among the responsibilities of the organization's managers is the assessment of the control processes in their respective areas. Internal and external auditors provide varying degrees of assurance about the state of effectiveness of the risk management and control processes in select activities and functions of the organization.
3. Senior management and the board normally expect that the chief audit executive (CAE) will perform sufficient audit work and gather other available information during the year so as to form a judgment about the adequacy and effectiveness of the risk management and control processes. The CAE should communicate that overall judgment about the organization's risk management process and system of controls to senior management and the audit committee. A growing number of organizations have included a management's report on the risk management process and system of internal controls in their annual or periodic reports to external stakeholders.
4. The CAE should develop a proposed audit plan normally for the coming year that ensures sufficient evidence will be obtained to evaluate the effectiveness of the risk management and control processes. The plan should call for audit engagements or other procedures to gather relevant information about all major operating units and business functions. It should include a review of the major risk management processes operating across the organization and a selection of the key risks identified from those processes. The audit plan should also give special consideration to those operations most affected by recent or expected changes. Those changes in circumstances may result from marketplace or investment conditions, acquisitions and divestitures, or restructures and new ventures. The proposed plan should be flexible so that adjustments may be made during the year as a result of changes in management strategies, external conditions, major risk areas, or revised expectations about achieving the organization's objectives.
5. In determining the proposed audit plan, the CAE should consider relevant work that will be performed by others. To minimize duplication and inefficiencies, the work planned or recently completed by management in its assessments of the risk management process, controls, and quality improvement processes as well as the work planned by the external auditors should be considered in determining the expected coverage of the audit plan for the coming year.
6. Finally, the CAE should evaluate the coverage of the proposed plan from two viewpoints: adequacy across organizational entities and inclusion of a variety of transaction and business-process types. If the scope of the proposed audit plan is insufficient to enable the expression of assurance about the organization's risk management and control processes, the CAE should inform senior management and the board of the expected deficiency, its causes, and the probable consequences.
7. The challenge for internal audit is to evaluate the effectiveness of the organization's system of risk management and controls based on the aggregation of many individual assessments. Those assessments are largely gained from internal audit engagements, management's self-assessments, and external auditor's work. As the engagements progress, internal auditors should communicate, on a timely basis, the findings to the appropriate levels of management so that prompt action can be taken to correct or mitigate the consequences of discovered control discrepancies or weaknesses.
8. Three key considerations in reaching an evaluation of the overall effectiveness of the organization's risk management and control processes are

   - Were significant discrepancies or weaknesses discovered from the audit work performed and other assessment information gathered?
   - If so, were corrections or improvements made after the discoveries?
   - Do the discoveries and their consequences lead to the conclusion that a pervasive condition exists resulting in an unacceptable level of business risk?

   The temporary existence of a significant risk management and control discrepancy or weakness does not necessarily lead to the judgment that it is pervasive and poses an unacceptable residual risk. The pattern of discoveries, degree of intrusion, and level of consequences and exposures are factors to be considered in determining whether the effectiveness of the whole system of controls is jeopardized and unacceptable risks exist.

9. The report of the CAE on the state of the organization's risk management and control processes should be presented, usually once a year, to senior management and the board. The report should emphasize the critical role played by the risk management and control processes in the quest for the organization's objectives, and it should refer to major work performed by internal audit and to other important sources of information that were used to formulate the overall assurance judgment. The opinion section of the report is normally expressed in terms of negative assurance; that is, the audit work performed for the period and other information gathered did not disclose any significant weaknesses in the risk management and control processes that have a pervasive effect. If the risk management and control deficiencies or weaknesses are significant and pervasive, the assurance section of the report may be a qualified or adverse opinion, depending on the projected increase in the level of residual risk and its impact on the organization's objectives.
10. The target audiences for the annual report are senior executives and board members. Because these readers have divergent understandings of auditing and business, the CAE's annual report should be clear, concise, and informative. It should be composed and edited to be understandable by them and targeted to meet their informational needs. Its value to these readers can be enhanced by focusing on the major risk areas and including major recommendations for improvement and information about current control issues and trends, such as technology and information security exposures, patterns of control discrepancies or weaknesses across business units, and potential difficulties in complying with laws or regulations.
11. Ample evidence exists of an "expectation gap" surrounding the internal audit activity's work in evaluating and providing assurance about the state of risk management and control processes. One such gap exists between management and the board's normally high expectations about the value of internal auditing services and the internal auditor's more modest expectations that derive from knowledge of practical limitations on audit coverage and from self-doubt about generating sufficient evidence to support an informed and objective judgment. The CAE should be mindful of the possible gap between what the report reader presumes and what actually happened during the year. He or she should use the report as another way to address different mental models and to suggest improving the capacity of the function or reducing the constraints to access and audit effectiveness.

IIA's Practice Advisory 2120.A1-2: Using Control Self-Assessment for Assessing the Adequacy of Control Processes

Nature of This Practice Advisory

Control self-assessment (CSA) methodology can be used by managers and internal auditors for assessing the adequacy of the organization's risk management and control processes. Internal auditors can utilize CSA programs for gathering relevant information about risks and controls; for focusing the audit plan on high-risk, unusual areas; and to forge greater collaboration with operating managers and work teams. *Compliance with Practice Advisories is optional.*

1. Senior management is charged with overseeing the establishment, administration, and evaluation of the processes of risk management and control. Operating managers' responsibilities include assessment of the risks and controls in their units. Internal and external auditors provide varying degrees of assurance about the state of effectiveness of the risk management and control processes of the organization. Both managers and auditors have an interest in using techniques and tools that sharpen the focus and expand the efforts to assess risk management and control processes that are in place and to identify ways to improve their effectiveness.
2. A methodology encompassing self-assessment surveys and facilitated workshops called CSA is a useful and efficient approach for managers and internal auditors to collaborate in assessing and evaluating control procedures. In its purest form, CSA integrates business objectives and risks with control processes. Control self-assessment is also referred to as control/risk self-assessment or CRSA. Although CSA practitioners use a number of differing techniques and formats, most implemented programs share some key features and goals. An organization that uses self-assessment will have a formal, documented process that allows management and work teams that are directly involved in a business unit function, or process to participate in a structured manner for the purpose of
    - Identifying risks and exposures
    - Assessing the control processes that mitigate or manage those risks

- Developing action plans to reduce risks to acceptable levels
- Determining the likelihood of achieving the business objectives

3. The outcomes that may be derived from self-assessment methodologies are

   - People in business units become trained and experienced in assessing risks and associating control processes with managing those risks and improving the chances of achieving business objectives.
   - Informal, "soft" controls are more easily identified and evaluated.
   - People are motivated to take ownership of the control processes in their units, and corrective actions taken by the work teams are often more effective and timely.
   - The entire objectives-risks-controls infrastructure of an organization is subject to greater monitoring and continuous improvement.
   - Internal auditors become involved in and knowledgeable about the self-assessment process by serving as facilitators, scribes, and reporters for the work teams and as trainers of risk and control concepts supporting the CSA program.
   - Internal audit activity acquires more information about the control processes within the organization and can leverage that additional information in allocating their scarce resources so as to spend a greater effort in investigating and performing tests of business units or functions that have significant control weaknesses or high residual risks.
   - Management's responsibility for the risk management and control processes of the organization is reinforced, and managers will be less tempted to abdicate those activities to specialists, such as auditors.
   - The primary role of the internal audit activity will continue to include the validation of the evaluation process by performing tests and the expression of its professional judgment on the adequacy and effectiveness of the whole risk management and control systems.

4. The wide variety of approaches used for CSA processes in organizations reflects the differences in industry, geography, structure, organizational culture, degree of employee empowerment, dominant management style, and the manner of formulating strategies and policies. This observation suggests that the success of a particular type of CSA program in one enterprise may not be replicated in another organization. The CSA process should be customized to fit the unique characteristics of each organization. Also, the observation suggests that a CSA approach needs to be dynamic and change with the continual development of the organization.
5. The three primary forms of CSA programs are facilitated team workshops, surveys, and management-produced analysis. Organizations often combine more than one approach.
6. Facilitated team workshops gather information from work teams representing different levels in the business unit or function. The format of the workshop may be based on objectives, risks, controls, or processes.

   - The objective-based format focuses on the best way to accomplish a business objective. The workshop begins by identifying the controls currently in place to support the objective and then determining the residual risks remaining. The aim of the workshop is to decide whether the control procedures are working effectively and are resulting in residual risks within an acceptable level.
   - The risk-based format focuses on listing the risks to achieving an objective. The workshop begins by listing all possible barriers, obstacles, threats, and exposures that might prevent achieving an objective and then examining the control procedures to determine if they are sufficient to manage the key risks. The aim of the workshop is to determine significant residual risks. This format takes the work team through the entire objective-risks-controls formula.
   - The control-based format focuses on how well the controls in place are working. This format is different from the two above because the facilitator identifies the key risks and controls before the beginning of the workshop. During the workshop, the work team assesses how well the controls mitigate risks and promote the achievement of objectives. The aim of the workshop is to produce an analysis of the gap between how controls are working and how well management expects those controls to work.
   - The process-based format focuses on selected activities that are elements of a chain of processes. The processes are usually a series of related activities that go from some beginning point

to an end, such as the various steps in purchasing, product development, or revenue generation. This type of workshop usually covers the identification of the objectives of the whole process and the various intermediate steps. The aim of the workshop is to evaluate, update, validate, improve, and streamline the whole process and its component activities. This workshop format may have a greater breadth of analysis than a control-based approach by covering multiple objectives within the process and supporting concurrent management efforts, such as reengineering, quality improvement, and continuous improvement initiatives.

7. The survey form of CSA utilizes a questionnaire that tends to ask mostly simple "Yes-No" or "Have–Have Not" questions that are carefully written to be understood by the target recipients. Surveys are often used if the desired respondents are too numerous or widely dispersed to participate in a workshop. They are also preferred if the culture in the organization may hinder open, candid discussions in workshop settings or if management desires to minimize the time spent and costs incurred in gathering the information.
8. The form of self-assessment called "management-produced analyses" covers most other approaches by management groups to produce information about selected business processes, risk management activities, and control procedures. The analysis is often intended to reach an informed and timely judgment about specific characteristics of control procedures and is commonly prepared by a team in staff or support role. The internal auditor may synthesize this analysis with other information to enhance the understanding about controls and to share the knowledge with managers in business or functional units as part of the organization's CSA program.
9. All self-assessment programs are based on managers and members of the work teams possessing an understanding of risks and controls concepts and using those concepts in communications. For training sessions, to facilitate the orderly flow of workshop discussions and as a check on the completeness of the overall process, organizations often use a control framework such as the COSO (Committee of Sponsoring Organizations of the Treadway Commision and CoCo (Criteria of Control) models.
10. In the typical CSA facilitated workshop, a report will be largely created during the deliberations. A group consensus will be recorded for the various segments of the discussions, and the group will review the proposed final report before the end of the final session. Some programs will use anonymous voting techniques to ensure the free flow of information and viewpoints during the workshops and to aid in negotiating differences between viewpoints and interest groups.
11. Internal audit's investment in some CSA programs is fairly significant. It may sponsor, design, implement, and, in effect, own the process, conducting the training, supplying the facilitators, scribes, and reporters, and orchestrating the participation of management and work teams. In other CSA programs, internal audit's involvement is minimal, serving as interested party and consultant of the whole process and as ultimate verifier of the evaluations produced by the teams. In most programs, internal audit's investment in the organization's CSA efforts is somewhere between the two extremes just described. As the level of internal audit's involvement in the CSA program and individual workshop deliberations increases, the chief audit executive should monitor the objectivity of the internal audit staff, take steps to manage that objectivity (if necessary), and augment internal audit testing to ensure that bias or partiality do not affect the final judgments of the staff. *Standard* 1120 states: "Internal auditors should have an impartial, unbiased attitude and avoid conflicts of interest."
12. A CSA program augments the traditional role of internal audit activity by assisting management in fulfilling its responsibilities to establish and maintain risk management and control processes and to evaluate the adequacy of that system. Through a CSA program, the internal audit activity and the business units and functions collaborate to produce better information about how well the control processes are working and how significant the residual risks are.
13. Although providing staff support for the CSA program as facilitator and specialist, the internal audit activity often finds that it may reduce the effort spent in gathering information about control procedures and eliminate some testing. A CSA program should increase the coverage of assessing control processes across the organization, improve the quality of corrective actions made by the process owners, and focus internal audit's work on reviewing high-risk processes and unusual situations. It can focus on validating the evaluation conclusions produced by the CSA process, synthesizing the information gathered from the components of the organization, and expressing its overall judgment about the effectiveness of controls to senior management and the audit committee.

IIA's Practice Advisory 2120.A1-3: The Internal Auditor's Role in Quarterly Financial Reporting, Disclosures, and Management Certifications

Nature of This Practice Advisory

Internal auditors should consider this guidance regarding quarterly financial reports, disclosures, and management certifications related to requirements of the US Securities and Exchange Commission (SEC). While such requirements are specifically directed to US registrants of the SEC, they are also applicable to over 1,300 foreign registrants. In order to provide a higher level of confidence to stakeholders, a growing number of non–publicly held organizations are voluntarily adopting selected SEC requirements to demonstrate best practices for disclosures and controls over quarterly reporting. Internal auditors are also directed to Practice Advisory 2120.A1, "Assessing and Reporting on Control Processes," for additional guidance. *Compliance with Practice Advisories is optional.*

1. The strength of all financial markets depends on investor confidence. Events involving allegations of misdeeds by corporate executives, independent auditors, and other market participants have undermined that confidence. In response to this threat, the US Congress and a growing number of legislative bodies and regulatory agencies in other countries passed legislation and regulation affecting corporate disclosures and financial reporting. Specifically in the United States of America the Sarbanes-Oxley Act of 2002 (the Sarbanes-Oxley Act) enacted sweeping reform requiring additional disclosures and certifications of financial statements by principal executive and financial officers.
2. The new law challenges companies to devise processes that will permit senior officers to acquire the necessary assurances on which to base their personal certification. A key component of the certification process is the management of risk and internal controls over the recording and summarizing of financial information.

New Statutory Requirements

3. Section 302 of the Sarbanes-Oxley Act outlines the corporate responsibility for financial reports, and the SEC has issued guidance to implement the act. As adopted, SEC Rules 13a-14 and 15d-14 require an issuer's principal executive officer or officers and the principal financial officer or officers, or persons performing similar functions, to certify in each quarterly and annual report, including transition reports, filed or submitted by the issuer under Section 13(a) or 15(d) of the Exchange Act that

    - He or she has reviewed the report.
    - Based on his or her knowledge, the report does not contain any untrue statement of a material fact or omit a material fact necessary to make a statement, in light of the circumstances under which such statements are made, not misleading with respect to the period covered by the report.
    - Based on his or her knowledge, the financial statements, and other financial information included in the report, fairly present in all material respects the financial condition, results of operations and cash flows of the issuer as of, and for, the periods presented in the report.
    - He or she and the other certifying officers
        - Are responsible for establishing and maintaining "disclosure controls and procedures" [a newly defined term reflecting the concept of controls and procedures related to disclosure embodied in Section 302(a)(4) of the Act] for the issuer.
        - Have designed such disclosure controls and procedures to ensure that material information is made known to them, particularly during the period in which the periodic report is being prepared.
        - Have evaluated the effectiveness of the issuer's disclosure controls and procedures as of a date within ninety days prior to the filing date of the report.
        - Have presented in the report their conclusions about the effectiveness of the disclosure controls and procedures based on the required evaluation as of that date.
    - He or she and the other certifying officers have disclosed to the issuer's auditors and to the audit committee of the board of directors (or persons fulfilling the equivalent function)
        - All significant deficiencies in the design or operation of internal controls (a preexisting term relating to internal controls regarding financial reporting) that could adversely affect the is-

suer's ability to record, process, summarize, and report financial data and have identified for the issuer's auditors any material weaknesses in internal controls
- Any fraud, whether or not material, that involves management or other employees who have a significant role in the issuer's internal controls
- Whether there were significant changes in internal controls or in other factors that could significantly affect internal controls subsequent to the date of their evaluation, including any corrective actions with regard to significant deficiencies and material weaknesses

Recommended Actions for Internal Auditors

4. The following actions and considerations are offered to internal auditors as value-added services that can be provided regarding quarterly financial reports, disclosures, and management certifications related to requirements of the SEC and the Sarbanes-Oxley Act. These recommended actions are also offered as best practices to non–publicly held companies and other organizations seeking to adopt similar processes over quarterly financial reporting.

   a. The internal auditor's role in such processes may range from initial designer of the process, participant on a disclosure committee, coordinator or liaison between management and its auditors, to independent assessor of the process.
   b. All internal auditors involved in quarterly reporting and disclosure processes should have a clearly defined role and evaluate responsibilities with appropriate IIA *Consulting and Assurance Standards* and with guidance contained in related Practice Advisories.
   c. Internal auditors should ensure that organizations have a formal policy and documented procedures to govern processes for quarterly financial reports, related disclosures, and regulatory reporting requirements. Appropriate review of any policies and procedures by attorneys, external auditors, and other experts can offer additional comfort that policies and procedures are comprehensive and accurately reflect applicable requirements.
   d. Internal auditors should encourage organizations to establish a "disclosure committee" to coordinate the process and provide oversight to participants. Representatives from key areas of the organization should be represented on the committee, including key financial managers, legal counsel, risk management, internal audit, and any area providing input or data for the regulatory filings and disclosures. Normally the chief audit executive (CAE) should be a member of the disclosure committee. Consideration should be given to CAE status on the committee. CAEs who serve as committee chairs or regular or "voting" members need to be aware of independence considerations and are advised to review IIA *Standards* and related Practice Advisories for guidance and required disclosures. Status as an "ex-officio" member normally would not create independence problems.
   e. Internal auditors should periodically review and evaluate quarterly reporting and disclosure processes, disclosure committee activities, and related documentation, and provide management and the audit committee with an assessment of the process and assurance concerning overall operations and compliance with policies and procedures. Internal auditors whose independence may be impaired due to their assigned role in the process should ensure that management and the audit committee are able to obtain appropriate assurance about the process from other sources. Other sources can include internal self-assessments as well as third parties, such as external auditors and consultants.
   f. Internal auditors should recommend appropriate improvements to the policies, procedures, and process for quarterly reporting and related disclosures based on the results of an assessment of related activities. Recommended best practices for such activities may include all, or components of, the following tools and procedures, depending on the specific process used by each organization:

      - Properly documented policies, procedures, controls, and monitoring reports
      - Quarterly checklist of procedures and key control elements
      - Standardized control reports on key disclosure controls
      - Management self-assessments (i.e., CSA)
      - Sign-offs or representation statements from key managers
      - Review of draft regulatory filings prior to submission
      - Process maps to document the source of data elements for regulatory filings, key controls, and responsible parties for each element
      - Follow-up on previously reported outstanding items

- Consideration of internal audit reports issued during the period
- Special or specifically targeted reviews of high-risk, complex, and problem areas, including material accounting estimates, reserve valuations, off-balance-sheet activities, major subsidiaries, joint ventures, and special-purpose entities
- Observation of the "closing process" for the financial statements and related adjusting entries, including waived adjustments
- Conference calls with key management from remote locations to ensure appropriate consideration of and participation by all major components of the organization
- Review of potential and pending litigation, and contingent liabilities
- CAE report on internal control, issued at least annually, and possibly quarterly
- Regularly scheduled disclosure and audit committee meetings

g. Internal auditors should compare processes for complying with Section 302 of the Sarbanes-Oxley Act (quarterly financial reporting and disclosures) to procedures developed to comply with Section 404 concerning management's annual assessment and public report on internal controls. Processes designed to be similar or compatible will contribute to operational efficiencies and reduce the likelihood or risk for problems and errors to occur or go undetected. While processes and procedures may be similar, it is possible that the internal auditor's role may vary. In some organizations, the work of internal auditors may form the basis for management's assertions about internal control, while in other organizations, internal auditors may be called on to evaluate management's assessment.

  - The nature of internal audit's work, and use thereof, can potentially affect the treatment or degree of reliance placed on the internal auditor's work by the external auditor. Internal auditors should ensure that each participant's role is clarified and activities are coordinated and agreed on with management and the external auditors.
  - In organizations where management conducts its own assessment of controls as the basis for an opinion, internal auditors should evaluate management's assessment and supporting documentation.
  - Internal auditors should evaluate how internal audit report comments are classified and ensure that comments that may be subject to disclosure in quarterly certifications or the annual report on internal controls are appropriately communicated to management and the audit committee. Extra care should be taken to ensure such comments are adequately resolved in a timely manner.

IIA's Practice Advisory 2120.A1-4: Auditing the Financial Reporting Process

Nature of This Practice Advisory

This Practice Advisory explores the internal audit's role and responsibilities in an organization's financial reporting process. The roles of senior management, external auditors, and internal auditors are

- Executive management is the owner of the control environment and financial information, including the notes accompanying the financial statements and the accompanying disclosures in the financial report.
- The external auditor assures the financial report user that the reported information fairly presents the financial condition and result of operations of the organization in accordance with generally accepted accounting principles.
- The internal auditor performs procedures to provide a level of assurance to senior management and the audit or other committee of the governing board that controls surrounding the processes supporting the development of financial report are effective.

Practice Advisory 2060-2, "Relationship with the Audit Committee," covers the internal auditor's interactions with the audit committee. Practice Advisory 2120.A1-1, "Assessing and Reporting on Control Processes," discusses the evidence needed to assess a system of internal controls and form an opinion. Practice Advisory 2120.A1-3, "The Internal Auditor's Role in Quarterly Financial Reporting, Disclosures, and Management Certifications," provides guidance on the requirements of US Sarbanes-Oxley Act and the related rules of the US Securities and Exchange Commission. This Practice Advisory focuses on internal auditor relationships with senior management and the external auditor regarding the financial reporting process. *Compliance with Practice Advisories is optional.*

1. The published reports of corporate governance failures in the United States of America and other countries underscore the need for change to achieve greater accountability and transparency by all organizations—profit making, nonprofit, and governmental. Senior management, boards of directors, internal auditors, and external auditors are the cornerstones of the foundation on which effective organizational governance is built. Internal audit activity plays a key role in support of good organizational governance; it has a unique position to assist in improving an organization's operations by evaluating and improving the effectiveness of risk management, control, and governance processes. Recent initiatives have put the spotlight on the need for senior management to be more accountable for the information contained in an organization's financial reports. Senior management and the audit committee of many organizations are requesting additional services from the internal audit activity to improve the governance and financial reporting processes. These requests include evaluations of the organization's internal controls over financial reporting and the reliability and integrity of its financial reports.

Reporting on Internal Control

2. An organization's audit or other board committee and internal auditing activity have interlocking goals. The core role of the chief audit executive (CAE) is to ensure that the audit committee receives the support and assurance services it needs and requests. One of the primary objectives of the audit committee is oversight of the organization's financial reporting processes to ensure their reliability and fairness. The committee and senior management typically request that the internal audit activity perform sufficient audit work and gather other available information during the year to form an opinion on the adequacy and effectiveness of the internal control processes. The CAE normally communicates that overall evaluation, on a timely basis, to the committee. The committee will evaluate the coverage and adequacy of the CAE's report and may incorporate its conclusion in the committee's report to the governing board.
3. Internal audit activity's work plans and specific assurance engagements begin with a careful identification of the exposures facing the organization, and internal audit's work plan is based on the risks and the assessment of the risk management and controls processes maintained by management to mitigate those risks. Among the events and transactions included in the identification of risks are

   - New businesses—including mergers and acquisitions
   - New products and systems
   - Joint ventures and partnerships
   - Restructuring
   - Management estimates, budgets, and forecasts
   - Environmental matters
   - Regulatory compliance

A Framework for Internal Control

4. The assessment of a system of internal control of an organization should employ a broad definition of control. The IIA believes that the most effective internal control guidance available today is the report *Internal Control—Integrated* Framework, published in 1992 and 1994 by the Committee of Sponsoring Organizations (COSO) of the Treadway Commission. While use of the COSO model is widely accepted, it may be appropriate to use some other recognized and credible model. Sometimes regulatory or legal requirements will specify the use of a particular model or control design for an organization or industry within a country.
5. Several conclusions in the *Internal Control—Integrated Framework* report are relevant to this discussion.

   - Internal control is defined broadly; it is not limited to accounting controls and is not narrowly restricted to financial reporting.
   - While accounting and financial reports are important issues, there are other important aspects of the business, such as resource protection, operational efficiency and effectiveness, and compli-

ance with rules, regulations, and organization policies. These factors also have an impact on financial reporting.

- Internal control is management's responsibility and requires the participation of all persons within an organization, if it is to be effective.
- The control framework is tied to the business objectives and is flexible enough to be adaptable.

Reporting on the Effectiveness of Internal Control

6. The CAE should provide to the audit committee the internal audit's assessment of the effectiveness of the organization's system of controls, including its judgment on the adequacy of the control model or design. A governing board must rely on management to maintain an adequate and effective internal control system. It will reinforce that reliance with independent oversight. The board or its audit (or other designated) committee should ask the following questions, and the CAE may be expected to assist in answering them.

   (a) Is there a strong ethical environment and culture?

   - Do board members and senior executives set examples of high integrity?
   - Are performance and incentive targets realistic, or do they create the excessive pressure for short-term results?
   - Is the organization's code of conduct reinforced with training and top-down communication? Does the message reach the employees in the field?
   - Are the organization's communication channels open? Do all levels of management get the information they need?
   - Is there zero tolerance for fraudulent financial reporting at any level?

   (b) How does the organization identify and manage risks?

   - Is there a risk management process, and is it effective?
   - Is risk managed throughout the organization?
   - Are major risks candidly discussed with the board?

   (c) Is the control system effective?

   - Are the organization's controls over the financial reporting process comprehensive, including preparation of financial statements, related notes, and the other required and discretionary disclosures that are an integral part of the financial reports?
   - Do senior and line management demonstrate that they accept control responsibility?
   - Is there an increasing frequency of "surprises" occurring at the senior management, board, or public levels from the organization's reported financial results or in the accompanying financial disclosures?
   - Is there good communication and reporting throughout the organization?
   - Are controls seen as enhancing the achievement of objectives or as a "necessary evil"?
   - Are qualified people hired promptly, and do they receive adequate training?
   - Are problem areas fixed quickly and completely?

   (d) Is there strong monitoring?

   - Is the board independent of management, free of conflicts of interest, well informed, and inquisitive?
   - Does internal audit have the support of senior management and the audit committee?
   - Do the internal and external auditors have and use open lines of communication and private access to all members of senior management and the audit committee?
   - Is line management monitoring the control process?
   - Is there a program to monitor outsourced processes?

7. Internal controls cannot ensure success. Bad decisions, poor managers, or environmental factors can negate controls. Also, dishonest management may override controls and ignore or stifle communications from subordinates. An active and independent governing board that is coupled with open and truthful communications from all components of management and is assisted by capable financial, legal, and internal audit functions is capable of identifying problems and providing effective oversight.

Roles for the Internal Auditor

8. The CAE needs to review internal audit's risk assessment and audit plans for the year, if adequate resources have not been committed to helping senior management, the audit committee, and the external auditor with their responsibilities in the upcoming year's financial reporting regimentation. The financial reporting process encompasses the steps to create the information and prepare financial statements, related notes, and other accompanying disclosures in the organization's financial reports.
9. The CAE should allocate the internal audit's resources to the financial reporting, governance, and control processes consistent with the organization's risk assessment. The CAE should perform procedures that provide a level of assurance to senior management and the audit committee that controls surrounding the processes supporting the development of financial reports are adequately designed and effectively executed. The controls should be adequate to ensure the prevention and detection of significant errors, irregularities, incorrect assumptions and estimates, and other events that could result in inaccurate or misleading financial statements, related notes, or other disclosures.
10. The following are suggested topics that the CAE may consider in supporting the organization's governance process and the oversight responsibilities of the governing board and its audit committee (or other designated committee) to ensure the reliability and integrity of financial reports.

    (a) Financial reporting

    - Providing information relevant to the appointment of the independent accountants.
    - Coordinating audit plans, coverage, and scheduling with the external auditors.
    - Sharing audit results with the external auditors.
    - Communicating pertinent observations with the external auditors and audit committee about accounting policies and policy decisions (including accounting decisions for discretionary items and off-balance-sheet transactions), specific components of the financial reporting process, and unusual or complex financial transactions and events (e.g., related-party transactions, mergers and acquisitions, joint ventures, and partnership transactions).
    - Participating in the financial reports and disclosures review process with the audit committee, external auditors, and senior management; evaluating the quality of the financial reports, including those filed with regulatory agencies.
    - Assessing the adequacy and effectiveness of the organization's internal controls, specifically those controls over the financial reporting process; this assessment should consider the organization's susceptibility to fraud and the effectiveness of programs and controls to mitigate or eliminate those exposures.
    - Monitoring management's compliance with the organization's code of conduct and ensuring that ethical policies and other procedures promoting ethical behavior are being followed; an important factor in establishing an effective ethical culture in the organization is when members of senior management set a good example of ethical behavior and provide open and truthful communications to employees, the board, and outside stakeholders.

    (b) Corporate governance

    - Reviewing corporate policies relating to compliance with laws and regulations, ethics, conflict of interests, and the timely and thorough investigation of misconduct and fraud allegations.
    - Reviewing pending litigation or regulatory proceedings bearing on organizational risk and governance.
    - Providing information on employee conflicts of interest, misconduct, fraud, and other outcomes of the organization's ethical procedures and reporting mechanisms.

    (c) Corporate control

    - Reviewing the reliability and integrity of the organization's operating and financial information compiled and reported by the organization.
    - Performing an analysis of the controls for critical accounting policies and comparing them with preferred practices (e.g., transactions in which questions are raised about revenue recognition or off-balance-sheet accounting treatment should be reviewed for compliance with appropriate general accepted accounting standards).

- Evaluating the reasonableness of estimates and assumptions used in preparing operating and financial reports.
- Ensuring that estimates and assumptions included in disclosures or comments are in line with underlying organizational information and practices and with similar items reported by other companies, if appropriate.
- Evaluating the process of preparing, reviewing, approving, and posting journal entries.
- Evaluating the adequacy of controls in the accounting function.

IIA's Practice Advisory 2120.A4-1: Control Criteria

Nature of This Practice Advisory

Internal auditors should consider these suggestions when evaluating control criteria. This guidance is not intended to represent all the considerations that may be necessary during such an evaluation, but simply a recommended set of items that should be addressed. *Compliance with Practice Advisories is optional.*

1. Before controls can be evaluated, management should determine the level of risk they want to take in the area to be reviewed. Internal auditors should identify what that level of risk is. This should be identified in terms of reducing the potential impact of the key threats to the achievement of the major objectives for the area under review.
2. If management has not identified the key risks and the level of risk they want to take, the internal audit may be able to help them through the facilitation of risk identification workshops or other techniques used by the organization.
3. Once the risk level is determined, the controls currently in place can be assessed to determine how successful they are expected to be in reducing the risk to the desired level.

3.4 Governance

2130—Governance—The internal audit activity should assess and make appropriate recommendations for improving the governance process in its accomplishment of the following objectives:

- Promoting appropriate ethics and values within the organization
- Ensuring effective organizational performance management and accountability
- Effectively communicating risk and control information to appropriate areas of the organization
- Effectively coordinating the activities of and communicating information among the board, external and internal auditors and management

2130.A1—The internal audit activity should evaluate the design, implementation, and effectiveness of the organization's ethics-related objectives, programs, and activities.
2130.C1—Consulting engagement objectives should be consistent with the overall values and goals of the organization.

IIA's Practice Advisory 2130-1: Role of the Internal Audit Activity and Internal Auditor in the Ethical Culture of an Organization

Nature of This Practice Advisory

Internal auditors should consider this guidance following in determining the role to play in the ethical culture of an organization. This role can vary depending on the existence, lack of, or degree of development of the organization's ethical culture. This guidance is not intended to represent all the procedures that may be necessary for a comprehensive assurance or consulting engagement related to an organization's ethics culture. *Compliance with Practice Advisories is optional.*

1. This Practice Advisory underscores the importance of organizational culture in establishing the ethical climate of an enterprise and suggests the role that internal auditors could play in improving that ethical climate. Specifically, the Practice Advisory
   - Describes the nature of the governance process
   - Links it to the ethical culture of the organization
   - States that all people associated with the organization, and specifically internal auditors, should assume the role of ethics advocates

- Lists the characteristics of an enhanced ethical culture

Governance and Organizational Culture

2. An organization uses various legal forms, structures, strategies, and procedures to ensure that it
   (a) Complies with society's legal and regulatory rules
   (b) Satisfies the generally accepted business norms, ethical precepts, and social expectations of society
   (c) Provides overall benefit to society and enhances the interests of the specific stakeholders in both the long term and the short term
   (d) Reports fully and truthfully to its owners, regulators, other stakeholders, and general public to ensure accountability for its decisions, actions, conduct, and performance

   The way in which an organization chooses to conduct its affairs to meet those four responsibilities is commonly referred to as its governance process. The organization's governing body (i.e., a board of directors or trustees or a managing board) and its senior management are accountable for the effectiveness of the governance process.
3. An organization's governance practices reflect a unique and ever-changing culture that affects roles, specifies behavior, sets goals and strategies, measures performance, and defines the terms of accountability. That culture impacts the values, roles, and behavior that will be articulated and tolerated by the organization and determines how sensitive—thoughtful or indifferent—the enterprise is in meeting its responsibilities to society. Thus, how effective the overall governance process is in performing its expected function largely depends on the organization's culture.

Shared Responsibility for the Organization's Ethical Culture

4. All people associated with the organization share some responsibility for the state of its ethical culture. Because of the complexity and dispersion of decision-making processes in most enterprises, each individual should be encouraged to be an ethics advocate, whether the role is delegated officially or merely conveyed informally. Codes of conduct and statements of vision and policy are important declarations of the organization's values and goals, the behavior expected of its people, and the strategies for maintaining a culture that aligns with its legal, ethical, and societal responsibilities. A growing number of organizations have designated a chief ethics officer as counselor of executives, managers, and others and as champion within the organization for "doing the right thing."

Internal Audit Activity as Ethics Advocate

5. Internal auditors and the internal audit activity should take an active role in support of the organization's ethical culture. They possess a high level of trust and integrity within the organization and the skills to be effective advocates of ethical conduct. They have the competence and capacity to appeal to the enterprise's leaders, managers, and other employees to comply with the legal, ethical, and societal responsibilities of the organization.
6. The internal audit activity may assume one of several different roles as an ethics advocate. Those roles include chief ethics officer (ombudsman, compliance officer, management ethics counselor, or ethics expert), member of an internal ethics council, or assessor of the organization's ethical climate. In some circumstances, the role of chief ethics officer may conflict with the independence attribute of the internal audit activity.

Assessment of the Organization's Ethical Climate

7. At a minimum, the internal audit activity should periodically assess the state of the ethical climate of the organization and the effectiveness of its strategies, tactics, communications, and other processes in achieving the desired level of legal and ethical compliance. Internal auditors should evaluate the effectiveness of the following features of an enhanced, highly effective ethical culture:
   (a) Formal code of conduct that is clear and understandable, and related statements, policies (including procedures covering fraud and corruption), and other expressions of aspiration
   (b) Frequent communications and demonstrations of expected ethical attitudes and behavior by the influential leaders of the organization

(c) Explicit strategies to support and enhance the ethical culture with regular programs to update and renew the organization's commitment to an ethical culture
(d) Several easily accessible ways for people to confidentially report alleged violations of the code, policies, and other acts of misconduct
(e) Regular declarations by employees, suppliers, and customers that they are aware of the requirements for ethical behavior in transacting the organization's affairs
(f) Clear delegation of responsibilities to ensure that ethical consequences are evaluated, confidential counseling is provided, allegations of misconduct are investigated, and case findings are properly reported
(g) Easy access to learning opportunities to enable all employees to be ethics advocates
(h) Positive personnel practices that encourage every employee to contribute to the ethical climate of the organization
(i) Regular surveys of employees, suppliers, and customers to determine the state of the ethical climate in the organization
(j) Regular reviews of the formal and informal processes within the organization that could potentially create pressures and biases that would undermine the ethical culture
(k) Regular reference and background checks as part of hiring procedures, including integrity tests, drug screening, and similar measures

MULTIPLE-CHOICE QUESTIONS (1-51)

1. Following a negative performance evaluation by a supervisor, a staff auditor went to the audit director to seek a change in the evaluation. The director was familiar with the auditor's performance and agreed with the evaluation. The director agreed to meet and discuss the situation. Which of the following is the best course of action for the director to take?

a. Have the supervisor participate in the meeting, so that there is no misunderstanding about the facts.
b. Have a human resources administrator present to ensure that improper statements are not made.
c. Meet privately with the employee. Tell the employee of the director's agreement with the performance evaluation and express interest in any additional facts the employee may wish to present.
d. Meet privately with the employee. Encourage discussion by asking for the employee's side of the issue and disclaiming any agreement with the supervisor.

2. The requirements for staffing level, education and training, and audit research should be included in

a. The internal auditing department's charter.
b. The internal auditing department's policies and procedures manual.
c. The annual plan for the internal auditing department.
d. Job descriptions for the various staff positions.

3. Which of the following activities is **not** included in determining the audit schedule?

a. Developing audit programs.
b. Assessing risk factors.
c. Planning workload requirements.
d. Identifying auditable locations.

4. The internal audit director of a multinational company must form an audit team to examine a newly acquired subsidiary in another country. Consideration should be given to which of the following factors?

I. Local customs.
II. Language skills of the auditor.
III. Experience of the auditor.
IV. Monetary exchange rate.

a. I, II, and III.
b. II, III, and IV.
c. I and III.
d. I and II.

5. A quality assurance program of an internal audit department provides reasonable assurance that audit work conforms to applicable standards. Which of the following activities are designed to provide feedback on the effectiveness of an audit department?

I. Proper supervision.
II. Proper training.
III. Internal reviews.
IV. External reviews.

a. I, II, and III.
b. II, III, and IV.
c. I, III, and IV.
d. I, II, III, and IV.

6. If the internal audit staff does **not** have the skills to perform a particular task, a specialist could be brought in from

I. The organization's external audit firm.
II. An outside consulting firm.
III. The department currently being audited.
IV. A college or university.

a. I and II.
b. II and IV.
c. I, II, and III.
d. I, II, and IV.

7. The **best** rationale for rotating internal auditors so that different individuals are assigned to consecutive audits of a given auditee is to

a. Prevent burnout on the part of the internal auditor, which may lead to excessive turnover in the internal audit department.
b. Promote rapid professional development on the part of internal auditors by exposing them to the full range of organizational activities.
c. Increase the diligence exercised by internal auditors who know that the quality of their work will be apparent to the next set of internal auditors.
d. Avoid the development of bias toward a given auditee.

8. Which of the following activities does **not** constitute audit supervision?

a. Preparing a preliminary audit program.
b. Providing appropriate instructions to the auditors.
c. Reviewing audit work papers.
d. Seeing that audit objectives are achieved.

9. The audit team leader is **least** likely to have a primary role in

a. Allocating budget audit hours among assigned staff.
b. Updating the permanent files.
c. Reviewing the working papers.
d. Preparing the critique sheet for the audit.

10. In which of the following duties would the audit director **least** likely have a primary role?

a. Determine the need for expanded testing.
b. Review the summary findings sheet.
c. Select or approve team members.
d. Organize and draft the audit report.

11. An element of authority that should be included in the charter of the internal auditing department is

a. Identification of the operational departments which the audit department must audit.
b. Identification of the types of disclosures which should be made to the audit committee.
c. Access to records, personnel, and physical properties relevant to the performance of audits.
d. Access to the external auditor's working papers.

12. Having been given the task of developing a performance appraisal system for evaluating the audit performance of a large internal auditing staff, you should

a. Provide for an explanation of the appraisal criteria methods at the time the appraisal results are discussed with the internal auditor.

b. Provide general information concerning the frequency of evaluations and the way evaluations will be performed without specifying their timing and uses.
c. Provide primarily for the evaluation of criteria such as diligence, initiative, and tact.
d. Provide primarily for the evaluation of specific accomplishments directly related to the performance of the audit program.

13. The key factor to the success of an audit organization's human resources program is
a. An informal program for developing and counseling staff.
b. A compensation plan based on years of experience.
c. A well-developed set of selection criteria.
d. A program for recognizing the special interests of individual staff members.

14. Which of the following would be the **best** source of an internal audit director's information for planning staffing requirements?
a. Discussions of audit needs with executive management and the audit committee.
b. Review of audit staff education and training records.
c. Review audit staff size and composition of similar-size companies in the same industry.
d. Interviews with existing audit staff.

15. Which of the following is most essential for guiding the audit staff in maintaining daily compliance with the department's standards of performance?
a. Quality control reviews.
b. Position descriptions.
c. Performance appraisals.
d. Policies and procedures.

16. You have been selected to develop an internal auditing department for your company. Your approach would most likely be to hire
a. Internal auditors each of whom possesses all the skills required to handle all audit assignments.
b. Inexperienced personnel and train them the way the company wants them trained.
c. Degreed accountants since most audit work is accounting related.
d. Internal auditors who collectively have the knowledge and skills needed to complete all internal audit assignments.

17. The director of a newly formed internal auditing department is in the process of drafting a formal written charter for the department. Which one of the following items, related to the operational effectiveness of the internal audit department, should be included in the charter?
a. The frequency of the audits to be performed.
b. The manner by which audit findings will be reported.
c. The procedures which the internal auditors will employ in investigating and reporting fraud.
d. The internal auditors' unlimited access to those records, personnel, and physical properties that are relevant to the performance of the audits.

18. A director of internal auditing has reviewed credentials, checked references, and interviewed a candidate for a staff position. The director concludes that the candidate has a thorough understanding of internal auditing techniques, accounting, and management. However, the director notes that the candidate has limited knowledge of economics and computer science. Which of the following actions would be **most** appropriate?
a. Reject the candidate because of the lack of knowledge required by the *Standards*.
b. Offer the candidate a position despite the lack of knowledge in certain essential areas.
c. Encourage the candidate to obtain additional training in economics and computer science and then reapply.
d. Offer the candidate a position if other staff members possess sufficient knowledge in economics and computer science.

19. Which audit planning tool is general in nature and is used to ensure adequate audit coverage over time?
a. The long-range schedule.
b. The audit program.
c. The department budget.
d. The department charter.

20. A professional engineer applied for a position in the internal auditing department of a high-technology firm. The engineer became interested in the position after observing several internal auditors while they were auditing the engineering department. The director of internal auditing
a. Should not hire the engineer because of the lack of knowledge of internal auditing standards.
b. May hire the engineer in spite of the lack of knowledge of internal auditing standards.
c. Should not hire the engineer because of the lack of knowledge of accounting and taxes.
d. May hire the engineer because of the knowledge of internal auditing gained in the previous position.

Items 21 through 23 are based on the following:

Upon being appointed, a new director of internal auditing found an inexperienced audit staff that was over budget on most audits. A detailed review of audit working papers revealed no evidence of progressive reviews by audit supervisors. Additionally, there was no evidence that a quality assurance program existed.

21. As a means of controlling projects and avoiding time-budget overruns, decisions to revise time budgets for an audit should normally be made
a. Immediately after the preliminary survey.
b. When a significant deficiency has been substantiated.
c. When inexperienced audit staff is assigned to an audit.
d. Immediately after expanding tests to establish reliability of findings.

22. Determining that audit objectives have been met is part of the overall supervision of an audit assignment and is the ultimate responsibility of the
a. Staff internal auditor.
b. Audit committee.
c. Internal auditing supervisor.
d. Director of internal auditing.

23. To properly evaluate the operations of an internal auditing department, a quality assurance program should include
a. Periodic supervision of internal audit work on a sample basis.
b. Internal reviews, by other than the internal audit staff, to appraise the quality of department operations.
c. External reviews at least once every three years by qualified persons who are independent of the organization.
d. Periodic rotation of audit managers.

24. The internal auditing department of a large corporation has established its operating plan and budget for the coming year. The operating plan is restricted to the following categories: a prioritized listing of all audits, staffing, a detailed expense budget, and the commencement date of each audit. Which of the following **best** describes the major deficiency of this operating plan?
a. Requests by management for special projects are not considered.
b. Opportunities to achieve operating benefits are ignored.
c. Measurability criteria and targeted dates of completion are not provided.
d. Knowledge, skills, and disciplines required to perform work are ignored.

25. The capabilities of individual staff members are key features in the effectiveness of an internal auditing department. Select the primary consideration used when staffing an internal auditing department.
a. Background checks.
b. Job descriptions.
c. Continuing education.
d. Organizational orientation.

26. Internal audit staff members should be afforded an appropriate means through which they can discuss problems and receive updates regarding departmental policies. The most appropriate forum for this objective is
a. The department's informal communication lines.
b. Intradepartment memoranda.
c. Staff meetings.
d. Employee evaluation conferences.

27. The peer review process can be performed internally or externally. A distinguishing feature of the external review is its objective to
a. Identify tasks that can be performed better.
b. Determine if audit activities meet professional standards.
c. Set forth the recommendations for improvement.
d. Provide an independent evaluation.

28. Exit conferences serve to ensure the accuracy of the information used by an internal auditor. A secondary purpose of an exit conference is to
a. Get immediate action on a recommendation.
b. Improve relations with auditees.
c. Agree to the appropriate distribution of the final report.
d. Brief senior management on the results of the audit.

29. The advantage attributed to the establishment of internal auditing field offices for work at remote locations is best described as
a. The possibility of increased objectivity of personnel assigned to a field office.
b. A reduction of travel time and related travel expense.
c. The increased ease of maintaining uniform company-wide standards.
d. More contact with senior audit personnel leading to an increase in control.

30. The director of internal auditing is preparing the work schedule for the next budget year and has limited audit resources. In deciding whether to schedule the purchasing or the personnel department for an audit, which of the following would be the **least** important factor?
a. There have been major changes in operations in one of the departments.
b. The audit staff has recently added an individual with expertise in one of the areas.
c. There are more opportunities to achieve operating benefits in one of the departments than in the other.
d. The potential for loss is significantly greater in one department than the other.

31. According to the IIA *Standards*, an internal auditing department's activity reports should
a. List the material findings of major audits.
b. List unresolved findings.
c. Report the weekly activities of the individual auditors.
d. Compare audits completed with audits planned.

32. The best means for the internal auditing department to determine whether its goal of implementing broader audit coverage of functional activities has been met is through
a. Accumulation of audit findings by auditable area.
b. Comparison of the audit plan to actual audit activity.
c. Surveys of management satisfaction with the internal auditing function.
d. Implementation of a quality assurance program.

33. Why should organizations require auditees to promptly reply and outline the corrective action that has been implemented on reported deficiencies?
a. To remove items from the "pending" list as soon as possible.
b. To effect savings or to institute compliance as early as possible.
c. To indicate concurrence with the audit findings.
d. To ensure that the audit schedule is kept up to date.

34. Which of the following factors serves as a direct input to the internal auditing department's financial budget?
a. Audit work schedules.
b. Activity reports.
c. Past effectiveness of the internal auditing department in identifying cost savings.
d. Auditing department's charter.

35. While attending a social function, an internal auditor described to a group of friends the elements of a sensitive audit on which he was working. The internal auditing director's best avenue for proceeding is to

a. Fire the auditor to set an example for other auditors.
b. Remove the auditor from all audits in that area or in other sensitive areas.
c. Reprimand the auditor for "talking shop" at a social function.
d. Explain that the act is an ethical violation of the profession and that further such action could result in dismissal or other serious effects.

36. The internal auditing department for a large corporation recently concluded an audit of sales department travel expenses. Which of the following groups should receive a copy of the audit report?
a. Sales director and vice president for marketing.
b. Chairman of the board, chief operating officer, and vice president for marketing.
c. Chairman of the board, controller, and sales director.
d. Chief financial officer, sales director, and chief executive officer.

37. External review of an internal auditing department is **not** likely to evaluate
a. Adherence to the internal auditing department's charter.
b. Compliance with the IIA *Standards.*
c. Detailed cost-benefit analysis of the internal auditing department.
d. Audit planning documents, particularly those submitted to senior management and the audit committee.

38. An internal auditing manager has a small team of employees, but each individual is self-motivated and could be termed a "high achiever." The audit manager has been given a particularly difficult assignment. Even for a high achiever, the probability that this job can be completed by one individual by the required deadline is low. Select the best course for the audit manager.
a. Assign one individual since high achievers thrive on high risks.
b. Assign two staff members to moderate the risk of failure.
c. Assign the entire staff to ensure the risk of failure is low.
d. Ask company management to cancel the job.

39. Recent criticism of an internal auditing department suggested that audit coverage was not providing adequate feedback to senior management on the processes used in the organization's key lines of business. The problem was further defined as lack of feedback on the recent implementation of automated support systems. Which two functions does the director of internal auditing need to improve?
a. Staffing and communicating.
b. Staffing and decision making.
c. Planning and organizing.
d. Planning and communicating.

40. In some cultures and organizations, managers insist that the internal auditing function is not needed to provide a critical assessment of the organization's operations. A management attitude such as this will most probably have an adverse affect on the internal auditing department's
a. Operating budget variance.
b. Charter.
c. Performance appraisals.
d. Policies and procedures.

41. Successful consultative communication in an internal audit is partially based on feedback from auditees about auditors' actions during the audit. This feedback
a. Should go only to senior management as a means of reviewing the auditors.
b. Should go only to the auditors to help them improve their audit performance.
c. Should go to both management and the auditors to ensure business value is being added.
d. Will keep auditees on the defensive regarding the auditors.

42. Which of the following components of the enterprise risk management (ERM) framework addresses processes and people in an organization?
a. Strategic risks.
b. Operational risks.
c. Financial risks.
d. Hazard risks.

43. Which of the following is **not** the goal of enterprise risk management (ERM) initiatives?
a. Integrating risks.
b. Creating shareholder value.
c. Protecting shareholder value.
d. Enhancing shareholder value.

44. The scope of enterprise risk management (ERM) encompasses which of the following:

I. Creating opportunities.
II. Derisking opportunities.
III. Analyzing strengths.
IV. Focusing on weaknesses.

a. I and II.
b. I and III.
c. III and IV.
d. I, III, and IV.

45. Enterprise risk management (ERM) focuses on which of the following:
a. Value-added potential.
b. Risk management process.
c. Asset management principles.
d. Management accountability.

46. The role and focus of the internal audit function in enterprise risk management (ERM) with the objective of improving corporate governance includes which of the following:

I. Follow-up on ERM scorecards.
II. Internal controls for ERM.
III. The IIA's *Standards* on ERM.
IV. Follow-up on ERM metrics.

a. I and II.
b. II and III.
c. I and IV.
d. III and IV.

47. Which of the following attributes of the internal audit department can hinder the implementation of enterprise risk management (ERM) in the auditor's organization?

I. Control-based audit approach.
II. Use of traditional auditing tools.
III. Consultant role.
IV. Facilitation skills.

a. I and II.
b. II and III.
c. I and IV.
d. III and IV.

48. Corporate governance is concerned with
a. The trend toward more women on boards of directors.
b. Hostile takeovers becoming the norm.
c. The legitimacy of state charters issued in Delaware.
d. The relative roles, rights, and accountability of such stakeholder groups as owners, board members, managers, employees, and others.

49. The major issue embedded in the structure of modern corporations that has contributed to the corporate governance problem has been
a. Excessive executive compensation.
b. Early retirement programs, such as the one implemented by IBM.
c. The separation of ownership from control.
d. Union domination of the proxy machinery.

50. The method by which a company exists and describes the basic terms of its existence is
a. Corporate governance.
b. Corporate charter.
c. Corporate ownership.
d. Compensation issues.

51. Which of the following is not a proper role of corporate board of directors?
a. Guardian.
b. Governance.
c. Guarantor.
d. Guidance.

MULTIPLE-CHOICE ANSWERS AND EXPLANATIONS

1. c __ __	12. d __ __	23. c __ __	34. a __ __	45. a __ __
2. c __ __	13. c __ __	24. c __ __	35. d __ __	46. c __ __
3. a __ __	14. a __ __	25. b __ __	36. a __ __	47. a __ __
4. a __ __	15. d __ __	26. c __ __	37. c __ __	48. d __ __
5. c __ __	16. d __ __	27. d __ __	38. b __ __	49. c __ __
6. d __ __	17. d __ __	28. b __ __	39. d __ __	50. b __ __
7. d __ __	18. d __ __	29. b __ __	40. b __ __	51. c __ __
8. a __ __	19. a __ __	30. b __ __	41. c __ __	
9. b __ __	20. b __ __	31. d __ __	42. b __ __	
10. d __ __	21. a __ __	32. b __ __	43. a __ __	1st: __/51 = __%
11. c __ __	22. d __ __	33. b __ __	44. a __ __	2nd: __/51 = __%

1. (c) A private conversation signals to the employee that the director is interested in what he or she has to say and will not be measuring his or her words against those of another. However, the director must establish a position and show support for the supervisor. There may be more than one valid viewpoint, but that does not necessarily mean that the employee's is valid. Choice (a) is incorrect. The supervisor, as author of a critical performance review, will only add to the element of management intimidation. Choice (b) is incorrect. Again, the presence of a third party would inhibit the director's listening effectiveness. Unless the director thinks the auditor's concerns are so serious that the human resources department must be informed, it is preferable to meet with the employee privately. Choice (d) is incorrect. It is never appropriate to mislead an employee in order to obtain information or to determine the employee's view on a matter.

Subject Area: Internal audit—organizational governance. Source: CIA 597, I-21.

2. (c) The annual plan should be comprised of both an audit schedule and a budget and, as such, should include all of these issues. Choice (a) is incorrect. The charter outlines the purpose, authority, and responsibilities of the department, not the details related to staffing and such. Choice (b) is incorrect. The policies and procedures manual spells out how audits should be conducted. It does not cover areas such as staffing levels. Choice (d) is incorrect. Job descriptions do not reflect staffing level requirements.

Subject Area: Internal audit—organizational governance. Source: CIA 590, II-8.

3. (a) The development of audit programs occurs during the planning phase of an individual audit. It is not included within the scope of developing the audit schedule. Choices (b), (c), and (d) are incorrect. Each choice is considered to determine the audit schedule.

Subject Area: Internal audit—organizational governance. Source: CIA 594, III-3.

4. (a) In addition to language skills, local customs must be considered. For example, gender and ethnic compatibility may be important in some Middle Eastern countries because religious restrictions and incompatibilities are relevant. As always, experience levels are relevant in making audit assignments. Choice (b) is incorrect. The Monetary Exchange Rate would not be a factor in determining the needed traits of the team members. Choice (c) is incorrect. Includes appropriate factors, but does not identify all the acceptable choices. Choice (d) is incorrect. It includes an incomplete answer. See choice (c).

Subject Area: Internal audit—organizational governance. Source: CIA 594, III-4.

5. (c) The purpose of a quality assurance program is to evaluate the operations of the internal audit department. The IIA *Standards* note that a program should include supervision, internal reviews, and external reviews. Choices (a), (b), and (d) are incorrect. Proper training is an important component of maintaining a current staff, but does not provide feedback.

Subject Area: Internal audit—organizational governance. Source: CIA 594, III-5.

6. (d) The key point is independence and objectivity. A specialist from the department currently being audited would not be independent due to his or her natural bias toward that department. Choices (a) and (b) are incorrect. They include acceptable consultants, but do not identify all the acceptable choices. Choice (c) is incorrect. A specialist from the same department is unacceptable since the person would not be either independent or objective.

Subject Area: Internal audit—organizational governance. Source: CIA 594, III-7.

7. (d) Choice (d) is the primary reason. The alternatives may be desirable, but they are not the basis for the rotation preference. Choice (a) is incorrect. It is a secondary reason. For example, auditor burnout can be reduced with less travel. Choice (b) is incorrect. It is a secondary reason. Professional development can be obtained in other ways, such as attending conferences, seminars, and taking the CIA exam. Choice (c) is incorrect. It is a secondary reason. This approach establishes a precedent or standard for others to follow.

Subject Area: Internal audit—organizational governance. Source: CIA 594, III-91.

8. (a) It is a planning task. Choices (b), (c), and (d) are incorrect. Each choice is a supervisory task.

Subject Area: Internal audit—organizational governance. Source: CIA 594, III-92.

9. (b) This is a task most likely performed by the audit staff. Choices (a), (c), and (d) are incorrect. Each choice is a common team leader task.

Subject Area: Internal audit—organizational governance. Source: CIA 594, III-93.

10. **(d)** It is a task most likely performed by the team leader. Choices (a), (b), and (c) are incorrect. Each choice is a common audit director task.

Subject Area: Internal audit—organizational governance. Source: CIA 594, III-94.

11. **(c)** The auditor must have access to all audit evidence in order to fulfill his or her obligations and responsibilities. Choice (a) is incorrect. The internal audit department should not specifically identify what activities will be audited. Choice (b) is incorrect. The auditor is obligated to make all needed disclosures to the audit committee. Choice (d) is incorrect. Access to the external auditor's working papers cannot be guaranteed in the charter.

Subject Area: Internal audit—organizational governance. Source: CIA 1193, I-3.

12. **(d)** The appraisal of audit performance should deal primarily with specific accomplishments related to audits. This provides a more objective appraisal than focusing on traits, which are largely subjective. Choice (a) is incorrect. The persons whose performance is being appraised should be made aware of the criteria and methods at the time they begin the employment, not at the time of the performance review. Choice (b) is incorrect. The frequency and use of the evaluation are important criteria that should be clearly communicated. Choice (c) is incorrect. The criteria named are traits, not accomplishments. Although traits are important, a performance evaluation system for evaluating audit performance should primarily focus on specific accomplishments not traits.

Subject Area: Internal audit—organizational governance. Source: CIA 591, I-9.

13. **(c)** Selection of individuals with the attributes and education needed for internal auditing is essential if the staff is to develop properly. In any organization, whether it is audit or nonaudit function, a well-developed set of selection criteria is important. Choice (a) is incorrect. The success of any training program will be heavily dependent on the attributes of those being trained. Choice (b) is incorrect. While compensation is an important factor in attracting and retaining staff, it is probably not the most important in staff development. Choice (d) is incorrect. It is not the best answer because such a program should be fair and equitable to all staff members.

Subject Area: Internal audit—organizational governance. Source: CIA 591, I-10.

14. **(a)** It is a good source of information concerning staff size or skill requirements. Choice (b) is incorrect. It is not the best choice since there is no obvious link with scheduled work. Choice (c) is incorrect. That would not account for the unique needs of a particular organization. Choice (d) is incorrect. It is not the best choice since there is no obvious link with scheduled work.

Subject Area: Internal audit—organizational governance. Source: CIA 591, I-11.

15. **(d)** Comprehensive policies and procedures provided by the director of internal audit guide the audit staff on a daily basis to ensure compliance with department's standards of performance. Choice (a) is incorrect. Quality control reviews would evaluate compliance and not serve as a daily guide to the audit staff. Choice (b) is incorrect. Position descriptions provide the purpose description and responsibilities of individual positions but are not effective in the day-to-day management of the function. Choice (c) is incorrect. Performance evaluations are a periodic function and will not be effective on a day-to-day basis.

Subject Area: Internal audit—organizational governance. Source: CIA 591, I-12.

16. **(d)** Having a collective mix of knowledge and skills is an integral part of the IIA's *Standards*. No internal audit department can have a credible program without this mix. Choice (a) is incorrect. The scope of internal auditing is so broad it is not possible for one individual to have the requisite expertise in all areas. Choice (b) is incorrect. It is desirable to have various skill levels to match auditors appropriately with varying assignment complexities. It is also necessary to have experienced auditors available to train and supervise less experienced staff members. Choice (c) is incorrect. Many skills are needed in internal auditing. Computer skills are widely needed in companies that perform IT audits. Many industries find it necessary to have the skills of engineers and other disciplines available on a regular basis.

Subject Area: Internal audit—organizational governance. Source: CIA 591, II-8.

17. **(d)** The IIA's *Standards* state that the charter should include the internal auditors' access to those records, personnel, and physical properties that are relevant to their work. Having limitations on such access would impact the operational effectiveness of the internal audit department because the internal auditor would not be able to conduct the audit in the proper approach that he designed it. Choice (a) is incorrect. The *Standards* state that "the charter should (a) establish the department's position within the organization; (b) authorize access to records, personnel, and physical properties relevant to the performance of audits; and (c) define the scope of internal auditing activities." Accordingly, not only is the frequency of audits not included in the charter, but also such information is not related to the operational effectiveness of the internal audit department. Choice (b) is incorrect. The manner of reporting audit findings (how they are reported, to whom they will be reported, etc.) is not included in the charter and is not related to operational effectiveness of the internal audit department. Choice (c) is incorrect. The procedures to be employed by internal auditors in investigating and reporting fraud are not included in the charter.

Subject Area: Internal audit—organizational governance. Source: CIA 1193, II-4.

18. **(d)** This is the most realistic way to address the department's staffing needs. Choice (a) is incorrect. The IIA S*tandards* state the general subjects that staff should possess knowledge of but clearly state that every auditor need not possess knowledge of all of them. Choice (b) is incorrect. The department's needs may be for additional expertise in economics or computer science. Choice (c) is incorrect. This may be good advice, but it does not adequately address the department's present needs.

Subject Area: Internal audit—organizational governance. Source: CIA 1193, II-5.

19. **(a)** The long-range program gives evidence of coverage of key functions at planned intervals. Choice (b) is incorrect. The audit program is limited in scope to a particular project. Choice (c) is incorrect. The department budget may be used to justify head count, but it is not used to ensure adequate audit coverage over time. Choice (d) is incorrect. The department charter is not an audit planning tool.

Subject Area: Internal audit—organizational governance. Source: CIA 592, I-4.

20. **(b)** Internal auditing standards are required to be known by the department collectively. Individual internal auditing staff members may, however, bring special skills to the department instead of specific knowledge of internal auditing standards. Choice (a) is incorrect. Each new employee of an internal auditing department is not required to have knowledge of internal auditing standards. It is required that the department collectively has this knowledge. Choice (c) is incorrect. Each individual internal auditor is not required to have knowledge of accounting or taxes. Choice (d) is incorrect. What knowledge that was acquired by observing is irrelevant to the skills necessary for internal auditing.

Subject Area: Internal audit—organizational governance. Source: CIA 592, I-5.

21. **(a)** Time budgets should be appraised for revision after the preliminary survey and preparation of the audit program. Choice (b) is incorrect. When a deficiency has been substantiated, no further audit work is required. Choice (c) is incorrect. The assignment of inexperienced staff should have no effect on the time budget. Choice (d) is incorrect. Expanded tests should have no effect on the time budget; the budget would have already been expanded as necessary.

Subject Area: Internal audit—organizational governance. Source: CIA 592, I-15.

22. **(d)** The director of internal auditing is responsible for supervision, including determining that audit objectives are being met. Choices (a), (b), and (c) are incorrect. According to the *Standards*, the director of internal auditing is responsible for supervision.

Subject Area: Internal audit—organizational governance. Source: CIA 592, I-16.

23. **(c)** External reviews should be conducted at least once every three years. Choice (a) is incorrect. Supervision should be carried out continually, not just on a periodic test basis. Choice (b) is incorrect. Internal reviews should be conducted by internal auditors and should focus on specific audit projects. Choice (d) is incorrect. Periodic rotation of audit managers is not required.

Subject Area: Internal audit—organizational governance. Source: CIA 592, I-17.

24. **(c)** This is a requirement of the *Standards.* Choices (a) and (b) are incorrect. Prioritizing audits would consider these factors. Choice (d) is incorrect. Staffing for each audit would include this consideration.

Subject Area: Internal audit—organizational governance. Source: CIA 592, II-20.

25. **(b)** Properly formulated job descriptions provide a basis for the identifying job qualifications (including training and experience). Choice (a) is incorrect. Background checks help assure that statements made by prospective employees are accurate. However, they are not the primary requisite. Choice (c) is incorrect. Continuing education occurs after the proper people are hired. Choice (d) is incorrect. A thorough orientation helps the new employee become productive more rapidly. However, it will not overcome hiring the wrong person.

Subject Area: Internal audit—organizational governance. Source: CIA 1192, II-8.

26. **(c)** Formal staff meetings provide the best opportunity for ensuring that issues are addressed timely and efficiently. Choice (a) is incorrect. Informal communication is not the most appropriate forum. Choice (b) is incorrect. Memoranda are generally impersonal and do not afford a good opportunity for maximum exchange of ideas. Choice (d) is incorrect. The employee evaluation conference is not a timely place to discuss problems and receive updates.

Subject Area: Internal audit—organizational governance. Source: CIA 1192, II-9.

27. **(d)** External review process will provide independent evaluation for management and the audit committee. Choice (a) is incorrect. Internal peer review process will identify things that can be done better. Choice (b) is incorrect. Internal review process will assess if audit activities meet professional standards. Choice (c) is incorrect. Internal review process will set forth recommendations for improvement.

Subject Area: Internal audit—organizational governance. Source: CIA 1192, II-10.

28. **(b)** The exit conference can be used to allow operating management to air their views and to present any operational objections to specific recommendations. Choice (a) is incorrect. An interim report would have been used to accomplish this. Choice (c) is incorrect. The distribution of reports is not a secondary purpose of an exit conference. Choice (d) is incorrect. Senior management should be given a greatly condensed view of the results of an audit.

Subject Area: Internal audit—organizational governance. Source: CIA 1192, II-14.

29. **(b)** Advantage of field office. Choice (a) is incorrect. Objectivity of field office personnel decreases. Choice (c) is incorrect. Disadvantage: decreases ease of maintaining standards. Choice (d) is incorrect. Senior audit personnel are expected to be at corporate level.

Subject Area: Internal audit—organizational governance. Source: CIA 1192, II-2.

30. **(b)** Audit needs, not auditor skill availability, should drive audit schedules. Choices (a), (c), and (d) are incorrect. Each is an important factor according to the *Standards*.

Subject Area: Internal audit—organizational governance. Source: CIA 592, II-11.

31. **(d)** This information is a status report to be provided to the audit oversight authority. Choices (a), (b), and (c) are incorrect. Each one of them is not an activity report as defined by the *Standards.*

Subject Area: Internal audit—organizational governance. Source: CIA 592, II-7.

32. **(b)** Comparison of the plan to actual activity will reveal if the planned breadth was achieved. Choice (a) is incorrect. The number of audit findings is not an indicator of audit breadth or quality. Choice (c) is incorrect. Management satisfaction does not directly relate to the expressed goal (broader audit coverage). Choice (d) is incorrect. Implementation of a quality assurance program has no bearing on the stated goal.

Subject Area: Internal audit—organizational governance. Source: CIA 1191, I-5.

33. **(b)** This is the objective of the audit. Choice (a) is incorrect. This is a mechanical immaterial aspect of the report process. Choice (c) is incorrect. The auditee may not concur with the finding. This may or may not be considered in closing the audit. Choice (d) is incorrect. This is an administrative function of the audit organization.

Subject Area: Internal audit—organizational governance. Source: CIA 1191, I-44.

34. **(a)** As specified in the IIA's *Standards*, audit work schedules determine both staffing plans and financial budgets. Choice (b) is incorrect. Activity reports compare actual performance with goals and schedules and compare actual expenditures with financial budgets. Choice (c) is incorrect. While past performance is an indicator of the value of internal auditing, it will not impact the funds committed to current operations. Choice (d) is incorrect. The charter for an internal auditing department defines the purpose, authority, and responsibility of the department.

Subject Area: Internal audit—organizational governance. Source: CIA 1191, I-7.

35. **(d)** This is an instructive solution and explains the defect in the actions of the internal auditor. Choice (a) is incorrect. There was no intent to do wrong. The sanction is probably too severe. Also, the staff may lose a good auditor. Choice (b) is incorrect. The single occurrence described does not warrant this action. Choice (c) is incorrect. This is partly correct but it has no instructive value.

Subject Area: Internal audit—organizational governance. Source: CIA 1191, II-49.

36. **(a)** Audit reports should be distributed to those members of the organization who are able to ensure that audit results are given due consideration, in this case, the sales director and vice president of marketing would be sufficient. Choice (b) is incorrect. The distribution should include only that shown in choice (a). The chairman of the board and chief operating officer need not be involved unless significant problems were revealed. Choice (c) is incorrect. The distribution should include only those people shown in choice (a). The chairman of the board and controller need not be involved unless significant problems were revealed. Choice (d) is incorrect. The distribution should include only those people shown in choice (a). Chief financial officer and chief executive officer involvement would not be needed.

Subject Area: Internal audit—organizational governance. Source: CIA 1191, II-40.

37. **(c)** The cost benefit of internal auditing is neither easily quantifiable nor the subject of an external review. Choice (a) is incorrect. Included in the evaluation of the performance of an internal auditing department per the IIA *Standards*. Choices (b) and (d) are incorrect. They are included in the evaluation of the performance of an internal auditing department per the IIA Standards.

Subject Area: Internal audit—organizational governance. Source: CIA 1191, II-3.

38. **(b)** High achievers thrive when the job provides for personal responsibility, feedback, and moderate risks. Choices (a), (c), and (d) are incorrect. High achievers prefer moderate risks. They perform best with moderate risks.

Subject Area: Internal audit—organizational governance. Source: CIA 595, III-25.

39. **(d)** The problem of lack of feedback indicates the director has problems in planning and allocating audit resources, and communicating this need to the audit staff. Choice (a) is incorrect. There is no indication that there are staffing problems (i.e., insufficient audit personnel) or that audit personnel lack necessary skills to provide feedback on automated support systems. Choice (b) is incorrect. There is no indication that staffing or decision making is a problem. Choice (c) is incorrect. There is no indication that organizing is a problem.

Subject Area: Internal audit—organizational governance. Source: CIA 595, III-33.

40. **(b)** In this type of situation, management is highly averse to analysis or possible criticism of their actions and will not grant the internal auditors an adequate charter. Choice (a) is incorrect. An operating budget variance report is a control device used to monitor actual performance versus budget. Management foot-dragging could cause unfavorable variances, but favorable variances could also occur if many audits were cut short due to scope impairments. Choice (c) is incorrect. An unbiased evaluation of audit staff would not be affected by lack of cooperation on the part of nonaudit management. Choice (d) is incorrect. Policies and procedures of the internal audit function are developed by the internal audit department and should not be affected by nonaudit management.

Subject Area: Internal audit—organizational governance. Source: CIA 1194, III-14.

41. **(c)** Both management and auditors should be involved in improving the image of internal audit in the organization. Choice (a) is incorrect. The auditors also need to know the feedback so they can improve relations with auditees for the next audit. Choice (b) is incorrect. Management should also know if communication is poor because of some auditor behavior. Choice (d) is incorrect. Involving the auditees should reduce conflict and defensiveness and make the audit more participative.

Subject Area: Internal audit—organizational governance. Source: CIA 1196, 1-2.

42. **(b)** The operational risk is related to the organization's internal systems, products, services, processes, technology, and people. Choice (a) is incorrect. The strategic risks include risks related to strategy, political, economic, regulatory, and global market conditions. It also includes reputation risks, leadership risks, brand management risks, and customer risks. Choice (c) is incorrect. The financial risk includes risks from volatility in foreign currencies, interest rates, and commodities. It also includes credit risk, liquidity risk, and market risk. Choice (d) is incorrect. The hazard risk includes risks that are insurable, such as natural disasters, various insurable liabilities, impairment of physical assets and property, and terrorism. The enterprise risk management (ERM) includes both upside and downside risks.

Subject Area: Internal audit—organizational governance. Source: Author.

43. (a) The ERM approach is more than just integrating risks where risks are a part of uncertainty. The goal of an ERM initiative is to create, protect, and enhance shareholder value by managing the uncertainties that could influence in achieving the organization's objectives.

Subject Area: Internal audit—organizational governance. Source: Author.

44. (a) According to the IIA Research Foundation, ERM defines risk as any event or action that could adversely influence an organization's ability to achieve its objectives. ERM encompasses the more traditional view of potential hazards (threats) as well as opportunities. Management must consider derisking the opportunities when creating and evaluating new opportunities. Risks and opportunities move together, and the key is to determine if the potential of a given opportunity exceeds the risks. Choices (b), (c), and (d) are incorrect. Items III and IV are part of the strength, weaknesses, opportunity, and threat (SWOT) analysis used in strategic management. When companies fail to manage risks, opportunities are missed and shareholder value can be lost, which creates great pressure on management to improve corporate governance.

Subject Area: Internal audit—organizational governance. Source: Author.

45. (a) According to the IIA Research Foundation, the chief audit executives (CAEs) of the study companies understand the value-added potential of ERM, which makes them very effective ERM champions. ERM adds value because it is both inward-looking and forward-thinking. Choices (b), (c), and (d) are incorrect. They are part of the value-added potential.

Subject Area: Internal audit—organizational governance. Source: Author.

46. (c) Traditionally, the internal audit's role has been to provide reliable, overall assessment of risks and internal control effectiveness. In light of ERM implementation in improving corporate governance, internal auditors now (1) take a more business-oriented approach to audit company's operations, (2) change their audit approach to focus on business risk, (3) perform more effective follow-up on open ERM scorecards and metrics to increase management accountability, and (4) review formal action plans developed by management as part of the ERM implementation. Scorecards, metrics, and formal action plans are key parts of the ERM infrastructure. Choices (a) and (b) are incorrect. Internal controls and the IIA's *Standards* on ERM, either individually or jointly, will not improve corporate governance. Choice (d) is incorrect. See the answer given for choices (a) and (b).

Subject Area: Internal audit—organizational governance. Source: Author.

47. (a) In order to meet the ERM implementation challenge, the internal auditor should (1) use a risk-based audit approach (not a control-based approach), (2) be a consultant to the ERM implementation team (not as a policeman), (3) focus on future events (not past events), and (4) acquire competent skills to become an ERM facilitator (not use traditional accounting and auditing tools and skills). Choice (b) is incorrect. The consultant role does not hinder the implementation of ERM. Choice (c) is incorrect. Facilitation skills do not hinder the implementation of ERM. Choice (d) is incorrect. See the responses given for choices (b) and (c).

Subject Area: Internal audit—organizational governance. Source: Author.

48. (d) Corporate governance refers to the methods by which a firm is being governed, directed, administered, or controlled and to the goals for which it is being governed. Corporate governance is concerned with the relative roles, rights, and accountability of such stakeholder groups as owners, boards of directors, managers, employees, and others who assert to be stakeholders. Choice (a) is incorrect. More women on the board is encouraged. Choice (b) is incorrect. Hostile takeovers are not the norm. Choice (c) is incorrect. Delaware is not the only state in which a company can incorporate.

Subject Area: Internal audit—organizational governance. Source: CBM, Volume 4.

49. (c) The major condition embedded in the structure of modern corporations that has contributed to the corporate governance problem has been the separation of ownership from control. Choices (a), (b), and (d) are incorrect. They are minor issues.

Subject Area: Internal audit—organizational governance. Source: CBM, Volume 4.

50. (b) The method by which a firm is being governed, directed, administered, or controlled and the goals for which it is being governed are based on the corporate charter. Choices (a), (c), and (d) are incorrect. They do not deal with a company's existence.

Subject Area: Internal audit—organizational governance. Source: CBM, Volume 4.

51. (c) The board of directors provides governance, guidance, and oversight. They are not guarantors for shareholders. Choices (a), (b), and (d) are incorrect. They are proper roles for the directors.

Subject Area: Internal audit—organizational governance. Source: CBM, Volume 4.

4 PERFORM OTHER INTERNAL AUDIT ROLES AND RESPONSIBILITIES (0–10%)

THEORY

4.1 Ethics/Compliance

(a) Role of Corporate Code of Ethics

Ethics is knowing what is right or wrong, proper or improper. Ethics forms basic ground rules for individuals to follow. It resides within a person and it is a personal matter. Since people run businesses, personal ethics is business ethics and vice versa. Also, ethics is indivisible or inseparable, that is, it is the whole thing or nothing.

CORPORATE CULTURE VERSUS CORPORATE ETHICS

Corporate culture is identified formally in written statements of corporate vision or mission statements, or as a set of basic qualities, values, beliefs, or commitments.

Corporate culture raises the overall sense of ethical behavior in a way that is easy to understand and accept. Corporate culture needs to include the ethical element.

A good corporate culture should incorporate a substantial part of corporate ethics—explicitly or implicitly.

A person's competence, integrity, and objectivity are the roots of ethical behavior. Professionals have stricter rules and higher expectations about their ethical behavior than others do. According to Stephen Landekich, professionalism means that a person acts and is expected to act as an expert at a reliable level of conduct.[1] A professional not only acts in a manner beyond reproach but also is careful about any related conditions and circumstances that possibly might appear improper or be so perceived by others. Consequently, a code of ethics is a distinct mark of an established profession.

(b) Conflicts of Interest

The conflict-of-interest policy often is considered a part of the overall ethics policies. Conflict-of-interest concerns sometimes constitute the main part of ethics standards. Landekich's research indicated that all major companies share the view that conflicts between an employee's activities or personal interests and the company interests are one of the most significant causes of concern with regard to proper business conduct. The guiding principle is that the best interests of the company must motivate the employee's acts. Anything that might be inconsistent with this principle constitutes an actual or potential conflict of interest or the appearance of a conflict of interest. For example, if a fund manager puts more time and energy into managing his own personal funds at the expense of his company's funds, it is a conflict-of-interest situation.

---

[1] *__Corporate Codes of Conduct__ by Stephen Landekich, The Institute of Management Accountants, Montvale, New Jersey, A Research Project, 1989.*

Companies uniformly prohibit conflicts of interest, unless an employee has obtained written company approval. Such a basic clause may appear within a code of ethics or in a separately issued policy. In either case, typical conflict-of-interest situations are described in considerable detail.

Landekich gathered a concise set of standards on conflict of interest taken from a company's corporate code of conduct. For example

- Employees are forbidden to have direct or indirect ownership interests (excluding publicly traded securities of large companies listed on stock exchange) or profit participation in organizations selling or buying goods or services to or from the company where such relationship may reasonably lead to a conflict of interest.
- Employees or members of their families may not receive compensation, services, gifts, or entertainment from such organizations which receipt could reasonably be construed to have influenced the employee in dealing with them on behalf of the company.

Ethics Policy

The ethics policy is contained in the corporate policies, internal auditing policies, or conflict-of-interest policies.

Only 5% of ethics are written. Ethics and quality are interrelated, that is, one needs the other to work more effectively.

- In accordance with the personnel policy concerning "Outside Employment," the company prohibits its employees from engaging in outside employment with a supplier, customer, competitor, or a firm that may become such in the foreseeable future where such a relationship may reasonably lead to a conflict of interest.
- Certain employees will be required to sign a "Conflict of Interest Statement" annually.
- Employees who have questions regarding what constitutes a conflict of interest should discuss the matter with their division management.
- Dittenhofer and Klemm undertook a research project for the IIA to determine attitudes of internal auditors relative to 20 ethics issues.[2] These 20 situations (issues) were grouped into eight ethics classifications. The general comments on the eight classifications follow.
  - **Confidentiality.** There is a definite agreement between employees' attitudes and the perceived positions of their employers. No substantial differences were noted as to staff level, location, or industry.
  - **Honesty and Objectivity.** Employees seem stricter about violating these areas of ethics than their employers violate. All were consistent about action to take.
  - **Loyalty.** The answers were not clear-cut. There was little agreement between auditors' and employers' positions. Whistle-blowing appears to cause differing attitudes about loyalty ties.
  - **Conflict of Interest.** Auditors and their employers agree as to the action to take. Auditors outside the United States seem to be more hard-line. There were no major differences in the other categories. However, the percentages in the industrial groups varied significantly.
  - **Gifts.** Internal auditors are stricter than their organizations. Generally, there is congruity in all classifications.
  - **Professional Competence.** This area dealt with evidence and disclosure. Auditors' opinions and their perceived employers' positions did not display a high degree of concern over this aspect. Attitudes were reflected in the categories of internal auditors. *Disclosure:* Auditors and their organizations (as perceived) showed more concern for these incidents. This attitude was shared by all other categories.
  - **Striving for Proficiency and Effectiveness.** There is less concern, and the perceived organizations' opinions are somewhat less concerned.
  - **High Standards of Morality and Dignity.** There was general disagreement about an internal auditor going to a city from an employer-paid training session to apply for a new job. It ap-

[2] ***Ethics and the Internal Auditor*** *by Mortimer Dittenhofer and Rebecca Klemm, IIA Monograph Series, IIA, Altamonte Springs, Florida, 1983.*

pears that there are less firm positions and that attitudes are less comparable as to the situation given.

In conclusion, there is an apparent awareness of unethical positions among audit practitioners. They recognize unethical behavior and, on an organizational basis, are prepared to take action and impose sanctions on those who act improperly.

(c) Factors Influencing Ethical Standards

In a study, Brenner and Molander asked a group of managers to list factors that they believed influenced ethical standards.[3] The replies, in order of importance, were

Factors causing *higher* ethical standards:

1. Public disclosure, publicity, media coverage, and better communication
2. Increased public concern, public awareness, consciousness and security, better-informed public, and societal pressures
3. Government regulation, legislation and intervention, and federal courts
4. Education of business managers, increase in manager professionalism, and education
5. New social expectation of the role that business is to play in society, and the attitudes of young adults
6. Greater sense of social responsibility on the part of organizations, and greater awareness of the implications of their actions
7. Business responsiveness, corporate policy changes, and top management's emphasis on ethical action

Factors causing *lower* ethical standards:

1. Society's lower standards, social decay, more permissive society, growth of materialism and hedonism, loss of church and home influence, and less quality, more quantity desires
2. Competition, pace of life, the stress of trying to succeed, current economic conditions, and the cost of doing business
3. Political corruption, loss of confidence in government, politics, political ethics, and climate
4. People being more aware of unethical acts, constant media coverage, and communications that create an atmosphere for crime
5. Greed, desire for gain, worship of the dollar as a measure of success, selfishness, and a lack of personal integrity and moral fiber
6. Pressure for profit from within the organization from superiors or stockholders, corporate influences on managers, and corporate policies

It is easy to rationalize unethical conduct in business because of the prevailing theory that executives must provide stockholders with the greatest possible return on their investments (i.e., profit). This leads us to believe that ethical practices are rarely rewarded when compared to profits.

KEY CONCEPTS TO REMEMBER: CORPORATE CODE OF ETHICS

- The best reason for establishing a code of conduct within an organization is that such codes express standards of individual behavior for members of the organization.
- An example of unacceptable behavior that should be included in a conflict-of-interest policy is providing a mailing list of company employees to a relative who is offering training that might benefit the organization. Conflict-of-interest policy should prohibit any activity contrary to the best interests and well-being of the organization.
- A conflict-of-interest policy should include, among other things: an employee shall not accept money, gifts, or services from a customer, an employee shall not borrow from or lend money to vendors, and an employee shall not use company information for private purposes. The conflict-of-interest policy for a private firm (e.g., manufacturing company) should **not** include that the employee not participate in the management of a public agency.

[3] ***Is the Ethics of Business Changing?*** *In Ethics in Practice by Steven N. Brenner and Earl A. Molander, Havard Business School Press, Boston, MA, 1989.*

- A firm's code of ethics contains the statement "Employees shall not accept gifts or gratuities over $50 in value from persons or firms with whom our organization does business." This provision is designed to prevent excessive sales allowances granted by an employee.
- Several years ago a large financial institution developed and distributed a code of conduct to all its officers and employees. The best audit approach to provide the audit committee with the highest level of comfort about the code of conduct would be to fully evaluate the comprehensiveness of the code and compliance therewith and to report the results to the audit committee.
- A review of an organization's code of conduct revealed that it contained comprehensive guidelines designed to inspire high levels of ethical behavior. The review also revealed that employees were knowledgeable of its provisions. However, some employees still did not comply with the code. To enhance its effectiveness, the code of conduct should contain provisions for disciplinary action in the event of violations.

(d) **Options for Facilitating Ethical Behavior**

An organization has several options to facilitate ethical behavior. The options require careful planning and proper implementation with sincere interest and commitment. According to Moore and Dittenhofer, the presentation of the code of conduct plays an important role in how employees view its importance.[4] If the code of conduct is presented casually to a new employee along with other material related to the employment entrance process, such as insurance forms, tax deduction forms, pension information, and so forth, it will be considered a perfunctory document with minimal importance or significance. However, if the code is covered in a training program, and top management attends and participates, the code will be seen as a major element of organizational governance and a positive guide to attitude and behavior.

An alternative to distributing the code in a training program is for the chief executive officer (CEO) to transmit it with a personal letter. This tone-from-the-top message should explain that the code governs conduct at all levels of the organization. The letter may include a statement that says infractions will be dealt with seriously. It should be made clear that the excuse "I did what was best for the organization" will not be acceptable.

Conflict-of-Interest Policy

A conflict-of-interest policy should state that employees should not do business with family members as a customer or supplier even though no fraud appears to have been committed.

Another successful method for introducing new employees to the code of conduct is in a workshop where they see examples of ethics in practice. This is a good way to expose them to role-playing exercises relating to the most common types of infractions and to the potential disciplinary action that could be taken as a result. In addition to an initial exposure to the code of conduct just mentioned, ongoing training is also needed. This may be most effective when done by individual supervisors, usually in conjunction with employee training, orientation, or professional development courses. An effective way to impress the concept of ethics on each new employee is for supervisors to explain that ethical conduct is a core value of the organization that employees are expected to comply with throughout their careers. This subject should be discussed each time the supervisor focuses on performance issues with an individual.

In some cases, code-of-conduct training can be done on a broader scale through a seminar or meeting. If properly designed, a session of this nature can be effective. In other cases, videotapes on the subject of ethics are used, either separately or as part of additional training. This type of presentation is most effective if the CEO or a member of top management participates in the videotape and

[4] ***How to Develop a Code of Conduct*** *by Wayne G. Moore and Mortmer A.Dittenhofer IIA Monograph Series, IIA, Altamonte Springs, Florida, 1992*

provides supportive comments. Also, the presentation is enhanced if a knowledgeable individual is available to answer questions.

To keep the ethics momentum going, the code-of-conduct document needs to be updated periodically. The updating team should consider such elements as infractions not originally or specifically covered in the original code of conduct, changes in the organization's policies, environmental and organizational changes with material impact on the organization and its employees, and definitions and descriptions that are not clear.

(e) **Monitoring Compliance with the Code of Conduct**

Compliance with the code of conduct is an ongoing responsibility of each employee and is primarily based on the honor system. Employees should be asked to certify or sign a form asserting that they have complied with the code or to list exceptions to such compliance. These surveys may be administered by operating management or a staff group, such as legal, employee relations (human resources), or internal auditing.

(f) **Fraud in Financial Reporting**

In 1987 the Report of the National Commission on Fraudulent Financial Reporting (Treadway Commission) made recommendations for the public company to improve the financial reporting process.[5] In it, the commission made specific recommendations on the Code of Corporate Conduct.

> *The public company should develop and enforce written codes of corporate conduct. Codes of conduct should foster a strong ethical climate and open channels of communication to help protect against fraudulent financial reporting. As a part of its ongoing oversight of the effectiveness of internal controls, a company's audit committee should review annually the program that management establishes to monitor compliance with the code.*

A strong corporate ethical climate at all levels is vital to the well-being of the corporation, all its constituencies, and the public at large. Such a climate contributes importantly to the effectiveness of company policies and control systems and helps influence behavior that is not subject to even the most elaborate system of controls. Consequently, a strong corporate ethical climate emphasizing accountability helps to protect a company against fraudulent financial reporting.

A written code of corporate conduct strengthens the corporate ethical climate by signaling to all employees standards for conducting the company's affairs. Well-defined ethical standards and guidelines for acceptable behavior promote ethical decision making at all levels of the organization and help resolve ethical dilemmas that arise.

To succeed, a code of corporate conduct must have the full support of management and the board of directors. The most influential factors in determining the code's effectiveness are the attitude and the behavior of the top officers and directors, who set the example for the entire company. The CEO, in particular, has a special role; the CEO's attitude, behavior, and expectations of others strongly influence the actions of other upper-level managers.

ACTIVITIES TO ENSURE A STANDARD LEVEL OF CONDUCT

Proper hiring practices
Competitive levels of compensation
Performance incentives
Company tradition and reputation
Control mechanisms
Proper organization structure

The development of a corporate code of conduct is not an overnight task. A company must invest the necessary time, energy, and resources to ensure that the code is tailored to its circumstances. Since those circumstances will evolve to meet changing demands, the company must update the code periodically.

Finally, the full support of management and the board is needed to ensure that the code receives widespread understanding and support. Employees representing all levels of the corporation should be

---

[5] *Report of the National Commission on Fraudulent Financial Reporting, October 1987*

encouraged to participate in the code's development and evolution in an appropriate fashion. Such collaboration can minimize cases of noncompliance due to lack of understanding and can promote acceptance and adherence. In addition, the code and any amendments must be publicized throughout the corporation.

A code of corporate conduct can also help establish an environment where open communication is expected, accepted, and protected. Management needs a free flow of information to assist it in directing the company's operations, especially in a large, decentralized business. This need is critical in assessing the risk of fraudulent financial reporting. An atmosphere of open communication allows an employee, when confronted with suspected fraud, to bring the problem to the attention of someone high enough in the corporation to solve it without fear of reprisal.

The code must also provide an accessible internal complaint and appeal mechanism. This mechanism should be designed to facilitate internal disclosure, particularly those involving allegations of fraudulent financial reporting or other misconduct. The mechanism could take a variety of forms, such as the use of an ombudsman

Such internal procedures offer a number of advantages. They allow management to correct inadvertent mistakes and mistakes that may result from bad judgment or failure to recognize a problem. They also encourage employees to act in good faith and tend to ensure the validity of any complaint. In addition, effective internal action may make external disclosures to government authorities or other third parties unnecessary.

BUSINESS PRACTICES THAT CONSTITUTE AREAS OF ETHICAL DILEMMA

Hidden defects in products
Unfair credit practices
Deceptive advertising
Overselling
Overcharging
Unreal delivery dates
Products that are unhealthy

The code of corporate conduct should protect employees who use these internal procedures against reprisal. Failure to adopt guarantees against reprisal as well as to provide an effective internal complaint procedure could undermine the vitality of codes of conduct and encourage a call for antiretaliatory legislation, for which there is ample precedent at the state and the federal level.

The Treadway Commission observed a great deal of diversity in written codes of corporate conduct. Some are general; others are specific in their content and direction. Corporate management should develop a code that fits the particular circumstances of its business. Nearly all codes of conduct, however, should include a conflict-of-interest policy, to prevent actual or apparent improprieties in connection with business transactions; a corporate policy of compliance with domestic and foreign laws affecting its business, including those laws relating to financial disclosures; and a policy of confidentiality relating to the company's proprietary information.

Tools to Monitor Compliance

Annual survey
A periodic query
An ethics review board
A policy guidance
Employee indoctrination
Periodic review by internal audit

Adequate monitoring and enforcement mechanisms are yet another element that is indispensable to the success of a code of conduct. Management is responsible for determining how best to establish adequate monitoring and enforcement mechanisms and for implementing them. This responsibility is typically carried out through the legal department, internal audit department, or a separate ombudsman function.

The board of directors should be responsible through the audit committee for reviewing the program that management establishes to monitor compliance with the code of conduct. Employees at all levels should understand that violating the law or compromising the company's code of conduct can result in serious disciplinary actions (including dismissal and criminal or civil proceedings where appropriate) and that no employee is exempt from the code.

Written codes of corporate conduct have further advantages. Such codes foster a strong ethical climate, helping to create a work environment that appeals to company personnel at all levels. With an effective code, a company's employees may be more highly motivated, and the company may be able to attract and retain better employees. In an era when loyalty between organizations and their customers seems less enduring, a company's concern for a strong ethical climate also may generate a positive image outside the organization, which can lead to increased business opportunities.

EXAMPLE: Content of a Code of Conduct

Although each organization is different in some respects, certain types of employee behavior can be expected in all organizations. The contents of a code of conduct are divided into three groups: (1) mandatory (those items that should always appear in a code-of-conduct document), (2) strongly suggested, and (3) desirable. Factors that determine what is appropriate for each specific code are based on a complete understanding of the business and corporate culture.

Mandatory

Tone at the top. *Most important, the code should convey a strong tone-at-the-top message. This is usually accomplished by including a letter from the chairman, president, and/or managing director that expresses the organization's strong commitment to ethical business conduct.*

Employee responsibilities. *The list of responsibilities expected from each employee should be broad and should establish a positive approach to what follows, for example, a shared set of common understanding setting forth the philosophy expected in the workplace.*

The most common responsibilities mentioned include honesty, fairness, integrity, loyalty, due care, compliance with laws and regulations, avoiding conflicts of interest, safeguarding the organization's assets, and maintaining the confidentiality of nonpublic information.

Business courtesies. *In profit-oriented organizations, the customer is number one, so that is a good place to start. How should the firm conduct itself in dealing with customers?*

The practice of giving gifts, granting favors, and providing entertainment is usually acceptable, but within certain limits. In general, guidelines such as these apply. The amounts: must not be excessive, and cannot be construed as a bribe or payoff, must be consistent with customary business practices, must be legal, and should not embarrass the organization or the employee if publicly disclosed.

On the other side of the gift, favor, and entertainment equation is the receipt of such courtesies. In some organizations, the receipt of a gift is reported and monitored closely; in others, including certain governmental units, the receipt of gifts of any kind is totally prohibited.

In most organizations, however, "token" gifts, favors, and entertainment are acceptable. These are usually in the form of advertising and promotional items emblazoned with the organization's logo, or they may be a business luncheon/dinner or entertainment.

Gift giving and receiving is an issue that generates considerable interest and discussion, and should be clearly understood. Many organizations have a "double standard." For example, marketing and salespeople may be permitted and even encouraged to entertain customers in as lavish a manner as possible to complete a "sale," yet the same organization's purchasing department personnel are not permitted to accept similar gratuities from someone else's sales force.

Clearly it is important to identify the reasons for this double standard because readers of the code will focus on it immediately. A clear explanation will prevent any feeling that this issue is being covered up or circumvented.

Cash gifts, either given or received, are not appropriate and should be prohibited due to the lack of an audit trail and accountability of funds. However, in some countries (e.g., Japan) cash gifts are the norm. Care should be exercised in explaining such cultural differences.

Conflicts of interest. *No code of conduct would be complete without a discussion of conflicts of interest. Broadly speaking, employees should avoid any situations involving a conflict between their personal interests and those of the organization. In dealings with current or potential customers, suppliers, contractors, and competitors, employees should act in the best interest of the organization to the exclusion of any personal advantage. When potential conflicts occur, employees should make prompt, full disclosure of these issues to management.*

Although conflicts of interest materialize in the "eyes of the beholder," their importance can vary significantly depending on the business. A list of common conflicts include

- ***Financial Interest.*** *This generally involves ownership by an employee or an employee's family member of a significant financial interest in an outside enterprise that does business with, or seeks to do business with, or is a competitor of, the organization.*
- ***Key Outside Role.*** *In this instance, an individual serves as a director, officer, partner, consultant, or in another key role, in any outside enterprise that does business with, or seeks to do business with, or is a competitor of, the organization.*
- ***Agent of a Third Party.*** *This position acts as broker, finder, or other intermediary for the benefit of a third party in transactions involving the organization.*
- ***Other.*** *This is any other arrangement or circumstance, including family or personal relationships, that might dissuade the employee from acting in the best interest of the organization.*

Control and use of assets. *Control and judicious use of the organization's assets, including proprietary information stored both on paper and electronically, is each employee's responsibility. Employees should safeguard physical property and other assets against unauthorized use or removal as well as any loss by criminal act or breach of trust. Data transmitted and/or stored electronically are particularly sensitive and may require unique protection.*

Recordkeeping and reporting. *All financial and operational reports, accounting records, research reports, expense accounts, sales reports, time sheets, and other documents should accurately and clearly represent the relevant facts or true nature of conditions and transactions. Improper, misleading, incomplete, or fraudulent accounting documentation or financial reporting is not permitted and may also be in violation of applicable laws. Intentional accounting misclassifications and improperly accelerating or deferring expenses or revenues would be examples of unacceptable reporting practices.*

Travel and entertainment. *Travel and entertainment should be consistent with the needs of the organization. An employee should neither lose nor gain financially as a result of organizational travel and/or entertainment. Employees should spend the organization's money as carefully as their own.*

Inside information. *Confidential information, such as business strategies, pending contracts, unannounced products, exploration or research results, financial projections, or customer lists, should not be released without proper authority to anyone not employed by the organization or to an employee who has no need for such information. Nonpublic information obtained as an employee should not be used for personal gain by the employee or by anyone as a result of association with the employee. Use for personal profit includes taking advantage of such information by trading or providing information for others to trade in securities of the organization or acquiring property of any kind.*

Ethics Implementation Procedures

An ethics committee
A hotline phone
A counsel for guidance
A compliance review board
An internal complaint and appeal mechanism
An ombudsman

Political contributions. *Employees should not make any contribution of organization funds, property, or services, or personal funds in the name of the organization to any political party or committee or to any candidate for or holder of any office of any government. In some cases, it is legal to participate in a political action committee (PAC) or for an organization to support or oppose public referenda or similar ballot issues. No direct or indirect pressure in any form should be directed toward employees to make any political contributions or participate in the support of a political party or the political candidacy of any individual.*

Equal employment opportunity. *While conducting business on behalf of the organization, employees should respect the rights and cultural differences of individuals. Employees should practice the principle of equal employment opportunity without regard to race, religion, national origin, sex, age, physical handicap, or political affiliation. In addition, harassment of any type should not be tolerated.*

Compliance with the code of conduct. *A periodic certification of compliance with the code of conduct is one way to ensure employees focus on the document. The act of signing one's name also tends to emphasize the personal nature of the responsibilities required by the code, and should encourage compliance. Providing a hotline, phone number, or ombudsman for people to call and report instances of violation of the policy is another effective method of encouraging compliance with the code. Organizations often use several of these methods.*

Strongly Suggested

In most organizations, these issues should be part of the code of conduct. In not-for-profit organizations, however, they may not be necessary.

Business inducements. *In this competitive world, a myriad of sales commission, rebate, discount, credit, and allowance programs exist. These inducements deserve close scrutiny to ensure they comply, in the spirit as well as in the letter, with tax regulations and currency exchange controls. Values should be reasonable, competitively justified, properly documented, and made to the business entity to which the original sales agreement or invoice was made or issued. Payments should not be made to individuals and should be made only in the country of the entity's place of business.*

Again, the mirror-image transaction should be covered. Commission payments for purchases should be made only to the seller in the country where the business is located or in the country to which the product was delivered.

The organization's policy on facilitating payments should be explained in this section. The Foreign Corrupt Practices Act of 1977 prohibited such payments, but the Omnibus Trade Act of 1988 amended this provision to a more liberal interpretation of facilitating payments. Payments are permitted if they are legal; are necessary; follow an established, well-recognized practice in the area; and are for administrative actions to which the organization is clearly entitled. Such payments should be properly approved and recorded.

In some countries, the concept of "facilitating payments" is unheard of, and omitting their mention in the code may be advisable. Care should be taken in multinational organizations to ensure such payments are accepted in a country before the code of conduct is assumed to permit them.

Antitrust laws. *Organizations in various countries are subject to antitrust laws or laws that prohibit agreements or actions that may restrain trade or reduce competition. Violations would include price fixing or agreements to control prices to boycott certain suppliers or customers or to limit the production or sale of products. Care must be taken to ensure that activities with representatives of other firms, even professional organizations, are not viewed as a violation of antitrust law. In matters involving antitrust, appropriate legal counsel should be consulted.*

Antiboycott laws. *Organizations in various countries also are subject to antiboycott laws. For US corporations, these laws prohibit participation in or cooperation with international boycotts that are not sanctioned by the US government. The mere receipt of a request to engage in any boycotting activity is a reportable event by law in some countries. Because of the complexity of antiboycott laws, any questions in this area should be referred to appropriate legal counsel.*

Government business. *In some organizations, doing business with foreign governments is an integral part of the operation. Sometimes standards and requirements for transactions with foreign governments differ from normal commercial practices, and a clear understanding of the rules governing such transactions is critical to staying out of trouble.*

An example is the giving, offering, or accepting of business courtesies, such as meals and entertainment. This may be standard practice in a commercial enterprise, yet prohibited in a governmental unit. Again, reference to legal counsel is recommended to ensure that all sensitive areas are properly considered.

Competitive intelligence. *Success in the highly competitive business world demands an understanding of competitors' strategies. Collecting data on competitors, while important, should be done ethically. The use of illegitimate resources and actions that may not be illegal but are in bad taste or may cause embarrassment should not be used. If any questions arise in this area, legal counsel should be consulted.*

Desirable

The list of desirable items could be endless, but included here are a few items that may be useful, depending on the type of organization or which code is being developed.

Political activities. *Relationships with potential and incumbent public officials can be very sensitive and potentially embarrassing to the organization unless guidelines specify what activities are appropriate. Particular care should be taken to ensure the organization does not make payments to political groups or members to influence sales or to induce them not to perform their duties.*

Purchase and sale of real estate and natural resources. *Employees should be prohibited from competing with the organization in real estate and natural resources activities, or from using the organization's information or equipment to enable them to profit either directly or indirectly in the acquisition or disposal of real estate or natural resources.*

Environment. *Protecting the environment requires the ongoing vigilance of all employees. All facilities should be operated in accordance with applicable environmental regulations and in a manner that conserves energy and natural resources and protects the environment.*

Sexual harassment. *Reinforcement in the code of conduct that the organization will not permit sexual harassment establishes this commitment to all.*

SOURCE: Wayne G. Moore and Mortimer A. Dittenhofer, ***How to Develop a Code of Conduct*** *(Altamonte Springs, FL: Institute of Internal Auditors (IIA), 1992).*

(g) Integrating Ethical Standards in Complex Situations

It is good to integrate ethical standards with company policies and procedures, conflict-of-interest statements, job/position descriptions, employee performance evaluations, vision/mission statements, posters and marketing/advertising materials, product packing materials, management employment contracts, legal contracts with outsiders, purchase orders and invoices, employment/job applications, and company annual reports.

Ethics-related statements should be included in so many places for reinforcement purposes and because not everyone will have access to the same ethics-related materials. For example, a consultant may not have access to job descriptions and employee performance evaluations that an employee would have. Similarly, outsiders such as investors and creditors would have more access to a company's annual report than to a company policy manual or job application or description.

Another way to integrate ethical standards in complex situations is to measure a manager's performance based on both quantitative and qualitative factors. Usually a managers' bonuses or other rewards are based on how well they meet their quantitative goals, such as increase in revenues or decrease in costs. While these goals are good, managers should also be measured on qualitative factors, such as quality; working relations with customers, suppliers, and employees; and productivity levels.

Double Standard for Ethics

Most businesspeople hold to ethical behavior in their private lives, but cease to be private persons in their organizational lives. This indicates that people have double standards as far as ethics are concerned: one standard for private lives and one standard for their organizational lives.

An organization's goals are interrelated. This fact should be considered during the establishment and evaluation of individual manager's goals and actual performance.

By placing emphasis on only one or a few goals, the other related goals may be in jeopardy. For example, focusing on increasing revenues or decreasing costs alone is not enough because these goals might have been achieved by jeopardizing or manipulating other related goals, such as too much inventory or too little inventory, or too much maintenance expense or too little maintenance expense, or expensing fixed asset acquisitions instead of capitalizing.

4.2 IIA's Performance Standards

2100—Nature of Work—The internal audit activity ***should*** evaluate and contribute to the improvement of risk management, control, and governance *processes using a systematic and disciplined approach.*
2110—Risk Management—The internal audit activity should assist the organization by identifying and evaluating significant exposures to risk and contributing to the improvement of risk management and control systems.

2110.A1—The internal audit activity should monitor and evaluate the effectiveness of the organization's risk management system.
2110.A2—The internal audit activity should evaluate risk exposures relating to the organization's governance, operations, and information systems regarding the

- Reliability and integrity of financial and operational information
- Effectiveness and efficiency of operations
- Safeguarding of assets
- Compliance with laws, regulations, and contracts

2110.C1—During consulting engagements, internal auditors should address risk consistent with the engagement's objectives and be alert to the existence of other significant risks.
2110.C2—Internal auditors should incorporate knowledge of risks gained from consulting engagements into the process of identifying and evaluating significant risk exposures of the organization.

(a) **Ethics/Compliance**

IIA's Practice Advisory 2100-5: Legal Considerations in Evaluating Regulatory Compliance Programs

Nature of This Practice Advisory

Internal auditors should consider these suggestions when evaluating an organization's regulatory compliance programs. This guidance is not intended to represent all the procedures that may be necessary for a comprehensive assurance or consulting engagement related to regulatory compliance. Compliance with Practice Advisories is optional.

Caution: Internal auditors are encouraged to consult legal counsel in all matters involving legal issues as requirements may vary significantly in different jurisdictions. The guidance contained in this Practice Advisory is based primarily on the legal system in the United States of America.

1. Compliance programs assist organizations in preventing inadvertent employee violations, detecting illegal activities, and discouraging intentional employee violations. They can also help prove insurance claims, determine director and officer liability, create or enhance corporate identity, and decide the appropriateness of punitive damages. Internal auditors should evaluate an organization's regulatory compliance programs in light of steps 2–8 for effective compliance programs
2. The organization should establish compliance standards and procedures to be followed by its employees and other agents that are reasonably capable of reducing the prospect of criminal conduct.
    - The organization should develop a written business code of conduct that clearly identifies prohibited activities. This code should be written in language that all employees can understand, avoiding legalese.
    - A good code provides guidance to employees on relevant issues. Checklists, a question-and-answer section, and a reference to additional sources for further information all help make the code user friendly.
    - The organization should create an organizational chart identifying board members, senior officers, the senior compliance officer, and department personnel who are responsible for implementing compliance programs.
    - Codes of conduct that are viewed as legalistic and "one-sided" by employees may increase the risk that employees will engage in unethical or illegal behavior, whereas codes that are viewed as straightforward and fair tend to decrease the risk that employees will engage in such activity.
    - Companies using reward systems that attach financial incentives to apparently unethical or illegal behavior can expect a poor compliance environment.
    - Companies with international operations should institute a compliance program on a global basis, not just for selected geographic locations. Such programs should reflect appropriate local conditions, laws, and regulations.
3. Specific individual(s) within high-level personnel of the organization should be assigned overall responsibility to oversee regulatory compliance with standards and procedures.
    - "High-level personnel of the organization" refers to individuals who have substantial control of the organization or who have a substantial role in the making of policy within the organization.
    - High-level personnel of the organization includes: a director; an executive officer; an individual in charge of a major business or functional unit of the organization, such as sales, administration, or finance; and an individual with a substantial ownership interest.
    - To be fully effective, the CEO and other senior management must have significant involvement in the program.
    - In some organizations, assigning chief compliance responsibilities to the company's general counsel may convince employees that management is not committed to the program and that the program is important to the legal department only, not the firm as a whole. In other organizations, the opposite may be true.

- In a large company with several business units, compliance responsibilities should be assigned to high-level personnel in each unit.
- It is not enough for the company to create the position of chief compliance officer and to select the rest of the compliance unit. The company should also ensure that those personnel are appropriately empowered and supplied with the resources necessary for carrying out their mission. Compliance personnel should have adequate access to senior management. The chief compliance officer should report directly to the CEO.

4. The organization should use due care not to delegate substantial discretionary authority to individuals whom the organization knows, or should know through the exercise of due diligence, have a propensity to engage in illegal activities.
   - Companies should screen applicants for employment at all levels for evidence of past wrongdoing, especially wrongdoing within the company's industry.
   - Employment applications should inquire as to past criminal convictions. Professionals should be asked about any history of discipline in front of licensing boards.
   - Care should be taken to ensure that the company does not infringe on employees' and applicants' privacy rights under applicable laws. Many jurisdictions have laws limiting the amount of information a company can obtain in performing background checks on employees.

5. The organization should take steps to communicate effectively its standards and procedures to all employees and other agents, for example, by requiring participation in training programs or by disseminating publications that explain in a practical manner what is required.
   - The effectiveness of a compliance program will depend on the ways in which it is communicated to employees. Generally, an interactive format works better than a lecture. Programs communicated in person tend to work better than programs communicated entirely through video or game formats. Programs that are periodically repeated work better than onetime presentations.
   - The best programs include employee training that allows employees to practice new techniques and use new information. Such activities are particularly appropriate with regard to management training, but are effective with regard to employees at all levels.
   - The language used by an organization's code of conduct and employee manual should be easy to understand. Alternative methods of communicating the code and the employee manual to employees lacking more formal education must be found and implemented.
   - Compliance tips, statements, and warnings should be disseminated to employees through a variety of available media: newsletters, posters, e-mail, questionnaires, and presentations.
   - Organizations should present the program on multiple occasions to different sets of employees, targeting the information presented to the areas important to each functional group of employees. The information should be tailored to that group's job requirements. For example, environmental compliance information should be directed to those departments, such as manufacturing or real property management, that have an increased likelihood of violating or detecting violations of such laws and regulations. Providing such training to a department with no such responsibilities could be detrimental, inspiring employee apathy or a belief that the program was not well constructed.
   - New employees should receive basic compliance training as part of their orientation. Later they can be incorporated into ongoing compliance efforts in their departments.
   - Agents of the organization should be asked to attend a presentation specifically geared toward them. It is important that an organization inform its agents of the organization's core values and that the actions of its agents that are attributable to the company will be monitored in connection with the compliance program. The organization should be prepared to cease doing business with agents who fail to adhere to the organization's compliance standards.

- Organizations should require employees to periodically certify that they have read, understood, and complied with the company's code of conduct. This information should be related annually to senior management and the board of directors.
- All ethics-related documents—codes of conduct, human resources policies/manuals, and so on—should be readily available to all employees. Continuous access availability, such as through the organization's intranet, is strongly encouraged.

6. The organization should take reasonable steps to achieve compliance with its standards, for example, by utilizing monitoring and auditing systems reasonably designed to detect criminal conduct by its employees and other agents and by having in place and publicizing a reporting system whereby employees and other agents can report criminal conduct by others within the organization without fear of retribution.

   - The organization should devote an amount of resources to the internal audit plan that is appropriate given the size of the company and the difficulty of the audit task. The audit plan should concentrate on the organization's activities in each of its businesses.
   - The audit plan should also include a review of the organization's compliance program and its procedures, including reviews to determine whether: written materials are effective, communications have been received by employees, detected violations have been appropriately handled, discipline has been evenhanded, whistle-blowers have not been retaliated against, and the compliance unit has fulfilled its responsibilities. The auditors should review the compliance program to determine whether it can be improved and should solicit employee input in that regard.
   - Each program should have a hotline or other reporting system under which employees can report activity that they believe to be unethical, illegal, or against the company's code of conduct. Employees must be free to report such behavior without fear of reprisal.
   - Although an attorney monitoring the hotline is better able to protect attorney-client and work-product privileges, one study observed that employees have little confidence in hotlines answered by the legal department or by an outside service. The same study showed that employees have even less confidence in write-in reports or an off-site ombudsman, but have the most confidence in hotlines answered by an in-house representative and backed by a nonretaliation policy.
   - Use of an on-site ombudsman is more effective if the ombudsman reports directly to the chief compliance officer or the board of directors, if the ombudsman can keep the names of whistle-blowers secret, if the ombudsman provides guidance to whistle-blowers, and if the ombudsman undertakes follow-up review to ensure that retaliation has not occurred. Additionally, some jurisdictions now recognize a limited ombudsman privilege, under which the ombudsman is protected from disclosing confidential communications made by whistle-blowers to the ombudsman.
   - An effective tool for uncovering unethical or illegal activity is the ethics questionnaire. Each employee of the organization should receive a questionnaire that asks whether he or she is aware of kickbacks, bribes, or other wrongdoing. To protect privilege, the questionnaire should be sent by organization counsel; contain a statement that the questionnaire is protected by privilege; require the employee to complete, sign, and return the questionnaire without making a copy; and contain a statement that the organization retains the right to disclose information provided to the company to government agencies or in litigation. Note that privilege will be lost if the questionnaire is disclosed to outside parties.

7. The standards should be consistently enforced through appropriate disciplinary mechanisms, including, as appropriate, discipline of individuals responsible for the failure to detect an offense. Adequate discipline of individuals responsible for an offense is a necessary component of enforcement; however, the form of discipline that will be appropriate will be case-specific.

   - The compliance program should contain a disciplinary system under which those who violate the organization's code of conduct receive punishment appropriate to the offense, such as warning, loss of pay, suspension, transfer, or termination. But if an employee is found to have committed some illegal act, the organization might have to terminate that employee, in keeping with the organization's obligation to use "due care not to delegate substantial discretionary authority to individuals whom the organization knew, or should have known through the exercise of due diligence, had a propensity to engage in illegal activities."

- Discipline under the program must be fair. The program has slight chance of succeeding if unethical or illegal activity goes unpunished, especially if tied to the activities of senior management or big producers. Ignored wrongdoing by such persons will encourage such behavior in the rest of the workforce.
- Termination or other discipline of employees may be limited by whistle-blower laws, exceptions to the employee-at-will doctrine, employee or union contracts, and employer responsibilities with regard to discrimination, wrongful discharge, and employer bad-faith laws/doctrines.
- The program should provide for the discipline of managers and other responsible persons who knew or should have known of misconduct and did not report it. Failure of the program to do so may cause a court to find that the program is not effective; the program will then have no beneficial effect on sentencing.
- Organizations should be scrupulous and thorough in documenting employee discipline. The organization should be able to prove that it made its best efforts to collect information with regard to any incident and took appropriate action based on the information available.

8. After an offense has been detected, the organization should take all reasonable steps to respond appropriately to the offense and to prevent further similar offenses—including any necessary modifications to its program to prevent and detect violations of law.

    - The organization should respond appropriately to each offense detected by the compliance program. Appropriate responses include disciplinary action taken with regard to those who engaged in misconduct.
    - In some circumstances, an appropriate response could require self-reporting the violation to the government, cooperation with governmental investigations, and the acceptance of responsibility for the violation. Note that similar to the existence of an effective compliance program, making these responses could result in a court lowering the amount of the organization's fine.
    - Failure to detect or prevent a serious violation could indicate that the compliance program needs a major overhaul. At a minimum, after any violation is detected, compliance personnel should examine the program to determine whether changes need to be made.
    - One change that may be required in light of a violation could be the replacement or shuffling of compliance personnel. In fact, the organization may need to discipline or replace any manager who fails to detect or prevent misconduct in the areas under the manager's supervision, especially if the violation is one that the manager should have detected.

(b) **Risk Management**

IIA's Practice Advisory 2100-3: The Internal Auditor's Role in the Risk Management Process

Nature of This Practice Advisory

The definition of internal auditing calls for "a disciplined approach to evaluate and improve the effectiveness of *risk management*, control, and governance processes." Internal auditors have a key role to play in an organization's risk management process in order to practice internal auditing in accordance with the IIA's *Standards*. This advisory seeks to provide internal auditors with guidance for determining their role in an organization's risk management process and for complying with the *Standards*. Additional considerations beyond those contained in this advisory may be necessary. *Compliance with Practice Advisories is optional.*

1. Risk management is a key responsibility of management. To achieve its business objectives, management should ensure that sound risk management processes are in place and functioning. Boards and audit committees have an oversight role to determine that appropriate risk management processes are in place and that these processes are adequate and effective. Internal auditors should assist both management and the audit committee by examining, evaluating, reporting, and recommending improvements on the adequacy and effectiveness of management's risk processes. Management and the board are responsible for their organization's risk management and control processes. However, internal auditors acting in a consulting role can assist the organization in identifying, evaluating, and implementing risk management methodologies and controls to address those risks.
2. Developing assessments and reports on the organization's risk management processes are normally a high audit priority. Evaluating management's risk processes is different than the requirement that auditors use risk analysis to plan audits. However, information from a comprehensive risk management process, including the identification of management and board concerns, can assist the internal auditor in planning audit activities.
3. The chief audit executive should obtain an understanding of management's and the board's expectations of the internal audit activity in the organization's risk management process. This understanding should be codified in the charters of the internal audit activity and audit committee.
4. Responsibilities and activities should be coordinated between all groups and individuals with a role in the organization's risk management process. These responsibilities and activities should be appropriately documented in the organization's strategic plans, board policies, management directives, operating procedures, and other governance-type instruments. Examples of some of the activities and responsibilities that should be documented include

    - Setting strategic direction may reside with the board or a committee.
    - Ownership of risks may be assigned at the senior management level.
    - Acceptance of residual risk may reside at the executive management level.
    - Identifying, assessing, mitigating, and monitoring activities on a continuous basis may be assigned at the operating level.
    - Periodic assessment and assurance to others should reside with the internal audit activity.

5. Internal auditors are expected to identify and evaluate significant risk exposures in the normal course of their duties.
6. The internal audit activity's role in the risk management process of an organization can change over time and may be found at some point along a continuum that ranges from

    - No role, to
    - Auditing the risk management process as part of the internal audit plan, to
    - Active, continuous support and involvement in the risk management process, such as participation on oversight committees, monitoring activities, and status reporting, to
    - Managing and coordinating the risk management process.

7. Ultimately, it is the role of executive management and the audit committee to determine the role of internal audit in the risk management process. Management's view on internal audit's role is likely to be determined by factors such as the culture of the organization, ability of the internal auditing staff, and local conditions and customs of the country.
8. Additional guidance can be found in these Practice Advisories.

    - PA 2100-4, "The Internal Auditor's Role in Organizations without a Risk Management Process"
    - PA 1130.A1-2, "The Internal Auditor's Responsibility for Other (Non-audit) Functions"
    - PA 2110-1, "Assessing the Adequacy of Risk Management Processes"
    - PA 2010-2, "Linking the Audit Plan to Risk and Exposure"

IIA's Practice Advisory 2100-4: The Internal Auditor's Role in Organizations without a Risk Management Process

Nature of This Practice Advisory

The definition of internal auditing calls for "a disciplined approach to evaluate and improve the effectiveness of risk management, control, and governance processes." Internal auditors have a key role to play in an organization's risk management process in order to practice internal auditing in accordance with the *Standards*. However, some organizations may not have an established risk management process. This advisory seeks to provide internal auditors with guidance for determining their role in an organization without an established risk management process. Additional considerations beyond those contained in this advisory may be necessary. *Compliance with Practice Advisories is optional.*

1. Risk management is a key responsibility of management. To achieve its business objectives, management should ensure that sound risk management processes are in place and functioning. Boards and audit committees have an oversight role to determine that appropriate risk management processes are in place and that these processes are adequate and effective. Internal auditors should assist both management and the audit committee by examining, evaluating, reporting, and recommending improvements on the adequacy and effectiveness of management's risk processes. Management and the board are responsible for their organization's risk management and control processes. However, internal auditors acting in a consulting role can assist the organization in identifying, evaluating, and implementing risk management methodologies and controls to address those risks.
2. Developing assessments and reports on the organization's risk management processes are normally a high audit priority. Evaluating management's risk processes is different from the requirement that auditors use risk analysis to plan audits. However, information from a comprehensive risk management process, including the identification of management and board concerns, can assist the internal auditor in planning audit activities.
3. The chief audit executive should obtain an understanding of management's and the board's expectations of the internal audit activity in the organization's risk management process. This understanding should be codified in the charters of the internal audit activity and audit committee.
4. If an organization has not established a risk management process, the internal auditor should bring this to management's attention along with suggestions for establishing such a process. The internal auditor should seek direction from management and the board as to the audit activity's role in the risk management process. The charters for the audit activity and audit committee should document the role of each in the risk management process.
5. If requested, internal auditors can play a proactive role in assisting with the initial establishment of a risk management process for the organization. A more proactive role supplements traditional assurance activities with a consultative approach to improving fundamental processes. If such assistance exceeds normal assurance and consulting activities conducted by internal auditors, independence could be impaired. In these situations, internal auditors should comply with the disclosure requirements of the *International Standards for the Professional Practice of Internal Auditing (Standards)*. Additional guidance can also be found in Practice Advisory 1130.A1-2, "The Internal Auditor's Responsibility for Other (Nonaudit) Functions."
6. A proactive role in developing and managing a risk management process is not the same as an "ownership of risks" role. In order to avoid an "ownership of risk" role, internal auditors should seek confirmation from management as to its responsibility for identification, mitigation, monitoring, and "ownership" of risks.
7. In summary, internal auditors can facilitate or enable risk management processes, but they should not "own" or be responsible for the management of the risks identified.

IIA's Practice Advisory 2110-2: The Internal Auditor's Role in the Business Continuity Process

Nature of This Practice Advisory

Internal auditors should consider these suggestions when evaluating an organization's activities related to business continuity. Many processes are required to ensure the continuity of an organization after a disaster occurs. The development of a comprehensive plan begins with assessing the potential impact and consequences of a disaster and understanding the risks. (The entire process of ensuring business continuity will incorporate, among other things, business continuity and disaster recovery plans.) Those plans should be constructed, maintained, tested, and audited to ensure that it remains appropriate for the needs of the organization. *Compliance with Practice Advisories is optional. This guidance is repeated in Part 1 and Part 2 for proper coverage of the subject matter.*

1. Business interruption can result from natural occurrences and accidental or deliberate criminal acts. Those interruptions can have significant financial and operational ramifications. Auditors should evaluate the organization's readiness to deal with business interruptions. A comprehensive plan would provide for emergency response procedures, alternative communication systems and site facilities, information systems backup, disaster recovery, business impact assessments and resumption plans, procedures for restoring utility services, and maintenance procedures for ensuring the readiness of the organization in the event of an emergency or disaster.
2. Internal auditing activity should assess the organization's business continuity planning process on a regular basis to ensure that senior management is aware of the state of disaster preparedness.
3. Many organizations do not expect to experience an interruption or lengthy delay of normal business processes and operations due to a disaster or other unforeseen event. Many business experts say that it is not *if* a disaster will occur, but *when* it will occur. Over time, an organization will experience an event that will result in the loss of information, access to properties (tangible or intangible), or the services of personnel. Exposure to those types of risks and the planning for business continuity is an integral part of an organization's risk management process. Advance planning is necessary to minimize the loss and ensure continuity of an organization's critical business functions. It may enable the organization to maintain an acceptable level of service to its stakeholders.
4. A crucial element of business recovery is the existence of a comprehensive and current disaster recovery plan. Internal auditors can play a role in the organization's planning for disaster recovery. Internal audit activity can (a) assist with the risk analysis, (b) evaluate the design and comprehensiveness of the plan after it has been drawn up, and (c) perform periodic assurance engagements to verify that the plan is kept up-to-date.

Planning

5. Organizations rely on internal auditors for analysis of operations and assessment of risk management and control processes. Internal auditors acquire an understanding of the overall business operations and the individual functions and how they interrelate with one another. This positions the internal audit activity as a valuable resource in evaluating the disaster recovery plan during its formulation process.
6. Internal audit activity can help with an assessment of an organization's internal and external environment. Internal factors that may be considered include the turnover of management and changes in information systems, controls, and major projects and programs. External factors may include changes in outside regulatory and business environment and changes in markets and competitive conditions, international financial and economic conditions, and technologies. Internal auditors can help identify risks involving critical business activities and prioritize functions for recovery purposes.

Evaluation

7. Internal auditors can make a contribution as objective participants when they review the proposed business continuity and disaster recovery plans for design, completeness, and overall adequacy. Auditors can examine the plan to determine that it reflects the operations that have been included and evaluated in the risk assessment process and contains sufficient internal control concerns and prescriptions. Internal auditors' comprehensive knowledge of the organization's business operations and applications enables them to assist during the development phase of the business continuity plan by evaluating the plan's organization, comprehensiveness, and recommended actions to manage risks and maintain effective controls during a recovery period.

Periodic assurance engagements

8. Internal auditors should periodically audit the organization's business continuity and disaster recovery plans. The audit objective is to verify that the plans are adequate to ensure the timely re-

sumption of operations and processes after adverse circumstances and that it reflects the current business-operating environment.

9. Business continuity and disaster recovery plans can become outdated very quickly. Coping with and responding to changes is an inevitable part of the task of management. Turnover of managers and executives and changes in system configurations, interfaces, and software can have a major impact on these plans. Internal audit activity should examine the recovery plan to determine whether (a) it is structured to incorporate important changes that could take place over time and (b) the revised plan will be communicated to the appropriate people, inside and outside the organization.
10. During the audit, internal auditors should consider
    - Are all plans up-to-date? Do procedures exist for updating the plans?
    - Are all critical business functions and systems covered by the plans? If not, are the reasons for omissions documented?
    - Are the plans based on the risks and potential consequences of business interruptions?
    - Are the plans fully documented and in accordance with organizational policies and procedures? Have functional responsibilities been assigned?
    - Is the organization capable of and prepared to implement the plans?
    - Are the plans tested and revised based on the results?
    - Are the plans stored properly and safely? Is the location of and access to the plans known to management?
    - Are the locations of alternate facilities (backup sites) known to employees?
    - Do the plans call for coordination with local emergency services?

Internal audit's role after a disaster

11. Internal auditors have an important role to play immediately after a disaster occurs. An organization is more vulnerable after a disaster has occurred, and it is trying to recover. During that recovery period, internal auditors should monitor the effectiveness of the recovery and control of operations. Internal audit activity should identify areas where internal controls and mitigating actions should be improved and recommend improvements to the entity's business continuity plan. Internal audit can also provide support during the recovery activities.
12. After the disaster, usually within several months, internal auditors can assist in identifying the lessons learned from the disaster and the recovery operations. Those observations and recommendations may enhance activities to recover resources and update the next version of the business continuity plan.
13. In the final analysis, it is senior management that will determine the degree of internal auditors' involvement in the business continuity and disaster recovery processes, considering their knowledge, skills, independence, and objectivity.

(c) **Privacy**

IIA's Practice Advisory 2100-8: The Internal Auditor's Role in Evaluating an Organization's Privacy Framework

Nature of This Practice Advisory

Internal auditors should consider these suggestions when evaluating an organization's activities related to its privacy framework. This guidance is not intended to represent all the procedures necessary for a comprehensive assurance or consulting engagement related to the privacy framework, but rather a recommended core set of high-level auditor responsibilities to complement related board and management responsibilities. Compliance with Practice Advisories is optional. *This guidance is repeated in Part 1 and Part 2 for proper coverage of the subject matter.*

1. Concerns relating to the protection of personal privacy are becoming more apparent, focused, and global as advancements in information technology and communications continually introduce new risks and threats to privacy. Privacy controls are legal requirements for doing business in most of the world.
2. Privacy definitions vary widely depending on country, culture, political environment, and legal framework. Privacy can encompass personal privacy (physical and psychological); privacy of

space (freedom from surveillance); privacy of communication (freedom from monitoring); and privacy of information (collection, use, and disclosure of personal information by others). "Personal information" generally refers to information that can be associated with a specific individual, or that has identifying characteristics that might be combined with other information to do so. It can include any factual or subjective information, recorded or not, in any form or media. Personal information might include, for example

- Name, address, identification numbers, income, or blood type
- Evaluations, comments, social status, or disciplinary actions
- Employee files, credit records, loan records

3. Privacy is a risk management issue. Failure to protect privacy and personal information with the appropriate controls can have significant consequences for an organization. For example, it can damage the reputation of individuals and the organization, lead to legal liability issues, and contribute to consumer and employee mistrust.
4. There are a variety of laws and regulations developing worldwide relating to the protection of personal information. As well, there are generally accepted policies and practices that can be applied to the privacy issue.
5. It is clear that good privacy practices contribute to good governance and accountability. The governing body (e.g., the board of directors, head of an agency or legislative body) is ultimately accountable for ensuring that the principal risks of the organization have been identified and the appropriate systems have been implemented to mitigate those risks. This includes establishing the necessary privacy framework for the organization and monitoring its implementation.
6. The internal auditor can contribute to ensuring good governance and accountability by playing a role in helping an organization meet its privacy objectives. The internal auditor is uniquely positioned to evaluate the privacy framework in an organization and identify the significant risks along with the appropriate recommendations for their mitigation.
7. In conducting such an evaluation of the privacy framework, the internal auditor should consider
   - The various laws, regulations, and policies relating to privacy in their respective jurisdictions (including any jurisdiction where the organization conducts business).
   - Liaison with in-house legal counsel to determine the exact nature of such laws, regulations, and other standards and practices applicable to the organization and the country/countries in which it does business.
   - Liaison with information technology specialists to ensure information security and data protection controls are in place and regularly reviewed and assessed for appropriateness.
   - The level or maturity of the organization's privacy practices. Depending on the level, the internal auditor may have differing roles. The auditor may facilitate the development and implementation of the privacy program, conduct a privacy risk assessment to determine the needs and risk exposures of the organization, or review and provide assurance on the effectiveness of the privacy policies, practices, and controls across the organization. If the internal auditor assumes a portion of the responsibility for developing and implementing a privacy program, the auditor's independence may be impaired.
8. Typically, the internal auditor could be expected to identify the types and appropriateness of information gathered by the organization that is deemed personal or private, the collection methodology used, and whether the organization's use of the information so collected is in accordance with its intended use and the laws, in the areas that the information is gathered, held, and used.
9. Given the highly technical and legal nature of the topic, the internal auditor should ensure that the appropriate in-depth knowledge and capacity to conduct any such evaluation of the privacy framework is available, using third-party experts, if necessary.

(d) **Information or Physical Security**

IIA's Practice Advisory 2100-2: Information Security

Nature of This Practice Advisory

Internal auditors should consider these suggestions when evaluating an organization's governance activities related to information security. This guidance is not intended to represent all the procedures necessary for a comprehensive assurance or consulting engagement related to information security, but simply a recommended core set of high-level auditor responsibilities to complement related board and management responsibilities. *Compliance with Practice Advisories is optional. This guidance is repeated in Part 1 and Part 2 for proper coverage of the subject matter.*

1. Internal auditors should determine that management and the board have a clear understanding that information security is a management responsibility. This responsibility includes all critical information of the organization regardless of media in which the information is stored.
2. The chief audit executive should determine that the internal audit activity possesses, or has access to, competent auditing resources to evaluate information security and associated risk exposures. This includes both internal and external risk exposures, including exposures relating to the organization's relationships with outside entities.
3. Internal auditors should determine that the board has sought assurance from management that information security breaches and conditions that might represent a threat to the organization will promptly be made known to those performing the internal audit activity.
4. Internal auditors should assess the effectiveness of preventive, detective, and mitigation measures against past attacks, as deemed appropriate, and future attempts or incidents deemed likely to occur. Internal auditors should confirm that the board has been appropriately informed of threats, incidents, vulnerabilities exploited, and corrective measures.
5. Internal auditors should periodically assess the organization's information security practices and recommend, as appropriate, enhancements to, or implementation of new, controls and safeguards. Following an assessment, an assurance report should be provided to the board. Such assessments can be conducted either as separate stand-alone engagements or as multiple engagements integrated into other audits or engagements conducted as part of the approved audit plan.

IIA's Practice Advisory 2100-6: Control and Audit Implications of E-commerce Activities

Nature of This Practice Advisory

Growth of e-commerce continues at a fast pace, both for business-to-business and business-to-consumer applications. Effective controls and processes are critical for successful development and implementation of an e-commerce strategy. Thus, an effective e-commerce assessment effort may be a key part of the annual audit plan for many companies. This Practice Advisory provides an overview of the control and audit implications. Additional resources for practitioners are: IIA's Systems Assurance and Control (SAC) product and other technology reports and publications of the Information Systems Audit and Control Association (ISACA). Both have developed guidelines and criteria for evaluation of electronic systems and models. *Compliance with Practice Advisories is optional. This guidance is repeated in Part 1 and Part 2 for proper coverage of the subject matter.*

1. Electronic commerce (e-commerce) is generally defined as "conducting commercial activities over the Internet." These commercial activities can be business-to-business (B2B), business-to-consumer (B2C), and business-to-employee (B2E). The growth of e-commerce has been dramatic and is anticipated to grow even more rapidly in the years ahead. The recent publication by the IIA Research Foundation, Systems Assurance and Control (SAC), and the success of the Web-based *www.ITAudit.org* and various e-mail IIA newsletters confirms that technology not only supports e-commerce strategies, but is an integral part. Web-based and other technology changes have a dramatic impact on society, governance, economics, competition, markets, organizational structure, and national defense. Clearly, these changes and the dramatic growth of e-commerce create significant control and management challenges that should be considered by internal auditors in developing and implementing their audit plans.

Understanding and Planning an E-Commerce Engagement

2. Continuous changes in technology offer the internal auditing profession both great opportunity and risk. Before attempting to provide assurance on the systems and processes, an internal auditor should understand the changes in business and information systems, the related risks, and the alignment of strategies with the enterprise's design and market requirements. The internal auditor should review management's strategic planning and risk assessment processes and its decisions about
   - Which risks are serious?

- Which risks can be insured?
- What current controls will mitigate the risks?
- Which additional compensating controls are necessary?
- What type of monitoring is required?

3. The major components of auditing e-commerce activities are
   - Assess the internal control structure, including the tone set by senior management.
   - Provide reasonable assurance that goals and objectives can be achieved.
   - Determine if the risks are acceptable.
   - Understand the information flow.
   - Review the interface issues (i.e., hardware to hardware, software to software, and hardware to software).
   - Evaluate the business continuity and disaster recovery plans.
4. The concerns of the chief audit executive (CAE) in performing an e-commerce engagement relate to the competency and capacity of the internal audit activity. Among the possible factors that may constrain the internal audit activity are
   - Does the internal audit activity have sufficient skills? If not, can the skills be acquired?
   - Are training or other resources necessary?
   - Is the staffing level sufficient for the near term and long term?
   - Can the expected audit plan be delivered?
5. Internal auditor's questions during risk assessment. The IIA's *SAC* publication can assist the internal auditor in audit planning and risk assessment. It includes a list of e-commerce areas that should be of interest to an internal auditor who is undertaking an engagement and assessing risks. The questions for internal auditors to consider are
   - Is there a business plan for the e-commerce project or program?
   - Does the plan cover the integration of the planning, design, and implementation of the e-commerce system with the strategies of the organization?
   - What will be the impact on the performance, security, reliability, and availability of the system?
   - Will the functionality meet the end user's needs (e.g., employees, customers, business partners) as well as management's objectives?
   - Have governmental and regulatory requirements been analyzed and considered?
   - How secure is the hardware and software, and will they prevent or detect unauthorized access, inappropriate use, and other harmful effects and losses?
   - Will transaction processing be current, accurate, complete, and indisputable?
   - Does the control environment allow the organization to achieve its e-commerce objectives as it moves from concepts to results?
   - Does the risk assessment include internal and external forces?
   - Have the inherent risks associated with the Internet and Internet provider (i.e., reliability of basic communications, authentication of users, and who has access) been addressed?
   - Have other issues been addressed (e.g., disclosures of confidential business information, misuse of intellectual property, violations of copyrights, trademark infringement, libelous statements on Web sites, fraud, misuse of electronic signatures, privacy violations, and reputation damage)?
   - If outside vendors are used, has a going-concern evaluation been conducted by a trusted third party who is qualified to certify the vendor?
   - If vendors provide hosting services, do they have a tested business contingency plan? Have they provided a recent SAS-70 report? (SAS-70 reports can offer valuable information about internal controls to user organizations.) Also, have privacy issues been resolved?
   - Does the contract include audit rights?

E-Commerce Risks and Control Issues

6. The e-commerce risk and control environment is complex and evolving. Risk can be defined as the uncertainty of an event occurring that could have a negative impact on the achievement of objectives. Risk is inherent to every business or government entity. Opportunity risks assumed by

management are often drivers of organizational activities. Beyond these opportunities may be threats and other dangers that are not clearly understood and fully evaluated and are too easily accepted as part of doing business. In striving to manage risk, it is essential to have an understanding of risk elements. It is also important to be aware of new threats and changes in technology that open new vulnerabilities in information security. For management purposes, the next seven key questions can serve to identify organizational risk and target potential ways to control or mitigate the exposures. (Risk practitioners use a variety of different risk management approaches; these questions illustrate one approach.) Risk elements associated with the questions are displayed in brackets.

(a) **Risk identification and quantification**

- What could happen that would adversely affect the organization's ability to achieve its objectives and execute its strategies? [Threat events]
- If it happens, what is the potential financial impact? [Single-loss exposure value]
- How often might it happen? [Frequency]
- How probable are the answers to the first three questions? [Uncertainty]

(b) **Risk management and mitigation**

- What can be done to prevent and avoid, mitigate, and detect risks and provide notification? [Safeguards and controls]
- How much will it cost? [Safeguard and control costs]
- How efficient would that be? [Cost/benefit or ROI analysis]

7. Some of the more critical risk and control issues to be addressed by the internal auditor are
   - General project management risks
   - Specific security threats, such as denial of service, physical attacks, viruses, identity theft, and unauthorized access or disclosure of data
   - Maintenance of transaction integrity under a complex network of links to legacy systems and data warehouses
   - Web site content review and approval when there are frequent changes and sophisticated customer features and capabilities that offer around-the-clock service
   - Rapid technology changes
   - Legal issues, such as increasing regulations throughout the world to protect individual privacy; enforceability of contracts outside the organization's country; and tax and accounting issues
   - Changes to surrounding business processes and organizational structures

Auditing E-Commerce Activities

8. The overall audit objective should be to ensure that all e-commerce processes have effective internal controls. Management of e-commerce initiatives should be documented in a strategic plan that is well developed and approved. If there is a decision not to participate in e-commerce, that decision should be carefully analyzed, documented, and approved by the governing board.
9. Audit objectives for an e-commerce engagement may include
   - Evidence of e-commerce transactions
   - Availability and reliability of security system
   - Effective interface between e-commerce and financial systems
   - Security of monetary transactions
   - Effectiveness of customer authentication process
   - Adequacy of business continuity processes, including the resumption of operations
   - Compliance with common security standards
   - Effective use and control of digital signatures
   - Adequacy of systems, policies, and procedures to control public key certificates (using public key cryptographic techniques)
   - Adequacy and timeliness of operating data and information
   - Documented evidence of an effective system of internal control

10. The details of the audit program used to audit e-commerce activities in specific organizations will vary depending on industry, country, and legal and business models. An outline of a possible e-commerce audit protocol for key areas follows.

    (a) **E-Commerce organization**—The internal auditor should

    - Determine the value of transactions.
    - Identify the stakeholders (external and internal).
    - Review the change management process.
    - Examine the approval process.
    - Review the business plan for e-commerce activities.
    - Evaluate the policies over public key certificates.
    - Review the digital signature procedures.
    - Examine service level agreements between buyer, supplier, and certification authority.
    - Ascertain the quality assurance policy.
    - Assess the privacy policy and compliance in e-commerce activities.
    - Assess the incident response capability.

    (b) **Fraud**—The internal auditor should be alert for

    - Unauthorized movement of money (e.g., transfers to jurisdictions where the recovery of funds would be difficult)
    - Duplication of payments
    - Denial of orders placed or received, goods received, or payments made
    - Exception reports and procedures, and effectiveness of the follow-up
    - Digital signatures: Are they used for all transactions? Who authorizes them? Who has access to them?
    - Protections against viruses and hacking activities (history file, use of tools)
    - Access rights: Are they reviewed regularly? Are they promptly revised when staff members are changed?
    - History of interception of transactions by unauthorized persons

    (c) **Authentication**—The internal auditor should review the policies for authenticating transactions and evaluating controls.

    - Evidence of regular reviews
    - Control self-assessment (CSA) tools used by management
    - Regular independent checks
    - Segregation of duties
    - Tools that management should have in place: firewalls (multilevel to partition e-commerce and other activities), password management, independent reconciliation, and audit trails

    (d) **Corruption of data**—The internal auditor should evaluate controls over data integrity.

    - Who can amend catalogs and prices or rates? What is the approval mechanism?
    - Can someone destroy audit trails?
    - Who can approve bulletin board amendments?
    - What are the procedures for ordering and recording?
    - Is the process of online tendering providing adequate documentation?
    - Tools that should be in place include intrusion management (monitoring software, automatic time-out, and trend analysis), physical security for e-commerce servers, change controls, and reconciliation.

    (e) **Business interruptions**—The internal auditor should review the business continuity plan and determine if it has been tested. Management should have devised an alternative means to process the transactions in the event of an interruption. Management should have a process in place to address these potential conditions.

    - Volume attacks
    - Denial of service attacks

- Inadequacies in interfacing between e-commerce and financial management systems
- Backup facilities
- Strategies to counter hacking, intrusion, cracking, viruses, worms, Trojan horses, and back doors

(f) **Management issues**—The internal auditor should evaluate how well business units are managing the e-commerce process. These are some relevant topics.

- Project management reviews of individual initiatives and development projects
- System development life cycle reviews
- Vendor selection, vendor capabilities, employee confidentiality, and bonding
- Postimplementation economic reviews: Are anticipated benefits being achieved? What metric is being used to measure success?
- Postimplementation process reviews: Are new processes in place and working effectively?

MULTIPLE-CHOICE QUESTIONS (1-21)

1. The proper organizational role of internal auditing is to
- a. Assist the external auditor in order to reduce external audit fees.
- b. Perform studies to assist in the attainment of more efficient operations.
- c. Serve as the investigative arm of the audit committee of the board of directors.
- d. Serve as an appraisal function to examine and evaluate activities as a service to the organization.

2. In some organizations, consideration is being given to the possibility of outsourcing internal audit functions. Management in a large organization should recognize that the external auditor might have an advantage, compared to the internal auditor, because of the external auditor's
- a. Familiarity with the organization. Its annual audits provide an in-depth knowledge of the organization.
- b. Size. It can hire experienced, knowledgeable, and certified staff.
- c. Size. It is able to offer continuous availability of staff unaffected by other priorities.
- d. Structure. It may more easily accommodate audit requirements in distant locations.

3. The status of the internal auditing function should be free from the impact of irresponsible policy changes by management. The most effective way to ensure that freedom is to
- a. Have the internal auditing charter approved by both management and the board of directors.
- b. Adopt policies for the functioning of the auditing department.
- c. Establish an audit committee within the board of directors.
- d. Develop written policies and procedures to serve as standards of performance for the department.

4. The internal auditor's responsibility for the prevention of fraud would include all of the following **except:**
- a. Determining if the organizational environment fosters control consciousness.
- b. Ensuring against the occurrence of fraud.
- c. Being aware of activities in which fraud is likely to occur.
- d. Evaluating the effectiveness of actions taken by management to deter fraud.

5. The consultative approach to auditing emphasizes
- a. Imposition of corrective measures.
- b. Participation with auditees to improve methods.
- c. Fraud investigation.
- d. Implementation of policies and procedures.

6. In some cultures and organizations, managers insist that the internal auditing function is not needed to provide a critical assessment of the organization's operations. A management attitude such as this will most probably have an adverse affect on the internal auditing function's
- a. Operating budget variance.
- b. Effectiveness.
- c. Performance appraisals.
- d. Policies and procedures.

Items 7 through 9 are based on the following:

A service company is currently experiencing a significant downsizing and process reengineering. Its board of directors has redefined the business goals and established initiatives using technology developed in-house to meet these goals. As a result, a more decentralized approach has been adopted to run the business functions by empowering the business branch managers to make decisions and perform functions traditionally done at a higher level.

The internal auditing staff is made up of the director, two managers, and five staff auditors, all with financial background. In the past, the primary focus of successful audit activities has been the service branches and the six regional division headquarters, which support the branches. These division headquarters are the primary targets for possible elimination. The support functions, such as human resources, accounting, and purchasing, will be brought into the national headquarters and technology will be enhanced to enable and augment these operations.

7. Based on the above changes and assuming those total audit resources remain the same, what activities should the internal auditing department perform to best serve the organization?

I. Increase audit time in systems development.
II. Increase audit time in service branches.
III. Increase audit time in functions being centralized.
IV. Continue the allocation of audit time as before.

- a. I and II.
- b. II and III.
- c. I and III.
- d. III and IV.

8. Up to this point, internal auditing has reported to the chief operating officer. Due to the significant changes, there has been some discussion as to changing this reporting relationship. What would be the best reporting relationship for internal auditing?
- a. Administrative and functional to the president.
- b. Administrative to the president, functional to the board.
- c. Administrative to the chief financial officer and functional to the president.
- d. Administrative and functional to the chief operating officer.

9. Branch managers view the internal auditing function as a watchdog for top management. What is the best way for internal auditing to change this view to one that is more cooperative?
- a. Increase focus on control responsibilities.
- b. Increase technical skills.
- c. Increase confidentiality of investigative audits to minimize fear.
- d. Increase solicitation of auditee concerns.

10. As part of the process to improve auditor-auditee relations, it is very important to deal with how internal auditing is perceived. Certain types of attitudes in the work performed will help create these perceptions. From a management perspective, which attitude is likely to be the **most** conducive to a positive perception?
- a. Objective.
- b. Investigative.

c. Interrogatory.
d. Consultative.

11. In planning a system of internal operating controls, the role of the internal auditor is to
a. Design the controls.
b. Appraise the effectiveness of the controls.
c. Establish the policies for controls.
d. Create the procedures for the planning process.

12. An audit committee should be designed to enhance the independence of both the internal and external audit functions and to insulate the audit functions from undue management pressures. Using these criteria, audit committees should be composed of
a. A rotating subcommittee of the board of directors or its equivalent.
b. Only members from the relevant outside regulatory agencies.
c. Members from all important constituencies, specifically including representatives from banking, labor, regulatory agencies, shareholders, and officers.
d. Only external members of the board of directors or its equivalent.

13. Accepting the concept that internal auditing should be an integral part of an organization can involve a major change of attitude on the part of top management. Which of the following would be the **best** way for internal auditors to convince management regarding the need for and benefits of internal auditing?
a. Persuading top managers to accept the idea of internal audits by contacting company shareholders and regulatory agencies.
b. Educating top managers about the benefits and communicating with them on a regular basis.
c. Negotiating with top management to provide them with rewards, such as favorable audits.
d. Involving top management in deciding which audit findings will be reported.

14. Which of the following features of a large manufacturing company's organization structure would be a control weakness?
a. The IT department is headed by a vice president who reports directly to the president.
b. The chief financial officer is a vice president who reports to the chief executive officer.
c. The audit committee of the board consists of the chief executive officer, the chief financial officer, and a major stockholder.
d. The controller and treasurer report to the chief financial officer.

15. Audit committees have been identified as a major factor in promoting independence of both the internal and external auditor. Which of the following is the most important limitation on the effectiveness of audit committees?
a. Audit committees may be composed of independent directors. However, those directors may have close personal and professional friendships with management.
b. Audit committee members are compensated by the organization and thus favor a stockholder's view.
c. Audit committees devote most of their efforts to external audit concerns and do not pay much attention to internal auditing and the overall control environment.
d. Audit committee members do not normally have degrees in the accounting or auditing fields.

16. Who should have the **least** influence on the appointment of the director of internal audit?
a. The controller.
b. The audit committee.
c. The external auditor.
d. The chief executive officer.

17. During discussions with top management, the director of internal auditing identified several strategic business issues to consider in preparing the annual audit schedule. Which of the following does **not** represent a strategic issue for this purpose?
a. A monthly budgeting process will be implemented.
b. An international marketing campaign will be started to develop product recognition and also to leverage the new corporate-based advertising department.
c. Joint venture candidates will be sought to provide manufacturing and sourcing capabilities in European and Asian markets.
d. A human resources database will be established to ensure consistent administration of policies and to improve data retention.

18. Audit committees are most likely to participate in approving
a. Staff promotions and salary increases.
b. Internal audit report findings and recommendations.
c. Audit work schedules.
d. Appointment of the internal audit director.

19. Audit committees are responsible for
a. Selecting the director of internal auditing.
b. Developing the internal auditing plan and budget.
c. Reviewing and approving the internal audit charter.
d. Selecting the independent accountants.

20. To avoid creating conflict between the chief executive officer (CEO) and the audit committee, the internal auditing director should
a. Submit copies of all audit reports to the CEO and audit committee.
b. Strengthen independence through organizational status.
c. Discuss all pending reports to the CEO with the audit committee.
d. Request board establishment of policies covering internal auditing relationships with the audit committee.

21. Which of the following would **not** be an appropriate member of an audit committee?
a. The vice president of the local bank used by the company.
b. An academic specializing in business administration.
c. A retired executive of a firm that had been associated with the corporation.
d. The firm's vice president of operations.

MULTIPLE-CHOICE ANSWERS AND EXPLANATIONS

1. d __ __	6. b __ __	11. b __ __	16. a __ __	21. d __ __
2. d __ __	7. c __ __	12. d __ __	17. a __ __	
3. a __ __	8. b __ __	13. b __ __	18. d __ __	
4. b __ __	9. d __ __	14. c __ __	19. c __ __	1st: __/21 = __%
5. b __ __	10. d __ __	15. a __ __	20. d __ __	2nd: __/21 = __%

1. (d) This alternative describes the basic role concept of internal auditing. Choice (a) is incorrect because reduction of external audit fees is a result of internal audit work but not a role. Choice (b) is incorrect because this does not represent a complete description of the proper role. Choice (c) is incorrect because this role is too limited for internal auditing. It also serves operations management and top management.
Subject Area: Internal audit—roles and responsibilities. Source: CIA 1196, III-30.

2. (d) The external auditor can offer better service in other geographical areas because of its dispersion of offices. Choice (a) is incorrect. The internal audit staff, not the external auditor, through its continuous auditing gains an in-depth knowledge of the organization. Choice (b) is incorrect. The internal audit staff is able to maintain an experienced knowledgeable and certified (CIA) staff, without the potential threat of staff reassignment. Choice (c) is incorrect. The internal staff is continuously available and not subject to greater priority work with other clients.
Subject Area: Internal audit—roles and responsibilities. Source: CIA 1196, III-34.

3. (a) Approval of the charter by the board of directors will protect the internal auditing function from management actions, which could weaken the status of the internal auditing department. Choice (b) is incorrect. While adoption of the *Standards* serves as a guide and a measure of internal auditing performance, it will not protect and preserve the department's status. Choice (c) is incorrect. The establishment of an audit committee does not ensure the status of internal auditing without its involvement in areas such as approval of the charter. Choice (d) is incorrect. Written policies and procedures serve to guide the audit staff but have little impact on management.
Subject Area: Internal audit—roles and responsibilities. Source: CIA 593, I-5.

4. (b) Auditor is not responsible for acting as an ensurer or guarantor against fraud. Choice (a) is incorrect. Internal auditing is responsible for evaluating the organization's control consciousness. Choice (c) is incorrect. Auditor should be aware of activities where fraud is likely to occur. Choice (d) is incorrect. Deterrence of fraud is the responsibility of management; evaluating the effectiveness of management efforts is the responsibility of internal auditing.
Subject Area: Internal audit—roles and responsibilities. Source: CIA 1192, I-50.

5. (b) Since auditors alone cannot implement audit recommendations, auditee participation and involvement makes improvements better. Choice (a) is incorrect. Imposition implies an adversarial relationship. Choice (c) is incorrect. Auditors, not consultants, investigate fraud. Choice (d) is incorrect. Due to the requirement for independence, auditors should never implement policies and procedures.
Subject Area: Internal audit—roles and responsibilities. Source: CIA 595, III-2.

6. (b) In this type of situation, management is highly averse to analysis or possible criticism of their actions and will inhibit the internal audit department's effectiveness. Choice (a) is incorrect. An operating budget variance report is a control device used to monitor actual performance versus budget. Management foot-dragging could cause unfavorable variances, but favorable variances could also occur if many audits were cut short due to scope impairments. Choice (c) is incorrect. An unbiased evaluation of audit staff would not be affected by lack of cooperation on the part of nonaudit management. Choice (d) is incorrect. Policies and procedures of the internal audit function are developed by the internal audit department and should not be affected by nonaudit management.
Subject Area: Internal audit—roles and responsibilities. Source: CIA 595, III-16.

7. (c) Due to the focus on technology, audit time spent reviewing systems development should be increased (Item I). More testing is needed at the central location due to concentration of functions (Item III). Choices (a) and (b) are incorrect. Item II is incorrect. While a small incremental increase in audit time may be feasible, the benefit derived would be minimal. Choice (d) is incorrect. Item IV is incorrect. Change to business goals, processes, and focus will also require proactive change by the internal auditing department.
Subject Area: Internal audit—roles and responsibilities. Source: CIA 1195, III-3.

8. (b) Independence is less likely to be impaired if the internal auditing department reports to the board. Choice (a) is incorrect. Independence is impaired because the president is responsible for the areas to be audited. Choice (c) is incorrect. Independence may be impaired in financial audits as well as audits of line functions. Choice (d) is incorrect. Independence may be impaired for all audits of operational areas.
Subject Area: Internal audit—roles and responsibilities. Source: CIA 1195, III-3, III-4.

9. (d) Two-way communication is important in fostering a cooperative relationship. Choice (a) is incorrect. Control has negative connotations and breeds antagonism with line personnel. Choice (b) is incorrect. Interpersonal skills are more important to fostering a cooperative relationship. Choice (c) is incorrect. Participation and cooperation are paramount in trying to improve auditor-auditee relations, especially in audits that require intense investigation.
Subject Area: Internal audit—roles and responsibilities. Source: CIA 1195, III-5.

10. (d) A consultative attitude leads to two-way communication. Choice (a) is incorrect. An objective attitude is desirable, but by itself will not lead to a more positive relationship. Choice (b) is incorrect. An investigative attitude is not likely to enhance the relationship. Choice (c) is incorrect. An interrogatory attitude is not likely to enhance the relationship.

Subject Area: Internal audit—roles and responsibilities. Source: CIA 1195, III-7.

11. (b) This is the proper role of the internal auditor, which is to report the results to management. Choices (a), (c), and (d) are incorrect because they are the roles of management.

Subject Area: Internal audit—roles and responsibilities. Source: CIA 1190, I-11.

12. (d) Audit committees should be made up of external members of the board of directors or other similar oversight committees. Choice (a) is incorrect. Rotating subcommittee members can be internal to a company and would not have independence. Choice (b) is incorrect. External members should represent different backgrounds, not just regulatory background. Choice (c) is incorrect. The size of the audit committee is limited and cannot include too many such as representatives from shareholders and labor.

Subject Area: Internal audit—roles and responsibilities. Source: CIA 1196, III-10.

13. (b) Education and communication, although lengthy and costly, are the only way to achieve long-term results. Choice (a) is incorrect. Manipulation is not an option since it can be done only if the party manipulating has power. Its effects are also short-lived and do not lead to long-term commitment. Choice (c) is incorrect. Negotiation is not an alternative since the two parties do not have equal power. Furthermore, internal auditors often do not have immediate rewards available to them to offer management. Choice (d) is incorrect. Involving top management in this manner is not appropriate.

Subject Area: Internal audit—roles and responsibilities. Source: CIA 597, III-33.

14. (c) The audit committee should be made up of independent directors. Choices (a), (b), and (d) are incorrect. These are strengths since they prevent the information technology operation from being dominated by a user.

Subject Area: Internal audit—roles and responsibilities. Source: CIA 1190, II-7.

15. (a) This is a major limitation that has hampered the effective operation of audit committees. Choice (b) is incorrect. Audit committee members are usually composed of outside directors. Many of these directors have a broad viewpoint and are not limited to a stockholder's view. Choice (c) is incorrect. Audit committees devote considerable time to the external audit function, but the evidence is that they are increasingly devoting time to internal audit reports. Choice (d) is incorrect. A committee member need not have an accounting degree to understand most reporting and control issues.

Subject Area: Internal audit—roles and responsibilities. Source: CIA 1196, I-26.

16. (a) The controller is an auditee, and as such should have the least influence. The highest levels of management and the audit committee are directly involved in the appointment. The external auditor has influence on the appointment because the external auditor requires an appropriate level of expertise and independence in order to rely on the work of the internal auditor. Choice (b) is incorrect. The audit committee participates in approving the selection and dismissal of the internal audit director. Choice (c) is incorrect. The external auditor is consulted on the appointment of the director of the internal audit. Choice (d) is incorrect. The director of internal audit administratively should report to the chief executive officer. Therefore, the CEO should have some say in the appointment of the director of internal audit.

Subject Area: Internal audit—roles and responsibilities. Source: CIA 594, III-6.

17. (a) Choice (a) is the correct answer. This is an operating decision to facilitate the budgeting process and improve information. Choice (b) is incorrect. The director will need to ensure that the new marketing process and the centralized advertising department are recognized and monitored in risk assessment and planning activities. Choice (c) is incorrect. The addition of joint-venture partners will add new or additional concerns for risk assessment and planning in the internal auditing department. Choice (d) is incorrect. Both the assumptions and ongoing activities related to human resources database would require consideration in the planning and programming of audit activity.

Subject Area: Internal audit—roles and responsibilities. Source: CIA 1193, I-6.

18. (d) The independence of the internal auditing department is enhanced when the audit committee participates in naming its director. Choice (a) is incorrect. The company's internal auditing director is responsible for staff promotions. Choice (b) is incorrect. The company's internal auditing director is responsible for approving internal audit reports. Choice (c) is incorrect. This is a part of the internal auditing department's planning function.

Subject Area: Internal audit—roles and responsibilities. Source: CIA 593, II-4.

19. (c) This is an oversight activity. It will ensure that internal auditors are carrying out their responsibilities. Choice (a) is incorrect. The audit committee should exercise an active oversight role. The actual decision, however, should be left to appropriate senior management of the organization. Choice (b) is incorrect. Developing the internal audit plan and budget is the responsibility of the audit director. Choice (d) is incorrect. Selecting the independent accountants is the responsibility of senior management of the organization. However, the audit committee approves the (1) selection of the internal audit director and independent accountants and (2) audit plan and budget.

Subject Area: Internal audit—roles and responsibilities. Source: CIA 593, I-4.

20. (d) The action the internal auditing director should take to avoid conflict between the CEO and the audit committee (IIA *Standards*). Choice (a) is incorrect. The CEO and audit committee most likely should receive summary reports. Top management and the board ordinarily are not involved in the details of audit work. Choice (b) is incorrect. Independence is not sufficient to avert conflict unless reporting relationships are well defined. Choice (c) is incorrect. See choice (a).

Subject Area: Internal audit—roles and responsibilities. Source: CIA 593, II-13.

21. (d) Audits may be conducted in the member's area of control and responsibility. Thus, the potential member is not independent of the audit function. The potential member is also not an outside director. Choices (a), (b), and (c) are incorrect. They are normally independent of the firm's internal operations and external to the firm.

Subject Area: Internal audit—roles and responsibilities. Source: CIA 593, II-13.

5 GOVERNANCE, RISK, AND CONTROL KNOWLEDGE ELEMENTS (15–25%)

THEORY

5.1 Corporate Governance Principles

(a) **Corporate Governance Defined.** To understand corporate governance, it is useful to understand the idea of legitimacy. Legitimacy is a somewhat abstract concept, but it is vital in that it helps explain the importance of the relative roles of a corporation's charter, shareholders, board of directors, management, and employees, all of which are components of the modern corporate governance system.

Whereas legitimacy is a condition, legitimization is a dynamic process by which business seeks to perpetuate its acceptance. The dynamic process aspect should be emphasized, because society's norms and values change and business must change if its legitimacy is to continue. It is also useful to consider legitimacy at both the micro, or company, level and the macro, or business institution, level.

The issue of corporate governance is a direct outgrowth of the question of legitimacy. For business to be legitimate and to maintain its legitimacy in the eyes of the public, its governance must correspond to the will of the people.

"Corporate governance" refers to the method by which a firm is being governed, directed, administered, or controlled and to the goals for which it is being governed. Corporate governance is concerned with the relative roles, rights, and accountability of such stakeholder groups as owners, boards of directors, managers, employees, and others who assert to be stakeholders.

(b) **Corporate Governance Principles and Issues**

(i) **Components of corporate governance.** To appreciate fully the legitimacy and corporate governance issues, it is important that we understand the major groups that make up the corporate form of business organization, because it is only by so doing that we can appreciate how the system has failed to work according to its intended design.

(ii) **Roles of four major groups.** The four major groups we need to mention in setting the stage are the (1) shareholders (owners/stakeholders), (2) board of directors, (3) managers, and (4) employees. Overarching these groups is the **charter** issued by the state, giving the corporation the right to exist and stipulating the basic terms of its existence.

Under US corporate law, **shareholders** are the owners of a corporation. As owners, they should have ultimate control over the corporation. This control is manifested primarily in the right to select the board of directors of the company. Generally, the number of shares of stock owned determines the degree of each shareholder's right.

Because large organizations may have hundreds of thousands of shareholders, they elect a smaller group, known as the **board of directors,** to govern and oversee the management of the business. The board is responsible for ascertaining that the manager puts the interests of the owners (i.e., shareholders) first. The third major group in the authority hierarchy is **management**—the group of individuals hired by the board to run the company and manage it on a daily basis. Along with the board, top management establishes overall policy. Middle- and lower-level managers carry out this policy and conduct the daily supervision of the operative employees. **Employees** are those hired by the company to perform the actual operational work. Managers are employees, too, but in this discussion we use the term "employees" to refer to nonmanagerial employees.

(iii) **Separation of ownership from control.** The social and ethical issues that have evolved in recent years focus on the *intended* versus *actual* roles, rights, responsibilities, and accountability of these four major groups. The major condition embedded in the structure of modern corporations that has contributed to the corporate governance problem has been the **separation of ownership from control**. In the precorporate period, owners were typically the managers themselves. Thus, the system worked the way it was intended; the owners also controlled the business. Even when firms grew larger and managers were hired, the owners often were on the scene to hold the management group accountable.

As the public corporation grew and stock ownership became widely dispersed, a separation of ownership from control became the prevalent condition. The dispersion of ownership into hundreds of thousands or millions of shares meant that essentially no one or no one group owned enough shares to exercise control. This being the case, the most effective control that owners could exercise was the election of the board of directors to serve as their representative and watch over management. The shareholders were owners in a technical sense, but most of them perceived themselves to be investors rather than owners.

The other factors that added to management's power were the corporate laws and traditions that gave the management group control over the **proxy process**—the method by which the shareholders elected boards of directors. Over time, it was not difficult for management groups to create boards of directors of like-minded executives who would simply collect their fees and defer to management on whatever it wanted. The result of this process was that power, authority, and control began to flow upward from management rather than downward from the shareholders (owners). **Agency problems** developed when the interests of the shareholders were not aligned with the interests of the manager, and the manager (who is simply a hired *agent* with the responsibility of representing the owner's best interest) began to pursue self-interest instead.

(iv) **Role of the board of directors.** It is clear from the preceding discussion that a potential governance problem is built into the corporate system because of the separation of ownership from control. It is equally clear that the board of directors is intended to oversee management on behalf of the shareholders. However, this is where the system had once broken down. For corporate governance to function as it was originally intended, the board of directors must be an effective, potent body carrying out its roles and responsibilities in ascertaining that management pursue the shareholders' best interests.

Although the governance battle has been won at large US companies, the war is not over. Often midsize and smaller companies and overseas boards still do not follow the guidelines for good governance. Dot-coms in particular have tended to have boards dominated by insiders, a combination of current management and others with connections to the company. Europe, too, is just entering the corporate governance battle. Mass stock ownership is a new phenomenon, but investors who feel stung by steep price drops are taking action. European shareholders are going to court and showing up en masse at annual meetings.

(v) **Need for board independence.** Board independence from management is a crucial aspect of good governance. It is here that the difference between **inside directors** and **outside directors** becomes most pronounced. Outside directors are independent from the firm and its top managers. In contrast, inside directors have some sort of ties to the firm. Sometimes they are top managers in the firm; other times insiders are family members or others with close ties to the chief executive officer (CEO). To varying degrees, each of these parties is "beholden" to the CEO and, therefore, might be hesitant to speak out when necessary.

Another problem is managerial control of the board processes. CEOs often can control board perks, such as director compensation and committee assignments. Board members who rock the boat may find they are left out in the cold.

(vi) **Issues surrounding compensation.**

(A) ***CEO compensation.*** The issue of executive pay was a lightning rod for the concern that managers place their own interests over those of their shareholders. Two issues are at the heart of the CEO pay controversy: (1) the extent to which CEO pay is tied to firm performance, and (2) the overall level of CEO pay.

The move to tie CEO pay more closely to firm performance grew in momentum when shareholders observed CEO pay rising as firm performance fell. Many executives had gotten staggering salaries, even while profits were falling, workers were being laid off, and shareholder return was dropping. Shareholders were assisted in their effort to monitor CEO pay by stricter disclosure requirements from the Securities and Exchange Commission (SEC). The revised compensation disclosure rule, adopted by the SEC in 1992, was designed to provide shareholders with more information about the relationship between firm performance and CEO compensation. According to the results of one study, it seems to have worked. Since the rule's implementation, compensation committees have met more frequently, lessened the number of insiders as members, and become more moderate in size. More important, largely through the use of stock options, CEO pay has become more closely aligned with accounting and market performance measures than it was before the rule's implementation. There is some evidence that boards of directors are becoming the watchdogs they are always supposed to be.

(B) ***Outside director compensation.*** It was suggested earlier that there might be some link between CEO and executive compensation and board members. Therefore, it should not be surprising that directors' pay is becoming an issue, too.

Eighty years ago, it was illegal to pay nonexecutive board members. The logic was that because board members represented the shareholders, paying them out of the company's (i.e. shareholders') funds would be self-dealing.

(vii) **Consequences of the merger, acquisition, and takeover wave.** Mergers and acquisitions are another form of corporate governance, ones that come from outside the corporation. The expectation is that the threat of a possible takeover will motivate top managers to pursue shareholder interest rather than self-interest. The merger, acquisition, and hostile takeover wave of the 1980s brought out many new issues related to corporate governance. The economic prosperity of the 1980s, coupled with the rise of junk bonds and other creative methods of financing, made it possible for small firms and individuals to buy large corporations. Many corporate CEOs and boards went to great lengths to protect themselves from these takeovers. A major criticism of CEOs and boards during this period was that they were overly obsessed with self-preservation rather than making optimal decisions on behalf of their owners/stakeholders. Three of the most questionable top management practices to emerge from the hostile takeover wave were greenmail, poison pills, and golden parachutes.

(viii) **Insider trading scandals.** Insider trading is the practice of obtaining critical information from inside a company and then using that information for one's own personal financial gain. Although insider-trading scandals of this magnitude have not recurred, the revelations and repercussions of the Wall Street scandal will be with us for years. Insider-trading scandals gave the financial industry on Wall Street the biggest black eye it has had in over 50 years. Not only are shareholders suspicious of what has been going on unbeknownst to them, but small investors and the general public have lost faith in what they thought was the stable and secure financial industry. In 2001 the SEC instituted new disclosure rules designed to aid the small investor who historically has not had access to the information large investor's hold. Regulation FD (fair disclosure) set limits on the common company practice of selective disclosure. When companies disclose meaningful information to shareholders and securities professionals, they must now do so publicly so that small investors can enjoy a more level playing field.

(ix) **Board member liability.** In the mid- to late 1980s, not many individuals wanted board director positions. Concerned about increasing legal hassles emanating from stockholder, customer, and employee lawsuits, directors were quitting such positions or refusing to accept them in the first place. Although courts rarely hold directors personally liable in the hundreds of shareholder suits filed every year, over the past several years there have been a few cases in which directors have been held personally and financially liable for their decisions.

(x) **Improving corporate governance.** Efforts to improve corporate governance may be classified into two major categories for discussion purposes. First, changes could be made in the composition, structure, and functioning of boards of directors. Second, shareholders—on their own initiative or on the initiative of management or the board—could assume a more active role in governance. Each of these possibilities deserves closer examination.

(A) ***Changes in boards of directors.*** In the past decade or so, changes have begun to be made in boards of directors. These changes have occurred because of the growing belief that CEOs and executive teams need to be made more accountable to shareholders and other stakeholders. These changes include composition of the board, use of board committees (audit committee, nominating committee, compensation committee, public issues [policy] committee, governance committee), and getting tough with CEOs.

The principal responsibilities of an audit committee are

- To ensure that published financial statements are not misleading
- To ensure that internal controls are adequate
- To follow up on allegations of material, financial, ethical, and legal irregularities
- To ratify the selection of the external auditor

In 2003 the National Association of Corporate Directors (NACD) issued a director's handbook titled *The Governance Committee*. Its purpose is to raise the bar of board performance through effective oversight of the board's governance practices, use of ethics, and the process for director recruitment and retention. It is hoped that this handbook will improve the corporate governance process through the **governance committee**.

(B) ***Increased role of shareholders.*** Prior to the 1980s, civil rights activists, consumer groups, and other social activist pressure groups insisted that companies join their causes. Today companies increasingly understand the stakeholder perspective, which has created a new dilemma for companies as they deal with two broad types of shareholders: the traditional shareholder groups (i.e., the large institutional investors, such as pension funds), which are primarily interested in the firm's financial performance, and growing numbers of social activist shareholders, groups that typically pressure firms to adopt their desired postures on social causes (i.e., third world employment practices, animal testing, affirmative action, and environmental protection).

A major problem seems to be that both groups of shareholders feel like neglected constituencies. Both groups are attempting to rectify this condition through a variety of means. They are demanding effective power. They want to hold management groups accountable. They want to make changes, including changes in management if necessary. Like companies' earlier responses to other stakeholder activist groups, many executives are resisting. The result is a battle between managers and shareholders for corporate control.

Shareholder initiatives. Two perspectives in an increased role for shareholders include (1) the perspective of shareholders themselves asserting their rights on their own initiative and (2) initiatives being taken by companies to make shareholders a true constituency. The shareholder initiatives may be classified into three major, overlapping areas: (1) the rise of shareholder activist groups, (2) the filing of shareholder resolutions and activism at annual meetings, and (3) the filing of shareholder lawsuits.

Company initiatives. The need for companies to reestablish a relationship with their owners/stakeholders is somewhat akin to parents having to reestablish relations with their children once the children have grown up. Over the years, the evidence suggests that corporate executives have neglected their owners rather than making them a genuine part of the family. As share ownership has dispersed, there are several legitimate reasons why this separation has taken place. But there is also evidence that management groups have been too preoccupied with their own self-interests. In either case, corporations are beginning to realize that they have a responsibility to their shareholders that cannot be further neglected. Owners are demanding accountability, and it appears that they will be tenacious until they get it.

Public corporations have obligations to their shareholders and to potential shareholders. **Full disclosure** is one of these responsibilities. Disclosure should be made at regular and frequent intervals and should contain information that might affect the investment decisions of shareholders. This information might include the nature and activities of the business, financial and policy matters, tender offers, and special problems and opportunities in the near future and in the longer term. Of paramount importance are the interests of the investing public, not the interests of the incumbent management team. Board members should avoid conflicts between personal interests and the interests of shareholders. Company executives and directors have an obligation to avoid taking personal advantage of information that is not disclosed to the investing public and to avoid any personal use of corporation assets and influence.

With regard to corporate takeovers, fair treatment of shareholders necessitates special safeguards, including candor in public statements on the offer made, full disclosure of all information, absence of undue pressure, and sufficient time for shareholders to make considered decisions. A constructive purpose, not a predatory one, should be served by takeovers. The firm's major stakeholders are its owners. They are interdependent with other stakeholders, and, therefore, management should carry out its obligations to other constituency groups within the context of shareholder concern.

Shareholder programs are not a substitute for keeping shareholders foremost in the minds of executives and boards when economic decisions are being made. However, they do demonstrate an attempt by executives to give serious consideration to corporate/shareholder relations. These types of programs help the corporate governance problem because they show the shareholders that they matter and that they are important to the firm.

(c) **Sarbanes-Oxley Act of 2002**

(i) **Overview.** As a result of recent corporate scandals resulting from management's "lack of integrity," management fraud, accounting firms' negligence, and use of earnings management techniques, both investors and creditors have lost confidence in corporate America. In light of this financial crisis and credibility gap, the US Congress passed new legislation entitled Sarbanes-Oxley Act of 2002 to reform the accounting profession and corporate management and governance.

Essentially, the Act creates a five-member Public Company Accounting Oversight Board, which has the authority to set and enforce auditing, attestation, quality control, and ethics (including independence) standards for auditors of public companies. It is also empowered to inspect the auditing operations of public accounting firms that audit public companies as well as impose disciplinary and remedial sanctions for violations of the board's rules, securities laws, and professional auditing and accounting standards.

Other provisions affecting the accounting profession include requiring the rotation of the lead audit partner and reviewing audit partner every five years and extending the statute of limitations for the discovery of fraud to two years from the date of discovery and five years after the act. The law restricts the consulting work public company auditors can perform for their publicly traded audit clients and establishes harsh penalties for securities law violations, corporate fraud, and document shredding. Regarding sanctions, fines range from $100,000 for individual negligent conduct to $15 million to a firm for knowing or intentional conduct, including recklessness and repeated acts of negligence.

The Act also requires CEOs and chief financial officers (CFOs) to certify their company's financial statements as part of the annual report to stockholders. They also have a greater duty to communicate and coordinate with corporate audit committees who are now responsible for hiring, compensating, and overseeing the independent auditors. There are new requirements regarding enhanced financial disclosures as well.

(ii) **Provisions of the Act.** Those sections of the Sarbanes-Oxley Act that apply to internal auditors include Sections 301, 302, 404, and 406. Section 301 focuses on public company audit committees. Section 302 deals with quarterly CEO/CFO certification of financial statements and disclosure controls. Section 404 addresses annual evaluation and management assessment of internal control over financial reporting. Section 406 covers code of ethics.

Section 301 of the Act requires the audit committee to directly oversee the company's external audit firm, be independent, establish procedures for handling complaints about accounting or auditing matters, have the authority to hire advisors, and be adequately funded. Chief audit executives are often key audit committee advisors. As such, they may be heavily involved in drafting the audit committee charter and developing procedures to support audit committee responsibilities.

Section 301.4 demands further attention. Audit committees are required to "establish procedures for (1) the receipt, retention, and treatment of complaints received by the issuer regarding accounting, internal accounting controls, or auditing matters; and (2) the confidential, anonymous submission by employees of the issuer of concerns regarding questionable accounting or auditing matters." This requires setting up a "whistle-blower'' program in the organization. According to Hernan Murdock,[1] there are four steps for building effective whistle-blower program, including assessment (step 1), building (step 2), program release (step 3), and performance monitoring (step 4). Activities in step 1 include evaluating needs, identifying staff, and selecting oversight board. Activities in step 2 include training operators (or train-the-trainer), updating policies and procedures, and developing charter. Activities in step 3 include distributing notices, meeting with employees, and selecting a facilitator. Activities in step 4 include reviewing performance reports, meeting with oversight board, and surveying employees. Choosing a sympathetic and knowledgeable facilitator will increase employee acceptance of the program and put employees at ease.

Section 302 of the Act requires CEOs and CFOs to personally certify in quarterly financial reports that they

- Know of no material financial misstatements
- Designed internal controls in such a way that they would know of such misstatements
- Evaluated internal controls within the last 90 days
- Presented their conclusions about the effectiveness of internal controls
- Disclosed to the external auditors and audit committee any significant deficiencies or material weaknesses in the design or operation of internal control, as well as any fraud involving people who have a significant role in internal controls
- Indicated in the report whether any significant changes in internal controls have occurred since their evaluation

Organizations need reliable processes to support these certifications, and internal auditors are playing key role in designing an/or evaluating these processes. The SEC coined the term "disclo-

[1] ***Internal Audit's Role in Corporate Governance: Sarbanes-Oxley Compliance*** *(Altamonte Springs, FL: Institute of Internal Auditors, 2003).*

sure controls and procedures" to limit the evaluation to internal controls over financial reporting and over material nonfinancial disclosures. A key element of the disclosure process is a disclosure committee, in which knowledgeable, high-level employees come together to rigorously examine financial information and other disclosures as they are being prepared.

Section 404 of the Act requires that annual reports contain

- A statement that management is responsible for maintaining an adequate internal control structure and procedures for financial reporting
- An assessment, as of the end of the most current fiscal year, of the effectiveness of the internal control structure and procedures for financial reporting
- Attestation to this assessment by the external audit firm

Organizations need reliable processes to support these assertions, and internal auditors are playing a key role in designing and/or evaluating these processes. Internal auditors perform the detailed documentation and testing of activity-level controls required to support the assertion.

To comply with the Section 404 of the act, many organizations are following COSO (Committee of Sponsoring Organizations) with a two-tiered evaluation of internal controls. The first tier is entry-wide management control evaluation, and the second tier is process- or activity-level control evaluation.

(A) ***Entity-wide management control evaluation.*** For the control environment and other soft controls, self-assessment is the only effective evaluation technique. Self-assessment questionnaires are the tools most often used for soft control evaluation in a Sarbanes-Oxley context. A self-assessment questionnaire can gather evidence from across the organization and it is efficient, and hence suitable to entity-wide assessment.

(B) ***Process- or activity-level control evaluation.*** Although soft controls are important at this level, more attention is normally paid to hard controls, such as detailed analysis, testing, and subtesting. Note that evidence produced by hard control testing is more reliable than that of the soft control. Self-assessment increases employees' knowledge and ownership of internal control, and it frees auditors to do more value-added activities than detailed testing. An attractive option is continuous monitoring of controls through the computer system.

Note that the control environment is an integrated whole, not a series of discrete controls. The individual pieces contribute to the whole, but it is the interaction among those pieces that makes up the control environment.

Internal audit should be the CEO's and CFO's best source of assurance about internal control. They should ask the chief audit executive to supply an annual opinion on internal control. The first step is to base the annual audit plan on the control model. The control-based audit plan should not replace a risk-based audit plan. The annual opinion should come after the risk assessment to ensure that audit coverage will support an opinion on control for the organization as a whole. Also, the COSO-based audit plan should not override the risk-based audit plan. The audit plan changes throughout the year, as risks and audit resources change. The COSO grid should be consulted periodically to ensure that changes do not prevent the chief audit executive from giving that overall opinion. The COSO grid is also useful for the audit department in aggregating and reporting results.

Winters recommended an internal control maturity framework model for evaluating and reporting internal controls.[2] The model has five levels, where the higher-numbered levels reflect greater efficiency and reduced risk to the organization:

Level 1: Unreliable. It is a reflection of unpredictable environment for which controls have not been designed or implemented.

Level 2: Informal. Controls are present but inadequately documented and largely dependent on manual intervention. There are no formal communications or training programs related to internal controls.

Level 3: Standardized. Controls are in place and documented, and employees have received formal communications about them. Undetected deviations from controls may occur.

---

[2] *Bruce I. Winters, "Choose the Right Tools for Internal Control Reporting," Journal of Accountancy (February 2004).*

Level 4: Monitored. Standardized controls are in place and undergo periodic testing to evaluate their design and operation; test results are communicated to management. Limited use of automated tools may support controls.
Level 5: Optimized. An integrated internal control framework with real-time monitoring by management is in place to implement continuous improvement. Automated processes and tools support the controls and enable the organization to quickly change the controls as necessary.

Section 406 of the act requires all publicly traded companies to have a code of ethics, or explain why they do not, for their CEO, CFO, and principal accounting officer. The act also requires that a full code of ethics be made publicly available via annual report, on public company's Web sites, or upon request. Subsequent changes to the code must be disclosed in SEC filings.

5.2 Alternative Control Frameworks

Seven control frameworks or models are discussed in this section, including (1) Committee of Sponsoring Organizations (COSO) of the Treadway Commission, which has been adopted in the United States; (2) the Criteria of Control (CoCo) in Canada; (3) the Control Self-Assessment (CSA) in the United States; (4) the Cadbury Report of the committee on the financial aspects of corporate governance in United Kingdom; (5) the Turnbull Model in United Kingdom; (6) the King Model in South Africa; and (7) the KonTraG Model in Germany.

(a) **COSO's Definition of Internal Control.** Internal controls have objectives, concepts, and components. According to the Committee of Sponsoring Organizations (COSO) of the Treadway Commission (1992) report, internal control is a process, effected by an entity's board of directors, management, and other personnel, designed to provide reasonable assurance regarding the achievement of objectives in the following three categories:

- Effectiveness and efficiency of operations
- Reliability of financial reporting
- Compliance with applicable laws and regulations

This definition reflects four fundamental **concepts**.

- Internal control is a process. It is a means to an end, not an end in itself.
- Internal control is affected by people. It is not merely a policy manual and forms, but people at every level of an organization.
- Internal control can be expected to provide only reasonable assurance, not absolute assurance, to an entity's management and board.
- Internal control is geared to the achievement of objectives in one or more separate but overlapping categories.

The three objectives and the four fundamental concepts of internal controls are shown in Exhibit 5.1.

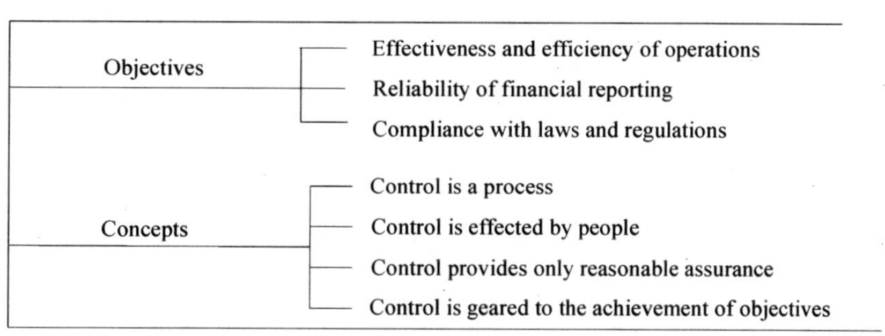

Exhibit 5.1: Internal control objectives and concepts

(i) **A process.** Internal control is not one event or circumstance, but a series of actions that permeate an entity's activities. These actions are pervasive and are inherent in the way management runs the business.

Business processes, which are conducted within, or across, organization units or functions, are managed through the basic management processes of planning, executing, and monitoring. Internal control is a part of these processes and is integrated with them. It enables them to function and monitors their conduct and continued relevancy. It is a tool used by management, not a substitute for management.

This conceptualization of internal control is very different from the perspective of some observers who view internal control as something added on to an entity's activities, or as a necessary burden, imposed by regulators or by the dictates of overzealous bureaucrats, or unnecessarily dependent on a person's attitude.

The internal control system is intertwined with an entity's operating activities and exists for fundamental business reasons. Internal controls are most effective when they are built into the entity's infrastructure and are part of the essence of the enterprise. They should be "built in" rather than "built on."

"Building in" controls can directly affect an entity's ability to reach its goals and supports businesses' quality initiatives. The quest for quality is directly linked to how businesses are run and how they are controlled. Quality initiatives become part of the operating fabric of an enterprise, as evidenced by

- Senior executive leadership ensuring that quality values are built into the way a company does business
- Establishing quality objectives linked to the entity's information collection and analysis and other processes
- Using the knowledge of competitive practices and customer expectations to drive continuous quality improvement

These quality factors parallel those in effective internal control systems. In fact, internal control is integrated not only with quality programs, but usually critical to their success.

Building in controls also has important implications to cost containment and response time.

- Most enterprises are faced with highly competitive marketplaces and a need to contain costs. Adding new procedures separate from existing ones adds costs. By focusing on existing operations and their contribution to effective internal control, and building controls into basic operating activities, an enterprise often can avoid unnecessary procedures and costs.
- A practice of building controls into the fabric of operations helps trigger development of new control necessary to new business activities. Such automatic reaction makes entities more nimble and competitive.

(ii) **People.** A board of directors, management, and other personnel in an entity effect internal control. The people of an organization accomplish it by what they do and say. People establish the entity's objectives and put control mechanisms in place.

Similarly, internal control affects people's actions. Internal control recognizes that people do not always understand, communicate, or perform consistently. Each individual brings to the work place a unique background and technical ability, and has different personal needs and priorities.

The realities affect, and are affected by, internal control. People must know their responsibilities and limits of authority. Accordingly, a clear and close linkage needs to exist between people's duties and the way in which they are carried out, as well as with the entity's objectives.

The organization's people include the board of directors, as well as management and other personnel. Although directors might be viewed as primarily providing oversight, they also provide direction and approve certain transactions or policies. As such, the board of directors is an important element of internal control.

(iii) **Reasonable assurance.** Internal control, no matter how well designed and operated, can provide only reasonable assurance to management and the board of directors regarding achievement of an entity's objectives. The likelihood of achievements is affected by limitations inherent in all internal control systems.

These limitations include the realities that human judgments in decision making can be faulty, persons responsible for establishing controls need to consider their relative costs and benefits, and breakdowns can occur because of human failures, such as a simple error or mistake. Additionally, controls can be circumvented by collusion of two or more people. Finally, management has the ability to override the internal control system.

(iv) **Objectives.** Every entity sets out on a mission, establishing objectives it wants to achieve and strategies for achieving them. Objectives may be set for an entity as a whole or be targeted to specific activities within the entity. Although many objectives are specific to a particular entity, some are widely shared. For example, objectives common to virtually all entities are achieving and maintaining a positive reputation within the business and consumer communities, providing reliable financial statements to stakeholders, and operating in compliance with laws and regulations.

An internal control system can be expected to provide reasonable assurance of achieving objectives relating to the reliability of financial reporting and compliance with laws and regulations. Achievement of those objectives, which are based largely on standards imposed by external parties, depends on how activities within the entity's control are performed.

However, achievement of operations objectives—such as a particular return on investment, market share, or entry into new product lines—is not always within the entity's control. Internal control cannot prevent bad judgment or decisions or external events that can cause a business to fail to achieve operations goals. For these objectives, the internal control system can provide reasonable assurance only that management and, in its oversight role, the board are made aware, in a timely manner, of the extent to which the entity is moving toward those objectives.

(v) **Internal control components.** Internal control consists of five interrelated components. These are derived from the way management runs a business and are integrated with the management process. The components presented by the COSO study include (see Exhibit 5.2).

Five Components of Internal Control

- Control environment
- Risk assessment
- Control activities
- Information and communication
- Monitoring

Exhibit 5.2: Five components of internal control

1. **Control environment.** The core of any business is its people—their individual attributes, including integrity, ethical values, and competence—and the environment in which they operate. They are the engine that drives the entity and the foundation on which everything rests.
2. **Risk assessment.** The entity must be aware of and deal with the risks it faces. It must set objectives, integrated with sales, production, marketing, financial, and other activities, so that the organization is operating in concert. It must also establish mechanisms to identify, analyze, and manage the related risks.
3. **Control activities.** Control policies and procedures must be established and executed to help ensure that the actions identified by management as necessary to address risks to achievement of the entity's objectives are effectively carried out. Examples of control activities include approvals, authorizations, verifications, reconciliations, reviews of operating performance, security of assets, and segregation of duties. Types of control activities can include preventive controls, detective controls, manual controls, computer controls, and management controls. Regardless of whether a policy is written, it must be implemented thoughtfully, conscientiously, and consistently. Controls are also classified into two categories: (1) hard controls and (2) soft controls. Hard controls are formal, tangible, and easier to measure and evaluate. Examples of hard controls include budgets, dual controls, written approvals, reconciliations, authorization levels, verifications, and segregation of duties. However, soft controls are informal, intangible, subjective, and difficult to measure and evaluate. Examples of soft controls include an organization's ethical climate, integrity, values, culture, vision, people's behaviors and attitudes, commitment to competence, tone at the top, management philosophy, management's operating style, level of understanding and commitment, and communication. Tools to evaluate hard controls include flowcharts, system narratives, testing, and counting. Tools to evaluate soft controls include self-assessments, questionnaires, interviews, and workshops. Generally speaking, senior managers most often use soft skills and soft controls to achieve their objectives; other managers most often use hard skills and hard controls. Soft skills include people skills such as interpersonal skills, motivation, leadership, and communications skills. Hard skills include technical skills such as functional skills, problem identification and solving skills, and decision-making skills.

4. **Information and communication.** Surrounding these activities are information and communication systems. These enable the entity's people to capture and exchange the information needed to conduct, manage, and control its operations.
5. **Monitoring.** The entire process must be monitored and modifications made as necessary. In this way, the system can react dynamically, changing as conditions warrant.

(vi) **Tiered approach to audits.** When there is a conflict between the choices, the COSO-based approach should not override the risk-based approach to audits. Self-assessment questionnaires, which are soft controls, can be applied at any organizational level (first tier). The second tier is the activity level (e.g., process, subprocess, function, or department). Hard controls, such as documenting and testing control activities, are evaluated during the second tier. The best approach is analytical, starting from objectives, identifying risks and controls, evaluating the design of the controls, and testing control effectiveness.

(vii) **Relationship of internal control objectives and components.** There is a direct relationship between objectives, which are what an entity strives to achieve, and the components, which represent what is needed to achieve the objectives. Information is needed for all three objective categories—to effectively manage business operations, to prepare financial statements reliably, and to determine compliance. All five components are applicable and important to achievement of operations objectives. Each component cuts across and applies to all three objectives categories. Examples are

- Financial and nonfinancial data generated from internal and external sources, which is part of the information and communication component, is needed to effectively manage business operations, develop reliable financial statements, and determine that the entity is complying with applicable laws.
- The establishment and execution of control policies and procedures to ensure that management plans, programs, and other directives are carried out—representing the control activities component—is also relevant to all three objectives categories.

WHAT INTERNAL CONTROLS CAN AND CANNOT DO

What internal controls do. Internal control can help an entity achieve its performance and profitability targets and can prevent loss of resources. It can help ensure reliable financial reporting. And it can help ensure that the enterprise complies with laws and regulations, avoiding damage to its reputation and other consequences. In sum, it can help an entity get to where it wants to go and avoid pitfalls and surprises along the way.

What internal controls cannot do. Unfortunately, some people have greater, and unrealistic, expectations. They look for absolutes, believing that

- Internal control can ensure an entity's success—that is, it will ensure achievement of basic objectives or will, at the least, ensure survival.

Even effective internal control can only help an entity achieve these objectives. It can provide management information about the entity's progress, or lack of it, toward their achievement. But internal control cannot change an inherently poor manager into a good one. And shifts in government policy or programs, competitor's actions, or economic conditions can be beyond management's control. Internal control cannot ensure success, or even survival.

- Internal control can ensure the reliability of financial reporting and compliance with laws and regulations.

This belief is also unwarranted. An internal control system, no matter how well conceived and operated, can provide only reasonable—not absolute—assurance to management and the board regarding achievement of an entity's objectives. The likelihood of achievement is affected by limitations inherent in all internal control systems. These limitations include the realities that judgments in decision making can be faulty and those control breakdowns can occur because of a simple error or mistake.

Additionally, controls can be circumvented by the collusion of two or more people, and management has the ability to override the system. Another limiting factor is that the design of an internal control system must reflect the fact that there are resource constraints, and the benefits of controls must be considered relative to their costs.

Thus, while internal control can help an entity achieve its objectives, it is not a panacea.

(viii) **Responsibility for internal control.** Who is responsible for establishing and ensuring an adequate and effective internal control environment within the organization? It is the management, the audit committee, and the board of directors—not the auditors. Auditors are responsible for ensuring an adequate and effective system of internal control in the organization. Here the term "management" refers to senior management, operating management, and department/section management. The term "auditors" refers to both internal and external (independent) auditors. For example, company management is responsible for ensuring the adequacy of disclosures in the financial statements of a publicly held company.

According to the COSO study, everyone in an organization has responsibility for internal control: management, board of directors, internal auditors, other personnel.

(A) ***Management.*** The chief executive officer is ultimately responsible and should assume ownership of the system. More than any other individual, the CEO sets the tone at the top that affects integrity and ethics and other factors of a positive control environment.

In a large company, the CEO fulfills this duty by providing leadership and direction to senior managers and reviewing the way they are controlling the business. Senior managers, in turn, assign responsibility for establishment of more specific internal control policies and procedures to personnel responsible for the unit's functions.

In a smaller entity, the influence of the CEO, often an owner-manager, is usually more direct. In any event, in a cascading responsibility, a manager is effectively a chief executive of his or her sphere of responsibility. Of particular significance are financial officers and their staffs, whose control activities cut across, as well as up and down, the operating and other units of an enterprise.

(B) ***Board of directors.*** Management is accountable to the board of directors, which provides governance, guidance, and oversight. Effective board members are objective, capable, and inquisitive. They also have knowledge of the entity's activities and environment, and commit the time necessary to fulfill their board responsibilities. Management may be in a position to override controls and ignore or stifle communications from subordinates, enabling a dishonest management that intentionally misrepresents results to cover its tracks.

A strong, active board, particularly when coupled with effective upward communications channels and capable financial, legal, and internal audit functions, is often best able to identify and correct such a problem.

(C) ***Internal auditors.*** Internal auditors play an important role in evaluating the effectiveness of a control system, and contribute to its ongoing effectiveness. Because of the organizational position and authority in an entity, an internal audit function often plays a significant monitoring role.

(D) ***Other personnel.*** Internal control is, to some degree, the responsibility of everyone in an organization and therefore should be an explicit or implicit part of everyone's job descriptions. Virtually all employees produce information used in the internal control system or take other actions needed to effect control. Also, all personnel should be responsible for communicating upward problems in operation, noncompliance with the code of conduct, or other policy violations or illegal actions.

A number of external parties often contribute to the achievement of an entity's objectives. External auditors, bringing an independent and objective view, contribute directly through the financial statement audit and indirectly by providing information useful to management and the board in carrying out their responsibilities. Others providing information to the entity useful in effecting internal control are legislators and regulators, customers, and others transacting business with the enterprise, financial analysts, bond raters, and the news media. External parties, however, are not responsible for, nor are they a part of, the entity's internal control system.

COSO'S INTERNAL CONTROL STANDARDS SUMMARY

Five component standards include control environment, risk assessment, control activities, information and communication, and monitoring. Each standard is presented along with its major factors or subcomponents.

Standard 1: Control Environment
1.1 Integrity and ethical values
1.2 Commitment to competence
1.3 Management's philosophy and operating style
1.4 Organizational structure
1.5 Assignment of authority and responsibility
1.6 Human resources policies and practices
1.7 Oversight groups

Standard 2: Risk Assessment
2.1 Risk identification
2.2 Risk analysis
2.3 Managing risk during change

Standard 3: Control Activities
3.1 Types of control activities
3.2 Integration with risk assessment
3.3 Control over information systems
3.4 Entity-specific control activities

Standard 4: Information and Communication
4.1 Information
4.2 Communications
4.3 Means of communicating

Standard 5: Monitoring
5.1 Ongoing monitoring activities
5.2 Separate evaluations
5.3 Internal reporting of deficiencies

(ix) **Limitations of internal control.** Internal control has been viewed by some observers as ensuring an entity will not fail—that is, the entity will always achieve its operations, financial reporting, and compliance objectives.[3] In this sense, internal control sometimes is looked on as a cure-all for all real and potential business ills. This view is misguided. Internal control is not a panacea.

In considering limitations of internal control, two distinct concepts must be recognized.

- Internal control—even effective internal control—operates at different levels with respect to different objectives. For objectives related to the effectiveness and efficiency of an entity's operations—achievement of its basic mission, profitability goals, and the like—internal control can help to ensure that management is aware of the entity's progress, or lack of it. But it cannot provide even reasonable assurance that the objectives themselves will be achieved. The first set of limitations acknowledges that certain events or conditions are simply outside management's control.
- Internal control cannot provide absolute assurance with respect to any of the three objectives categories (i.e., effectiveness and efficiency of operations, reliability of financial reporting, and compliance with applicable laws and regulations). The second set of limitations has to do with the reality that no system will always do what it is intended to do. The best that can be expected in any internal control system is that reasonable assurance is obtained.

(x) **Factors to be considered when understanding limitations of internal control.** Six factors need to be considered when understanding limitations of internal controls. These include reasonable as-

[3] *Committee of Sponsoring Organizations of the Treadway Commission (COSO), "Internal Control—Integrated Framework," 1992.*

surance, judgment, control breakdowns, management override, collusion, and costs versus benefits (see Exhibit 5.3).

Factors to Be Considered When Understanding Limitations of Internal Control

- Reasonable assurance (not absolute assurance)
- Judgment
- Control breakdowns
- Management override of internal controls
- Collusion
- Costs vs. benefits

Exhibit 5.3: Factors to be considered when understanding limitations of internal control

1. **Reasonable assurance.** Reasonable assurance certainly does not imply that an internal control system will frequently fail. Many factors, individually and collectively, serve to provide strength to the concept of reasonable assurance. The cumulative effect of controls that satisfy multiple objectives and the multipurpose nature of controls reduce the risk that an entity may not achieve its objectives. However, because of the inherent limitations discussed above, there is no guarantee that, for example, an uncontrollable event, a mistake, or an improper reporting incident could never occur. In other words, even an effective internal control system can experience a failure. *Reasonable assurance is not absolute assurance.*
2. **Judgment.** The effectiveness of controls will be limited by the realities of human frailty in the making of business decisions. Such decisions must be made with human judgment in the time available, based on information at hand, and under the pressures of the conduct of business. Some decisions based on human judgment may later, with the clairvoyance of hindsight, be found to produce less than desirable results, and may need to be changed.

   The nature of internal control-related decisions that must be made based on human judgment is described further below in the discussion of breakdowns, management override, and costs versus benefits.
3. **Control breakdowns.** Even if internal controls are well designed, they can break down. Personnel may misunderstand instructions. They may make judgment mistakes. Or they may commit errors due to carelessness, distraction, or fatigue. Temporary personnel executing control duties for vacationing or sick employees might not perform correctly. System changes may be implemented before personnel have been trained to react appropriately to signs of incorrect functioning.
4. **Management override.** An internal control system can be only as effective as the people who are responsible for its functioning can. Even in effectively controlled entities—those with generally high levels of integrity and control consciousness—a manager might be able to override internal control.

   The term "management override" is used here to mean overruling prescribed policies or procedures for illegitimate purposes with the intent of personal gain or an enhanced presentation of an entity's financial condition or compliance status. Override practices include deliberate misrepresentations to bankers, lawyers, accountants, and vendors, and intentionally issuing false documents such as purchase orders and sales invoices.

   Management override should not be confused with management intervention, which represents management's action to depart from prescribed policies or procedures for legitimate purposes. Management intervention is necessary to deal with nonrecurring and nonstandard transactions or events that otherwise might be handled inappropriately by the control system.

   Provision for management intervention is necessary in all internal control systems because no system can be designed to anticipate every condition. Management's actions to intervene are generally overt and commonly documented or otherwise disclosed to appropriate personnel, whereas actions to override usually are not documented or disclosed, with an intent to cover up the actions.

MANAGEMENT OVERRIDE VS. MANAGEMENT INTERVENTION

- *Management override* is departing from prescribed policies or procedures for illegitimate purposes and is not documented or disclosed.
- *Management intervention* is departing from prescribed policies or procedures for legitimate purposes and is documented or disclosed.

5. **Collusion.** The collusive activities of two or more individuals can result in control failures. Individuals acting collectively to perpetrate and conceal an action from detection often can alter financial data or other management information in a manner that cannot be identified by the control system. For example, there may be collusion between an employee performing an important control function and a customer, supplier, or another employee. On a different level, several layers of sales or divisional management might collude in circumventing controls so that reported results meet budgets or incentive targets.
6. **Costs versus benefits.** Resources always have constraints, and entities must consider the relative costs and benefits of establishing controls. In determining whether a particular control should be established, the risk of failure and the potential effect on the entity are considered along with the related costs of establishing a new control.

   Costs and benefit measurements for implementing controls are done with different levels of precision. Generally, it is easier to deal with the cost side of the equation, which, in many cases, can be quantified in a fairly precise manner. The benefit side often requires an even more subjective valuation. Nevertheless, certain factors can be considered in assessing potential benefits: the likelihood of the undesired condition occurring, the nature of the activities, and the potential financial or operating effect the event might have on the entity.

   The complexity of cost-benefit determination is compounded by the interrelationship of controls with business operations. Where controls are integrated with, or "built in" to, management and business processes, it is difficult to isolate either their costs or benefits.

   Similarly, many times a variety of controls may serve, individually or together, to mitigate a particular risk. Cost-benefit determinations also vary considerably depending on the nature of the business. High-risk activities definitely require cost-benefit analysis while low-risk activities might not.

   The challenge is to find the right balance. Excessive control is costly and counterproductive. For example, customers making telephone orders will not tolerate order acceptance procedures that are too cumbersome or time-consuming. Too little control, however, presents undue risk of bad debts. An appropriate balance is needed in a highly competitive environment. And, despite the difficulties, cost-benefit decisions will continue to be made.

(b) **CoCo Model in Canada.** The Canadian Institute of Chartered Accountants (CICA) has issued 20 "criteria of control" (CoCo) as a framework for making judgments about control. The term "control" has a broader meaning than internal control over financial reporting. CoCo defines control as "those elements of an organization (including its resources, systems, processes, culture, structure, and tasks) that, taken together, support people in the achievement of the organization's objectives." It defines three categories of objectives.

- Effectiveness and efficiency of operations
- Reliability of internal external reporting
- Compliance with applicable laws, regulations, and internal policies

The criteria of control are the basis for understanding control in an organization and for making judgments about the effectiveness of control. The criteria are formulated to be broadly applicable. The effectiveness of control in any organization, regardless of the objective it serves, can be assessed using these criteria. The criteria are phrased as goals to be worked toward over time; they are not minimum requirements to be passed or failed.

CoCo defines four types of criteria: purpose, commitment, capability, and monitoring and learning. The *purpose* type groups criteria that provide a sense of the organization's direction and address objectives (including mission, vision, and strategy); risks (and opportunities); policies; planning; and performance targets and indicators. The *commitment* type groups criteria that provide a sense of the organization's identity and values and address ethical values, including integrity, human resource policies, authority, responsibility, accountability, and mutual trust. The *capability* type groups criteria that provide a sense of the organization's competence and address knowledge, skills, and tools; communication processes; information; coordination; and control activities. The *monitoring and learning* type groups criteria that provide a sense of the organization's evolution and address monitoring internal and external environment, monitoring performance, challenging assumptions, reassessing information needs and information systems, follow-up procedures, and assessing the effectiveness of control.

(c) **Control Self-Assessment Model.** Control self-assessment (CSA) deals with evaluating the system of internal control in any organization. CSA is a shared responsibility among all employees in the organization, not just internal auditing or senior management. The examination of the internal control environment is conducted within a structured, documented, and repetitive process. The formal assessment approach takes place in workshop sessions with business users as participants (process owners) and internal auditors as facilitators (subject matter experts) and as nonfacilitators (note takers). The purpose of the sessions is conversation and mutual discovery and information sharing.

(i) **Elements of CSA.** CSA has five elements: (1) up-front planning and preliminary audit work, (2) the gathering of process owners with a meeting facilitator, (3) a structured agenda to examine the process's risks and controls, (4) a note taker and electronic voting technology to input comments and opinions, and (5) reporting the results and the development of corrective action plans.

(ii) **Scope of CSA.** CSA can be done either as a stand-alone project or as a supplement to traditional audit work. CSA is not suitable to situations such as finding fraud or compliance reviews (e.g., regulatory audits), or when participants have conflicting objectives, as in third-party contracts. CSA can be applied to numerous situations, business issues, and industries, regardless of size. It is a management tool that has equal application to horizontal (organization-wide), vertical (single department), or diagonal (process inquiries) issues.

(iii) **Effect on auditors.** CSA can be used to assess business and financial statement risks, control activities, ethical values, and control effectiveness; the controls that mitigate those risks; and overall compliance with policies and procedures.

During the assessment process, there is a constant interactive dialogue between the auditor and the auditee, as well as between the auditees. This interaction increases communication and builds trust and confidence between each party. At the same time, it is educational to both parties because there is a knowledge transfer between the auditor and the auditee. The auditors will have a greater knowledge of business functions, while the auditees will have a better understanding of and appreciation for controls and the business process of which they are a part.

The increased communication and the knowledge transfer adds value to the organization in the following ways:

- Auditors accomplish control assessment.
- Auditees understand the purpose of controls.
- Management takes responsibility for the development and maintenance of the control environment.
- Process improvement issues are identified and resolved (i.e., implemented or deferred).

(iv) **Interrelationships between CSA, CoCo, and COSO.** CSA can be an effective tool for accomplishing the objectives of both CoCo and COSO. CSA acts as a link to the CoCo and COSO.

The CSA audit can address the four elements of the CoCo framework (i.e., purpose, commitment, capability, and monitoring and learning). Both commitment and capability are examples of soft controls (e.g, risk assessment, the achievement of business objectives and goals, and the attitude of people toward controls).

(v) **Conclusion.** CSA is a dynamic business process improvement and control-enhancing technique. The CSA in relation to internal auditing is like total quality management and continuous process improvement techniques in relation to other parts of the organization. The only difference is how the CSA program is implemented in each organization, but the benefits are real and long lasting.

(d) **Cadbury Report in the United Kingdom.** The Cadbury Report of the committee on the financial aspects of corporate governance issued in December 1992 consists of internal controls, fraud, audit (internal and external), financial reporting practices, audit committees, shareholders, corporate governance, the board of directors, and the code of best practice.

Regarding internal controls, the report says that directors maintain a system of internal control over the financial management of the company, including procedures designed to minimize the risk of fraud. The directors should make a statement in the report and accounts on the effectiveness of their system of internal control and the auditors should report thereon.

Regarding fraud, the report says that prime responsibility for the prevention and detection of fraud and other illegal acts is that of the board, as part of its fiduciary responsibility for protecting the assets of the company. The auditor's responsibility is to properly plan, perform, and evaluate his or her audit work so as to have a reasonable expectation of detecting material misstatements in the financial statements.

Regarding the internal audit, the report states that the function of the internal auditors is complementary to, but different from, that of the external (outside) auditors. The committee regards the internal audit as good practice for companies to establish internal audit function to undertake regular monitoring of key controls and procedures. Such regular monitoring is an integral part of a company's system of internal control and helps to ensure its effectiveness. An internal audit function is well placed to undertake investigations on behalf of the audit committee and to follow up any suspicion of fraud. It is essential that heads of internal audit should have unrestricted access to the chairman of the audit committee in order to ensure the independence of their position.

Regarding the external audit, the report says that an essential first step is to be clear about the respective responsibilities of directors and external auditors for preparing and reporting on the financial statements of companies, in order to begin to narrow the "expectation gap." This gap is due to lack of understanding of the nature and extent of the external auditors' role. The gap is the difference between what audits do achieve and what it is thought they achieve or should achieve. The expectations gap is damaging not only because it reflects unrealistic expectations of audits but also because it has led to disenchantment with the value of audits to the various interested parties.

The external auditors' role is to report whether the financial statements give a true and fair view, and the audit is designed to provide a reasonable assurance that the financial statements are free of material misstatements. The auditors' role is not (to cite a few of the misunderstandings) to prepare the financial statements, or to provide absolute assurance that the figures in the financial statements are correct, or to provide a guarantee that the company will continue to exist.

(e) **Turnbull Model in the United Kingdom.** In 1998 the London Stock Exchange developed a Combined Code for corporate governance. The code requires that company directors should, at least annually, conduct a review of the effectiveness of the system of internal control and should report to shareholders that they have reviewed the effectiveness of all three types of controls, including financial, operational, and compliance control.

(f) **King Model in South Africa.** The Institute of Directors in South Africa has established the King Committee on Corporate Governance that produced the King Report in 1994. The committee has developed a Code of Corporate Practices and Conduct, and compliance with the code is a requirement to be listed in the Johannesburg stock exchange (JSE) Securities Exchange in South Africa.

(g) **KonTraG Model in Germany.** In 1998 the German government proposed changes for the reform of corporate governance. The model affects control and transparency in business. Specifically, it impacts the board of directors, supervisory board, corporate capitalization principles, authorization of no-par-value shares, small nonlisted stock corporations, banks investing in industrial companies, and the acceptance of internationally recognized accounting standards.

5.3 Enterprise Risk Management Vocabulary, Concepts, and Techniques

(a) **Risk Management Defined.** Traditionally, corporate risk management has focused on partial portfolio of risks (silo approach), specifically on financial and hazard risks. The scope was narrow, ignoring all the other risks impacting the organization. It did not exploit the "natural hedges" and "portfolio effects" in the collective. It tended to treat risk as downside phenomenon. Now enterprise risk management (ERM) focuses on total portfolio of risks, including financial, hazard, strategic, and operational risks. The scope of ERM is much broader than the traditional view with the objective of creating, protecting, and enhancing shareholder value. The ERM treats risk as both upside and downside phenomenon since it integrates all risks.

When creating the shareholder value, management needs to understand risks and opportunities go together. The key is to determine the potential benefits of a given opportunity exceed the risks. During this exercise, management needs to consider derisking opportunities, meaning becoming a market leader by reducing the risks. This will lead to earnings growth, revenue growth, and expense control/reduction followed by earnings consistency from year to year.

ERM is defined as "a rigorous and coordinated approach to assessing and responding to all risks that affect the achievement of an organization's strategic and financial objectives. This includes both upside and downside risks." ERM risks are classified as

- **Financial risk.** These are risks arising from volatility in foreign currencies, interest rates, and commodities. They include credit risk, liquidity risk (bankruptcy risk), and market risk.
- **Hazard risk.** These are risks that are insurable, such as natural disasters, various insurable liabilities, impairment of physical assets, and terrorism.
- **Strategic risk.** This is a high-level and corporate-wide risk, which includes political risk, regulatory risk, reputation risk, leadership risk, and market brand risk. It is also related to failure of strategy and changing customer needs and business conditions.
- **Operational risk.** This is a risk related to the organization's systems, processes, technology, and people.

ERM VOCABULARY

- **Hazard** is a condition that creates or increases the probability of a loss. Three types of hazards exist: (1) physical hazard, (2) moral hazard, and (3) morale hazard. Physical hazard is a condition of the subject of insurance that creates or increases the chance of loss, such as structural defects, occupancy, or similar conditions. Moral hazard is a dishonest predisposition on the part of an insured that increases the chance of loss. Morale hazard is a careless attitude on the part of an insured that increases the chance of loss or causes losses to be greater than would otherwise be the case.
- **Hedging** is taking a position opposite to the exposure or risk. This can be done with financial derivatives, such as futures contracts, forward contracts, options, and swaps. A perfect hedge is not possible because financial derivatives used to hedge do not move together, leaving some risk. The idea behind hedging is to minimize risk. A value is created for shareholders if corporate hedging does not duplicate the shareholders' "homemade" hedging.
- **Insurance** is an economic device whereby an individual or a corporation substitutes a small certain cost (the premium) for a large uncertain financial loss (the claim, or contingency insured against) that would exist if it were not for the insurance policy (contract).
- **Insurable interest** is an interest that might be damaged if the peril insured against occurs; the possibility of a financial loss to an individual or a corporation that can be protected against through insurance.
- **Natural hedges** are created from the relationship between revenues and costs of a business unit or a subsidiary. The more revenues over the cost, the better protection is. The key is the extent to which cash flows adjust naturally to currency changes due to exchange-rate fluctuations. One way to explore the likelihood of a natural hedge is to determine whether a subsidiary's revenue and cost functions are sensitive to domestic or global business conditions.

  Many types of risks may be relatively correlated with each other. Consequently, combining these risks produces a form of natural hedging. The traditional silo approach could actually reduce the overall efficiency of the firm's risk management activities by destroying the natural hedging that exists at the enterprise-wide level.
- **Peril** is the cause of possible loss, the event insured against. "Open peril" is a term used to describe a broad form of property insurance in which coverage applies to loss arising from any fortuitous cause other than those perils or causes specifically excluded.

- **Portfolio effect** considers risk and return of a firm when it is investing in acquisition or expansion projects. Management needs to find the relationship between the net present values (NPVs) for new projects and the NPVs for existing projects. In a portfolio framework, the trade-off between risk and expected NPV for different combinations of investments can be analyzed.
- **Risk** is a possibility of loss. Many types of risks exist, including pure risk, speculative risk, static risk, dynamic risk, subjective risk, and objective risk.
- **Pure risk** is a condition in which there is the possibility of loss or no loss. Risk management is a scientific approach to the problem of dealing with the pure risks facing an individual or an organization in which insurance is viewed as simply one of several approaches for dealing with such risks. The techniques of insurance and self-insurance are commonly limited to the treatment of pure risks, such as fire, product liability, and worker's compensation. Traditionally, the risk management tools—avoidance, loss control, and transfer—have been applied primarily to the pure or hazard risks facing a firm.
- **Speculative risk** exists when there is uncertainty about an event that could produce either a profit or a loss.
- **Static risks,** which can be either pure or speculative, stem from an unchanging society that is in stable equilibrium. Examples of pure static risk include the uncertainties due to such random events as lightning, windstorms, and death. Business undertakings in a stable economy illustrate the concept of speculative static risk.
- In contrast, **dynamic risks** are produced because of changes in society. Dynamic risks also can be either pure or speculative. Examples of sources of dynamic risk include urban unrest, increasingly complex technology, and changing attitude of legislatures and courts about a variety of issues.
- **Subjective risk** refers to the mental state of an individual who experiences doubt or worry as to the outcome of a given event. In addition to being subjective, a particular risk may be either pure or speculative and either static or dynamic.
- **Objective risk** differs from subjective risk primarily in the sense that it is more precisely observable and therefore measurable. In general, objective risk is the probable variation of actual from expected experience.
- **Risk assessment (risk analysis)** is the process of identifying the risks and determining the probability of occurrence, the resulting impact, and additional safeguards that would mitigate this impact. It includes risk measurement and prioritization.
- **Risk financing** includes internal funding for risks (self-insurance and residual risk) and external transfer of risks, such as insurance and hedging. It can be unfunded or funded retention. The unfunded retention is treated as part of the overall cost of doing business. A firm may decide to practice funded retention by making various preloss arrangements to ensure that money is readily available to pay for losses that occur. Examples of funded retention include use of credit, reserve funds, self-insurance, and captive insurers.
- **Risk management** is the total process of identifying, controlling, and mitigating risks as it deals with uncertainty. It includes risk assessment (risk analysis); cost-benefit analysis; and the selection, implementation, test, and evaluation of safeguards (risk mitigation); risk financing (risk funding); and risk monitoring (reporting and feedback).

$$\text{Risk Management} = \text{Risk Assessment} + \text{Risk Mitigation} + \text{Risk Financing} + \text{Risk Monitoring}$$
$$\text{Residual Risk} = \text{Total Risk} - \text{Risk Mitigation}$$

- **Risk mitigation** includes designing and implementing controls and control-related procedures to minimize risks.
- **Risk monitoring** includes internal and external reporting and feedback into risk assessment, continuing the loop.

- **Risk transfer** involves payment by one party (the transferor) to another party (the transferee, or risk bearer). Five forms of risk transfer are (1) hold-harmless agreements, (2) incorporation, (3) diversification, (4) hedging, and (5) insurance.
- **Self-insurance** is a risk-retention program that incorporates elements of the insurance mechanism where the self-insured organization pays the claims rather than an insurance company.

(b) **IIA Survey Results.** The Institute of Internal Auditors Research Foundation (IIARF) conducted a multi-industry global survey of chief financial officers, chief audit executives, chief corporate counsels, and chief risk officers to understand trends and emerging practices in ERM.

The following list is a summary of major survey results:

- Key drivers of ERM are a desire for a unifying framework and corporate governance regimes.
- The top five motivating factors driving ERM activity identified were (1) desire for a unifying framework (more than 50% of respondents), (2) corporate governance guidelines (38%), (3) mandate from board of directors, (4) competitive pressures, and (5) desire for earnings stability.
- Organizations view ERM as a tool to help manage their most important business issues, such as corporate governance, value management, change management, capital management, and contingency planning.
- The chief financial officer is the most likely senior executive to coordinate and oversee risk management or compliance activities (90%).
- The chief audit executive will be responsible for overseeing ERM activities (30%), the chief financial officer (24%), and the chief risk officer (21%).
- Organizational barriers need to be overcome to implement ERM. The top five barriers include (1) organizational culture; (2) unclear benefits; (3) lack of formalized process, language, and definitions" (4), organizational "turf"; and (5) lack of tools.
- More than 60% of organizations identify implementing risk management programs through a change management model (high-level key lever). Low-level use of key levers, such as personnel management or compensation, may make ERM implementation very difficult.
- Most organizations include financial or operational risks in their internal auditing plan, but less than half consider strategic risks. For example, 63% of respondents reported that the finance function had a formal risk assessment process. In contrast, only 21% of respondents reported activity related to the human resource function.
- ERM may initially be more of a management information tool than a driver of corporate performance may. ERM is seen as an analytical tool rather than as a performance management system.
- A variety of tools and metrics are used, such as risk mapping or optimization software. Risk metrics includes value at risk and earnings at risk.

(c) **Approaches to ERM.** An ERM approach can be viewed in three dimensions. The first represents the range of organization operations. This includes business units or locations, starting small as pilot projects and eventually rolling out to the entire enterprise (i.e., institutionalization). The second dimension represents the sources of risk (hazard, financial, operational, and strategic). This may include property catastrophe risk and currency risk. The third dimension represents the types of risk management activities or processes (risk identification, risk measurement, risk mitigation, and risk monitoring).

Within this ERM universe, two general models of ERM have emerged that are not mutually exclusive. These models are a measurement-driven approach and a process-control approach. A measurement-driven approach focuses on identifying the key risk factors facing an organization and understanding their materiality and probability of occurrence. Risk mitigation activities are focused on the most material risks with appropriate mitigation strategies. Specific steps in the measurement-driven model include assess risk (risk factors and profiles), shape risk (impacts, mitigate, and finance), exploit risk (plans and opportunities), and keep ahead (monitor change and loop). A process-control approach focuses on key business processes and accompanying uncertainties in the execution of the business plan. The emphasis is on linking the process steps, reporting relationships, methodologies, and data collection and reporting to ensure informed decision making. The goal is to manage risk events by achieving consistency of application across the business process spectrum thereby limiting the possibility of surprise occurrence. The process-control model assumes that good processes can control risks.

Some organizations are approaching ERM in two ways: (1) push approach and (2) pull approach. In the push approach, corporate or division management tries to implement the ERM throughout the organization. In the pull approach, individual business units will adopt the ERM at their own pace.

Scorecards, action plans, and monitoring are part of the ERM approach. The scorecards include metrics, a time frame for managing the risk, and a link to shareholder value. Action plans include identifying a risk champion and determining milestones. Monitoring includes progress reviews and review for validity of metrics.

(d) **ERM Tools.** Five alternative risk-transfer tools, other than traditional insurance, include: (1) captives, (2) financial insurance, (3) multiline/multiyear insurance, (4) multiple-trigger policies, and (5) securitization. Multiple-trigger policies and securitization tools are more commonly used. Alternative risk-transfer tools include

- Captives, where a noninsurance firm for the purpose of accepting the risk of the parent firm owns an insurer. Captives combine risk transfer and risk retention.
- Financial insurance contracts, which are based on spreading risk over time, as opposed to across a pool of similar exposures. These contracts usually involve a sharing of the investment returns between the insurer and the insured.
- Multiline/multiyear insurance contracts, which combine a broad array of risks (multiline) into a contract with a policy period that extends over multiple years (multiyear). For example, a pure risk may be combined with a financial risk.
- Multiple-trigger policies, which reflect that source of the risk is not as important as the impact of the risk on the earnings of the firm. A pure risk is combined with a financial risk. The policy is "triggered," and payment is made, only upon the occurrence of an adverse event.
- Securitization, which involves the creation of securities such as bonds, or derivatives contracts, options, swaps, futures, which have a payout or price movement that is linked to an insurance risk. Examples include catastrophe options, earthquake bonds, catastrophe bonds, and catastrophe equity puts.

(e) **Implementation of ERM.** First, senior management support and commitment is needed to properly implement the ERM program in the organization. A dedicated group of cross-functional staff is needed to push it through the organization. Employees should see the ERM program as an enhancement to existing processes, rather than as a new, stand-alone process. The implementation should proceed incrementally and leverage "early wins."

Most organizations are implementing the ERM program incrementally. Some are beginning by layering additional sources of risk, one at a time, into their exiting processes for risk assessment and risk mitigation. Some are embracing all sources of risk at the outset, but are tackling the processes one at a time, with most starting with risk assessment. Others are taking on all risk sources and all processes, but on a small, manageable subset of their operations as a pilot project. Most all are seeking "early wins" that will help build momentum and confidence and promote further development toward their ideal ERM process.

(f) **Role of Internal Auditing in ERM Implementation.** The chief audit executive (CAE) is an ERM champion and should use risk-based audit plans that are consistent with the organization's goals. Internal auditing is the implementation arm of an ERM program. Internal auditors act as facilitators in cross-functional risk assessment workshops conducted in the business units. Best practices in running workshops include length of the workshop, preparation for the workshop, risk agreement, capturing the discussion, software selection, anonymous voting, instantaneous reporting and feedback, and selection and training of the facilitator.

Internal auditors must be process owners and subject matter experts. Both internal auditors and other employees of the organization should view the ERM as a value-added activity since it is both inward-looking and forward-thinking.

Internal auditors should think like managers and focus on business objectives rather than an audit universe. This requires new skill levels for internal auditors, including facilitation skills, skills in risk scorecards, and developing risk frameworks and metrics.

Traditional audit tools, such as checklist approaches and internal control questionnaires, may not work in implementing the ERM program. Internal auditors should move away from the perception of being policemen. ERM can improve the efficiency of internal auditing function since they accomplish more with less.

Some organizations have set up ERM committees, consisting of representatives from strategic planning, human resource, internal auditing, risk management, and loss prevention.

When companies fail to manage risk, opportunities are missed and shareholder value can be lost. Consequently, both internal pressures and external pressures develop to improve corporate governance. With respect to corporate governance, internal auditors can play an important role in ensuring that senior management, the audit committee, and the board of directors are fully informed of the organization's risk profiles and exposures.

5.4 Risk/Control Implications of Different Organizational Structures

(a) Organization Defined

(i) **What is an organization?** Organization and management theorists such as Chester Barnard define an organization as "a system of consciously coordinated activities or forces of two or more persons." In other words, when people gather together and formally agree to combine their efforts for a common purpose or goal, an organization is the result.

The purpose of the management process is to achieve organizational objectives in an effective and efficient manner. According to Edgar Schein, a prominent organizational psychologist, all organizations share four characteristics (see Exhibit 5.4).

Common characteristics of organizations
- Coordination of effort
- Common goal or purpose
- Division of labor
- Hierarchy of authority

Exhibit 5.4: Common characteristics of organizations

Coordination of effort is based on the idea that two heads are sometimes better than one. Individuals who join together and coordinate their mental and/or physical efforts can accomplish great things. There is a synergy here in that coordination of effort multiplies individual contributions.

Common goal or purpose gives organization members a rallying point. Coordination of effort is enhanced when employees join together to strive for something of mutual interest.

Division of labor breaks **complex** tasks into specialized jobs so those employees become more proficient by repeatedly doing the same specialized task.

Hierarchy of authority is needed to see that the intended goals are carried out effectively and efficiently. Authority is the right to direct the actions of others. People who promote flatter organizational structure (fewer levels of management) do not favor the traditional hierarchy of authority. However, there are people who encourage hierarchy of authority, as shown in Exhibit 5.5.

Proponents of flatter organizations	*Proponents of hierarchy of authority*
• Advocate fewer levels of management	• Hierarchy is the most efficient, the hardiest, and the most natural structure
• Hierarchy connotes bureaucracy	• Hierarchy can release energy and creativity, rationalize productivity, and improve morale
• Believe that managerial hierarchy kills initiativeness and crushes creativity	
• Speed up communications	

Exhibit 5.5: Proponents of flatter organizations and hierarchy of authority

(ii) **Classifying organizations.** Organizations can be classified according to their intended purposes. Four categories exist, although some large and complex organizations have overlapping categories. These categories include: (1) business organizations, (2) nonprofit service organizations, (3) mutual-benefit organizations, and (4) commonweal organizations. The primary goals of these organizations include

- **Business organizations.** Must make a profit to survive. Focus on satisfying the demand for products and services and earning profits.

- **Nonprofit service organizations.** Focus is on service, not profits. Specific service is the goal as long as the organization is solvent. Greater pressure to operate more efficiently in light of limited funds available. Serves a specific segment of the society.
- **Mutual-benefit organizations.** Focus is on serving the needs of the members, be it a labor union or other association. Individuals join together to press for their own self-interests. Greater pressure to operate effectively and efficiently to survive. Examples include professional associations such as IIA and unions.
- **Commonweal organizations.** Focus is on offering standardized public services without attempting to earn a profit. Serve all segments of the society, such as fire and police departments and public schools. Their great size makes them unwieldy and difficult to manage.

(iii) **Organization charts.** An organization chart is a visual display of an organization's structural skeleton. Such charts show how departments are tied together along the principal lines of authority. They show reporting relationships, not lines of communication. Organization charts are tools of management to deploy human resources and are common in both profit and nonprofit organizations.

Every organization chart has two dimensions—vertical hierarchy and horizontal hierarchy—and two types—formal and informal, as shown in Exhibit 5.6.

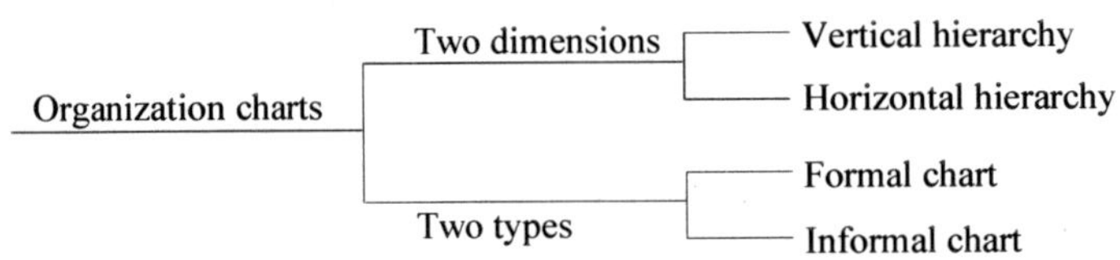

Exhibit 5.6: Organization charts

A typical organization chart, displaying the managerial pyramid, will have two dimensions: horizontal and vertical. These dimensions represent the division of labor and chain of command respectively.

Vertical hierarchy establishes the chain of command, or who reports to whom. It does not show responsibilities, cannot show informal organization, and cannot show all lines of communication. A person with a lower job rank may be shown at a higher level on the chart (e.g., administrative secretary or assistant).

Horizontal hierarchy establishes the division of labor and specialization, such as marketing, production, and finance. Generally, specialization is achieved at the expense of coordination when designing organizations. A workable balance between specialization and coordination can be achieved through contingency design. The horizontal hierarchy does not show responsibilities, cannot show informal organization, cannot show all lines of communication, and does not show reporting channels or hierarchy of authority. A person with a lower job rank may be shown at a higher level on the chart (e.g., administrative secretary or assistant). Networking is accomplished through horizontal hierarchy where the interaction of persons of equal status is taking place for the purpose of professional or moral support.

Formal chart is the documented, official map of the company's departments with appointed leaders who get things done through power granted by their superiors. Formal charts have job titles.

The **informal chart** is not documented and is composed of natural leaders who get things done through power granted by peers. Informal charts have no job titles.

KEY CONCEPTS TO REMEMBER: ORGANIZATION CHARTS

- Job title does not necessarily indicate everything about that person's level of authority
- Nominal power lies in formal organization charts
- Real power lies in informal organization charts
- Even supervisors need to use the informal power network to get things done

The formal organization chart serves as a guideline, but it may not always keep track of changes in power relationships. One of the reasons why natural leaders evolve is that modern organizations are complex; they require the close cooperation of many people doing jobs that the formal organization chart cannot accommodate. *There is at least one person available with people skills and technical skills that make him or her a natural leader. There may be more than one informal leader; there is only one formal leader in each area of the company.*

Natural leadership is intangible. It can cause factions, but it can also build a positive team spirit. It is important for the formal leader to be tuned in to informal power to get things done. Formal leaders have the nominal power, and most subordinates obey to it. But it will make the formal leader's job easier if he or she can influence the informal employee leadership network and win its support. This may even lay the foundation for establishing real rapport and motivating employees.

Management consultant Gareth Morgan made an interesting observation about organization charts.[4] He said that organization charts are useful tools, but they can also be extremely limiting because they entrench the idea that an organization is a structure that can be engineered and reengineered to produce appropriate results. A new organization chart is often seen as a solution to an organization's problems. But, more often than not, it can leave the basic problems unchanged. Morgan says, for example, that when a large bureaucracy is reshaped or "downsized," the result is a smaller bureaucracy. When moved to matrix structure, the result is bureaucratic management in another form. Morgan's main concern is that this restructuring does not create an organization that can flow and self-organize along with the changes faced. The same old organization is reshaped with similar problems and weaknesses.

Organization charts, clearly defined systems, flow diagrams, and other engineered blueprints have provided effective models for systematizing organizational activity. They still do if one is organizing a routine, predictable task. However, they do not work in a new era of nonroutine, unpredictable task environments.

As information technology takes us into a world where old structures and forms of organization dissolve and at times become almost invisible, the old approach no longer works. Through the use of telephone, facsimile machines, electronic mail, computers, and video conferencing, employees and their organizations are becoming disembodied. They can act as if they are completely connected while remaining far apart. Employees can transcend traditional barriers of space and time, continually creating and re-creating themselves through changing networks of interconnection based on real-time communication. As one network comes into being, others dissolve. Organizations do not have to be organizations anymore.

Nowadays, mechanistic thinking breaks down, and managers have to find fresh images for understanding and shaping what they are doing. Morgan suggests designing organizations as if they were spider plants or dandelion seeds blowing in the wind. He proposes that the management of change is the process of imaginization, which invites creativity.

(b) **Theories of Organization.** Basically two theories exist: the traditional view and the modern view. The traditional view has closed-system thinking, while the modern view incorporates open-system thinking (see Exhibit 5.7).

Theories of organization
- Traditional view (closed-system thinking, variables are known and controllable, less uncertain environment)
- Modern view (open-system thinking, variables are difficult to predict or control, more uncertain environment)

Exhibit 5.7: Theories of organization

The **traditional view** assumes that the surrounding environment is fairly predictable and that uncertainty within the organization can be eliminated through proper planning and strict control. The primary goal is economic efficiency. All goal-directed variables are known and controllable.

[4] *Gareth Morgan, Imaginization:* ***The Art of Creative Management*** *(Newbury Park, CA:Sage Publications, 1993).*

The **modern view** assumes that both the organization and its surrounding environments are filled with variables that are difficult to predict or control. The organization interacts continuously with an uncertain environment. The primary goal is survival in an environment of uncertainty and surprise. The modern view deals with more variables that cannot be controlled or predicted.

Next, we explore the evolution of traditional organization theory and its challenges followed by system characteristics.

(i) **Traditional view of organizations.** Henri Fayol and Frederick Taylor treated organizing as a subfield of management. They believed that close supervision, obedience, orders, and rules were the norm. Four traditional principles of organization have emerged: (1) a well-defined hierarchy of authority (to ensure the coordinated pursuit of organizational goals); (2) unity of command (each individual answered to only one superior); (3) authority equal to responsibility (Authority is the right to get subordinates to accomplish objectives, and responsibility is the obligation to accomplish those objectives. Individuals should be accountable for getting something done only when they were given formal authority to get it done.); and (4) downward delegation of authority but not of responsibility (the obligation for getting something done remains with the superior although the authority and responsibility were passed along to subordinates).

Later Max Weber termed bureaucracy as efficient because of the following four characteristics: (1) division of labor, (2) hierarchy of authority, (3) a framework of rules, and (4) impersonality (hiring and promoting people on the basis of what they know, not who they know). Bureaucracy is a matter of degree, and a moderate degree of bureaucratization can enhance organizational efficiency while extreme cases can hinder efficiency. However, trying to eliminate bureaucracy is impractical.

The traditionalists' rigid recommendations for organizing and managing were challenged since they did not work in all situations. Experience has proved that organizing was more than just strict obedience to authority and that bureaucracy has become the epitome of inefficiency. In addition, bottom-up authority and environmental complexity and uncertainty also challenged the traditional thinking about organizations.

(A) ***Authority.*** Is authority top-down or bottom-up? Traditionalists believed that authority was tied to property ownership and therefore naturally flowed from the top of the organization to the bottom. Chester Barnard questioned the traditional assumption about the automatic downward flow of authority. Instead, he proposed a more democratic *acceptance theory of authority* in which a leader's authority is determined by subordinates' willingness to comply with it.

Acceptance theory of authority. The acceptance theory of authority opened the door for upward communication and the informal organization that is based on friendship rather than work rules. Subordinates are viewed as active controllers of authority, not mere passive recipients.

Barnard believes that a subordinate recognizes a communication from a superior as being authoritative and decides to comply with it only when

1. The message is understood,
2. The subordinate believes it is consistent with the organization's purpose,
3. It serves the subordinate's interest, and
4. The subordinate is able to comply.

(B) ***Uncertainty.*** Charles Perrow observed that the increasing complexity of markets, variability of products, increasing number of branch plants, and changes in technology all required more adaptive organizations, not rigid structure. Plans usually have to be made on the basis of incomplete or imperfect information and, consequently, things do not always work out according to plan.

(ii) **Modern view of organizations.** Proponents of open-systems views realize that system-to-system interactions are often as important as the systems themselves. Here the "system" includes social, political, legal, and economic systems. A highly organized and vigorously interactive world needs realistically dynamic models, which is a characteristic of open-system thinking.

CLOSED SYSTEMS VS. OPEN SYSTEMS

Traditional closed-system thinking emphasizes rigid organization structure. It largely ignores environmental influences. Closed-system thinking does not have permeable boundaries. It assumes that all organizations are systems with common characteristics.

Modern open-system thinking emphasizes the need for flexibility and adaptability in organization structure. It fosters a more realistic view of the interaction between an organization and its environment. Open systems have permeable boundaries. All organizations are open systems.

Four characteristics that emphasize the adaptive and dynamic nature of all modern open systems are (1) interaction with the environment, (2) synergy, (3) dynamic equilibrium, and (4) equifinality (see Exhibit 5.8).

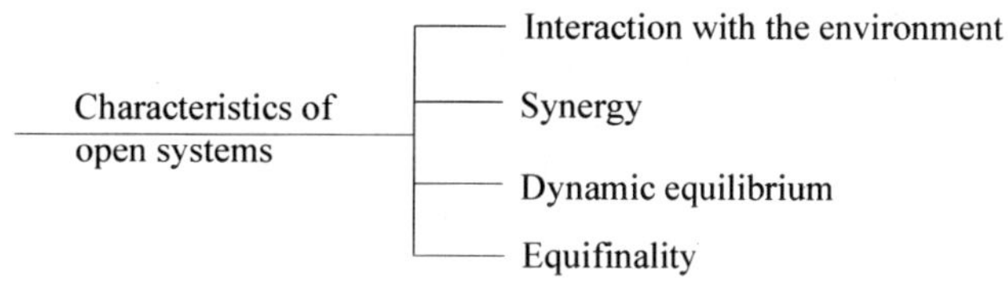

Exhibit 5.8: Characteristics of open systems

Since open systems are not self-sufficient, they depend on the environment for survival (i.e., **interaction with the environment**). An open system adds up to more than the sum of its parts (i.e., **synergy**). A successful business is more than the factors of production: labor, land, and capital.

In open systems, dynamic equilibrium is the process of maintaining the internal balance necessary for survival by importing needed resources from the environment (i.e., **dynamic equilibrium**). **Equifinality** means reaching the same result by different means. It indicates that there is more than one way to get the job done.

Another way of looking at the open systems is in relation to subsystems. If a system is made up of subsystems, *three organizational subsystems would include technical, boundary spanning, and managerial.* The technical subsystem (production function) physically transforms raw materials into finished goods and services. Boundary-spanning subsystems facilitate the organization's interaction with its general environment. Most boundary-spanning jobs (interface functions) are easily identified by their titles. The managerial subsystem controls and directs the other subsystems in the organization.

KEY CONCEPTS TO REMEMBER: OPEN SYSTEMS

- Technical subsystems are the very core of the organization.
- Boundary-spanning subsystems are directed outward toward the general environment.
- The managerial subsystem serves as a bridge between the other two subsystems.

Many traditional theories of organizing exist, including bureaucracy, administrative theory, scientific management theory, and human relations theory. The latter topic is discussed briefly.

(c) **Human Relations Theory.** Many management philosophers rejected the individualism, which was emphasized in the theories of bureaucracy, administrative theory, and scientific management. These new philosophers deplored competition between individuals in the organization and supported the idea of a cooperative group ethic. Emphasis was placed on the relations between people who are members of groups.

Mary Parker Follett and **George Elton Mayo** were two prominent philosophers associated with the **human relations movement**. Mary Parker Follett proposed the idea that individual freedom must be subordinated to the interest of the group. She was concerned with the individual but thought that the individual finds his or her creative self only by relating to others in groups. Follett thought that all authority rested on the consent of those who are directed. Therefore, she proposed that demands should arise from the situation rather than from the superior. Follett proposed that superiors should give reasons for their orders to subordinates. Participative management style is most likely to produce subordinates with management skills.

George Elton Mayo was very concerned with groups in the organization. He attempted to employ scientific methods to study the behavior of groups. He is most famous for his experiments at the Hawthorne Electric Plant in 1928, which in part investigated the influence of the degree of illumination on the productivity of workers. According to the Hawthorne studies, worker behavior is a complex system of forces that include personalities of the workers, nature of their jobs, and formal measurement and reward practices of the organization.

Closely related to the human relations movement is the **behavioral science** approach. Both of these approaches deal with the individual and his interaction in groups. However, the behavioral science approach arose because of the discontent with the methodology of researchers such as Mayo. Behavioral scientists deplored the small amount of data gathered by human relations advocates and the unsystematic examination of the data gathered.

Also, behavioral scientists thought that human relations writers overemphasized group behavior at the expense of individual behavior. Finally, behaviorists rejected the overriding concern with cooperation, when conflict may result in such benefits as innovation. It is easy to see that behavioral scientists emphasize the scientific method in investigating the individual and groups so that conclusions can be objective.

Behavioral scientists use three primary methods to study individuals and groups so that management can learn better ways of handling people. These methods are the case study, the sample survey, and the experiment. These three methods are inductive approaches since they involve studying a small number of persons or one organization and generalizing the results to other persons and organizations.

There are two primary criticisms of the behavioral science approach. First, it is not as precise a science as physics or chemistry because people are not as predictable as the nature of the universe. Second, behavioral science conclusions are useful, but since people and the environment in each organization are different, the application of findings may produce different results in different settings.

Douglas McGregor outlined a set of highly optimistic assumptions about human nature. He recommended Theory Y, which is a set of assumptions for his optimistic perspective about people. This is in contrast with the traditional view of people by managers (Theory X). He criticized Theory X for being pessimistic, stifling, and outdated. Exhibit 5.9 shows the comparison between Theory X and Theory Y assumptions about people from the manager's perspective.

McGregor Theory X/Y Assumptions

Theory X assumptions	*Theory Y assumptions*
• Most people are lazy, dislike or avoid work	• Work is a natural activity, and people are creative, energetic, and imaginative
• Most people must be coerced and threatened, and are unwilling to take responsibility	• The average person is willing to take responsibility
• Most people prefer to be directed	• People are capable of self-direction and self-control
• Most people are interested only in job security	• People are committed to do a good job if they are rewarded adequately

Exhibit 5.9: McGregor Theory X/Y assumptions

Senior management believes employees will volunteer to serve on committees because: (1) they want to play a greater role in the operation of their company, (2) they want to receive more from their jobs than just a paycheck, and (3) they have interests that extend beyond the boundaries of their specific jobs and will welcome the opportunity to pursue those interests. The motivational strategy that management has adopted is McGregor's Theory Y.

William Ouchi discovered a type of organization that exhibited a style of management that effectively combines the traits of typical American and Japanese companies. He called these hybrid companies **Theory Z organizations**. These companies focus on the employee in areas such as: long-term employment, relatively slow evaluation and promotion, cross-functional career paths, participative decision making, individual responsibility, concern for employee, and emphasis on employee self-control. Theory Z is an organizational culture based on a participative decision-making process.

Theory T and Theory T+ are complementary theories based on Southeast Asian assumptions that: work is a necessity but not a goal itself; people should find their rightful place in peace and harmony with their environment; absolute objectives exist only with God; in the world, persons in authority positions represent God, so their objectives should be followed; people behave as members of a family and/or group; and those who do not are rejected by society.

(d) **Contingency Design Theory.** Organizing is the structuring of a coordinated system of authority relationships and task responsibilities. It spells out who does what and who reports to whom. Organizational structure can translate strategy into an ongoing productive operation (see Exhibit 5.10).

Strategy → (leads to) → structure

Strategy → (determines) → technology required

Strategy → (determines) → resources available

Exhibit 5.10: Strategy and structure

Contingency design is an extension of the modern open-system view where it permits the custom tailoring of organizations to meet unique external and internal situational demands. Contingency design is based on the assumption that there is no single best way to structure an organization. It is the process of determining the degree of environmental uncertainty and adapting the organization and its subunits to the situation. *Contingency design is fitting the organization's strategy to its internal and external environment.*

Two popular contingency models that validate the contingency approach by systematically matching structural characteristics with environmental demand include the Burns and Stalker model and the Lawrence and Lorsch model.

(i) **Burns and Stalker model.** Behavioral scientists Tom Burns and G.M. Stalker proposed a typology for categorizing organizations by structural design. They distinguished between mechanistic and organic organizations (see Exhibit 5.11).

Structural design of organizations

Mechanistic organizations

Characteristics of mechanistic organizations

- Rigid in design
- Have strong bureaucratic qualities
- Communication tends to be formal, command-and-control type
- Narrow task definition
- Low task flexibility
- High reliance on instructions
- Narrow knowledge requirements
- Suitable for relatively stable and certain environments

Organic organizations

Characteristics of organic organizations

- Flexible in structure
- Adaptive to change
- Communication tends to be participative
- Broad task definition
- Low reliance on instructions
- Broader knowledge requirements
- Suitable for unstable and uncertain environments

Exhibit 5.11: Structural design of organizations

(ii) **Lawrence and Lorsch model.** Paul Lawrence and Jay Lorsch documented the relationships between two opposing structural forces (differentiation and integration) and environmental complexity. **Differentiation** resulting from a division of labor and technical specialization is the tendency among specialists to think and act in restricted ways. Differentiation tends to fragment and disperse the organization.

Integration, in opposition to differentiation, is the collaboration among specialists that is needed to achieve a common purpose. Integration is a unifying and coordinating force and is partially achieved through hierarchical control, standard policies and procedures, departmentalization, cross-functional teams and committees, better human relations, and liaison individuals and groups.

According to Lawrence and Lorsch, every organization requires an appropriate dynamic equilibrium (an open-system theme) between differentiation and integration. *They demonstrated that in successful firms, both differentiation and integration increased as environmental complexity increased.* These findings are equally applicable to the overall organization, departments, or divisions. They also found that the more differentiated an organization, the more difficult it is to achieve integration. These findings suggest that organizational failure in the face of environmental complexity probably results from a combination of high differentiation and inadequate integration. Under these conditions, specialists work at cross-purposes and become involved in counterproductive conflicts.

Contingency design models conclude that there is no single best organization design and the more uncertain the environment, the more flexible and adaptable the organization structure must be.

KEY CONCEPTS TO REMEMBER: VARIOUS THEORIES OF MANAGEMENT

- Bureaucratic organization is characterized by division of labor, hierarchy (top-down) authority, a framework of rules, impersonality, formal policies and procedures, and a competency level for hiring and promotions. Bureaucracies focus on organizational tasks rather than people and emphasize productivity of human behavior and task results. Bureaucracies tend to be stable in the long run. Division of work deals with specialization of labor to achieve organizational objectives.
- The classical view of an early theory of management includes the universality concept. "Esprit de corps," one of 14 of Fayol's universal principles of management, emphasizes teamwork, communications, and harmonious effort among individuals. An example is "employees of a small retail outlet are highly motivated and genuinely concerned about the store's prosperity."
- The universal process is based on the belief that a single management process can be applied in all organizations. It believes that good managers are interchangeable among organizations. It uses a rigid, inflexible organizational structure regardless of the external environment.
- The operational approach, also known as scientific management or operations research, is concerned with technical, quantitative, and objective means of achieving efficiency in production operations. The manager is production-oriented, and his or her primary interest is in improving efficiency and reducing waste. Standardization of work is a goal of the scientific school of management.
- Behavioral approaches to management primarily focus on people. They imply that it is in management's best interest to be concerned about employees' well-being. The behavioral approach to management most likely to resulted from the prospect of unionization.
- Operations management is a management process that designs, operates, and controls production systems. The focus of productive systems is to transform physical resources and human talent into needed goods and services. The operations management theory or approach views organizations as productive systems consisting of inputs, a transformation process, and outputs.
- In general systems theory, the term "subsystem" is used to describe the relationship of each system component to the next higher component. In the opinion of general systems theorists, all organizations are identified as being open. The systems approach to management views the organization as a system of interconnected and interdependent parts. It believes that the whole is greater than the sum of its parts. The systems approach to management is demonstrated by a chief executive officer who stresses the importance of the interdependencies among the various components of the organization.

- Contingency management approach is practiced by a member who assigns responsibility and delegates authority based on the task to be performed and the individual available for assignment. Contingency management theory uses multivariate analysis to determine how a grouping of variables react together to produce an outcome.
- According to contemporary management thought, managers should be given training in a course linking key staffing issues with organizational strategy and structure. Such a course should include human resources planning, selection, training, and performance appraisal.
- The principle of equity is concerned with fairness and justice.
- Under the scalar chain principle (the chain of command), there is a chain of direct authority relationship from superior to subordinate. The scalar principle of management has been violated when an employee goes over the head of the supervisor and receives special permission from the departmental manager to, for example, take an extra week of vacation.
- The unity of command principle is violated when an employee answers to several bosses.
- Unity of direction requires the focus of all efforts aimed toward accomplishing the same goal, that is, in the same direction.

(e) **Types of Departmentalization.** Two common forms of integration are through the hierarchical chain of command and departmentalization. Some integration is needed to offset the negative effects of differentiation. It is through departmentalization that related jobs, activities, or processes are grouped into major organizational subunits such as departments, divisions, groups, or units.

Four basic types of departmentalization include (see Exhibit 5.12)

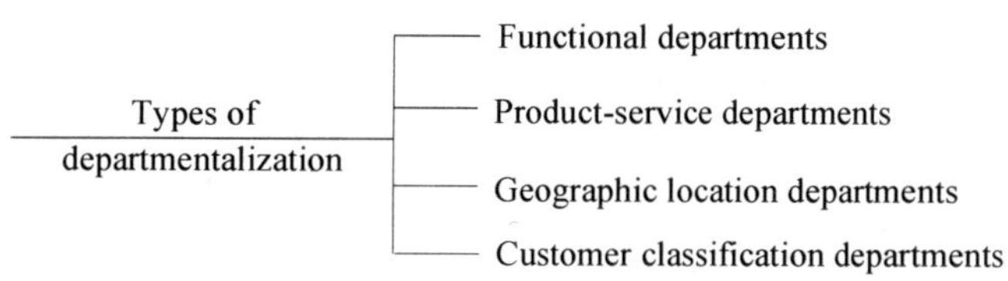

Exhibit 5.12: Types of departmentalization

Functional departments. Functional departments, in both profit and nonprofit organizations, categorize jobs according to the activity performed. Manufacturing, marketing, and finance are some examples of functional departments, and this type of categorization is popular because it permits those with similar technical expertise to work in a coordinated subunit. It becomes unpopular when departmental concerns tend to override more important organizational concerns. Functional departments can encourage differentiation at the expense of integration. A small, single, standard product line may be organized as functional departmentalization such as manufacturing, accounting, and sales. When organizational and reporting lines are unbroken, it is an indication of functional departmentalization.

CHARACTERISTICS OF ORGANIZATION STRUCTURES

Organization structures such as functional departments, product-service departments, geographic location departments, and customer classification departments are in their pure form. In practice, a combination of these structures is found.

Organization structures such as product-service, geographic location, and customer classification departments can create costly duplication of personnel and facilities. However, functional departments do not create duplication of personnel and facilities.

Product-service departments. In the product-service department category, a product or service, rather than a functional category of work, is the unifying theme. Ideally, those working in a product-service department have a broad "business" orientation rather than a narrow functional orientation. One weakness of the product-service approach is that inefficient and costly duplication of effort may take place. A product departmentalization may be good for a firm making multiple products. An example would be a computer manufacturer that organizes into mainframe computers, minicomputers, and personal computers.

Geographic location departments. Geography dictates the structure and format of the organization and is based on the concept that managers should be closer to the action. Advantages include knowledge of local business and customers and disadvantages include long lines of communication. The force behind the geographical lines is global competition. *"Think global and act local" is the catchphrase for companies operating in a global market.*

Customer classification departments. Customers have different needs and are of different types, such as business versus residential; retail versus wholesale; industrial versus commercial. The rationale behind organizing the company into customer classification is to better service the distinctly different needs of each customer type.

(f) **Contingency Design Alternatives.** Contingency design requires managers to select from a number of situationally appropriate alternatives instead of blindly following fixed principles of organization. Design alternatives include span of control, centralization and decentralization, line and staff organizations, and matrix organization (see Exhibit 5.13).

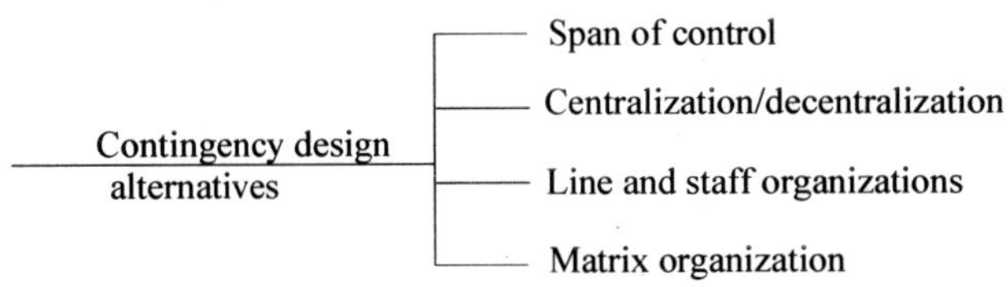

Exhibit 5.13: Contingency design alternatives

(i) **Span of control.**

(A) ***Narrow and wide.*** The number of people who report directly to a manager represents that manager's span of control or span of management. The optimal size of a span of control in a work area is dependent on the department's function, organizational levels, changes in the nature of the work, and the clarity of instructions given employees. The optimal span of control is not dependent on the total number of employees in the department or company.

NARROW SPAN OF CONTROL VS. WIDE SPAN OF CONTROL

"Narrow span of control" means few people to oversee, which in turn creates many hierarchical levels (tall organizations), which in turn requires many managers. The number of subordinates supervised is small. Workers are geographically dispersed.

"Wide span of control" means many people to oversee, which in turn creates few hierarchical levels (flat organizations), which in turn requires few managers. Jobs are similar, procedures are standardized, all workers are in the same work area, and tasks are simple and repetitive. An upper limit of the number of employees supervised must exist.

Obviously, a balance between too little and too much supervision is required. The ideal span of control ranges from 4 subordinates at the top of the organization to 12 at the lowest level. The reason for the difference is that top-level managers are supervising people and lower-level managers are responsible for supervising specific tasks.

(B) ***Tall and flat.*** A tall organization has many levels of hierarchy and a narrow span of control. A flat organization structure is one with relatively few levels of hierarchy and is characterized by a wide span of management control (see Exhibit 5.14).

Characteristics of tall organization structure	Characteristics of flat organization structure
• Tasks are highly complex and varied.	• Tasks require little direction and control of subordinates.
• Work areas are geographically dispersed.	• Employees must be able to work with little or no supervision.
• Subordinates perform distinctly different tasks.	• More timely and efficient in decision making.
• Good at problem resolution due to discipline imposed by hierarchy.	• Information flows fast from top to bottom.
• Information flows slowly from top to bottom.	

Exhibit 5.14: Characteristics of tall and flat organization structures

(ii) **Centralized and decentralized organizations.** Two methods of organizing are centralized and decentralized. In a **centralized organization,** decisions are made at the higher levels of management. Decisions in a decentralized organization are made at the lower levels. Authority is delegated to lower levels of the organization.

Centralization versus decentralization. The extent of an organization's centralization or decentralization is determined by the span of control, the number of levels in the hierarchy, and the degree of coordination and specialization.

Centralization is typically used in those organizations that emphasize coordination of decisions that must be applied uniformly to a set of known or common problems. In planning an audit of a highly decentralized operation, an auditor assumes that the authority to make significant risk decisions has been delegated to the unit managers.

Companies that allow managers a great deal of autonomy are described as utilizing decentralized management. The following factors are considered in determining whether a centralized or decentralized design should be adopted (see Exhibit 5.15).

Factors	Decentralization	Centralization
Number and kind of decisions	Many unique decisions	Generic or uniform decisions
Culture of the organization	Less formal	More formal
Value of uniform procedures and rules	Rapidly changing products and industries	Slowly changing products and industries
Skills of lower-level managers	Must be generalists	Do not require as much training
Size and growth rate of the firm	Larger organizations and/or rapid growth rate	Smaller organizations and/or less rapid growth rate
Strategy	Emphasis on new product development through company research	Emphasis on production of standard products in large volume

Exhibit 5.15: Factors for decentralization and centralization

(A) ***Two approaches to achieve decentralization: functional and divisional.*** **Functional decentralization** occurs when related activities or functions are grouped within an organization. For instance, all functions relating to marketing are grouped under one head. The main advantage of functional decentralization is that it allows specialists to work in areas where they contribute the most to the firm. This is very important in industries that survive mainly because of technical expertise.

However, once the specialists can make decisions on their own, coordination with other areas such as production may suffer. Another problem is that when one group is created, it is difficult to measure the performance of the individual specialists. As the firm grows, this problem also will grow.

Divisional decentralization is the creation of units whose managers are in charge of producing and marketing a certain product, a group of related products, or activities for a geographic region. A division thus created will involve many if not all of the functions engaged in by the entire organization. Divisionalization results in many semi-independent units equivalent to small organizations within the larger parent.

The main advantage of divisionalization is that it enables decision making that is closer to the activities of the organization in contrast to decision making that arises from a central office far away. A second advantage is that responsibility can be assigned easily to the manager of a division so that the manager's contribution to the company can be evaluated. A third advantage of divisionalization is that greater unity of command is achieved. The primary disadvantage is that divisionalization can lead to suboptimization.

Divisionalization can create a feeling of autonomy in division managers which results in dysfunctional competition between them. As a result, the entire firm will suffer. Some managers will emphasize short-run gains to promote their careers to the detriment of the long-run interests of the organization.

(B) ***Decentralizaton: advantages and disadvantages.*** The **advantages** are said to arise from the greater autonomy assumed by lower-level management and workers. Top management is free to concentrate on more important problems, such as long-range planning, because lower-level management is handling many of the detailed matters on its own. The general speed of business activity is increased since lower-level management does not have to wait for upper-level approval. Probably the greatest advantage claimed for decentralization is that it supplies freedom to think boldly and creatively, stimulates a sense of personal freedom, raises morale, and provides an excellent training ground for future top executives.

The greater autonomy also gives rise to the **disadvantages** of decentralization. With each unit making its own decisions, activities are likely to be duplicated. Normally, it would be cheaper to perform some activities centrally (e.g., finance, accounting). The managers of autonomous units may possibly ignore the advice of specialists. Decentralization can lead to suboptimization. In the interest of the whole organization, top management should install some controls to attempt to correct some of the disadvantages of decentralization.

(iii) **Line and staff organizations.** Line and staff organization structure is designed to maximize the unity-of-command principle by giving only the managers the authority to make decisions affecting those in the chain of command. There is no crossover between line and staff organization structure since each structure has its own chain of command.

Line managers have the authority to make decisions and give orders to all subordinates in the chain of command. Staff authority is generally limited to subordinates within its department. There is a natural conflict between these two parties due to power differences and different backgrounds.

One important source of conflict is the fact that line employees have formal authority while staff employees have informal power. Line managers tend to emphasize decisiveness, results, costs, and implementation, whereas staff members advise and prefer completeness, controls, adherence to policies and procedures, and systematic analysis to solve organizational problems. Staff function supports the line function but does not control it.

(iv) **Matrix organization.** In a matrix organization, people with vertical (down) and horizontal (across) lines of authority are combined to accomplish a specific objective. This design is suitable to a project environment where the project manager is responsible for completing a project without a formal line authority. Under these conditions, project managers tend to use negotiation skills, persuasive ability, technical competence, and the exchange of favors to complete a project in order to compensate for their lack of formal authority (see Exhibit 5.16).

Advantage of Matrix Organizations	*Disadvantages of Matrix Organizations*
Efficient use of resources, project integration, improved information flow, flexibility, discipline, and improved motivation and commitment	Power struggles, conflict, slow reaction time, difficulty in controlling and monitoring tasks and people, overhead, stress due to dual reporting

Exhibit 5.16: Advantages and disadvantages of matrix organization

A matrix organization structure will likely have unity-of-command problems unless there is frequent and comprehensive communication between the various functional managers and project managers.

A large internal auditing department employs specialists in areas such as computer auditing and statistical sampling. All specialists report directly to the assistant manager for technical services. When needed on a specific audit, they report to the audit supervisor responsible for the assignment. The matrix form of organizational structure exists in relation to the specialists.

5.5 Risk/Control Implications of Different Leadership Styles

(a) **Overview.** The control environment has a pervasive influence on the way business activities are structured, objectives are established, and risks are assessed.[5] It also influences control activities, information and communication systems, and monitoring activities. This is true not only of their design, but also the way they work day to day. The entity's history and culture influence the control environment. It influences the control consciousness of its people. Effectively controlled entities strive to have competent people, instill an enterprise-wide attitude of integrity and control consciousness, and set a positive tone at the top. They establish appropriate policies and procedures, often including a written code of conduct, which foster shared values and teamwork in pursuit of the entity's objectives.

If management style is autocratic and the level of formality is highly structured, one can expect a strong control consciousness. Similarly, if management style is empowered and the level of formality is loose or informal, one can expect a weak control consciousness.

(b) **Control Environment Factors.** The control environment encompasses seven factors (see Exhibit 5.17). Although all are important, the extent to which each is addressed will vary with the entity. For example, the chief executive of an entity with a small workforce and centralized operations may not establish formal lines of responsibility and detailed operating policies, but could nevertheless have an appropriate control environment.

Seven Factors Contributing to Strong Control Environment

- Integrity and ethical values
- Commitment to competence
- Board of directors or audit committee
- Management's philosophy and operating style
- Organizational structure
- Assignment of authority and responsibility
- Human resource policies and practices

Exhibit 5.17: Seven factors contributing to strong control environment

(i) **Integrity and ethical values.** An entity's objectives and the way they are achieved are based on preferences, value judgments, and management styles. Those preferences and value judgments, which are translated into standards of behavior, reflect management's integrity and its commitment to ethical values.

The effectiveness of internal controls cannot rise above the integrity and ethical values of the people who create, administer, and monitor them. Integrity and ethical values are essential elements of the control environment, affecting the design, administration, and monitoring of other internal control components. *Integrity is a prerequisite for ethical behavior in all aspects of an enterprise's activities. The CEO usually is the dominant personality in an organization and individually often sets its ethical tone.*

INCENTIVES AND TEMPTATIONS

Incentives cited for engaging in fraudulent or questionable financial reporting practices and, by extension, other forms of unethical behavior are

- Pressure to meet unrealistic performance targets, particularly for short-term results
- High performance-dependent rewards
- Upper and lower cutoffs on bonus plans

Temptations for employees to engage in improper acts include

- Nonexistent or ineffective controls, such as poor segregation of duties in sensitive areas, that offer temptations to steal or to conceal poor performance

[5] *COSO, "Internal Control—Integrated Framework."*

- High decentralization that leaves top management unaware of actions taken at lower organizational levels and thereby reduces the chances of getting caught
- A weak internal audit function that does not have the ability to detect and report improper behavior
- An ineffective board of directors that does not provide objective oversight of top management
- Penalties for improper behavior that are insignificant or unpublicized and thus lose their value as deterrents

SOURCE: Kenneth A. Merchant, ***Fraudulent and Questionable Financial Reporting: A Corporate Perspective*** *(Morristown, NJ: Financial Executives Research Foundation, 1987).*

Narrow span of control vs. wide span of control. An auditor should consider the control environment factor "integrity and ethical values" in determining whether a positive and effective control environment exists. Some issues that an auditor might focus on during a control evaluation include

- Existence and implementation of codes of conduct and other policies regarding acceptable business practice, conflicts of interest, or expected standards of ethical and moral behavior
- Dealings with employees, suppliers, customers, investors, creditors, insurers, competitors, and auditors (e.g., whether management conducts business on a high ethical plane, and insists that others do so, or pays little attention to ethical values)
- Pressure to meet unrealistic performance targets—particularly for short-term results—and extent to which compensation is based on achieving those performance targets

(ii) **Commitment to competence.** Competence should reflect the knowledge and skills needed to accomplish tasks that define the individual's job. There often is a trade-off between competence and cost. Management needs to specify the competence levels for particular jobs and to translate those levels into requisite knowledge and skills. The necessary knowledge and skills may in turn depend on the individuals' intelligence, training, and experience. There often can be a trade-off between the extent of supervision and the requisite competence level of the individual.

An auditor should consider the control environment factor "commitment to competence" in determining whether a positive and effective control environment exists. Some issues on which an auditor might focus during control evaluation include

- Formal or informal job descriptions or other means of defining task that comprise particular jobs
- Analyses of the knowledge and skills needed to perform jobs adequately

(iii) **Board of directors or audit committee.** The entity's board of directors and audit committee influences the control environment and tone at the top significantly. Factors include the board or audit committee's independence from management, experience and stature of its members, extent of its involvement and scrutiny of activities, and the appropriateness of its actions. Another factor is the degree to which difficult questions are raised and pursued with management regarding plans or performance. Interaction of the board or audit committee with internal and external auditors is another factor affecting the control environment.

An auditor should consider the control environment factor "board of directors or audit committee" in determining whether a positive and effective control environment exists. Some issues on which an auditor might focus during control evaluation include

- Independence from management, such that necessary, even if difficult and probing, questions are raised
- Frequency and timeliness with which meetings are held with chief financial and/or accounting officers, internal auditors, and external auditors
- Sufficiency and timeliness with which information is provided to board or committee members, to allow monitoring of management's objectives and strategies, the

entity's financial position and operating results, and terms of significant agreements

- Sufficiency and timeliness with which the board or audit committee is appraised of sensitive information, investigations and improper acts (e.g., travel expenses of senior officers, significant litigation, investigation of regulatory agencies, defalcations, embezzlement or misuse of corporate assets, violations of insider trading rules, political payments, illegal payments)

KEY CONCEPTS TO REMEMBER: CONTROL ENVIRONMENT

- The primary purpose of an internal auditor's evaluation of internal controls is to determine if management has planned and implemented activities needed to attain goals and objectives.
- Control by management is the result of proper and effective planning, organizing, and directing of organizational activities.
- Adequate control is defined as a state that exists if management has planned and organized in a manner which provides reasonable assurance that the organization's objectives and goals will be achieved efficiently and economically.
- Controls provide assurance to management that desired actions will be accomplished when objectives are established in writing, standards are adopted, results are compared with the standards, and corrective actions are undertaken.
- Corporate directors, management, external auditors, and internal auditors all play important roles in creating a proper control environment. Senior management is primarily responsible for establishing a proper environment and specifying an overall internal control structure.
- Corporate management has a role in the maintenance of internal control. In fact, management sometimes is a control. For example, supervision of employees is a control device.
- An adequate system of internal controls is most likely to detect an irregularity perpetrated by a single employee, not a group of employees in collusion.
- It is control weakness when the audit committee of the board consists of the chief executive officer, the chief financial officer, and a major stockholder.
- Accounting and auditing are control-oriented functions in an organization. While management accountants prepare reports to senior management detailing the funds expended and the expenses incurred by each department in the company, the internal auditors would identify inadequate controls that increase the likelihood of unauthorized expenditures.
- A control strength environment is where the treasurer's office prepares checks for suppliers based on vouchers prepared by the accounts payable department.
- The internal audit's overall responsibility is to act as an independent appraisal function to review operations as a service to management by measuring and evaluating the effectiveness of controls.

(iv) **Management's philosophy and operating style.** Management's philosophy and operating style affect the way the enterprise is managed, including the kinds of business risks accepted. An entity that has been successful taking significant risks may have a different outlook on internal control than one that has faced harsh economic or regulatory consequences as a result of venturing into dangerous territory. An informally managed company may control operations largely by face-to-face contact with key managers. A more formally managed one may rely more on written policies, performance indicators, and exception reports.

Other elements of management's philosophy and operating style include attitudes toward financial reporting, conservative or aggressive selection from available alternative accounting principles, conscientiousness and conservatism with which accounting estimates are developed, and attitudes toward data processing and accounting functions and personnel.

An auditor should consider the control environment factor "management's philosophy and operating style" in determining whether a positive and effective control environment exists. Some issues on which an auditor might focus on during control evaluation include

- Nature of business risks accepted, for example, whether management often enters into particularly high-risk ventures or is extremely conservative in accepting risks
- Frequency of interaction between senior management and operating management, particularly when operating from geographically removed locations
- Attitudes and actions toward financial reporting, including disputes over application of accounting treatments (e.g., selection of conservative versus liberal accounting policies; whether accounting principles have been misapplied, important financial information not disclosed, or records manipulated or falsified)

(v) **Organizational structure.** An entity's organizational structure provides the framework within which its activities for achieving entity-wide objectives are planned, executed, controlled, and monitored. Activities may relate to what is sometimes referred to as the value chain: inbound (receiving) activities, operations, or production, outbound (shipping), marketing, sales and service.

Significant aspects of establishing a relevant organizational structure include defining key areas of authority and responsibility and establishing appropriate lines of reporting. An entity develops an organizational structure suited to its needs. Some are centralized, others are decentralized. Some have direct reporting relationships; others are more of a matrix organization. Some entities are organized by industry or product line, by geographical location, or by a particular distribution or marketing network. Other entities, including many state and local governmental units and not-for-profit institutions, are organized on a functional basis.

An auditor should consider the control environment factor "organizational structure" in determining whether a positive and effective control environment exists. Some issues on which an auditor might focus during control evaluation include

- Appropriateness of the entity's organizational structure and its ability to provide the necessary information flow to manage its activities
- Adequacy of definition of key managers' responsibilities and their understanding of these responsibilities
- Adequacy of knowledge and experience of key managers in light of responsibilities

(vi) **Assignment of authority and responsibility.** This includes assignment of authority and responsibility for operating activities and establishment of reporting relationships and authorization protocols. It involves the degree to which individuals and teams are encouraged to use initiative in addressing issues and solving problems, as well as limits of their authority. It also deals with policies describing appropriate business practices, knowledge and experience of key personnel, and resources provided for carrying out duties.

Employee Empowerment

There is a tendency to push authority downward to bring decision making closer to front-line personnel. An entity may take this tack to become more market-driven or quality focused—perhaps to eliminate defects, reduce cycle time, or increase customer satisfaction.

Alignment of authority and accountability often is designed to encourage individual initiative, within limits. Delegation of authority, or "empowerment," means surrendering central control of certain business decisions to lower echelons—to the individuals who are closest to everyday business transactions. This may involve empowerment to sell products at discount prices; negotiate long-term supply contracts, licenses, or patents; or enter alliances or joint ventures.

A critical challenge is to delegate only to the extent required to achieve objectives. This requires ensuring that risk acceptance is based on sound practices for identification and minimization of risk, including sizing risks and weighing potential losses versus gains in arriving at good business decisions.

Another challenge is ensuring that all personnel understand the entity's objectives. It is essential that each individual know how his or her actions interrelate and contribute to achievement of the objectives.

The control environment is greatly influenced by the extent to which individuals recognize that they will be held accountable. This holds true that all the way to the chief executive, who has ultimate responsibility for all activities within an entity, including the internal control system.

An auditor should consider the control environment factor "assignment of authority and responsibility" in determining whether a positive and effective control environment exists. Some issues on which an auditor might focus on during control evaluation include

- Assignment of responsibility and delegation of authority to deal with organizational goals and objectives, operating functions, and regulatory requirements, including responsibility for information systems and authorizations for changes
- Appropriateness of control-related standards and procedures, including employee job descriptions
- Appropriate numbers of people, particularly with respect to data processing and accounting functions, with the requisite skill levels relative to the size of the entity and nature and complexity of activities and systems

(vii) **Human resources policies and practices.** Human resources practices send messages to employees regarding expected levels of integrity, ethical behavior, and competence. Such practices relate to hiring, orientation, training, evaluating, counseling, promoting, compensating, and remedial actions. For example

- Standards for hiring the most qualified individuals, with emphasis on educational background, prior work experience, past accomplishments, and evidence of integrity and ethical behavior, demonstrate an entity's commitment to competent and trustworthy people.
- Recruiting practices that include formal, in-depth employment interviews and informative and insightful presentations on the entity's history, culture, and operating style send a message that the entity is committed to its people.
- Training policies that communicate prospective roles and responsibilities and include practices such as training schools and seminars, simulated case studies, and role-play exercises illustrate expected levels of performance and behavior.
- Rotation of personnel and promotions driven by periodic performance appraisals demonstrate the entity's commitment to the achievement of qualified personnel to higher levels of responsibility.
- Competitive compensation program that include bonus incentives serve to motivate and reinforce outstanding performance.
- Disciplinary actions send a message that violations of expected behavior will not be tolerated.

It is essential that personnel be equipped for new challenges as issues that enterprises face change and become more complex—driven in part by rapidly changing technologies and increasing competition. Education and training, whether classroom instructions, self-study, or on-the-job training, must prepare an entity's people to keep pace and deal effectively with the evolving environment. They will also strengthen the entity's ability to effect quality initiatives. Hiring of competent people and one-time training are not enough. The education process must be ongoing.

An auditor should consider the control environment factor "human resource policies and practices" in determining whether a positive and effective control environment exists. Some issues on which an auditor might focus during control evaluation include

- Extent to which policies and procedures for hiring, training, promoting, and compensating employees are in place
- Appropriateness of remedial action taken in response to departures from approved policies and procedures
- Adequacy of employee candidate background checks, particularly with regard to prior actions or activities considered being unacceptable by the entity

- Adequacy of employee retention and promotion criteria and information-gathering techniques (e.g., performance evaluations) and relation to the code of conduct or other behavioral guidelines

5.6 Change Management

(a) **Agents of Change.** Organizations must change to survive in a competitive environment. This requires everyone in the organization believing in and accepting the change. Ideally, managers need to be architects or agents of change rather than the victims of change. When introducing changes, managers often are surprised that things do not turn out as planned. This is because the change process is not carried out properly. The change itself is not the problem. When managers are acting as agents of change, their company will be much more responsive, flexible, and competitive. In addition to managers, internal auditors can act as change agents due to their nature of work. Auditors facilitate change through their recommendations to management. Each recommendation auditors make requires some change in the existing policies, procedures, and practices or creation new ones.

(b) **How to Change.** A corporation can change by reengineering business policies, processes, jobs, and procedures; outsourcing nonstrategic activities; partnering with major suppliers and customers; implementing total quality management programs; redesigning the organizational structure to fit the business strategy; renovating physical plants and facilities; installing computer-based systems and technologies; understanding one's own products, services, markets, and customers and those of competitors; and installing performance measurement methods and reward systems.

PROMOTERS VS. RESISTORS OF CHANGE

People at the top of the organization usually promote change because they have clear vision and better goals to achieve.

People at the bottom of the organization usually resist change the **least** because they know how bad things really are at their level.

People at the middle of the organization usually resist change the **most** because they neither know top management goals nor know how bad things really are at the bottom. They are in a confused stage since they neither know the top nor the bottom.

(c) **Types of Organizational Change.** Organization psychologists David Nadler and Michael Tushman developed an instructive typology of organizational change describing four types of changes (see Exhibit 5.18).[6]

	Incremental	*Strategic*
Anticipatory	Tuning 1	Reorientation 3
Reactive	Adaptation 2	Re-creation 4

Exhibit 5.18: Typology of organizational change

As the exhibit shows, **anticipatory changes** are any systematically planned changes intended to take advantage of expected situations (e.g., following demographics). **Reactive changes** are those necessitated by unexpected environmental events (e.g., responding to competitor's action). **Incremental changes** involve the subsystems adjustments needed to keep the organization on its chosen path (e.g., adding a third shift in a manufacturing plant). **Strategic changes** alter the overall shape or direction of the organization (e.g., switch from building houses to apartments by a construction contractor).

The four specific resulting types of organizational change from the previous model are tuning, adaptation, reorientation, and re-creation (see Exhibit 5.19).

---

[6] *Robert Kreitner, **Management**, 9th edition (Boston: Houghton Mifflin, 2004).*

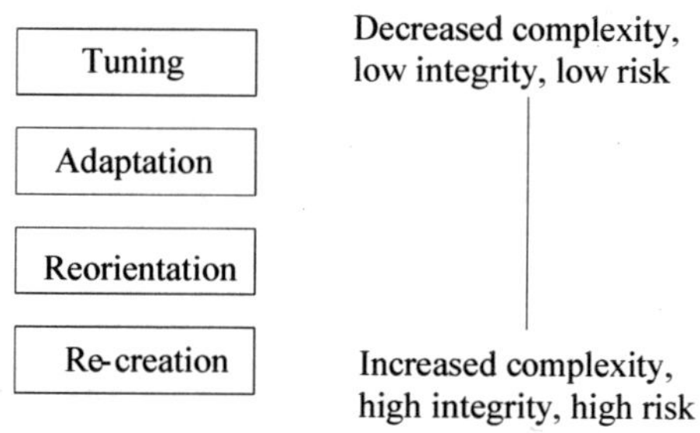

Exhibit 5.19: Specific types of organizational change

In this exhibit, **tuning** is the most common form of organizational change covering preventive maintenance and continuous improvement. The major thrust of tuning is to actively anticipate and avoid problems rather than passively waiting for things to go wrong before taking action. *Managers should seek the change, not just expect the change.*

Adaptation, like tuning, involves incremental changes. The difference is that the changes are in reaction to external problems, events, or pressures. **The reorientation** change is anticipatory and strategic in scope. It is also called "frame bending" because the organization is significantly redirected, while continuing its original mission. **Re-creation** is a type of change that is reactive and strategic in scope. It is also called "frame breaking" because the new organization is completely different from the past.

(d) **Resistance to Change.** Organizational change comes in all forms, sizes, shapes, and with various degrees of impacts and consequences for employees. Among the most common reasons for resistance to change are: surprise, inertia, misunderstanding, emotional side effects, lack of trust, fear of failure, personality conflicts, lack of tact, threat to job status or security, and breakup of work groups. *Management faces the challenge of foreseeing and neutralizing resistance to change, as the resistance is both rational and irrational.*

Management theorists have offered at least six options to overcome resistance to change. These options include: (1) education and communication, (2) participation and involvement, (3) facilitation and support, (4) negotiation and agreement, (5) manipulation and co-optation, and (6) explicit and implicit coercion. Situational appropriateness is the key to success.

Education and communication. This option promotes prevention rather than cure. The idea here is to help employees understand the true need for a change as well as the logic behind it. Various media may be used, including face-to-face discussions, formal group presentations, and special reports or publications. Advantages: Once persuaded, employees will help with the implementation of the change. Drawbacks: Education and communication can be time-consuming if many employees are involved.

Participation and involvement. Personal involvement through participation tends to defuse rational and irrational fears about a workplace change. Involvement in the design and implementation of a change makes one become an owner of the change process and its success. Advantages: Participation and involvement lead to commitment from employees. Drawbacks: Participation and involvement can be time-consuming if participators design an inappropriate change.

Facilitation and support. Support from management in the form of special training, job stress counseling, and compensatory time off can be helpful when fear and anxiety are responsible for resistance to change. Advantages: No other approach works as well with adjustment problems. Drawbacks: Facilitation and support can be time-consuming, expensive, and still fail.

Negotiation and agreement. Management can neutralize resistance to change by exchanging something of value for cooperation. Advantages: It is a relatively easy way to avoid major resistance. Drawbacks: Negotiation and agreement can be too expensive in many cases if others are alerted to negotiate for compliance.

Manipulation and co-optation. Manipulation occurs when managers selectively withhold or dispense information and consciously arrange events to increase the chance that a change will be successful. Co-optation normally involves token participation, and the impact of their input is negligible. Advantages: It can be a relatively quick and inexpensive solution to resistance problems. Drawbacks: The process can lead to future problems if people feel manipulated.

Explicit and implicit coercion. Managers who cannot or will not invest the time required for the other strategies can force employees to go along with a change by threatening them with termination, loss of pay raises or promotions, transfer, and so forth. Advantages: It is speedy, and can overcome any kind of resistance. Drawbacks: This process can be risky if it leaves employees mad at the initiators.

(e) **Dos and Don'ts of Change Process.** Internal auditors should consider the following dos and don'ts of change process during their audit work:

- A real paradigm shift is needed for changes to take place. Excuses like "It is our company policy" and "We have no resources" no longer work. Forward-looking people are needed.
- Motivating stakeholders (employees, customers, and suppliers) can have a multiplier effect on the change initiative. Their involvement in problem solving and knowledge sharing is vital.
- The active performance measures are not always obvious. They should be made explicit.
- During the change implementation process, expect setbacks and roadblocks. Address them on a case-by-case basis.
- Communicating honestly is important. Act straightforward with all stakeholders.
- Use the grapevine to a project's advantage; do not let the project be abused by it.
- Empower employees so they feel that they have real influence over standards of production, quality, and service. This brings significant changes in employees' behavior. However, this requires that managers who do the empowering must also change. Empowerment means that employees have the correct knowledge and appropriate tools to do things well, not just have the authority to do the job.
- Identify the barriers to change. If possible dismantle them, but at least deal with them.
- Today's change projects require "border crossing" of departments, divisions, suppliers, and customers. Borderless projects should be encouraged since border-bound projects like to maintain their own turf.
- A goal-focused and results-oriented performance measurement system is needed to institutionalize the changes since performance measures are a primary strategy deployment tool. Do not settle for a single measurement; instead, opt for a "set of measures."
- Understand and consider the cultural differences at the workplace. Do not discount them.

(f) **Organizational Development.** Organizational development (OD) is a systematic approach to planned change programs intended to help employees and organizations function more effectively. OD combines the knowledge from various disciplines, such as behavioral science, psychology, sociology, education, and management. OD is a process of fundamental change in an organization's culture. For OD programs to be effective, not only must they be tailored to unique situations, but they also must meet the seven common objectives in order to develop trust. *Problem-solving skills, communication, and cooperation are required for success.*

1. Deepen the sense of organizational purpose and align individuals with that purpose.
2. Strengthen interpersonal trust, communication, cooperation, and support.
3. Encourage a problem-solving rather than a problem-avoiding approach to organizational problems.
4. Develop a satisfying work experience capable of building enthusiasm.
5. Supplement formal authority with authority based on personal knowledge and skill.
6. Increase personal responsibility for planning and implementing.
7. Encourage personal willingness to change.

Organization development brings out pros and cons.

Pros: General management lacks a systematic approach and is often subject to haphazard, bits-and-pieces management style. OD gives managers a vehicle for systematically introducing change by applying a broad selection of management techniques as a unified and consistent package. This approach leads to greater personal, group, and organizational effectiveness.

Cons: The seven common objectives listed above are not new. They have been addressed by one or another management techniques.

(i) ***OD process.*** Social psychologist Kurt Lewin recommended that change agents unfreeze, change, and then refreeze social systems related to three major phases or components of OD.[7]

Unfreezing phase -----> Change phase -----> Refreezing phase

Unfreezing involves neutralizing resistance by preparing employees for change. Change involves implementing the change strategy. Refreezing involves systematically following up a change program for permanent results.

(ii) ***Unfreezing phase.*** The objective of unfreezing phase is to assess the situation and suggest an appropriate change strategy. The scope of work includes making announcements, holding meetings, and launching a promotional campaign in the organization's newsletter and on bulletin boards. The goal is to deliver a clear message to employees about the change. Management needs to avoid creating unrealistic expectations such as miracles.

During the unfreezing phase, management may choose to diagnose the situation by using several approaches, such as: (1) requiring records (personnel or financial) for signs of excessive absenteeism, cost overruns, budget variances, (2) interviewing employees with specific questions about their job and the organization, (3) mailing survey questionnaires for opinions and suggestions, and (4) observing employees at work since people tend to say one thing and do another. After the data are collected and compiled, it is good to compare the results with past results to see how things have changed. This would help in mapping a future course of action.

(iii) ***Change phase.*** The objective of the change phase is to implement the change strategy through enhanced collaboration and cooperation. In this phase of intervention, the wheels of change are set in motion. Intervention here means that a systematic attempt will be made to correct an organizational deficiency uncovered through diagnosis.

Six popular OD interventions designed to increase effectiveness include: (1) life and career planning, (2) skill development, (3) role analysis, (4) team building, (5) survey feedback, and (6) grid OD. These six interventions are grouped into three categories: (1) individual, (2) group, and (3) entire organization targets, as shown in Exhibit 5.20.

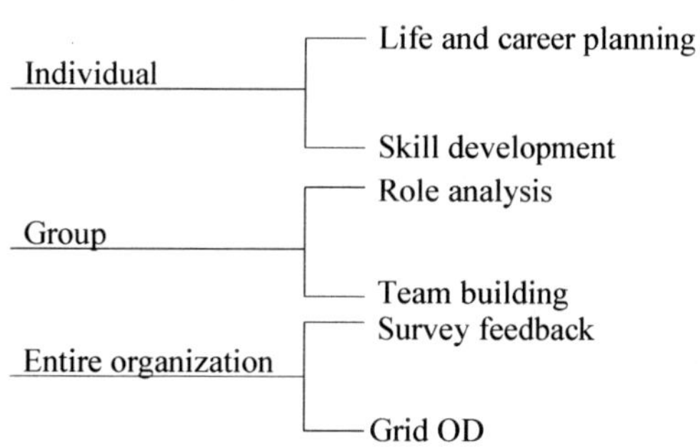

Exhibit 5.20: OD interventions

(A) ***Individual interventions.*** The overall objective of *life and career planning* is to get individuals to define their personal goals for growth and development and to plan ways to achieve them. Here an assumption is made that organizational growth and development is a function of individual growth and development. The overall objective of *skill development* is to place emphasis on learning how to do it in terms of delegation, problem solving, conflict resolution, and leading. Skill development deals with content rather than process.

(B) ***Group interventions.*** The overall objective of *role analysis* is to define a prescribed way of behaving. A systematic clarification of interdependent task and job behavior is made. The overall objective of *team building* is to place emphasis on interactive group processes, the "how" of effective group behavior. This intervention is the most widely used human resource development technique.

(C) ***Entire organization interventions.*** The overall objective of *survey feedback* is to inform employees where they stand in relation to others on important organizational issues so that constructive problem solving can take place. Effective feedback should be relevant, understand-

---

7 *Ibid.*

able, descriptive, verifiable, controllable, comparative, and inspiring. The overall objective of *grid OD* is to present a package covering several OD interventions arranged in an orderly and coherent fashion. OD grid is based on Blake and Mouton's leadership grid—a popular OD approach.

(iv) ***Refreezing phase.*** The objective of the refreezing phase is to address unanticipated problems and side effects and to maintain positive changes. The effectiveness of change strategy is also evaluated. The scope includes follow-up and monitoring to ensure lasting change.

(A) ***Maintaining positive changes.*** The goal is to induce employees to behave differently and positively. This calls for more cooperation, more collaboration, and more productivity among employees. Some of the items for maintaining positive changes include: top management support, peer group support, a formal reward and punishment system—a supportive climate for change on the job.

(B) ***Evaluating the OD program.*** An objective evaluation of results is desired even though it is difficult, time-consuming, and expensive. According to a recent statistical analysis conducted by Neuman, Edwards, and Raju

- Combined interventions were more effective at improving employee attitudes and satisfaction than were single-technique interventions
- Team building was the most effective OD intervention for improving attitudes and satisfaction
- OD interventions tend to have a stronger influence on attitudes than on satisfaction.
- The empirical linkages between OD interventions and productivity are not strong.[8]

5.7 Conflict Management

(a) **What Is Conflict Management?** Social scientists say that conflict is inevitable between people, and without conflict there is no major personal change or social progress. Conflict management involves accepting or even encouraging constructive conflict as necessary. The key point is to minimize the destructive form of conflict.

To be human is to experience conflict. This conflict arises due to differences in personal values, opinions, desires, habits, and needs of people. It is impossible for people to rise completely above selfishness, betrayals, misrepresentations, anger, and strain. The best way to depict conflict is on a scale of disruptive and destructive dimensions (see Exhibit 5.21).

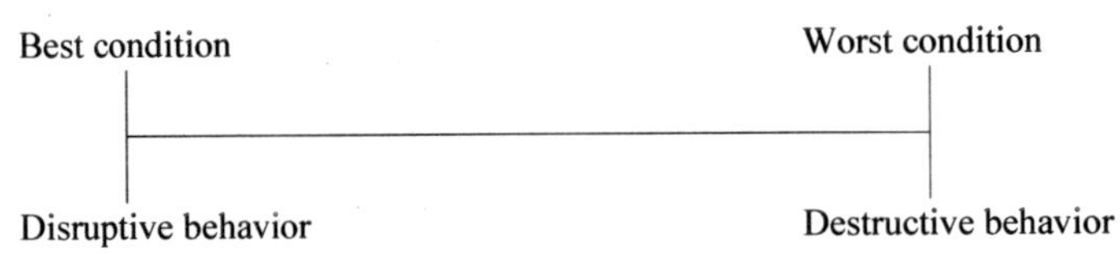

Exhibit 5.21: Scale of disruptive and destructive dimensions

Conflict at best is disruptive and at worst it is destructive. Once it erupts, conflict is difficult to control. Destructive conflict has a tendency to expand until it consumes all the things and people it touches.

When two or more people are together for any length of time, some conflict will be generated. That is inevitable. Social scientists make an important distinction between two types of conflict: realistic conflict and nonrealistic conflict (see Exhibit 5.22).

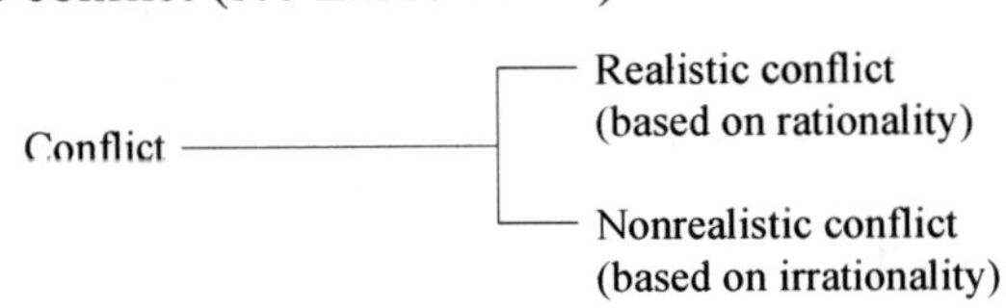

Exhibit 5.22: Types of conflicts

[8] ***Personal Psychology*** *(Autumn 1989).*

In realistic conflict, there are opposed needs, goals, means, values, or interests. Nonrealistic conflict arises from ignorance, error, tradition, prejudice, dysfunctional organizational structure, win/lose types of competition, hostility, or the need for tension release. Realistic conflict can be resolved by focusing on the emotions first followed by substantive issues and using collaborative problem-solving methods. Unrealistic conflict creates unwarranted tension between people and can cause unnecessary destruction. Unrealistic conflict should be handled very carefully; it can be prevented to some extent.

(b) **Benefits of Conflict.** Despite its drawbacks, conflict has benefits. It can spur technological development, encourage personal and intellectual growths, and help renew business organizations. Professor Richard Walton of Harvard University's Graduate School of Business noted the positive impact that conflict can have on business and other organizations. According to Walton

> *A moderate level of interpersonal conflict may have the following constructive consequences. First, it may increase the motivation and energy available to do tasks required by the social system. Second, conflict may increase the innovativeness of individuals and the system because of the greater diversity of the viewpoints and a heightened sense of necessity. Third, each person may develop increased understanding of his own position, because the conflict forces him to articulate his views and to bring forth all supporting arguments. Fourth, each party may achieve greater awareness of his own identity. Fifth, interpersonal conflict may be a means for managing the participants' own internal conflicts.*

(c) **Personal Conflict Prevention and Control Methods.** Although it is impossible to totally eradicate conflict, personal conflict prevention and control can avert much needless strife (unrealistic conflict). Both individuals and institutions need to develop prevention and control methods. Robert Bolton recommends[9]

- One way of diminishing the amount of conflict is to **use fewer roadblocks**. Ordering (dominating), threatening, judging, name-calling, and other roadblocks are conflict-promoting interactions.
- **Reflective listening** to another person when he or she has a strong need or a problem helps the other person dissipate "negative" emotions.

Ways to Increase One's Tolerance and Acceptance of Others

- Greater assertiveness
- Increased emotional support in our lives
- Effective courses in communication skills

- **Assertion skills** enable a person to get needs met with minimal strife. By asserting when needs arise, one can prevent the buildup of emotions that so often cause conflict. Both assertion and listening skills help to clear up two major sources of conflict: errors and lack of information.
- **Awareness** of which behaviors are likely to start a needless conflict between people can eliminate many confrontations. Certain words, looks, or actions tend to "trigger" specific people into conflict. These behaviors may be rooted in early childhood experiences. Some people can sense that a storm is brewing.

How to Handle Differing Point of Views?

When another person expresses a differing point of view on a tense topic, many of us have a strong tendency to disagree argumentatively, put the other person down, or angrily denounce the person. This behavior is difficult to control, but it must be done, especially when the other person is underassertive.

- **"Dumping one's bucket" of tension without filling the other's bucket** is another important conflict prevention and control method. Strenuous exercise, competitive athletics, and sexual activities also can drain off one's tensions without adding to other people's stress.

[9] *Robert Bolton, **People Skills** (New York: Simon & Schuster, 1979).*

- **Increased emotional support** from family and friends can decrease one's proneness to unnecessary conflict. In general, the more we are loved and cared for, the less we need to fight.
- **Heightened tolerance and acceptance of others** also tends to diminish unrealistic conflict. Some say that these tolerances and acceptances are conditioned by upbringing and even by genetic factors. But each of us can become more tolerant and accepting than we now are.
- "**Issues control**" is another important way of managing conflicts. It is often preferable to deal with one issue at a time, to break issues down into smaller units rather than deal with enormous problems with many parts, to start with easily resolved issues (i.e., start with points of agreement), and to define the dispute in nonideological terms. Try to find how your needs and the other's needs can be satisfied (i.e., win/win situation) through jointly identifying the cause of disagreement.
- **A careful appraisal of the full consequences and the cost of a conflict** may deter you from involving yourself in needless disputes. It is difficult to estimate the cost of a conflict, because emotional interactions are unpredictable and frequently get out of hand.

(d) **Group or Organizational Conflict Prevention and Control Methods.** Individual actions alone are not enough. Group and/or organizational actions are needed to prevent and control the conflict that occurs in the workplace. The way an organization is structured has a bearing on the amount of conflict generated in it. The potential for conflict tends to be greater in centralized, bureaucratic organizations than in decentralized organizations. The more rigid institutions, according to Rensis Likert, have less effective communication and are less adept at managing conflict constructively than are the organizations at the other end of the continuum.

Bolton suggests[10]

- The personality and methods of the **leader** are important. Managers who have low levels of defensiveness and who are supportive tend to help people in their organizations avert unnecessary strife. A person who is in a position of power, one who has great charisma, or one who has developed effective communication skills tends to have the greatest influence on the way conflict is handled.
- The **climate** of a group also influences the amount of conflict it generates. Although some kinds of competition can be healthy, research evidence suggests that win/lose competition fosters needless conflict and diminishes the ability to resolve disputes effectively. However, cooperating to achieve goals that could not be accomplished without joint effort promotes more genuine harmony.
- Well-conceived and clearly stated **policies and procedures** that have the understanding and support of the relevant individuals create orderly processes that can help mitigate unnecessary chaos and conflict. When policies and procedures do not match the needs of the organization or its members, when they are arrived at arbitrarily and administered high-handedly, they can add to the level of unrealistic conflict in the organization.
- The **degree of change and the method by which change is introduced** into a family or an organization influences the amount and severity of disputes in that institution. A certain amount of change is necessary in all institutions, but too rapid a change or changes utilizing inadequate methods of communications can create significant and needless conflict.
- **Mechanisms to settle grievances** need to be established. A mechanism is practiced when resolving disputes between labor and management of an organization.
- **Training for conflict management** is necessary both for the prevention of needless conflict and for the resolution of the conflicts that are inevitable in any relationship or organization.

WHAT IS THE BEST WAY TO HANDLE CONFLICT?

Conflict management skills should be taught as part of training program that includes listening, assertion, and collaborative problem-solving skills.

[10] *Ibid.*

Agreed-on ways of preventing and resolving conflict, adequate channels of communication, and mechanisms for handling grievances, when combined with proper training in the above areas, provide a comprehensive program of conflict management.

Much conflict needs to be faced and resolved at the earliest possible moment. When prevention and control strategies are used improperly and unwisely, they merely postpone the inevitable. The final result is worse than an early, direct resolution of the strife.

When some people want to dodge conflict altogether, they tend to misuse the prevention and control strategies listed above. Others use denial, avoidance, capitulation, or domination as mechanisms for keeping their lives free of the unpleasantness of strife.

5.8 Management Control Techniques

(a) **Management Controls Defined.** Management controls, in the broadest sense, include the plan of organization, methods, and procedures adopted by management to ensure that its goals and objectives are met. Management controls, also known as internal controls, include accounting and administrative controls.

Management control systems must be integrated with ongoing management practices and, where appropriate and effective, with other management initiatives, such as productivity improvement, quality improvement, business process improvement, reengineering, and performance measures and standards. Examples of management practices include periodic staff meetings, quarterly management reviews, budget planning and execution, and variance analysis.

Management control systems must be effective and efficient—balancing the costs of control mechanisms and processes with the benefits the systems are intended to provide or control. They should identify who is accountable and provide accountability for all activities.

(b) **Traditional Management Controls.** Management controls include the process for planning, organizing, directing, and controlling the entity's operations. They include the management control systems for measuring, reporting, and monitoring operations. Specifically, they include automated and manual systems, policies and procedures, and other ongoing management activities that help ensure risks are managed and controlled. Internal auditing is an important part of management control.

Managerial control can be divided into feed-forward and feedback controls. A feed-forward control is a proactive control such as defect prevention, inspection, training, and budgeting. A feedback control is used to evaluate past activity to improve future performance. It measures actual performance against a standard to ensure that a defined result is achieved. Examples of feedback controls include surveys and variance analysis.

(c) **Contemporary Management Controls.** Many new management controls have evolved over the years, including economic-value-added (EVA), market-value-added (MVA), activity-based costing (ABC), open-book management, and the balanced scorecard system.

EVA is a financial control technique that is defined as a company's net (after-tax) operating profit minus the cost of capital invested in the company's tangible assets. It captures all the things a company can do to add value from its activities, such as running the business more efficiently, satisfying customers, and rewarding shareholders. Each job, department, or process in the organization is measured by the value added.

MVA measures the stock market's estimate of the value of a company's past and projected capital investment projects. For example, when a company's market value (the value of all outstanding stock plus the company's debt) is greater than all the capital invested in it from shareholders, bondholders, and retained earnings, the company has a positive MVA, an indication that it has created wealth. A positive MVA usually goes hand-in-hand with a high EVA measurement.

ABC attempts to identify all the various activities needed to provide a product or service and allocate costs accordingly. Because ABC allocates costs across business processes, it provides a more accurate picture of the cost of various products and services. In addition, it enables managers to evaluate whether more costs go to activities that add value or to activities that do not add value. They can then focus on reducing costs associated with non-value-added activities.

Open-book management first allows employees to see for themselves—through charts, computer printouts, meetings, and reports—the financial condition of the company. Second, it shows individual employees how their job fits into the big picture and affects the financial future of the organization. Finally, it ties employee rewards to the company's overall success. The goal of open-book management is to get every employee thinking like a business owner rather than like a hired hand—what money is coming in and where it is going. Open-book management helps employees appreciate why efficiency is important to the organization's success. It turns the traditional control on its head.

The balanced scorecard system is a comprehensive management control system that balances traditional financial measures with measures of customer service, internal business processes, and the organization's capacity for learning and growth. The financial perspective reflects a concern that the organization's activities contribute to improving short- and long-term financial performance (e.g., net income and return on investment). Customer service indicators measure such things as how customers view the organization, as well as customer retention and satisfaction. Internal business process indicators focus on production and operating statistics, such as order fulfillment or cost per order. The learning and growth indicator focuses on how well resources and human capital are being managed for the company's future. Metrics may include employee retention and the introduction of new products.

5.9 Types of Control

(a) **Control Characteristics.** Control is any positive and negative action taken by management that would result in accomplishment of the organization's goals, objectives, and mission. Controls should not lead to compulsion or become a constraint on employees. Controls should be natural and should be embedded in the organizational functions and operations. More so, controls should be accepted by the employees using or affected by them. Use and implementation of controls should be inviting, not inhibiting. Controls should be seen as beneficial from the employee's personal and professional viewpoints. Ideally, controls should facilitate the achievement of employee's and organizational goals and objectives. In other words, any control that does not help or promote in achieving the goals and objectives should not be implemented. Controls should be effective and efficient. Controls should not cost more than the benefits derived.

(b) **Control Requirements.** The auditor needs to understand the control requirements of an application system or a business operation before assessing control strengths and weaknesses. In other words, there should be a basis or baseline in place (i.e., standards, guidelines, and benchmarks) prior to control measurement and assessment. In the absence of a baseline of standards, auditor's findings, conclusions, and recommendations will be questioned and will not be accepted by the auditee. Usually the basis is

- Internal control principles
- Operating standards for manual and automated operations both in system-user areas and Information Systems areas
- Application system development or maintenance methodology standards
- Technical standards
- Operations standards
- Administrative standards
- Industry standards
- Auditee's operating standards
- Generally accepted accounting principles
- Generally accepted information technology standards
- Generally accepted auditing standards
- Generally accepted government auditing standards
- Generally accepted IS control objectives and techniques
- Generally accepted system security principles
- Organization's policies and procedures
- Control philosophy of management
- Risk and exposure levels of the system or operation under consideration
- Management's tolerance to risk levels
- The nature and type of industry (i.e., financial, regulated)
- Government, tax, legal, accounting, regulatory requirements
- Management's directives and circulars
- Good business and management practices

(c) **Combination, Complementary, and Compensating Controls.** Controls or control measures should prevent, reduce, or even eliminate potential risks and exposures. Controls should also prevent and detect errors, omissions, and irregularities. Controls are needed within and around a computer-based application system as well as in computer operations. Controls are additive.

(i) **Combination controls.** Rarely would a single control suffice to meet control objectives. Rather, a combination of controls or complementary controls is needed to make up a whole and to provide a synergistic effect.

Some examples of combination controls include

- Supervisory reviews and approvals are combined with organization's policies, procedures, and standards
- A combination of controls from the five types of controls (i.e., directive, preventive, detective, corrective, and recovery)
- A specific general control (e.g., full-volume backups) combined with another specific general control (e.g., incremental backups)
- A specific general control combined with one or more application system controls
- A specific application system control combined with one or more general controls
- System-user controls in one user department combined with controls in other system-user departments
- IS controls in one IS section or department combined with controls in other IS sections or departments
- System-user controls combined with IS controls
- Manual controls combined with automated controls
- One-application system controls combined with other and related application system controls
- Application system controls combined with operating systems software controls
- Application system controls combined with database system controls
- Application system controls combined with automated program library management system controls
- Application system controls combined with automated access-control security system controls
- Application system controls combined with automated data file management system (e.g., tape, cartridges, and disk) controls
- Application system controls combined with automated documentation system controls
- Application system controls combined with automated report balancing system controls
- Application system controls combined with data communication system controls
- Application system controls combined with data dictionary system controls
- Application system controls combined with telecommunication system controls
- Application system controls combined with general data processing controls
- Physical-access security controls combined with logical-access security controls
- A user identification code combined with a password code to make user authentication more assured

An example of a combination of controls is a situation where fire-resistant materials are used in the computer center (a preventive control) to prevent a fire, while smoke and fire detectors are used to detect smoke and fire (a detective control), and fire extinguishers are used to put out the fire (a corrective control). Here a single preventive control would not be sufficient. All three controls are needed to be effective.

(ii) **Complementary controls.** Complementary controls (hand-in-hand controls) have an important place in both the manual and the automated control environment. Complementary controls are different from compensating controls in that, in the latter, category weak controls in one area or function are balanced by strong controls in other areas or functions, and vice versa. A function or an area need not be weak to use complementary controls. Complementary controls can enhance the effectiveness of two or more controls when applied to a function, program, or operation. These individual, complementary controls are effective as stand-alones and are maximized when combined or integrated with each other. In other words, complementary controls have a synergistic effect.

Some examples of complementary controls include

- External security software functions can complement the security features available in applications software and vice versa.
- Security features within a database management system can complement the security functions available in the applications software.
- External security software functions can complement the security features available in the following systems software products: tape/disk management system, report distribution system, operator console automation system, job-control validation system, job-scheduling system, problem/change management system, online program development facilities, online teleprocessing monitors, database management systems, and job rerun software.
- External security software functions can complement the security features available in hardware devices (access keys, smart cards, access cards) and biometrics devices.
- Data editing and validation routines operating during data entry into the computer system can complement the same routines operating during data updating into the master files.
- Manual controls can complement automated controls and vice versa.
- The following areas can complement each other: administrative controls, physical security controls, personnel security controls, technical security controls, emanations security controls, operations controls, applications controls, procedural controls, environmental controls (heat, humidity, air-conditioning), and telecommunications security controls.

(iii) **Compensating controls.** Normally the auditor will find more control-related problems if it is a first-time audit of an area. Generally the more frequently an area is audited, the less the probability of many control weaknesses. Therefore, determining the nature of efficient and effective operations needs both audit instinct and business judgment. During the control evaluation process, the auditor should consider the possibility of availability of compensating controls as a way to mitigate or minimize the impact of inadequate or incomplete controls. In essence, the concept of compensating controls deals with balancing of weak internal controls in one area with strong internal controls in other areas of the organization. Here the word "area" can include a section within a user or IS department.

An example of a weak control is a situation where data control employees in the IS department are not reconciling data-input control totals to data-output control totals in an application system. This control weakness in the IS department can be compensated for by strong controls in the user department where end users reconcile their own control totals with those produced by the application system. Sometimes automated compensating controls and procedures are needed to shorten the lengthy manual controls and procedures (e.g., replacing a manual report balancing system with an automated report balancing system).

Compensating controls are needed whenever

- Manual controls are weak.
  Solution: Look for strong computer controls or other.
- Computer controls are weak.
  Solution: Look for strong manual controls or other.
- Interface controls between manual and automated systems are weak.
  Solution: Look for strong controls in either the receiving or the sending system,
- Functional (system) user controls are weak.
  Solution: Look for strong IS controls or other.
- IS controls are weak.
  Solution: Look for strong controls in system-user departments or other IS departments.
- Third-party manual controls are weak.
  Solution: Look for strong controls in the in-house system in either the manual or the automated part.

- Third-party computer controls are weak.
  Solution: Look for strong controls in the in-house system in either the manual or the automated part.
- Physical-access security controls are weak.
  Solution: Look for strong logical-access security controls.
- Logical-access security controls are weak.
  Solution: Look for strong physical-access security controls, supervisory reviews, or more substantive testing.
- A specific general control is weak.
  Solution: Look for a strong and related application control(s).
- An application system control is weak.
  Solution: Look for a strong and related general control(s).
- Employee performance is weak.
  Solution: Look for strong supervisory reviews and more substantive testing.

(d) **Control Assessment.** During an assessment of control strengths and weaknesses, the auditor might run into situations where a business function, system, or manual/automated procedure is overcontrolled or undercontrolled. This means that there may be too many controls in one area and not enough controls in other areas. Also, there may be duplication or overlapping of controls between two or more areas. Under these conditions, the auditor should recommend to eliminate either some user controls, some IS controls, some manual controls, some automated controls, or a combination of them. The same may be true of situations where a system or operation is oversecured or undersecured, and where an application system is overdesigned or underdesigned. This assessment requires differentiating between relevant and irrelevant information; considering compensating controls, which is discussed later; considering interrelationships of controls, which is also discussed later; and judging materiality and significance of audit findings taken separately and as a whole.

Control Assessment Challenge

The key issues are to know how much control is needed, how to measure it, how to evaluate whether a control is deficient or sufficient, and how to balance it.

Rarely can a single finding lead to the conclusion of an unacceptable audit or uncontrolled area. Usually a combination of control weaknesses is required to call an area unacceptable. For example, a finding such as "housekeeping is poor in the data center" alone or in combination with "there are no smoking or eating signs in the data center" will not qualify for giving an unacceptable or uncontrolled audit rating. The audit findings must be significant. The nature of the operation (e.g., automated or manual and sensitive or routine), criticality of the system (high risk versus low risk), costs to develop and maintain controls, and the materiality (significance) of the finding are more important criteria to consider than simple observation of control weaknesses. Note that materiality is relative, not absolute. What is material to one organization may not mean the same to another. Audit judgment plays an important role in deciding what is material, what is a significant control weakness, what is an efficient operation, what is an effective system, and which should be considered separately and as a whole. In other words, the auditor needs to focus on the entire environment of the audited operation or system and take a big-picture approach instead of taking a finding-by-finding approach. A cost-benefit analysis might help the auditor in the process of evaluating controls.

(e) **Cost-Benefit Analysis.** A cost-benefit analysis is advised during the process of designing each type of control into an application system during its development and maintenance as well as during its operation. Ideally, costs should never exceed the benefits to be derived from installing controls. However, costs should not always be the sole determining factor because it may be difficult or impractical to quantify benefits such as timeliness, improved quality and relevance of data and information, and improved customer service and system response time. When controls are properly planned, designed, developed, tested, implemented, and followed, they should meet one or more of the following 12 attributes: (1) practical, (2) reliable, (3) simple, (4) complete, (5) operational, (6) usable, (7) appropriate, (8) cost-effective, (9) timely, (10) meaningful, (11) reasonable, and (12) consistent.

(f) **Costs versus Controls versus Convenience.** Costs of controls vary with their implementation time and the complexity of the system or operation. Control implementation time is important to realize benefits from installing appropriate controls. For example, it costs significantly more to correct a design problem in the implementation phase of an application system under development than it does to address in the early planning and design phases.

There are **trade-offs** among costs, controls, and convenience factors. The same is true between system usability, maintainability, auditability, controllability, and securability attributes of systems. For example

- High-risk systems and complex systems and operations require more controls.
- Excessive use of tight-security features and control functions can be costly and may complicate procedures, degrade system performance, and impair system functionality, which could ultimately inhibit the system's usability.
- System users prefer as few integrity and security controls as possible, only those needed to make the system really usable.
- The greater the maintainability of the system, the easier it is for a programmer to modify it. Similarly, the greater the maintainability of the system, the less expensive it is to operate in the long run.

(g) **Controls by Dimension.** Control can be viewed through three different dimensions of timing: precontrol, concurrent control, and postcontrol (see Exhibit 5.23).

Types of control
- Precontrol (proactive control)
- Concurrent control (ongoing control)
- Postcontrol (reactive control)

Exhibit 5.23: Types of control

Precontrol (e.g., policy) anticipates problems and is proactive in nature. Concurrent control is exercised through supervision and monitoring. Postcontrol identifies deviations from standards or budgets and calls for corrective action, and is similar to feedback control. Precontrol and feed-forward control are interrelated since they deal with future-directed actions. Forecasting, budgeting, and real-time computer systems are examples of feed-forward controls. Precontrol is the most preferred action; the least preferred action is postcontrol. The difference is when a corrective action is taken—the sooner the better.

A feedback control is used to evaluate past activity in order to improve future performance. It measures actual performance against a standard to ensure that a desired result is achieved. Feedback control has been criticized because corrective action takes place after the fact (reactive).

Feedback control can allow costs to build up due to their back-end position. An example is human resource managers holding exit interviews with employees who have resigned to go to work for competitors. Management tabulates the interviewee's responses and uses the information to identify problems with training, compensation, working conditions, or other factors that have caused increased turnover. Other examples include customer surveys, increased finished goods inspections, increased work-in-process (WIP) inspections, variance analysis, postaction controls, monitoring product returns, and evaluating customer complaints.

A feed-forward control attempts to anticipate problems and effect timely solutions (proactive), and hence is important to management. An example is when a key auditee employee will not be available for a few weeks for audit work due to illness, and the audit supervisor reschedules the audit work to be done in this auditable area. Other examples include: defect prevention by quality control inspection of raw materials and WIP, quality control training programs, budgeting, forecasting inventory needs, and advance notice of a purchase.

(h) **Specific Types of Controls.** Controls prevent the adverse effects of risks. Many different types of control activities have been described, including directive controls, preventive controls, detective controls, corrective controls, manual controls, computer controls, and management controls (see Exhibit 5.24).

The complexity of an entity and the nature and scope of activities affect its control activities. Complex organizations with diverse activities may face more difficult control issues than simple organizations with less varied activities. An entity with decentralized operations and an emphasis on local autonomy and innovation presents different control circumstances than a highly centralized one. Other factors that influence an entity's complexity and, therefore, the nature of its controls include location and geographical dispersion, the extensiveness and sophistication of operations, and information processing methods. All these factors affect an entity's control activities, which need to be designed accordingly to contribute to the achievement of the entity's objectives.

Control activities can also be classified by specified control objectives, such as ensuring completeness, timeliness, accuracy, and authorization of transactions, which are applicable to both manual and computer processing environments (see Exhibit 5.24).

Control Categories by Function and Objectives

- Controls by function
  - Directive controls
  - Preventive controls
  - Detective controls
  - Corrective controls
  - Manual controls
  - Computer controls
- Controls by objectives
  - Data completeness
  - Data timeliness
  - Data accuracy
  - Data authorization

Exhibit 5.24: Control categories by function and objective

(i) **Controls by function.** Controls can be classified according to the function they are intended to perform. **Directive controls** ensure the occurrence of a desirable event. Specific examples of directive controls include: requiring all members of the internal auditing department to be Certified Internal Auditors and providing management with assurance of the realization of specified minimum gross margins on sales. Other examples include policies, directives, guidance, and circulars.

Preventive controls are needed to avoid the occurrence of an unwanted event. Examples include segregation of duties, use of checklists, use of systems development methodology, competent staff, use of passwords, authorization procedures, and documentation. Segregation of duties means duties are divided among different people to reduce the risk of error or inappropriate actions. For example, it includes dividing the responsibilities for authorizing transactions, recording them, and handling the related asset. A manager authorizing credit sales would not be responsible for maintaining accounts receivable records or handling cash receipts. Similarly, salespersons would not have the ability to modify product price files or commission rates. It calls for a separation of the functional responsibilities of custodianship, record keeping, operations, and authorization.

Detective controls are needed to discover the occurrence of an unwanted event. The installation of detective controls is necessary to provide feedback on the effectiveness of the preventive controls. Examples include reviews and comparisons, bank reconciliations, account reconciliations, and physical counts.

Corrective controls are needed to correct after an unwanted event has occurred. They fix both detected and reported errors. Examples include correction procedures, documentation, and control and exception reports.

Manual controls include budgets, forecasts, policies and procedures; reporting; physical controls over equipment, inventories, securities, cash, and other assets, and periodically counted and compared with amounts shown on control records.

Computer controls include general controls and application controls. General controls include data center operations controls, system software controls, access security controls, and application system development and maintenance controls. Application controls are designed to control application processing, helping to ensure the completeness and accuracy of transaction processing, authorization, and validity. Many application controls depend on computerized edit checks. These edit checks consist of format, existence, reasonableness, and other checks on the data, which are built into each application during its development. When these checks are designed properly, they can help provide control over the data being entered into the computer system. Computer controls are performed to check accuracy, completeness, and authorization of transactions.

(ii) **Controls by objectives.** Examples of data completeness controls include use of prenumbered forms, obtaining transaction authorization, and system logging of transactions. Examples of data timeliness controls include use of electronic mail to send urgent messages instead of phone and use of facsimile to send urgent letters instead of regular mail. Examples of data accuracy controls include use of batch and hash totals, check digits, balance controls, and system-assigned numbers to documents. Examples of data authorization controls include management approvals, two-person controls, and overrides.

KEY CONCEPTS TO REMEMBER: HOW MANY CONTROLS ARE THERE?

- Accounting controls are well defined with a body of professional standards published. They help ensure there is full accountability for physical assets and that all financial transactions are recorded and reported timely and accurately.
- Administrative controls help ensure resources are safeguarded against waste, loss or fraud, and misappropriation, and support the accomplishment of organization's goals and objectives. These controls include accurate and timely management information, and effective and efficient processes for planning, productivity improvement, quality control, legal and regulatory compliance, and improving economy and efficiency.
- Auditing controls are the system of checks and balances in effect throughout the organization.
- Operating controls include segregation of duties, dual controls, joint custody, rotation of duties, adherence to prescribed policies and procedures, and employees taking vacations.
- Operational controls include controls that are not clearly defined and completely communicated due to constant changes and several functional departments involved in the operating chain. They are not supported by clear standards and are subject to greater misinterpretation.
- Input controls prevent or detect the entry of inaccurate or incomplete data into a computer system.
- Output controls ensure that computer outputs (reports, files, and listings) are distributed only to authorized people.
- Hardware controls must have existing rigid and clear standards in order to operate in different operating environments.
- Physical security controls are rigid, well defined, and subject to less misinterpretation.
- An organizational control system's components include objectives, standards, and an evaluation-reward system.
- A financial control system's components include budgeting, financial ratio analysis, and cash management.
- A managerial control is the result of proper planning, organizing, and directing. Its ultimate objective is to promote organizational effectiveness, which is the degree to which the organization achieves its short-term and long-term objectives. Components of managerial controls include forestalling management fraud and protecting assets.
- Components do not include implementing plans.

(i) **Controls in Business Application Systems.** The scope of business application system controls include controls over data origination, preparation, and data input; data processing; system-related file maintenance; data output; application system documentation; spreadsheet work; data integrity; and user satisfaction assessment. Each area is discussed next.

(i) **Data origination, preparation, and data input controls.** There are several approaches to data preparation and data entry into the application system. In some cases, the data are captured on a paper (source) document like a sales or purchase order. The source documents are batched into small groups and entered into the system either by functional users or central data-entry operators through the use of terminals. In other cases, there is no externally generated source document since the customer calls in and places an order with the organization.

Other approaches include use of factory data collection devices for factories; automated teller machine recorders for banks; point-of-sale (POS) recorders for the retail business with or without bar codes; magnetic ink character recognition devices for the banking industry for customer checks and deposit tickets; optical character recognition devices to read credit card statements, insurance premium notices, and utility company billings; optical mark reading devices to read pencil marks made in specific locations on preprinted forms to be used in grading structured examination questions; scanners for document image processing; and voice recognition input devices used to recognize human voice in airline and parcel industries to route packages.

Regardless of the method used to capture the data, the entered data are edited and validated for preventing or detecting errors and omissions. Therefore, access controls and data editing and validation controls are important to ensure that quality data are entering into the application system.

WHAT CAN GO WRONG IN DATA PREPARATION AND ENTRY?

- Adequate separation of duties may not be maintained over data origination, data preparation, data input, data update, and data output activities between and among system users and data processors.
- Design of forms and documents used for data input preparation and the design of input terminal screens may not match or may be too complex for the skill level of the system user. Consequently, data are entered incorrectly and improperly.
- Source transactions may be inaccurate, unauthorized, or lost during movement from department to department, during data entry, and/or during data processing.
- Transaction errors may not be properly prevented, detected, or corrected and resubmitted in a timely manner.
- Data input errors, irregularities, omissions, and data alterations are the most common computer-related problems leading to fraud, crime, and abuse.

The following are red flags that suggest vulnerability to data errors: old application system with high program maintenance, large volume of data for processing, frequent processing and updating activity, numerous transaction types and sources, large number of coded data elements, high employee turnover (e.g., data entry clerks, operators, programmers, system analysts), inadequate training, complex data structures, and lack of standards related to security, access, and program-change control.

(ii) **Data processing controls.** Although there are some common controls, controls will be different between batch and online processing. Similar to data input, data editing and validation controls are important during computer processing. Therefore, more use of program-based processing controls is needed to ensure data integrity and security. These controls include limit check, range test, validity check, table lookup, reasonableness test, sequence check, comparison test, check digit test, ratio test, and relationship test.

WHAT CAN GO WRONG IN PROCESS VALIDATION AND EDITING?

- Transactions may be processed in the wrong fiscal period.
- Transactions may be improperly classified, valued, summarized, or reported.
- Adequate data editing and validation controls may not be available in application program processing logic to prevent or detect errors, omissions, or irregularities.
- Application program processing jobs may take longer due to inefficient data file structures, poor choice of design techniques, poor selection of data file access methods, poorly structured program logic, and/or ineffective program statements.

- Backout or fallback procedures may not be available for programs, causing abnormal termination, or due to other operational problems during computer-job processing.

(iii) **System-related file maintenance controls.** The auditor will encounter many system-related files during an audit of the application system. These files contain valuable data for audit analysis and reporting purposes. Major concerns for the auditor should be who can access and update these files. Some examples of these files are

- **Master files.** Examples of master files are customer files, vendor files, employee files, account files.
- **Transaction files.** Transaction files are detail files used with the master files. Routine and repeat transactions are collected into transaction files and then used to update the master data files.
- **Backup files.** Backup files contain program or data files.
- **Program files.** Program files contain source, object, or executable code.
- **Table files.** Table files contain data such as office codes, state codes, postal zip codes, department codes, tax codes, and plant codes. These tables are used during program execution for data editing, validation, and referencing purposes.
- **Summary/history files.** Summary files contain a history of transactions such as month-to-date, quarter-end, year-end, or last five years' data. These transactions are maintained in a summary form.
- **Archive files.** Archive files contain data or programs that are infrequently used and yet important to store for many useful reasons.
- **Control files.** Control files contain parameter-related information such as dates, cycles, and reports. These parameters are used in processing computer jobs.
- **Print files.** Print files contain data and program files waiting to be printed. These files are stored in a spool area and wait until the current print job is completed. When their turn comes up, these files are printed.
- **Report files.** Report files contain report records for each application system–generated output.
- **Command files.** Command files contain certain key commands (e.g., execute, copy, delete, write) required by an application program, operating system, or other support systems software. Commands are supplied to various programs during their execution.
- **Work files.** Work files are any files that are created, used, and then deleted at the end of one job step. Work files are also called scratch files. Normally work files are used to sort data files. Application programs create these files as needed. Work files are temporary in nature.
- **Temporary files.** A temporary file is one that lasts for the duration of the job regardless of the successful completion or termination of the job. The operating system automatically deletes all such files when the job terminates. Sometimes programmers have the application program create a temporary cross-reference file from an input file and then use it in the downstream (subsequent job) processing.
- **Log files.** A log file is a data file or command file that contains data and commands that are logged during computer job and program processing. Log files can be created by an operating system, application system, database system, telecommunication system, or security system. For example, a database system may create before-and-after images of records during an update process in a database log file. Log files are also temporary in nature.
- **Document image files.** An image file is created out of a document such as a loan, credit, or employment application; payment invoice; and purchase order. These documents are then stored and retrieved as needed. An image file can be downloaded or uploaded to and from the host computer and the microcomputer.
- **User files.** User files are created by each user of the system for the user's personal library and use.
- **Transmission files.** Transmission files are the ones waiting to be transmitted from one location to the other, from one computer system to the other, from one entity to the other, or from one time zone to the other.

WHAT CAN GO WRONG IN FILE MAINTENANCE?

- A computer file may be lost or damaged due to bad write/read head error or disk failure on an input/output device.
- Both the original and backup file may be stored on the same magnetic media (e.g., disk, tape, cartridge) or physical area, thus losing both.
- System files may be erased, destroyed, or unlogged intentionally or accidentally.
- Before (from) and after (to) image record reporting may not be available when database or data files are updated, thus losing accountability.
- Identification of production data files could be difficult because file names may not consistently indicate whether files are related to production application systems.

(iv) **Data output controls.** There are many output devices in use. Some examples are terminals, printers, plotters, microfilm, microfiche, and voice recognition (VR) units. System output documents are photographed onto a roll of film and stored on microfilm, microfiche, and optical disk. Audio response systems will help people inquire about a customer's bank balance, get time and temperature readings, and obtain a telephone number from a directory. Usually system outputs are in the form of hard-copy reports. Trends indicate that paper will be replaced by online viewing of reports on a terminal.

WHAT CAN GO WRONG IN SYSTEM OUTPUT ACTIVITIES?

- Exception reporting may not be available to focus on deviations.
- Report balancing rules may not be documented or may be changed without authorization.
- Unneeded reports may be sent to system users.
- System output reports may be delivered to wrong users.
- System outputs (i.e., reports, lists, screens) may be lost, delayed, or truncated due to incorrect sizes between receiving and sending data fields.
- System users may not clearly understand the system outputs.
- System outputs may not be accurate or complete.

Balancing, distribution, and retention of system outputs are of major concern to the auditor since they affect the quality and timeliness of data and usefulness of the system.

(v) **Application system documentation controls.** System documentation is a key element of audit evidence. Without correct and complete documentation, new users cannot be trained properly, programmers cannot maintain the system correctly, users of the system cannot make any meaningful references to the system functions and features, management or anyone cannot understand the system functions and features, and reviewers of the systems (e.g., auditors) cannot make an objective evaluation of the system functions and controls.

Six types of documentation manuals (systems, user, program, computer operations, help-desk, and network control) can be expected in a well-run IS organization. Each type of documentation is targeted for a specific individual or department, sometimes more than one department. For example, help-desk and network control manuals are very much needed by both end users and help-desk staff for an online system or one that is connected to outside third-party data-processing services for access during in-house processing. See Exhibit 5.25 for details of these six types of documentation manuals, which would be developed during system development work.

Documentation type	*Documentation contents*
Systems manual	System flowchart; systems requirements; system functions; design specifications; screen layouts; sample reports
Program manual	Program flowcharts; program functions; file layouts; program specifications
Computer operations manual	Job setup procedures; job narratives; job rerun and restart procedures; file backup procedures; report distribution procedures

User manual	System functions; sample screen and report layouts; report balancing procedures; file maintenance procedures; error correction procedures
Help-desk manual	Contact names and phone numbers of users and IS staff; problem diagnostic and reporting procedures; problem escalation procedures; problem logging, tracking, and closing procedures
Network control manual	Information about circuits, nodes, line, modems; problem diagnostic procedures; problem reporting and resolution procedures; network backup and contingency procedures

Exhibit 5.25: Application system documentation types and contents

WHAT CAN GO WRONG IN APPLICATION DOCUMENTATION?

- User manuals/guides or documentation may not be available to understand how the system works, or it may not be current.
- System/program documentation may not be available to facilitate system/program maintenance, or it may not be current.
- Help-desk/network documentation may not be available to facilitate system/network diagnosis and troubleshooting, and it may not be current.
- Operations documentation may not be available to operators to facilitate operations and troubleshooting of operational problems, and it may not be current.

(vi) **Spreadsheet controls.** Spreadsheet software is getting more powerful and simpler to use. Some applications include financial budgeting, project/product costing, payroll, word processing, analytical comparison, and others. Problems can arise: (1) through improper usage of spreadsheet software; (2) due to inadequate planning, design, and documentation of spreadsheet application; and (3) due to human errors. The consequences of these problems and errors are significant as the outputs of spreadsheet are used in decision making.

WHAT CAN GO WRONG IN SPREADSHEET SOFTWARE AND ITS USE?

- Applicable quality control techniques such as author verification (desk checking) and supervisory review may not be available over spreadsheets to ensure that they are error-free.
- Spreadsheet work may not be documented clearly and completely.
- Formulas and key data may not be protected from writing over.
- The most frequent errors in spreadsheets occur during data entry and formulation.
- Errors or mistakes during data entry may not have been noticed or corrected in a timely manner.
- Assumptions and instructions related to the planning, operation, and interpretation of the spreadsheet application may not be documented clearly and adequately.

(vii) **Data integrity controls.** Data integrity is the heart of any application. Data integrity controls ensure the reliability and usability of data and information in making management decisions. The higher the integrity of controls, the greater the credibility and reliability of the application system. Here the term "data integrity" refers to five control attributes: completeness, accuracy, authorization, consistency, and timeliness. The interrelationships of the five control attributes are shown in Exhibit 5.26.

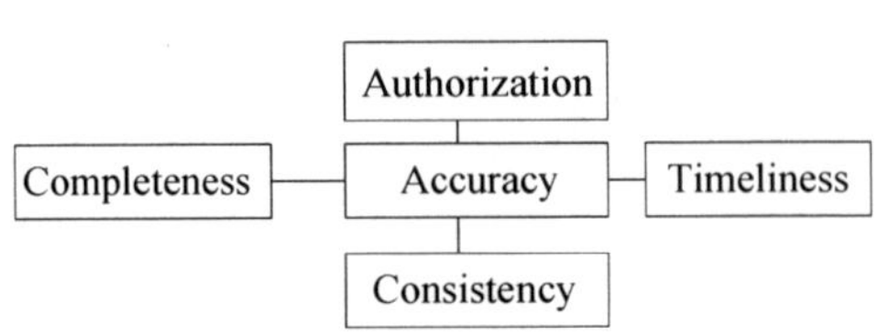

Exhibit 5.26: Interrelationships of control attributes

The objectives of a data integrity review are to ensure that basic internal controls such as documented procedures, access controls, management reviews, audit trails, and automated program-processing controls are established and to verify that they are functioning properly and effectively. Directive, preventive, detective, corrective, and recovery controls should be established in each application system during system development, system maintenance, and system operations activities to achieve the five control attributes of data integrity.

DATA INTEGRITY RULES AND CONTROLS

- A directive control will ensure that people follow data integrity rules consistently.
- A preventive control will stop a data integrity violation from happening.
- A detective control will recognize a data integrity violation.
- A corrective control will fix or repair the damage done by a data integrity violation.
- A recovery control will help in recovering or restoring from a disaster caused by a data integrity violation.

Specifically

- **Data completeness** refers to the presence or absence of information. All required data elements must be present for a transaction or record to be complete. Examples include all numeric places should be filled and a check cannot be issued unless all fields have a valid value.
- **Data accuracy** asks whether data values have been entered into the system correctly and whether data values have been distorted during processing. The sources of the data in terms of where they came from and incorruptibility of data are also important here. This means that the received data are unchanged (no additions, changes, and deletions from the original order, without repetition and omission) with positive assurance and an acceptable degree of confidence. Examples include checking for numeric ranges, spelling errors, data duplication, and data omission.
- **Data authorization** looks at whether transactions are authorized by appropriate personnel for proper accountability. The person who is approving the transactions is also important here. Moreover, authorization function should be tailored or responsive to the requirements of the application system.
- **Data consistency** asks whether policies, procedures, and standards have been uniformly applied. This refers to the relation between intradata elements and intra- and interrecords and files. Examples include a Requestor's name cannot equal an Approver's name, and an Approver's name cannot equal a Signatory's name in a check-approval scenario. The causes of data inconsistencies can be due to invalid, untimely, incomplete, and inaccurate data.
- **Data timeliness** means that data are not stale for intended use and that they are current. Management needs to understand the need for establishing controls to ensure data integrity. This understanding makes the system more effective and useful.

(viii) **User satisfaction assessment.** Assessment of system user satisfaction is a very important part of the audit of an application system. This is because it is the system user who paid for the system, who owns the system, and who uses the system.

In fact, the system is not successful and useful if the system user is not satisfied with system functions and results. One way to assess user satisfaction is to conduct user surveys periodically. System usability should be a major concern for the user and the auditor.

ISSUES IN USER SATISFACTION

- The application system may not be user-friendly, that is, may not be easy to use.
- System users may not be satisfied with the performance of the system, that is, online system response time may be too slow or batch job turnaround time may be too long.
- The application system may not be available to system users for use when it is needed and where it is needed.

- The application system may not be providing the right kind of information needed to run business operations.
- The application system may not be giving users control reports, exception reports, summary reports, aging reports, error reports, productivity reports, and audit trail reports.
- Functional users may not have documented and tested plans and procedures for operating their application systems during a power outage, natural disaster, or system failure.
- Access to an application system may take a longer time due to too many screens, menus, submenus, or steps to get into programs. Usually the greater the number of screens, the longer it takes to move from one screen to the other.

(j) **Inventory of Controls in Business Application Systems.** Application controls are designed to control computerized application systems, helping to ensure the completeness and accuracy of transaction processing, authorization, and validity. The following list provides the nature of each control (preventive, detective, and corrective); the type of control (completeness, accuracy, continuity, authorization, consistency, and security) is indicated where necessary.

Preventive Controls

- **Brevity codes.** A shortened form of standardized messages that reduces the amount of input required by valid users while often hiding the message type, or other information obtained from the user interface, from unauthorized users. This control increases data accuracy.
- **Data attribute checks.** Verification that data have particular attributes (e.g., length, type, content).
- **Validity checks.** These are tests for the validity of codes such as state, tax rates, social security number, customer number, vendor number, or employee number. Usually table lookups are performed for data comparison. This accuracy control is a preventive and a detective control.
- **Compatibility tests.** Compatibility tests are used to determine whether an acceptable user is allowed to proceed in the system. This test focuses on passwords, access rules, and system privileges. This is a security control.
- **Processing parameters.** The flexible use of parameters facilitates operation and customized reporting features can be used to specify dates (beginning and ending), processing frequency and cycles (daily, weekly, monthly), report numbers, computer-job numbers, and locations (plant numbers, office numbers, or store numbers). This is a continuity control.
- **Prenumbered forms.** Sequential numbers on individual source documents or input forms (i.e., purchase orders or invoices) are preprinted to allow subsequent detection of loss or misplacement of documents and forms. This is a completeness control.
- **System-assigned numbers.** These are the same as prenumbered forms except that the system automatically assigns the sequential numbers. This is an accuracy control.
- **Precoded forms/screens.** Fixed data elements or fields are entered or printed on input forms, source documents, terminal screen menus, or report listings to prevent errors in data coding and data entry, for example, on turnaround documents such as utility bills. A variation of this is called **preformatting,** where the display of a document with blanks for data items to be entered by the system user or the data entry operator. This is an accuracy control.
- **Turnaround documents.** Source documents and input forms can be designed in such a way that they achieve two purposes: (1) to serve as a bill, invoice, or notice to a customer or a user and (2) to use the same document when returned as an input document for entering the necessary data into the computer system. This is an accuracy control.
- **Reference values or codes kept outside the program.** For ease of system or program maintenance, it is better to keep frequently used or changing values or codes (i.e., social security numbers, tax rates, pay classes) outside the program as an external table or other means (LEVEL 88 values in COBOL programs), and not embedded in the programming statements. Table lookups are provided. This is a continuity control.
- **Transaction cancellation.** The system can be designed in such a way as to cancel each transaction record after it is used in order to prevent its repeated use. Examples are purchase orders, receiving reports, invoices, sales returns, and the like. The system flags repeated use of the same document number; this is analogous to manual stamping of "paid" or "processed." Cancellation

also can be used to reverse or back-out previous transactions for any reason. This is a completeness control.

- **Management approvals.** Supervisors or managers should be required to approve sensitive and important transactions that others entered into the system or calculated using the system. This is achieved by entering a secret keyword or number as a means of authorization. This is an authorization control.
- **Concurrent access controls.** For database systems, concurrent access (updates) to the same record or file by multiple users is a concern as it affects data integrity. Usually automatic file/record locking facilities are used to prevent concurrent accesses. These controls are required to minimize the possibility of destroying data records. This is a security control.
- **Two-person controls.** Two individuals review or approve the work of each other. Examples are: one person initiates a transaction and the other person approves it, one person counts inventory or cash while other person observes it. The purpose is to provide accountability or accuracy in dealing with sensitive or high-risk transactions or activities to minimize fraud or other irregularities. This is an accuracy control.
- **Overrides.** Overrides can include manual and system-based overrides. The system should prevent unauthorized individuals overriding exceptions or errors. A report should be produced showing who did what. This is a security and authorization control.

Detective Controls

- **Summary integrity check.** This is a method for checking the correctness of data by comparing data with a "summary" of the data. It is similar to a batch-control technique.
- **Batch totals.** To ensure accuracy in data entry and processing, control totals can be compared by the system with manually calculated and entered control totals using the data fields such as quantities, line items, documents, or dollars. This is a completeness control.
- **Hash totals.** This is a technique for improving data accuracy, whereby totals are obtained on identifier (meaningless) data fields such as account number, social security number, part number, or employee number. These totals have no significance other than for internal system control purposes. This is an accuracy control.
- **Limit check.** The program tests specified data fields against defined high- or low-value limits (e.g., quantities or dollars) for acceptability before further processing. This is an accuracy control. Examples of error messages: transaction is over $30,000, purchase order is over $50,000, or multiple price change number cannot be higher than 9999. The limits can be based on transaction values and times.
- **Reasonableness test.** This test can be used to determine whether input data, updated data, calculated data, or output data are reasonable. Ascending/descending checks for numeric and alphabetic data can be performed. Tolerance tests measuring dollar or percentage deviation of vendor invoice from purchase-order amount can be designed. This test is specific to an application-system function. This is an accuracy control. Examples of error messages: Airline passenger departure flight time is not reasonable with arrival flight time for the same day or customer order quantity is not reasonable with historical order.
- **Check digit.** This is a digit, derived by a mathematical formula, that is a function of the other digits within a word or number. It is a checksum calculated on each digit of a numeric string. It is used for testing accuracy of transcription, transposition, data entry, and data processing, and detects such errors. Part numbers, stock-keeping numbers, credit card numbers, employee numbers, and account numbers can be check-digited. This is an accuracy control. Examples of error messages: Invalid check-digit must be zero through six. Invalid check digit on transfer number. Check digits can be operated on any part of the number as long as they are applied consistently.
- **Overflow check.** This is a limit check based on the capacity of a computer memory or data file area to accept data. This programming technique can be used to detect the truncation of a financial or quantity data-field value after computation (e.g., addition, multiplication, and division). Usually the first digit is lost. This is an accuracy control.
- **Format checks.** These are used to determine that data are entered in the proper mode, as numeric or alphabetical characters, within designated fields of information. The proper mode in

each case depends on the data record definition. These are accuracy controls. Examples of error messages: Invalid transaction format. Invalid date format, date must be mm-dd-yy.

- **Date checks.** These can be used to record transactions in the proper accounting (fiscal) month; they relate to logical consistencies between transaction dates and events. These are continuity controls. Examples of error messages: Merchandise date received should be after the date shipped. Budget transaction date out of range. Control card "to" date is less than "from" date the job canceled.
- **Label check.** This is a processing control whereby a computer application program verifies internal file labels for tapes to ensure that the correct data file is used in the processing. This is a continuity control. Example of error message: Wrong file is mounted.
- **Completeness test.** This is a programming test to determine whether data entries have been made in data fields that should be left blank. It can be used to detect missing data fields or records. This is a completeness control.
- **Range test.** This is the same as "limit check," but this term is used when both high and low values are used for testing. It can also define include and exclude values. This is an accuracy control. Examples of error messages: Percentage must be between 10 and 75 inclusive or price change number must be in range 1000 through 1999.
- **Range check.** This is a verification that data are within a certain range of values.
- **Discrete value check.** This is verification that data have either certain permissible values or do not have other restricted values, out of a wider set of possible values.
- **Record count.** This is a processing control whereby information such as maximum, active, inactive, and available record counts will ensure proper size of the file and avoid loss of records. This is a continuity control. Example of error message: Transaction counts and actual record counts do not agree.
- **Sign test.** This is a test for a numeric data field containing a designation of an algebraic sign such as + or -, which can be used to denote, for example, debits or credits for financial data fields. This is an accuracy control. Example of error message: Sign is inconsistent with transaction type.
- **Size test.** This test can be used to test the full size of the data field. For example, a social security number in the United States should have nine digits. This is a completeness control. Examples of error messages: Line quantity or total may not be more than five digits long, or numeric postal zip code must be either five or nine digits.
- **Sequence check.** This is a way of testing for a certain sequence of record types or transaction numbers during computer processing. It can also be used to test the sequence of purchase orders, receiving reports, invoices, and the like. It is also called "anticipation control" and depends on the system and its design logic. This is a completeness control. Examples of error messages: Missing transaction No. 06 or missing record type 09.
- **Duplicate checks.** These are the same as sequence checks but look for duplication. These are completeness controls. Examples of error messages: multiple tax records or multiple account records.
- **Cross-field editing.** Cross-field editing tests for the validity of multiple data fields simultaneously with a logical and predefined relationship to each other in the same record. This is a consistency control. Examples of error messages: No tax on taxable department. Tax amount received or paid on a nontaxable item or department. Incorrect telephone area code compared to postal zip code.
- **Cross-record editing.** This is the same as cross-field editing, but the tests are performed among multiple records. This is a consistency control. Examples of error messages: Account number in a transaction record does not match with the master file. Department number not on file for the store/plant/office.
- **System matching.** The system matches certain transactions, such as purchase order numbers to receiving report numbers to vendor invoices or shipping advices to billing numbers, and lists unmatched transactions for review and follow-up. This is completeness control. Examples of error messages: Account number does not match with the recording code. Tax percentage calculated does not match with tax tables.

- **Field combination tests.** One or more data fields are tested for the right combination. These are accuracy controls. Examples of error messages: invalid plant number for the business division; city and/or state cannot have city code; no price found for the given item/style; if the style number is entered, then the house number must also be entered; invalid employee number for the location; or invalid payclass for the given subclass.
- **Run-to-run totals.** These are processing controls whereby output control totals resulting from one process (cycle, program, or module) are used as input control totals over subsequent processing. The control totals are used as a verification mechanism (automatically or manually) and link one process or cycle to another in a sequence. The control totals can be grouped by dollars, records, or in some other way. This control ensures program-processing accuracy. These are continuity controls. Examples of error messages: Database-beginning records total plus transaction activity records total is not equal to ending-records total, or net amount is not equal to total cost plus transportation cost minus discount.
- **Suspense file.** In this technique, computer files are designed to contain unprocessed or partially processed transactions awaiting further action. All pending or rejected transactions (errors) can be maintained in a suspense file for later review and correction. This will ensure that all errors are corrected. This is a completeness control. Examples of error messages: Transaction is rejected or transaction is incomplete or suspended.
- **Header and trailer record verification.** This is a processing-control technique used to verify the accuracy of header information in a first record of a file and to verify the accuracy of a control total in the trailer or last record for comparison with accumulated counts or values of records processed. This is an accuracy control. Examples of error messages: Wrong file entered for processing or trailer record counts do not equal accumulated counts.
- **Balance controls.** The system can be designed to balance transactions using a system- or function-dependent technique whereby an out-of-balance condition is automatically detected and reported. This is an accuracy control. Examples of error messages: The total sum of units or dollars must equal the sum of units or dollars for each location.
- **System logging of transactions.** This is a processing control whereby the system maintains a log to record user ID, password, transaction number, department number, terminal ID, date, and time to provide an electronic audit trail. This is a security control.
- **Comparison controls.** The program is designed to compare certain values in the same or different records to determine accuracy and reasonableness. These are consistency controls. Examples are: listing of differences between prices on purchase orders and purchase invoices, listing of differences between stock-status dollar values and general-ledger amounts, listing of shipment values and billed amounts, comparison of merchandise total plus freight plus tax amount with purchase-invoice total, comparison of quantities of product sold in the last quarter with quantities in inventory and reports of slow-moving inventory based on criteria built into the program, and comparison of debit-dollar totals with credit-dollar totals for financial accounting journal entry transactions. This technique is dependent on the application system's function.
- **Computation controls.** The program logic includes columnar footing and cross-footing, extensions, and postings to ensure mathematical and processing accuracy. Most techniques described here are dependent on the application system's functions. These are accuracy controls. Examples of error messages: Total quantity must be the sum of all line quantities.
- **Ratio test.** This is a mathematical calculation whereby one data element is divided into another to yield a ratio value. This is a consistency control. An example is: Return on investment/assets (ROI/ROA) is calculated as dividing the data element "operating or net income" in the numerator by the data element "investment or assets" in the denominator.
- **Rounding technique.** For financial and accounting calculations such as multiplication and division, the system analyst or programmer should decide how to handle rounding calculations and decimal point rounding rules consistently across and within all programs and systems. This is an accuracy control.
- **Relationship test.** This is a comparison of values to validate a logical or defined correlation; it is also referred to as a conditional test. For example, an invoice date must be the same as or earlier than the related payment date. This is a consistency control.

- **Descriptive read-back.** This is a design technique whereby a code or number is converted to its description and appears on the computer terminal screen for human inspection to determine its accuracy and completeness. This is an accuracy control. An example is when a customer number is entered, his or her name and address will appear on the screen to ensure that the right customer record is accessed.
- **Data checks.** The system analyst or programmer should test for the presence of blank spaces when numeric data are expected to be received in a numeric data field or should test for division by zero when a division is expected with a nonzero value. This prevents program failure during processing as a result of missing or improper data. These are accuracy controls.
- **Key verification.** Important data elements or fields need to be key verified by rekeying to verify data entry accuracy. This is an accuracy control. Example of error message: Incorrect account number, check it.
- **One-for-one checking.** Critical reports or input documents should be compared one-for-one with subsequent outputs to ensure accuracy and completeness of data entry and computer processing.
- **Cross footing.** Cross footing compares horizontal (rows) and vertical (columns) totals in a table or report to be equal. This is an accuracy control.

Corrective Controls

- **Program comments.** The consistent inclusion of English comments in the program will help programmers understand the program's functions and features during its maintenance. This is a consistency control.
- **Job control comments.** The consistent inclusion of English comments in the job control language will help the maintenance programmer and the data control analyst understands the purpose of job control language. This is a consistency control.
- **Automatic error correction.** The system is designed to correct errors automatically on the basis of predefined criteria and in cases where human intervention is not immediately needed. This is a continuity control.
- **Overrides by supervisors.** The system should be designed so that the ability to override certain critical and sensitive errors is limited to supervisors and managers using a password control. This is both a continuity control and an authorization control.
- **Audit trail report.** The system should provide a clear and complete listing of audit trail reports for tracing and verification purposes. This is an accuracy control.
- **Control report.** The system should provide a clear and complete listing of batch control and system logging reports for user balancing and verification purposes. This is an accuracy control.
- **Exception report.** This is a report produced on request or in response to certain specified conditions and highlights exceptions or deviations from the anticipated situation. The type of report and its details depend on the application system's function. This is an accuracy control.
- **Error report.** A report showing all rejected transactions in error, indicating the severity level of the error and the required action to correct the error. This is an accuracy control.
- **Before/after image record reporting for file maintenance.** To ensure data integrity, the system must report the data field values both before and after the changes so functional users can detect data-entry and update errors. This is an accuracy control.
- **Clear and complete error messages.** To facilitate error correction, all error messages should be easy to understand and meaningful. They should neither be cryptic or negative, nor use code numbers. This is a continuity control.
- **Error total.** To facilitate error correction and increase employee productivity, error totals should be provided by error type, department, position, transaction, plant, store, or company. Errors can be totaled as dollars, quantities, or records. This is an accuracy control.
- **Documentation.** Correct, up-to-date system, programming, computer operations, network control, help desk, and user manuals (documented procedures) will help system analysts, programmers, computer operators, network control analysts, and functional users correct errors, answer questions, and resolve problems during maintenance, operation, and use of the system. This is a continuity control.

- **Automatic backup and recovery.** The system is designed to provide automated periodic backup of all required disk files, as opposed to needing human intervention to ensure timely recovery from a disaster. In some systems, file restoration and recovery are automatic. This is a continuity control.
- **Journaling.** All application system transactions should be captured on a journal file so that recovery can be made should a system failure occur. This is a continuity control.
- **Checkpoint control.** All application system batch jobs requiring more than one hour of CPU processing time need to be designed with a checkpoint control so that automatic backup of files is made at every 15 or 30 minutes to facilitate a recovery should a disaster occur. This is a continuity control.
- **Transaction back-out.** All application systems (database or not) should have the ability to back-out or reverse invalid or improper transaction data should a processing problem or error occur. This is a continuity control.
- **Recovery logging.** For database systems, a recovery log can be used to record system status information as well as information describing the changes made to the database. Both before images and after images of the database pages affected by an update can be stored in the recovery log, which can be accessed by means of rollback and roll-forward techniques. This is a continuity control.
- **Fallback procedure.** In the event of a failure of transactions or the system, the program has the ability to fall back to the original or alternate method for continuation of processing. This is a continuity control.

(k) **Summary of Controls**

(i) **Operational application system controls.** Exhibit 5.27 provides a summary of preventive, detective, and corrective controls as they relate to information systems in operation. See section 5.9(j) for a definition of these control terms. Implementation of these controls would help information technology (IT) management in strengthening overall controls.

Preventive controls	*Detective controls*	*Corrective controls*
Data dictionary	Batch control totals	Program comments
Structured techniques	Hash totals	Job control comments
Programming and documentation standards	Limit checks	Automatic error correction
Processing parameters	Reasonableness checks	Overrides by supervisors
Online prompting	Check digits	Audit trail reports
Self-help features	Overflow checks	Control reports
Default options	Format checks	Exception reports
Good screen design	Date checks	Productivity reports
Field highlighting	Label checks	Aging reports
Screen diagnostic messages	Completeness tests	Error reports
Prenumbered forms	Range tests	Before/after image reporting
System-assigned numbers	Record counts	Clear and complete error messages
Precoded forms and screens	Sign test	Error totals
Turnaround documents	Size test	Documentation
Data ownership	Sequence checks	Automated backup and recovery mechanisms
Data classification	Duplicate checks	Journaling
Table lookups	Cross-field checking	Data retention
Passwords	Cross-record checking	Checkpoint controls
Transaction cancellation	System matching	Transaction backout
Data encryption	Field combination tests	Recovery logging
Management approvals	Validity checks	Fallback procedures
	Run-to-run totals	

Concurrent access controls	Suspense files
Two-person controls	Header/trailer record verifications
Fault-tolerant controls	Balance controls
System or manual overrides	System logs
	Comparison controls
	Computation controls
	Ratio tests
	Rounding techniques
	Descriptive readback
	System walk-throughs
	Data checks
	Key verification
	One-for-one checking
	Crossfooting

Exhibit 5.27: Operational application system preventive, detective, and corrective controls summary

(ii) **Information technology management.** Operating management has the ultimate responsibility for the implementation of cost-effective controls in manual or automated systems. Management activities range from strategic planning to operational control. Strategic planning requires external, very broad, future-oriented data whereas operational control requires information that is largely internal, narrow, and current.

Feed-forward controls help management in anticipating problems. Exhibit 5.28 presents a summary of preventive, detective, and corrective controls as they relate to information systems environment. Implementation of these controls would help IT management in strengthening overall controls.

Preventive controls	Detective controls	Corrective controls
Policies, procedures, standards	Project management tools	Exception reports
Separation of duties	Control parameters	Progress reports
Job (position) descriptions	Operating/capital budgets	Control reports
Short-range plans	Tolerance limits	Error reports
Long-range plans		Special reports
System access rules		

Exhibit 5.28: Information systems environment preventive, detective, and corrective controls summary

(iii) **Information technology operations.** Exhibit 5.29 presents a summary of preventive, detective, and corrective controls as they relate to functional areas of IT operations. Implementation of these controls would help IT management in strengthening overall controls.

Preventive controls	Detective controls	Corrective controls
Establish IT steering committee	Install smoke and fire detectors and fire alarms	Automate the report balancing procedures
Establish service-level agreements	Require system logging of transactions	Use comments in job execution language
Establish and enforce computer center policies, procedures, and standards	Reduce computer operator intervention by installing console management system	Provide periodic backup of data and programs, and rotate them through off-site storage
Establish a problem, change, and configuration management function	Review system activity logs, journals, and exception reports	Facilitate system recovery and restart procedures
Install help-desk function to support system users	Rotate key employees in the computer center	Install automated job recovery software
Establish a separate and centralized network control function		

Require periodic audits of the computer center	Require employees to take vacations	Develop fall-back systems and procedures
Establish a chargeback system	Acquire or develop an automated job accounting information system	Install fault-tolerant devices and software to recover from a system failure
Eliminate manual job scheduling practices	Ensure running of correct version of production programs	
Discourage printing of hardcopy reports	Compare production resource usage	
Install automated tape and disk management systems	Install water detection measures and environmental control devices	
Install computer capacity management function		

Exhibit 5.29: Functional areas of IT operations preventative, detective, and corrective controls summary

(iv) **Data and network communications.** Exhibit 5.30 presents a summary of preventive, detective, and corrective controls as they relate to data and network communications. Implementation of these controls would help IT management in strengthening overall controls.

Preventive controls	Detective controls	Corrective controls
Policies, procedures, and standards	Contingency plan testing	Contingency plan maintenance and update
Encryption techniques	Network line utilization statistics	Network diagnostic data collection tools with automatic corrective action
Transborder data transmission laws	Network diagnostic tools	Network routing capabilities
Training and education plans	Network testing capabilities	Networking monitoring tools
Problem and change management system	Test cables and connectors prior to power-up for each node	Recovery mechanisms such as checkpoints, roll-back and roll-forward features in the database
Fault-tolerance network design practices	Periodic inventory of network equipment	Recovery techniques from computer viruses
Resilient network design principles such as redundant equipment and components; alternate paths, routes, nodes, and circuits and lines; and parallel links	Install physical security devices	
Contingency plan development	Implement logical security mechanisms	
Network management tools	Message sequence numbers	
Install quality cables for LAN network	Checksum techniques	
	Computer viruses detection tools	

Exhibit 5.30: Network communications preventive, detective, and corrective controls summary

(v) **System security and information protection.** Privacy of information is important and is protected by logging and analyzing system usage, implementing program change controls, and separating personal/personnel data from operating or statistical data. Both management and auditors can be equally liable for security breaches occurred in the organization. Situational pressures (e.g., gambling, drugs), opportunities to commit for fraud (e.g., weak system of controls), and personal characteristics (e.g., lack of integrity, honesty) are major causes of fraud, whether computer-related or not. There is nothing new about the act of committing fraud. There is no new way to commit fraud because someone somewhere has already tried it.

Exhibit 5.31 presents a summary of preventive, detective, and corrective controls as they relate to security function. Implementation of these controls would help IT management in strengthening overall controls.

Preventive controls	*Detective controls*	*Corrective controls*
Establish a computer security management (steering) committee	Require all employees to wear badges	Provide application system generated error reports to users for review
Establish a computer security function	Provide last activity/sign-on data on computer terminals	Provide periodic backup of data and programs, and rotate through off-site storage
Assign asset responsibility to employees and exact accountability	Inform the user of any unauthorized attempts to guess his password	Establish system recovery/restart guidelines in applications and systems software
Distribute job descriptions with security responsibility	Install continuous area surveillance mechanisms	Implement vital records retention programs
Generate a security awareness among employees	Review system activity logs, journals, and exception reports to detect security violations	
Encourage legal ownership of software and protection of copyrighted (intellectual) property	Conduct periodic security audits	
Provide guidelines to protect confidentiality of data and information	Require that employees take vacations	
Establish a quality control technique for computer security function	Insert dummy names and known addresses as decoys into financially related mailing lists to detect their unauthorized use	
Require audits of data processing systems and operations by auditors	Provide dummy data files for intruders to trap while reviewing the data	
Issue guidelines for software development and maintenance methodology focusing on computer security design	Control program changes to ensure that only authorized changes are made	

Exhibit 5.31: Security function preventive, detective, and corrective controls summary

(vi) **Contingency planning.** Exhibit 5.32 presents a summary of preventive, detective, and corrective controls as they relate to contingency planning. Implementation of these controls would help IT management in strengthening overall controls.

Preventive controls	*Detective controls*	*Corrective controls*
Conduct risk analysis	Establish recovery organization with clearly defined responsibilities	Provide periodic backup of data and programs, and rotate through off-site storage
Establish the planning committee	Establish recovery logging procedures	Test the disaster recovery plan
Prioritize application systems	Conduct disaster recovery training	Install automated job recovery software
Revisit the data storage and retention practices	Conduct recovery testing	Test the emergency procedures
Install electronic vaulting	Conduct periodic fire drills	Obtain sufficient insurance coverage
Purge data and program files periodically	Maintain a problem log during plan testing	Implement vital records retention programs
Issue guidelines on how to discard/dispose of used paper records, mechanical records, and electronic records		Develop fallback systems and procedures
Develop disaster awareness among employees		Update the planning document
Establish system recovery/restart guidelines in applications and systems software		Issue a report of lessons learned from testing

Exhibit 5.32: Contingency planning preventive, detective, and corrective controls summary

(vii) **Application Development.** Exhibit 5.33 presents a summary of preventive, detective, and corrective controls as they relate to information systems acquisition, development, and maintenance. Implementation of these controls would help IT management in strengthening overall controls.

Preventive controls	*Detective controls*	*Corrective controls*
Establish a software development management (steering) committee	Practice peer reviews	Design automated error correction features into applications software
Establish a software quality assurance function	Use program tracing tools and techniques	Produce before and after image (from and to) reports for correction errors during data file maintenance activities
Issue software development methodology guidelines	Practice structure walk-throughs	Design audit trail reports, control reports, aging reports, and exception reports for user and auditor review
Establish a data administration and database administration function	Use automated documentation aids	Use preprocessors to make programs more readable
Encourage auditor and management participation and reviews	Practice software verification and validation techniques	Use interactive program debugging tools
Require active user participation and receiver user sign-off letters	Use software debugging tools during testing	Use comments in computer programs and job execution language
Issue guidelines for software usability, maintainability, securability, auditability, and controllability criteria	Design data-editing and validation control routines into the software	Design checkpoint, recovery/restart procedures into the software
Implement good project management techniques	Inspect and test software independently	
Use structured techniques for analysis, design, programming, and testing		
Inspect and test software independently		

Exhibit 5.33: Information systems acquisition, development, and maintenance preventive, detective, and corrective controls summary

(viii) **End-user computing.** Lack of adequate separation of duties is a potential control weakness in a microcomputer or minicomputer environment. Direct supervision and frequent work reviews should be conducted to balance the control weaknesses.

When uploading data to a host computer, the data conversion programs residing on the host computer should reject inaccurate or incomplete data before updating any host-resident data files. Control totals should be developed between the micro- and the host computer and reconciled automatically by the program. Uploading is one source of computer viruses, and its effects on other programs and data files are unknown.

Exhibit 5.34 presents a summary of preventive, detective, and recovery controls as they relate to small computers and end-user computing. Implementation of these controls would help IT management in strengthening overall controls.

Preventive controls	*Detective controls*	*Corrective controls*
Establish a PC or microcomputer support function	Install physical security devices	Develop control reports
Issue policies, procedures, and standards	Implement logical security mechanisms	Develop audit trail reports
Establish controls in application programs used for mini and midrange computers (e.g., label checking, recovery procedures, batch and file balancing, audit trails)	Test end user–developed software	Develop exception reports
Require a user ID and a password prior to accessing the PC system		Develop error reports
		Develop activity aging reports

Initiate a preventive maintenance program for the PCs		
Install program change controls for end user–developed systems		
Require documentation for end user–developed and maintained systems		

Exhibit 5.34: Small computer and end-user computing preventive, detective, and corrective controls summary

(ix) **Third-party services.** Almost every IT department uses third-party service providers such as outsourcing. Management should be cautious about knowing what to outsource and when.

Exhibit 5.35 presents a summary of preventive, detective, and corrective controls as they relate to third-party services. Implementation of these controls would help IT management in strengthening overall controls.

Preventive controls	*Detective controls*	*Corrective controls*
Legal contracts with right to audit clauses	Periodic review and modification of contracts	Periodic progress reporting
Nondisclosure agreements	Logical access and physical access security controls	Exit interviews
Noncompeting agreements	Time reporting	Ad hoc or regular reports to monitor third-party vendor's work
Work proposals with clear and measurable deliverables	Review of work products and deliverables	
Copyright protection awareness		

Exhibit 5.35: Third-party services preventive, detective, and corrective controls summary

MULTIPLE-CHOICE QUESTIONS (1-184)

Corporate Governance Principles

1. Effective whistle-blower programs can help organizations meet the requirements of Section 301 of the Sarbanes-Oxley Act's Audit Committees. Which of the following is **not** an element of the whistle-blower program?
 a. Collecting employee concerns.
 b. Improving internal communication.
 c. Collecting information about emerging issues.
 d. Improving external communication.

2. The most effective way of releasing the whistle-blower program throughout the organization is to have
 a. Hard-copy memos.
 b. Electronic-mails.
 c. Face-to-face meetings.
 d. Computer-based training programs.

3. The "train-the-trainer" approach is implemented in which phase of the whistle-blower program?
 a. Assessment.
 b. Building.
 c. Program release.
 d. Performance monitoring.

4. The selection of the facilitator is made in which phase of the whistle-blower program?
 a. Assessment.
 b. Building.
 c. Program release.
 d. Performance monitoring.

5. Employee surveys are conducted in which phase of the whistle-blower program?
 a. Assessment.
 b. Building.
 c. Program release.
 d. Performance monitoring.

6. A key element of the implementation of Section 302 of the Sarbanes-Oxley Act's Quarterly CEO and CFO Certifications is
 a. Disclosure controls.
 b. Disclosure procedures.
 c. Disclosure committee.
 d. Disclosure policies.

7. According to Section 404 of the Sarbanes-Oxley Act's Management Assessment of Internal Controls, assessment and assertion of an organization's control environment should focus on which of the following?
 a. Integrated controls.
 b. Discrete controls.
 c. Soft controls.
 d. Hard controls.

Alternate Control Frameworks

8. According to the Committee of Sponsoring Organizations (COSO) report, which of the following is the most important component of internal control?
 a. Risk assessment.
 b. Control environment.
 c. Control activities.
 d. Monitoring.

9. When evaluating control self-assessment, most of the time should be spent on reviewing hard controls in which of the following areas?
 a. Organizational level.
 b. Activity level.
 c. Process level.
 d. Department level.

10. Which of the COSO components include many soft controls?

I. Control environment.
II. Risk assessment.
III. Control activities.
IV. Information and communication.
V. Monitoring.

 a. I and II.
 b. I and III.
 c. II and V.
 d. I, III, and IV.

11. COSO users adopt which of the following control evaluation processes?
 a. Single-tiered.
 b. Two-tiered.
 c. Three-tiered.
 d. Four-tiered.

12. The COSO-based audit approach should **not** override which of the following?
 a. Risk-based approach.
 b. Transaction-based approach.
 c. Management-based approach.
 d. Audit committee-based approach.

13. According to the COSO report, audit plan changes as

I. Risks change.
II. Audit resources change.
III. Board change.
IV. Policies change.

 a. I only.
 b. I and II.
 c. III and IV.
 d. I, II, III, and IV.

14. According to the COSO report, the annual audit plan should be based on which of the following?

I. Control model.
II. Risk model.
III. Resource model.
IV. Management model.

 a. I only.
 b. II only.
 c. I and II.
 d. III and IV.

15. According to the COSO report, the internal control framework consists of which of the following?
 a. Processes, people, objectives.
 b. Profits, products, processes.
 c. Costs, revenues, margins.
 d. Return on investment, earnings per share, market share.

16. According to the COSO report, an entity's internal control system is built into all of the following basic management processes **except:**
- a. Planning.
- b. Execution.
- c. Monitoring.
- d. Risk.

17. According to the COSO report, the correct sequence is
- a. Risks, objectives, actions.
- b. Actions, objectives, risks.
- c. Objectives, risks, actions.
- d. Objectives, actions, risks.

18. According to the COSO report, the core of an organization is which of the following?
- a. Products.
- b. Processes.
- c. People.
- d. Profits.

19. According to the COSO report, the effectiveness of an internal control system depends on which of the following?
- a. Authorization of the process.
- b. Approval of the process.
- c. Condition of the process.
- d. Description of the process.

20. According to the COSO report, an entity's objectives are based on all of the following **except:**
- a. Preferences.
- b. Profits.
- c. Value judgments.
- d. Management style.

21. An effective relationship between risk level and internal control level is which of the following?
- a. Low risk and strong controls.
- b. High risk and weak controls.
- c. Medium risk and weak controls.
- d. High risk and strong controls.

22. The concept of control should be viewed as
- a. Accomplishing an objective.
- b. Limiting an operation.
- c. Blocking a process.
- d. Inhibiting a person.

23. The purpose of control is to
- a. Control employee behavior.
- b. Determine who is in charge of a department.
- c. Ensure that the goals of a firm are being achieved.
- d. Determine whether an operation is a cost or profit center.

24. Which of the following levers of control create positive and inspirational forces in an organization?

- I. Belief systems.
- II. Interactive control systems.
- III. Boundary systems.
- IV. Diagnostic control systems.

- a. I and II.
- b. II and III.
- c. III and IV.
- d. II and IV.

25. Usually control decisions do **not** include
- a. What measures to implement.
- b. How to evaluate performance.
- c. What type of punishments to impose.
- d. What type of incentives to use.

26. Senior managers most often use which of the following to achieve their business objectives?
- a. Hard controls, third-party reviews, and hard skills.
- b. Soft controls, self-assessments, and soft skills.
- c. Soft controls, third-party reviews, and soft skills.
- d. Hard controls, self-assessments, and hard skills.

27. According to the COSO report, for a policy to be implemented, it need **not** be
- a. Written.
- b. Thoughtful.
- c. Clear.
- d. Consistent.

28. According to the COSO report, which of the following is **not** a precondition to internal control?
- a. Objective setting.
- b. Strategic planning.
- c. Risk management.
- d. Monitoring.

29. According to the COSO report, an effective internal control system requires an ultimate
- a. User.
- b. Sponsor.
- c. Owner.
- d. Customer.

30. According to the COSO report, the threshold level for a "reportable condition" is
- a. Higher than that of a material weakness.
- b. A yardstick for determining whether the internal control system is effective.
- c. Lower than that of a material weakness.
- d. A yardstick for determining whether the internal control system is ineffective.

31. Auditors regularly evaluate controls and control procedures. Which of the following best describes the concept of control as recognized by internal auditors?
- a. Management regularly discharges personnel who do not perform up to expectations.
- b. Management takes action to enhance the likelihood that established goals and objectives will be achieved.
- c. Control represents specific procedures that accountants and auditors design to ensure the correctness of processing.
- d. Control procedures should be designed from the bottom up to ensure attention to detail.

32. Which group has the primary responsibility for the establishment, implementation, and monitoring of adequate controls in the posting of accounts receivable?
- a. External auditors.
- b. Accounts receivable staff.
- c. Internal auditors.
- d. Accounting management.

33. Corporate directors, management, external auditors, and internal auditors all play important roles in creating a proper control environment. Top management is primarily responsible for

a. Establishing a proper environment and specifying an overall internal control structure.
b. Reviewing the reliability and integrity of financial information and the means used to collect and report such information.
c. Ensuring that external and internal auditors adequately monitor the control environment.
d. Implementing and monitoring controls designed by the board of directors.

34. Corporate management has a role in the maintenance of internal control. In fact, management sometimes is a control. Which of the following involves managerial functions as a control device?

a. Supervision of employees.
b. Use of a corporate policies manual.
c. Maintenance of a quality control department.
d. Internal auditing.

Risk Management Concepts and Techniques

35. Expressed as a percentage, what is the degree of objective risk if a company owns 1,000 cars, has averaged 30 collision losses per year, the collision losses will very likely range between 35 and 45, and last year's loss experience was 25?

a. 25.0%
b. 30.0%
c. 33.3%
d. 40.0%

36. Which of the following are steps in the four-step risk management process?

a. Select risk-management techniques and purchase insurance on selected risks.
b. Select risk-management techniques and identify risks.
c. Select risk-management techniques, purchase insurance on selected risks, and identify risks.
d. Identify risks and analyze severity of expected losses.

37. Risk is defined as

a. Uncertainty concerning loss.
b. The probable variation of actual from expected experience.
c. The long-run chance of occurrence or relative frequency of loss.
d. A specific contingency that may cause loss.

38. Risk can be categorized as

a. Objective-subjective and perils-hazards.
b. Objective-subjective, physical-moral-morale, and pure-speculative.
c. Static-dynamic, subjective-objective, and pure-speculative.
d. Objective-subjective, physical-moral-morale, pure-speculative, and perils-hazards.

39. Risk managers do **not** use which of the following approaches to identify risks?

a. Contract analysis.
b. Statistical analysis.
c. Financial engineering.
d. On-site inspections.

40. In the past, Tracie's Ceramics has averaged 5 injuries among its 30 employees per year. What is the probability of an employee injury this year?

a. 0.1667.
b. 16.67.
c. 6.67.
d. 1.67.

41. Sharon, the risk manager of Tracie's Ceramics, wants to know more about the 5 injuries among her 30 employees. One loss was a wrist sprain that has a probability of 0.06. Another was a back sprain with a probability of 0.07. Yet another was overinhalation of a hazardous substance with a probability of 0.02. The other two were slips and falls with a probability of 0.13. If the amounts of the losses were $700, $3,000, $2,500, $950, and $1,000, respectively, what is the expected value of an employee injury loss for that year?

a. $500.5
b. $432.0
c. $555.5
d. $513.5

42. The three most commonly used methods of loss control are

a. Risk retention, risk avoidance, and risk transfer.
b. Self-insurance, diversification, and risk transfer.
c. Frequency reduction, severity reduction, and cost reduction.
d. Insurance transfers, frequency reduction, and severity reduction.

43. Self-insurance differs from the establishment of a reserve fund in that

a. Establishing a reserve fund is a form of risk retention.
b. Self-insurance involves prefunding of expected losses through a fund specifically designed for that purpose.
c. Self-insurance requires the existence of a group of exposure units large enough to allow accurate loss prediction.
d. Self-insurance requires the formation of a subsidiary company.

44. The purchase of insurance is a common form of

a. Risk retention.
b. Risk transfer.
c. Risk avoidance.
d. Loss control.

45. Risk transfer is most likely ideal for a risk with a

a. High degree of diversification and a low potential severity.
b. High expected frequency and a low potential severity.
c. High expected frequency and a high potential severity.
d. Low expected frequency and a high potential severity.

46. Which of the following is **not** an example of risk retention?

a. Use of credit.
b. Use of reserve funds.
c. Incorporation.
d. Self-insurance.

47. Which of the following does **not** have to be present in order to start a self-insurance program?

a. A weak general financial condition so that the savings of insurance premiums will be material to the firm.
b. A sufficient number of exposure units to enable accurate loss prediction.
c. The establishment of a fund for the specific purpose of prefunding expected losses.
d. Accurate records of past losses.

48. Regarding risk management, captive insurers combine which of the following?

I. Risk retention.
II. Risk transfer.
III. Risk mapping.
IV. Risk profiling.

a. I and II.
b. II and III.
c. III and IV.
d. I and IV.

49. Which of the following is **not** an example of risk retention?

a. Self-insurance.
b. Using a disclaimer of warranties clause on product packaging.
c. Unplanned retention.
d. Use of a reserve fund to prefund physical damage to company cars.

50. The first step in selecting available risk management techniques is to

a. Implement appropriate loss control measures.
b. Select the optimal mix of risk retention and risk transfer.
c. Avoid risks if possible.
d. Determine the availability of risk management tools.

51. Which of the following is **not** an example of risk transfer?

a. Diversification.
b. Hedging.
c. Self-insurance.
d. Hold-harmless agreements.

52. Which statement is true about risk management?

a. Capital budgeting and statistical analysis cannot be used to select the best mix of risk retention and transfer.
b. Deductibles and self-insurance cannot be used together.
c. Capital budgeting and statistical analysis can be used to select the best mix of risk retention and transfer.
d. Risk transfer is the same thing as insurance.

53. A tool that generally is **not** used to manage subjective risk is

a. Obtaining more information.
b. Group discussion.
c. Systematically identifying and analyzing appropriate methods for dealing with risks.
d. Severity reduction.

54. Regarding risk management, "high" and "low" loss frequency and severity are

a. Considered the same for all firms.
b. Defined differently for different firms.
c. Identifiable by industry standards.
d. Unimportant when considering risk avoidance.

55. Regarding risk management, insurance should be purchased for losses in excess of the firm's

a. Risk avoidance level.
b. Short-term assets.
c. Expected losses.
d. Retention level.

56. All of the following conditions are suggestive of the types of situations where self-insurance by a business is both possible and feasible **except:**

a. Objects at risk are not subject to simultaneous destruction.
b. The firm must administer the plan with existing, in-house personnel.
c. The firm has accurate records or has access to satisfactory statistics regarding the probability of loss.
d. The firm is in satisfactory financial condition.

Control Implications of Different Structures and Styles

57. In organizations where new product groups are often created, a structure that combines functional and product departmentalization and creates dual lines of authority would be optimal. The best structure for this organization would be

a. Professional bureaucracy.
b. Mechanistic.
c. Matrix.
d. Machine bureaucracy.

58. The following principles characterize certain organizational structures

I. A superior can delegate the authority to make decisions but cannot delegate the ultimate responsibility for the results of those decisions.
II. A supervisor's span of control should not exceed seven subordinates.
III. Responsibility should be accompanied by adequate authority.
IV. Employees at all levels should be empowered to make decisions.

Which of these principles are shared by both hierarchical and open organizational structures?

a. I and III.
b. I and IV.
c. II and III.
d. III and IV.

59. The relationship between organizational structure and technology suggests that in an organization using mass production technology (e.g., automobile manufacturing), the best structure would be

a. Organic, emphasizing loose controls and flexibility.
b. Matrix, in which individuals report to both product and functional area managers.

c. Mechanistic, that is, highly formalized, with tight controls.
d. Integrated, emphasizing cooperation among departments.

60. Routine tasks, which have few exceptions and problems that are easy to analyze, are conducive to
a. Formalized structure, where procedure manuals and job descriptions are common.
b. Decentralized decision making, where decisions are pushed downward in the organization.
c. Organic structures that emphasize adaptability and flexibility to changing circumstances.
d. High degrees of job satisfaction on the part of employees performing them.

61. Which of the following theories predicts that employee behavior depends on the belief that good performance will be rewarded by continued employment?
a. Equity theory: Employees compare their job inputs and outcomes with those of others and then react to eliminate inequities.
b. Expectation theory: The strength of a tendency to act in a certain way depends on the strength of an expectation that an act will be followed by a given outcome.
c. Goal-setting theory: Specific and difficult goals lead to higher performance.
d. Reinforcement theory: Behavior is a function of its consequences.

62. If a supervisor uses a supportive management approach, evidenced by positive feelings and concern for subordinates, a problem might result because
a. An approach based on pure power makes it difficult to motivate staff.
b. This approach depends on material rewards for the worker.
c. This approach depends on people who want to work, grow, and achieve.
d. The manager must believe in the teamwork approach.

63. Which particular type of organizational structure will likely have unity-of-command problems unless there is frequent and comprehensive communication between the various functional and project managers?
a. Line and staff.
b. Strategic business unit.
c. Centralized.
d. Matrix.

64. Some management scholars have credited Douglas McGregor with founding the field of organizational behavior by arriving at a modern set of assumptions about people. Identify the basic assumption(s) underlying McGregor's theory Y.
a. Employees are lazy and unambitious.
b. Employees are concerned only with higher wages.
c. Employees are component parts of the organizational system.
d. Employees are energetic and creative individuals.

65. A major aerospace company is organized so that vertical and horizontal lines of authority are combined. The company has found that this organizational structure is more conducive to the completion of major projects. Select the organizational form used by this company
a. Line and staff.
b. Matrix.
c. Functional.
d. Bureaucratic.

66. An organization chart depicts the official positions and formal lines of authority within a company. Such charts usually have two dimensions to describe: (1) the chain of command and (2) the division of labor. These two dimensions are called
a. Vertical hierarchy and horizontal specialization.
b. Staff and line functions.
c. Product and service departmentalization.
d. Functional departmentalization and specialized staff.

67. A specific type of organization is characterized by division of labor, hierarchy of authority, a framework of rules, and impersonality. Identify the organization type
a. Bottom-up.
b. Synergistic.
c. Bureaucratic.
d. Equifinal.

68. While conducting a routine audit, an auditor found the following symptoms of a dysfunctional work environment: high levels of absenteeism and turnover; strict adherence to policies and procedures without an understanding of their purpose; and employees who felt they were treated like numbers, not like people. These problems are most likely to occur in an organization that practices
a. Scientific management.
b. Classical bureaucracy.
c. Theory Y management.
d. The contingency approach to management.

69. For the past several years, many organizations have attempted to reduce administrative costs and respond more rapidly to customer and competitive demands. One method is to eliminate layers of middle management. The element of organizational structure affected by such reductions is
a. Spatial (geographic) differentiation.
b. Formalization.
c. Vertical differentiation.
d. Formalization of jobs.

Items 70 and 71 are based on the following:

The structure of an organization generally follows its overall strategy. At one end are loosely structured, organic organizations. At the other end are highly centralized, tightly controlled, mechanistic organizations. The following questions present the strategies for two different companies.

70. A company is a pioneer in the combination of laser and robotic technologies. The company's scientists and engineers hold many patents. They are continually looking for ways to improve their products as well as to introduce new ones. Identify the most appropriate structural option for this organization
a. Mechanistic.
b. Imitative.
c. Organic.
d. Holistic.

71. A company maintains a chain of warehouse-style outlets. These outlets sell high volumes of food, office supplies, and other relatively inexpensive commodities. Marketing expenses are minimized, and each store is plainly furnished. Select the structural option best suited to this organization.

a. Mechanistic.
b. Imitative.
c. Organic.
d. Holistic.

72. In what form of organization does an employee report to multiple managers?

a. Bureaucracy.
b. Matrix.
c. Departmental.
d. Mechanistic.

73. If an organization were to change from an inflexible organizational structure with many layers in its hierarchy to a more flexible streamlined structure as a result of change in its external environment, the company would be adhering to which view of management?

a. Contingency.
b. Open systems.
c. Universality.
d. Classical.

74. The assistant director of internal auditing requires strict adherence by staff to prewritten audit programs and prescribed audit schedules; no exceptions are tolerated. Audit work is scheduled based on a firm three-year cycle. Monthly statistics are compiled and mailed to all staff. These statistics are used to evaluate performance, show budget versus actual data on job time, issuing reports, and six other measures. This assistant director's management approach is best described as

a. Operational.
b. Behavioral.
c. Systems.
d. Contingency.

75. Centralization and decentralization are defined according to the relative delegation of decision-making authority by top management. Many managers believe that decentralized organizations have significant advantages over centralized organizations. A major advantage of a decentralized organization is that

a. Decentralized organizations are easier to control.
b. Decentralized structures streamline organizations and eliminate duplication of resources.
c. Decentralized organizations have fewer managers than centralized organizations.
d. Decentralized organizations encourage increased initiative among employees.

76. A large manufacturing firm operates many business units serving different markets in different regions of a country. Which of the following organization structures is suitable for this firm?

a. Functional organization.
b. Product organization.
c. Matrix organization.
d. Divisional organization.

77. An organization that combines strict adherence to the unity of command with high division of labor may cause problems for customers trying to obtain information. Of the following, which is the most probable type of internal environment this structure creates?

a. Networked and formal.
b. Compartmentalized and informal.
c. Networked and informal.
d. Compartmentalized and formal.

78. With the shift in some countries' economies toward service industries, a new form of organization has developed. This organization structure is referred to as the professional bureaucracy. While this structure resembles the machine bureaucracy (which relies on standardized work processes) in several respects, it is different in one key aspect. This significant difference is that in a professional bureaucracy

a. Senior management has had to give up a substantial amount of control.
b. Tasks are accomplished with a high degree of efficiency.
c. There is strict adherence to rules.
d. There is a tendency for subunit conflicts to develop.

79. A project team combining employees from several departments was pulled together as a temporary organization within a large laboratory to accomplish a specific mission in outer space. This is an example of

a. The sociotechnical approach.
b. Matrix organization.
c. Management by objective.
d. Decentralized organization.

80. Many organizations make concerted efforts to ensure that job titles have no negative connotations. Attainment of a job title that is perceived to be prestigious addresses which of the following needs?

a. Physiological.
b. Esteem.
c. Love.
d. Safety.

81. Which of the following statements best describes the contingency approach in selecting an organizational structure?

a. The most efficient and effective organizations have a hierarchical structure based on a legalized, formal authority.
b. The key to a successful organizational structure is its fit with the strategy and its internal and external environment.
c. A successful organizational structure has two objectives: economic effectiveness and employee satisfaction.
d. People are differentiated less vertically according to rank and more flexibly according to current contribution.

82. In a dynamic organization, a manager analyzes problem situations and responds to each situation. The management theory that best describes this approach is

a. General systems.
b. Behavioral.
c. Operations.
d. Contingency.

83. A "flat" organization structure is one with relatively few levels of hierarchy and characterized by wide spans of management, while a "tall" organization has many levels of hierarchy and narrow spans of management. Which of the following situations is consistent with a flat organization structure?

a. Tasks where little direction and control of subordinates is required.
b. Work areas that are geographically dispersed.
c. Tasks that are highly complex and varied.
d. Subordinates perform distinctly different tasks.

84. What mechanisms do **not** help to coordinate the division of tasks in an organization?

a. Division of labor.
b. Departmentalization.
c. Standard operating procedures.
d. Administrative hierarchy.

85. Which of the following is **not** true with regard to matrix structures for organizations?

a. They are akin to functional structures in that they foster specialization.
b. They are akin to divisional structures in that they have an explicit focus on results.
c. They work well only when the organization's projects or products have a short life cycle.
d. The major disadvantage of matrix structures is their potential for creating confusion and power struggles.

86. If an organization were to change from an inflexible organization structure with many layers in its hierarchy to a more flexible, streamlined structure as a result of a change in its external environment, the company would be adhering to which view of management?

a. Contingency.
b. Open systems.
c. Universality.
d. Classical.

87. A manager who is production-oriented and whose primary interest is in improving efficiency and reducing waste would be using which of the following approaches to management?

a. Behavioral approach.
b. Systems approach.
c. Contingency approach.
d. Operational approach.

88. During the preliminary survey, an internal auditor reviewed an organizational chart that depicted the chief executive officer (CEO) in the top box with the second-level boxes designating the vice presidents of manufacturing, marketing, finance and accounting, and administration. The vice-presidential level boxes are tied to the CEO box by an unbroken line. This indicates to the internal auditor that the form of departmentalization of this organization at the second level is

a. Staff.
b. Matrix.
c. Functional.
d. Project.

89. An employee in production planning gave the following description of the job: "I really like working here. All employees try to do their best and there is a sense of teamwork. The supervisors are more like senior partners than bosses are." Which of Fayol's universal principles of management is being addressed?

a. Equity.
b. Unity of direction.
c. Initiative.
d. Esprit de corps.

90. An approach to management based on the assumption that the parts of an organization operate interdependently and that "the whole is greater than the sum of its parts" is called the

a. Universal process approach.
b. Operational approach.
c. Behavioral approach.
d. Systems approach.

91. An approach to management that is an effort to determine, through research, which managerial practices and techniques are appropriate and can be generalized to specific situations is the

a. Contingency approach.
b. Aldag/Dunham approach.
c. Behavioral approach.
d. Operational management approach.

92. A matrix organization structure is probably most appropriate for which of following business situations?

a. A manufacturer producing a single product for only a few customers.
b. A grocer operating a chain of stores nationwide.
c. An automobile dealership.
d. A construction company with several large projects.

93. An auditor was having trouble adjusting to a new supervisor. When a job-related problem arose, the auditor went directly to the audit director without consulting the supervisor. Identify Fayol's principle of management that the auditor violated.

a. Order.
b. Division of work.
c. Scalar chain.
d. Unity of direction.

94. An audit director wants to encourage the managerial development of a promising auditor. Select the task that is best delegated to develop this promising subordinate.

a. Resolving a disagreement between two audit supervisors.
b. Acting as audit liaison on a special task force.
c. Drafting a pro forma departmental budget for the coming year.
d. Negotiating with senior management for additional staff.

Items 95 and 96 are based on the following:

The president of a firm asked for help to clearly define the managerial approach the firm should take. The following four statements were among the responses:

1. Management is the same in all organizations and includes the functions of organizing, staffing, directing, and controlling.
2. For us to remain competitive, we must focus on using our resources efficiently and effectively. That is the key to managerial success.

3. Employees are important. To be successful, we must ensure that they are properly trained and motivated, and we must keep the communication channels open.
4. Organizations are complex, dynamic, integrated organisms. We need to recognize this fact and focus our attention on developing synergistic interrelationships.

95. Which statement reflects the **operational approach** to management?
   a. 1.
   b. 2.
   c. 3.
   d. 4.

96. Which statement reflects the **behavioral approach** to management?
   a. 1.
   b. 2.
   c. 3.
   d. 4.

97. An organization chart is a visual display of an organization's structural skeleton. Two essential dimensions of all organization charts are
   a. Lines of communication and horizontal specialization.
   b. Vertical hierarchy and horizontal specialization.
   c. Vertical hierarchy and relative importance of organization members.
   d. Lines of communication and relative importance of organization members.

98. The optimal span of control of a manager is contingent on several situational variables. For instance, a manager supervising workers within the same work area who are performing identical tasks that are simple and repetitive would best be able to supervise
   a. An unlimited number of employees.
   b. Only a few workers and this would be described as having a narrow span of control.
   c. A relatively large number of employees and this would be described as having a wide span of control.
   d. Fewer workers than if the workers were geographically dispersed.

99. A typical organization chart displaying the managerial pyramid will have two dimensions: horizontal and vertical. These dimensions represent
   a. The formal and informal organizations.
   b. Responsibility and authority.
   c. The division of labor and chain of command.
   d. Reporting channels and hierarchy of authority.

100. A retired university professor, concerned about the rights of the elderly, formed an association with others sharing similar views. The association raised funds through membership dues and lobbied government officials to have their views enacted into law. This organization is classified as a
   a. Business.
   b. Not-for-profit service.
   c. Mutual benefit.
   d. Commonweal.

101. The traditional vertical orientation of organizational hierarchies is yielding to horizontal linkages based on need and convenience. That trend is best described as
   a. Synthesis perspective.
   b. Decentralization.
   c. Networking.
   d. Self-reliance.

102. Which of the following factors is **least** likely to affect a manager's direct span of control?
   a. Frequency of supervisor-subordinate contact.
   b. Manager's willingness to delegate authority.
   c. Manager's training and communication skills.
   d. Number of people in the corporation.

103. A small furniture-manufacturing firm with 100 employees is located in a two-story building and does not plan to expand. The furniture manufactured is not special-ordered or custom-made. Considering these facts, the most common structure for this organization would be
   a. Functional departmentalization.
   b. Product departmentalization.
   c. Matrix organization.
   d. Divisional organization.

104. In general, as organizations grow in size, their strategies
   a. Become more ambitious, and they often expand their activities within their industry.
   b. Focus on vertical integration, and their structures consequently must become more centralized.
   c. Change from a focus on a diverse set of products to a focus on a single product line.
   d. Follow and are determined by their internal structures.

105. Discount stores and sellers of generic grocery products keep prices low and innovate only where there are low-risk, high-payback projects. They are pursuing a(n)
   a. Innovation-minimization strategy.
   b. Imitation strategy.
   c. Cost-minimization strategy.
   d. Initiation strategy.

106. A bias for action, frequent contact with customers, autonomy, entrepreneurship, simple form, and minimal overhead are all elements of an organization that focuses on
   a. Continuously updating its technology.
   b. Taking a contingency view of organizational performance.
   c. Paying close attention to business basics.
   d. Continuous strategic planning.

107. Management of a financial services company is considering a strategic decision concerning the expansion of its existing local area network (LAN) to enhance the firm's customer service function. Which of the following aspects of the expanded system is the **least** significant strategic issue for management?
   a. How the expanded system can contribute to the firm's long-range business plan.
   b. How the expanded system would support daily business operations.
   c. How indicators can be developed to measure how well the expanded system achieves its business objectives.
   d. How the expanded system will contribute to the reduction of operating costs.

108. As an organization increases the number of employees, its structure becomes more complex. Rules become more formalized, and more supervisors are hired to direct the increased numbers of subordinates. What is the nature of the size-structure relationship?

a. The size-structure relationship is linear.
b. The structure becomes fixed once an organization attains a level of about 200 employees.
c. The size-structure relationship is concave.
d. None of the above.

109. Internal auditors need to be aware of the advantages and disadvantages of various organizational structures. A substantial duplication of functions characterizes which of the following structures?

a. Simple structure.
b. Divisional structure.
c. Machine bureaucracy.
d. Professional bureaucracy.

110. Controlling production and administrative cost is critical for an organization to thrive in today's markets. Which of the following are positive traits of a cost-conscious manager?

a. Awareness of short- and long-term cost trade-offs and seeking opportunities for cost synergy.
b. Taking personal responsibility for reducing overhead and obtaining budget changes by seeking incremental increases.
c. Imaginative about direct and indirect costs and being goal displaced.
d. Trying hard to keep what was in the prior budget and seeking opportunities for cost synergy.

111. Organizational restructuring has been successfully accomplished by setting up strategic business units (SBUs). Which of the following is **not** a criterion for an organizational unit to qualify as an SBU? An SBU should

a. Serve a specific market outside the parent organization.
b. Be a profit center.
c. Be risk averse.
d. Be faced with outside competition.

112. A consumer product manufacturer is organized into five major departments: (1) production, (2) engineering, (3) marketing, (4) finance, and (5) administration. In addition, to ensure coordination for each product, there is a product management department. This organization structure is an example of

a. Matrix organization.
b. Decentralization.
c. Product-service departmentalization.
d. Organic organization.

113. A business that is organized into several semiautonomous units—each with its own financing, marketing, and production effort—is using a method of organizing known as

a. Functional departmentalization.
b. Organic departmentalization.
c. Product-service departmentalization.
d. Strategic business unit departmentalization.

114. How a firm's structure relates to the environment in which the firm operates is important to the success of a firm. A firm's structure can be mechanistic (a rigid pyramid-shaped organization) or organic (a flexible and adaptive organization). Which of the following items is **not** characteristic of the interaction between a firm's environment and its structure?

a. The more dynamic the environment, the more the firm's structure should be organic.
b. The more complex the environment, the more the firm's structure should be mechanistic.
c. The more stable the environment, the more the firm's structure should be mechanistic.
d. The more scarce the environment, the more the firm's structure should be organic.

115. Which particular type of organization structure will likely have unity-of-command problems unless there is frequent and comprehensive communication between the various functional and project managers?

a. Line and staff.
b. Strategic business unit.
c. Centralized.
d. Matrix.

116. A vertically integrated company is best described as one that

a. Owns all of its production facilities.
b. Manufactures the component parts used in its product.
c. Is departmentalized by product or service.
d. Fosters very narrow span of control.

Change and Conflict Management

117. The adoption of a new idea or behavior by an organization is known as organizational

a. Development.
b. Change.
c. Structure.
d. Intervention.

118. If top managers select a goal of rapid company growth, which of the following will have to be changed first to meet that growth?

a. Competitive actions.
b. Internal actions.
c. External actions.
d. Environmental actions.

119. What is the least intense and least risky type of change?

a. Tuning.
b. Reorientation.
c. Re-creation.
d. Adaptation.

120. Which of the following types of organizational change involves incremental change?

I. Tuning.
II. Reorientation.
III. Re-creation.
IV. Adaptation.

a. I only.
b. I and II.
c. IV only.
d. I and IV.

121. Which of the following types of organizational change is called frame bending?
 a. Tuning.
 b. Reorientation.
 c. Re-creation.
 d. Adaptation.

122. Which of the following types of organizational change is called frame breaking?
 a. Tuning.
 b. Reorientation.
 c. Re-creation.
 d. Adaptation.

123. Which of the following strategies for overcoming resistance to change should be used when the concern is prevention?
 a. Education and communication.
 b. Participation and involvement.
 c. Facilitation and support.
 d. Negotiation and agreement.

124. Which of the following strategies for overcoming resistance to change should be used when a speedy change is necessary?
 a. Manipulation and co-optation.
 b. Explicit and implicit coercion.
 c. Facilitation and support.
 d. Negotiation and agreement.

125. What is the **best** description of organization development?

I. Planned effort.
II. Planned change.
III. Frame bending.
IV. Frame breaking.

 a. I only.
 b. II only.
 c. I and II.
 d. III and IV.

126. During which phase of the organization development does diagnosis occur?
 a. Unfreezing.
 b. Change.
 c. Refreezing.
 d. Intervention.

127. Which of the following holds a change effort together in an organization?
 a. Leader.
 b. Manager.
 c. Trust.
 d. Change agent.

128. Conflict involves which of the following?
 a. Negative behaviors.
 b. Destructive behaviors.
 c. Incompatible behaviors.
 d. Competitive behaviors.

129. Status differentials and unrealized expectations are part of which of the following?
 a. Conflict triggers.
 b. Communication triggers.
 c. Personality triggers.
 d. Time pressure triggers.

130. Faced with three years of steadily decreasing profits despite increased sales and a growing economy, which of the following is the healthiest course of action for a chief executive officer to take?
 a. Set a turnaround goal of significantly increasing profits within two months. Set clear short-term objectives for each operating unit, which together should produce the turnaround.
 b. Reduce staff by 10% in every unit.
 c. Classify all job functions as either: (1) adding value in the eyes of the customer (i.e., production and sales), or (2) not adding value in the eyes of the customer (i.e., accounting and human resources). Reduce staff in the non-value-adding functions by 20%.
 d. Implement a plan to encourage innovation at all levels. Use early retirement and reemployment programs to trim staff size.

131. A major corporation is considering significant organizational changes. Which of the following groups would **not** be responsible for implementing these changes?
 a. Employees.
 b. Top management.
 c. Common stockholders.
 d. Outside consultants.

132. Negotiation, manipulation, coercion, employee education, and increased communication are all ways in which managers can
 a. Improve employee morale.
 b. Overcome resistance to change.
 c. Maintain control of information.
 d. Demonstrate their power to both their supervisors and subordinates.

133. Lack of skills, threats to job status and security, and fear of failure have all been identified as reasons why employees often
 a. Want to change the culture of their organization.
 b. Are dissatisfied with the structure of their organization.
 c. Are unable to perform their jobs.
 d. Resist organizational change.

134. In many jobs, excessive specialization can eventually lead to poor motivation, boredom, and alienation. In order to cope with the potential problems in such a situation, managers should
 a. Focus on their employees' higher-level needs in order to help them achieve self-actualization.
 b. Remove dissatisfiers such as low salary, bad supervision, lack of job security, and poor working conditions.
 c. Implement an optimal organizational rewards system and provide all needed training to keep employees up to date on technology.
 d. Change the jobs to fit the employees' needs or rotate employees to jobs that satisfy their needs.

135. Following a decision to change the composition of audit teams, management encounters significant resistance to the change from members of the auditing department. The most likely reason for the resistance is
 a. Possible inefficiencies of the new schedule.
 b. The breakup of existing audit teams.

c. Understaffing for the tasks involved.
d. Selection of a more costly approach to performing the audit.

136. In order to achieve organizational goals, a manager is required to consider an overall force affecting the company. This force can best be identified as

a. The universal process.
b. Standardization.
c. Changing environment.
d. Strategic planning.

137. An organization's management perceives the need to make significant changes. Which of the following factors is management **least** likely to be able to change?

a. Organization's members.
b. Organization's structure.
c. Organization's environment.
d. Organization's technology

138. A printing company changes its type of ink to a non-toxic variety due to unfavorable publicity by a local environmental group. This is an example of an organizational change called

a. Anticipatory.
b. Reactive.
c. Incremental.
d. Strategic.

139. Which one of the following is **not** a characteristic of an innovative manufacturing company?

a. Emphasis on continuous improvement.
b. Responsiveness to the changing manufacturing environment.
c. Emphasis on existing products.
d. Improved customer satisfaction through product quality.

140. For several years, the internal audit department had been using character-based software on its laptop computers to complete assigned audits. After performing extensive research, the director of internal audit determined that a change to software with a graphical user interface (GUI) would be beneficial to the department. When the subject was announced at a regular departmental meeting, several of the internal audit staff expressed concern about the extra time it would take to learn new software, the slowness of GUI software, and the fact that the character-based software was familiar and had caused no problems. Which of the following approaches would be best suited to changing the staff auditors' attitudes?

I. Inform the staff auditors about the research completed.
II. Impose the decision on the audit staff.
III. Offer time off and departmental funds for training.
IV. Negotiate the dates for the introduction of the software.
V. Tell the employees that if they do not accept the new software, they may be fired.

a. I, II, III, and IV only.
b. I, III, and IV only.
c. II, III, and V only.
d. II, IV, and V only.

141. An internal auditor is conducting an operational review that affects several different functional units. The auditor believes that the process under review can be improved, but the operating managers are resistant to suggestions for change. There are several methods the auditor could use to overcome the operating managers' resistance. Identify the technique that will produce the highest probability of success with the fewest negative side effects.

a. Negotiation with the operating managers.
b. Participation by the managers in the decision process.
c. Coercion of the managers through threats.
d. Cooperation by approaching each manager individually.

142. Internal auditors can be considered as leading agents for change within an organization. Which of the following is **not** a good way to promote this concept?

a. A directive from top management, stating that internal auditors will be used for all process-improvement projects.
b. A brochure describing what internal auditing can do and the qualifications of the auditors.
c. Postaudit questionnaires to obtain information on how auditees perceive the audit operation.
d. Bulletins that highlight widespread or universal applications of audit findings.

143. Following a decision to change the composition of production teams, management encounters significant resistance to the change from members of the department. The most likely reason for the resistance is

a. Inefficiencies of the new structure.
b. Concerns about changes in working relationships.
c. Understaffing for the tasks involved.
d. Selection of a more costly approach to performing production work.

144. When management is faced with resistance to change and severe time constraints, what are the best tactics to ensure that tasks are accomplished?

a. Participation and involvement.
b. Facilitation and support.
c. Negotiation and agreement.
d. Explicit and implicit coercion.

145. When microcomputers were first introduced on a large-scale basis in the mid-1980s, many people resisted using these new machines. Select the most probable reason these individuals resisted change.

a. Habit.
b. Job security.
c. Fear of the unknown.
d. Selective information processing.

146. Which of the following is **not** a principal reason for organizational members resisting organizational change?

a. Member's relative position in the hierarchy.
b. Uncertainty.
c. Concern over personal loss.
d. Belief that the change is not in the organization's best interest.

147. An organization's management perceives the need to change fundamentally. Which of the following factors is management **least** likely to change?

a. Organization's members.
b. Organization's structure.
c. Organization's environment.
d. Organization's technology.

148. The process of organizational change can be impeded if the organization has a strong culture in place. Which of the following is **not** an effective step for changing a strong organizational culture?

a. Prepare a comprehensive cultural "audit" to identify the existing dimensions of the organization's culture.
b. Provide assurance to existing executives that their positions and prospects are secure.
c. Create awareness that the organization is faced with a serious crisis.
d. Revamp selection and reward criteria to promote a different set of organization values.

149. Identify the management technique in which employees assist in setting goals, making decisions, solving problems, and designing and implementing organizational changes.

a. Total quality control.
b. Participative management.
c. Kanban.
d. Just-in-time technology.

150. Organizational development (OD) is one of the major approaches to proactive management of change in organizations. One of the major objectives of OD is to

a. Increase the power of leaders.
b. Align the organization's and the employees' goals.
c. Attract better employees to the organization.
d. Provide the organization and its managers with ways to increase efficiency.

Control Types and Techniques

151. Which of the following management control systems measures performance in terms of operating profits minus the cost of capital invested in tangible assets?

a. Open-book management system.
b. Economic-value-added system.
c. Activity-based costing system.
d. Market-value-added system.

152. A comprehensive management control system that considers both financial and nonfinancial measures relating to a company's critical success factors is called a(n)

a. Balanced scorecard system.
b. Economic-value-added system.
c. Activity-based costing system.
d. Market-value-added system.

153. An exception report for management is an example of which of the following?

a. Preventive control.
b. Detective control.
c. Corrective control.
d. Directive control.

154. Which of the following management practices involves concentrating on areas that deserve attention and placing less attention on areas operating as expected?

a. Management by objectives (MBO).
b. Responsibility accounting.
c. Benchmarking.
d. Management by exception (MBE).

155. Organizational procedures allow employees to anticipate problems. This type of control is known as

a. Feedback control.
b. Strategic control.
c. Feed-forward control.
d. Performance appraisal.

156. As part of a total quality control program, a firm not only inspects finished goods but also monitors product returns and customer complaints. Which type of control best describes these efforts?

a. Feedback control.
b. Feed-forward control.
c. Production control.
d. Inventory control.

157. One particular type of control is frequently criticized because corrective action takes place after the fact. What type of control exhibits that trait?

a. Automatic control.
b. Feedback control.
c. Strategic control.
d. Feedforward control.

158. The operations manager of a company notified the treasurer of that organization 60 days in advance that a new, expensive piece of machinery was going to be purchased. This notification allowed the treasurer to make an orderly liquidation of some of the company's investment portfolio on favorable terms. Select the type of control that this example describes

a. Feedback.
b. Strategic.
c. Budgetary.
d. Feed-forward.

159. To be successful, large companies must develop means to keep the organization focused in the proper direction. Organization control systems help keep companies focused. These control systems consist of which of the following components?

a. Budgeting, financial ratio analysis, and cash management.
b. Objectives, standards, and an evaluation-reward system.
c. Role analysis, team building, and survey feedback.
d. Coaching, protection, and challenging assignments.

160. Control has been described as a closed system consisting of six elements. Identify one of the six elements.

a. Setting performance standards.
b. Adequately securing data files.
c. Approval of audit charter.
d. Establishment of independent audit function.

161. An organization's policies and procedures are part of its overall system of internal controls. The control function performed by policies and procedures is

a. Feed-forward control.
b. Implementation control.
c. Feedback control.
d. Application control.

162. The comment card filled out by a customer in a restaurant is a control device used by management to improve the level of service and the quality of food. Controls of this type are classified as

a. Feed-forward controls.
b. Steering controls.
c. Concurrent controls.
d. Feedback controls.

163. The three basic components of all organizational control systems are

a. Objectives, standards, and an evaluation-reward system.
b. Plans, budgets, and organizational policies and procedures.
c. Statistical reports, audits, and financial controls
d. Inputs, objectives, and an appraisal system.

164. The internal auditing function of an organization is an integral part of the organization's overall system of internal control. Select the type of control provided when an auditing function conducts a systems development review.

a. Feedback control.
b. Strategic plans.
c. Policies and procedures.
d. Feed-forward control.

165. The internal auditing function of an organization is an integral part of the organization's overall system of internal control. Select the type of control emphasized by an operational audit.

a. Feedback control.
b. Strategic plans.
c. Policies and procedures.
d. Feed-forward control.

166. Internal auditors can evaluate the management function of controlling by determining if

a. The grouping of activities in a department meets departmental objectives.
b. Management is provided with prompt feedback on performance variances.
c. Employee turnover rates are analyzed for trends and investigations are made for adverse trends.
d. Anticipated problems are discussed, identified, and evaluated with possible solutions provided.

167. When planning the controls review of the end-user computing (EUC) application, the internal auditor chose to include the general control environment in the scope. Which one of the following statements regarding general controls is the auditor most likely to find true?

a. The effectiveness of the general controls is influenced by the application controls.
b. Identifying the person or function responsible for the general controls may be easier here than in a traditional mainframe environment.
c. The need for specific general controls is relatively constant across EUC environments.
d. General controls must be in place before application controls can be relied on.

168. A payroll clerk with authorized access to the local area network (LAN) was able to directly update personnel files independent of the application programs. The best control to prevent a clerk from doing this would be to

a. Restrict access to LAN workstations by such means as automatic lockup after a predefined period of keyboard inactivity.
b. Restrict access to and monitor installation of software products or tools having powerful update capabilities.
c. Use password security to authenticate users as they attempt to log on to the LAN.
d. Establish a security policy for the department that prohibits direct updating of data files.

169. The auditor used the reporting capabilities of the fourth-generation (4GL) to analyze the data files for unusual activity such as excessive overtime hours, unusual fluctuations in pay rates, or excessive vacation time. The application controls being verified by this analysis are

a. Edit and validation controls.
b. Rejected and suspense item controls.
c. Controls over update access to the database.
d. Programmed balancing controls.

170. Which of the following input controls or edit checks would catch certain types of errors within the payment amount field of a transaction?

a. Record count.
b. Echo check.
c. Check digit.
d. Limit check.

171. When assessing application controls, which one of the following input controls or edit checks is most likely to be used to detect a data input error in the customer account number field?

a. Limit check.
b. Validity check.
c. Control total.
d. Hash total.

172. An internal auditor is reviewing the adequacy of existing policies and procedures concerning end user computing activities. The auditor is testing

a. An application control.
b. An organizational control.
c. An environmental control.
d. A system control.

173. To ensure the completeness of a file update, the user department retains copies of all unnumbered documents submitted for processing and checks these off individually against a report of transactions processed. This is an example of the use of

a. Established batch totals.
b. One-for-one checking.
c. Computer sequence checks.
d. Computer matching.

174. Rejection of unauthorized modifications to application systems could be accomplished through the use of

a. Programmed checks.
b. Batch controls.
c. Implementation controls.
d. One-for-one checking.

175. The best control for detecting processed data totals that do not agree with input totals is

a. Run-to-run checking.
b. Existence checking.
c. Key verification.
d. Prerecorded inputs.

176. To ensure that goods received are the same as those shown on the purchase invoice, a computerized system should

a. Match selected fields of the purchase invoice to goods received.
b. Maintain control totals of inventory value.
c. Calculate batch totals for each input.
d. Use check digits in account numbers.

177. Which of the following controls would be most efficient in reducing common data input errors?
a. Keystroke verification.
b. Set of well-designed edit checks.
c. Balancing and reconciliation.
d. Batch totals.

178. To ensure that a computer file is accurately updated in total for a particular field, the best control is
a. Computer matching.
b. Check digit.
c. Transaction log.
d. Run-to-run totals.

179. To ensure that a particular data field is properly maintained, manual postings of batch totals for that field to a control account
a. Are of no value in file maintenance.
b. Should be periodically compared to the computer master file.
c. Stand alone as a control.
d. Should be used in combination with hash totals.

180. A new auditor is being briefed on various types of audits by the audit supervisor. The supervisor states that some areas within the organization are more difficult to audit because the controls generally are not as clearly defined as in other departments. Select the type of control that is usually most difficult to assess.
a. Operational.
b. Hardware.
c. Accounting.
d. Physical security.

181. Due to the vulnerability to fraud, the trust department of a bank required that an officer other than the trust officer verifies income distribution orders and sign disbursement checks. Which type of control is typified by such segregation of duties?
a. Input.
b. Auditing.
c. Corrective.
d. Operating.

182. Monitoring is an important component of internal control. Which of the following items would not be an example of monitoring?
a. Management regularly compares divisional performance with budgets for the division.
b. Data processing management regularly generates exception reports for unusual transactions or volumes of transactions and follows up with investigation as to causes.
c. Data processing management regularly reconciles batch control totals for items processed with batch controls for items submitted.
d. Management has asked internal auditing to perform regular audits of the control structure over cash processing.

183. An adequate system of internal controls is most likely to detect an irregularity perpetrated by a
a. Group of employees in collusion.
b. Single employee.
c. Group of managers in collusion.
d. Single manager.

184. Controls can be classified according to the function they are intended to perform; for example, to discover the occurrence of an unwanted event (detective), to avoid the occurrence of an unwanted event (preventive), or to ensure the occurrence of a desirable event (directive). Which of the following is a directive control?
a. Performing monthly reconciliation of bank statements.
b. Requiring dual signatures on all disbursements over a specific dollar amount.
c. Recording every transaction on the day it occurs.
d. Requiring all members of the internal auditing department to be Certified Internal Auditors.

MULTIPLE-CHOICE ANSWERS AND EXPLANATIONS

1. d __ __	40. a __ __	79. b __ __	118. b __ __	157. b __ __
2. c __ __	41. c __ __	80. b __ __	119. a __ __	158. d __ __
3. b __ __	42. c __ __	81. b __ __	120. d __ __	159. b __ __
4. c __ __	43. c __ __	82. d __ __	121. b __ __	160. a __ __
5. d __ __	44. b __ __	83. a __ __	122. c __ __	161. a __ __
6. c __ __	45. d __ __	84. a __ __	123. a __ __	162. d __ __
7. a __ __	46. c __ __	85. c __ __	124. b __ __	163. a __ __
8. b __ __	47. a __ __	86. a __ __	125. c __ __	164. d __ __
9. b __ __	48. a __ __	87. d __ __	126. a __ __	165. d __ __
10. a __ __	49. b __ __	88. c __ __	127. c __ __	166. b __ __
11. b __ __	50. c __ __	89. d __ __	128. c __ __	167. d __ __
12. a __ __	51. c __ __	90. d __ __	129. a __ __	168. b __ __
13. b __ __	52. c __ __	91. a __ __	130. d __ __	169. a __ __
14. c __ __	53. d __ __	92. d __ __	131. c __ __	170. d __ __
15. a __ __	54. b __ __	93. c __ __	132. b __ __	171. b __ __
16. d __ __	55. d __ __	94. b __ __	133. d __ __	172. b __ __
17. c __ __	56. b __ __	95. b __ __	134. d __ __	173. b __ __
18. c __ __	57. c __ __	96. c __ __	135. b __ __	174. c __ __
19. c __ __	58. a __ __	97. b __ __	136. c __ __	175. a __ __
20. b __ __	59. c __ __	98. c __ __	137. c __ __	176. a __ __
21. d __ __	60. a __ __	99. c __ __	138. b __ __	177. b __ __
22. a __ __	61. b __ __	100. c __ __	139. c __ __	178. d __ __
23. c __ __	62. c __ __	101. c __ __	140. b __ __	179. b __ __
24. a __ __	63. d __ __	102. d __ __	141. b __ __	180. a __ __
25. c __ __	64. d __ __	103. a __ __	142. a __ __	181. d __ __
26. b __ __	65. b __ __	104. a __ __	143. b __ __	182. c __ __
27. a __ __	66. a __ __	105. c __ __	144. d __ __	183. b __ __
28. d __ __	67. c __ __	106. c __ __	145. c __ __	184. d __ __
29. c __ __	68. b __ __	107. d __ __	146. a __ __	
30. c __ __	69. c __ __	108. d __ __	147. c __ __	
31. b __ __	70. c __ __	109. b __ __	148. b __ __	
32. d __ __	71. a __ __	110. a __ __	149. b __ __	
33. a __ __	72. b __ __	111. c __ __	150. b __ __	
34. a __ __	73. a __ __	112. a __ __	151. b __ __	
35. c __ __	74. a __ __	113. c __ __	152. a __ __	
36. b __ __	75. d __ __	114. b __ __	153. c __ __	
37. a __ __	76. d __ __	115. d __ __	154. d __ __	
38. c __ __	77. d __ __	116. b __ __	155. c __ __	1st: __/184 = __%
39. c __ __	78. a __ __	117. b __ __	156. a __ __	2nd: __/184 = __%

Corporate Governance Principles

1. (d) The whistle-blower program can act as a means of collecting employee concerns, improving internal communication, collecting information regarding emerging issues before they become crises, and enhancing the organization's overall system of internal controls. The program does not improve external communications because it focuses on internal communication. Choices (a), (b), and (c) are incorrect. They all do help the organization to meet the requirements of the act. Choices (a), (b), and (c) help to improve the implementation of whistle-blower program because they focus on improving internal communication.

Subject Area: Governance, risk, and control knowledge elements—corporate governance principles. Source: Author.

2. (c) While a hard-copy memo, an e-mail, video conferencing, voice conferencing, or even preparing a computer-based training program is a viable option to release the whistle-blower program throughout the organization, the most effective way is to have face-to-face meetings with employees. This shows management's commitment to the program. Choices (a), (b), and (c) are incorrect. They are not effective ways.

Subject Area: Governance, risk, and control knowledge elements—corporate governance principles. Source: Author.

3. (b) The building phase trains operators. An approach that is widely used in other settings and practical in the whistle-blower program is the "train-the-trainer" approach. Choice (a) is incorrect because the assessment phase evaluates the needs. Choice (c) is incorrect because the program release phase introduces the whistle-blower program throughout the organization. Choice (d) is incorrect because the performance monitoring phase surveys employees.

Subject Area: Governance, risk, and control knowledge elements—corporate governance principles. Source: Author.

4. (c) The selection of the facilitator for the whistle-blower program release sessions is made in the program release phase. Choosing a sympathetic and knowledgeable facilitator will increase employee acceptance of the program and put employees at ease. Choice (a) is incorrect. The assessment phase identifies staff. Choice (b) is incorrect. The building phase updates polices and procedures. Choice (d) is incorrect. The performance-monitoring phase meets with oversight board.

Subject Area: Governance, risk, and control knowledge elements—corporate governance principles. Source: Author.

5. (d) Performance monitoring requires verifying compliance with the program's protocol to ensure quality control. Surveys should be conducted to obtain feedback and to make sure that employees remain aware that the program is in place and working effectively. Choice (a) is incorrect. The assessment phase selects oversight board. Choice (b) is incorrect. The building phase trains the oversight board. Choice (c) is incorrect. The program release phase distributes notices.

Subject Area: Governance, risk, and control knowledge elements—corporate governance principles. Source: Author.

6. (c) Section 302 of the Sarbanes-Oxley Act requires CEOs and CFOs to personally certify in quarterly financial reports. To implement this section, the SEC introduced the term "disclosure controls and procedures," which limits the evaluation to internal controls over financial reporting and over material nonfinancial disclosures. A key element of the disclosure process is a disclosure committee, in which knowledgeable, high-level people come together to rigorously examine financial information and other disclosures as they are being prepared. Choice (a) is incorrect. "Disclosure controls" is a part of the term introduced by the SEC and is not a key element. Choice (b) is incorrect. "Disclosure procedures" is a part of the term introduced by the SEC, and is not a key element. Choice (d) is incorrect. The disclosure policies are neither a part of the term introduced by the SEC nor a key element.

Subject Area: Governance, risk, and control knowledge elements—corporate governance principles. Source: Author.

7. (a) The control environment of an organization does not exist as series of discrete controls, like the steps in a transaction processing systems. It is an integrated whole. The individual pieces contribute to the whole, but it is the interaction among the pieces that make up the control environment. Thus, the organization's assessment and assertion of the control environment should be treated as a whole and in an integrated manner. Choice (b) is incorrect. Discrete controls are used in transaction processing systems. Choice (c) is incorrect. Soft controls are subjective aspects of control, like tone at the top. Choice (d) is incorrect. Hard controls like testing are performed in traditional auditing work.

Subject Area: Governance, risk, and control knowledge elements—corporate governance principles. Source: Author.

Alternate Control Frameworks

8. (b) According to the COSO's report, five components of internal control include control environment, risk assessment, control activities, information and communication, and monitoring. Control environment is the foundation on which everything rests and is the basis for assessing integrity and ethical values, management's philosophy, and operating style (soft controls). Choice (a) is incorrect because risk assessment identifies risks and suggests controls. Choice (c) is incorrect because control activities need control procedures. Choice (d) is incorrect because monitoring includes management reviews and comparisons.

Subject Area: Governance, risk, and control knowledge elements—alternate control frameworks. Source: Author.

9. (b) Most of the time, hard controls should be evaluated at the activity level; this is in addition to the soft controls. The focus of the hard controls should be on detailed documentation and testing of control activities. Activity level includes process level, functional level, and department level. Choice (a) is incorrect because soft controls should be evaluated at the organizational level. Choice (c) is incorrect because process level is a part of the activity level. Choice (d) is incorrect because department level is a part of the activity level.

Subject Area: Governance, risk, and control knowledge elements—alternate control frameworks. Source: Author.

10. (a) The two of the five components of the COSO "control environment and risk assessment" includes many soft controls that are intangibles, such as evaluating tone at the top, management's philosophy, operating style, integrity, and the organization's ethical climate. Choice (b) is incorrect because control activities focus on hard controls. Choice (c) is incorrect because monitoring includes both soft and hard controls. Choice (d) is incorrect because control activities, information, and communication include both soft and hard controls.

Subject Area: Governance, risk, and control knowledge elements—alternate control frameworks. Source: Author.

11. (b) COSO users often adopt a two-tiered control evaluation process. This includes entity-wide assessment (organizational level) followed by process or activity level (second-tier). Choice (a) is incorrect because a single-tiered evaluation process is not as strong as the two-tiered one. Choice (c) is incorrect because there is no such thing as the three-tiered evaluation. Choice (d) is incorrect because there is no such thing as the four-tiered evaluation.

Subject Area: Governance, risk, and control knowledge elements—alternate control frameworks. Source: Author.

12. (a) The COSO-based audit approach should not override the risk-based audit approach where the latter should receive high priority. Where there are gaps, the two approaches should be reconciled. Choice (b) is incorrect because a transaction-based approach can be overridden. Choice (c) is incorrect because a management-based approach can be overridden. Choice (d) is incorrect because the audit committee would not be involved in the detailed audit approaches.

Subject Area: Governance, risk, and control knowledge elements—alternate control frameworks. Source: Author.

13. (b) The audit plan changes throughout the year as risks and audit resources change. Choice (a) is incorrect because audit resources do change frequently. Choice (c) is incorrect because the changes occurring in the board's composition and polices should not directly impact the audit plan. Choice (d) is incorrect this choice mixes the correct and incorrect answers.

Subject Area: Governance, risk, and control knowledge elements—alternate control frameworks. Source: Author.

14. (c) The annual audit plan should be based on the control model. This should not replace a risk-based model. Choice (a) is incorrect because risk should be considered.

Choice (b) is incorrect because control should be considered. Choice (d) is incorrect because resources and management model could be part of the control and risk model.

Subject Area: Governance, risk, and control knowledge elements—alternate control frameworks. Source: Author.

15. **(a)** The core of any business is its people—their individual attributes, including integrity, ethical values, and competence and the environment in which they operate. They are the engine that drives the entity and the foundation on which everything else rests. The entity will have its objectives and the processes to achieve those objectives. Choice (b) is incorrect because profits and products are not part of the internal control. Choice (c) is incorrect because costs, revenues, and margins are not part of the internal control. Instead, they are part of financial control. Choice (d) is incorrect because ROI, EPS, and market share are not part of the internal control. Instead, they are part of financial and marketing control.

Subject Area: Governance, risk, and control knowledge elements—alternate control frameworks. Source: Author.

16. **(d)** According to the COSO report, there is a synergy and linkage among planning, execution, and monitoring, forming an integrated system that reacts dynamically to changing conditions. However, risk to an entity comes from internal and external sources, which must be identified, analyzed, measured, and managed. Risk varies with time, competition, and other factors. Choice (a) is incorrect because planning is a part of the internal control system. Choice (b) is incorrect because execution is a part of the internal control system. Choice (c) is incorrect because monitoring is a part of the internal control system.

Subject Area: Governance, risk, and control knowledge elements—alternate control frameworks. Source: Author.

17. **(c)** According to the COSO report, objectives provide the organization's targets. To be in control, risks potentially affecting the achievement of an entity's objectives must be identified and analyzed. Then actions must be put in place to mitigate the identified risks. Choice (a) is incorrect because objectives should be first since they drive everything else. Choice (b) is incorrect because actions should come last. Choice (d) is incorrect because risks come before actions.

Subject Area: Governance, risk, and control knowledge elements—alternate control frameworks. Source: Author.

18. **(c)** According to the COSO report, the core of an organization is people. Profits result from products and processes, and it is the people who make things happen. Choice (a) is incorrect because people make products. Choice (b) is incorrect because people are involved in processes. Choice (d) is incorrect because profits come from products.

Subject Area: Governance, risk, and control knowledge elements—alternate control frameworks. Source: Author.

19. **(c)** Deficiencies in an entity's internal control system can surface from any of a number of sources. A "deficiency" may represent a perceived, potential, or real shortcoming, or an opportunity to strengthen the internal control system to provide a greater likelihood that the entity's objectives will be achieved. The condition of the process is either deficient or not. Authorization, approval, and description of the process are steps in the internal control system, whereas the condition is the result of the process. Choice (a) is incorrect because authorization of the process is a part of the internal control system. Choice (b) is incorrect because approval of the process is a part of the internal control system. Choice (d) is incorrect because description of the process is a part of the internal control system.

Subject Area: Governance, risk, and control knowledge elements—alternate control frameworks. Source: Author.

20. **(b)** Objective setting begins at the entity level, encompassing mission and value statements, preferences, and management style, which leads to overall strategy. Profits are the result of specific goals, where goals are derived from objectives. Choice (a) is incorrect because preferences should be considered in setting an entity's objectives. Choice (c) is incorrect because value judgments should be considered in setting an entity's objectives. Choice (d) is incorrect because management style should be considered in setting an entity's objectives.

Subject Area: Governance, risk, and control knowledge elements—alternate control frameworks. Source: Author.

21. **(d)** According to the COSO report, there is a direct relationship between the risk level and the control level. That is, high-risk situations require stronger controls, low-risk situations require weaker controls, and medium-risk situations require medium controls. Choice (a) is incorrect because low risk requires weak controls. Choice (b) is incorrect because high risk requires strong controls. Choice (c) is incorrect because medium risk requires medium controls.

Subject Area: Governance, risk, and control knowledge elements—alternate control frameworks. Source: Author.

22. **(a)** Controls should facilitate the achievement of an organization's goals, and they should not limit operational practices, processes, and people's actions. According to the COSO report, a control is defined as the policies, practices, and organizational structure designed to provide reasonable assurance that business objectives will be achieved and that undesired events could be prevented or detected and corrected. Choice (b) is incorrect because controls should not limit an operation. Choice (c) is incorrect because controls should not block a process. Choice (d) is incorrect because controls should not inhibit a person.

Subject Area: Governance, risk, and control knowledge elements—alternate control frameworks. Source: Author.

23. **(c)** The purpose of a control mechanism is to ensure that goals of a firm are being achieved. Choice (a) is incorrect because rewards and punishments control employee behavior. Choice (b) is incorrect because management determines who is in charge of a department. Choice (d) is incorrect because responsibility accounting determines cost or profit center.

Subject Area: Governance, risk, and control knowledge elements—alternate control frameworks. Source: Author.

24. **(a)** Belief systems and interactive control systems create positive and inspirational forces. Boundary systems and diagnostic control systems create negative forces such as rules and constraints. Choice (b) is incorrect because boundary systems are part of negative forces. Choice (c) is incorrect because boundary system and diagnostic control systems are part of negative forces. Choice (d) is incorrect because diagnostic control systems are part of negative forces.

Subject Area: Governance, risk, and control knowledge elements—alternate control frameworks. Source: Author.

25. **(c)** Control involves the use of incentives and rewards and to motivate employees in order to help them accomplish organizational goals and objectives. Controls should be seen as positive actions, not so much of negative actions (punishments). People prefer positive things rather than negative things. Choice (a) is incorrect because what measures to implement is a part of the control decision. Choice (b) is incorrect because how to evaluate performance is a part of the control decision. Choice (d) is incorrect because incentives are part of the control decision.

Subject Area: Governance, risk, and control knowledge elements—alternate control frameworks. Source: Author.

26. **(b)** Generally speaking, senior managers most often use soft skills and soft controls to achieve their business objectives. Self-assessment is a tool to implement soft control. Choice (a) is incorrect because hard controls, third-party reviews, and hard skills are used by lower-level managers. Choice (c) is incorrect because lower-level managers depend on third-party reviews such as contractors and consultants. Choice (d) is incorrect because lower-level managers use hard controls and hard skills.

Subject Area: Governance, risk, and control knowledge elements—alternate control frameworks. Source: Author.

27. **(a)** Many policies and controls are informal and undocumented yet are regularly performed and highly effective. However, the unwritten policy must be thoughtful, clear, and consistent for others to understand and implement it. Choice (b) is incorrect because policies must be thoughtful to be useful. Choice (c) is incorrect because policies must be clear to be useful. Choice (d) is incorrect because policies must be consistent to be useful.

Subject Area: Governance, risk, and control knowledge elements—alternate control frameworks. Source: Author.

28. **(d)** Monitoring comes after developing strategic plans, setting objectives, and conducting risk assessment. Monitoring will assess the current performance of controls and their adequacy over time. Choices (a), (b), and (c) are incorrect because they are essential to internal control systems and should be done prior to monitoring.

Subject Area: Governance, risk, and control knowledge elements—alternate control frameworks. Source: Author.

29. **(c)** An effective control system requires an ultimate owner. The only truly effective owner of the control system is the chief executive officer (CEO). The CEO is the only person who can establish the right tone at the top of the organization and who has the power to ensure that all parts of the enterprise effectively communicate and coexist. The ownership responsibility cannot be delegated to an accountant or an auditor. Choice (a) is incorrect because a user does not have the power and authority to implement controls. Choice (b) is incorrect because a sponsor is a person who funds a control system. Choice (d) is incorrect because customer could be internal or external to an internal control system.

Subject Area: Governance, risk, and control knowledge elements—alternate control frameworks. Source: Author.

30. **(c)** Auditors are required to communicate only those findings meeting a specified threshold of seriousness or importance. Reportable conditions are defined as "significant deficiencies in the design or operation of the internal control structure, which could adversely affect the organization's ability to record, process, summarize, and report financial data consistent with the assertions of management in the financial statements." Choice (a) is incorrect. The threshold level for a reportable condition is lower than that of material weaknesses for reporting matters identified during an audit to the entity's audit committee. Choice (b) is incorrect. It does not serve as a yardstick for determining whether an internal control system is "effective." Choice (d) is incorrect. The need to report a finding to an entity's audit committee does not necessarily mean that the internal control system is ineffective.

Subject Area: Governance, risk, and control knowledge elements—alternate control frameworks. Source: Author.

31. **(b)** This is the definition of control contained in the IIA *Standards*. Choice (a) is incorrect. This is an example of a show of power, but is not a comprehensive definition or example of the concept of control. Choice (c) is incorrect. Control as a concept is broader than processing controls and is designed by management, not by auditors. Choice (d) is incorrect. Some control procedures may be designed from the bottom up, but the concept of control flows from management down through the organization.

Subject Area: Governance, risk, and control knowledge elements—alternate control frameworks. Source: CIA 1195, I-67.

32. **(d)** Management is responsible for controls. Choice (a) is incorrect. External auditors are responsible for audit of financial statements. Choice (b) is incorrect. Accounts receivable staff are responsible for daily transaction handling. Choice (c) is incorrect. See choice (d).

Subject Area: Governance, risk, and control knowledge elements—alternate control frameworks. Source: CIA 1195, III-1.

33. **(a)** This is the best description of top management's responsibility. Choice (b) is incorrect. This is a function assigned to internal auditing. Choice (c) is incorrect. Management cannot pass its responsibilities for control to auditors. Choice (d) is incorrect. The board may establish criteria but it usually does not design controls as such.

Subject Area: Governance, risk, and control knowledge elements—alternate control frameworks. Source: CIA 1193, II-8.

34. **(a)** The best form of control over the performance of individuals is supervision. This is a managerial function. Choice (b) is incorrect. This does not control; it only advises. Choice (c) is incorrect. A quality control department is a form of internal review. The manager of quality control should be independent of the operations reviewed. Choice (d) is incorrect. Internal reviews (i.e., internal auditing) should be independent of the operations reviewed and are not a managerial function.

Subject Area: Governance, risk, and control knowledge elements—alternate control frameworks. Source: CIA 592, II-22.

Risk Management Concepts and Techniques

35. **(c)** Objective risk is probable variation of actual from expected losses divided by expected losses. (45 – 35)/30 = 10/30 = 33.3%. The loss experience information is not relevant here. Choice (a) is incorrect because it assumes the loss experience is same as the objective risk. Choice (b) is incorrect because it assumes collision losses are same as the objective risk. Choice (d) is incorrect because it takes the average of collision losses of 35 and 45 and results in 40%.

Subject Area: Governance, risk, and control knowledge elements—risk management concepts and techniques. Source: CBM, Volume 4.

36. **(b)** The risk-management process involves identifying risks, evaluating risks, selecting risk-management techniques, and implementing and reviewing decisions. Choice (a) is incorrect because companies can be self-insured and do not need to purchase insurance. Choice (c) is incorrect because companies can be self-insured and do not need to purchase insurance. Choice (d) is incorrect because analyzing severity of expected losses is a part of identifying risks.

Subject Area: Governance, risk, and control knowledge elements—risk management concepts and techniques. Source: CBM, Volume 4.

37. **(a)** Risk means uncertainty. Risk regarding the possibility of loss can be especially problematic. It is when there is uncertainty about the occurrence of a loss that risk becomes an important problem. Choice (b) is incorrect because it defines the objective risk. Choice (c) is incorrect because it defines the probability. Choice (d) is incorrect because it relates contingencies to risks.

Subject Area: Governance, risk, and control knowledge elements—risk management concepts and techniques. Source: CBM, Volume 4.

38. **(c)** Risks can be classified into three types: static versus dynamic, subjective versus objective, and pure versus speculative. Choice (a) is incorrect. It is a partial answer. Choice (b) is incorrect. It is a partial answer. Choice (d) is incorrect. It is a partial answer. Pure risk is a condition in which there is the possibility of loss or no loss only. Peril is the cause of possible loss. Hazard is a condition that creates or increases the probability of loss.

Subject Area: Governance, risk, and control knowledge elements—risk management concepts and techniques. Source: CBM, Volume 4.

39. **(c)** Flowcharts, contract analysis, statistical analysis, on-site inspections, and others are used to identify risks. Financial engineering is used to reduce financial risk. This includes options, calls, and puts. Choice (a) is incorrect. Contract analysis is used to identify risks. Choice (b) is incorrect. Statistical analysis is used to identify risks. Choice (d) is incorrect. On-site inspections provide a direct observation of activities and are used to identify risks.

Subject Area: Governance, risk, and control knowledge elements—risk management concepts and techniques. Source: CBM, Volume 4.

40. **(a)** This question is based on probability calculation, which ranges from 0 to 1. The probability of an employee being injured is defined as the chance of injury in terms of number of injuries divided by the number of employees. 5/30 equals 0.1667. Choice (b) is incorrect. It multiplies the 0.1667 with 100, resulting in 16.67. Choice (c) is incorrect. It misplaces the decimal point, resulting in 6.67. Choice (d) is incorrect. It multiplies 0.1667 with 10 resulting in 1.67.

Subject Area: Governance, risk, and control knowledge elements—risk management concepts and techniques. Source: CBM, Volume 4.

41. **(c)** The expected value is defined as the probability of loss multiplied by the amount of loss. 0.06 × \$700 + 0.07 × \$3,000 + 0.02 × \$2,500 + 0.13 × \$950 + 0.13 × \$1,000 = \$42 + \$210 + \$50 + \$123.5 + \$130 = \$555.5. Choice (a) is incorrect. It forgets to add \$50, resulting in \$500.5. Choice (b) is incorrect. It forgets to add \$123.5, resulting in 432.0. Choice (d) is incorrect. It forgets to add \$42, resulting in \$513.5.

Subject Area: Governance, risk, and control knowledge elements—risk management concepts and techniques. Source: CBM, Volume 4.

42. **(c)** Common methods of loss control include reducing the probability of losses or decreasing the cost of losses that do occur. Probability of losses is related to frequency and severity. Cost reduction is also a method of controlling losses. Choice (a) is incorrect because risk retention, risk avoidance, and risk transfer are risk-management techniques focusing on risk financing methods. Risk avoidance is different from loss control, because the firm or individual is sill engaging in operations that gave rise to particular risks. Choice (b) is incorrect because self-insurance, diversification, and risk transfer are not loss control methods. Instead, they are risk financing methods. Choice (d) is incorrect because it mixes both correct and incorrect answers.

Subject Area: Governance, risk, and control knowledge elements—risk management concepts and techniques. Source: CBM, Volume 4.

43. **(c)** Self-insurance by a firm is possible and feasible when it has accurate records or has access to satisfactory statistics to enable it to make good estimate of expected losses. The general financial condition of the firm should be satisfactory and the firm's management must be willing and able to deal with large and unusual losses. Choice (a) is incorrect because a reserve fund may not be enough for large losses. Choice (b) is incorrect because it is a necessary element of self-insurance. Choice (d) is incorrect because self-insurance does not require the creation of a subsidiary company.

Subject Area: Governance, risk, and control knowledge elements—risk management concepts and techniques. Source: CBM, Volume 4.

44. **(b)** The most widely used form of risk transfer is insurance. Choice (a) is incorrect because risk retention is a technique for managing risk and does not involve insurance. Choice (c) is incorrect because risk avoidance is best if it can be done and does not involve insurance. Choice (d) is incorrect because loss control involves risk reduction or risk mitigation and does not involve insurance.

Subject Area: Governance, risk, and control knowledge elements—risk management concepts and techniques. Source: CBM, Volume 4.

45. **(d)** As a rule, risk retention is optimal for losses that have a low expected severity, with the rule becoming especially appropriate when expected frequency is high. Another general guideline applies to risks that have a low expected frequency but a high potential severity. In this situation, risk transfer often is the optimal choice. Finally, when losses have both high expected severity and high expected frequency, it is likely that risk transfer, risk retention, and loss control all will need to be used in varying degrees. Choice (a) is incorrect because the degree of diversification is not related to frequency or severity. Choice (b) is incorrect because it is an example of risk retention. Choice (c) is incorrect because it is an example of risk avoidance.

Subject Area: Governance, risk, and control knowledge elements—risk management concepts and techniques. Source: CBM, Volume 4.

46. **(c)** Incorporating an organization is an example of risk transfer. The other three choices are examples of risk retention. Choice (a) is incorrect because the use of credit is an example of risk retention. Choice (b) is incorrect because use of reserve fund is an example of risk retention. Choice (d) is incorrect because self-insurance is an example of risk retention.

Subject Area: Governance, risk, and control knowledge elements—risk management concepts and techniques. Source: CBM, Volume 4.

47. **(a)** The following conditions are suggestive of the types of situations where self-insurance by a business is both possible and feasible: (1) The firm should have a sufficient number of objects so situated that they are not subject to simultaneous destruction; (2) The firm must have accurate records or have access to satisfactory statistics to enable it to make good estimates of expected losses; (3) The firm must make arrangements for administering the plan and managing the self-insurance fund; and (4) The general financial condition of the firm should be satisfactory, and the firm's management must be willing and able to deal with large and unusual losses. Choices (b), (c), and (d) are incorrect because each is one of the conditions for a self-insurance.

Subject Area: Governance, risk, and control knowledge elements—risk management concepts and techniques. Source: CBM, Volume 4.

48. **(a)** Captive insurers combine risk retention and risk transfer. Captive insurers is a form of funded risk retention. Choice (b) is incorrect because risk mapping is not an example of captive insurer. Choice (c) is incorrect because risk mapping and risk profiling are the same. Choice (d) is incorrect because risk profiling is not part of captive insurer.

Subject Area: Governance, risk, and control knowledge elements—risk management concepts and techniques. Source: CBM, Volume 4.

49. **(b)** Using a disclaimer of warranties clause on product packaging is an example of risk avoidance. Choice (a) is incorrect because self-insurance is an example of risk retention. Choice (c) is incorrect because unplanned retention is an example of risk retention. Choice (d) is incorrect because use of a reserve fund is an example of risk retention. Risk retention can be planned or unplanned, funded or unfunded. Self-insurance and reserve funds are examples of risk retention.

Subject Area: Governance, risk, and control knowledge elements—risk management concepts and techniques. Source: CBM, Volume 4.

50. **(c)** The steps for selecting among available risk-management techniques for a given situation may be summarized as: (1) avoid risks if possible, (2) implement appropriate loss control measures, and (3) select the optimal mix of risk retention and risk transfer. Choice (a) is incorrect because it is the second step. Choice (b) is incorrect because it is the third step. Choice (d) is incorrect because it is a part of the third step.

Subject Area: Governance, risk, and control knowledge elements—risk management concepts and techniques. Source: CBM, Volume 4.

51. **(c)** Self-insurance is an example of risk retention. Risk transfer methods include diversification, hedging, and hold-harmless agreements. Choice (a) is incorrect because diversification is an example of risk transfer. Choice (b) is incorrect because hedging is an example of risk transfer. Choice (d) is incorrect because hold-harmless agreement is an example of risk transfer.

Subject Area: Governance, risk, and control knowledge elements—risk management concepts and techniques. Source: CBM, Volume 4.

52. **(c)** Both capital budgeting and statistical procedures may be used in selecting an appropriate retention level (a mix consisting of risk retention and transfer), with insurance purchased for losses in excess of that level. Choice (a) is incorrect because capital budgeting and statistical analysis can be used in risk management. Choice (b) is incorrect because deductibles and self-insurance can be used together. Choice (d) is incorrect because risk transfer is more than insurance.

Subject Area: Governance, risk, and control knowledge elements—risk management concepts and techniques. Source: CBM, Volume 4.

53. **(d)** Severity reduction is used to manage objective risk due to its quantitative nature. Because objective and subjective risks are often both present in the same situation, some consideration must also be given to managing subjective risk. In one sense, the techniques applied to objective risk should also affect subjective risk. Choice (a) is incorrect because more information is obtained to manage subjective risk. Choice (b) is incorrect because group discussion is used to manage subjective risk due to its consensus approach. Choice (c) is incorrect. If risks have been systematically identified and analyzed, and if decisions have been made regarding the appropriate methods for dealing with those risks, then in most cases subjective risk can be expected to decrease.

Subject Area: Governance, risk, and control knowledge elements—risk management concepts and techniques. Source: CBM, Volume 4.

54. **(b)** What constitutes "high" and "low" loss frequency and severity must be established on an individual basis. What is low loss severity for a multimillion-dollar company may be quite high for a small firm or an individual. In this regard, concepts such as total assets, net worth, and expected future income all are relevant. Choice (a) is incorrect because the degree of loss frequency and severity are not the same for all firms. Choice (c) is incorrect because they are not identifiable by industry standards. Choice (d) is incorrect because they are important when considering risk avoidance.

Subject Area: Governance, risk, and control knowledge elements—risk management concepts and techniques. Source: CBM, Volume 4.

55. **(d)** Because in many situations both risk retention and risk transfer will be used in varying degrees, it is important to determine the appropriate mix of these two risk-management techniques. Both capital budgeting methods and statistical procedures may be used in selecting an appropriate retention level, with insurance purchased for losses in excess of that level. Choice (a) is incorrect because insurance is not needed if risk can be avoided. Choice (b) is incorrect because short-term assets are not relevant, but total assets are. Choice (c) is incorrect because expected losses come into play in computing frequency and severity levels.

Subject Area: Governance, risk, and control knowledge elements—risk management concepts and techniques. Source: CBM, Volume 4.

56. (b) Self-insurance can be contracted out to a third-party administrator so there is no need to have an in-house staff to administer it. The following conditions are suggestive of the types of situations where self-insurance by a business is both possible and feasible: (1) The firm should have a sufficient number of objects so situated that they are not subject to simultaneous destruction; (2) The firm must have accurate records or have access to satisfactory statistics to enable it to make good estimates of expected losses; (3) The firm must make arrangements for administering the plan and managing the self-insurance fund; and (4) The general financial condition of the firm should be satisfactory, and the firm's management must be willing and able to deal with large and unusual losses. Choices (a), (c), and (d) are incorrect because each is one of the conditions for a self-insurance.

Subject Area: Governance, risk, and control knowledge elements—risk management concepts and techniques. Source: CBM, Volume 4.

Control Implications of Different Structures and Styles

57. (c) A matrix organizational structure combines functional and product departmentalization, creates a dual reporting structure, and is optimal where product groups are necessary. Choice (a) is incorrect. A professional bureaucracy is a structure with high complexity and low formalization in which professionals are required. Choice (b) is incorrect. A mechanistic structure is one that is highly formalized and standardized and that has no dual authority structure. It is not the optimal structure. Choice (d) is incorrect. In a machine bureaucratic structure, rules and regulations permeate the entire structure and tasks are highly routine.

Subject Area: Governance, risk, and control knowledge elements—control implications of different structures and styles. Source: CIA 597, III-2.

58. (a) This principle applies to both types of organizational structure (items I and III). Choice (b) is incorrect. Item IV is incorrect. This principle does not apply in a hierarchical organization. Choice (c) is incorrect. Item II is incorrect. This principle does not apply in an open organization. Choice (d) is incorrect. See choice (b).

Subject Area: Governance, risk, and control knowledge elements—control implications of different structures and styles. Source: CIA 597, III-7.

59. (c) Mass production would be best matched with a mechanistic, highly formalized structure. Choice (a) is incorrect. Mass production technology should not be matched with an organic structure. Choice (b) is incorrect. Matrix is not a type of structure, but rather a type of departmentalization and should not be used with mass production.

Choice (d) is incorrect. There is no such thing as integrated structure, and integration is not conducive to mass production.

Subject Area: Governance, risk, and control knowledge elements—control implications of different structures and styles. Source: CIA 1196, III-3.

60. (a) Routine tasks are conducive to formalized structure. Choice (b) is incorrect. Routine tasks are conducive to centralization. Choice (c) is incorrect. Routine tasks are conducive to mechanistic, not organic, structures. Choice (d) is incorrect. Job satisfaction is often low in tasks that are routine and repetitive.

Subject Area: Governance, risk, and control knowledge elements—control implications of different structures and styles. Source: CIA 1196, III-4.

61. (b) The strength of a tendency to act in a certain way depends on the strength of an expectation that an act will be followed by a given outcome. Choice (a) is incorrect. In equity theory, the employees compare their job inputs and outcomes with others and then respond to eliminate inequities. Choice (c) is incorrect. Goal-setting theory postulates that specific and difficult goals lead to higher performance. Choice (d) is incorrect. Reinforcement theory states that behavior is a function of its consequences.

Subject Area: Governance, risk, and control knowledge elements—control implications of different structures and styles. Source: CIA 1196, II-12.

62. (c) If the people do not want to work, grow, and achieve, the manager will be unsuccessful when using this approach. Choice (a) is incorrect. The autocratic model is based on pure power. Choice (b) is incorrect. The custodial model depends on material rewards for staff. Choice (d) is incorrect. The manager's beliefs alone will not be enough.

Subject Area: Governance, risk, and control knowledge elements—control implications of different structures and styles. Source: CIA 1196, II-26.

63. (d) This structure allows authority to flow both vertically and horizontally. Choice (a) is incorrect. This structure is designed to maximize unity of command by giving only line managers the authority to make decisions affecting those in their chain of command. Choice (b) is incorrect. This is merely a method of dividing an organization into more homogeneous units to better serve specific markets. Choice (c) is incorrect. A centralized structure need not have unity-of-command problems if management is organized in a line and staff fashion.

Subject Area: Governance, risk, and control knowledge elements—control implications of different structures and styles. Source: CIA 1196, II-29 and 1190, III-6.

64. (d) This is the basis for Theory Y. Choices (a) and (b) are incorrect. They are traditional theories. Choice (c) is incorrect. This relates to Barnard and systems theory.

Subject Area: Governance, risk, and control knowledge elements—control implications of different structures and styles. Source: CIA 590, III-10.

65. (b) Matrix structures are found in construction and aerospace firms that work on large projects. Choice (a) is incorrect. Lines of authority are vertical in this situation, with staff positions acting as advisors. Choice (c) is incorrect. Under this format, staff's positions can temporarily assume line functions. Choice (d) is incorrect. Authority is hierarchical in this structure.

Subject Area: Governance, risk, and control knowledge elements—control implications of different structures and styles. Source: CIA 590, III-8.

66. (a) The chain of command is called vertical hierarchy while the division of labor is called horizontal specialization. Choice (b) is incorrect. Staff and line does not discuss the chain of command. Choice (c) is incorrect. Departmentalization does not discuss chain of command. Choice (d) is incorrect. The answer does not discuss chain of command.

Subject Area: Governance, risk, and control knowledge elements—control implications of different structures and styles. Source: CIA 590, III-15.

67. (c) The characteristics listed are typical of a bureaucracy as defined by Weber. Choice (a) is incorrect. A hierarchy of authority implies top-down authority. Choice (b) is incorrect. Synergy is a characteristic of open systems. It results when components combine to form more than their sum. Choice (d) is incorrect. Equifinality is a characteristic of open systems in which the same result is achieved through different means.

Subject Area: Governance, risk, and control knowledge elements—control implications of different structures and styles. Source: CIA 1190, III-3.

68. (b) These are all symptoms of a dysfunctional bureaucracy. Choices (a), (c), and (d) are incorrect. These are all symptoms of a dysfunctional bureaucracy.

Subject Area: Governance, risk, and control knowledge elements—control implications of different structures and styles. Source: CIA 1196, III-29.

69. (c) This refers to the vertical depth of the organizational hierarchy. Choice (a) is incorrect. This refers to the degree of geographic separation between facilities and personnel. Choice (b) is incorrect. This refers to the degree of job standardization through descriptions and rules. Choice (d) is incorrect. This term refers to the variety of jobs within an organization that require specialized knowledge or skills.

Subject Area: Governance, risk, and control knowledge elements—control implications of different structures and styles. Source: CIA 596, III-4.

70. (c) Innovative strategy organizations operate best with a loose structure, low division of labor, and low formalization. Choice (a) is incorrect. A mechanistic structure is appropriate for organizations focusing on cost minimization through tight controls, extensive division of labor, and high formalization. Choice (b) is incorrect. This is not a true structural option. Imitative strategies are best suited to a mechanistic and organic structure. Choice (d) is a distracter.

Subject Area: Governance, risk, and control knowledge elements—control implications of different structures and styles. Source: CIA 596, III-15.

71. (a) A mechanistic structure is appropriate for organizations focusing on cost minimization through tight controls, extensive division of labor, and high formalization. Choice (b) is incorrect. This is not a true structural option. Imitative strategies are best suited to a mechanistic and organic structure. Choice (c) is incorrect. An organic structure exhibits an innovative strategy and operates best with a loose structure, low division of labor, and low formalization. Choice (d) is incorrect. It is a distracter.

Subject Area: Governance, risk, and control knowledge elements—control implications of different structures and styles. Source: CIA 596, III-16.

72. (b) In a matrix organization, project managers may "borrow specialists from line managers..." Choice (a) is incorrect. In a bureaucracy, each subordinate reports to only a single manager. Choice (c) is incorrect. Departmental organization structures represent the "typical organization" with unified and thus clear-cut single lines of authority. Choice (d) is incorrect. Mechanistic organization structure is another term referring to bureaucracy.

Subject Area: Governance, risk, and control knowledge elements—control implications of different structures and styles. Source: CIA 595, III-9.

73. (a) The key to the contingency approach is that different types of organization structures are appropriate in different situations or external environments. Choice (b) is incorrect. Open systems involve a continual interaction between the organization and its external environment. Choice (c) is incorrect. It is based on the belief that a single management process can be applied in all organizations. Choice (d) is incorrect. The emphasis is on principles distilled from past organizational experience.

Subject Area: Governance, risk, and control knowledge elements—control implications of different structures and styles. Source: CIA 1194, III-1.

74. (a) The operational approach serves to make work as efficient as possible, and is characterized by technical and quantitative terms. Choice (b) is incorrect. The behavioral approach is humanistic, emphasizing the manager's ability to understand and work with people. Choice (c) is incorrect. The systems approach recognizes the many organizational and environmental variables in the manager's role and responsibilities. Choice (d) is incorrect. The contingency approach advocates research to determine which managerial practices and techniques are appropriate in specific situations.

Subject Area: Governance, risk, and control knowledge elements—control implications of different structures and styles. Source: CIA 1194, III-5.

75. (d) This advantage is normally associated with decentralized organizations. Choice (a) is incorrect. Centralized organizations are generally easier to control. Choice (b) is incorrect. This advantage is usually associated with centralized organizations. Choice (c) is incorrect. The number of managers is not related to the degree of centralization or decentralization but is a function of the "span of control."

Subject Area: Governance, risk, and control knowledge elements—control implications of different structures and styles. Source: CIA 1194, III-9.

76. (d) Divisional organization structure is appropriate for large firms operating in different markets and different regions with many business units. Each business unit can be a separate division. Choice (a) is incorrect because it is suitable for many traditional firms as it avoids duplication of effort and allows or specialization of tasks and simplified training. Choice (b) is incorrect because it is appropriate for multiproduct and multiline firms. Choice (c) is suitable for company's heavily engaged in research and development and project management work.

Subject Area: Governance, risk, and control knowledge elements—control implications of different structures and styles. Source: Author.

77. (d) A high division of labor results in compartmentalization. Strict adherence to unity of command results in formal relationships. Choices (a), (b), and (c) are incorrect because they are inappropriate or incompatible combinations. For example, compartmentalization cannot be informal in nature.

Subject Area: Governance, risk, and control knowledge elements—control implications of different structures and styles. Source: CIA 1195, III-21.

78. (a) For the professionals to accomplish their jobs, they must be afforded substantial autonomy. Choice (b) is incorrect. The machine bureaucracy can accomplish routine tasks in a highly efficient manner. A professional bureaucracy can accomplish its tasks very efficiently also. Choice (c) is incorrect. Both organization structures thrive on rules. Choice (d) is incorrect. This is a characteristic of both organization structures.

Subject Area: Governance, risk, and control knowledge elements—control implications of different structures and styles. Source: CIA 1195, III-26.

79. (b) Employees working in a matrix organization will have two supervisors and two job duties. Choices (a), (c), and (d) are incorrect. None of them meets the criteria described.

Subject Area: Governance, risk, and control knowledge elements—control implications of different structures and styles. Source: CIA 1190, III-9.

80. (b) Esteem addresses the self-respect and self-worth of an individual. Choice (a) is incorrect. This is a lower-level need, including the needs for food, water, and sleep. Choice (c) is incorrect. This relates to the desire to belong with others. Choice (d) is incorrect. Safety needs are just above the physiological needs and deal with safety from the elements and from enemies.

Subject Area: Governance, risk, and control knowledge elements—control implications of different structures and styles. Source: CIA 1190, III-12.

81. (b) Choice (b) recognizes that different organizational structures and processes are required for effectiveness in different kinds of environments. Choice (a) is incorrect. It describes a mechanistic approach. Choice (c) is incorrect. It basically describes an organic approach but is not the "best" answer. Choice (d) is incorrect. It describes a matrix organization.

Subject Area: Governance, risk, and control knowledge elements—control implications of different structures and styles. Source: CIA 1190, III-60.

82. (d) This scenario is essentially a definition of the contingency approach to management. Choice (a) is incorrect. Systems theory is based on the premise that everything is a component of a larger, interdependent system. Choice (b) is incorrect. This theory focuses on the causes of human work behavior and how management techniques can best influence positive results. Choice (c) is incorrect. Operations theory frequently uses complex models and other quantitative techniques to simulate and predict the workings of production systems.

Subject Area: Governance, risk, and control knowledge elements—control implications of different structures and styles. Source: CIA 590, III-1.

83. (a) In order for a flat structure to be successful, employees must be able to work unsupervised much of the time since the manager with many employees has little time for each one. Choice (b) is incorrect. Geographically dispersed work areas are very difficult to control by a manager with many subordinates. Choice (c) is incorrect. Tasks that are highly complex and varied are more appropriate for narrow spans. Choice (d) is incorrect. Narrow spans are more appropriate where the similarity of work performed by subordinates is identical or slightly different.

Subject Area: Governance, risk, and control knowledge elements—control implications of different structures and styles. Source: CIA 594, III-79.

84. (a) It is not a coordinating mechanism; it helps create the need for coordination. Choices (b), (c), and (d) are incorrect. Each choice is an example of coordinating mechanisms.

Subject Area: Governance, risk, and control knowledge elements—control implications of different structures and styles. Source: CIA 594, III-82.

85. (c) Matrix can work regardless of whether the product life cycle is long or short. Choice (a) is incorrect. True, members are assigned to work groups based on their specialization. Choice (b) is incorrect. True, members are also organized around specific products/projects. Choice (d) is incorrect. True, the dual reporting systems in matrix structures enhance these risks.

Subject Area: Governance, risk, and control knowledge elements—control implications of different structures and styles. Source: CIA 594, III-84.

86. (a) In the contingency view, the manager's alternative course of action depends on his or her assessment of various situational variables. In this case, responding to a change in the external environment. Choice (b) is incorrect. The systems view is a way looking at organizations and assumes that all organizations are systems with common characteristics. This answer is a good distracter since an "open" system interacts with its environment. Choice (c) is incorrect. The universality view would call for a rigid, inflexible structure regardless of the external environment. Choice (d) is incorrect. The classical view is an early theory of management and should include the universality concept.

Subject Area: Governance, risk, and control knowledge elements—control implications of different structures and styles. Source: CIA 591, III-4.

87. (d) The focus of the operational approach is on improving efficiency and reducing waste. Over the years this approach has been identified with the fields of scientific management, management science, operations research, and operations management. Choice (a) is incorrect. The central focus of the behavioral approach is on the human resource and success is largely dependent on the manager's ability to understand and work with people. Choice (b) is incorrect. The focus of the systems approach is on the total environment of the organization, especially the external component and the effect it has upon the success of the organization.

Choice (c) is incorrect. The focus of the contingency approach is on making adjustments in management decisions making that are based on changes in situational variables.

Subject Area: Governance, risk, and control knowledge elements—control implications of different structures and styles. Source: CIA 593, III-4.

88. (c) This is an example of the use of the functional form of departmentalization. Choice (a) is incorrect. This is an example of a line rather than staff activity. Further, the line/staff question is an example of the delegation of authority rather than an example of departmentalization. Choice (b) is incorrect. The matrix form of departmentalization is a compromise between the functional and product forms of departmentalization. Choice (d) is incorrect. The project form of departmentalization is used for specific organizational tasks that are usually large, experimental, or unique.

Subject Area: Governance, risk, and control knowledge elements—control implications of different structures and styles. Source: CIA 593, III-9.

89. (d) Harmonious efforts (esprit de corps) make this the correct choice according to Fayol's universal principles of management. Choice (a) is incorrect because equity refers to fairness and justice. Choice (b) is incorrect because unity of direction refers to coordinated efforts in same direction. Choice (c) is incorrect because initiative refers to formulating and executing plans.

Subject Area: Governance, risk, and control knowledge elements—control implications of different structures and styles. Source: CIA 1192, III-4.

90. (d) This answer represents a completely different style of thinking about organizations. The assumption is that managers affect, and in turn are affected by, many other organizational and environmental variables. Choice (a) is incorrect. The universal process approach is also known as the universalist or functional approach. This approach assumes the parts of an organization operate independently and that "the whole is equal to the sum of its parts." Choice (b) is incorrect. The operational approach is a system of management that focuses on production oriented issues. An early form of this approach is scientific management. This approach also assumes the parts of an organization operate independently and that "the whole is equal to the sum of its parts." Choice (c) is incorrect. The behavioral approach is based on the belief that people deserve to be the central focus of organized activity. The assumptions of this approach are the same as the first two answers.

Subject Area: Governance, risk, and control knowledge elements—control implications of different structures and styles. Source: CIA 592, III-1.

91. (a) The contingency approach believes that the relationships between management techniques and situations can be categorized and an appropriate course of action selected depending on the outcome of the analysis. Choice (b) is incorrect. This answer refers only to researchers who have done work in the area. Choice (c) is incorrect. The behavioral approach is not necessarily situational in nature. Choice (d) is incorrect. An operational management technique deals with actual management practice rather than research.

Subject Area: Governance, risk, and control knowledge elements—control implications of different structures and styles. Source: CIA 592, III-2.

92. (d) Since each project might have its own situational and technical demands as well as budget and profit targets, this type of business is well suited to the matrix structure. Choice (a) is incorrect. A manufacturer of this type would probably adopt a functional (marketing, production, engineering, etc.) structure. Choice (b) is incorrect. A national grocer would probably use a regional or geographic structure. Choice (c) is incorrect. The most appropriate type of structure for this type of business would probably a divisional structure (new car sales, used car sales, service, etc.).

Subject Area: Governance, risk, and control knowledge elements—control implications of different structures and styles. Source: CIA 1191, III-7.

93. (c) The scalar chain requires that the chain of command be followed. Choice (a) is incorrect. This principle deals with the proper placement of materials and personnel. Choice (b) is incorrect. This principle deals with specialization of labor to achieve organizational success. Choice (d) is incorrect. This principle requires the focus of all efforts in the same direction.

Subject Area: Governance, risk, and control knowledge elements—control implications of different structures and styles. Source: CIA 592, III-4.

94. (b) This would give the auditor experience as a spokesperson for the audit department and as a horizontal link with other areas. Choice (a) is incorrect. These individuals are senior to the auditor, who would be perceived as lacking authority. Choice (c) is incorrect. The auditor does not have the knowledge or experience to present a reasonably comprehensive budget. This role cannot be delegated so far down the chain of command. Choice (d) is incorrect. This task resides solely with the audit director and cannot be delegated.

Subject Area: Governance, risk, and control knowledge elements—control implications of different structures and styles. Source: CIA 592, III-5.

95. (b) Choice (b) reflects the operational approach, which stresses efficiency. Choice (a) is incorrect. It reflects the universal approach to management. Choice (c) is incorrect. It reflects the behavioral approach. Choice (d) is incorrect. It reflects the systems approach to management.

Subject Area: Governance, risk, and control knowledge elements—control implications of different structures and styles. Source: CIA 1192, III-5.

96. (c) Choice (c) reflects the behavioral approach. Choice (a) is incorrect. It reflects the universal approach to management. Choice (b) is incorrect. It reflects the operational approach, which makes people its control focus. Choice (d) is incorrect. It reflects the systems approach to management.

Subject Area: Governance, risk, and control knowledge elements—control implications of different structures and styles. Source: CIA 1192, III-6.

97. (b) Vertical hierarchy and horizontal specialization are the two dimensions of all organization charts. Choice (a) is incorrect. While organization charts indicate some of the relationships requiring communication, by no means does an organization chart show all lines of communication in an organization. Choice (c) is incorrect. While in most cases the more important people (to the mission of the organization) are listed at the top of an organization chart, it is possible, even likely, that a person with lower organizational rank might be shown at a higher position on the chart. For example, an administrative assistant to the president might be shown nearer the top of the chart than the vice president of sales. Choice (d) is incorrect. See choices (a) and (c).

Subject Area: Governance, risk, and control knowledge elements—control implications of different structures and styles. Source: CIA 1192, III-7.

98. (c) These conditions support a wide span of control. Choice (a) is incorrect. While a manager under these conditions would be able to supervise a large number of employees, there is an upper limit. Choice (b) is incorrect. The conditions described in the stem support a wide span rather than a narrow span. Choice (d) is incorrect. Geographical dispersion would decrease the span of control rather than increase it.

Subject Area: Governance, risk, and control knowledge elements—control implications of different structures and styles. Source: CIA 1192, III-9.

99. (c) The division of labor (horizontal dimension) indicates who does what, and the chain of command (vertical dimension) shows who reports to whom. It shows formal structure only. Choice (a) is incorrect. Informal organization not shown. Choice (b) is incorrect. Responsibility is not defined on the chart. Choice (d) is incorrect. Both refer to the vertical dimension.

Subject Area: Governance, risk, and control knowledge elements—control implications of different structures and styles. Source: CIA 592, III-11.

100. (c) A mutual benefit organization is one in which individuals join together strictly in pursuit of self-interests. Choice (a) is incorrect. The organization described is not a business; it is not profit seeking. Choice (b) is incorrect. The organization described provides no direct service to customers. Choice (d) is incorrect. A commonweal organization offers standardized service to all members of a given population, not true of the organization described here.

Subject Area: Governance, risk, and control knowledge elements—control implications of different structures and styles. Source: CIA 592, III-12.

101. (c) Networking is the interaction of persons of essentially equal status for the purpose of information transfer or support. Choice (a) is incorrect. Synthesis perspective refers to the struggle between stability and change in a society. Choice (b) is incorrect. Decentralization refers to the delegation of decision-making authority. Choice (d) is incorrect. Self-reliance defines a person's conviction that self-help is preferable to that of the institution.

Subject Area: Governance, risk, and control knowledge elements—control implications of different structures and styles. Source: CIA 1191, III-2.

102. (d) The number of people in an organization has no impact on the number of individuals that a manager can control effectively. Choice (a) is incorrect. Managers who can contact subordinates frequently are able to control more people than those who have relatively infrequent contact with subordinates. Choice (b) is incorrect. Managers who delegate authority have more time to control the subordinates who report to them. These individuals can therefore supervise more people than managers who prefer not to delegate authority. Choice (c) is incorrect. Managers who have received effective training and are skillful communicators are equipped to control more individuals than managers who are untrained and/or have deficient communication skills.

Subject Area: Governance, risk, and control knowledge elements—control implications of different structures and styles. Source: CIA 1191, III-3.

103. (a) Organization by function is common to almost all firms at some level. It avoids duplication of effort and allows for specialization and supplied training. Choice (b) is incorrect. Product departmentalization is appropriate for multiline firms. Choice (c) is incorrect. Matrix organization is used in research and development and project management. Choice (d) is incorrect. Divisional organization is appropriate for large firms.

Subject Area: Governance, risk, and control knowledge elements—control implications of different structures and styles. Source: CIA 597, III-9.

104. (a) As organizations grow, their strategies become more ambitious and elaborate. Companies often expand their activities within their industry. Choice (b) is incorrect. Vertical integration depends on the industry. Larger organizations normally implement a decentralized (divisional) strategy. Choice (c) is incorrect. The change is from a single product line to a more diverse set of products. Choice (d) is incorrect. Structures follow strategies; strategies do not follow structures.

Subject Area: Governance, risk, and control knowledge elements—control implications of different structures and styles. Source: CIA 1196, III-6.

105. (c) A cost-minimization strategy tightly controls costs, refrains from incurring unnecessary innovation or marketing expenses, and cuts prices in selling a discount product. This describes the strategy pursued by the sellers of generic grocery products. Choice (a) is incorrect. Innovation minimization is not a type of strategy. An innovation strategy is one type that emphasizes the introduction of new products or services, but it does not describe discount stores or sellers of generic grocery products. Choice (b) is incorrect. Imitation strategy describes one such as the imitator of designer styles, a strategy seeking to move into new products only after their viability has been proven elsewhere. Choice (d) is incorrect. There is no strategy described as initiation strategy.

Subject Area: Governance, risk, and control knowledge elements—control implications of different structures and styles. Source: CIA 1196, III-7.

106. (c) The four elements are part of the eight attributes of excellence as defined in Peters and Waterman's book *In Search of Excellence.* Choice (a) is incorrect. The attributes listed place an emphasis of people over technology. Choice (b) is incorrect. A contingency approach would suggest that what is important for any business depends on a number of internal and external factors. Choice (d) is incorrect. Continuous strategic planning is not a major focus of such an organization.

Subject Area: Governance, risk, and control knowledge elements—control implications of different structures and styles. Source: CIA 1196, III-21.

107. (d) Cutting costs, per se, is the least important issue. Payoff, or return on costs, is a more relevant strategic consideration. Choice (a) is incorrect. Long-range business plans are a central aspect of strategic decisions. Choice (b) is incorrect. Support of daily business operations is an important aspect of strategic decisions. Choice (c) is incorrect. Measurement of plan fulfillment is essential to management's evaluation of the system.

Subject Area: Governance, risk, and control knowledge elements—control implications of different structures and styles. Source: CIA 1194, III-20.

108. (d) The size-structure relationship may be linear at some point, but it will not remain linear indefinitely. Size affects structure at a decreasing rate. Choice (a) is incorrect. Size affects structure at a decreasing rate. Choice (b) is incorrect. The organization will become fixed once it has around 2,000 employees. Choice (c) is incorrect. See choice (d).

Subject Area: Governance, risk, and control knowledge elements—control implications of different structures and styles. Source: CIA 1195, III-24.

109. (b) Since each division is essentially a self-contained organization, there is substantial duplication of functions compared to more centralized structures. Choice (a) is incorrect. The small size and simplicity of these organizations generally precludes significant inefficiency in the use of resources. Choices (c) and (d) are incorrect. The central tendencies of a bureaucracy minimize the duplication of functions found in a divisional structure.

Subject Area: Governance, risk, and control knowledge elements—control implications of different structures and styles. Source: CIA 1195, III-25.

110. (a) These are positive characteristics that should be encouraged. Choice (b) is incorrect. Taking personal responsibility for reducing overhead is a positive characteristic. However, seeking incremental budget increases is a frequently used budget game and should be discouraged. Choice (c) is incorrect. Imagination in addressing direct and indirect costs should be encouraged, but goal displacement is a management problem that is exhibited when the means become more important then the ends. Choice (d) is incorrect. Seeking opportunities for cost synergy is a good managerial characteristic. However, trying hard to keep the prior budget intact is a budget game that should be discouraged.

Subject Area: Governance, risk, and control knowledge elements—control implications of different structures and styles. Source: CIA 595, III-13.

111. (c) The purpose of a strategic business unit (SBU) is to allow for entrepreneurial risk taking, which is generally limited by the parent organization's bureaucratic structure and concomitant reluctance to take risks. Choice (a) is incorrect. SBUs should not impact the market of the parent company. Choice (b) is incorrect. SBUs must operate as profit centers in order to provide a measure of their effectiveness independent of the original organization. Choice (d) is incorrect. The requirement of coping effectively with competition means that the SBU is a more appropriately sized unit for dealing with competition (as opposed to the larger parent, which makes decisions more slowly and hence less competitively).

Subject Area: Governance, risk, and control knowledge elements—control implications of different structures and styles. Source: CIA 596, III-31.

112. (a) It is the correct definition of matrix organization, which is applicable to new product management project, system development project, software package evaluation, and so on. Choice (b) is incorrect. The basic functional structure is not decentralized. Choice (c) is incorrect. The basic structure described is functional. Choice (d) is incorrect. It is classical, not organic.

Subject Area: Governance, risk, and control knowledge elements—control implications of different structures and styles. Source: CIA 1192, III-3.

113. (c) Product-service organizations use products or services provided by the firm as the unifying theme in organizing. Under this option, functions are subordinate to product grouping. Choice (a) is incorrect. Functional departmentalization is when the major activities of a firm are organized by function (marketing, finance, etc.) and products or services are subordinate to the functional level. Choice (b) is incorrect. "Organic" is not a method of departmentalization. Instead it is a category of organizations, which is defined as being fluid and flexible in structure. Choice (d) is incorrect. The term "strategic business unit" is not a type of departmentalization. However, this answer is a good distracter because the semiautonomous units created may be treated as SBUs in the planning process.

Subject Area: Governance, risk, and control knowledge elements—control implications of different structures and styles. Source: CIA 1192, III-8.

114. (b) Complex environments are best matched with an organic firm structure. Choice (a) is incorrect. Dynamic environments are best matched with an organic firm structure. Choice (c) is incorrect. Stable environments are best matched with a mechanistic firm structure. Choice (d) is incorrect. Scarce environments are best matched with an organic firm structure.

Subject Area: Governance, risk, and control knowledge elements—control implications of different structures and styles. Source: CIA 594, III-52.

115. (d) This structure allows authority to flow both vertically and horizontally. Choice (a) is incorrect. This structure is designed to maximize unity of command by giving only line managers the authority to make decisions affecting those in their chain of command. Choice (b) is incorrect. This is merely a method of dividing an organization into more homogeneous units to better serve specific markets. Choice (c) is incorrect. A centralized structure need not have unity-of-command problems if management is organized in a line and staff fashion.

Subject Area: Governance, risk, and control knowledge elements—control implications of different structures and styles. Source: CIA 594, II-22.

116. (b) This is the best description of a vertically integrated company. Choice (a) is incorrect. It is a company that owns all of its production facilities and still depend on suppliers for component parts. Choice (c) is incorrect. Departmentalization by product or service is the grouping of organizational subsystems that permits extensive authority for a division executive over a given product or product line or over a service or group of services. Choice (d) is incorrect.

A narrow span of control limits the number of subordinates to a minimum that each individual supervises.

Subject Area: Governance, risk, and control knowledge elements—control implications of different structures and styles. Source: CIA 1191, III-4.

Change and Conflict Management

117. (b) Organizational change is defined as the adoption of a new idea or behavior by an organization. Choice (a) is incorrect because organizational development is planned change programs intended to help people and organization function more effectively. Choice (c) is incorrect because organizational structure refers to who reports to whom in the company. Choice (d) is incorrect because organizational intervention refers to management's degree of involvement in the day-to-day operation.

Subject Area: Governance, risk, and control knowledge elements—change and conflict management. Source: Author.

118. (b) Internal forces for change arise from internal activities and decisions. If top managers select a goal of rapid company growth, internal actions will have to be changed first to meet that growth. Choice (a) is incorrect because competitive actions are external actions to a company. Choice (c) is incorrect because external actions include competitive and regulatory actions. Choice (d) is incorrect because environmental actions are external actions.

Subject Area: Governance, risk, and control knowledge elements—change and conflict management. Source: Author.

119. (a) Tuning is the most common, least intense, and least risky type of change. Choice (b) is incorrect. Reorientation change is anticipatory and strategic in scope. Choice (c) is incorrect. Re-creation is most intense and most risky change. Choice (d) is incorrect. Adaptation changes are in reaction to external pressures, events, or problems.

Subject Area: Governance, risk, and control knowledge elements—change and conflict management. Source: Author.

120. (d) Both tuning and adaptation involve incremental change or continuous improvement (kaizen). Choice (a) is incorrect because tuning is a partial answer. Choice (b) is incorrect because reorientation change is anticipatory and strategic in scope. Choice (c) is incorrect because adaptation is a partial answer.

Subject Area: Governance, risk, and control knowledge elements—change and conflict management. Source: Author.

121. (b) Reorientation is anticipatory and strategic change. It is called *frame bending* because the organization is significantly redirected. Choice (a) is incorrect because tuning is anticipatory and incremental change. Choice (c) is incorrect because re-creation is reactive and strategic change. Choice (d) is incorrect because adaptation is reactive and incremental change.

Subject Area: Governance, risk, and control knowledge elements—change and conflict management. Source: Author.

122. (c) Re-creation is reactive and strategic change. It is called *frame breaking* because it puts organizations to competitive pressures. Choice (a) is incorrect because tuning is anticipatory and incremental change. Choice (b) is incorrect because reorientation is anticipatory and strategic change. Choice (d) is incorrect because adaptation is reactive and incremental change.

Subject Area: Governance, risk, and control knowledge elements—change and conflict management. Source: Author.

123. (a) According to Kreitner (*Management*, 9th edition [Boston: Houghton and Mifflin Company, 2004]), there are six strategies for overcoming resistance to change, including education and communication, participation and involvement, facilitation and support, negotiation and agreement, manipulation and co-optation, and explicit and implicit coercion. Education and communication strategy is appropriate because it teaches prevention rather than cure. Choice (b) is incorrect because participation and involvement increase the stake in success and do not prevent the resistance to change. Choice (c) is incorrect because facilitation and support help to reduce fear and anxiety and do not prevent the resistance to change. Choice (d) is incorrect because negotiation and agreement neutralize potential or actual resistance and do not prevent the resistance to change.

Subject Area: Governance, risk, and control knowledge elements—change and conflict management. Source: Author.

124. (b) When management does not have time, they can force employees to go along with a change by threatening them with termination, loss of pay raises, or promotions, transfers, and the like. It uses explicit and implicit coercion techniques. Choice (a) is incorrect because manipulation and co-optation strategies take time to change. Choice (c) is incorrect because facilitation and support help to reduce fear and anxiety and take time to change. Choice (d) is incorrect because negotiation and agreement neutralize potential or actual resistance and take time to change.

Subject Area: Governance, risk, and control knowledge elements—change and conflict management. Source: Author.

125. (c) Organization development (OD) consists of planned efforts or planned changes in an organization's culture. Choices (a) and (b) are incorrect because they are partial answers. Choice (d) is incorrect because frame bending is reorientation while frame breaking is re-creation.

Subject Area: Governance, risk, and control knowledge elements—change and conflict management. Source: Author.

126. (a) The organization development (OD) process consists of three phases, such as unfreezing, change, and refreezing. Diagnosis occurs in the unfreezing phase. Choice (b) is incorrect because intervention occurs in the change phase. Choice (c) is incorrect because follow-up occurs in the refreezing phase. Choice (d) is incorrect because intervention is not one of the phases of OD.

Subject Area: Governance, risk, and control knowledge elements—change and conflict management. Source: Author.

127. (c) Trust is the glue that holds a change effort together in an organization. Usually employees are afraid of change, and trust is the solution. Choice (a) is incorrect because a leader can facilitate change efforts. Choice (b) is incorrect because a manager can implement change efforts.

Choice (d) is incorrect because a change agent turns ideas into actions.

Subject Area: Governance, risk, and control knowledge elements—change and conflict management. Source: Author.

128. (c) Conflict involves incompatible behaviors that make other people less effective and productive. There are two faces of conflict, including competitive and cooperative conflict. There are two sets of tools for managing conflict, including conflict triggers to stimulate conflict and conflict resolution to solve destructive conflict. Choice (a) is incorrect because negative behaviors are not necessarily incompatible behaviors. Choice (b) is incorrect because destructive behaviors are nonproductive. Choice (d) is incorrect because competitive behavior is one face of conflict.

Subject Area: Governance, risk, and control knowledge elements—change and conflict management. Source: Author.

129. (a) According to Kreitner (*Management*, 9th edition [Boston: Houghton and Mifflin Company, 2004]), conflict triggers include ambiguous or overlapping jurisdictions, competition for scarce resources, communication breakdowns, time pressures, unreasonable standards, personality clashes, status differentials, and unrealized expectations. Choice (b) is incorrect because communication trigger is a part of conflict trigger. Choice (c) is incorrect because personality trigger is a part of conflict trigger. Choice (d) is incorrect because time pressure trigger is a part of conflict trigger.

Subject Area: Governance, risk, and control knowledge elements—change and conflict management. Source: Author.

130. (d) This is a long-term solution, which contains the elements needed to counter organizational decline. Choice (a) is incorrect. This response illustrates two of the characteristics of organizational decline: increased centralization of decision making and lack of long-term planning. The exclusive emphasis on short-term results is likely to be counter-productive. Choice (b) is incorrect. Another characteristic of organizational decline is nonprioritized cuts. Downsizing, by itself, rarely turns a company around. Choice (c) is incorrect. This is too crude a method of prioritizing cuts. Reducing staff disproportionately in control functions could have disastrous consequences.

Subject Area: Governance, risk, and control knowledge elements—change and conflict management. Source: CIA 597, III-5.

131. (c) Common stockholders are not responsible for implementing decisions within the organization. If members of the management team are also common stockholders, they must make decisions using the stewardship function and separate their ownership interests from their managerial responsibilities. Choice (a) is incorrect. Organizational change is conducted through change agents, which include employees of the organization. Choice (b) is incorrect. Organizational change is conducted through change agents, which include all levels of management. Choice (d) is incorrect. Outside consultants often act as change agents because they can offer an objective, independent view of the organization.

Subject Area: Governance, risk, and control knowledge elements—change and conflict management. Source: CIA 597, III-15.

132. (b) The five items listed in the question are generally recommended as means of overcoming resistance to change. Each technique is recommended in different situations and is likely to address specific resistance to change factors. Choice (a) is incorrect because all five items listed may either increase or decrease morale. Choice (c) is incorrect because all five items listed may either increase or decrease a manager's control over information or the organization. Choice (d) is incorrect. Although use of manipulation and coercion may help a manager demonstrate power, education, communication, and negotiation would not.

Subject Area: Governance, risk, and control knowledge elements—change and conflict management. Source: CIA 1196, III-5.

133. (d) The 3 factors listed are among the 11 most common reasons employees resist change in organizations. Choice (a) is incorrect. The three factors listed do not lead to a desire to change the culture—as a matter of fact, they would inhibit culture change. Choice (b) is incorrect. The three factors are also not typically related to satisfaction with organizational structure, although they all may, in some cases, lead to dissatisfaction. Choice (c) is incorrect. They are not generally identified as inhibitors of performance.

Subject Area: Governance, risk, and control knowledge elements—change and conflict management. Source: CIA 1196, III-16.

134. (d) Job design theories of motivation are the ones that specifically address the issue of overspecialization. These theories focus on the match between the person and the job as the key to motivation. If there is overspecialization and boredom, the recommendation is to either enrich the job or move the employee to a job that provides the appropriate level of challenge. Choice (a) is incorrect. Focus on employees' higher-level needs in order to help them achieve self-actualization would be a recommendation based on Maslow's hierarchy of needs. Maslow's theories do not address the job itself as source of motivation. Additionally, given the complexity of self-actualization, Maslow's theory does not focus on self-actualization as the core of practical motivation. Choice (b) is incorrect. These actions would not address the issue of overspecialization although they may remove some of the obstacle to proper motivation. Choice (c) is incorrect. Implementing an optimal organizational rewards systems and providing extensive training to keep employees up to date would not, once again, address the job and the issue of overspecialization. Good reward systems are key to motivation. However, they would not address the source of the problem as presented in the question and therefore would only provide an incomplete solution.

Subject Area: Governance, risk, and control knowledge elements—change and conflict management. Source: CIA 1196, III-28.

135. (b) "Members of cohesive work groups often exert ...pressure... to resist changes that threaten to break up the group." Choice (a) is incorrect. Complaints about "why it will not work" virtually always represent an "acceptable" roadblock to a plan that has unacceptable behavioral consequences. Choice (c) is incorrect. Issues of under- or overstaffing for a task represent symptoms of resistance to change but not the actual or root cause of the problem. Choice (d) is incorrect. Citing cost factors also represents an "acceptable" rationale to block the implementation of a new approach.

Subject Area: Governance, risk, and control knowledge elements—change and conflict management. Source: CIA 1194, III-18.

136. (c) Change is of primary concern, and the environment is composed of factors within and outside of the organization. Choice (a) is incorrect because this is a management approach first espoused by Henri Fayol. Choice (b) is incorrect because this is a component of the scientific school of management. Choice (d) is incorrect because strategic planning is a function of top management.

Subject Area: Governance, risk, and control knowledge elements—change and conflict management. Source: CIA 590, III-3.

137. (c) Environment is often determined by external forces, outside direct control of the organization. Choices (a), (b), and (d) are incorrect. Each is a factor that managers seek to change.

Subject Area: Governance, risk, and control knowledge elements—change and conflict management. Source: CIA 596, III-24.

138. (b) Reactive changes are necessitated by unexpected environmental events or pressures. Choice (a) is incorrect. Anticipatory changes are any systematically planned changes intended to take advantage of expected situations. Choice (c) is incorrect. Incremental changes involve subsystem adjustments needed to keep the organization on its chosen path. Choice (d) is incorrect. Strategic changes alter the overall shape or direction of the organization.

Subject Area: Governance, risk, and control knowledge elements—change and conflict management. Source: CIA 596, III-19.

139. (c) Maintaining and manufacturing the existing products over introducing new ones may not be consistent with product quality and continuous improvement. If an existing product is not of high quality, it should be dropped. Choice (a) is incorrect. Continuous improvement is important to be sure high levels of performance are achieved. Choice (b) is incorrect. More and more manufacturers are automating every day to achieve high quality, deliver customized products on time, minimize inventory, and increase flexibility. Choice (d) is incorrect. Customers are the final judges and most important people for the enterprise. Customer needs must be satisfied by providing services and products that were made right the first time.

Subject Area: Governance, risk, and control knowledge elements—change and conflict management. Source: CIA 596, III-20.

140. (b) All the activities will help to change employees' attitudes. Choices (a), (c), and (d) are incorrect. Imposing the decision (II) is unlikely to change attitudes, and threats (V) are unlikely to change attitudes.

Subject Area: Governance, risk, and control knowledge elements—change and conflict management. Source: CIA 1196, II-35.

141. (b) Participation of the operating managers in the decision process can improve the overall decision, reduce resistance, and actually obtain their commitment to the change. Choice (a) is incorrect. Negotiation presents a scenario where at least one party sacrifices rather than producing a win-win situation. Also, if significant concessions are made to one manager, the others will try to gain a similar advantage. Choice (c) is incorrect. Coercion can be a temporary solution, but resistance will only be subdued, not eliminated. In addition, future cooperation between the auditor and operating managers will be severely restricted. Choice (d) is incorrect. This approach with the managers could produce a solution, but it would not be optimal because the auditor would have acquiesced on some points to obtain manager agreement.

Subject Area: Governance, risk, and control knowledge elements—change and conflict management. Source: CIA 1195, III-29.

142. (a) The directive would not *sell* if it directs employees. Thus, it is not a true statement. Choice (b) is incorrect. The use of the brochure is a recommended procedure. Choice (c) is incorrect. The questionnaire allows the auditee to participate in the conduct of the audit organization. Choice (d) is incorrect. The bulletins disclose the beneficial results of the internal audit process.

Subject Area: Governance, risk, and control knowledge elements—change and conflict management. Source: CIA 1196, III-32.

143. (b) "Members of cohesive work groups often exert ...pressure... to resist changes that threaten to break up the group." Choice (a) is incorrect. Complaints about "why it will not work" virtually always represent an "acceptable" roadblock to a plan that has unacceptable behavioral consequences. Choice (c) is incorrect. Issues of under or overstaffing for a task represent symptoms of resistance to change but not the actual or root cause of the problem. Choice (d) is incorrect. Citing cost factors also represent an "acceptable" rationale to block the implementation of a new approach.

Subject Area: Governance, risk, and control knowledge elements—change and conflict management. Source: CIA 1196, III-33.

144. (d) Explicit and Implicit coercion are particularly good where speed is essential and the initiators possess considerable power. Choice (a) is incorrect. It is too time consuming under the circumstances. Choice (b) is incorrect. It is time consuming, expensive and still prone to failure. Choice (c) is incorrect. It alerts others to begin negotiations, thus increasing the delay.

Subject Area: Governance, risk, and control knowledge elements—change and conflict management. Source: CIA 595, III-11.

145. (c) This is a reason to resist change, and the individuals feared they would be unable to learn to work with the new machines. Choices (a), (b), and (d) are incorrect. Each is a valid reason to resist change, but it is not consistent with the scenario.

Subject Area: Governance, risk, and control knowledge elements—change and conflict management. Source: CIA 595, III-28.

146. (a) This is not a principal reason as both low- and high-ranking individuals may resist change. Choices (b), (c), and (d) are incorrect. Each choice is a principal reason for resisting change.

Subject Area: Governance, risk, and control knowledge elements—change and conflict management. Source: CIA 594, III-80.

147. (c) Sometimes an organization becomes a victim of its environment. External forces are beyond the control of any manager and hence are difficult to change by the manager. Choices (a), (b), and (d) are incorrect. Each choice is a factor that managers seek to change. Changing the environment is less frequently observed.

Subject Area: Governance, risk, and control knowledge elements—change and conflict management. Source: CIA 594, III-83.

148. (b) This step would tend to further entrench the existing culture. Choices (a), (c), and (d) are incorrect. Each choice would be helpful in changing the existing organizational culture.

Subject Area: Governance, risk, and control knowledge elements—change and conflict management. Source: CIA 594, III-85.

149. (b) With participative management, employees participate in these four key areas. Choice (a) is incorrect. This is a quality control program in which everyone sees quality control as his or her job. Choice (c) is incorrect. This is a just-in-time inventory control technique. Choice (d) is incorrect. Just-in-time refers to inventory control methods that minimize production inventories while providing needed materials and parts just in time.

Subject Area: Governance, risk, and control knowledge elements—change and conflict management. Source: CIA 592, III-7.

150. (b) Organizational development (OD) is one of the major approaches to a proactive management of change in organizations. Among its major guiding principles is the alignment of individual and organizational goals. Choice (a) is incorrect. OD does not aim at increasing the leader's power. To the contrary, it often focuses on participation and power sharing. Choice (c) is incorrect. Attracting better applicants to an organization is not a major goal of OD, although a strong culture and high employee satisfaction, which can result from successful OD efforts, may become powerful recruiting tools for an organization. Choice (d) is incorrect. Providing an organization and its managers with means of increasing efficiency is not the primary goal of OD. As is the case with choice (c), increased efficiency may result from a healthier organization; however, OD can be considered successful if higher effectiveness but not better efficiency is achieved.

Subject Area: Governance, risk, and control knowledge elements—change and conflict management. Source: CIA 1196, III-18.

Control Types and Techniques

151. (b) The economic-value-added system is a new system to measure corporate performance. The open-book management system focuses on sharing company's financial information to all employees. The activity-based costing system identifies various activities needed to produce a product or service and determines the cost of those activities. The market-value-added system determines the market value of a firm based on its market capitalization rate.

Subject Area: Governance, risk, and control knowledge elements—control types and techniques. Source: Author.

152. (a) The balanced scorecard system is a comprehensive management control system that balances the traditional accounting (financial) measures with the operational (nonfinancial) measures.

Subject Area: Governance, risk, and control knowledge elements—control types and techniques. Source: Author.

153. (c) Detecting an exception in a business transaction or process is detective in nature, but reporting it is an example of corrective control. Both preventive and directive controls do not either detect or correct an error; they simply stop if possible.

Subject Area: Governance, risk, and control knowledge elements—control types and techniques. Source: Author.

154. (d) Management by exception involves the actions described in the question. Choice (a) is incorrect. In management by objectives, subordinates and their managers jointly formulate the subordinate's set of objectives and the plans for attaining those objectives for a subsequent period. Choice (b) is incorrect. Responsibility accounting is a technique to allocate cost and expense. Choice (c) is incorrect. Benchmarking involves looking at best practices in other companies.

Subject Area: Governance, risk, and control knowledge elements—control types and techniques. Source: CIA 597, III-19.

155. (c) Procedures provide guidance on how tasks should be accomplished. Choice (a) is incorrect. This is a retrospective control based on the outcome of a completed activity. Choice (b) is incorrect. This is a broader based control that should go hand-in-hand with strategic planning. Choice (d) is incorrect. This is a retrospective control.

Subject Area: Governance, risk, and control knowledge elements—control types and techniques. Source: CIA 1196, III-2.

156. (a) Feedback control makes sure past mistakes are not repeated. Choice (b) is incorrect. The controls mentioned are after processing and therefore cannot provide feed-forward control. Choice (c) is incorrect. Complaints are not part of production control. Choice (d) is incorrect. The question is not limited to inventory.

Subject Area: Governance, risk, and control knowledge elements—control types and techniques. Source: CIA 592, III-17.

157. (b) Feedback controls can allow costs to build up due to their back-end position. Choice (a) is incorrect. Organizations are artificial open systems and do not have automatic controls. Natural open systems, such as the human body, have automatic controls to maintain balance and sustain life. Choice (c) is incorrect. This is a planning-type control and, as such, would be a feed-forward control. Choice (d) is incorrect. A feed-forward control attempts to anticipate problems and effect timely solutions.

Subject Area: Governance, risk, and control knowledge elements—control types and techniques. Source: CIA 1193, III-13.

158. (d) Feed-forward control provides for the active anticipation of problems so that they can be resolved in a timely manner. Choice (a) is incorrect. Feedback controls deal with decision making based on evaluations of past performance. Choice (b) is incorrect. Strategic controls are broad based and effect an organization over a long period of time. Choice (c) is incorrect. Control of budgeted expenditures is not mentioned in the example.

Subject Area: Governance, risk, and control knowledge elements—control types and techniques. Source: CIA 1191, III-11.

159. (b) These items are the basic components of complex organizational control systems in large companies. Choice (a) is incorrect. These are means of financial control. Choice (c) is incorrect. These are several types of organizational development interventions. Choice (d) is incorrect. Mentoring fulfills several types of career enhancement functions, including these.

Subject Area: Governance, risk, and control knowledge elements—control types and techniques. Source: CIA 1191, III-10.

160. (a) Setting performance standards is one of the six elements. Choice (b) is incorrect. Securing data files is not one of the elements of a closed control system. Choice (c) is incorrect. Approving of the audit charter is not one of the control elements. Choice (d) is incorrect. Establishing the audit function is not one of the closed system control elements.

Subject Area: Governance, risk, and control knowledge elements—control types and techniques. Source: CIA 1191, II-10.

161. (a) Policies and procedures provide guidance on how an activity should be performed to best ensure that an objective is achieved (feed-forward). Choice (b) is incorrect. Implementation controls refer to controls applied during systems development. Choice (c) is incorrect. Policies and procedures provide primary guidance before and during the performance of some task rather than give feedback on its accomplishment. Choice (d) is incorrect. Application controls apply to specific applications, such as payroll or accounts payable.

Subject Area: Governance, risk, and control knowledge elements—control types and techniques. Source: CIA 1195, III-17.

162. (d) Controls that evaluate the final product or output are feedback controls. Choice (a) is incorrect. Feed-forward controls precede the production of the product or delivery of the service. Inspection of raw material would be a feed-forward control. Choice (b) is incorrect. Steering controls is another name for feed-forward controls. Choice (c) is incorrect. Concurrent controls are controls that occur during the process. An example might be the inspection of component parts.

Subject Area: Governance, risk, and control knowledge elements—control types and techniques. Source: CIA 590, III-21.

163. (a) These are the three basic components of a control system. Choice (b) is incorrect. These three terms are all used to describe subsystems of a control system. Choice (c) is incorrect. These three terms are used to describe either a subsystem of a control process or a tool used in a control system. Choice (d) is incorrect. While "objectives" is a correct answer, the other two are incorrect. "Inputs" is a good distracter because it is part of the "input-process-output" relationship used to describe a system.

Subject Area: Governance, risk, and control knowledge elements—control types and techniques. Source: CIA 590, III-22.

164. (d) A feed-forward control provides information on potential problems so that corrective action can be taken in anticipation of rather than as a result of a problem. Choice (a) is incorrect. A feedback control provides information on the results of a completed activity. Choice (b) is incorrect. Strategic plans are developed by senior management and provide a long-range path for the organization. Choice (c) is incorrect. Policies and procedures are developed by management and are the most basic control subsystem of an organization.

Subject Area: Governance, risk, and control knowledge elements—control types and techniques. Source: CIA 595, III-15.

165. (d) A feed-forward control provides information on potential problems so that corrective action can be taken in anticipation of rather than as a result of a problem. Choice (a) is incorrect. A feedback control provides information on the results of a completed activity. Choice (b) is incorrect. Strategic plans are developed by senior management and provide a long-range path of the organization. Choice (c) is incorrect. Policies and procedures are developed by management and are the most basic control subsystem of an organization.

Subject Area: Governance, risk, and control knowledge elements—control types and techniques. Source: CIA 1194, III-11.

166. (b) Verifying that the prompt feedback on variances is provided to management is one way internal auditors facilitate the management function of controlling. Choice (a) is incorrect. This relates to the management function of organizing. Choice (c) is incorrect. This relates to the management function of directing. Choice (d) is incorrect. This relates to the management function of planning.

Subject Area: Governance, risk, and control knowledge elements—control types and techniques. Source: 596, III-25.

167. (d) The relationship between the application controls and the general controls is such that general controls are needed to support the functioning of application controls, and both are needed to ensure complete and accurate information processing. Choice (a) is incorrect. Application controls are dependent on the general controls. Choice (b) is incorrect. In an EUC environment, responsibility for general controls may be shared by several individuals in different departments or locations. Choice (c) is incorrect. The need for specific general controls varies with the complexity and importance of the application.

Subject Area: Governance, risk, and control knowledge elements—control types and techniques. Source: CIA 596, I-30.

168. (b) Sophisticated software packages may inadvertently threaten data security by allowing users to bypass existing system level security. Choice (a) is incorrect. Restricting access to LAN workstations is a control to prevent unauthorized persons from gaining access to the network. Choice (c) is incorrect. Password security when logging on may not prevent authorized users of the LAN from accessing unauthorized functions. Choice (d) is incorrect. A security policy may establish responsibility but will not prevent inappropriate update of information.

Subject Area: Governance, risk, and control knowledge elements—control types and techniques. Source: CIA 596, I-31.

169. (a) Edit or validation routines should be present in the application to reject or flag these unusual items. Choice (b) is incorrect. Rejected and suspense item controls are relevant only if the data are first subject to edit and validation checks. Choice (c) is incorrect. Controls over update access to the database are general controls rather than application controls. Choice (d) is incorrect. Programmed balancing controls are designed to identify errors in the processing of data rather than in the data itself.

Subject Area: Governance, risk, and control knowledge elements—control types and techniques. Source: CIA 596, I-32.

170. (d) A limit test is a test of whether a field amount fits within a predetermined upper and/or lower limit. It can catch only certain errors (i.e., those that exceed the acceptable range). Choice (a) is incorrect. A record count provides the number of documents entered into a process. Choice (b) is incorrect. An echo check is designed to check the reliability of computer hardware. Choice (c) is incorrect. A self-checking number contains digits that are a formula of the other digits. Account numbers with a self-checking digit reduce data input errors.

Subject Area: Governance, risk, and control knowledge elements—control types and techniques. Source: CIA 596, I-57.

171. (b) A validity test can compare the value of a customer account number field with a master file containing valid customer accounts. Choice (a) is incorrect. A limit test is a test of whether a field amount fits within a predetermined upper and/or lower limit. It can catch only certain errors (i.e., those that exceed the acceptable range). Choice (c) is incorrect. A control total is the number of transactions in a batch. Choice (d) is incorrect. A hash total is the number obtained from totaling the same field value for each transaction in a batch. The total has no meaning or value other than as a comparison with another hash total.

Subject Area: Governance, risk, and control knowledge elements—control types and techniques. Source: CIA 596, I-58.

172. (b) Policies and procedures are part of the administration of EUC, which is defined at an organizational level. Choice (a) is incorrect. Application controls are specific to the flow of transactions. Choice (c) is incorrect. Environmental controls influence the effective operation of all internal controls. Choice (d) is incorrect. System control is not a specific response; it is too broad.

Subject Area: Governance, risk, and control knowledge elements—control types and techniques. Source: CIA 593, I-22.

173. (b) One-for-one checking is as described. Choice (a) is incorrect. Batch totals require numerical control. Choice (c) is incorrect. Computer sequence checks require that transactions be numbered. Choice (d) is incorrect. Computer matching is performed under program control and not by the user.

Subject Area: Governance, risk, and control knowledge elements—control types and techniques. Source: CIA 592, I-33.

174. (c) Implementation controls are designed to ensure that only authorized program procedures are introduced into the system. Choice (a) is incorrect. Programmed checks are used to check the potential accuracy of input data (e.g., a range check). Choice (b) is incorrect. Batch control is used to ensure the completeness and accuracy of input and update. Choice (d) is incorrect. One-for-one checking is a technique used to check individual documents for accuracy and completeness of data input or update.

Subject Area: Governance, risk, and control knowledge elements—control types and techniques. Source: CIA 591, I-36.

175. (a) During each program run in a series, the computer accumulates the totals of transactions that have been processed and reconciles them with the totals forwarded from the previous program run. Choice (b) is incorrect. Existence checking ensures that individual data codes agree with valid codes held in a file or a program. Choice (c) is incorrect. Key verification ensures the completeness and accuracy of selected fields on individual documents. Choice (d) is incorrect. Prerecorded input (turnaround document) is used to ensure accuracy and completeness of input.

Subject Area: Governance, risk, and control knowledge elements—control types and techniques. Source: CIA 591, I-37.

176. (a) Computer matching of fields such as goods received number, product code, supplier code, and quantity assures agreement between goods received and goods invoiced. Choice (b) is incorrect. Control totals do not identify specific item-by-item differences. Choice (c) is incorrect. Batch totals provide only a total value for a field and do not allow for detail matching. Choice (d) is incorrect. Check digits provide only for validation of predefined account numbers.

Subject Area: Governance, risk, and control knowledge elements—control types and techniques. Source: CIA 591, I-41.

177. (b) A combination of edit checks, resulting in exception reports, would be the most efficient way of reducing errors. Choice (a) is incorrect. Keystroke verification (a labor-intensive procedure) consists of entering data a second time, with differences detected by a mechanical signal. Choice (c) is incorrect. Balancing and reconciliation make tests of equality and analyze differences. Like choice (a), it is laborious. Choice (d) is incorrect. Batch totals are used to control input via agreement of preestablished totals and are better suited for completeness control.

Subject Area: Governance, risk, and control knowledge elements—control types and techniques. Source: CIA 591, II-34.

178. (d) Run-to-run totals are used to ensure completeness of update. Choice (a) is incorrect. Computer matching is used to ensure that data are completely entered. Choice (b) is incorrect. Check digits are used to determine if a number has been keyed incorrectly. Choice (c) is incorrect. A transaction log is used in conjunction with special programs to reperform processing and compare results.

Subject Area: Governance, risk, and control knowledge elements—control types and techniques. Source: CIA 591, II-35.

179. (b) To be of benefit, manual postings of batch totals must be agreed to the master file. Choice (a) is incorrect. When agreed, batch totals are useful. Choice (c) is incorrect. Unless agreed or reconciled, batch totals in a control account do not serve as a control. Choice (d) is incorrect. Hash totals are not required or appropriate in this situation.

Subject Area: Governance, risk, and control knowledge elements—control types and techniques. Source: CIA 591, II-36.

180. (a) Operational controls frequently are not supported by clear criteria or standards. There is no firm external procedural framework for operational controls such as generally accepted accounting principles provide for accounting controls. Choice (b) is incorrect. Computer hardware controls are relatively obvious physical processing controls. Choice (c) is incorrect. These controls are well defined by the framework of GAAP. Choice (d) is incorrect. Physical controls, and the objectives, are apparent. They are not subject to any significant degree of misinterpretation.

Subject Area: Governance, risk, and control knowledge elements—control types and techniques. Source: CIA 1190, III-13.

181. (d) Operating controls include all those that promote safe, accurate, and timely processing of the bank's transactions, for example, dual control, joint custody, rotation of employees, and segregation of duties. Choice (a) is incorrect. An example of a bank's input controls is an edit test of the bank. Choice (b) is incorrect. Auditing controls are the system of checks and balances in effect throughout the bank. Choice (c) is incorrect. Corrective controls are those that correct errors discovered.

Subject Area: Governance, risk, and control knowledge elements—control types and techniques. Source: CIA 1190, III-4.

182. (c) This is an example of a processing control procedure. Choice (a) is incorrect. This is a typical example of a monitoring control. Choice (b) is incorrect. This is a monitoring control, which is deployed by lower-level management to determine when operations may be out of control. Choice (d) is incorrect. Effective internal auditing can be recognized as a form of effective monitoring, that is, it represents an analysis of the integrity of management's other controls. When audits or reviews are performed on a regular basis, such as the control reviews over cash, they provide an effective monitoring control.

Subject Area: Governance, risk, and control knowledge elements—control types and techniques. Source: CIA 1195, I-66.

183. (b) A good system of internal controls is likely to expose an irregularity if one employee perpetrates it without the aid of others. Choice (a) is incorrect. A group has a better chance of successfully perpetrating an irregularity than does an individual employee. Choice (c) is incorrect. Management can override controls, singly or in groups. Choice (d) is incorrect. Management can override controls, singly or in groups.

Subject Area: Governance, risk, and control knowledge elements—control types and techniques. Source: CIA 592, II-17.

184. (d) This is a directive control. The control is designed to encourage a desirable event to occur, that is, to enhance the professionalism and level of expertise of the internal auditing department. Choice (a) is incorrect. This is a detective control. The events under scrutiny have already occurred. Choices (b) and (c) are incorrect. They are preventive controls. The controls are designed to deter an undesirable event.

Subject Area: Governance, risk, and control knowledge elements—control types and techniques. Source: CIA 1192, I-18.

6 PLAN ENGAGEMENTS (15–25%)

THEORY

6.1 Audit Process

Conducting an audit is a process with a series of activities to be reviewed and with a series of procedures to be followed. A structured methodology, consisting of audit phases or stages, can be used during the audit process to ensure quality and to ensure that all required activities are accomplished—starting from the beginning of an audit to the completion of the audit. Each phase has defined tasks to be completed. Five such phases include (1) the preliminary survey, (2) the audit program, (3) fieldwork, (4) reporting, and (5) monitoring and follow-up. The audit report is the end product of the audit process. The audit process described is linked to three overall audit areas: preaudit, during the audit, and postaudit.

The preliminary survey → The audit program → Fieldwork
Monitoring and follow-up ← Reporting ←

Exhibit 6.1: Sequence of the audit phases

(a) **Preliminary Survey.** The preliminary survey is the first step in the audit process and its purpose is familiarization, which is essential to a well-balanced and well-conducted audit. The survey activities include touring of facilities and operations, conducting audit inquiries, and performing analytical reviews. The audit scope and audit objectives are developed. Potential risks and exposures, goals, and standards for the audited area are identified and gathered.

Controls related to the activity being examined are identified. Questionnaires for mail survey and for personal interview are prepared to obtain background information and to understand the control-related problems and issues from the auditees. The audit program is not developed in this phase.

KEY CONCEPTS TO REMEMBER: PRELIMINARY SURVEY

- Personal observation, physical inspection of equipment, review of documents, inquiries, flowcharts, analytical reviews, and walk-throughs are the major tools used in the preliminary survey phase.
- A flowcharting approach used in evaluating internal controls during the preliminary

review provides the auditor with the best visual grasp of a system and a means for analyzing complex operations. Other approaches that do not provide such visual grasp include a questionnaire approach, matrix approach, and detailed narrative approach.

- Activities typically performed in the preliminary survey phase include: interviewing operating personnel, identifying the objectives of the auditee, identifying standards used to evaluate performance, and assessing the risks inherent in the auditee's operations. Time budgeted for the audit should be determined after completion of the preliminary survey.
- When the audit resources are limited and the results of the preliminary survey and limited audit testing conducted reveal that an operating function is working as intended and no major deficiencies are noted, the auditor should send a memo to all interested parties summarizing the preliminary survey results and indicating that the audit has been canceled.
- During the preliminary survey phase of an audit of production cycle, management stated that the sale of scrap was well controlled. The best evidence to verify that assertion can be obtained by comparing the quantities of scrap expected from the production process with the quantities sold.
- During a preliminary survey an auditor notes that several accounts payable vouchers for major suppliers show adjustments for duplicate payments of prior invoices. This would indicate a need for additional testing to determine related controls and the current exposure to duplicate payments made to suppliers.
- An example of preaudit work is conducting an entrance conference with the auditee.
- Agenda items for discussion at a preaudit meeting would be purpose and scope of the audit, records and auditee personnel needed, and expected starting and completion dates. It does not include the sampling plan and key criteria.
- The auditor in charge has just been informed of the next audit assignment and the audit team has been assigned. The audit budget will be finalized after the preliminary survey.

(b) **Audit Program.** In the second phase of the audit process, audit procedures are developed to accomplish audit objectives. The audit procedures describe which activities to review and which transactions to examine. Writing an audit program is a documentation of audit planning. More is said about the audit program later in this section.

(c) **Fieldwork.** The audit procedures included in the audit program are carried out in the third phase of the audit process. Fieldwork is examining records and evaluating information.

Evidence is collected in this phase to draw audit conclusions. The effectiveness of controls is evaluated here also. Working papers are prepared to document the results of the audit work.

KEY CONCEPTS TO REMEMBER: FIELDWORK

- Fieldwork has been defined as "a systematic process of objectively gathering evidence about an entity's operations, evaluating it, and determining if those operations meet acceptable standards." Tasks in the fieldwork include expanding or altering audit procedures if circumstances warrant, applying the audit program to accomplish audit objectives, and creating working papers that document the audit.
- If an auditor used an internal control questionnaire during the survey phase and received positive responses, the auditor will confirm these responses in the fieldwork phase.
- The preliminary audit survey discloses a prior audit deficiency was never corrected. Subsequent fieldwork confirms that the deficiency still exists. The auditor should discuss the issue with the person(s) responsible for the problem, who should know how to solve the problem.

CONTROL STATUS DURING THE SURVEY AND THE FIELDWORK PHASES

- In the preliminary survey phase, the existence of controls is determined.
- In the fieldwork phase, the effectiveness of controls is tested.
- In the fieldwork phase, the adequacy of controls is evaluated.

(d) **Reporting.** In the fourth phase of the audit process, audit results are communicated to the auditee both orally and in writing with a clear and professional opinion rendered. An exit conference is conducted to review the audit reports with auditees.

(e) **Monitoring and Follow-up.** Monitoring and follow-up, the last phase, can be sophisticated or simple depending on a number of factors, including the size and complexity of the audit organization. Regardless of the type of audit chosen, each audit should include a firm basis for monitoring and follow-up actions, active status monitoring, and a determination of the results of actions taken on recommendations. The director of internal auditing should ensure follow-up of prior audit findings and recommendations to determine if corrective action was taken and is achieving the desired results.

Auditee responses to the audit report are reviewed to assess their adequacy and timeliness and the appropriateness of proposed corrective actions. Auditee responses and their corrective actions are monitored to ensure their timely completion. Effective follow-up is essential to get the full benefits of audit work. If monitoring and follow-up disclose that action on major recommendations is not progressing, additional steps should be considered promptly. Follow-up should be elevated to progressively higher levels of management of the organization to obtain prompt action. Continued attention is required until expected results are achieved. At this point, audit recommendations are closed.

Audit recommendations should be closed for only one of these reasons: the recommendation was effectively implemented, an alternative action was taken that achieved the intended results, circumstances have so changed that the recommendation is no longer valid, or the recommendation was not implemented despite the use of all feasible strategies. When a recommendation is closed for the last reason, a judgment is made on whether the objectives are significant enough to be pursued at a later date in another assignment.

Auditing is a process similar to a manufacturing process. The audit process has a clear beginning and ending points with activities falling in between. The process accepts inputs (e.g., auditor time and effort, management input) and transforms them into meaningful outputs (e.g., audit reports, audit working papers). The audit process can be further explained in terms of "what happens when" and "who does what."

Exhibit 6.2 presents "what happens when," that is, activities conducted in three overall audit areas such as preaudit, during the audit, and postaudit, and ties the audit process to three such areas.

Activities during preaudit	*Activities during audit*	*Activities during postaudit*
Opening the audit project, short-term audit planning (scope, objectives, resources, and time frames), entrance conference, preliminary survey, audit program development, application of computer-assisted audit techniques, working paper preparation.	Fieldwork, observations, testing, examinations, control evaluations, interim written reports, interim oral reports, working paper preparation, application of computer-assisted audit techniques, final audit report, correction of major findings.	Exit conference, management (auditee) responses, correction of audit findings, monitoring of corrective actions, closing the audit project, auditor performance evaluation, customer satisfaction survey (i.e., obtaining feedback from auditees), project quality review (e.g., lessons learned), follow-up audit.

Exhibit 6.2: Audit activities

A description of "who does what" in the audit process follows. Different players (auditors) have different roles to fulfill in the process. Some common audit titles, in the order of hierarchy, include audit director, audit manager/supervisor, team leader/auditor in charge, and staff/senior auditor.

- *Job duties or responsibilities of an audit director* in a specific audit project would include selecting or approving project team members, approving project resources, attending entrance and exit conferences as needed, determining the need for expanded testing, reviewing the summary audit findings, monitoring the corrective action taken on reported audit findings, conducting auditor performance appraisals, obtaining feedback from audit customers, and closing the audit.

- *Job duties or responsibilities of an audit manager/supervisor* in a specific audit project would include opening an audit by approving the project budget, attending entrance and exit conferences, approving the audit program, providing instructions to auditors, reviewing the audit working papers, ensuring that audit objectives are achieved, reviewing the draft audit report, developing follow-up audit plans, conducting auditor performance appraisals, and closing the audit.
- *Job duties or responsibilities of an audit team leader/auditor-in-charge* in a specific audit project would include allocating the budgeted audit hours among assigned staff, attending entrance and exit conferences, preparing a preliminary audit program, reviewing the audit working papers and preparing a review point sheet from a quality control viewpoint, organizing and drafting the audit report, and conducting auditor performance appraisals.
- *Job duties or responsibilities of a staff/senior auditor* in a specific audit project would include conducting a preliminary survey, developing an audit program, attending entrance and exit conferences, executing the audit program, collecting audit evidence, preparing the working papers, updating the permanent audit files, and providing input to the draft audit report.

6.2 Audit Planning

Two kinds of audit plans exist: (1) staff plans and (2) audit plans.

(a) **Staff Plans.** Staff planning should include assigning staff with the appropriate skills and knowledge for the job, assigning an adequate number of experienced staff and supervisors to the audit (consultants should be used when necessary), and providing for on-the-job training of staff.

The availability of staff and other resources is an important consideration in establishing the objectives, scope, and methodology of an audit. For example, limitations on travel funds may preclude auditors from visiting certain locations, or lack of an expertise in a particular methodology may preclude auditors from undertaking certain objectives. Auditors may be able to overcome such limitations by use of staff from local offices or by engaging consultants with the necessary knowledge, skills, and expertise.

(b) **Audit Plans.** A written audit plan should be prepared for each audit and is essential to conducting audits efficiently and effectively. The form and content of the written audit plan will vary among audits. The plan generally should include an audit program and a memorandum or other appropriate documentation of key decisions about the objectives, scope, and methodology of the audit and of the auditors' basis for those decisions.

Documenting the audit plan is an opportunity for the auditors to review the work done in planning the audit to determine whether the proposed audit objectives are likely to result in a useful report, the proposed audit scope and methodology are adequate to satisfy the audit objectives promptly, and sufficient staff and other resources have been made available to perform the audit.

Written audit plans should generally include this information.

- **Introduction and background.** To the extent necessary, information should be provided about the legal authority for the audited organization, program, activity, operation, or function; its history and current objectives; its principal locations; and similar information needed by auditors to understand and carry out the audit plan.
- **Scope and objectives.** A clearly described scope and clearly stated objectives should indicate what the audit is to accomplish.
- **Audit methods.** The audit methodology should be clearly described and should present suggested steps, procedures, and sampling plans, which should be included in the audit program. For coordinated audits, the audit organization planning the work should ensure that comparable audit methods and procedures are followed to ensure that the data obtained from participating locations will be complete. Auditors should design the methodology to provide sufficient, competent, and relevant evidence to achieve the objectives of the audit. Methodology includes not only the nature of the auditors' procedures, but also their extent (e.g., sample size).
- **Special instructions.** The auditors should clearly understand and reach early agreement on the responsibilities in each audit. This agreement is especially important when the work is to be directed by a central audit organization with work to be conducted at several different locations. This section of the plan may be used to list the responsibilities of each audit organization, such

as preparing audit programs, conducting audit work, supervising audit work, drafting reports, handling auditee comments and questions, and processing the final report.

- **Report.** To the extent possible, the audit plan should set forth the general format of the audit report, cite the types of information to be included, and list the recipients of the report.

KEY CONCEPTS TO REMEMBER: PLANNING AN AUDIT ASSIGNMENT

- Documentation required to plan an internal auditing project should include evidence that the resources needed to perform the audit have been considered. The requirements for staffing levels, education and training, and audit research, along with others, should be included in the annual audit plan.
- In audit planning, internal auditors should review all relevant information. Audit planning should be documented, and the planning process should include obtaining background information about the activities to be audited, establishing audit objectives and scope of work, and determining how, when, and to whom the audit results will be communicated. Audit planning should not include collecting audit evidence on all matters related to the audit objectives—this is done in fieldwork after the audit program is written.
- The audit plan should include a detailed schedule of areas to be audited during the coming year; an estimate of the time required for each audit; risk, exposure, and potential loss to the organization; and the approximate starting date for each audit.
- When assigning individual staff members to actual audits, internal auditing managers are faced with a number of important considerations related to needs, abilities, and skills. The most important criteria are the complexity of the audit, the experience level of the auditor, and special skills possessed by the staff auditor. The least important are the staff auditor's desire for training in the audit area or the fact that the audit topic is the same as the auditor's major subject in college.
- The audit department of a large corporation has established its operating plan and budget for the coming year. The operating plan should include a prioritized listing of all audits, staffing, a detailed expense budget, and the targeted start date and completion date of each audit along with measurability criteria.
- An internal auditor judged an item to be immaterial when planning an audit. However, the auditor may still include the item if it is subsequently determined that adverse effects related to the item are likely to occur.
- When auditors are transferred from an operating department of the company, they should not be assigned to an audit of their previous department.
- The audit department can engage an engineering consulting firm to perform the work when an internal auditing department has scheduled an audit of a construction contract. The audit work involves comparing materials purchased to those specified in the engineering drawings. The audit department does not have anyone on staff with sufficient expertise to complete this audit work.
- Audit objectives, an element in the audit planning process, typically take a long-term perspective, while audit staffing, audit programs, and audit procedures are short term.
- The long-range schedule as an audit-planning tool is general in nature and is used to ensure adequate audit coverage over time.
- A strategic audit plan covers audits identified to be performed over the next three to five years.

6.3 Analytical Reviews

As a part of fieldwork, the internal auditor should perform analytical reviews to understand the relationships between various data. The focus is on determining the reasonableness of data. Techniques such as regression analysis, simple ratio analysis, and trend analysis can be used to provide insights into the financial and operational data. The outcome of the review is to provide a "red flag" to the auditor so that he or she can adjust the audit scope and the audit procedures accordingly. For example, analytical reviews can be used to indicate the possible existence of fraud.

The key is not to view the data and its relations individually but to integrate that information with other related data to provide greater insights into the dynamics of the data. *Some examples of application of analytical reviews follow:*

- Inventory turnover rates are compared with established industry standards to assess the performance of a business unit or division.
- Regular analytical review of operating divisions would include analysis of sales, cash flow, and profit statistics. Specifically, use of accelerated depreciation methods and sale of capital assets to obtain larger performance bonuses should be looked at in detail.
- The most persuasive means of assessing production quality control is to evaluate the number and reasons for sales adjustments and to perform trend analysis.
- Change analysis and trend analysis of buyer or vendor activity are analytical techniques to detect irregularities in purchasing. Purchases from two new vendors are increased dramatically after a new buyer was hired. Based on sales volume, it can be concluded that the buyer was obtaining kickbacks from the two new vendors.
- Analytical procedures in which current financial statements are compared with budgets or previous statements are primarily intended to determine overall reasonableness of statement contents.
- An unexpected decrease in total asset turnover ratio could indicate that fictitious inventory has been recorded.
- Accounts payable schedule verification may include the use of analytical evidence. An example is comparing the balance on the schedule with the balances of prior years.
- Workers' compensation claims can be analyzed for injuries by type of personal computer equipment and extensiveness of use of computers by individual employees.
- Analysis of loan default ratios by a loan officer in a bank should provide good trend analysis of that officer's loan activities and intentions.
- Analytical procedures revealed an extraordinary increase in account balances in maintenance supplies during the past year. These data need to be analyzed further before reaching conclusions. The increase could be a common indicator of fraud.
- A decrease in the accounts receivable turnover rate indicates a more liberal credit policy; an increase in the accounts receivable turnover rate indicates a conservative (tight) credit policy.
- During an operational audit, an auditor compares the inventory turnover rate of a subsidiary with established industry standards to assess the performance of the subsidiary and to indicate where additional audit work may be needed.
- A regression analysis technique is used to find a correlation between the operating conditions and age of water meters for a municipality.
- An aging analysis is prepared to evaluate the adequacy of the company's allowance for doubtful accounts.
- A comparison of cost data with current market quotations would be a reliable test of the valuation of marketable equity securities.

6.4 Planning Materiality

Material errors, irregularities, and illegal acts will have a direct and material effect on financial statement amounts. Materiality is defined as the magnitude of a misstatement that would influence the judgment of a reasonable user of financial statements. Audit procedures must be designed to provide reasonable assurance of detecting material financial statement misstatements (i.e., material errors and irregularities). Thus, materiality refers to the level of precision (or accuracy) of the financial statements; the lower the materiality, the greater the precision and vice versa.

From an internal audit viewpoint, materiality refers not only to the financial statements but also to the business operations and computer systems. Consider

- From a financial statement standpoint, materiality is to be evaluated in relation to the financial statements as a whole.
- From an operations standpoint, materiality is to be evaluated in relation to a specific operation under consideration as well as all other operations affected by it.
- From a computer system standpoint, materiality is to be evaluated in relation to a specific information system under consideration as well as all other interfacing systems affected by it.

- Material weaknesses in either business operations or computer systems may or may not directly affect the financial statements.

For example, heavy use of pirated software may become a sensitive and material issue if it was known to software vendors or other interested third parties that existed to monitor software piracy situations in companies. Subsequent fines and penalties imposed could be high and the acquisition of software through official sources would cost money. In addition, loss of image and bad reputation is a major factor to think about.

FACTORS AFFECTING THE EXTENT OF AUDIT TESTING

- Materiality
- Audit risk
- Business risk
- Cost and time

Similarly, unauthorized dissemination of product formulas, process knowledge, and secret recipes to competitors would have a material effect when the competitor decides to take advantage of the newfound information. Another example is impact of poor-quality products and possible environmental control-related violations by the organization.

Material weaknesses in business operations and computer systems have a business risk. The risk of adverse publicity and injury to the organization's reputation is of concern here. Business risk (exposure risk) is different from audit risk. From an internal auditor's perspective, audit risk is best defined as the risk that the auditor may fail to detect a significant error or weakness during an examination and performance of an audit. AICPA SAS 47, *Audit Risk and Materiality in Conducting an Audit*, defines audit risk as the probability that an auditor will issue an unqualified (clean) opinion on financial statements that actually contain material misstatements. Audit risk is therefore the complement of the level of assurance; *the lower the audit risk, the greater the assurance and vice versa.* Since audits are performed on a test or sampling basis, audit risk cannot be reduced to zero except at prohibitive cost. The concepts of materiality and audit risk suggest that the financial statements are accurate only within reasonable and practical limits.

In practice, decisions relating to materiality and the extent of audit testing are left to the professional judgment of the individual auditor. Increased audit testing would reduce both the business risk and the audit risk (and possibly the level of materiality) and at the same time would increase the cost of conducting the audit. This is because even small reductions in materiality and/or audit risk can result in disproportionately large increases in sample sizes and hence audit costs. *Short of 100% verification, audit risk cannot be reduced to zero.*

About 53% of respondents in a survey of government auditors indicated that they ordinarily attempt to quantify audit risk in determining the extent of audit testing.[1] Audit risk and materiality are important considerations in planning an audit and evaluating its results. Materiality plays a major role in planning the scope of an audit, the extent of audit testing, and in evaluating the sufficiency of audit evidence. As a practical matter, the materiality threshold is a gray area that separates what is very likely material from what is very likely not material.

(a) **Types of Errors.** Three types of errors can exist: (1) known errors, (2) likely errors, and (3) possible errors (see Exhibit 6.3). Errors are defined as financial statement misstatements that are either intentional or unintentional. Since audits are performed on a test or sampling basis, it is helpful to distinguish between three types of errors.

Types of errors
- Known errors (detected errors)
- Likely errors (estimated errors)
- Possible errors (errors implicit in sampling work)

Exhibit 6.3: Types of errors

[1] *K. K. Raman and Relmond P. Van Daniker,* ***Materiality and Audit Risk in Governmental Auditing, A Research Monograph*** *(Alexandria, VA: Association of Government Accountants, 1990).*

Known errors are errors that have actually been detected by the auditor during substantive testing. **Likely** errors are estimated errors obtained by projecting to the population the same proportion of known errors observed in representative samples. Likely errors include known errors. **Possible errors** represent the amount of error at the upper limit of the confidence interval obtained in projecting sample results to the population. Possible errors are implicit in both statistical and nonstatistical sampling, although they can be quantified using only statistical sampling. Possible errors include both likely and known errors.

AUDIT PLANNING AND EVALUATION

In planning the audit, the scope of the audit should be large enough so that possible errors will not exceed the materiality threshold at a reasonable level of assurance.

In forming the audit opinion at the evaluation stage of the audit, if possible errors exceed the materiality threshold, the auditor must either issue an adverse opinion or collect more evidence to reduce uncertainty.

Many auditors use their estimated (planning) materiality to evaluate only known errors. These auditors may be underestimating the amount of error in financial statements since possible errors exceed known errors.

The auditor needs to identify the potential users of the financial statements or audit reports before determining the appropriate level of assurance or materiality. This is because the user is the one being affected by the auditor's work.

Although there are no authoritative guidelines on what should be the maximum acceptable level of audit risk, usually a 95% assurance level (i.e., a 5% level of audit risk) would be reasonable. *Assurance level is the complement of audit risk.*

More auditors base their decisions on known and likely errors; fewer auditors base their decision on possible errors. The information about errors helps to evaluate the sufficiency of audit evidence and to decide whether additional audit testing is needed before issuing an opinion.

In determining the materiality of errors, most auditors take into consideration the combined effect of diverse errors not judged to be material individually, net out material and immaterial errors that have opposite effects, and take into account unadjusted errors from prior periods.

(b) **Who Should Set the Materiality Level?** The auditor and the auditee should arrive at an understanding about the levels of materiality and the assurance level to be applied in an audit. This understanding should be based on cost-benefit considerations.

A structured audit approach will be more effective in controlling audit risk and audit costs than an unstructured one. A structured approach is one that relies on statistical sampling and/or formal decision aids for integrating audit evidence.

Auditor judgment plays an important role in determining materiality, in determining the amount of audit work to be performed, and in evaluating the evidence that is collected. Providing formal guidance to auditors may increase judgment consensus.

(c) **What Is Material and Immaterial?** Due professional care requires that the auditor consider the relative materiality or significance of matters to which audit procedures are applied. Various studies suggest that the magnitude of an error as a percentage of income is the most important factor in determining its materiality; items that have a more than 10% effect on income would normally be considered material, while items constituting less than 5% of income would normally be considered immaterial.

An auditor would most likely judge an error in an account balance to be material if the error involves a large percentage of net income. Least likely to be material are clerical mistakes that are unlikely to occur again, unverified routine transactions, and unusual transactions for the company. When a related party is involved, such as a major stockholder, an error would be considered material when the stockholder's receivables balance accounts for less than 1% of the company's receivables.

Other factors of materiality, besides income effect of the error, include effect on earnings trend, effect on working capital, and effect on total assets. Legal and political factors are important, and compliance with laws and regulations is also crucial.

As a practical matter, assurance level cannot be separated from materiality. Given the same sample size, an auditor with a lower materiality level will have a higher level of audit risk; for audit risk to be comparable across auditors, the assurance level must be related to a materiality level.

(d) **Qualitative vs Quantitative Materiality.** Sometimes the nature of disclosure (sensitive or not) and the evidence of a desire to mislead (accidental or deliberate) are more important than quantitative factors. The auditor should weigh more toward human behavior.

Quantitative and qualitative materiality. Quantitative materiality is applicable during the planning stage of an audit. Qualitative materiality is applicable during the evaluation stage of an audit since it is not practical to plan the audit to detect qualitative misstatements.

In addition to quantitative materiality, the auditor should consider qualitative materiality. Qualitative materiality may include the cumulative effect of immaterial items or the needs of users.

The materiality threshold should vary for each audit project and for each audit type (i.e., operational audit, financial audit, compliance audit, information technology audit).

Legal and political factors and environmental factors may affect the determination of qualitative materiality. Irregularities, fraud, illegal acts, legal covenants, and account misclassifications would likely be considered qualitatively material.

The auditor needs to strike a balance between cost-effectiveness and preferences of user groups for financial statements completely free of errors.

(e) **How to Compute Materiality.** Materiality is computed by taking a base and multiplying that by a percentage. The base, in declining order of importance, includes total revenues, total expenditures, total assets, retained earnings, and income. The percentage used can be a flat percentage or one obtained from a sliding scale. A flat percentage is based on the notion that materiality is completely relative; a sliding scale is based on the notion that some amounts are large enough to be always material.

In the government auditors' survey, it was noted that a majority (65%) of the respondents use a flat percentage while 35% use a sliding scale to compute materiality.

6.5 Detailed Risk Assessment

Audit resources are limited and expensive, and hence they should be properly allocated and scheduled for maximum utilization. Risk models or risk analysis is often used in conjunction with development of long-range audit schedules. Performing risk analysis and risk assessment is a major step in audit planning work. A **risk** is defined as the probability that an unfavorable event occurs that could lead to a financial or other form of loss. The potential occurrence of such an event is called **exposure**. Risks are caused by exposures. Controls can reduce or eliminate risks and exposures.

STEPS INVOLVED IN A RISK ASSESSMENT MODEL

- Identifying risk factors
- Judging the relative importance of the risk factors
- Measuring the extent to which each risk factor is present in an audit unit
- Quantifying and evaluating the risk level
- Allocating the audit resources according to the risk level

Risks are inherent when business activities and transactions are processed in either a manual or an automated manner. Intentional or unintentional errors, omissions, and irregularities (e.g., theft, fraud) do occur when people handle transactions during analyzing, recording, approving, classifying, computing, processing, summarizing, posting, and reporting activities. These risks represent potentially damaging events that can produce losses.

(a) **Audit Risk Factors.** High-risk areas should receive high priority and low-risk areas should be given low priority. A systematic risk assessment approach is better than a haphazard, trial-and-error, approach. An IIA survey[2] identified 19 potentially important audit-risk factors. Each factor might be related to the risk or to the allocation of internal audit resources when the objective is to minimize losses to the firm.

---

[2] *Patton, Evans, and Lewis,* ***Audit Risk Assessment*** *(Altamonte Springs, FL: Institute of Internal Auditors, 1982).*

1. **Quality of internal control system (most important factor).** The design and past performance of an internal control system is important in judging the probability of errors in the system. Audit units with a weak system of internal controls pose a higher risk of loss. Consequently, units with weak internal control should receive a larger share of audit resources.
2. **Competence of management.** Although difficult to measure objectively, the competence of a unit's management influences the confidence that the internal auditor has in the operations of the unit. The less competent the management, the higher the risk of losses to the firm.
3. **Integrity of management.** Even more difficult to assess or measure, the integrity of management bears an obvious relationship to the probability of losses to the firm through overrides of the control system.
4. **Size of unit.** The size of a unit will normally affect the magnitude of its potential losses. Thus, the larger an audit unit (in terms of total assets, revenue, cash flow, etc.), the larger the demand for audit resources.
5. **Recent change in accounting system.** A recent change in systems may invalidate past performance as a measure of control strength and usually increases the probability of errors during its "break-in" period.
6. **Complexity of operations.** As the operating complexity of an audit unit increases, the information and control system will also become more complex. This complexity can increase both the probability of error and the effort required to monitor the system.
7. **Liquidity of assets.** Highly liquid assets normally receive more audit attention than their asset size alone would indicate. Liquid assets are active, mobile resources that are an attractive target for defalcations. Thus, the more liquid the resources of an audit unit, the greater the level of internal auditing.

AUDIT RISK FACTORS

IIA Professional Standards—Planning suggests these risk factors be considered during the risk assessment process.

- Ethical climate and pressure on management to meet objectives
- Competence, adequacy, and integrity of personnel
- Asset size, liquidity, or transaction volume
- Financial and economic conditions
- Competitive conditions
- Complexity or volatility of activities
- Impact of customers, supplier, and government regulations
- Degree of computerized information systems
- Geographical dispersion of operations
- Adequacy and effectiveness of the system of internal control
- Organizational, operational, technological, or economic changes
- Management judgments and accounting estimates
- Acceptance of audit findings and corrective action taken
- Date and results of previous audits

---

8. **Recent change in key personnel.** Control systems depend on competent judgments by key personnel. A lack of continuity in personnel may mean the control system is less effective than in previous periods.
9. **Economic condition of unit.** Because of pressure on management to produce improved economic results, the risk of control breakdowns is often greater in units with poor economic performance. In addition, poor economic performance may be a signal of such breakdowns. Thus, units with poor economic conditions are likely to pose more risk for the firm.

RISK FACTORS

Factors to be used in risk analysis include (1) financial exposure and potential loss, (2) results of prior audits, and (3) major operating changes. Skills available on the audit staff is not a risk factor since missing skills can be obtained from elsewhere unless too costly that risk may be accepted.

Factors that should be considered when evaluating audit risk in a functional area would include: (1) volume of transactions, (2) dollar value of "assets at risk," and (3) average value per transaction.

---

10. **Rapid growth.** Rapid growth stretches the personnel and the management control system of an operation. While growth provides significant opportunities for profit, it also provides the opportunity for control problems to emerge.
11. **Extent of computerized data processing.** Computer processing provides a central hub through which much essential management information passes. In some cases, this hub is viewed as a "black box"; and great potential exists for the loss of asset control as well as the loss of significant information.
12. **Time since last audit.** Because the internal audit detects and deters inappropriate activity, the effects of internal auditing will likely be greatest just before and just after an audit. As the time since the last audit increases, the risk of loss of internal control increases.
13. **Pressure on management to meet objectives.** For the same reasons discussed in item 9, increased performance pressure increases the pressure to circumvent controls.
14. **Extent of government regulation.** This factor reflects the fact that the firm may be subject to some unpredictable forces, which may serve to increase risk.
15. **Level of employees' morale.** This factor may be important because low morale may indicate significant differences between the objectives of the top management and those of individuals at lower levels. Such differences can lead to increased risk.
16. **Audit plans of independent auditors.** Although internal and external auditors have differing concerns and objectives in auditing, their activities do overlap. The plans of external auditors can influence individuals in units, which might be subject to external and internal auditing.
17. **Political exposure.** Risk comes in many forms. The cost of events can be direct (i.e., lost profits and fraud losses) or indirect (i.e., reputation).
18. **Need to maintain appearance of independence by internal auditor.** This factor was included to see if the internal auditor's resource allocation would be significantly affected by the need to maintain the appearance (in addition to the substance) of independence within the firm. Given its low rating, this factor apparently is not a significant influence.
19. **Distance of unit from home office (least important factor).** This factor was included to determine if the out-of-sight, out-of-mind approach applied to internal audit risk. It may also reflect the foreign versus domestic aspects of relative risk.

(b) **Approaches to Risk Assessment.** The purposes of risk analysis and assessment are to identify risks and exposures, calculate the damage or loss, and make cost-effective control recommendations. Several risk assessment techniques and approaches are available to quantify risks. Some of them, used in combination, are

- Judgment and intuition
- Scoring approach
- Delphi technique
- Quantitative methods

Judgment and intuition always play an important role in risk assessment. The auditor calls on personal and professional experience and education. This is often called a gut-feel approach. Under this approach, risks may be labeled as high, medium, or low.

The **scoring approach** assigns a weight factor and a risk level to each characteristic. The product of these two numbers is the weighted risk score of the characteristic, and the sum over the risk scores

of an area yields the area risk score. These areas can be ranked according to the weighted risk score. For example, a simplistic, five-factor scoring approach is shown in Exhibit 6.4.

Quality of internal control	Weight factor 30%	Risk level: good control (0), poor control (4)
Liquidity of assets involved	Weight factor 25%	Risk level: none (0), cash (4)
Complexity of operations and systems	Weight factor 20%	Risk level: simple (0), very complex (4)
Stability of organization and systems	Weight factor 15%	Risk level: very stable (0), very unstable (4)
Time since last internal audit	Weight factor 10%	Risk level: continuous (0), more than three years ago (4)

Exhibit 6.4: Risk scoring approach

The weight factors can be derived from using the **Delphi technique**. The audit department can use the Delphi technique to get the weights from the audit staff using their expertise in operational audits, financial audits, compliance audits, program audits, and computer system audits. The rationale for using the Delphi technique is that it is sometimes difficult to get a consensus on the cost or loss value and the probabilities of occurrence.

An example of a **quantitative method,** as recommended by Federal Information Processing Standards (FIPS) Publications (PUB) 65, involves calculating an annual loss exposure value based on estimated costs and potential losses. The annual loss exposure values are considered in the cost-effective selection of controls and safeguards. The essential elements of risk analysis are an assessment of the damage, which can be caused by an unfavorable event, and an estimate of how often such an event may happen in a period of time. Quantitative means of expressing both potential impact and estimated frequency of occurrence are necessary in performing a quantitative risk analysis. The annual loss exposure is calculated as

$$\text{ALE} = \text{I} \times \text{F}$$

where **ALE** is annual loss exposure, **I** is estimated impact in dollars, and **F** is the estimated frequency of occurrence per year.

6.6 Determining Audit Objectives and Scope

(a) **Audit Objectives.** Audit objectives are what the audit project is going to accomplish. Clearly defining the audit assignment objective(s) is a must at the beginning of each audit since it guides the extensiveness of internal control assessment, as well as the scope and methodology of the audit work. Audit assignments with broad objectives are generally more difficult to accomplish and require more staff resources and time than do assignments with specific objectives. Therefore, to the extent possible, audit objective(s) should be defined as precisely as possible to preclude unnecessary work, while concomitantly meeting the assignment's purpose.

For example, this audit objective might require extensive data gathering based on a random statistical sample: "Determine what percentage of program recipients are ineligible for benefits." In this case, one needs to find out the total recipients, eligible recipients, and ineligible recipients. Statistical projections are required based on the sample results.

In contrast, this audit objective might be accomplished with less extensive statistical sampling: "Determine if the agency consistently uses reasonable controls to ensure that only eligible recipients receive benefits." In this case, one needs to assess the controls using different methods (e.g., review of controls over beneficiary enrollment), in which a sampling procedure is a part of the audit procedures.

There should be a meeting of the minds as to objectives between the auditor and the auditee at the beginning of an audit in order to have a useful audit at the end. In all cases, the objectives, scope, and methodology section of the audit report should clearly describe the audit objectives, scope, and the assumptions and basis for auditor conclusions.

(b) **Audit Scope.** The scope of an internal audit is initially defined by the audit objectives. Preliminary survey, audit programs, audit project scheduling, and time estimates are driven by audit objectives. An example of an audit objective is evaluating whether cash receipts are adequately safeguarded.

AUDIT SCOPE

The scope of the internal audit function should not include reviewing the strategic management process, assessing the quality of management decision making both quantitatively and qualitatively, and reporting the results to the audit committee. Other than that, the scope can include anything from the mailroom to the shipping room. The reason is that strategic planning and decision making are the core duties of senior management. The internal auditor should not second-guess senior management; the auditor may not be qualified to perform such reviews.

Scope is the boundary of the audit. Determining the scope of the audit is part of audit planning. It addresses such things as the period and number of locations to be covered. The audit scope should include financial, operational, and compliance audits. The eight steps in determining the scope of the audit would include

- Considering the significance and the needs of potential users of the audit report.
- Obtaining an understanding of the area to be audited.
- Considering legal and regulatory requirements.
- Considering internal control structure.
- Identifying criteria needed to evaluate matters of subject to the audit.
- Identifying significant findings and recommendations from previous audits that could affect the current audit objectives. Auditors should determine if management has corrected the conditions causing those findings and implemented those recommendations.
- Identifying potential sources of data that could be used as audit evidence and the reliability of these data, including data collected by the audited entity, data generated by the auditors, or data provided by third parties.
- Considering whether the work of other auditors or of experts may be used to satisfy some of the auditors' objectives.

Neither audit objectives and audit scope nor audit methodology is determined in isolation. Auditors determine these three elements of the audit plan together, as the considerations in determining each often overlap.

(c) **Considerations for Audit Scope.** Determining the audit scope normally involves matters such as the number of locations to be visited, time frames to be covered, and the type and depth of work needed to ensure that assignment objectives are accomplished and that all applicable audit standards are met.

In establishing an audit scope, the audit team or the supervisor should consider questions such as

- What elements of a finding are required? Is disclosing a particular condition enough, or is it necessary to establish cause and effect? Will it be necessary to evaluate the condition against criteria?
- Will assignment findings relate only to the samples or cases reviewed, or will it be necessary to generalize them to a larger universe?
- What are the relevant sources of data? Who/what holds the data (people, data tapes, and files)? Will the data be available? Are they likely to be reliable?
- What kind of information will be required? For example, will a judgmental sample be acceptable, or will a statistically projectable random sample be required?
- When are audit work results (i.e., audit reports) required?

Determining scope may require trade-offs. For example, a more narrow scope may result in a less powerful message. But it may be the best that can be done considering available resources and time. Is the more narrow scope acceptable?

(d) **Audit Scope Impairments.** During the audit engagement, auditors may find scope impairments. When factors external to the audit organization and the auditor restrict the audit scope or interfere with the auditor's ability to form objective opinions and conclusions, the auditor should attempt to remove the limitation or, failing that, report the limitation. For example, under these conditions an audit will be adversely affected and the auditor will not have complete freedom to make an objective judgment.

- Interference or influence that improperly or imprudently limits or modifies the scope or type of an audit
- Interference with the selection or application of audit procedures or the selection of transactions to be examined
- Denial of access to sources of information, such as books, records, and supporting documents, or denial of opportunity to obtain explanations by officials and employees of the organization, or activity under audit
- Unreasonable restrictions on the time allowed to complete an audit competently

KEY CONCEPTS TO REMEMBER: AUDIT SCOPE

- When faced with an imposed scope limitation, the director of internal auditing should communicate the potential effects of the scope limitation to the audit committee of the board of directors.
- When an internal auditor is auditing the financial operations of an organization, the audit scope does not include a review of the financial decision-making process. The scope includes reviewing the reliability and integrity of financial information; reviewing systems established to ensure compliance with applicable policy, plans, procedures, and other types of authority; and appraising economy, efficiency, and effectiveness of the employment of resources.
- Internal auditors should review the means of safeguarding assets from losses arising from exposure to the elements.

6.7 Audit Work Program

Preparing an audit program is the next step after completing the preliminary survey work. An audit program serves as a road map for the auditor. The audit program provides the auditor the necessary guidance to proceed with the detailed audit work in terms of audit procedures to be conducted and required audit evidence to be collected during the audit. The audit program should focus on major activities and key controls within and around such activities.

The audit program development should take a structured approach where the audit project is broken down into phases, tasks, and steps. Audit programs provide a description of the methodology and suggested steps and procedures to accomplish the audit objectives, a systematic basis for assigning work to audit supervisors and staff, and the basis for a summary record of work.

Audit procedures are the detailed steps, instructions, or guidelines provided for the auditor for the collection and accumulation of a particular type of audit evidence during the audit. Audit procedures can be verbal or written; the latter are preferred and are developed by auditors and approved by audit supervisors. They should be clear to enable auditors to understand what is to be accomplished.

An example of an audit procedure might be "obtain physical inventory sheets, verify the accuracy of inventory extension by multiplying the quantity with cost/price figures. Note any exceptions." Usually audit procedures start with using action words, such as review, verify, look, observe, analyze, confirm, interrelate, construct, reconstruct, prove, read, identify, inquire, determine, reconcile, ascertain, examine, scan, foot, cross-foot, compute, recompute, compare, count, trace, and retrace.

Written audit programs should not be used merely as a checklist of steps to be conducted. Effective work on operational or performance audits require that the staff understand the objectives of the audit and use initiative and creativity in applying the audit program and in assessing the results of the work.

Two types of audit programs exist: (1) standard audit program and (2) customized audit program. Exhibit 6.5 compares each of these programs.

Standardized audit programs

- Inexperienced auditors can execute the programs
- Do not require a great knowledge of the operating environment to develop the programs
- Not much work is required to develop the programs
- Would be appropriate for use in a minimum changing operating environment

Customized audit programs

- Experienced auditors required to execute the programs
- Require lots of knowledge of the operating environment to develop good programs
- Significant amount of time and effort are required to develop the programs

Standardized audit programs	Customized audit programs
• Would be appropriate for use in multiple locations with similar operations • Useful in conducting repeat, routine audits • Would not be appropriate for a complex or changing operating environment	• Would be appropriate for a complex or changing operating environment • Cannot be used in multiple locations with dissimilar operations • Useful in conducting unique, nonroutine audits • Would not be appropriate for a simple or unchanging operating environment

Exhibit 6.5: Standardized vs. customized audit programs

KEY CONCEPTS TO REMEMBER: AUDIT PROGRAMS

- The primary role of an audit program is to serve as a tool for planning, directing, and controlling audit work.
- The primary purpose of developing a written audit program is to help ensure that the audit work is properly planned and documented.
- Audit program should be designed for each individual audit and should include audit steps and procedures to provide assurances that the objectives of the audit are met. To achieve established objectives of the audit department, the best criterion with respect to audit programs is to tailor each audit program to meet the needs of the specific audit assignment.
- These items should be considered essential criteria for developing audit programs: description of the objectives of the auditee operations as agreed to by the auditee, specificity as to the controls to be tested, and specificity as to audit work steps to be followed. The methodology to be used for the audit work steps is not a consideration.
- In the preparation of an audit program, these items are essential: the performance of a preliminary survey, a review of materials from prior audit reports, a review of performance standards set by management. Preparation of a budget identifying the costs of resources needed is not essential during the audit program phase. It would be essential during the planning stage of the audit.
- Upon discovering that an audit area was omitted from the audit program, the auditor should evaluate whether completion of the audit as planned will be adequate.
- Audit programs that test internal controls should be tailored for the audit of each operation.
- The audit program focuses on audit objectives and related audit procedures required to achieve those objectives.
- An example of an audit objective is to ensure that an update of a master file is performed accurately. Example of a related audit procedure is to reconcile computer-generated totals with totals on the updating reports.
- An example of an audit objective is to determine whether inventory stocks are sufficient to meet projected sales.
- An example of an audit procedure is to observe the procedures used to identify defective units produced.
- An example of an audit objective is to determine whether current company policies and procedures are sufficient to provide adequate control over employee additions and deletions to the payroll master file.
- Due professional care standards require that the auditor consider the relative materiality or significance of matters to which audit procedures are applied.

6.8 Planning the Audit Work

Planning and managing an audit assignment starts from developing work plans to completing the audit engagement. The majority of the audit work takes place in the fieldwork phase. In planning, auditors define the audit's objectives, scope, and methodology. Planning continues throughout the audit, and auditors should document their plan and changes to it. The most important task is to make sure that sufficient staff and other resources are available to do the audit work. The audit work can be done either at the headquarters (home office) and/or at the field offices. Exhibit 6.6 summarizes advantages and disadvantages of headquarters and field office work.

At headquarters	*At field offices*
Advantages • More avenues to recruit new auditors • Availability of qualified auditors due to location and ability to recruit auditors due to corporate name • Auditors with special skills can be hired	Advantages • Reduction of travel time and expenses • Auditors will be familiar with local operations and people
Disadvantages • Headquarters auditors are not familiar with field office operations and people • Requires more travel time and expenses • Auditors will be away from home and family • Auditors will have "burnout" feeling	Disadvantages • More expensive to operate a separate office • Lack of qualified auditors due to location • Lack of specific skills among the audit staff • Auditors will not be familiar with the corporate culture • Auditors will not have management insight due to lack of ongoing contact

Exhibit 6.6: Audit work at headquarters and field offices

6.9 IIA'S *Performance Standards*

(a) **Engagement Planning.**

2200—Engagement Planning—Internal auditors should develop and record a plan for each engagement, including the scope, objectives, timing, and resource allocations.

2201—Planning Considerations—In planning the engagement, internal auditors should consider

- The objectives of the activity being reviewed and the means by which the activity controls its performance
- The significant risks to the activity, its objectives, resources, and operations, and the means by which the potential impact of risk is kept to an acceptable level
- The adequacy and effectiveness of the activity's risk management and control systems compared to a relevant control framework or model
- The opportunities for making significant improvements to the activity's risk management and control systems

2201.A1—When planning an engagement for parties outside the organization, internal auditors should establish a written understanding with them about objectives, scope, respective responsibilities, and other expectations, including restrictions on distribution of the results of the engagement and access to engagement records.

2201.C1—Internal auditors should establish an understanding with consulting engagement clients about objectives, scope, respective responsibilities, and other client expectations. For significant engagements, this understanding should be documented.

IIA's Practice Advisory 2200-1: Engagement Planning

Nature of This Practice Advisory

Internal auditors should consider these suggestions when planning engagements. This guidance is not intended to represent all the considerations that may be necessary, but simply a recommended set of items that should be addressed. *Compliance with Practice Advisories is optional.*

1. The internal auditor is responsible for planning and conducting the engagement assignment, subject to supervisory review and approval. The engagement program should
   - Document the internal auditor's procedures for collecting, analyzing, interpreting, and documenting information during the engagement.
   - State the objectives of the engagement.
   - Set forth the scope and degree of testing required to achieve the engagement objectives in each phase of the engagement.
   - Identify technical aspects, activity objectives, risks, processes, and transactions that should be examined.
   - State the nature and extent of testing required.
   - Be prepared prior to the commencement of engagement work and modified, as appropriate, during the course of the engagement.
2. The chief audit executive is responsible for determining how, when, and to whom engagement results will be communicated. This determination should be documented and communicated to man-

agement, to the extent deemed practical, during the planning phase of the engagement. Subsequent changes, which affect the timing or reporting of engagement results, should also be communicated to management, if appropriate.

3. Other requirements of the engagement, such as the engagement period covered and estimated completion dates, should be determined. The final engagement communication format should be considered, since proper planning at this stage facilitates preparing the final engagement communication.
4. All those in management who need to know about the engagement should be informed. Meetings should be held with management responsible for the activity being examined. A summary of matters discussed at meetings and any conclusions reached should be prepared, distributed to individuals, as appropriate, and retained in the engagement working papers. Topics of discussion may include
   - Planned engagement objectives and scope of work
   - The timing of engagement work
   - Internal auditors assigned to the engagement
   - The process of communicating throughout the engagement, including the methods, time frames, and individuals who will be responsible
   - Business conditions and operations of the activity being reviewed, including recent changes in management or major systems
   - Concerns or any requests of management
   - Matters of particular interest or concern to the internal auditor
   - Description of the internal auditing activity's reporting procedures and follow-up process

IIA's Practice Advisory 2320-1: Analysis and Evaluation

Nature of This Practice Advisory

Internal auditors should consider these suggestions when using analysis and evaluation to reach conclusions. This guidance is not intended to represent all the considerations that may be necessary during such an evaluation, but simply a recommended set of items that should be addressed. *Compliance with Practice Advisories is optional. This guidance is repeated in Part 1 and 2 for proper coverage of the subject matter.*

1. Analytical audit procedures provide internal auditors with an efficient and effective means of assessing and evaluating information collected in an engagement. The assessment results from comparing information with expectations identified or developed by the internal auditor. Analytical audit procedures are useful in identifying, among other things
   - Differences that are not expected
   - The absence of differences when they are expected
   - Potential errors
   - Potential irregularities or illegal acts
   - Other unusual or nonrecurring transactions or events
2. Analytical audit procedures may include
   - Comparison of current period information with similar information for prior periods
   - Comparison of current period information with budgets or forecasts
   - Study of relationships of financial information with the appropriate nonfinancial information (e.g., recorded payroll expense compared to changes in average number of employees)
   - Study of relationships among elements of information (e.g., fluctuation in recorded interest expense compared to changes in related debt balances)
   - Comparison of information with similar information for other organizational units
   - Comparison of information with similar information for the industry in which the organization operates
3. Analytical audit procedures may be performed using monetary amounts, physical quantities, ratios, or percentages. Specific analytical audit procedures include, but are not limited to, ratio, trend, and regression analysis, reasonableness tests, period-to-period comparisons, comparisons with budgets, forecasts, and external economic information. Analytical audit procedures assist in-

ternal auditors in identifying conditions that may require subsequent engagement procedures. Internal auditors should use analytical audit procedures in planning the engagement in accordance with the guidelines contained in Section 2200 of the *International Standards for the Professional Practice of Internal Auditing (Standards)* (Practice Advisory 2210-1).

4. Analytical audit procedures should also be used during the engagement to examine and evaluate information to support engagement results. Internal auditors should consider the factors listed next in determining the extent to which analytical audit procedures should be used. After evaluating these factors, internal auditors should consider and use additional audit procedures, as necessary, to achieve the engagement objective.
   - The significance of the area being examined
   - The assessment of risk and effectiveness of risk management in the area being examined
   - The adequacy of the system of internal control
   - The availability and reliability of financial and nonfinancial information
   - The precision with which the results of analytical audit procedures can be predicted
   - The availability and comparability of information regarding the industry in which the organization operates
   - The extent to which other engagement procedures provide support for engagement results
5. When analytical audit procedures identify unexpected results or relationships, internal auditors should examine and evaluate such results or relationships. This examination and evaluation should include making inquiries of management and the application of other engagement procedures until internal auditors are satisfied that the results or relationships are sufficiently explained. Unexplained results or relationships from applying analytical audit procedures may be indicative of a significant condition, such as a potential error, irregularity, or illegal act. Results or relationships that are not sufficiently explained should be communicated to the appropriate levels of management. Internal auditors may recommend appropriate courses of action, depending on the circumstances.

(b) **Engagement Objectives and Scope.**

2210—Engagement Objectives—Objectives should be established for each engagement.

2210.A1—Internal auditors should conduct a preliminary assessment of the risks relevant to the activity under review. Engagement objectives should reflect the results of this assessment.
2210.A2—The internal auditor should consider the probability of significant errors, irregularities, noncompliance, and other exposures when developing the engagement objectives.
2210.C1—Consulting engagement objectives should address risks, controls, and governance processes to the extent agreed on with the client.

2220—Engagement Scope—The established scope should be sufficient to satisfy the objectives of the engagement.

2220.A1—The scope of the engagement should include consideration of relevant systems, records, personnel, and physical properties, including those under the control of third parties.
2220.A2—If significant consulting opportunities arise during an assurance engagement, a specific written understanding as to the objectives, scope, respective responsibilities, and other expectations should be reached and the results of the consulting engagement communicated in accordance with consulting standards.
2220.C1—In performing consulting engagements, internal auditors should ensure that the scope of the engagement is sufficient to address the agreed-on objectives. If internal auditors develop reservations about the scope during the engagement, these reservations should be discussed with the client to determine whether to continue with the engagement.

IIA's Practice Advisory 2210-1: Engagement Objectives

Nature of This Practice Advisory

Internal auditors should consider these suggestions when establishing engagement objectives. This guidance is not intended to represent all the considerations that may be necessary, but simply a recommended set of items that should be addressed. *Compliance with Practice Advisories is optional.*

1. Planning should be documented. Engagement objectives and scope of work should be established. Engagement objectives are broad statements developed by internal auditors and define what the engagement is intended to accomplish. Engagement procedures are the means to attain engagement objectives. Engagement objectives and procedures, taken together, define the scope of the internal auditor's work.
2. Engagement objectives and procedures should address the risks associated with the activity under review. The term "risk" is the uncertainty of an event occurring that could have an impact on the achievement of objectives. Risk is measured in terms of consequences and likelihood. The purpose of the risk assessment during the planning phase of the engagement is to identify significant areas of activity that should be examined as potential engagement objectives.

IIA's Practice Advisory 2210.A1-1: Risk Assessment in Engagement Planning

Nature of This Practice Advisory

Internal auditors should consider these suggestions when assessing risk during engagement planning. This guidance is not intended to represent all the considerations that may be necessary during such an evaluation, but simply a recommended set of items that should be addressed. Internal auditors use their judgment to decide which items are needed to gain sufficient confidence that relevant risks are identified for a specific engagement. *Compliance with Practice Advisories is optional.*

1. The internal auditor should consider management's assessment of risks relevant to the activity under review. The internal auditor will want to take into account
    - The reliability of management's assessment of risk
    - Management's monitoring and reporting of risk issues
    - Management reports of events that have exceeded the agreed limits for risk toleration
    - Whether there are risks identified by management elsewhere in the organization in related activities or supporting systems that may be relevant to the activity under review
    - Management's own assessment of controls related to risks
2. Background information should be obtained about the activities to be reviewed. A review of background information should be performed to determine the impact on the engagement. Relevant items may include
    - Objectives and goals
    - Policies, plans, procedures, laws, regulations, and contracts, which could have a significant impact on operations and reports
    - Organizational information, for example, number and names of employees, key employees, job descriptions, and details about recent changes in the organization, including major system changes
    - Budget information, operating results, and financial data of the activity to be reviewed
    - Prior engagement working papers
    - Results of other engagements, including the work of external auditors, completed or in process
    - Correspondence files to determine potential significant engagement issues
    - Authoritative and technical literature appropriate to the activity
3. If appropriate, a survey should be conducted to become familiar with the activities, risks, and controls, to identify areas for engagement emphasis, and to invite comments and suggestions from engagement clients. A survey is a process for gathering information, without detailed verification, on the activity being examined. The main purposes are to
    - Understand the activity under review
    - Identify significant areas warranting special emphasis
    - Obtain information for use in performing the engagement
    - Determine whether further auditing is necessary
4. A survey permits an informed approach to planning and carrying out engagement work and is an effective tool for applying the internal auditing activity's resources where they can be used most effectively. The focus of a survey will vary depending on the nature of the engagement. The scope

of work and the time requirements of a survey will vary. Contributing factors include the internal auditor's training and experience, knowledge of the activity being examined, the type of engagement being performed, and whether the survey is part of a recurring or follow-up assignment. Time requirements will also be influenced by the size and complexity of the activity being examined and by the geographical dispersion of the activity.

5. A survey may involve use of these procedures.
   - Discussions with the engagement client
   - Interviews with individuals affected by the activity, for example, users of the activity's output
   - On-site observations
   - Review of management reports and studies
   - Analytical auditing procedures
   - Flowcharting
   - Functional "walk-through" (tests of specific work activities from beginning to end)
   - Documenting key control activities
6. The internal auditor should prepare a summary of results from the reviews of management's assessment of risk, the background information, and findings from any survey work carried out. The summary should identify
   - Significant engagement issues and reasons for pursuing them in more depth
   - Pertinent information acquired from all sources
   - Engagement objectives, engagement procedures, and special approaches, such as computer-assisted audit techniques
   - Potential critical control points, control deficiencies, and/or excess controls
   - Preliminary estimates of time and resource requirements
   - Revised dates for reporting phases and completing the engagement
   - When applicable, reasons for not continuing the engagement

(c) **Engagement Resource Allocation.**

2230—Engagement Resource Allocation—Internal auditors should determine appropriate resources to achieve engagement objectives. Staffing should be based on an evaluation of the nature and complexity of each engagement, time constraints, and available resources.

IIA's Practice Advisory 2230-1: Engagement Resource Allocation

Nature of This Practice Advisory

Internal auditors should consider these suggestions when determining engagement resource allocation. This guidance is not intended to represent all the considerations that may be necessary, but simply a recommended set of items that should be addressed. *Compliance with Practice Advisories is optional.*

In determining the resources necessary to perform the engagement, evaluation of these areas is important

- The number and experience level of the internal auditing staff required should be based on an evaluation of the nature and complexity of the engagement assignment, time constraints, and available resources.
- Knowledge, skills, and other competencies of the internal audit staff should be considered in selecting internal auditors for the engagement.
- Training needs of internal auditors should be considered, since each engagement assignment serves as a basis for meeting developmental needs of the internal auditing activity.
- The use of external resources should be considered in instances where additional knowledge, skills, and other competencies are needed.

(d) **Engagement Work Program.**

2240—Engagement Work Program—Internal auditors should develop work programs that achieve the engagement objectives. These work programs should be recorded.

2240.A1—Work programs should establish the procedures for identifying, analyzing, evaluating, and recording information during the engagement. The work program should be approved prior to *its implementation*, and any adjustments should be approved promptly.
2240.C1—Work programs for consulting engagements may vary in form and content depending on the nature of the engagement.

IIA's Practice Advisory 2240-1: Engagement Work Program

Nature of This Practice Advisory

Internal auditors should consider these suggestions when developing engagement work programs. This guidance is not intended to represent all the considerations that may be necessary, but simply a recommended set of items that should be addressed. *Compliance with Practice Advisories is optional.*

1. Engagement procedures, including the testing and sampling techniques employed, should be selected in advance, where practicable, and expanded or altered if circumstances warrant. More detailed guidance is described in Practice Advisory 2210.A1-1.
2. The process of collecting, analyzing, interpreting, and documenting information should be supervised to provide reasonable assurance that the auditor's objectivity is maintained and engagement goals are met. More detailed guidance is described in Practice Advisory 2340-1.

IIA's Practice Advisory 2240.A1-1: Approval of Work Programs

Nature of This Practice Advisory

Internal auditors should consider these suggestions when approving work programs. This guidance is not intended to represent all the considerations that may be necessary, but simply a recommended set of items that should be addressed. *Compliance with Practice Advisories is optional.*

1. In obtaining approval of the engagement work plan, such plans should be approved in writing by the chief audit executive or designee prior to the commencement of engagement work, where practicable. Initially, approval may be obtained orally, if factors preclude obtaining written approval prior to commencing engagement work. Adjustments to engagement work plans should be approved in a timely manner.

MULTIPLE-CHOICE QUESTIONS (1-66)

1. During a preliminary survey, an auditor notes that several accounts payable vouchers for major suppliers show adjustments for duplicate payment of prior invoices. This would indicate

a. A need for additional testing to determine related controls and the current exposure to duplicate payments made to suppliers.
b. An unrecorded liability for the amount of purchases that are not processed while awaiting supplier master file address maintenance.
c. A lack of control in the receiving area that prevents timely notice to the accounts payable area that goods have been received and inspected.
d. The existence of a sophisticated accounts payable system that correlates overpayments to open invoices and therefore requires no further audit concern.

2. Which of the following best describes a preliminary survey?

a. A standardized questionnaire used to obtain an understanding of management objectives.
b. A statistical sample of key employee attitudes, skills, and knowledge.
c. A "walk-through" of the financial control system to identify risks and the controls that can address those risks.
d. A process used to become familiar with activities and risks in order to identify areas for audit emphasis.

Items 3 through 5 are based on the following:

The following information is available from the financial statements of a manufacturing division. The director of internal auditing is reviewing the data to identify potential risks as a basis for planning the audit. The division has not been audited by the internal auditing department in the past three years. The division conducts most of its business autonomously. The division has historically relied on one major product. However, that product is aging and will soon lose its patent protection.

Ratio	*(20X3)* Current year	*(20X2)* Previous year	*(20X1)* Prior year	*Industry* average
Current ratio	1.94	1.89	2.28	2.13
Quick ratio	0.66	0.88	1.22	1.4
Days sales in receivables	112	93	72	69
Days sales in inventory	148	167	92	73
Cost of goods sold as % of sales	0.375	0.402	0.412	0.445
Sales/tangible assets	2.89	2.58	2.53	3.01
Sales/total assets	1.33	1.31	2.53	2.78
Sales growth	0.03	0.16	0.02	0.045
Net income (thousands)	($7,600)	$985	($1,200)	$4,500

3. The division had a large increase in sales in the previous year (20X2). Which of the following hypotheses would the data support regarding the potential cause of the sales increase? The division

a. Reduced its selling price for most of its product line.
b. Acquired another company and accounted for the purchase as a purchase transaction, not a pooling.
c. Liquidated a substantial part of its older inventory.
d. Sold off most of its intangible assets, realizing a profit on the sale.

4. Which of the following would **not** explain the decrease in cost of goods sold as a percentage of sales ratio? The division

a. Liquidated inventory in conjunction with a plan to bring its current ratio more in line with the industry average.
b. Increased the selling price of its products by selling to less creditworthy customers.
c. Recorded subsequent year's sales in the current year, but adjusted inventory to actual goods on hand at year-end.
d. Is incorrectly capitalizing certain production costs.

5. The current ratio increased during the past year while the quick ratio decreased. Which of the following explanations would best explain the reason that the current ratio increased while the quick ratio decreased?

a. A substantial increase in accounts payable that affects the current ratio but not the quick ratio.
b. The significant buildup of inventory.
c. The substantial increase in accounts receivable.
d. The large increase in the amount of intangible assets that affects the current ratio but not the quick ratio.

6. Writing an audit program occurs at which stage of the audit process?

a. During the planning stage.
b. Subsequent to testing internal controls to determine whether to rely on the controls or audit around them.
c. As the audit is performed.
d. At the end of each audit, the standard audit program should be revised for the next audit to ensure coverage of noted problem areas.

7. In planning an audit, an on-site survey could assist with all of the following **except:**

a. Obtaining auditee comments and suggestions on control problems.
b. Obtaining preliminary information on internal controls.
c. Identifying areas for audit emphasis.
d. Evaluating the effectiveness of the system of internal controls.

8. Fieldwork has been defined as "a systematic process of objectively gathering evidence about an entity's operations, evaluating it, and determining if those operations meet acceptable standards." Which of the following is **not** part of the work performed during fieldwork?

a. Expanding or altering audit procedures if circumstances warrant.
b. Applying the audit program to accomplish audit objectives.
c. Creating working papers that document the audit.
d. Developing a written audit program.

9. The IIA *Standards* require auditors to discuss conclusions and recommendations at appropriate levels of management before issuing final written reports. Auditors usually accomplish this by conducting exit conferences. Which of the following **best** describes the purpose of exit conferences?

a. To allow auditees to get started implementing recommendations as soon as possible.
b. To allow auditors to explain complicated findings before a written report is issued.
c. To allow auditors to "sell" findings and recommendations to management.
d. To ensure that there have been no misunderstandings or misinterpretations of facts.

10. The advantage attributed to the establishment of internal auditing field offices for work at foreign locations is best described as

a. The possibility of increased objectivity of personnel assigned to a field office.
b. A reduction of travel time and related travel expense.
c. The increased ease of maintaining uniform company-wide standards.
d. More contact with senior audit personnel leading to an increase in control.

11. In the preparation of an audit program, which of the following items is **not** essential?

a. The performance of a preliminary survey.
b. A review of material from prior audit reports.
c. The preparation of a budget identifying the costs of resources needed.
d. A review of performance standards set by management.

12. A primary purpose of the closing conference is to

a. Implement audit findings.
b. Gather audit evidence.
c. Resolve remaining issues.
d. Determine the scope of the audit.

13. What action should an internal auditor take on discovering that an audit area was omitted from the audit program?

a. Document the problem in the work papers and take no further action until instructed to do so.
b. Perform the additional work needed without regard to the added time required to complete the audit.
c. Continue the audit as planned and include the unforeseen problem in a subsequent audit.
d. Evaluate whether completion of the audit as planned will be adequate.

14. In order to determine the extent of audit tests to be performed during fieldwork, preparing the audit program should be the next step after completing the

a. Preliminary survey.
b. Survey of company policies.
c. Assignment of audit staff.
d. Time budgets for specific audit tasks.

15. Which of the following is a step in an audit program?

a. The audit will commence in six weeks and include tests of compliance.
b. Determine whether the manufacturing operations are effective and efficient.
c. Auditors may not reveal findings to nonsupervisory, operational personnel during the course of this audit.
d. Observe the procedures used to identify defective units produced.

16. Audit programs testing internal controls should

a. Be tailored for the audit of each operation.
b. Be generalized to fit all situations without regard to departmental lines.
c. Be generalized so as to be usable at all locations of a particular department.
d. Reduce costly duplication of effort by ensuring that every aspect of an operation is examined.

17. An auditor begins an audit with a preliminary evaluation of internal control, the purpose of which is to decide on the extent of future auditing activities. If the auditor's preliminary evaluation of internal control results in a finding that controls may be inadequate, the next step would be

a. An expansion of audit work prior to the preparation of an audit report.
b. The preparation of a flowchart depicting the internal control system.
c. An exception noted in the audit report if losses have occurred.
d. To implement the desired controls.

18. An internal auditor has just completed an on-site survey in order to become familiar with the company's payroll operations. Which of the following should be performed next?

a. Assign audit personnel.
b. Establish initial audit objectives.
c. Write the audit program.
d. Conduct fieldwork.

19. Interviewing operating personnel, identifying the objectives of the auditee, identifying standards used to evaluate performance, and assessing the risks inherent in the auditee's operations are activities typically performed in which phase of an internal audit?

a. The fieldwork phase.
b. The preliminary survey phase.
c. The audit programming phase.
d. The reporting phase.

20. The auditor-in-charge has just been informed of the next audit assignment and the assigned audit team. Select the appropriate phase for finalizing the audit time budget.

a. During formulation of the long-range plan.
b. After the preliminary survey.
c. During the initial planning meeting.
d. After the completion of all fieldwork.

21. Many administrative audit tasks are performed during the course of an audit. Various audit tasks are shown below and given a number. In the answers, the numbered tasks are grouped as being done primarily by a staff auditor, audit manager, or director of audit. Only one of the following groupings is correct. Select the answer in which listed tasks are **most** appropriately grouped according to the auditor position.

1. The auditee is selected and the scope of the audit assigned.
2. An initial interview is held with the auditee explaining the scope of the audit.
3. Working papers are prepared showing audit work performed.
4. Audit work is supervised during the fieldwork.

5. Working papers are reviewed.
6. Inquiry is made of auditee management to explain unusual findings.
7. Working papers are finalized and a preliminary report is prepared.
8. Review draft audit report prior to discussion with management.
9. After the audit report has been discussed with auditee management, the report and working papers receive a final review before the audit report is signed, published, and distributed.

Not all tasks are listed in each answer and some of the numbered tasks could be done by more than one of the three auditing personnel.

	Staff auditor	*Audit manager*	*Audit director*
a.	3, 6, 7	2, 5, 8	1, 8, 9
b.	2, 4, 7	3, 4, 8	1, 6, 9
c.	3, 7, 9	2, 4, 6	2, 3, 8
d.	2, 7, 9	4, 6, 8	1, 5, 6

22. A governmental agency constrained by scarce audit and human resources wishes to know the status of its program for licensing automobiles. In particular, management is concerned about the possibility of

- A backlog in new license applications, and
- Poor controls over the collection and processing of application fees.

The results of the preliminary survey and limited audit testing conducted by the internal auditing department revealed that the licensing process was operating as intended. No major deficiencies were noted. How should the internal auditing department proceed?

a. Perform no further audit work, issue a formal audit report with the survey results, and discuss the results with management.
b. Perform no further audit work, discuss pertinent issues with management and the executive director, and prepare an audit program for future use so that another survey will not be necessary.
c. Complete the audit as scheduled to ensure that other issues do not exist that were not noted during the survey phase.
d. Send a memorandum report to the executive director and other concerned parties summarizing the preliminary survey results and indicating that the audit has been canceled.

23. Which of the following would **not** be considered an objective of the audit closing or exit conference?

a. To resolve conflicts.
b. To discuss the findings.
c. To identify concerns for future audits.
d. To identify management's actions and responses to the findings.

24. During an exit conference, an auditor and an auditee disagreed about a well-documented audit finding. Which of the following would describe an appropriate manner to handle the situation, assuming that it cannot be resolved prior to issuing the audit report?

a. Present the finding giving all of the facts and conclusions resulting from the testing.
b. Present both the audit finding and auditee's position on the finding.
c. Defer reporting the item and plan to perform more detailed work during the next audit.
d. Change the finding to agree with the auditee's position.

25. An audit of an automated accounts receivable function for a single-plant furniture manufacturing company has just been completed. Significant findings include late posting of customers' payments, late mailing of monthly invoices, and erratic follow-up on past-due accounts. Which of the following managers should attend the exit conference for this audit?

a. Director of internal auditing, chief operating officer, and controller.
b. Head of the audit team, controller and vice president of information systems.
c. Head of the audit team, manager of the accounts receivable department, and manager of the data processing department.
d. Director of internal auditing, chief financial officer, chief executive officer, and vice president of information systems.

26. One of the primary roles of an audit program is to

a. Serve as a tool for planning, directing, and controlling audit work.
b. Document an auditor's understanding of the internal control system.
c. Provide for a standardized approach to the audit engagement.
d. Delineate the audit risk accepted by the auditor.

27. The IIA *Standards* require that internal auditors discuss conclusions and recommendations at appropriate levels of management before issuing final written reports. Which of the following is the primary reason that a closing conference should be documented by the auditor?

a. The information may be needed if a dispute arises.
b. The *Standards* require that closing conferences be documented.
c. The information may be needed to revise future audit programs.
d. Closing conference documentation becomes a basis for future audits.

28. The preliminary survey discloses that a prior audit deficiency was never corrected. Subsequent fieldwork confirms that the deficiency still exists. Which of the following courses of action should the internal auditor pursue?

a. Take no action. To do otherwise would be an exercise of operational control.
b. Discuss the issue with the director of internal auditing. The problem requires an ad hoc solution.
c. Discuss the issue with the person(s) responsible for the problem. They should know how to solve the problem.
d. Order the person(s) responsible to correct the problem. They have had long enough to do so.

29. The **best** control over the work on which audit opinions are based is

a. Supervisory review of all audit work.
b. Preparation of time budgets for auditing activities.
c. Preparation of working papers.

d. Staffing of audit activities.

30. A standardized internal audit program would **not** be appropriate for the following situation:
  a. A stable operating environment undergoing only minimal changes.
  b. A complex or changing operating environment.
  c. Multiple locations with similar operations.
  d. Subsequent inventory audits performed at same location.

31. An audit program for a comprehensive audit of a purchasing function should include
  a. Work steps arranged by relative priority based on perceived risk.
  b. A statement of the audit objectives of the operation under review with agreement by the auditee.
  c. Specific methods to accomplish audit objectives.
  d. A focus on risks impacting the financial statements as opposed to controls.

32. The finance department of a governmental unit has a computer-based model for forecasting tax revenue to use in preparing annual budgets. The internal audit group has been asked to audit the model. A reasonable objective of the audit would be to
  a. Verify that for varying input values the model gives results consistent with revenue behavior.
  b. Confirm that the model forecasts each kind of revenue within a small percentage of actual revenue.
  c. Determine whether the programs used for this year's forecast were identical to those used in the previous year.
  d. Ensure that the model was modified so that it would have forecasted the previous year's actual revenue.

33. An internal auditing department has scheduled an audit of a construction contract. One portion of this audit will include comparing materials purchased to those specified in the engineering drawings. The auditing department does not have anyone on staff with sufficient expertise to complete this audit step. Select the best alternative for the director of internal auditing.
  a. Delete the audit from the schedule.
  b. Perform the entire audit using current staff.
  c. Engage an engineering consultant to perform the comparison.
  d. Accept the contractor's written representations.

34. One purpose of the exit conference is for the internal auditor to
  a. Require corrective action for deficiencies found.
  b. Review and verify the appropriateness of the audit report based on auditee input.
  c. Review the performance of audit personnel assigned to the engagement.
  d. Present the final audit report to management.

35. At a meeting with audit managers, the director of internal auditing is allocating the audit work schedule for next year's plan. Which of the following methods would ensure that each audit manager receives an appropriate share of both the work schedule and internal auditing department resources?
  a. Auditable units are assigned to each manager based on risk and skill analysis.
  b. Each of the audit managers selects the individual audit assignments desired, based on preferences for the audit area and the management personnel involved in the audit.
  c. Each audit manager chooses audit assignment preferences based on the total staff hours that are currently available to each manager within the department.
  d. The full list of scheduled audits is published for the audit staff, and work assignments are made based on career interests and travel requirements.

36. An internal auditor would most likely judge an error in an account balance to be material if the error involves a(n)
  a. Clerical mistake that is unlikely to occur again.
  b. Large percentage of net income.
  c. Unverified routine transaction.
  d. Unusual transaction for the company.

37. An internal auditor judged an item to be immaterial when planning an audit. However, the auditor may still include the item if it is subsequently determined that
  a. Sufficient staff is available.
  b. Adverse effects related to the item are likely to occur.
  c. Related evidence is reliable.
  d. Miscellaneous income is affected.

38. In the performance of an audit, audit risk is best defined as the risk that an auditor
  a. Might not select documents that are in error as part of the examination.
  b. May not be able to properly evaluate an activity because of its poor internal accounting controls.
  c. May fail to detect a significant error or weakness during an examination.
  d. May not have the expertise to adequately audit a specific activity.

39. An internal auditor discovered an error in a receivable due from a major stockholder. The receivable's balance accounts for less than 1% of the company's total receivables. Would the auditor be likely to consider the error to be material?
  a. Yes, if relative risk is low.
  b No, if there will be further transactions with this stockholder.
  c. Yes, because a related party is involved.
  d. No, because a small dollar amount is in error.

Items 40 through 43 are based on the following:

A manufacturing company has been expanding rapidly and is considering adding a new production line. Employees are currently working double shifts and receiving large amounts of overtime pay. Demand for all of the company's products is currently high, but management worries about demand fluctuations with changes in the economy and technological developments by competitors. Management is concerned with such issues as whether it is efficiently using its resources, whether it is expanding too rapidly or not rapidly enough, whether employee morale is decreasing, and whether future expansion should be financed internally or through debt.

40. Of the following management requests, which is within the normal audit scope as stated in the IIA *Standards*?

a. Perform an independent evaluation of management's planning process as a basis for making recommendations.
b. Talk with banks to identify financing alternatives and negotiate contract alternatives, which would be presented to management for their evaluation.
c. Analyze financing alternatives and present the alternatives to the audit committee.
d. Undertake a make-or-buy decision analysis to determine whether the company should subcontract for part of its manufacturing versus adding capacity. Report the recommendation to management for approval.

41. Which of the following factors might best indicate the possibility of fraudulent activity in the production process?

a. Employee overtime has increased 50% during the past year.
b. Although scrap is generated, there is no income reported from scrap sales.
c. Interviews with employees indicate they have a general dissatisfaction with management and believe that productivity could be greatly improved if management listened to the employees.
d. Inventory, per accounting records, has decreased at the same time that the cost of goods sold has increased.

42. Management requests the auditor to examine factors that would help improve the efficiency with which resources are used in the purchasing and production processes. Which of the following procedures would be the **least** effective in addressing management's concern?

a. Perform an evaluation of the planning process to determine goods to be ordered and the method of purchasing goods.
b. Perform a comparison of production costs over the past three years. Identify any large deviations and investigate causes.
c. Interview personnel involved in the production process to gain insight on production or acquisition problems.
d. Compare the company's total cost of goods sold, as a percentage of total sales, with industry averages.

43. Management is concerned that employee productivity and morale may be decreasing even though production workers are being paid more overtime wages. Which of the following audit procedures would be **least** effective in addressing this concern?

a. Develop a schedule of employee pay and analyze changes in overtime pay.
b. Develop a schedule of production per employee over the past two years stratified by production during standard work shifts and production during overtime periods.
c. Take a statistical sample of employees and interview selected employees regarding their morale, productivity, and views on methods to improve efficiency.
d. Obtain "best practices" production data from a comparable industry and identify areas of differences. Follow-up with interviews of production supervisors.

Items 44 through 50 are based on the following:

An internal auditor is assigned to perform an audit of the company's insurance program, including the appropriateness of the approach to minimizing risks to the company. The company self-insures against large casualty losses and health benefits provided for all its employees. The company is a large national firm with over 15,000 employees located in various parts of the country. It uses an outside claims processor to administer its health care program. The company's medical costs have been rising by approximately 8% per year for the past five years, and management is concerned with controlling them.

44. The auditor needs to determine the scope of the proposed audit of insurance coverage by the company. Which of the following statements are correct regarding the potential scope of the audit?

I. Since it is an internal audit, the audit department should concentrate on processing that occurs within the company and not on auditing the correctness of transaction processing by the health care processor.
II. The auditor should interview management prior to beginning the audit to understand (1) its concerns and (2) the underlying assumptions made and rationale used when making the self-insurance decision.
III. The auditor should consider engaging an actuarial consultant to better understand the risks involved in order to help determine the scope of the audit.

a. I only.
b. II only.
c. Both I and II.
d. II and III.

45. Which of the following analytical review procedures would provide the most insight into the reasonableness of the increase in health care costs?

a. Develop a comparison of the costs incurred with similar costs incurred by other companies.
b. Obtain the government index of health care costs for the comparable period of time and compare the rate of increase with that of the cost per employee incurred by the company.
c. Obtain a bid from another health care administrator to provide the same administrative services as the current health care administrator.
d. Develop a comparison of overall health insurance costs incurred by the company with similar costs incurred by companies in the same industry.

46. Assume that the auditor wishes to test whether the health care processor is meeting contract requirements regarding the proper payment or denial of employee claims. The best audit approach would be to take a sample of

a. Employees and interview them regarding their health care experiences with proper and timely payment by the health care processor.
b. Claims paid by the health care processor and determine whether all the payments were proper.
c. Claims filed with the health care processor and determine whether they were either appropriately paid or denied.
d. Claims paid by the health care processor and engage an outside expert to analyze whether the claims were appropriately processed.

47. When the audit was assigned, management asked the auditor to evaluate the appropriateness of using self-insurance to minimize risk to the organization. Given the scope of the audit requested by management, should the auditor engage an actuarial consultant to assist in the audit if these skills do not exist on staff?

a. No. The audit department is skilled in assessing controls, and the insurance control concepts are not distinctly different from other control concepts.
b. No. It is a normal audit function to assess risk; this audit engagement is therefore not unique.
c. Yes. An actuary is essential to determine whether the health care costs are reasonable.
d. Yes. The actuary has skills not usually found in auditors to identify and quantify self-insurance risks.

48. Assume the auditor becomes concerned that significant fraud may be taking place by dentists who are billing the health care processor for services that were not provided. For example, employees may have their teeth cleaned, but the dentist charges the processor for pulling teeth and developing dentures. The most effective audit procedure to determine whether such a fraud exists would be to

a. Develop a schedule of payments made to individual dentists. Verify that payments were made to the dentists by confirming the payments with the health care processor.
b. Take a random sample of payments made to dentists and confirm the amounts paid with the dentists' offices to determine that the amounts agree with the amounts billed by the dentists.
c. Take a random sample of claims submitted by dentists and trace through the system to determine whether the claims were paid at the amounts billed.
d. Take a discovery sample of employee claims that were submitted through dentist offices and confirm the type of service performed by the dentist through direct correspondence with the employee who had the service performed.

49. The health care processor wishes to implement controls that would help prevent the type of fraud described in the prior question. Assume further that all the claims are submitted electronically to the health care processor. Which of the following control procedures would be the most effective?

a. Develop a program that identifies procedures performed on an individual in excess of expectations based on: the age of the employee, whether a similar procedure was performed recently, or the average cost per claim.
b. Require all submitted claims to be accompanied by a signed statement by the dentist testifying to the fact that the claimed procedures were performed.
c. Send confirmations to the dentists requesting them to confirm the exact nature of the claims submitted to the health care processor.
d. Develop an integrated test facility and submit false claims to verify that the system is detecting such claims on a consistent basis.

50. Assume that the auditor's preliminary findings indicate that certain dentists are billing the health care processor for services that were not provided and that this practice is not being detected or prevented by the health care processor. The auditor wishes to present to management an estimate of the amounts involved. The auditor chooses an approach that will sample claims by dentists and will verify whether the claims are appropriate. The best audit sampling approach would be

a. Discovery sampling based on a low to moderate level of fraud expectation.
b. Dollar unit sampling of all dentists to determine if the fraud might exceed a predetermined limit.
c. Attribute sampling classifying the existence of a nonvalid claim as a deviation.
d. Classical variables estimation of claims submitted by the suspected dentists stratified by dollar amount of services performed.

51. An internal auditor is assigned to conduct an audit of security of a local area network (LAN) in the finance department of the organization. Investment decisions, including the use of hedging strategies and financial derivatives, use data and financial models that run on the LAN. The LAN is also used to download data from the mainframe to assist in the decisions. In determining the scope of the audit, which of the following items should be considered **outside the scope** of the security audit?

a. Investigation of the physical security over access to the components of the LAN.
b. The ability of the LAN application to identify data items at the field or record level and implement user access security at that level.
c. Interviews with users to determine their assessment of the level of security in the system and the vulnerability of the system to compromise.
d. The level of security of other LANs in the company that also utilize sensitive data.

52. An internal auditor conducts a preliminary survey and identifies a number of significant audit issues and reasons for pursuing them in more depth. The auditee informally communicates concurrence with the preliminary survey results and asks that the auditor not report on the areas of significant concern until the auditee has an opportunity to respond to the problem areas. Which of the following audit responses would **not** be appropriate?

a. Keep the audit on the audit time schedule and discuss with management the need for completing the audit on a timely basis.
b. Consider the risk involved in the areas involved, and if the risk is high, proceed with the audit.
c. Consider the audit to be terminated with no report needed since the auditee has already agreed to take constructive action.
d. Work with the auditee to keep the audit on schedule and address the significant issues in more depth, as well as the auditee's responses, during the course of the audit.

53. The auditor has planned an audit of the effectiveness of the quality assurance function as it affects the receiving of goods, the transfer of the goods into production, and the scrap costs related to defective items. The auditee argues that such an audit is not within the scope of the internal auditing function and should come only under the purview of the quality assurance department. What would be the **most** appropriate audit response?

a Refer to the audit department charter and the approved audit plan, which includes the area designated for audit in the current time period.
b. Since quality assurance is a new function, seek the approval of management as a mediator to set the scope of the audit.
c. Indicate that the audit will only examine the function in accordance with the standards set, and approved, by the quality assurance function before beginning the audit.
d. Terminate the audit because an operational audit will not be productive without the auditee's cooperation.

Items 54 through 56 are based on the following:

The internal auditing department of an organization has been in existence for ten years. It has established a charter, which has not yet been approved by the audit committee. However, the audit committee is chaired by the chief executive officer (CEO) and includes the controller and one outside board member. The director reports directly to the controller who approves the internal audit work plan. Thus, the auditing department has never felt the need to push for a formal approval of the charter. The organization is publicly held and has nine major divisions. The previous director of internal auditing was recently dismissed following a dispute between the director and a major auditee. The CEO accused the director of not operating "in the best interests of the organization." A new director with significant experience in both public accounting and internal auditing has just been hired. Within the first month, the new director encountered substantial resistance from an auditee regarding the nature of an audit and the audit department's access to records.

54. Which of the following combinations best illustrates a scope limitation and the appropriate response by the director of internal auditing?

	Nature of Limitation	*Internal Auditing Action*
a.	Auditee limits scope of audit based on proprietary information.	Report only to the controller
b.	Auditee will not provide access to records needed for approved audit work plan.	Report to the board
c.	Auditee requests that the audit be delayed for two weeks to allow them to close their books.	Report directly to the CEO and controller
d.	Auditee will not allow auditor to contact major customers as part of a performance audit to measure efficiency of operations.	No reporting needed since it is an operational audit.

55. In considering the internal auditing department's independence, which of the following facts, by themselves, could contribute to a lack of internal audit independence?

I. The CEO accused the previous director of not operating "in the best interests of the organization."
II. The majority of audit committee members come from within the organization.
III. The internal audit charter has not been approved by the board or the audit committee.

a. I only.
b. II only.
c. II and III only.
d. I, II, III.

56. Given the current dispute with an auditee regarding audit scope, which of the following internal auditing actions is **not** appropriate?

a. Meet with the board to obtain approval of the audit charter to mitigate the existence of this problem and similar problems that may occur in the future.
b. Report the dispute, if it remains unresolved, to the board.
c. Review the approved work plan with the CEO and controller and ask for immediate guidance in dealing with the auditee.
d. Indicate to the auditee that if the resistance continues, the auditing department will not be available to perform cost/benefit audits for the department in the future.

57. During the course of an audit, the auditor makes a preliminary determination that a major division has been inappropriately capitalizing research and development expense. The audit is not yet completed, and the auditor has not documented the problem or determined that it really is a problem. However, the auditor is informed that the director of internal auditing has received the following communication from the president of the company:

> *The controller of Division B informs me that you have discovered a questionable account classification dealing with research and development expense. We are aware of the issue. You are directed to discontinue any further investigation of this matter until informed by me to proceed. Under the confidentiality standard of your profession, I also direct you not to communicate with the outside auditors regarding this issue.*

Which of the following would be an appropriate action for the director to take regarding the questionable item?

a. Immediately report the communication to the Institute of Internal Auditors and ask for an ethical interpretation and guidance.
b. Inform the president that this scope limitation will need to be reported to the chairperson of the audit committee.
c. Continue to investigate the area until all the facts are determined and document all the relevant facts in the audit work papers.
d. Immediately notify the external auditors of the problem to avoid aiding and abetting a potential crime by the organization.

58. The internal auditing department encounters a scope limitation from senior management that will affect its ability to meet its goals and objectives for a potential auditee. The nature of the scope limitation should be

a. Noted in the audit work papers, but the audit should be carried out as scheduled and the scope limitation worked around, if possible.
b. Communicated to the external auditors so they can investigate the area in more detail.
c. Communicated, preferably in writing, to the board.

d. Communicated to management stating that the limitation will not be accepted because it would impair the audit department's independence.

59. It is important that the auditor be able to carefully distinguish between a scope limitation and other limitations on the audit. According to the IIA *Standards*, which of the following would **not** be considered a scope limitation?

a. The divisional management of an auditee has indicated that the division is in the process of converting a major computer system and has indicated that the IT portion of the planned audit will have to be postponed until next year.
b. The audit committee reviews the audit plan for the year and deletes an audit that the director thought was important to conduct.
c. The auditee has indicated that certain customers cannot be contacted because the organization is in the process of negotiating a long-term contract with them and does not want to upset the customers.
d. None of the above.

60. According to the IIA *Standards*, an internal auditor's role with respect to operating objectives and goals includes

a. Approving the operating objectives or goals to be met.
b. Determining whether underlying assumptions are appropriate.
c. Developing and implementing control procedures.
d. Accomplishing desired operating program results.

61. The scope of an internal audit is initially defined by the

a. Audit objectives.
b. Scheduling and time estimates.
c. Preliminary survey.
d. Audit program.

62. An outside consultant is developing a system to be used for the management of a city's capital facilities. An appropriate scope of an audit of the consultant's product would be to

a. Review the consultant's contract to determine its propriety.
b. Establish the parameters of the value of the items being managed and controlled.
c. Determine the adequacy of the controls built into the system.
d. Review the handling of idle equipment.

63. Assume your company is considering purchasing a small toxic waste disposal company. As internal auditors, you are part of the team doing a due diligence review for the acquisition. Your scope (as auditors) would most likely **not** include

a. An evaluation of the merit of lawsuits currently filed against the waste company.
b. A review of the purchased company's procedures for acceptance of waste material and comparison with legal requirements.
c. Analysis of the company's compliance with, and disclosure of, loan covenants.
d. Assessment of the efficiency of the waste company's operations and profitability.

64. The **major** purpose of an exit conference is

a. Communication with all affected parties.
b. Correction of deficiencies found.
c. Assessment of audit staff's performance.
d. Presentation of the final audit report.

65. Which of the following is a proper step in an audit program?

a. Notification of the audit.
b. Observation of procedures.
c. Definition of audit objectives.
d. Planning for audit reporting.

66. An internal auditor suspects fraud in the purchasing department. To whom should the auditor communicate this first?

a. The board of directors.
b. The audit committee.
c. The vice president of purchasing.
d. The audit management.

MULTIPLE-CHOICE ANSWERS AND EXPLANATIONS

1. a __ __	15. d __ __	29. a __ __	43. a __ __	57. b __ __
2. d __ __	16. a __ __	30. b __ __	44. d __ __	58. c __ __
3. b __ __	17. a __ __	31. c __ __	45. b __ __	59. b __ __
4. a __ __	18. c __ __	32. a __ __	46. c __ __	60. b __ __
5. b __ __	19. b __ __	33. c __ __	47. d __ __	61. a __ __
6. a __ __	20. b __ __	34. b __ __	48. d __ __	62. c __ __
7. d __ __	21. a __ __	35. a __ __	49. a __ __	63. a __ __
8. d __ __	22. d __ __	36. b __ __	50. d __ __	64. a __ __
9. d __ __	23. c __ __	37. b __ __	51. d __ __	65. b __ __
10. b __ __	24. b __ __	38. c __ __	52. c __ __	66. d __ __
11. c __ __	25. c __ __	39. c __ __	53. a __ __	
12. c __ __	26. a __ __	40. a __ __	54. b __ __	
13. d __ __	27. a __ __	41. b __ __	55. c __ __	1st: __/66 = __%
14. a __ __	28. c __ __	42. d __ __	56. d __ __	2nd: __/66 = __%

1. (a) This preliminary survey information should prompt the auditor to identify the magnitude of such duplicate payments. Choice (b) is incorrect. This situation is not identified in the question. Choice (c) is incorrect. The existence of duplicate payments is not related to a problem in the receiving area. Choice (d) is incorrect. Duplicate payments are not overpayments; they are exceptions and should be handled as such.

Subject Area: Internal audit—plan audit engagements. Source: CIA 597, I-3.

2. (d) It is the most complete per the IIA *Standards*. Choices (a), (b), and (c) are incorrect. Each may be used, but it is only one means in fulfilling the objective of a preliminary survey.

Subject Area: Internal audit—plan audit engagements. Source: CIA 597, I-30.

3. (b) This is shown by the dramatic change between the sales/total assets ratio (large decrease) and the relatively small change in sales/tangible assets ratio. The company must have acquired a large amount of intangible assets during the year. Since purchase accounting also incorporates the results of the acquired company, it is the most likely explanation for the increase. Choice (a) is incorrect. There is no evidence that the company reduced its sales prices. If anything, it may have raised sales prices since the COGS/Sales ratio decreased. Choice (c) is incorrect. Inventory is increasing, not decreasing. Choice (d) is incorrect. This is not likely since intangible assets went up not down.

Subject Area: Internal audit—plan audit engagements. Source: CIA 595, I-49.

4. (a) This is not a potential explanation because (1) there has been an increase in inventory, and (2) a liquidation would have resulted in a write-down of the costs of inventory, which would have caused the ratio to move the other way. Choice (b) is incorrect. This is a potential explanation. Although not the most likely, there is a large increase in the number of days sales in accounts receivable, which could indicate the possibility of less creditworthy customers. Choice (c) is incorrect. This is a potential explanation. Recording subsequent year's sales in the current year, while adjusting inventory to goods actually on hand, would cause the ratio to increase. Choice (d) is incorrect. This is a potential explanation. Incorrectly capitalizing production costs would cause the number of day's sales in inventory to increase and the cost of goods ratio to decrease.

Subject Area: Internal audit—plan audit engagements. Source: CIA 595, I-50.

5. (b) Inventory affects the current ratio, but not the quick ratio. The division is facing liquidity problems as indicated by the quick ratio. Choice (a) is incorrect. It is likely that accounts payable has increased and the increase would affect the quick ratio more so than the current ratio. However, the increase in accounts payable would affect both ratios and would not constitute an explanation for the major differences in the two ratios. Choice (c) is incorrect. The substantial increase in accounts receivable affects both ratios. Moreover, the increase in receivables would have also caused the quick ratio to increase. Choice (d) is incorrect. The amount of intangibles does not affect either ratio.

Subject Area: Internal audit—plan audit engagements. Source: CIA 595, I-51.

6. (a) Planning should include writing the audit program. Choice (b) is incorrect. The external auditor may use this approach in designing substantive tests of balances. (AICPA SAS No. 55) Choice (c) is incorrect. The program is prepared in advance and modified, as appropriate, during the course of the audit. Choice (d) is incorrect. While choice (d) could be done, the program should be updated during the planning process.

Subject Area: Internal audit—plan audit engagements. Source: CIA 1194, I-13.

7. (d) Determining the effectiveness of internal controls would require testing. Choice (a) is incorrect. Survey would assist in obtaining auditee comments. Choice (b) is incorrect. Survey would assist in obtaining information on internal controls. Choice (c) is incorrect. Survey would assist in identifying areas for audit emphasis.

Subject Area: Internal audit—plan audit engagements. Source: CIA 1194, I-14.

8. (d) This is a requirement of the audit-planning standard. The audit program should be developed before the fieldwork begins. Choice (a) is incorrect. This is a requirement of the standards that relates to fieldwork. Choice (b) is incorrect. This statement concerning fieldwork is true, and it is in harmony with the standards. Choice (c) is incorrect. Working paper preparation is a requirement of the IIA standards, which should be met during fieldwork.

Subject Area: Internal audit—plan audit engagements. Source: CIA 1190, I-12.

9. (d) This is the primary purpose of exit conferences. Choice (a) and (c) are incorrect. These are secondary benefits of exit conferences. Choice (b) is incorrect. Complicated findings must be explained thoroughly in written reports.

Subject Area: Internal audit—plan audit engagements. Source: CIA 590, I-39.

10. (b) This choice is an advantage of field office. Choice (a) is incorrect. Objectivity of field office personnel decreases which is a disadvantage. Choice (c) is incorrect. It decreases ease of maintaining uniform standards, which is a disadvantage. Choice (d) is incorrect. It creates greater difficulty in maintaining adequate control, which is a disadvantage.

Subject Area: Internal audit—plan audit engagements. Source: CIA 590, I-10.

11. (c) Resources to be used is necessary. However, conversion to funds needed is not essential for the program. Choice (a) is incorrect. It is needed to determine audit objectives and controls in use. Choice (b) is incorrect. To get background on the audit. Choice (d) is incorrect. This refers to obtaining information on the validity of criteria to be used or to be evaluated during the audit.

Subject Area: Internal audit—plan audit engagements. Source: CIA 1190, I-30.

12. (c) A major purpose of the closing conference is to resolve remaining issues. Choice (a) is incorrect. Audit findings are not implemented. Audit recommendations are implemented. Choice (b) is incorrect. Audit evidence is gathered prior to the closing conference. Choice (d) is incorrect. The engagement scope is determined prior to the closing conference.

Subject Area: Internal audit—plan audit engagements. Source: CIA 1190, I-44.

13. (d) Changes are often needed in the audit plan as work progresses. The auditor should review the plan with his or her supervisor since revised budgets may be needed. Choice (a) is incorrect. Although the finding should be documented, it should be determined whether any changes may need to be made to the audit plan. Choice (b) is incorrect. The budgeted hours should be reviewed and increases approved prior to undertaking any additional steps. Choice (c) is incorrect. The unforeseen area may have an impact on the planned audit and need to be incorporated into the plan.

Subject Area: Internal audit—plan audit engagements. Source: CIA 590, II-2.

14. (a) During the preliminary survey, the internal auditor becomes acquainted with the auditee. He decides how much reliance he can place on the internal control system. This allows him to initially determine whether to extend or limit audit tests. He then prepares the audit program. Choice (b) is incorrect. The survey of company policies may be a segment of the preliminary survey. However, completing the survey of company policies is not sufficient to begin preparing the audit program; the entire preliminary survey must be completed. Choice (c) is incorrect. Audit staff are usually assigned to specific assignments before completing either the preliminary survey or the audit program. Choice (d) is incorrect. Specific tasks to be performed are determined during the audit program preparation.

Subject Area: Internal audit—plan audit engagements. Source: CIA 1190, II-12.

15. (d) This is an audit step because it is a procedure to be followed to obtain necessary evidence. Choice (a) is incorrect. This is simply the proposed starting time and partial scope. Choice (b) is incorrect. This is an audit objective. Choice (c) is incorrect. This is a rule for the conduct of the audit personnel.

Subject Area: Internal audit—plan audit engagements. Source: CIA 592, I-13.

16. (a) A tailor-made program will be more relevant to an operation than a generalized program. Choice (b) is incorrect. A generalized program cannot take into account variations resulting from changing circumstances and varied conditions. Choice (c) is incorrect. A generalized program cannot take into account variations in circumstances and conditions. Choice (d) is incorrect. Every aspect of an operation need not be examined—only those likely to conceal problems and difficulties.

Subject Area: Internal audit—plan audit engagements. Source: CIA 592, II-18.

17. (a) If the preliminary findings indicate control problems, the auditor usually decides to do some expanded testing. Choice (b) is incorrect. If a flowchart were necessary, the auditor would have prepared one during the preliminary evaluation. Choice (c) is incorrect. The auditor is not ready to make a report until more work has been performed. Choice (d) is incorrect. Auditors do not implement controls; that is a function of management.

Subject Area: Internal audit—plan audit engagements. Source: CIA 592, II-19.

18. (c) The audit program is normally prepared after the on-site survey. The on-site survey allows the auditor to become familiar with the auditee, and thus provides input to the audit program. Choice (a) is incorrect. Audit personnel are normally assigned before the on-site survey takes place. Choice (b) is incorrect. Initial audit objectives are established at the beginning of the planning process. They should be specified before the on-site survey takes place. Choice (d) is incorrect. Fieldwork can be performed only after the audit program has been written. Thus, fieldwork could not immediately follow the on-site survey.

Subject Area: Internal audit—plan audit engagements. Source: CIA 1192, I-21.

19. (b) These activities are normally accomplished during the preliminary survey phase. Choice (a) is incorrect. The activities described must be performed before the audit program can be developed, the fieldwork completed, or reporting can be undertaken. Choice (c) is incorrect. The activities described must be performed before the audit programming phase. Choice (d) is incorrect. The reporting phase is the last phase of the four choices given, hence it comes after the preliminary survey phase.

Subject Area: Internal audit—plan audit engagements. Source: CIA 593, II-14.

20. (b) The preliminary survey establishes the subject of the review, the theory of the audit approach, and the structure of the project. If the survey discloses significant differences from the project that was placed in the long-range plan, budget adjustments should be requested and authorized. Choice (a) is incorrect. An initial budget is determined at this time, but revisions, based on the preliminary survey, may be required. Choice (c) is incorrect. The audit project is not sufficiently well defined at this point to complete the budget. Choice (d) is incorrect. At this point, the bulk of the audit hours have been expended and the usefulness of the budget as a control and evaluation tool would be negated.

Subject Area: Internal audit—plan audit engagements. Source: CIA 1192, I-12.

21. (a) All tasks could be accomplished by the personnel in whom the tasks are grouped. Choice (b) is incorrect. Audit work is not supervised (4) by the staff auditor, nor are detailed working papers prepared (3) generally by the audit manager. Choice (c) is incorrect. Final review and signing of the report (9) is not done by the staff auditor, nor are detailed working papers prepared (3) by the audit director. Choice (d) is incorrect. Final review and signing of the report (9) is not done by the staff auditor, nor is the initial review of working papers (5) done by the audit director.

Subject Area: Internal audit—plan audit engagements. Source: CIA 594, I-7.

22. (d) This is the proper level of reporting in light of the results of the preliminary survey and limited testing. Choice (a) is incorrect. Since no further audit work was performed beyond the preliminary survey and limited testing, it would not be appropriate to issue a formal audit report or to discuss it with management. Choice (b) is incorrect. No audit program need be prepared for the future. Because events may occur, or compliance with policies and procedures may change, an audit program written now may be outdated for future use. Also, an audit report summarizing survey results should be prepared. Choice (c) is incorrect. It is not necessary if the survey and limited testing was conducted with due professional care. Also it is a poor use of audit resources.

Subject Area: Internal audit—plan audit engagements. Source: CIA 593, I-2.

23. (c) Identifying concerns for future audits is not a primary objective of the exit conference. Choice (a) is incorrect. Resolving conflicts is an objective of the exit conference. Choice (b) is incorrect. Reaching an agreement on the facts is an objective of the exit conference. Choice (d) is incorrect. Determining management's action plan and responses is an objective of the exit conference.

Subject Area: Internal audit—plan audit engagements. Source: CIA 593, II-39.

24. (b) This is a requirement per the IIA *Standards*. Choice (a) is incorrect. However, it is assumed that in compliance with *Standards*, the auditor discussed the matter with the auditee and that there were no problems. Choice (c) is incorrect. The report should present the findings (results) of the audit. Deferral of reporting would be unprofessional per the *Standards*. Choice (d) is incorrect. This could be correct if the auditor was in error. However, it evades the question and infers agreement with the auditee.

Subject Area: Internal audit—plan audit engagements. Source: CIA 1191, I-9.

25. (c) The managers of the accounts receivable and data processing departments should be informed of the findings by the head of the audit team and given an opportunity to clarify any misunderstandings that might arise. Those managers are in the best positions to resolve the problems that were noted, and their corrective action should be mentioned in the final report. Choice (a) is incorrect. It is neither necessary nor appropriate for these executives to be involved at this phase of the audit. Choice (b) is incorrect. The controller and vice president of information systems need not be involved at this phase of the audit. Choice (d) is incorrect. These executives, like those in choices (a) and (b), should not be involved in an exit conference. The exit conference should discuss audit findings with those who are directly responsible for problems and who are best positioned to take corrective action.

Subject Area: Internal audit—plan audit engagements. Source: CIA 1191, I-42.

26. (a) This is the primary purpose of an audit program. Choice (b) is incorrect. The internal control system should be documented in the work papers by means of narratives, flowcharts, internal control questionnaires, and so on—not in the audit program itself. Choice (c) is incorrect. The audit program should be logical, but it may not be consistent from year to year due to changing conditions encountered by the auditee. The audit program should be tailored to the current year's situation; thus, consistency may not be the most appropriate description. Choice (d) is incorrect. While audit risk should be considered in planning the audit, the nature and extent of audit risk should be documented in the audit work papers, specifically in the planning section.

Subject Area: Internal audit—plan audit engagements. Source: CIA 591, II-32.

27. (a) Notes taken during the course of a closing conference can be valuable in resolving disputes. Choice (b) is incorrect. Documentation of closing conferences is not specifically required by the *Standards*. Choice (c) is incorrect. Notes taken during the closing conference may lead to revised audit program, but that is not the primary use. Choice (d) is incorrect. Information obtained during the closing conference may provide the impetus for future audits, but this is not the primary reason for documenting the closing conference.

Subject Area: Internal audit—plan audit engagements. Source: CIA 1191, I-43.

28. (c) Obtaining auditee cooperation (or at least understanding) is a vital part of the solution of any problem. Choice (a) is incorrect. A deficiency finding places the firm at risk until the situation changes or the deficiency is corrected. Choice (b) is incorrect. Deficiency findings that have not been corrected are not unique, so they do not require ad hoc solutions. Choice (d) is incorrect. The internal auditor should have no line authority over the auditee. To exercise such authority impairs the internal auditor's objectivity.

Subject Area: Internal audit—plan audit engagements. Source: CIA 1191, I-45.

29. (a) As in other activities, the best control is surveillance by knowledgeable supervisors. Choice (b) is incorrect. Although useful in controlling audit time, time budgets do not assure the adequacy of work supporting opinions. Choice (c) is incorrect. Working papers provide the basis for audit opinions, but review is necessary to assure the adequacy of work. Choice (d) is incorrect. Although staffing is required, audit work reviews are essential to ensure an adequate basis for audit opinions.

Subject Area: Internal audit—plan audit engagements. Source: CIA 592, I-26.

30. (b) A standard audit program would not be appropriate for a complex or changing operating environment because the audit objectives and related work steps may no longer have relevance. Choice (a) is incorrect. Standard audit program would be appropriate for use in a minimum changing operating environment. Choice (c) is incorrect. Standard audit program could be used to audit multiple locations with similar operations. Choice (d) is incorrect. Standard audit program would be acceptable for conducting subsequent inventory audits at same location.
Subject Area: Internal audit—plan audit engagements. Source: CIA 592, I-28.

31. (c) Specific methods are included in an audit program. Choice (a) is incorrect. The program should normally be arranged in an order that would most efficiently complete the audit steps. Choice (b) is incorrect. Audit objectives should be stated, but they do not need to be agreed to by the auditee. Choice (d) is incorrect. In a comprehensive audit, there should be a focus on controls as opposed to risks.
Subject Area: Internal audit—plan audit engagements. Source: CIA 1192, I-13.

32. (a) An essential component of the audit approach would be to verify that for varying input values, the model gives results consistent with prior revenue behavior. Choice (b) is incorrect. There is no forecast technique that would always forecast all the different kinds of revenue this precisely; the overall behavior of the model is more important than the forecasting of individual revenue components. Choice (c) is incorrect. There is no reason to believe that the programs used for this year's forecast should be identical to those used in the previous year due to continually evolving circumstances in a state or country. Choice (d) is incorrect. Since the model is a forecasting tool, there is no reason to require that it predict the previous year's actual revenue, especially as conditions and tax regulations change.
Subject Area: Internal audit—plan audit engagements. Source: CIA 1193, I-34.

33. (c) A properly qualified and adequately supervised consultant may be used as needed according to the IIA *Standards*. Choice (a) is incorrect. It would be inappropriate to delete the audit. Choice (b) is incorrect. This is a direct violation of the *Standards*. Choice (d) is incorrect. Accepting the contractor's representations without adequate testing or disclosure of such would violate the *Standards*.
Subject Area: Internal audit—plan audit engagements. Source: CIA 593, I-6.

34. (b) The exit conference provides an opportunity for all parties to communicate their views. This may lead to modifications in the audit report, if justified. Choice (a) is incorrect. The internal auditor cannot require corrective action; only management can. Choice (c) is incorrect. Audit personnel performance is reviewed in private with the individual employee, not at the exit conference. Choice (d) is incorrect. The exit conference is normally based on draft reports. The final report is subject to modification based on the results of the exit conference.
Subject Area: Internal audit—plan audit engagements. Source: CIA 1192, II-44.

35. (a) Assignment on the basis of risk and skill analysis ensures high-risk areas are audited by people with the skills to do it. Choice (b) is incorrect. There is no objective basis in the audit manager's preference for an audit area or the management involved. Choice (c) is incorrect. Available staff hours are not an indicator of risk or composite skills necessary for individual audit assignments. Choice (d) is incorrect. Although career interests and travel requirements are considerations for staffing audit assignments, these factors are not objective in making assignments.
Subject Area: Internal audit—plan audit engagements. Source: CIA 1193, II-6.

36. (b) Materiality is judged based on the significance of the error compared to other items, such as net income. Choice (a) is incorrect. This factor alone does not suggest materiality, since the error is not compared to other items. It also suggests a low amount of relative risk, since the error is not likely to occur again. It appears to be a random error. Choice (c) is incorrect. This factor alone does not indicate materiality, but it does suggest high relative risk. Thus, the auditor may extend auditing procedures for the transaction, even if the error is judged to be immaterial. Choice (d) is incorrect. Again, this factor alone does not indicate materiality. However, the transaction may involve a large amount of relative risk. If so, auditing procedures should be extended even if the error is judged to be immaterial when compared to other items.
Subject Area: Internal audit—plan audit engagements. Source: CIA 1190, I-13.

37. (b) This indicates that auditing procedures may have to be extended because of the item's relative risk, despite the item's lack of materiality. Choice (a) is incorrect. If the auditor does not expect high relative risk, extending auditing procedures for an immaterial item would be an inefficient use of audit resources. This is because costs would exceed benefits. Choice (c) is incorrect. Auditing procedures might be extended if evidence were **unreliable** in hope of finding reliable evidence. Choice (d) is incorrect. This indicates that the item is material. The statement states the item is **immaterial**.
Subject Area: Internal audit—plan audit engagements. Source: CIA 1190, II-3.

38. (c) The failure to communicate an error or weakness in an audit is the overall audit risk. There may be several different reasons why the failure occurred, and these may be classified as in risk categories such as sampling risk, detection risk, or control risk. Choice (a) is incorrect. It describes only sampling risk. Choice (b) is incorrect. It describes only control risks. Choice (d) is incorrect. It describes the competency risk, which is a control risk.
Subject Area: Internal audit—plan audit engagements. Source: CIA 1192, I-3.

39. (c) The transaction probably represents high relative risk since a related party is involved, even though the error is small in dollar amount. The error may be significant enough to be considered material; materiality is based on more than just the dollar amount. Choice (a) is incorrect. Relative risk and materiality are two separate, but overlapping, concepts. If relative risk is low, the auditor would be less likely to consider the error to be material. Choice (b) is incorrect. This suggests that relative risk may be high, and the auditor would thus be likely to consider the error to be material. Choice (d) is incorrect. Since this is a related party transaction, even a small error may indicate s significant risk. The auditor would be likely to consider the error to be material.

Subject Area: Internal audit—plan audit engagements. Source: CIA 591, I-26.

40. (a) The planning process is part of the management control system, and its evaluation is part of the normal scope of the auditor's activities. Choice (b) is incorrect. Although such action may be requested, the activities are a normal management function, not an audit function. It also has the potential to impair the auditor's independence. Choice (c) is incorrect. The auditor should concentrate on management's planning and evaluation process and report on that process to audit committee. The auditor may respond to a management request for such an evaluation, but it is unlikely to be an audit committee request. Choice (d) is incorrect. This is a management function. The auditor may undertake the activity as a management request, but it is not consistent with the normal scope of activities defined in the IIA *Standards*.

Subject Area: Internal audit—plan audit engagements. Source: CIA 1196, I-56.

41. (b) If scrap is generated, there should be some evidence of scrap sales taking place. Choice (a) is incorrect. It appears that fluctuations in demand could have caused the overtime pay increase. Choice (c) is incorrect. The interviews indicate dissatisfaction with management's ability, but do not indicate a fraud. Choice (d) is incorrect. This would not necessarily be a fraud indicator given all the other problems identified. Cost of goods sold could be increasing because of higher sales, which is drawing down inventory.

Subject Area: Internal audit—plan audit engagements. Source: CIA 1196, I-57.

42. (d) While such a comparison may provide useful information, it does not directly address management's directive that the auditor identifies ways in which the efficiency of resource usage could be improved. Also, since different products will have different gross margins, the product mix will affect the results. Choice (a) is incorrect. Proper planning of the purchasing process is a significant influence on the efficiency of resources. Choice (b) is incorrect. This procedure would allow the auditor to focus on situations where costs have fluctuated and would allow the auditor to gain insight as to the causes of the fluctuations. Choice (c) is incorrect. Interviews with appropriate personnel should allow the auditor to gain insight on potential problems.

Subject Area: Internal audit—plan audit engagements. Source: CIA 1196, I-58.

43. (a) This would be the least effective procedure because it only analyzes overtime costs. It does not relate the costs to underlying production data. Choice (b) is incorrect. This procedure would be effective in determining whether productivity decreases during overtime periods. Choice (c) is incorrect. Interviews with employees would be effective in understanding morale issues as well as gathering suggestions for improvement. Choice (d) is incorrect. Best practices, where available, can be useful in providing insight on potential areas of improvement.

Subject Area: Internal audit—plan audit engagements. Source: CIA 1196, I-59.

44. (d) Both Statements II and III are correct. The audit department needs to have sufficient skills or use consultants to understand the risks associated with a proposed audit. In order to conduct the proposed audit, the auditor needs to assess the risks and may need the help of an actuary to better understand the risks to which the organization is exposed. Choice (a) is incorrect. One concern related to increased costs is the accuracy with which the health care processor is handling claims. It should be considered as an integral part of the audit. The internal auditor is not confined to activities only within the organization. Choice (b) is incorrect. Statement II is correct. However, Statement III is also correct, thus making it a preferred response. Choice (c) is incorrect. Statement I is not correct. See choice (a) above.

Subject Area: Internal audit—plan audit engagements. Source: CIA 1196, I-44.

45. (b) This is the best response because it considers that the number of employees covered may have changed. Choice (a) is incorrect. This approach does not consider that the number of employees covered may have changed during the time period considered. Choice (c) is incorrect. This approach is not an analytical review procedure. Further, it considers only one aspect of the total health costs (the cost of processing) and does not consider the underlying health care coverage. Choice (d) is incorrect. This would be effective if it were scaled by the number of employees and the coverage provided. It is a good step, but not as good as choice (b).

Subject Area: Internal audit—plan audit engagements. Source: CIA 1196, I-45.

46. (c) This would provide evidence on both the appropriateness of claim payments as well as whether claims are being denied as specified in the contract with the health care processor. Choice (a) is incorrect. This procedure provides data regarding the satisfaction of the employees with the processor, but does not provide unbiased information about the appropriateness of claim payments. Choice (b) is incorrect. This is a good procedure and will provide evidence on the proper payment of claims that were paid. However, it does not provide any information on claims that should have been paid, but were not paid. Choice (d) is incorrect. This procedure provides evidence only on the claims that were paid.

Subject Area: Internal audit—plan audit engagements. Source: CIA 1196, I-46.

47. (d) Management explicitly asked the auditor to assess the risks that the organization had incurred by moving to self-insurance. Auditors normally do not have these abilities. If necessary, the audit staffing should be expanded to include the expertise of an actuary. Choice (a) is incorrect. An actuary should be used. See choice (d). Choice (b) is incorrect. An actuary should be used. See choice (d). Choice (c) is incorrect. An auditor can determine if costs reasonable. See response (d).

Subject Area: Internal audit—plan audit engagements. Source: CIA 1196, I-47.

48. (d) The problem is that the dentist is submitting a claim on behalf of the employee for services that were not provided. The employee would be the best source of evidence as to whether the service was provided. Discovery sampling would be appropriate in this circumstance. Choice (a) is incorrect. This procedure would only provide evidence that payments were made, not whether the payments were proper. Choice (b) is incorrect. This only provides evidence about the amounts of the claims. The dentist is making the false claims; thus, confirmation with the dentist does not provide objective evidence. Choice (c) is incorrect. This would primarily provide evidence that all claims submitted were processed. It might provide additional evidence on types of claims that were denied, but it would not provide meaningful information on claims that were inappropriately paid.

Subject Area: Internal audit—plan audit engagements. Source: CIA 1196, I-48.

49. (a) This would be the most effective procedure because it would highlight unusual transactions that could be followed up with customer inquiry or other procedures aimed at determining whether claims are fictitious. Choice (b) is incorrect. This would slow down processing, but would not prevent the dentist who submitted the fraudulent claim from continuing to submit such claims. Choice (c) is incorrect. If fraud were involved, the service provider would confirm that the work was done even when it was not. Choice (d) is incorrect. The integrated test facility (ITF) would provide evidence on the correctness of the processing, not whether the claims that were submitted were proper. Also, the health care processor may not allow an ITF access to the provider's system.

Subject Area: Internal audit—plan audit engagements. Source: CIA 1196, I-49.

50. (d) This would be the best sampling technique to estimate the potential dollar amount of fraud by the dentists most likely to be making the false claims. Choice (a) is incorrect. The auditor wishes to estimate a dollar amount. Discovery sampling is best utilized to determine whether a fraud might be existing, not to estimate the dollar amount. Choice (b) is incorrect. Stratified classical variables estimation would be more efficient in this situation because it takes advantage of existing knowledge of the population. Choice (c) is incorrect. Attribute sampling does not provide dollar information.

Subject Area: Internal audit—plan audit engagements. Source: CIA 1196, I-50.

51. (d) The level of computer security at other locations in the company may be interesting for comparative purposes, but it has no effect on the level of security or the scope of examination needed at this location. Choice (a) is incorrect. This would be an appropriate procedure since exposures exist if the assets are not physically protected. Choice (b) is incorrect. LAN applications are becoming increasingly sophisticated and should provide the type of security suggested in this response. Choice (c) is incorrect. Interviews with users are often effective in identifying potential security breaches or other problems that should be addressed.

Subject Area: Internal audit—plan audit engagements. Source: CIA 1195, I-37.

52. (c) It would not be appropriate to consider the audit completed because the auditor has completed only a preliminary survey. The constructive action by the auditee may be a delaying tactic to hide additional problems. Choice (a) is incorrect. This would be an appropriate response consistent with the IIA *Standards.* Choice (b) is incorrect. The auditor should always consider the risk associated with the potential findings as a basis for determining the need for more immediate audit attention. Choice (d) is incorrect. This would be an appropriate response by the auditor because the issues may be more pervasive than shown by the preliminary survey.

Subject Area: Internal audit—plan audit engagements. Source: CIA 1195, I-38.

53. (a) This is the most appropriate response. The audit department charter should specify the broad responsibilities of the department, and the approved audit plan for the year should indicate management and the audit committee's approval for the process. Choice (b) is incorrect. It would not be appropriate to ask management to resolve every potential scope disagreement between the auditor and auditee. The audit charter and audit plan already communicate management's approval. Choice (c) is incorrect. There may be other objectives that have been set by management and the auditor. The audit should not be limited to the specific standards set by the quality assurance department, but should consider such standards in the development of the audit program. Choice (d) is incorrect. This would not be an appropriate response.

Subject Area: Internal audit—plan audit engagements. Source: CIA 1195, I-40.

54. (b) This is a scope limitation, which should appropriately be reported to the board. Choice (a) is incorrect. According to the *Standards*, a scope restriction such as this should be reported to the board. Choice (c) is incorrect. This would not generally be considered a scope limitation unless there was some specific reason for a "surprise audit." Choice (d) is incorrect. This is a scope limitation that should be communicated to the board. It does not make a difference that it is a performance or operational audit.

Subject Area: Internal audit—plan audit engagements. Source: CIA 1195, I-44.

55. (c) The charter enhances the auditor's independence because it clearly specifies, in advance, the authority, scope, and responsibility of the internal auditing function. Having outside directors on an audit committee enhances the independence of the internal auditing department. This is consistent with the research report on the best practices of audit committees. Choice (a) is incorrect. The statement that the CEO accused the previous director of not operating "in the best interests of the company" does not necessarily indicate a lack of independence, although it might be corroborating evidence if there are other factors present. Choice (b) is incorrect. According to the referenced report by the IIARF on audit committees, the independence of all audit functions is enhanced when the audit committee is made up of a majority of outside members. However, item III is also correct. Choice (d) is incorrect because only two items (II and III) are correct. Item I, by itself, may indicate a problem, but does not constitute evidence of an independence problem.

Subject Area: Internal audit—plan audit engagements. Source: CIA 1195, I-45.

56. (d) This would not be an appropriate action. Future audits should be based on the risk analysis performed by the internal audit department and the audit plan approved by the board. Choice (a) is incorrect. This would be an appropriate action since approval of a charter by the board explicitly defines the scope of activities by the audit department and expected cooperation from the auditees. Choice (b) is incorrect. This would be an appropriate action since the *Standards* require significant scope limitations be reported to the board. Choice (c) is incorrect. This would be an appropriate short-term response since management would have approved the audit program and should be in a position to secure auditee cooperation.

Subject Area: Internal audit—plan audit engagements. Source: CIA 1195, I-46.

57. (b) The director should communicate the scope limitation to the board. However, it would be appropriate to ensure that the president is aware of this. Choice (a) is incorrect. There are other factors that should be considered, such as the organization's code of conduct. Further, choice (b) should be pursued before seeking ethical interpretations from the IIA. Choice (c) is incorrect. The director should first consult the audit committee. The director provides value by serving the organization, and management may, in fact, be fully aware of the problem and may not want to incur additional costs. Choice (d) is incorrect. In this situation, the audit work is preliminary and the auditor has not yet formed a basis for an opinion. Thus, it would be too early to contact the external auditors. However, if an inquiry would be made by the external auditors, the internal auditors should share the extent of work completed to date.

Subject Area: Internal audit—plan audit engagements. Source: CIA 1195, I-55.

58. (c) This is required per the IIA *Standards*. Choice (a) is incorrect. The limitation should be communicated first to the board. Choice (b) is incorrect. There is no requirement or need to communicate the limitation to the external auditor. Choice (d) is incorrect. Internal auditing exists to serve the organization. Thus, the auditor's alternative is to communicate with the board, not threaten senior management.

Subject Area: Internal audit—plan audit engagements. Source: CIA 595, I-54.

59. (b) This is not a scope limitation. Rather, it is the audit committee's responsibility to review and approve the planned scope of activities for the year. Choice (a) is incorrect. This would be a scope limitation because it restricts the performance of an audit. Some scope limitations may be justified. The *Standards* identify scope limitations and do not distinguish between those that are justified and not justified. The limitations are reported to senior management and the board for their determination of the justification of the limitation. Choice (c) is incorrect. This is a scope limitation because it restricts the performance of specific procedures. Choice (d) is incorrect. Choices (a) and (c) are scope limitations.

Subject Area: Internal audit—plan audit engagements. Source: CIA 595, I-56.

60. (b) Internal auditors can provide assistance to managers who are developing objectives and goals by determining if the underlying assumptions are appropriate. Choice (a) is incorrect. The approval of objectives and goals to be met is a line function; internal auditing is a staff function. Choice (c) is incorrect. Management is responsible for developing and implementing controls. Choice (d) is incorrect. Management is responsible for accomplishing desired program results.

Subject Area: Internal audit—plan audit engagements. Source: CIA 590, I-1.

61. (a) The scope of the audit is specified by the audit objectives. Choice (b) is incorrect. The scheduling and time estimates are based on the audit objectives and the scope of the audit. Choice (c) is incorrect. The preliminary survey is performed after the audit objectives are determined. Choice (d) is incorrect. The audit program is developed based on the audit objectives and the scope of the audit.

Subject Area: Internal audit—plan audit engagements. Source: CIA 1192, II-22.

62. (c) This is a normal area of internal audit expertise. Choice (a) is incorrect. This aspect is related to a procurement action. Choice (b) is incorrect. This is a top management financial decision. Choice (d) is incorrect. This is a management policy. Some equipment may be retained for emergency use.

Subject Area: Internal audit—plan audit engagements. Source: CIA 1191, II-9.

63. (a) The merit of a lawsuit is a matter of legal judgment, beyond the expertise of internal audit. Choice (b) is incorrect. Comparison of procedures to legal requirements is within scope and expertise of internal audit. Choice (c) is incorrect. Compliance with loan covenants is within scope and expertise of internal audit. Choice (d) is incorrect. Assessing efficiency is a common practice of internal audit.

Subject Area: Internal audit—plan audit engagements. Source: CIA 594, I-27.

64. (a) The major purpose of an exit conference is to discuss problems, conclusions, and recommendations. This communication ensures that there have been no misunderstandings or misinterpretation of facts. It is not the time to correct deficiencies, which comes later. The audit staff's performance should not be brought up at this point since it will divert the audit findings. The final report is presented after incorporating the auditee's viewpoints expressed during the exit conference.

Subject Area: Internal audit—plan audit engagements. Source: Author.

65. (b) Techniques such as observation and inspection are part of an audit program, which describes specific actions (steps) to be taken by the auditor. The actions mentioned in the other three choices are taken prior to the development of an audit program. Choice (a) is incorrect. Notification of the audit is done during audit planning. Choice (c) is incorrect. Definition of audit objectives is done during audit planning. Choice (d) is incorrect. Planning for audit reporting is also done during audit planning.

Subject Area: Internal audit—plan audit engagements. Source: Author.

66. (d) In situations of suspected fraud, the auditor should handle the matter very carefully so as not to antagonize other members of the organization. First, the auditor should talk to audit management to see if audit management knows something more about the situation. The audit management should move the case forward. The auditor should never contact the other parties directly. Choice (a) is incorrect. It is too early to contact the board of directors. Choice (b) is incorrect. It is not appropriate to contact the audit committee. Contact should be done only after the fraud is investigated and found true. Choice (c) is incorrect. The auditor is only suspecting the fraud, it has not yet been proved, and the auditor should not contact the vice president of purchasing. Early and inappropriate notification could backfire on the auditor.

Subject Area: Internal audit—plan audit engagements. Source: Author.

A

B

C

O

P

Q

Printed in the United States of America
ED-10-05-11